THE AMERICAN COLONIES

THE AMERICAN COLONIES

From Settlement to Independence

R. C. Simmons

W · W · NORTON & COMPANY
New York · London

Printed in the United States of America.

First published as a Norton paperback 1981

Library of Congress Cataloging in Publication Data
Simmons, R. C.
The American Colonies.
(A Norton paperback)
Originally published by Longman, London.
Bibliography: p.
Includes index.
1. United States—History—Colonial period, ca. 1600–1775.
2. United States—History—Revolution, 1775–1783. I. Title.
E188.S59 1980 973.2 80–17527

ISBN 0-393-00999-8

W. W. Norton & Company, Inc., 500 Fifth Avenue, New York, NY 10110
W. W. Norton & Company Ltd., 10 Coptic Street London WC1A 1PU

8 9 0

For my parents

Contents

Preface

In the following pages, I have tried to combine a narrative introduction to early American history with the findings of recent scholarship. My debts to the writings of others are therefore many, as my bibliography acknowledges. This testifies to the variety and vitality of American scholarship concerned with the colonial period.

A general synthesis is bound to reflect such recent scholarship as well as the interests of the author, and I should state that some of the areas of early American life which seem to me of particular importance but which are only now being systematically treated are only briefly mentioned. Early American law and legal institutions; crime and punishment; treatment of the poor; and aspects of family life, of wealth distribution, and of social structure may be referred to. I should like to note that this book was begun and written without any bicentennial expectations, and that it is published in 1976 as the result of chance, not of design.

I owe my colleague, Professor A. E. Campbell, a particular word of thanks for reading my manuscript and saving me from a number of stylistic errors and infelicities. Professors John Shy and Jack P. Greene, while visiting England in 1975-1976, were also kind enough to read my manuscript; their comments saved me from a number of mistakes of fact and interpretation. But I must take responsibility for remaining mistakes, and for the general structure of and particular interpretations in this book. I also wish to acknowledge the generosity of several scholars in answering my queries about certain points of detail. I shall not name them in case I seem to be trying to lend their authority to my work.

A visit to the United States in 1968-1969 as an American Studies Fellow of the American Council of Learned Societies and a fellowship at the Charles Warren Center, Harvard University, allowed me to pursue specific research in early American history only indirectly connected with this present book. Nevertheless, some of the reading I then pursued has, I believe, helped in its preparation. I am grateful to both institutions. I must record my gratitude to Miss B. Ronchetti and the staff of the Inter-Library Loans Service of the University of Birmingham, who cheerfully and efficiently obtained a large number of books and articles for me.

University of Birmingham, England R. C. SIMMONS
1 January 1976

Prologue

Europeans and North America to 1620

A. The beginnings

For nearly a century after the voyages of Columbus, Europeans envisaged America primarily in terms of the Indies and the Hispano-Portuguese empire of South America. The reason is not hard to understand, since from those parts came the great wealth of the New World in silver, gold, sugar, tobacco, pearls, brazil wood, quicksilver, hides, and salt; and to them went a profitable supply of manufactured goods, cloth, and slaves. This creation of a new trade that eventually joined Europe, America, Asia, and Africa buoyed up men's imaginations and their greed. Spaniards and Portuguese sought to partition the New World and to exclude the rest of Christendom with paper treaties and iron guns. French, Dutch, and English pushed in, as first a few hardy privateers and adventurers sailed over American waters and then governments supported expeditions of plunder and trade.

The attack on the Indies, on Brazil, on New Spain and New Mexico began in the early sixteenth century and lasted into the eighteenth. French privateers were active off the Brazilian coast and in the Portuguese-African trade before 1510. By the 1530s they had begun to operate off the Azores as well as in Brazilian waters and to penetrate the Caribbean, attacking Hispaniola before 1538 and the eastern Caribbean in the 1540s. The famous French sailor François Le Clerc sacked Santiago de Cuba in 1554 and burned Havana to the ground a year or so later. English raiders appeared later, although William Hawkins, father of the famous John, took slaves from Africa to Brazil in the 1530s. Proposals made in England for trade expansion in the 1550s included an assault on the coast of Peru in association with French privateers. But the great age of English depredations in Spanish America began in 1563 with the arrival of John Hawkins at Hispaniola, where he exchanged slaves taken from Portuguese Africa for pearls, gold, hides, and sugar. From the 1590s the Dutch also joined the armed descent on the New World, as their shipping and sea power rapidly expanded.

In the meantime, North America was relatively neglected. Portuguese seamen in particular had made extensive voyages along the Atlantic coast during the early sixteenth century, a movement that reached its height with a systematic survey from the Grand Banks south to Florida by Estevan Gomez in 1524-1525. About a year earlier, the Florentine Giovanni da Verrazano had explored what are now New York harbor, Narragansett Bay, and the coast of Maine under orders from Francis I of France. On the Pacific coast, Juan Cabrillo had sailed north to San Francisco Bay in 1542, and Bartolomé Ferrelo continued on to Oregon a year later. Spanish would-be conquistadores had trekked through the interior of the continent, notably Narvaez's ill-fated expedition, which started from Florida in 1528, and those of Hernando de Soto in 1539 and Francisco Vasquez de Coronado in 1540. De Soto's great overland expedition took him from Tampa Bay to the Savannah River, from there along the Alabama River, then northwest almost to the Mississippi. The party subsequently reached the Mississippi south of modern Memphis, then went on to the Arkansas River, near its junction with the Canadian River, before striking southeast to the Mississippi down the Arkansas valley, where de Soto died. The expedition finally sailed down the Mississippi after an abortive march west beyond the Red River to the Brazos River. Coronado traveled through eastern Arizona, to the Grand Canyon, the Texas plains, and eastern Kansas, returning down the Rio Grande River to Mexico. By 1567 Spaniards had also explored the Alabama River and west of it toward the Mississippi and had penetrated to the southern Appalachians. The reports that all these men brought back spoke not of new riches and trade goods but of tough and warlike Indians, and vast emptinesses. To the merchants and bureaucrats whose support was needed for new schemes of settlement or colonization, these regions offered little, and they were left in peace.

Columbus had sailed west in the hope of reaching Asia; indeed he died in the belief that his voyages had brought him to an outlying part of the rich East Indies. John Cabot, who sailed west into the Atlantic from Bristol in 1497, similarly believed that the ocean was a gateway rather than a barrier to the spices of Cathay and Cipango. A strong tradition among Bristol seafarers also spoke of mysterious islands in the Atlantic, which several expeditions had searched for in the 1480s. On his first voyage, Cabot reached Newfoundland; possibly he went as far south as New England. For him, the cold North Atlantic coast was the edge of the eastern continent, and on his second voyage in 1498 he hoped to cruise south, expecting to reach the tropics and Cipango. Cabot died at sea on this expedition. It was generally believed that the lands he had reached were not Asia; now men hoped to find a navigable passage through or around them to the fabled continent. So the first discovery of North America brought initial disappointment: instead of the wealth of Asia, the rocky coasts of Newfoundland; instead of a rich spice trade, a possible haul of fish.

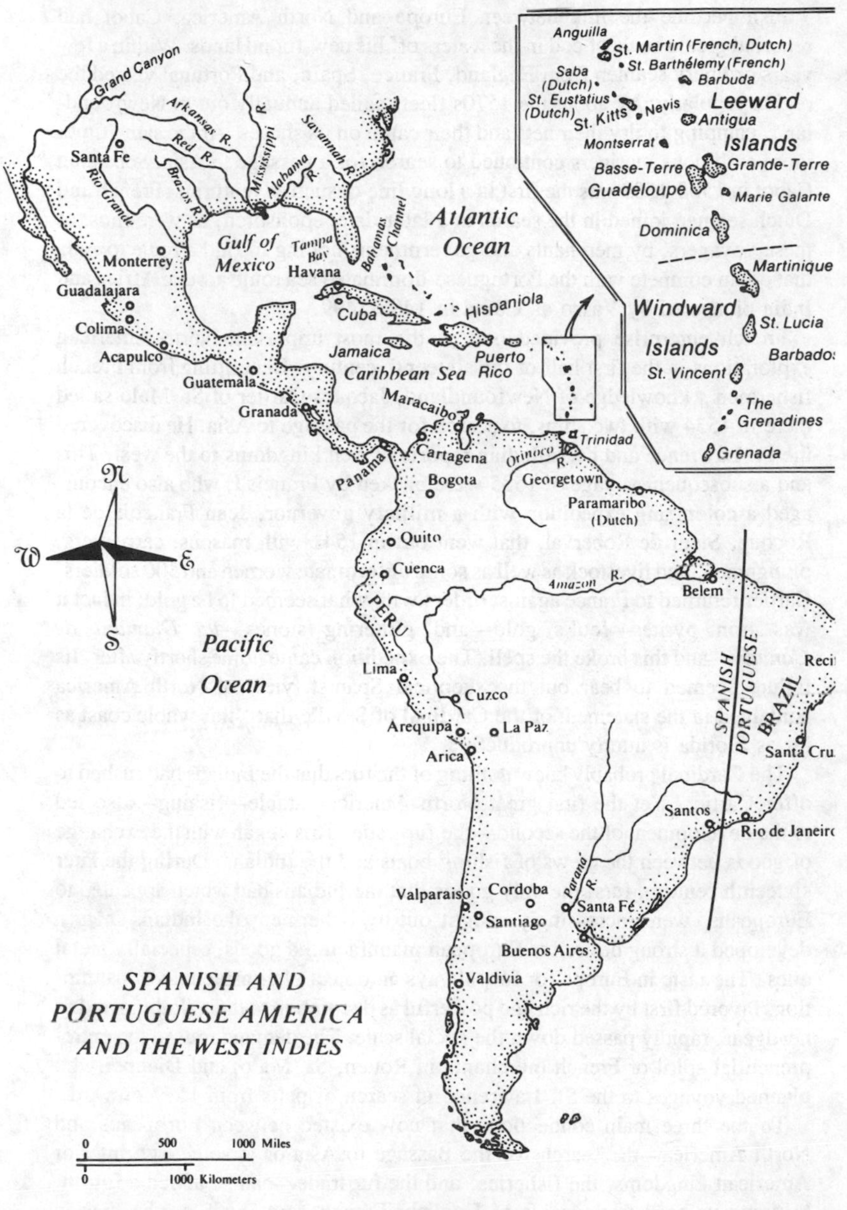

Grand Canyon
Arkansas R.
Mississippi R.
Savannah R.
Red R.
Santa Fe
Rio Grande
Brazos R.
Alabama R.
Gulf of Mexico
Tampa Bay
Bahamas Channel
Atlantic Ocean
Monterrey
Guadalajara
Havana
Cuba
Hispaniola
Colima
Acapulco
Jamaica
Caribbean Sea
Puerto Rico
Guatemala
Granada
Maracaibo
Panama
Cartagena
Orinoco R.
Trinidad
Bogota
Georgetown
Paramaribo (Dutch)
Quito
Cuenca
Amazon R.
Belem
PERU
Pacific Ocean
Lima
Cuzco
Arequipa
La Paz
Arica
SPANISH
PORTUGUESE
BRAZIL
Reci
Santa Cru
Santos
Rio de Janeir
Parana R.
Valparaiso
Cordoba
Santa Fé
Santiago
Buenos Aires
Valdivia
Anguilla
St. Martin (French, Dutch)
St. Barthélemy (French)
Saba (Dutch)
Barbuda
St. Eustatius (Dutch)
St. Kitts
Nevis
Leeward Islands
Antigua
Montserrat
Basse-Terre
Grande-Terre
Guadeloupe
Marie Galante
Dominica
Martinique
Windward Islands
St. Lucia
Barbado
St. Vincent
The Grenadines
Grenada
N
W
E
S
SPANISH AND PORTUGUESE AMERICA AND THE WEST INDIES
0
500
1000 Miles
0
1000 Kilometers

Fish became the link between Europe and North America. Cabot had reported great shoals of cod in the waters off his new-found lands. Within a few years ordinary seamen from England, France, Spain, and Portugal visited the region regularly; by about the 1570s fleets sailed annually out to Newfoundland, camping to dry their nets and their catch on its shores. At the same time, more ambitious mariners continued to search for a passage to Asia. Sebastian Cabot in 1508-1509 was the first in a long line of such adventurers. French and Dutch seamen joined in the search at a later date, sponsored, as were most of these voyagers, by merchants and governments hoping to find a route to Asia that could compete with the Portuguese-dominated sea route around Africa and India pioneered by Vasco da Gama in 1497-1499.

French enterprise provided one of the most important North American explorations in the first half of the sixteenth century. Benefitting from French fishermen's knowledge of Newfoundland, Jacques Cartier of St. Malo sailed there in 1534 with two ships, to search for the passage to Asia. He discovered the St. Lawrence and heard Indian reports of rich kingdoms to the west. This and a subsequent voyage of 1535 were backed by Francis I, who also encouraged a colonizing expedition with a military governor, Jean François de la Rocque, Sieur de Roberval, that went out in 1541 with masons, carpenters, ploughmen, and livestock as well as some unfortunate women and 300 soldiers. Cartier returned to France against orders with what seemed to be gold; in fact it was iron pyrites—fool's gold—and glittering stones—*un Diamant de Canada*—and this broke the spell. The expedition came home shortly after. Its failure seemed to bear out the skeptical Spanish view of North America contained in the statement of the Cardinal of Seville that "this whole coast as far as Florida is utterly unproductive."

The Cardinal probably knew nothing of the furs that the Indians had rushed to offer Cartier. Yet the first great North American staple—fishing—also led to the development of the second—the fur trade. This began with the exchange of goods between the crews of fishing boats and the Indians. During the later sixteenth century, furs, the only goods that the Indians had which appealed to Europeans, were increasingly sought out by fishermen; the Indians in turn developed a strong desire for European manufactured goods, especially metal ones. The taste in Europe for fur, always an object of conspicuous consumption, favored first by the rich and powerful as decoration to their clothing and as headgear, rapidly passed down the social scale. The demand roused the entrepreneurial spirit of French merchants in Rouen, St. Malo, and Dieppe, who planned voyages to the St. Lawrence in search of pelts from 1577 onward.

To the three main connections that now existed between Europeans and North America—the search for the passage to Asia or to some rich interior American kingdoms, the fisheries, and the fur trade—can be added a fourth, bringing us back to the raids of English, French, and Dutch on the Iberian empires of the New World. Although these were launched from European seaports, strategists and statesmen soon began to consider the possibility of establishing armed bases in or near Spanish America. These were conceived as permanent outposts for aggressive trade or privateering, with facilities for the supply and repair of ships and men and the storage and transhipment of goods and plunder. The first mature development of such ideas—in reality the forerunner of a strategy that encompassed the Old and the New World—was that of the French Huguenot statesman Admiral Gaspar de Coligny. Not surprisingly, given its open and unsettled coasts, North America seemed suitable for the establishment of such bases. Jean Ribault led a French Huguenot expedition to modern South Carolina in 1562 which disease, starvation, and Indian attack destroyed; in 1564 a second Huguenot colony farther south on the St. John's River was annihilated by Spanish forces. Ribault had visited England in 1562-1563 and tried to persuade the Queen to support his ventures. Whether or not directly inspired by Huguenot example, Englishmen in the next twenty years produced several plans for military colonies in the Americas.

Economic considerations and developments explain much of the combination of neglect and sporadic activity in North America. Spain and Portugal, fully extended by the demands of their other American territories and their world trade, had little interest in it except for the fisheries. Spain, it is true, established a military base at St. Augustine, Florida, in 1565, but this was a fortress rather than a colony, planned to protect the route of the treasure fleet through the Bahama channel and to exclude privateers from Florida. England's merchants, prosperous until the late 1540s, sought new trade only after the death of Henry VIII, but they directed their major attention to Morocco, Africa, and the search for a northeast passage around Russia to Asia. They returned to the idea of a northwest passage only in the 1570s. Francis I of France at first encouraged Cartier because he hoped to break Portugal's hold on the spice trade by the discovery of a northwest passage. The exploits of Ribault and other privateers reflected the rise of North Atlantic ports whose merchants invested in North American fishing and furs.

B. Early settlement attempts

The idea of settlement was not completely absent from even the earliest voyages of the northern Europeans. John Cabot's, and other early English patents, had contained general instructions for the government of any new lands that might be discovered; it was stated in a patent of 1501 that "all and singular as well as men as women of this our kingdom and the rest of our subjects wishing and desiring to visit these lands and islands thus newly found, and to inhabit the same, shall be allowed to and have power to go freely and safely. . . ." The first English book containing a section on America, published in 1517, also mentioned colonization, lamenting in verse the English failure to "have taken possession/And made first building and habitacion/A memory perpetuall" in a region where the natives "which as yet live all beastly" awaited instruction in the knowledge of heaven, hell, and the scriptures. Cartier's last voyage also had a colonizing element, as described above.

In England, less fragmentary arguments for colonization appeared in the 1550s, indirect and unfocused on particular territory, conscious above all of Spanish settlement and wealth in the New World. The best-known early propagandist, Richard Eden, a London lawyer, prefaced a translation of Peter Martyr's *Decades of the New World* with a reproach to Englishmen for their poverty, exhorting them to learn from the Spanish. Eight years later, in 1563, Ribault published *The whole and true discoverye of Terra Florida*, a direct incitement to English colonization within Spanish-claimed territory, dwelling on its precious metals, abundance of fruits and animals, and Indians awaiting Christianity, probably the topics which were most frequently mentioned in English sixteenth-century arguments for colonization. Similar publications appeared in France; indeed there was close contact between Huguenot and English expansionists at this time. A translation of a work by a leading exponent of French colonization, André Thevet, appeared in London in 1568, while John Florio translated accounts of Cartier's expeditions into English in 1580.

French maritime activity was severely curtailed by the outbreak of the Wars of Religion in 1562. Yet the fur trade carried on; together with memories of Cartier it kept alive French interest in North America and the Newfoundland-St. Lawrence region. Now groups of merchants and gentry in the west of France tried increasingly to monopolize the supply of American furs, an ambition that underlay frequent requests for royal grants and patents to Canadian territory in the last twenty-five years of the sixteenth century. The first such grants went to a Breton nobleman, the Marquis de la Roche, in 1577 and 1578, although the circumstances surrounding them are obscure. These closely resembled the original patents issued to Cartier and his associate, Roberval, more than thirty years before, mentioning the two men by name. They also gave La Roche vice-regal powers over New France, the first to be granted by the Crown. At this time La Roche made no attempt to act on his patent. In 1588 the King responded to requests from a nephew of Cartier, Jacques Noel of St. Malo, for a twelve-year monopoly of the trade, making a grant with grandiose phrases about colonization similar to those in Cartier's and Roberval's commissions. Yet this licence was very soon virtually revoked because of the objections of other St. Malo merchants. By the end of the sixteenth century, several other patents had also been issued and revoked, showing no clear policy or interest on the part of the Crown. Two patentees, La Roche, who had gained a renewal of his grant in 1598, and Pierre Chauvin, given a conflicting monopoly in 1599, did, however, send men to North America. These went as employees rather than as colonizers, the former to Sable Island and the latter to Tadoussac.

Neither of these settlements long survived. But the ideas of colonization then in evidence in France reveal a clear, early division of opinion. La Roche probably thought in terms of peopling his colony rather than establishing a mere factory (i.e. trading post) for furs. This ambition for settlement definitely gripped Pierre de Guast, Comte De Monts, a Huguenot gentleman of the Saintonge region, who in 1604 received a patent from the Crown conferring on him the King's authority as lieutenant governor of the "coasts, lands and confines of Acadia, Canada and other places in New France" and requiring him to "people, cultivate and settle the said lands." But French merchants, operating De Monts's monopoly on condition that they transported settlers to the colony, showed great hostility to this provision, preferring to maintain factories rather than establish settlers who might interfere with the fur trade. However, when De Monts sailed for North America in 1604, about 120 settlers went with him, and he established a base on Sainte Croix (modern Dochet) Island off the coast of Acadia. About half of his men died during the winter, and in 1605 he moved the remainder to a site near Port-Royal (modern Annapolis, Nova Scotia).

French interest in North America colonization seems to have come later than that of the English and to have lacked one great emphasis that marked the development of English colonizing ideas, an emphasis on colonies as a refuge for a surplus or unemployed population. In England, this view reflected sixteenth-century economic and social thinking concerned with agrarian changes, rising prices, and a general belief that Englishmen were overnumerous and underemployed. The same kind of concern is barely discernible in sixteenth-century France, and its absence probably removed one important stimulus to propaganda for large-scale colonization. In England, the introduction of these ideas into colonizing literature occurred in the 1560s and 1570s in connection not with North America but with Ireland, where English settlement was then proceeding. Frenchmen had no equivalent to the whole English experience of Irish colonization, and this may well have been a second reason for differences in English and French attitudes to North America.

The first English interest in American colonization, we have seen, sprang from rivalry with Spain and resulted in the advocacy, particularly in the 1570s, of fortified military settlements. Yet at the same time, the belief that Ireland could be subjugated by the establishment of English military plantations gave way to the view that proper colonies, made up of settlers from a wide cross section of English society—families of craftsmen, small and large landowners, traders and other representative Englishmen—should be encouraged. To promote migration, Irish promoters issued great quantities of persuasive literature dwelling on questions of English overpopulation, housing shortages, the rising prices of food and clothing, and other economic difficulties. They also stressed

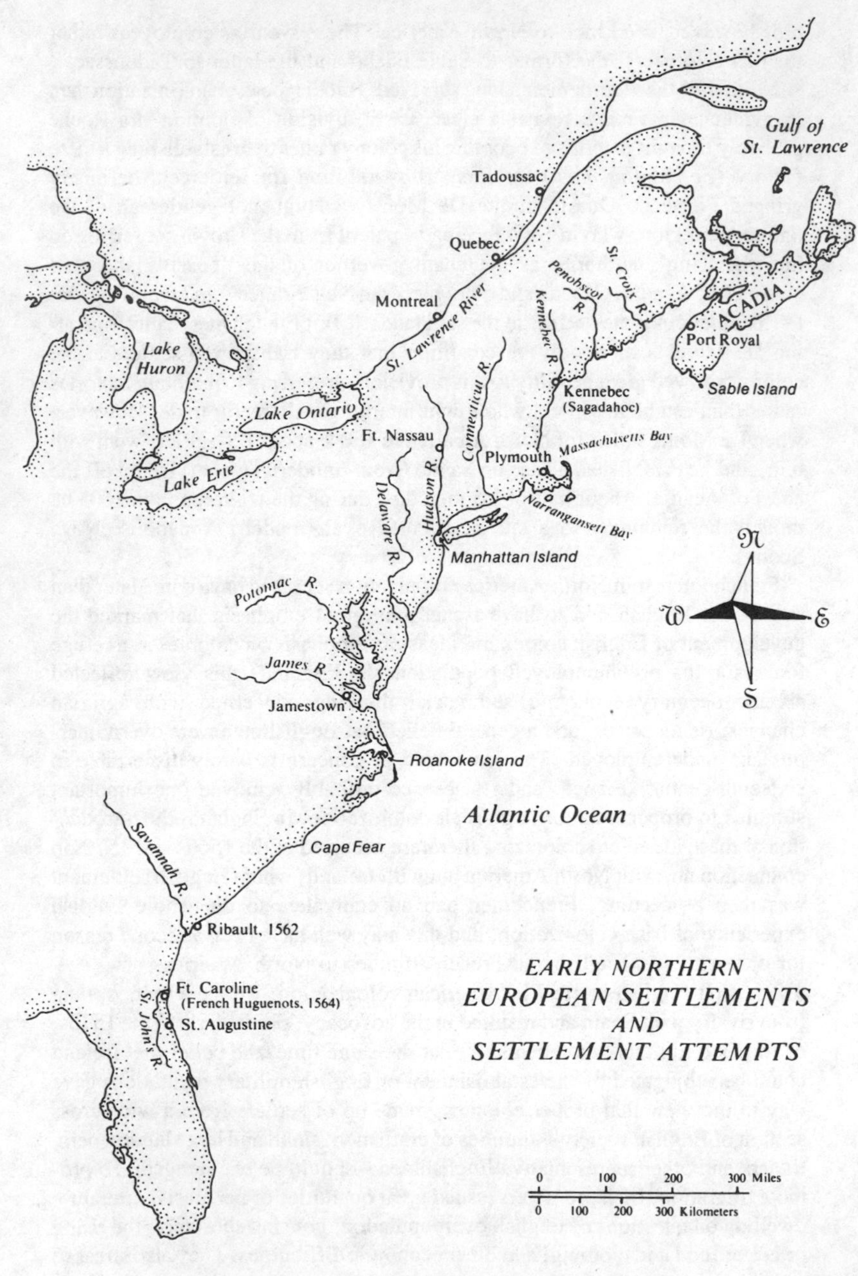

EARLY NORTHERN EUROPEAN SETTLEMENTS AND SETTLEMENT ATTEMPTS

the particular disabilities of younger sons of gentry families, trained for government and landholding since birth but deprived of the chance to exercise their vocation by the workings of primogeniture. Cheap land in Ireland, it was argued, benefitted the better sort of Englishmen as well as the poor.

Such arguments shortly afterward made their appearance in propaganda tracts aimed at convincing Englishmen of the need to colonize North America. Nor was this the only connection between Irish and American schemes. Many of the same men, often the seagoing gentry of southwest England, moved from one to the other. The renewal of interest in North America itself probably came about through the well-publicized exploits of John Frobisher, who in 1570 revived the search for the Northwest Passage and a year later set out to establish a gold-mining venture on Baffin Island. In 1577 another adventurer, Sir Humphrey Gilbert, previously involved in Irish and in Huguenot affairs, presented a plan for a military expedition to North America or the West Indies to establish a base there. This advice was rejected, but Gilbert received a patent in June 1578 allowing him to take possession of uninhabited North American lands within the next six years. Later in the same year he organized an American voyage, but this disintegrated into an attack on Spanish shipping.

Gilbert, a Devon soldier connected with the west country families who were in the vanguard of most Elizabethan maritime enterprise, returned to the idea of American colonization in about 1582. He then began to act on the idea that America should be considered not as a way station on the route to Asia, nor as a base for privateering against Spain, but as an end in itself, an empty continent open for settlement. By 1583 he had disposed of eight million acres of his projected colony, including substantial grants to a group of Catholic gentry led by Sir George Peckham and Sir Thomas Gerrard. Gilbert sailed to claim his new territories in June 1583, but he took possession only of a region around St. John's, Newfoundland, a rather pathetic gesture, since this was a well-known coast for fishermen of all nationalities. Although he then sailed south to seek more territory, his largest vessel was lost and further exploration abandoned. In early September 1583 Gilbert's own ship foundered, and he was drowned; the remnants of his fleet struggled back to England.

Gilbert's enterprise, ineffectual though it was, had great significance. First, his grants to Catholics, while financial in motive, anticipated the association of America with the idea of a refuge where religious dissidents could enjoy freedom of conscience—an important prelude to later colonizing schemes. Second, Gilbert's own plans for settlement show that he had moved far away from the prevailing idea of a garrison base. His plans for emigration of the poor with state subsidies, for the establishment of civil government, for churches, and for institutions of learning and charity in the New World reflected reforming ideas then prevalent in England. Again, Gilbert's vision anticipated that of later North American enterprisers who sought reforms in America that could not be achieved at home. Finally, it may well be that Gilbert's colonizing plans prompted the younger Richard Hakluyt's interest in the settlement of North America, for this was to be a consistent theme in the famous editor's many-sided endeavors during the rest of his life. Hakluyt's *Divers Voyages touching the discoverie of America* of 1582 may have shaped itself "from a series of small propaganda tracts [in support of Gilbert] with specific purposes into a book which combined all of them."

Gilbert's death left his half-brother, Sir Walter Raleigh, as an advocate of American colonization, though Raleigh's schemes once again reverted to the plan of establishing a strong military base near Spanish territory. In April 1585 his associate, Sir Richard Grenville, left England with seven vessels, arriving off the American mainland in July. In September the last vessel departed from the site of the new colony—Roanoke Island in present-day North Carolina—leaving 107 men there under the command of Ralph Lane. They wintered in America: the first intending permanent English settlers to do so. But in 1586 Lane and his men, fearing starvation, sailed back to England with Sir Francis Drake a few weeks before Grenville returned with supplies. Grenville left only a small party of some 15 men who later disappeared, presumably killed or driven away to their deaths by the hostile Indians. The colony had not lasted two years.

One of the colonists of 1585 had been John White, a surveyor by profession and a fine artist, whose job had been to sketch the flora, fauna, and other sights of the New World. On his return he contracted with Raleigh to go back to North America, suggesting a site on Chesapeake Bay. This colony, to be called the City of Raleigh, was planned from the first as one of settlement. Ships went out in 1587. Seventeen women and 9 children were included in the party of 110 persons that remained in America, but the settlers landed at Roanoke Island and not on the Chesapeake. White himself was forced to depart for England one month later, in August 1587, to negotiate for supplies. He was not to return until August 1590; these were the years of the Armada, which badly disrupted English shipping. In 1590 White found the Roanoke site deserted and the only clue to the colonists' fate the word CROATOAN carved on a post at the entrance to the fort and the letters CRO carved on a tree. He thought these might mean that the colonists had gone to Croatoan Island to the southeast of Roanoke. But White himself failed to get to the island as a result of accidents and storms. So ended the first real English colony of settlement in North America.

The late 1570s and the 1580s nevertheless constituted an important period for the colonization of North America, for in these years English attention became firmly focused on the settlement of the continent. Cooperation between propagandists and promoters resulted in numerous books and tracts stressing the necessity of American colonization which, while they could not have reached a wide audience, were read by influential men. Two publications were a eulogy of Frobisher and Gilbert by Thomas Churchyard, a hack poet, printed in 1578, and a translation by Thomas Nicholas, an English merchant to Spain, of Lopez de Gomara's history of Spanish colonization. The first dwelt on the idea of transporting poor persons; the second appealed for English emulation of Cortes. In 1580 Richard Hakluyt the younger published his first work, Florio's translation of Cartier's voyages, penning a preface that recommended settlement of the northeast. Hakluyt sat at the center of the North American group. His *Principal Navigations, Voyages, Traffiques and Discoveries of the English Nation . . . within the compasse of these 1600 Yeres* occupies the same position in the literature of Elizabethan maritime expansion as Foxe's *Book of Martyrs* in that of Elizabethan Protestantism. A paper of 1584 by Hakluyt on American colonization, now known as "A Discourse on Western Planting," written to win the support of the Queen and her ministers for Raleigh's American colony, was certainly the most important statement about North American colonization yet produced. It encapsulated each argument in its favor. Newfoundland also continued to be written about in several tracts published after Gilbert's voyage and death as a site for permanent English settlement.

After about 1580 the arguments for North American colonization were fairly standard. It was now generally agreed that North America, claimed by England as a result of Cabot's discovery, left vacant by Spain and Portugal, and geographically accessible to England (especially Newfoundland), had been providentially reserved for English possession. The great bounty of America—fish and furs, hides, potash, cordage, timber, minerals, tars and other kinds of naval stores in the northern part, fruits, vegetables, grapes, olives, oranges, and probably gold and silver in the warmer region—awaited the English. Moreover, the existing Indian population, when reduced to "civilitie" would be a market for English goods, and the new English settlers would eventually become great consumers of all English articles, especially woolens. This positive boost to the English economy would be reinforced by the departure of the poor and workless from the kingdom to find wealth and happiness in the New World. True, one writer added, it might need a great fleet of ships to transport them, but plenty of fishing boats sailed empty to Newfoundland each year. Given the success of these plans, English wealth and power would rapidly increase to surpass that of Spain.

In fact, because of the war with Spain, the 1590s proved unproductive of colonies. Actual capital investment in the ventures that have so far been mentioned was low, for men of means had less dangerous ways of placing their money. The 1590s drew merchant and gentry capital into a great anti-Spanish privateering war, when groups of investors buying shares in privateering expeditions stood a very good chance of making large profits. Although privateering and colonization had always been closely linked, with both Gilbert and Raleigh trying to raise prize money for their ventures, privateering now displaced schemes of settlement. It has been argued that the capital gained in privateering in the 1590s might eventually have supported some of the colonizing schemes of the early seventeenth century. The English gentry, as much or more than the English merchants, interested themselves in colonial schemes, valuing the idea of extending English glory and power as well as hoping for profit.

The threads of prior English involvement in North America were drawn together in the opening years of the seventeenth century. Two main groups of would-be promoters emerged after the signing of peace with Spain checked privateering missions. The first consisted of Londoners headed by Richard Hakluyt and Sir Thomas Smith, a leading merchant, who had taken up Raleigh's Roanoke rights. The London group's interest remained the Chesapeake and North Carolina region favored by Raleigh. The second group, mainly west-country men, looked toward northern New England, probably inspired by reports of a voyage in 1605 to Maine by Captain George Waymouth under the patronage of the Earl of Southampton, as well as by the fishing links between the west of England and Newfoundland. Certainly the two groups were jealous of each other, carrying on the traditional rivalry of the "outports" for the port of London and vice versa; presumably they thought it wise to combine in appealing for a royal grant in America, despite these feelings. They won a charter on 10 April 1606—but it carefully distinguished between a London group and a Plymouth one, authorizing the former to colonize between 34° and 41° north, (modern Cape Fear to New York City), the latter between 38° and 45° (roughly from the Potomac to Bangor, Maine). While these areas overlapped, each group was forbidden to establish itself within 100 miles of the other. Although the charter obviously recognized that permanent settlement would be attempted, there is no doubt that many of those involved still thought in commercial and strategic terms rather than of populous colonies of settlement. Government of the new colonies was to rest in a royal council in England, which was to commission subsidiary councils in America. Those going to the new colonies were to do so as company employees.

The first ships dispatched by the London group sailed in December 1606 with 144 men and boys as colonists and arrived in Virginia in April 1607. A site given the name of Jamestown was chosen in May 1607, and attempts were made to explore, build a fort, and plant food. But by September 1607 about half of the 104 or 105 who had finally remained in Virginia had died, possibly because a search for gold and precious minerals suddenly made the little society neglect to grow food, possibly because of the ravages of unfamiliar diseases. Moreover, it seems clear that the settlers—especially the more gentlemanly ones—argued among themselves about the exercise of authority, and this quickly led to intrigue and noncooperation. The arrival of more men and supplies—the first "supply" arrived in January 1608 with 120 new planters, the second in September with 70 (including 2 women), and the third in August 1609 with some 600 persons—should have helped. Yet mortality was staggering. Many more died than lived.

The precariousness of the Jamestown settlement resembled that of De

Monts's Acadian colony of 1604, though after the initial expedition, the French failed to send out the large numbers of people and supplies the Virginians received. The second Virginia Company colony—that of the Plymouth group—had even less success. Two ships carrying about 120 men left England in the middle of 1607 and sailed to the Sagadahoc River in Maine, where a primitive village was built. But "childish factions" also arose there, and food rapidly ran out. However, the death rate seems to have been slight compared with that of Virginia, and supplies did arrive from England—but not more settlers. Apparently the colonists became disillusioned and decided to return home. Half of them left in 1608, the rest in 1609 when the only remaining convincing leader, Raleigh Gilbert, youngest son of Sir Humphrey Gilbert, went back to claim an inheritance. Sagadahoc probably failed when it became obvious that no new settlers or strong leaders were likely to arrive. This reflected the lack of resources and organizing ability of the Plymouth group compared with its richer London rival.

C. English, French, and Dutch

The first months, even the first years of these infant settlements of the English and the French saw only fitful survival. The most cosseted plantation, Virginia, provided an awful reminder of the fragility of life in the New World, and early reports from the colony shocked its English backers to a careful reconsideration of its government and purpose. They determined to seek a new charter for Virginia and to change the nature of Virginia society by sending out "under the conduct of one able and absolute governor, a large supply of five hundred men, with some number of families, of wife, children and servants, to take faste holde and roote in that land." In May 1609 the Crown granted a second charter, vesting control of the colony in the "Treasurer and Company of Adventurers and Planters of the City of London for the first Colony of Virginia," a joint stock company with authority lodged in the treasurer, as the chief executive was known, and the Company Council. The charter also enlarged Virginia's boundaries. Sir Thomas Smith, now one of the most powerful merchants in London, became its treasurer, immediately launching a great appeal for funds that had a moderate response. These new funds financed a relatively large migration of about 800 persons, though that that many of these went in family groups is doubtful. Also, Lord De la Warr, a member of the Council and a man of influence, was appointed governor. He could not sail at once and reached the colony only in 1610.

These plans were misjudged. The arrival of hundreds of settlers threw the tiny semi-derelict plantation into chaos, and food supplies rapidly dwindled. About half the population died in 1609, a crisis in which illness and lack of food again worked together to bring an appalling mortality. Virginia officials continued to complain of the unwillingness or inability of the early settlers to grow food in an orderly way. These and other reports finally impelled the Virginia Company to impose martial law in the settlement, a state of affairs lasting from 1611 to 1618 and one that produced some improvement in agriculture. A momentous development came with the successful cultivation of tobacco—from West Indian and Orinoco plants and not the feeble Virginia stock—that produced exports of about fifty thousand pounds in 1618, a figure that rose more than sixfold by 1626. Yet in the short term this brought further suffering, as men neglected to grow food in order to raise the profitable narcotic. In 1619 a critic told the Virginia Company that overconcentration on tobacco and sassafras, a medicinal plant, had led the settlers "into an extremity of being ready to starve (unless the Magazine this last year had supplied them with Corne and Cattle from hence) to the stopping and great discouragement of many hundreds of people who were providing themselves to plant in Virginia." In fact, twelve years after initial settlement, the Virginia Company in England still strained its resources in order to send supplies and colonists.

Other changes resulted from these early difficulties of Company and colony. In 1612 the Company's government was again reorganized with a new charter that provided for more stockholder control, boundaries that included the Bermuda islands, greater powers over employees and colonists, and the right to raise money through lotteries. These brought in considerable but still insufficient sums, and the Company ran into debt. From about 1614 it gradually allowed settlers to work their own land rather than to produce for the public stock. A few years later it began to solicit further English investment by granting large areas of land to groups of men as particular or "private" plantations that were to be virtually self-governing, almost manorial estates with their own political representation. The introduction of private land ownership probably lessened friction between settlers and Company officials in the colony, and the particular plantations brought settlers and investment; but the reforms were born out of weakness, not strength. Virginia's population in 1618 numbered only some 600 persons, and the failure of the colony to develop split leading members of the Virginia Company into opposing groups with different ideas about what ought to be done.

One such group was led by Sir Edwin Sandys, who displaced Smith as treasurer in 1619. Sandys's grandiose plans included the diversification of the economy by the introduction of iron, silk, and glass making; the establishment of a stable social base by building schools, colleges, hospitals, churches, and inns; the remodeling of the colony's government and the ending of military rule; and the financing of these improvements by negotiating a contract to monopolize the supply of tobacco to England. Of these reforms, only the change in Virginia's government had lasting results. In 1618 a charter of grants and liberties was ratified for Virginia and sent out with a new governor, Sir

George Yeardley. The main thrust of its proposals, Yeardley proclaimed, was to replace the "cruell" military laws by "those free lawes which his Majesty's subjects live under in England." So that the inhabitants "might have a hande in the governinge of themselves, it was granted that a generall assemblie should be helde yearly once whereat were to be present the Governor and Counsell with two Burgesses [from each "town" or "particular plantation"] freely to be elected by the inhabitants thereof: this assembly to have power to make and ordaine whatsoever lawes and orders should by them be thought good and proffittable for our subsistence."

The first Virginia assembly met on 30 July 1619 in the church at Jamestown with twenty-two burgess members. Besides settling its own organization, the assembly ratified the privileges given the colony by the Virginia Company and passed some local laws. It also petitioned the Company for modifications to its privileges, requesting that no company laws made in London should bind Virginians unless approved by the assembly in Virginia. This motion, accepted by the Virginia Company in 1621, voiced the first quiet assertion of local rights and privileges against the authority of an English-based government. Yet, however significant and prophetic these proceedings now seem, to many in Virginia and England there was then still only the bare assurance that the colony would survive. Although perhaps in 1619 and early 1620 some 1,400 settlers arrived to join the 700 there, the death rate remained calamitous, and the colony's population numbered about 867 in March 1620.

By 1620 Virginians were not the only English settlers in North America. Bermuda had attracted attention after the shipwreck of the flagship of a Virginia supply fleet on the island in July 1609. The Somers Islands or Bermuda Company, formed as a subsidiary of the Virginia Company by 150 members in 1612, sent out 50 settlers in 1612 and several hundred more by 1615, investing perhaps £20,000 for which the Company received little or no return. The Bermuda Company was also reorganized, becoming independent of the Virginia Company. A governor and assistants met in London while a deputy governor presided on the island; law courts and parishes were also ordered set up. In fact, until the arrival of Governor Nathaniel Butler in 1619 carrying orders for reform of the government similar to those just made for Virginia, there was considerable civil disorder and disaffection in the colony. Nor was any cash commodity produced until about 1617, when tobacco growing became widespread. In 1620 a hurricane caused extensive destruction and a severe food shortage. Yet the 1,500 or so persons on the island had reasonable chances of survival without the threat of Indian attack that imperiled the Virginians.

A third English colony was established in Newfoundland, where 39 colonists landed in 1610 under the auspices of the Newfoundland Company, an association of Bristol and London merchants. Here, the formative idea was the establishment of a permanent base to protect the fisheries, although many mariners believed that the Newfoundland Company's object was to monopolize the best drying beaches and eventually the whole Newfoundland fishing industry. The settlement remained tiny for many years. Yet other colonial promoters interested themselves in the region: notably William Vaughan, an eccentric Welshman who sent out settlers in 1617-1618, and Henry Cary, Lord Falkland, who, with plans for a colony of Irishmen, received land both from Vaughan and, in 1620, from the Newfoundland Company. But these minute outposts, where they survivied, remained desolate fishing villages.

The fourth and final English colony in North America, at Plymouth in New England, had barely been initiated at the end of 1620. Two English agents of a large company of English then living in Leyden, Holland, had applied to the Virginia Company for land in Virginia as early as 1617. No patent was given until 1620, when the Englishmen also found a merchant backer, Thomas Weston, who agreed to underwrite some of their expenses. Weston drove a hard bargain, insisting that the new settlers virtually become his employees, paying him any profits made in America for seven years. The Leyden group's ancestry can be traced directly back to the year 1607 and the place of Scrooby in Nottinghamshire near the boundaries with Lincolnshire and Yorkshire. There, a number of men and women had withdrawn from their parish churches, coming together as an illegal separate "church." For some of the leaders of this movement, these acts brought fines and imprisonment. Many members of the Scrooby church decided to join other radical English Protestants in exile in Holland, where the state enforced the practice of religious toleration. They finally settled in Leyden, losing and gaining members as the years passed. Their most notable addition was the Reverend John Robinson, a scholarly Oxford graduate, whose extreme religious views had lost him a prosperous living and forced him into exile in 1608. The decision of some members of his church to go to America in 1617 was an admission of their Englishness and poverty. However much they feared the Batavianization of their children and suffered as mostly unskilled, rural outsiders in the urban bustle of Leyden, they still could not return safely to their native land. English America was the next best thing.

The emigrants are, of course, now better known as the Pilgrims, although of the 102 passengers on the *Mayflower* in 1620, only 35 were from Leyden and only a handful had Scrooby roots. The rest were miscellaneous persons recruited in London or Southampton. Yet the Pilgrims managed to avoid the severe disorders that harassed Sagadahoc and Virginia, probably because they were well organized under effective leaders: Governor William Bradford, a thirty-year-old yeoman of simple genius, and William Brewster, an older and well-educated gentleman, an experienced administrator who became the chief official of the Plymouth church. The first indication of the effectiveness of Pilgrim authority came with the signing of the famous Mayflower Compact on board that ship in November 1620, before the settlers landed. This was no great organic constitutional document but a simple agreement of the male settlers to "covenant, and combine ourselves togeather into a civill body politick; for our better ordering, and preservation . . . and by vertue hearof to enacte, constitute, and frame and such just and equall Lawes, ordinances, Act, constitutions, and offices, from time to time, as shall be thought most meete and convenient for the generall good of the colonie: unto which we promise all due submission and obedience." The agreement served in place of a formal charter—which Plymouth did not have and never received—allowing the community to suppress dissident or unruly elements.

The landing at Plymouth was also unpremeditated. After two false starts, the Pilgrims finally sailed late in the year for Virginia and arrived at Massachusetts Bay in November 1620. Suggestions of running down the coast toward Virginia finally ended with the decision to remain in New England. The occasion was momentous; the results cruel. In December 1620 the settlers, wrote Bradford, "took better view of the place, and resolved where to pitch their dwelling; and the 25th day began to erect the first house for common use to receive them and their goods." But "that which was most sad and lamentable was, that in two or three months' time half of their company died, especially in January and February, being the depth of winter and wanting houses and other comforts; being infected with scurvy and other diseases in which this long voyage and their inaccomodation had brought on them."

The arrival of the Pilgrims in Plymouth can be seen in retrospect as one turning point in English colonization, for it marked the beginning of a voluntary movement of religiously discontented persons to America, a movement that would swell to a flood in the late 1620s and the 1630s. Yet in 1620 the total number of English colonists living at different points from Bermuda north to Newfoundland could hardly have numbered more than 2,500, and their circumstances remained precarious. The beginnings of English colonization had sucked money and people out of England, and most of this investment was lost. The prologue to English colonization was no great epic of glory and success but an accumulation of distress, disease, and death.

French settlement in North America involved equal hardships, though its scale was small and its nature ambiguous. De Monts, whose Acadian venture has already been mentioned, faced the hostility of fur-trading merchants. Those associated with him in France disliked sending out settlers, and their rivals disliked the monopoly of the trade that he held. In 1607 he lost this; the handful of men in Acadia then left. In 1610 Jean de Poutrincourt returned to Port Royal with new settlers and supplies and worked hard to establish a proper colony, planting crops and erecting a gristmill. Poutrincourt's son took over the settlement in 1611, and men and supplies were sent out. In 1614 an English force from Virginia sacked Port Royal, claiming that it infringed on English territory. A handful of French remained, but they acted as middlemen in fur and fish for La Rochelle merchants. No new settlers arrived between 1618 and 1623.

By this time, a second French colony existed in North America. Quebec, inextricably linked with the name of its founder, Samuel Champlain, was established in 1608 by a small party sent out by De Monts. Champlain, their leader, had turned to extraordinary maritime ventures at the end of the Wars of Religion. In 1599 he sailed with the Spanish treasure fleet to the West Indies, returning to make himself an authority on trade and colonization. His initial interest in Canada sprang from a fascination with the old problem of a northwest passage to the Pacific, perhaps via some inland sea accessible from the St. Lawrence, to which he went in 1603. A year later he sailed with De Monts's party to Acadia, subsequently exploring its coasts. He persuaded De Monts to subsidize the Quebec expedition in order to set up a fur-trading base and a center for further explorations of the "route to China by the north." In 1608-1609 he wintered at Quebec with 28 men, 20 of whom died. Supplies sent from France revived the little base, but its numbers were always small, perhaps some 16 men in 1616 and some 60 persons in 1620. No French family went to Quebec until 1617. The King named important noblemen as lieutenant-generals and viceroys of Canada, but they and the various merchant companies involved with it did little in France to foster the colony. Champlain himself presented ambitious schemes for sending families and soldiers to Canada in 1618; they received royal approval but little else.

In short, Quebec, like Acadia, survived merely as a fur-trading base and had none of the attributes of a true settlement. Indeed, the tension between the fur trade and schemes of colonization explains much early Canadian history. Many of the seigneurs—the gentry and lesser nobility—who interested themselves in North America, men like De Monts and Poutrincourt, had colonial ambitions, seeing themselves as successful landlords over a French colonial tenantry. The earliest complete survey of French activity in Canada, Charles Lescarbot's ***History of New France***, certainly endorsed the idea of colonization, though nowhere did the author marshall a reasoned and coherent statement in support of it. Rather he made incidental, scattered remarks about its value. Generally, too, French religious orders, whose representatives went to Canada as early as 1610, favored the idea of populous colonies from which they could draw sustenance in attempts to convert the Indians. Yet the gentry had to depend on merchant capital for the dispatch of settlers. This they could obtain only by gaining a monopoly of the fur trade which they sold to the merchants. The modest measure of the seigneurs' success is indicated by the fact that in 1620 one condition on which two merchants received the monopoly of Quebec's trade was that they should transport only the merest handful of families to Canada over fifteen years. The merchant point of view was positively hostile to colonization; they wished to restrict migration to their own employees, fearing that free settlers would establish their own trading connections with the Indians or otherwise interfere with their monopoly.

The other Europeans directly concerned in North America by 1620 were the

Dutch. Their interest resembled that of the French more than the English, for they wished to exploit the rich fur trade rather than erect populous colonies. Some Dutch merchants had begun to trade in Newfoundland fish and French furs not long after 1600. Henry Hudson's Dutch-sponsored voyage up the river named after him in 1609 and his report of the abundance of furs brought to him by New York Indians attracted men to the Hudson from that year onward. From 1613 there was a gradual rise in the number of traders left behind in New York to man a factory there, established first at Fort Nassau on Castle Island. Several groups of merchants held monopolies of the trade in these years, but none thought in terms of colonization. So, while Dutchmen lived in New York in 1620, they did so as temporarily expatriate traders and not as settlers.

Chapter One
The English Colonies Established

A. The vital years

By the end of 1620 England's American colonies consisted of the weak and unstable settlements along the James River in Virginia, about 1,500 more comfortably situated men and women on the island of Bermuda, and the hard-pressed Pilgrims at Plymouth. As an outcome of the efforts expended on colonization, in terms of money spent and lives lost, this was no very considerable achievement. Yet optimism and activity had persisted despite setbacks. The idea of colonization now gripped mens' imaginations, and the conviction that Virginia and other settlements could become profitable and prestigious was growing in influence. The years after 1620 were to be vital ones that saw the translation of these hopes into results. Hakluyt's vision of an English seaborne empire became reality. Many new English settlements were established in the New World and thousands of English crossed over the Atlantic; some survived to people them.

In the 1620s the main thrust of English effort turned to the Caribbean, where the Elizabethans had fought but not settled. The lure of gold had taken would-be colonists to Guiana and the Amazon. One of these, Thomas Warner, landed on St. Christopher in 1622 during his homeward journey. His favorable report of the island's potential for tobacco and other tropical crops brought him the backing of English merchants, and he returned there in 1624, establishing the first English settlement in the West Indies. Shortly afterward, Barbados was explored by men from St. Christopher. A syndicate headed by the wealthy Anglo-Dutch merchant Sir William Courteen then financed its colonization. Most of the first inhabitants were laborers sent out to work for wages rather than settlers receiving land grants. The rapid success of these and other early West Indian colonies arose from their tobacco production, profitably sold by Dutch and English merchants.

From these two bases, Nevis was settled in 1628 and Antigua and Montserrat in 1632. The same years saw fruitless expeditions to other West Indian islands, also under the aegis of English promoters anxious to profit from the weakening Spanish surveillance of the Caribbean, itself the result of Dutch attacks. Indeed, the 1620s and 1630s were marked by a general European onslaught on Spanish power, in which the revival of English colonial fortunes, spearheaded by anti-Spanish Protestant enterprisers, was but one part.

Many English colonial schemes did not succeed. Permanent settlements arose only where initial efforts were followed by substantial English migration. What was remarkable about the 1620s and 1630s was the exodus of thousands of English to the New World. Rough calculations suggest that some 25,000 or 30,000 English went to the new Caribbean possessions by about 1640. Thousands also embarked for Virginia and Massachusetts, where a new colony was established in 1629. This great increase in the numbers of English stands, of course, in marked contrast to the years before 1620.

The "great migration," as it has been labeled, of 1620-1642 was, in the words of Carl Bridenbaugh, its best and most recent chronicler, a swarming of the English, some 58,000 of whom "ventured across the Atlantic Ocean to the strange new lands on the continent of North America or to certain small, hitherto unoccupied islands in the Caribbean Sea." In fact, the significance of this migration can be exaggerated, for it averaged only about 2,600 per year over twenty-two years, with (from 1629-1640) an average of some 1,600 per year going to New England. Migration from Spain to its empire probably averaged 2,000 per year through the whole of the sixteenth century. Figures for French migration are incomplete. In 1650 the French in the West Indies were stated by a contemporary to number 15,000 to 16,000. Our general knowledge suggests these were the survivors of the many more who had probably made the journey.

The great migration has been viewed by some historians as the result of extraordinary dislocations in English society causing men and women to seek an escape to the New World. Yet much evidence suggests that a major part of this migration can be better explained as the outcome of increased efforts by merchants, sea captains, and other entrepreneurs to attract and tranship new settlers to the Americas. In 1619, for example, purely by the use of vigorous recruiting methods, the Virginia Company brought 1,200 immigrants to that colony. After 1620, methods of promoting migration became businesslike and effective in response to demands for settlers from old and new colonies. The demand for migrants was a demand for laborers to grow cash crops, especially in the West Indies and the Chesapeake. In the early stages of the migration, attempts were made to avoid payment for labor. English authorities were solicited to empty their poorhouses and prisons and ship their inmates to America. Once tobacco planting became profitable in Virginia and the potential of West Indian agriculture apparent, investors were willing to advance capital to pay for the recruitment of workers. Growing demand for shipping and labor benefited European commercial interests and led to further efforts to promote migration. To the money provided by English investors, colonial planters later contributed funds for the recruitment and shipping of additional workers, using either their cash profits, commodities, personal or borrowed capital, or colonial lands provided for the purpose by the governments they controlled.

In Virginia from 1618, fifty acres of land were granted under the "head-right" system to every settler or to every person who imported a settler or servant into the colony. Many false claims seem to have been allowed, and the practice was virtually abolished in 1699. Yet the availability of land in Virginia during the seventeenth century meant that most males might eventually hope to become freeholders; there were few nonservile, landless men.

In Barbados, early development was financed by a commercial syndicate that paid for the export of workers. Although a policy of land grants was later introduced, relatively few men benefitted. By 1638 some eighty-five thousand acres had been granted to about 764 planters; by 1680 only some 3,000 men held land. Given the value and shortage of cultivatable land, few of the tens of thousands who came as servants can have received the ten acres each that their indentures promised them on completion of their time. True, in the Leeward Islands there was more land for distribution, and in Jamaica's early years every settler was entitled to thirty acres plus thirty acres for each member of his household, including servants. But on the whole, the later conversion of the West Indies to sugar production meant their end as colonies of true settlement and their development as slave societies. By the end of the seventeenth century at the latest, North America, rather than the Caribbean, beckoned settlers from Europe.

Of the English end of the migration business, too little is known. The Virginia Company certainly used handbills, ballads, sermons by friendly ministers, and other means of cheap mass advertising to persuade the ordinary man and woman that the crock of gold could be found in America. The large merchants doubtless had their own methods. The majority of emigrants were probably recruited and shipped by individual or small merchant partnerships using pack-horse men, peddlers, carriers, and other agents to reach the villages and towns of England with news of the benefits to be gained by venturing overseas. Probably, too, many young men were recruited in the seaports where they had already drifted in search of adventure and employment. One vital point to remember is that the English were not a particularly settled nation. For most emigrants, the distance across the Atlantic and the virgin soils to be expected there were "the only new factors. . . . They and their families were already accustomed to migration; emigration held few additional terrors."

The argument that an unusual deeper crisis made emigration attractive has to be considered. Of course, social, political, and religious discontents did exist. Economic depression, decline in the traditional cloth industry, epidemic disease, and unemployment all joined with political and religious grievances to form the subject of contemporary comment. Their relevance, at least to the stream of migration to the Chesapeake and the West Indies, is uncertain. That they were grave enough in their effects or in the way men saw them to bring about the great migration is unlikely. The absence of distress might have inhibited migration—as it did in the United Provinces—but its presence is hardly a complete explanation of why migration took place. The active promotion of migration as a business seems to explain much of the exodus, leaving particular economic, social, political, and religious causes to account only for portions of it, particularly the exodus to New England.

Yet a considerable literature of tracts and books did exist, dwelling pessimistically on overpopulation, unemployment, high prices, crime, poverty, and other social ills. England, the propagandists plausibly claimed, would benefit by the departure of a "great and superfluous multitude" who might themselves prosper in a brave new world. These assumptions continued, of course, the Elizabethan propaganda for colonies and, published in writings often paid for by colonial promoters, were highly selective in their arguments. Aimed at the clergy and gentry and other members of the governing class—not to make them emigrate but to persuade them to encourage the humble and unfortunate whom they ruled to do so—they must have created a climate of opinion favorable to migration.

It is necessary to divide broadly the migrants to the New World into two sorts. By far the largest category was *servants*. These were usually young people—mostly boys and youths—without means who were shipped free of charge to the Americas after signing a deed or *indenture* which assigned their labor to their shipper for a period of years. In America the contract was sold for money or land to established planters and merchants. The servant received board and lodging and usually was also promised a grant of land and sometimes one of money and equipment at the end of his term. Like many other seventeenth-century colonial commercial developments, this was a successful adaptation of older forms—the apprenticeship system and the annual hiring-out of servants—to the new demands of English expansion. A similar system prevailed in France, where the *engagés* were sometimes known as *trente-six mois* (thirty-six monthers), the term for which they were indentured.

A second group of emigrants, smaller in numbers, though exact figures are lacking, were the *planters*, sometimes known also as *adventurers*. These paid their own way, "adventuring" their persons, money, and equipment. Many took their families and servants with them. The land that they purchased or, more often, were granted in America was theirs to farm as they wished. Some went to the Chesapeake; few went to the West Indies. The majority settled in New England; contemporaries record that households or even parishes departed in distinct groups from the same English town or village. Indeed, the New England authorities encouraged family cohesion, requiring single men to live in families and married men to bring their wives to the colony. These settlers, as we shall see, were probably persuaded to leave England less by the recruiting activities of commercial promoters and agents than by other considerations.

ESTIMATED POPULATION

1620–1660

Showing decennial percentage increases

W = White Population
N = Negro Population
% = decennial percentage increase

	N.H.	%	Mass.	%	R.I.	%	Conn.	%	N.Y.	%	Dela.	%	Md.	%	Va.	%	N.C.	%	Totals
1620 W	–	–	102	–	–	–	–	–	–	–	–	–	–	–	2,180	–	–	–	2,282
N	–	–	–	–	–	–	–	–	–	–	–	–	–	–	20	–	–	–	20
1630 W	500	–	506	*396*	–	–	–	–	340	–	–	–	–	–	2,450	*12*	–	–	3,796
N	–	–	–	–	–	–	–	–	10	–	–	–	–	–	50	*150*	–	–	60
1640 W	1,025	*105*	8,782	*1,635*	300	–	1,457	–	1,698	*399*	–	–	563	–	10,292	*320*	–	–	24,117
N	30	–	150	–	–	–	15	–	232	*222*	–	–	20	–	150	*200*	–	–	597
1650 W	1,265	*23*	13,742	*56*	760	*153*	4,119	*183*	3,616	*113*	170	–	4,204	*647*	18,326	*78*	–	–	46,202
N	40	*33*	295	*97*	25	–	20	*33*	500	*116*	15	–	300	*1,400*	405	*170*	–	–	1,600
1660 W	1,505	*19*	19,660	*43*	1,474	*94*	7,955	*93*	4,336	*20*	510	*200*	7,668	*82*	26,070	*42*	980	–	70,158
N	50	*25*	422	*43*	65	*160*	25	*25*	600	*20*	30	*100*	758	*153*	950	*135*	20	–	2,920

B. The settlement of New England

The progress of the Plymouth colony was steady rather than spectacular. At first, all the settlers worked for the colony rather than for themselves. Private land ownership was introduced in 1627 when the population numbered 156, including forty families. A profitable beaver trade developed, and after 1630 livestock was sold to the incoming Massachusetts settlers. Although the colony's debts were not finally paid off until 1642, prosperity marked the years between about 1626 and 1636. Nor were there any serious internal crises. Bradford's firm but fair rule brought him the confidence of the majority, and a potential dispute revolving around an Anglican clergyman, John Lyford, who arrived in 1624, did not have serious effects. By 1632 a second plantation, or town, had been established across Massachusetts Bay at Duxbury, and settlers' growing demands for land grants showed a vigorous society in the making.

While Plymouth grew slowly but steadily, other groups attempted permanent settlements elsewhere on America's North Atlantic coast. Sir George Calvert, high official and secretary of state to James I, resigned this office in 1625 when he declared himself a Catholic. At the same time, he was created first Baron Baltimore. In 1620 he had purchased land from the unsuccessful Welsh promoter of Newfoundland colonization, Sir William Vaughan. By 1622 Calvert sent men and supplies to a spot that he named Ferryland, south of St. John's, Newfoundland. In 1623 he obtained a royal charter for his projected Newfoundland province, now grandly entitled Avalon "in imitation of old Avalon in Somersetshire, where Glastonbury stands, the first-fruits of Christianity in Britain, as the other was in that part of America." Although the settlement survived fitfully, the proprietor in 1628-1629 transferred his activities to the Chesapeake. Ferryland was left deserted. A Scottish enterprise headed by Sir William Alexander, later first Earl of Stirling (and Viscount Canada!), a courtier, royal servant, and prolific poet, also received a royal charter in 1621. But the intended colony at Novia Scotia, as this region was patriotically called, did not thrive in spite of the creation of Novia Scotia baronetcies to finance it and an expedition which in 1629 repeopled Port Royal. In 1632, as part of a peace treaty, it was handed over to the French, the original colonizers of this area.

A third and more important promoter was Sir Ferdinando Gorges, a west-country gentleman-soldier, for many years "governor of the forts and island of Plymouth" who sought to revive the almost defunct Virginia Company of Plymouth. Gorges obtained a royal charter in 1621, incorporating some 40 men under the name of the Council for New England. The Council received the territory from 40° to 48° latitude, roughly the lands held by the original Plymouth Virginia Company. Gorges made intermittent attempts to send out actual settlers; these mainly failed for lack of capital. The Council acted predominantly as a land-granting agency to would-be colonial promoters; from it the Plymouth colony received grants in 1621 and later. Other notable grants, providing the basis for the later colonies of Maine and New Hampshire, went to John Mason, an East Anglian merchant who had been appointed governor of Newfoundland in 1615 and became a propagandist for the settlement of northern New England, and to Gorges himself. By and large, however, such transactions stimulated little actual colonization, rather leading to confusion over land titles within New England. Yet seen with developments in the Caribbean, they are evidence of rising interest during these years in fresh schemes of expansion.

Two grants by the Council for New England led to the establishment of Massachusetts. The first went to representatives of a group of Dorchester merchants. Dorchester, a small Dorset town, lay in a west-country area where interest in America had been strong for many years, largely as the result of its fishermen's annual visits to the Newfoundland grounds. The original land grant was at Cape Ann, present-day Gloucester, Massachusetts, where its recipients hoped to establish a permanent fishing village. Then the scheme broadened to include farming as well as fishing as the economic mainstay. An association of west-country notables, the Dorchester Company, organized to plan and frame the enterprise. Twenty of its 119 members were clergymen, and they introduced a firm missionary emphasis. Cape Ann was to become a Christian settlement from which the gospel could be taken to the Indians and to the miscellaneous English of the New England coast. Although two or three groups of settlers went out, the venture failed. But its governor, Roger Conant, led about 30 men, women, and children to a site some 30 miles south, later to be named Salem.

The leading figure in the Dorchester Company was the Reverend John White, rector of the Church of Holy Trinity in the town. Supporting Conant's move, he stressed that Salem should become a godly community, "a receptacle for such as upon the account of religion" would go to a "foreign plantation." White's continuing efforts again led to an important grant from the Council for New England. In March 1628 a new organization, the New England Company, superseded the Dorchester Company, receiving an area running "from ocean to ocean" from three miles north of the Merrimack to three miles south of the Charles River. The Company had some 90 members, including west-country, London, and East Anglian Puritans as well as conventional merchants. The formal history of the New England Company was not a long one. Less than a year after its foundation, it was transformed into an incorporated joint-stock company, receiving a royal charter and a new name: "The Governor and Company of the Massachusetts Bay in New England." The rights of self-government and the land title that now depended not on the Council of New England but on the Crown removed doubts about the validity of the original land grants and safeguarded the position of several hundred migrants who had already been sent out to join Conant's "old planters" of Salem.

There is no doubt that White's success arose from his contacts with influential men of similar religious views, Puritans who sought reforms in the Church of England, attacking what they considered relics of Romish rituals and church government that had not been expunged by the Henrician Reformation and which found growing official approbation in the reigns of James I and Charles I. Basic to the Puritan cause was an unswerving determination to promote disciplined piety and godliness, of a Calvinistic kind, among the English people; all hoped for the installation of learned, godly, and resident ministers in each parish. More extreme Puritans also wished for the ending of episcopacy and of ecclesiastical law courts and the erection of new forms of church government. Puritans could be found throughout England. The informal connections and relationships that existed among its leaders made Puritanism a national movement.

From the time of the founding of the Dorchester Company, more and more important English Puritans became involved with these New England affairs. White himself was a moderate, conforming Puritan. John Humfry, treasurer of the Dorchester Company, his close associate, also a Puritan, worked with him to set up the New England Company. Humfry later married the sister of the Earl of Lincoln, a Puritan peer and member of the New England Company. Lincoln's other brothers-in-law were Isaac Johnson, a fellow member and early migrant to Massachusetts, and John Gorges, son of Sir Ferdinando. Lincoln's father-in-law was the Viscount Say and Sele, another pious peer, whose "cordial advice and true affection" smoothed these transactions. Another prominent Puritan peer, the freebooting Earl of Warwick, promoter of numerous naval and colonial enterprises, was a friend to the New England schemes. Puritan clergy—including Hugh Peters, later Cromwell's chaplain, Francis Higginson, John Cotton, John Davenport, Philip Nye, Samuel Skelton, and others—were closely connected with the proceedings.

Within the ranks of the Massachusetts Bay Company, Puritan influence soon became decisive. To earlier Elizabethan views that "the countryes lying north of Florida" had been reserved by God "to be reduced unto civility by the English nation" and that "by the revolution and cause of God's work and religion, which from the beginning hath moved from the East, towards and at last unto the West, where it is like to end," English Puritans of the 1620s and 1630s added a special gloss. Under pressure from Laudian elements in the Church of England, they increasingly feared that church reform of the kind they desired was now unobtainable. Of New England they asked "whether God hath provided this place to be a refuge for many whom he meanes to save out of the generall calamity, and seeing the Church hath none place to left to flie into but the wildernesse what better work can there be, then to goe and provide tabernacles and foode for her against she comes thither." Possibly associated with such sentiments were millenarian expectations. Certainly many English Puritans believed that human history had now entered a final phase, and that great and portentous events connected with the second coming of Jesus Christ were underway.

Some of these opinions were shared by a group of East Anglians who met to discuss migrating to New England in 1629. One of them, John Winthrop, has left a unique record of these years. Winthrop was a Suffolk landowner, lord of the manor of Groton. His Suffolk estates were insufficient to meet the needs of his large family, and like other poor gentry, Winthrop sought employment in London and became a minor government official, afterward losing his post. So economic considerations joined with religious to bring him to Cambridge in August 1629. There, he and eleven other influential East Anglian Puritans pledged that they would go to the Massachusetts Bay Company's settlement in New England. They made this promise conditional on receiving permission to take the Company's charter and government with them. Shortly after, this was agreed. In October 1629 Winthrop was elected governor of the Massachusetts Bay Company; in March 1630 he boarded the *Arbella*, ready to sail to America. He took the Massachusetts charter with him.

In 1630 nearly 1,000 men, women, and children followed Winthrop to New England to join the Salem planters and the migrants of 1628-1629. Here was the beginning of an outflow that lasted to 1642. Initially, the movement may have been strongly East Anglian. Part of the strength of Winthrop and his circle was their skill as recruiting agents, arising from their intimate contacts among the Puritan gentry and clergy of the region. Yet later migrants came from all over Britain. One historian was able to trace nearly 3,000, of whom roughly 20 percent came from East Anglia, 18 percent from the Midlands, 19 percent from the west country, 26 percent from London and the southern counties, and the remainder from Lincolnshire, Lancashire, and Yorkshire. The family nature of the migration, with wives, children, and old people making the journey, stands in sharp contrast to the migration of young males to the Chesapeake and the West Indies. The New England settlers were generally staid and orderly, some migrating in groups from the same parish or community. With them went a high proportion of clergy. Most of the heads of families paid their own passages, taking their money and possessions with them, boldly investing their futures in the American wilderness.

In Massachusetts, because of the homogeneity of its early population, a firm structure of government and society emerged very quickly. In part, also, this resulted from the transfer of the royal charter to the colony. At the beginning, Winthrop and the other leaders suppressed its exact terms, but they never wholly rejected its governmental provisions, and after 1634 these became one basis of the Massachusetts constitution. The charter provided for the Company's administration by a governor, his deputy, and 18 assistants, annually elected by the stockholders or freemen; these officers and stockholders were to meet quarterly as a general court to make these elections and to pass necessary laws and regulations. By abolishing the requirement that freemen had to hold stock in the Company and by deciding that they should be able to send representatives—deputies—to the General Court, the path was smoothed for the transformation of a trading company charter into a frame of government for a populous colony. Where it could not be easily adapted, it was ignored. The full number of eighteen assistants was not chosen until much later in the colony's history; the assistants assumed a veto power over legislation; the government levied taxes, exercised civil and criminal jurisdiction, created corporations, and made war and peace. None of these powers were given or even implied in the charter. Nor were the freemen's election of representative deputies or a decision, made in 1631, that the qualification for freemanship should be membership in a gathered church, part of the charter. So, secure at least for the time being from English supervision, the colony's leadership constructed on the royal charter a complete and self-governing commonwealth. In the opinion of many historians and in the words of one, this represented a conscious effort to "establish a state of their own which should be free of all alien control . . . of [the] king and the English parliament." In doing this, their pre-eminent aim was not independence for its own sake but for that of godly religion and the protection of their churches against outside interference. The religious sentiments of the leading settlers were very rapidly translated into institutional forms. How far, in fact, a definite scheme of church government and ecclesiastical organization had been specifically envisaged by them in England is uncertain. What is known is that the practices—to a limited extent—and the ideas—to a greater extent—that became integral to the Massachusetts church way did spring immediately from England. A form of Congregationalism– originally a probably secret congregating of those who felt they were elect or saved in a separate group as a true church away from the ungodly parishioners—seems to have existed within some English parish churches. This paralleled some theologians' claims that the scriptures ordained self-ruling congregations of elect Christians as independent churches, views that were common among a section of Puritans. In America these ideas were extended and refined. The practice of Congregationalism, extraordinary and secret in England, became ordinary and open in Massachusetts.

The first church associated with the Massachusetts Puritans was founded at Salem in 1629 before the migration of Winthrop and his fellows. Some churches were established in the summer of 1630 after the coming of the Winthrop fleet. These were followed by numerous other creations as the number of towns grew; by 1645 there were twenty-three churches in the colony. From the beginning, the idea of the independence of each individual church and an agreed form of church government for individual churches seems to have been generally accepted. But the precise qualifications and privileges of membership took some years to define. By or soon after 1636 it was usual in most churches to restrict membership to the "godly" or "visible saints." To qualify as a "visible saint" one needed special proof, not merely of good behavior and belief, but of an active conviction, tested by cross-examination, that the applicant had received personal assurances of salvation in a conversion "experience." In this way, the sanctified members were set off from the ordinary congregation. They alone could receive communion and have their children baptized; the male saints constituted the ultimate governing body of the church. When the numbers of church members made up a large percentage of the population, as they did during the early years, this state of affairs could bring stability, discipline, and harmony.

Internally, authority in each church was committed to its officers. Whether these could finally be overruled by the body of members was not immediately a problem, and the officers, once chosen, had considerable powers. In theory, the officers were to be the minister, teacher, ruling elder, and deacon. The minister's function was pastoral, the teacher's doctrinal, and the elder joined with them "in those acts of spiritual Rule which are distinct from the ministry of the words and Sacraments." Admitting and expelling church members, ordaining officers, and presiding over church meetings were among his main tasks. The deacon had responsibility for the temporal life of the church—its money and other similar matters. In practice, there was often only a minister, and there might be two elders. The office of deacon never became very important. Uniformity in church government was imposed by the civil authorities, who also legislated to enforce church attendance and the payment of church taxes in the towns by all the inhabitants, not just the church members. In all these ways most of the features that the English rulers of the Church of England insisted were central to its existence—episcopacy and the episcopal ordination of ministers, the prayer book, and open communion—were rejected in Massachusetts. So were church courts, tithes, and all matters connected with lay control and presentation to livings. Yet the first settlers continued to claim to be loyal, "nonseparating" members of the Church of England, in communion with the godly within it and hopeful of its full reformation on the Massachusetts—the scriptural—model.

Simultaneously with the foundation of the churches came the shaping of communities and of local government. Although Winthrop himself had once imagined that one great town might be formed to accommodate the first settlers, this proved impossible. Many men indeed showed no particular desire even to join in forming smaller group settlements, preferring haphazard and individualistic planting. Others, perhaps coming from the same place in England, desired to remain together. The government quickly insisted on regulated settlement within discrete communities with clear boundaries. By the end of 1630 there were seven of these: Boston, Medford, Salem, Watertown, Charlestown, Dorchester, and Roxbury, and the number almost trebled in the next ten years. From the beginning these towns developed as political and administrative as well as social and communal entities. Some town constables were appointed in 1630, and all towns were gradually ordered and authorized by the

General Court to regulate their own internal affairs. A law of 1636 summarized these requirements, stating that the towns' freemen could "dispose of their owne lands, and woods . . . grant lotts, and make such orders as may concerne the well-ordering of their owne townes, not repugnant to the lawes [of] . . . the General Court; as also lay . . . penalties for the breach of their orders." They could also "chuse their own particular officers, as constables, surveyors for the high wayes, and the like; and because much business is like to ensue to the constables of several townes, by reason they are to make distress, and gather ffynes, therefore every town shall have two constables, where there is need, that soe there office may not be a burthen to them, and they may attend more carefully upon the discharge of their office, for which they shalbe lyeable to give their accompts to this Court when they shalbe called thereunto."

Most Massachusetts towns remained no more than agricultural villages for many years. Yet their boundaries were far-flung. With a population of about 500, Dedham, for example, had lands extending to about 200 square miles during most of the seventeenth century. The towns themselves had to regulate land grants carefully, therefore, or their tiny populations might disperse over these wide areas. On the whole, at least during the first decades, this was successfully done, and population growth was matched by orderly expansion and orderly division of communities. It was common practice for the inhabitants' dwellings to be constructed in a small nucleus of "house-lots" of less than an acre each. Outside this central grouping lay the lands granted to the villagers, usually in open fields divided into individual lots. One series of these would be provided for ploughlands and arable farming, another for meadowland and grazing, others were of marsh or woodland. Common lands were also set aside for general use. Since this distribution of land was made over several years, many men found they had several separate holdings in different "divisions," often at some distance from each other. In short, many of the traditional, even obsolescent, farming practices of the English countryside were re-created in New England.

As transplanted Englishmen from manorial, village, or town communities, the early settlers also re-established other English practices. Foremost among these was the agrarian self-government to be found in some English villages. In lordless communities men had met for generations to legislate village bylaws, fix agricultural procedures, and elect officers to carry out their orders. Even on manorial estates much self-government of this type existed. Since Massachusetts entirely lacked manorial lords or established gentry families, communal self-government rapidly developed there, continuing the habits of late medieval agrarian life in the New World. The adaptation and modification of English models, for example, resulted in the selection of a number of men—at first known as "Townsmen" or "Prudentiall men" or "chosen men for managing the prudentiall affairs of the town"—as a ruling body over the town. Their powers and modes of appointment varied from town to town. In time they came to be called selectmen and to be elected on an annual basis. Here the experience of Englishmen with select parish vestries and manorial and village offices provided the basis of a famous New England institution. Such familiar petty officials as town constables and surveyors of highways were also re-created in the New England towns, although the traditional office of church-warden, with its multitude of secular responsibilities, was not. A host of specialized town offices also emerged—surveyors of fences, overseers of the commons, surveyors of the pound, and others—in response to the particular needs of the new communities.

The New England towns stand in sharp contrast to the more dispersed farms and plantations of Virginia and the later southern colonies. They also diverged in character from types of settlement found in many parts of England, where either the nucleated village was not known or where enclosure and commercial farming had resulted in the growth of more compact and specialized farms at a distance from village centers. Indeed, as farming and landholdings became established, many New Englanders also became unhappy with the nucleated village-open field system. Marlborough was founded in 1656-1657 by men from Sudbury, one of the first New England towns, who now chose to establish compact farms. Eventually the sale and exchange of lands and other factors resulted in the general consolidation of landholding in New England and the disappearance of open fields.

While the New England town is recognized as a distinctive feature of the region, various explanations have been sought for its rapid establishment. A need for strong community defense against Indians now seems the most likely primary reason. But human preference for neighbors and neighborliness; a Christian emphasis on social cohesion and mutual brotherliness; a special Puritan desire to provide populous communities as the basis for gathered churches; and a special Puritan vision of a closely settled and therefore easily regulated, godly society rather than a disorderly and therefore potentially irreligious one straggling over a hostile wilderness have all been mentioned. One earlier historian fancifully argued that Anglo-Saxons carried the germs of this type of community around with them. Another countered that the towns "grew by the exercise of English common sense combined with the circumstances of the place." Most early European settlers in America preferred to live in groups rather than to spread themselves thinly over a hostile land. In New England, unlike the Chesapeake, the West Indies, or the St. Lawrence, there were no early economic reasons why they should not do so.

The idea of the ordered community may also have arisen from a nostalgic, incomplete vision of an Elizabethan society. For with other Englishmen of their day, Winthrop and his fellows regretted the passing of the great age of the Virgin Queen, seeing their own time as one of troubled decline. Was the myth of an orderly community with its open fields an antidote to the commercial farming and enclosure that was increasingly evident in seventeenth-century

England and much disliked by many unsuccessful gentry of Winthrop's type? Certainly the leaders of Massachusetts valued social order, emphasizing that the creation of a new commonwealth was not to deprive the better sort of their authority. A famous speech of Winthrop's on the *Arbella* emphasized hierarchy and subordination, while the colony's leaders disliked both annual elections and the number of elective offices under the charter. Hierarchical ideas were indeed especially attractive to men beset by anxieties of purse and status in England, as Winthrop was. Even the decision to link church membership and the franchise—a blow to the traditional correlation of property with political rights—can be seen as an attempt to buttress order with godliness. For most holders of property were also church members. The Puritan reformer's vision of the good society looked backward to a disappearing or imaginary age even while it called for the creation of a new and godly Zion in the wilderness.

C. The New England colonies

The growth of Massachusetts, impressive in terms of numbers and the successful institution of church and civil government, did not lack controversy and dissension. As Englishmen as much as Puritans, the first inhabitants had a healthy interest in political forms and powers. In 1634 the freemen forced Winthrop and his fellow assistants to publish the Massachusetts charter and to govern more in line with its provisions. From 1636 onward the freemen's representatives to the General Court, the deputies, pressed for greater powers in government. The governor and assistants tended to claim complete executive and judicial control as the colony's permanent rulers. They also sought a substantial voice in legislation as members of the General Court. The division of the General Court into an upper and lower house in 1644 recognized that legislative powers—even in a godly society—ought to be limited. But the assistants continued for some years to exercise extensive authority; their members generally included the wealthier, better-born, and better-connected Englishmen in the colony who expected and often received general deference.

Much political and constitutional thinking in Massachusetts rested on broader English ideas rather than on Puritan thought *per se*. In arguing that the governor and assistants received their power as rulers directly from God, Winthrop and his colleagues repeated seventeenth-century commonplaces. So, too, were the statements that government ought to be "mixt," with the "monarchical" and "aristocratic" prerogatives and authority of the chief officeholders checked only by the need for the "democratic" consent of the governed. To this argument, used to exclude them from other than legislative activity, the deputies could find few answers, particularly since the clergy generally supported the proposition with citations to the scriptures. Until the

1660s, at least, the lower house remained largely subordinate to the governor and assistants. Its members, however, had increasing opportunities to enter the ranks of the assistants, whose own political claims and social standing became less pronounced as the years passed.

This informal reconciliation between deputies and assistants also drew sustenance from more tangible matters. In 1641 the authorities consented to the codifying of a "body of grounds of law, in resemblance to Magna Carta" to be "received for fundamental laws." This "Body of Liberties," passed by the General Court in December 1641, did not affirm new principles for a remade, godly commonwealth as much as it did a suitably modified adaptation of various English rights to the new conditions in the colony. Indeed, an earlier attempt to impose a body of biblically inspired laws had been rejected, although their author was the revered minister of the Boston church, John Cotton. In 1648 the printing of the colony's actual laws was agreed to. Both measures lessened the apprehension of some freemen and deputies that the assistants wished to govern arbitrarily.

These laws clearly spelled out the rights of all groups in the colony. A basic political—although not legal—distinction remained between freemen, who still had to be church members, and nonfreemen. Yet even here an original tendency to restrict all political management to church member-freemen lost direction in the years before 1660. Nonfreemen were allowed a role—one that they probably played anyway—in town government, and proposals, though unrealized, were made in 1645-1646 to allow non-church members of substantial estates to become freemen. A basic difficulty for the supporters of godly politics was that the number of male church members declined in proportion to the adult males in the colony, leaving fewer men with more power and more burdensome and not always welcome duties. This also meant an increase in the numbers of propertied non-church members with cause to claim that they were being denied political rights to which their social and economic position entitled them. Yet among the godly, the belief remained strong that an end to the political supremacy of the church members would endanger the churches and destroy the distinctive character of a sacred commonwealth by opening government to the unholy. While in 1658 the General Court affirmed certain local rights of nonfreemen, two years later it restated the position that only church members in full communion might become freemen.

Potentially more serious was the threat of religious schism, itself often creating political strife. This even more directly menaced the chief end of the colony, its churches and godly unity. Roger Williams, an early critic of the religious establishment in Massachusetts, alleged that the churches there were impure and unscriptural since they remained willing to accept communion with the Church of England. Williams also argued that in their zeal to link church membership with political rights and in their exercise of civil authority over ecclesiastical matters, the colony's government attempted to match the unmatchable, the Jewish state of Old Testament times. He could have been a dangerous opponent but dissipated his efforts with attacks on other basic institutions, the charter and land purchases from the Indians. Without any real following, he left the colony in 1636, correctly anticipating a sentence of banishment. His attacks did serve to force the colony's leaders to define more precisely their civil and ecclesiastical position.

A more insidious and popular movement, hence more dangerous, was the spread of antinomianism in the colony following the arrival of a highly intelligent and skillful woman, Anne Hutchinson, in 1634. Antinomianism, basically a belief that the elect or saved Christian is not subject to the same constraints as the ordinary man and woman, can take several forms. Mrs. Hutchinson persuaded many persons that large numbers of church members, including leading officeholders and many clergy, were unsaved. This belief came to divide the important Boston church, attracted the governor—then the young but well-born Sir Henry Vane—and irritated those unfavorably regarded, particularly John Winthrop. Many of Mrs. Hutchinson's supporters were Boston merchants who probably also resented the government's restrictions on their commercial activities. There is no doubt that Winthrop and many clergy, including finally John Cotton, whom Mrs. Hutchinson greatly admired, rightly saw that antinomianism would lead to a serious schism in the churches and an upheaval that would have political as well as ecclesiastical ramifications. In a complicated series of events in 1637-1638, the movement was supressed and Mrs. Hutchinson and some of her chief supporters exiled.

Both Williams and Hutchinson exemplified a kind of radical Protestantism that flourished in extreme forms in England during the civil wars. There, a religious toleration, freedom of the press, and unsettled social and political conditions provided a hothouse for the proliferation of prophets and sects. In Massachusetts, calls for religious toleration were always resisted. Nor did the more creative and radical fringe of the English civil-war sects spread to Massachusetts, except perhaps for Samuel Gorton, known in New England as a "familist," who agitated against the Massachusetts authorities after 1642. Another threat came not from the radicals but from the staid and learned scientist John Childe, who joined other Presbyterians in petitioning the Massachusetts government for religious and political changes, particularly the enfranchisement of non-church members. Both men hoped to persuade the English government to intervene against Massachusetts intolerance. In this they failed. Their actions, like those of the Quakers after 1656, further convinced the colony's authorities of the need for orthodoxy and vigilance. By 1660 a politico-ecclesiastical ideology had evolved that provided consistent arguments against internal and external threats.

One of the greatest insurances against internal dissensions in the Bay colony was the ease with which dissatisfied groups could move out beyond its borders. This fact was anticipated by the scholarly recluse William Blackstone, who alone had previously occupied the site of Boston. He left the colony in 1634 or 1635 with the heartfelt cry that he departed Massachusetts to avoid the rule of the Lords-brethren as he had left England to avoid that of the Lords Bishop. Blackstone went to an unsettled region north of present-day Providence, Rhode Island. Roger Williams and a few other men founded Providence itself in 1636. Portsmouth was settled in 1638 by followers of Mrs. Hutchinson, who argued among themselves a year later, causing one of their chief men, William Coddington, and his supporters to leave the settlement and establish themselves at what later became Newport. A fourth plantation, Warwick, was established in 1642-1643 by Samuel Gorton, the quarrelsome familist who had been refused sanctuary in both Providence and Portsmouth because he challenged their incipient governments as he had that of Massachusetts.

These four towns, separated by local and personal rivalries, did not become formally associated for many years. In 1644 Roger Williams obtained a patent from the English government in which all except Warwick were mentioned together as legal civil governments. In 1647 all four sent representatives to a general assembly at Portsmouth; here a series of "Acts and Orders" were passed that provided for a sort of weak federal government, under which the towns continued to be very independent. At the same time, a common judicial authority was recognized. Yet Coddington led a secessionist movement from 1651 to 1654 that was briefly successful. Not until after 1660, as we shall see, did a basic unity return. Even so, the Rhode Island towns did have one very important common denominator—their inhabitants repudiated the New England practice of religious intolerance, holding that the civil authorities should not enforce conformity to particular churches or beliefs. For this they received the enmity of their Puritan neighbors, whose attacks on Rhode Island helped to promote the cooperation of its towns.

The origins of Connecticut also belong to the earliest decade of Massachusetts history. The Connecticut River valley was first entered by English fur traders from Plymouth against the opposition of the Dutch, who claimed the region. Later, in 1634, several men from Massachusetts also sought furs in the valley. Reports of the availability of good land there, probably combined with dissatisfaction over land grants in their own towns, led to the migration of groups from Massachusetts. These early migrants, with others sent out from England by Sir Richard Saltonstall, a leading member of the Massachusetts Bay Company, settled in and around the town of Windsor. A separate group from Newtown (Cambridge) also went to the Connecticut valley in 1635, beginning what became the town of Hartford. At the same time, in 1635-1636, a substantial group of other Newtowners and of families from Dorchester and Watertown also prepared to leave Massachusetts. Many of these wished to go for the same economic reasons as previous migrants seeking fertile river land. But political and religious discontents also underlay this movement. The leader of the Newtown group was the town's minister, the Reverend Thomas Hooker, who then disagreed with John Cotton's apparent approval of Mrs. Hutchinson and certain of her antinomian tenets. Hooker was also uneasy about the stricter admissions procedure for church members then developing in Massachusetts as well as the limitation of the franchise to these elect Christians. He preferred voting rights to be held by all professed Christian freeholders. Associated with Hooker were several other important men who seem to have disliked the powers that Winthrop, and those assistants who thought like him, sought for their order. From the emigration of this period eventually came the settlements of Wethersfield and Springfield and the strengthening of Hartford.

The beginning of Connecticut, like that of Rhode Island, consisted therefore of the settlement of several separate towns. It was complicated by English developments. In 1632 the Earl of Warwick granted land that he hoped to receive from the Council for New England to an influential body of Puritans then contemplating emigration to New England. On behalf of the grantees, John Winthrop, Jr., the son of the Massachusetts leader, was appointed to establish a colony at the mouth of the Connecticut River. Here he built a fort, naming the settlement Saybrook, a composite of the names of its most prominent sponsors, Lord Say and Sele and Lord Brooke. Warwick's grant was in fact recognized in Massachusetts by Hooker and his colleagues. They therefore cooperated in late 1636 with John Winthrop, Jr., in designing a temporary form of government for all the new settlements.

This 1636 form of government underlined the differences between the intending Connecticut settlers' ideas and those prevailing in Massachusetts, since it gave political rights to the undefined "inhabitants" rather than to godly freemen. But a similar form of "general court"—governor, assistants, and deputies—to that of Massachusetts was called in 1637 and 1638. Also in 1638, when it became clear that the English Puritans had lost interest in Connecticut, its leading men decided to erect a more permanent government. After dissensions lasting some months, what became known as the "Fundamental Orders" were passed in January 1639. This document, consisting of a preamble and eleven orders, remained the basic constitutional frame for Connecticut until 1662. Its differences from the Massachusetts charter again underline the dissatisfaction felt by many Connecticut men with the Bay colony's government.

A general court continued as the chief legislative, administrative, and judicial body in Connecticut. But the governor's terms of office was set at one year, although he could be re-elected after another year. Moreover, the deputies were given a larger voice in the choice of assistants than they had in practice in Massachusetts, and the assistants did not have a veto over legislation. At town level all "admitted inhabitants" had the franchise and could vote for deputies to the General Court. But to be chosen as a deputy, or to vote for, or to sit as an assistant, men had to be made freemen by the General Court. Both "admitted inhabitants" and freemen had to be "substantial and godly householders" but not necessarily church members.

These provisions undoubtedly reflected the ideas of Hooker given in a famous sermon in 1638 in which he stressed the godly authority of magistrates less than the "free consent of the people." For him as for most other seventeenth-century men, the "people" meant not the masses but the respectable and propertied. So while Connecticut's form of government was hardly democratic, it did give greater weight than that of Massachusetts to the idea of representation. In other ways, Connecticut resembled the older colony. Its towns and town government were modeled fairly closely on the Bay colony's, while its church order differed importantly only in the fact that the very restrictive admissions policy adopted around 1636 in Massachusetts was not necessarily followed there.

New Haven, on the mainland coast of Long Island Sound, also remained an independent colony from its founding until after 1660. Its origins lay in the migration to Massachusetts of a London clergyman, the Reverend John Davenport, and several of his parishioners, with their families and servants. Davenport, until he fled to Holland to escape Laud's ministrations, had been vicar of St. Stephen's, Coleman Street, a famous Puritan church in the mercantile quarter of the City of London. Many of those who accompanied him to America hoped to continue their commercial activities in a Massachusetts coastal town. By 1636, the date of their arrival, there were no suitable spots left for an independent plantation, and Long Island Sound was selected as an alternative. The main body of migrants, with families from Yorkshire and Hertfordshire who had now joined them, sailed to the spacious harbor at the mouth of the Quinnipaic River in 1638. Here New Haven was set up. In 1639-1640 the Hertfordshire group amicably left the town to found an independent settlement at Milford. At about the same time, a group of English migrants from Surrey landed in New Haven, moving on to establish the town of Guilford. Other new settlements in the same period were partly under New Haven's control—Stamford, Southold, and Branford. In 1643, for reasons of defense and security, four of these five towns—Southold joined Connecticut—confederated with New Haven to form the New Haven colony.

Economic considerations rather than political or religious differences had thus led to the third exodus from Massachusetts to result in the eventual establishment of another New England colony. Politically, New Haven's colonial government repeated the familiar pattern of governor, deputy governor and assistants, and town deputies. However, the General Court never became bicameral, and the deputies had no speaker. Church membership, a prerequisite for freemanship, was perhaps even more strictly regulated in New Haven than in Massachusetts, and large sections of John Cotton's biblically inspired laws, rejected in his own colony, were incorporated into New Haven's fundamental laws. The fact that New Haven refused to allow trials by jury in its town or colony courts has often been mentioned but seems not to have been explained. Town and church affairs generally followed the Massachusetts pattern.

Plymouth's early history after 1630 also reflected the influence of the

Massachusetts colony. Before 1638 a system of annual elections had developed in which the governor and a number of assistants had been chosen; the male settlers met as a kind of legislative body. After this date, "all the males who had taken the oath of allegiance and were heads of families and settled residents" could vote both for the governor and assistants and for a newly formed body, consisting of representatives, or deputies, from the various towns. But only freemen could be elected as deputies or vote for the governor and assistants. Here the Bay colony's institutions counted. But unlike Massachusetts, Plymouth never adopted a church-based franchise, and its churches probably admitted any applicant of good behavior rather than insisting on evidence of saving grace. Nor did its early legislation include the severe measures used in Massachusetts to safeguard its church practices, probably because these were largely unchallenged in the smaller colony. Sterner laws, based on those of Massachusetts, were passed later; in 1650 the profanation of the Sabbath and slandering of churches and ministers, and in 1651 failure to attend church, became punishable offenses.

The development of northern New England does not fit into the pattern of expansion so far described. The patents granted to Ferdinando Gorges by the Council for New England resulted in little actual settlement. But in 1639 Gorges obtained a royal charter for his lands as the Province of Maine and sent over a deputy governor. From 1641 to 1649, Gorges's officials exercised an active authority over Kittery and York, two very small villages. Then the proprietor died, and control from England disappeared in the confusion of the civil wars. In 1652, after a brief period of self-government, these settlements were taken over by Massachusetts. Maine's inhabitants generally consisted of west-country fishermen and a few gentry of no pronounced religious feeling. But if Gorges had had his way, the whole province would have become a great Anglican proprietary, with its capital at "Gorgeana," as he named the little hamlet of Agamentus on the York River. Indeed, in 1635, he had made a determined effort to have the Massachusetts charter revoked and to assume the general government of New England—under Laudian auspices. New Hampshire's origins can be dated back to 1629, when Robert Mason and Gorges divided their joint holdings, giving Mason the territory south of the Piscataqua River. This had been settled by a few fishermen in 1623 under the direction of Gorges's and Mason's Laconia Company. Mason died in 1635, leaving his estates to a grandson, Robert Tufton Mason, whose claims were virtually abandoned until forty years later. During the intervening years, Massachusetts gradually extended its government over New Hampshire.

The solid center of New England, influential whether it provoked resistance, willing imitation, or grudging compliance, remained Massachusetts, a giant among the other colonies in population, in the wealth and numbers of her educated and ruling groups, with the region's major town and seaport. Among the colony's leaders, the large numbers of Puritan clergy were of special importance. Most were Oxford and Cambridge trained, some of great learning, some with other talents, some with a special interest in education. All were committed to the idea of a godly society as one in which literacy was general and opportunities existed for the transmission of learning. Mainly the products of an English Puritan insistence on an educated ministry, the clergy enjoined discipline, civility, and the hope of making New England an orderly society, a purer version of Protestant England. Not the least of their functions was the support of civil government and the suppression of both religious and political dissent. While this meant intolerance and repression, it also brought relative stability and an avoidance of much of the chaos that attended the early years of other colonies.

The particular concern of the ministers, the churches, were on the whole stable and effective nuclei of organization within the Puritan colonies. Here the gradual emergence of a supra-Congregational authority was relevant. Strictly speaking, each Congregational church was independent of all others; hence the importance of godly civil magistrates before whom church disputes might end. Yet churches were not slow to send each other advice. This went, for example, to the Salem church in large quantities when it supported Roger Williams. Indeed, the government frequently asked the ministers and elders of the churches to confer and report on difficult points of law and politics as well as of religion. During the Hutchinson crisis, an actual assembly or synod of "all the teaching elders through the country, and some new come out of England" was held by direction of the General Court and found eighty-two principles ascribed to Mrs. Hutchinson to be wrong. In 1646 the ministers of several churches successfully appealed to the General Court for another synod to consider problems of baptism, and representatives from Connecticut, Plymouth, and New Haven were invited to it. This Cambridge Synod resulted in the publication of "The Platform of Church Discipline" in 1648-1649, a document that "is the most important monument of early New England Congregationalism, because it is the clearest reflection of the system as it lay in the minds of the first generation on our soil after nearly twenty years of practical experience." In it a basic pattern of church relationships was set down and the power of the magistrates or the churches to call synods upheld. Any synod's directions, the Cambridge Platform recommended, were "so farr as consonant with the word of God . . . to be received with reverence and submission." It also affirmed the civil ruler's duty to "put forth his coercive power" in religious matters. So the independence of the Congregational churches was in theory and in practice generally limited by the overriding interest of clergy and magistracy in exercising a restraining, anti-schismatic authority.

A second important sphere of cooperation between clergy and civil government also lent distinctiveness and influence to Massachusetts. In 1636 the General Court appropriated £400 "towards a school or colledge." In 1637 a mixed group of magistrates and ministers was appointed a Board of Overseers, and a house and land purchased in Cambridge. In the same year John Harvard died, leaving a library of about 400 volumes and about £400 to the school that then took his name. Gradually, Harvard developed from a boarding school to an institution resembling an Oxford or Cambridge college. In 1650 it received a charter from the General Court incorporating the president and fellows. "The dynamic motive, to be sure, was to train up a learned ministry to take the place of Oxford and Cambridge graduates in New England, as they died off," Harvard's foremost historian has written. To which he added that the perpetuation of learning in its broadest sense was also intended, including history, law, medicine, philosophy, languages, and mathematics. Other scholars have contested this view, arguing that Harvard was first and foremost a Puritan seminary. Yet the evidence of its curriculum and the record of its graduates suggests that it was more than this, although something less than the Renaissance, humanistic academy that Professor Morison has sometimes seemed to depict. Harvard's early teachers gave instruction in several subjects—botany, astronomy, arithmetic, geometry, and Greek poetry, for example—but the core of the curriculum dealt with systematic divinity and ancillary studies. New England's stock of clerical and lay graduates was continuously replenished from within. Outside New England there was no similar institution for many years. Massachusetts, Connecticut, and New Haven, also, with mixed success, led the way in attempting to establish elementary and grammar schools. By 1660, in fact, the Puritan colonies had a high level of literacy and their standards of formal education and literary culture far surpassed what was to be found elsewhere in English America; no poet, for example, rivaled Anne Bradstreet, whose later writings are fine expressions of a quiet Puritan lyricism.

Church and town, government and governed, rested on the economic activities of the New England population. Of these, farming was naturally the mainstay, encouraged at first in Plymouth and Massachusetts by the need for food of the thousands of migrants who arrived until 1642. The end of the migration brought a slump. But Boston's merchants, active from the 1630s, discovered a demand for foodstuffs in Spain, the Canaries, Madeira, and ultimately the Caribbean, a commerce that was firmly established by 1660. Since this trade necessitated dependence on contacts in London, its development provided a counterweight to the notion of Massachusetts independence developed by politicians and clergy. Plymouth had no such overseas trade and never grew prosperous. Connecticut also failed to foster its own overseas commerce but exported produce through Boston. In many ways, New Haven contained the most ambitious merchants. They sought to extend their influence over Long Island and as far as the Delaware, sponsoring trading settlements on that river from about 1640 to 1660. These attempts proved fruitless, and the considerable original capital resources of New Haven's leading settlers suffered accordingly. Although some overseas and a coastal trade grew up, the great dreams of the firstcomers were unrealized. Rhode Island also remained predominantly a community of subsistence farmers, partly because of the isolation that the other New England colonies imposed on her and despite trade from Newport to the West Indies that began in the 1650s.

D. The development of the Chesapeake

For most Virginians, the years after 1620, in spite of the new, high rate of immigration from England, proved difficult and unhappy. From 1618 to 1624 "Virginia killed off between three and four thousand Englishmen. An estimated thirty-five hundred to four thousand immigrants increased the colony's population from about one thousand in 1618 to probably no more than fifteen hundred in 1624." In the rush to grow and sell tobacco, food planting continued to be neglected. All men who could afford them sought laborers to till their grounds, and a few rich men with many servants made fortunes. Others died from malnutrition and disease. In 1622 a devastating Indian raid killed 350 persons, and for the next two years the whites retaliated with equal savagery. A "census" of 1625 listed only some 1,218 inhabitants, 270 of whom were female. This unusual demographic balance meant that families remained scarce and that men, probably young and wild, made up a majority of the population; 58 percent of male Virginians were less than twenty-five years of age in 1625, and 454 of the 934 males and 52 of the 270 females in the colony were indentured or Negro servants. Moreover, by the 1630s many of Virginia's original leaders, men of gentlemanly birth, had died or returned home. Into their places as officeholders and local notables, rising from the ranks of the ordinary settlers, moved the tougher and more successful planters. With little gentility or social authority as yet, they were uneasy in their new roles, neither giving nor attracting deference. Not until late in the century would Virginia's social structure, either demographically or hierarchically, take on a more normal shape.

Political difficulties compounded these problems. In England disagreements between two powerful members, Sir Edwin Sandys and Sir Thomas Smith, and their followers split the Virginia Company. Members joined battle over a proposed contract between the English government, Virginia, and Bermuda for the supply of tobacco to England. The violent passions aroused attracted official concern, led to a royal investigation, and finally in 1624 to the dissolution of the Company. This drastic act recognized the inability of the Company's members to control both their own affairs and those of Virginia, whose progress had been so lackluster. In the place of company rule came a reversion to royal government—but to royal government without a royal charter. In Virginia under the new system, the colony's government was carried on by a royally appointed governor and council answering to the Privy Council.

No mention was made of a colonial assembly. (After the death of James I, two new English committees were appointed by the Privy Council, one to consider Virginia's government, the other its tobacco trade.) Henceforward, the Crown, through its commissions and instructions to the governors of Virginia, regulated the constitutional structure of the colony.

Yet the transition to royal government did not create great changes in Virginia itself. The assembly had first met in 1619. It probably did so in 1620, certainly in 1621, possibly in 1622 and 1623, and certainly in 1624. Already championing the cause of local self-government, its members begged commissioners sent by the Crown, in connection with the dissolution of the Virginia Company, that the council might continue to advise and the assembly to exist under the new royal governor. The assembly, its members suggested, should be able to authorize both the levying and the utilization of "any taxes or ympositions upon the colony, their lands or commodities." Although no formal assembly now met for several years, the governor did in fact summon conventions of settlers in 1625, in 1628, and in most years afterward. At first, these acted not as legislative bodies but as forums to discuss special questions, such as tobacco exports to England. After about 1630 there is evidence that the conventions gradually transmuted themselves into houses of burgesses, passing laws and doing some business on their own initiative. The King showed a willingness to accept this state of affairs and in 1639 instructed the governor to summon a representative assembly every year, reserving a veto power to himself. In doing this, Charles I was certainly meeting the wishes of Virginians. Requests and petitions had been drawn up on many occasions after 1624 asking for a restoration of the assembly and the colony's "old" privileges. Self-government, in other words, had early become a Virginian ideal.

While the assembly remained weak and doubtful of its authority, the Virginia council asserted itself against the royal governor. Although appointed by the Crown, its members were ambitious planters, ready to push local interests, especially their own. The rising tobacco barons who sat on the council favored territorial expansion, private acquisitions of colony lands, and local government untrammeled by English regulations. In this they pursued their own prosperity, for tobacco ate up the fertility of the soil and made the cultivation of new lands necessary. The most striking evidence of this situation occurred during the governorship (1630-1639) of Sir John Harvey, who sought to control tobacco planting, introduce new crops and—partly to pacify the Indians—prevent the expansion of settlement. The council opposed Harvey vigorously, treating him merely as a chairman, never as a governor, he complained. In 1635 Harvey was forced out of office and sailed for England; the council illegally chose an interim successor. Although Harvey later returned, his remaining years of office were also spent in disputes with his councillors.

A rapidly increasing population and pressures for the expansion of settlement provided the context of these arguments. By 1630 Virginia's population had almost doubled from that of 1625 to about 3,000 persons. In 1640 it numbered perhaps 10,000 and twenty years later some 27,000, a growth one authority has called "explosive and uncontrolled." For by the 1630s, food supplies kept up with population mainly because Harvey had forced agricultural production and diversification on the planters. Moreover, an acceptable form of local government evolved during the same years; eight counties became the main units of local administration in 1634. Central to each of them was a county court, able to hear a variety of common and less serious cases both civil and criminal. As in England, the county justices of the peace also sat as a virtual board of administrators, enforcing legislation dealing with routine matters of local government. The sheriff, whose office tended to be occupied in turn by the county J.P.s, exercised not only police functions but collected taxes, some royal or proprietary revenues, supervised elections and made election returns, and generally administered the county courts. His was an office of considerable power and profit. By law the county militia was controlled by a separate officer. In fact, the ordinary militia officers, often themselves J.P.s or burgesses, tended to run its affairs, an indication of the way in which a county elite—often the same men held positions as J.P.s, militia officers, representatives to the assembly, and vestrymen—now tended to appear.

The office of vestryman came with the creation of Church of England parishes in Virginia, a process beginning around 1618. Both the Company and the Crown gave some support to the growth of the church, and acts of the council and assembly gradually provided a legal structure for it. Yet there was no great fervor for its rites and organization in the colony. Many early settlers were Puritans, and the Anglican church emerged with many low church features. That no pressing demand for Congregational or Presbyterian government developed was probably due less to the attractions of the Anglican system than to the paucity of clergy and to a general indifference to religion. The first parishes were extremely large and the numbers of clergy very small, making any form of church organization difficult. But the parishes did have an official governing body, the vestry, which also became a force in local government, responsible for the collection of parish taxes and the supervision of aspects of parish life under the authority of the county court and the assembly. The greatest break with English precedents came as the vestry assumed the power of appointing and dismissing the parish clergyman, who, in England, was officially inducted by the bishop, often had a freehold in his incumbency, and was certainly formally independent of the vestry. Yet most English church livings in fact were owned by lay patrons whose clerical nominees received semi-automatic episcopal sanction and usually paid attention to the prejudices of their benefactors. In Virginia the vestry soon came to include the leading gentlemen of the parish, and it is possible to see it as a kind of more powerful lay patronate than the English one.

The geographical expansion of Virginia before 1660 can be closely traced.

Seven of the original eight counties of 1634 were on the James River and one on the eastern shore of Chesapeake Bay. Westward expansion was temporarily checked after this. The next two counties formed in 1637, Nansemond and lower Norfolk, were south of the James and east of the Chowan rivers. By the 1640s settlement began to build up between the Potomac and Rapahannock rivers. From Northumberland County, created in 1645, came three subdivisions: Lancaster County (1651), Westmoreland (1653), and Rapahannock (1656). At the same time, the area north of the York River also attracted settlers, becoming Gloucester County in 1651. Inevitably, this expansion brought clashes with the Powhatan Confederacy of Indians in Virginia, with whom the settlers always had uneasy relations, with killings on both sides. The 1622 Indian attack had resulted in the death of about a third of the settlers. This gave strength to those white leaders who opposed suggestions that the Indians be respected and converted to Christianity. They now saw, wrote John Smith, "just cause to destroy them by all meanes possible," and bitter reprisals followed. Another major conflict in 1644 and years of harassment brought an abrupt decline in Indian numbers.

While Virginia's settled areas gradually expanded in the 1640s and 1650s, one part of the Chesapeake was no longer available to the colony. In 1632 the King had made Cecilius Calvert, second Baron Baltimore, proprietor of a territory with its southern boundary on the south bank of the Potomac River and from there extending eastward across Chesapeake Bay. Its northern line passed along the fortieth parallel from Delaware Bay west to the source of the Potomac. In this way, the ambition of several Virginians to occupy Chesapeake Bay and to extend their colony northward was thwarted, and a second government established in the region. "Mariland," according to its founder, was so called "in memory and honor of the Queene." The name was also emblematic, since the Calvert family was Catholic. Their intention of making Maryland a Catholic refuge looked back, perhaps knowingly, to the schemes associated with the first great individual American proprietor, Sir Humphrey Gilbert.

The real founder of Maryland was Cecilius Calvert's father, George, the first baron. His abortive Newfoundland venture of Avalon has been described previously. In 1628 he visited Virginia, where he was refused a land grant because of his religion. His death in 1632, a few months before the King's grant, prevented this active promoter from realizing his many years' strivings. But Cecilius carried out his father's intentions. In November 1633 the ships *Ark* and *Dove* set sail from Cowes, carrying two or three hundred persons, including Cecilius's brother, Leonard Calvert, as his deputy governor. The ships arrived first in Virginia, then sailed on to the Potomac, then to an Indian town later named St. Mary's, which the settlers made their headquarters. With them were two Jesuits; mass had already been celebrated when the ships arrived on the Potomac. Yet these first flowers of Catholicism in English America did not bloom in entirely sympathetic circumstances. Some of the first settlers were undoubtedly Protestants. And from the beginning, the Calverts recognized that any substantial emigration from England—on which the future of Maryland depended—must include many Protestants. For this reason Cecilius instructed his brother to maintain good relations with the Protestant colonies in New England, New Amsterdam, and Virginia and not to allow Catholics to enter into debates over religion.

The establishment of a Catholic colony meant a new departure in the English settlement of America. Baltimore's plans for landholding and government also differed from those of other existing colonies. First, his charter constituted him proprietor of Maryland, holding his lands and his authority in the same manner as the lord bishop of Durham had "at any time heretofore." This gave him the virtually absolute, princely powers of a fourteenth-century lord palatine, with justice and administration stemming not from the King but from the proprietor. Baltimore could also grant land in feudal style with himself rather than the Crown as effective seigneur. In short, he had greater powers in Maryland than a seventeenth-century monarch in England and little to fear from that monarch's direct interference with his authority. Second, Baltimore determined to allot land and responsibility to his colonists so as to create a system of manors and freeholds held from him in feudal tenure. The old religion and the old forms of landholding, both declining in England, thus found a brave new world. Baltimore in his ways was as utopian as Pilgrims and Puritans had been, or at a later date, Quaker visionaries would be.

Baltimore granted some sixty or so manors, together with others laid out for members of his own family. With them were associated the manorial courts—courts leet and courts baron—now entering an era of decay in England, and other manorial practices. The proprietor also allocated many freehold tenements for ordinary settlers. In this way the title of freeholder, soon to take on anti-manorial and anti-magnate connotations, appeared in early Maryland. Moreover, Baltimore's charter specified that the proprietor call an assembly of freemen (or their deputies) and make laws with their advice and consent. Here lay the seeds of proprietary weakness. As early as 1635 an "unofficial" assembly tried to contravene the proprietor's insistence that he announce legislation and the assembly either assent or dissent. Although the first legal assembly and later ones were dominated by Calvert's own followers, freemen delegates in the assembly as early as 1642 asked to sit separately from the proprietor's councillors and appointees and conducted themselves in parliamentary fashion.

By 1640 Maryland's population numbered about 2,000; it grew mainly by immigration to about 8,000-12,000 in the next twenty years. Its economy resembled Virginia's, although tobacco growing was perhaps accompanied by more general farming than was the case in the southern colony. Besides the uncertain jurisdiction of the manorial courts—losing their importance by 1660—the colony was gradually divided, like Virginia, into counties which were subdivided into the hundreds, a type of administrative unit found but not much utilized in Virginia. While the manorial system survived, the county court probably had a judicial rather than administrative function. But by 1650, writes the leading historian of the southern colonies, "the institution had acquired a position in the government of the Maryland colony comparable in all important particulars to that of the county court in Virginia," and the administration of each new county was entrusted to a chief magistrate and board of commissioners.

The government of the proprietor over Maryland was a troubled one. Early opposition to the Maryland grant by Protestant Virginians, spearheaded by William Claiborne, an ambitious merchant, led to armed disputes within the colony as well as to challenges to Baltimore in the English courts. On the Catholic side, the Jesuit order tried to enlarge its influence in Maryland with land purchases and moves toward establishing the Catholic church and canon law that threatened the proprietor's wish for toleration. Most challenging of all was the growth in the numbers and assertiveness of Protestant settlers who gained an early superiority in the assembly and soon became aggressively anti-Catholic. Since the Catholic proprietor, his family, and friends held more or less all the chief offices in the colony, forming a closed oligarchy, the resentment of propertied and rising planters was to be expected. It resembled the opposition of similar Virginians to Harvey and other governors. In both colonies, internal strains and conflicts soon became enmeshed with new tensions caused by the outbreak of civil war in England.

E. The colonies and the English civil wars

The outbreak of civil war in England in 1642 caused many men from New England and some from the Chesapeake to return to the mother country eager for a part in the struggle. But only in Virginia did the colonial authorities take sides. There Charles I's previous generosity in permitting the re-establishment of the Virginia assembly, rather than any real understanding of the English issues, brought him support. In England, the colonies were far from men's thoughts. Although the Earl of Warwick had become president of a commission, appointed in 1643 by Parliament to take charge of the colonies and their trade, it was not until the King's execution and the appointment in 1649 of a new Council of State that any real colonial policy emerged. Virginia's government was then ordered to obey the new English authority but refused. In Maryland, the example of the Long Parliament may well have caused the assembly to press for more independence in 1642. In England, Baltimore almost lost his charter in 1647 through Puritan pressures.

In 1651 the English government sent emissaries to the southern colonies. These met with the Virginia assembly in the following year. The result was the peaceful "surrender" of Virginia but on very favorable terms, for administration and legislation were left to the assembly, which also gained the right to appoint the governor and councillors. In Maryland, too, the assembly benefitted from the renewal of English interest. Baltimore had attempted to protect Catholics by passing an "Act Concerning Religion" in 1649 which forbade religious persecution and formally stated that any believer in Jesus Christ would be free from molestation. He also appointed a Protestant governor. The English commissioners, however, supported the proprietor's opponents, recently enlarged by the migration of several hundred Virginia Puritans who settled in Providence (later Annapolis) near the mouth of the Severn River, and dismissed the proprietary governor. Subsequently, in 1654 an exclusively Protestant assembly met and declared Baltimore's authority invalid, substituting a violent anti-Catholic edict for the Act Concerning Religion. The Puritans then defeated the proprietor's forces in an armed struggle in 1655, executed four of their opponents, expelled Catholic priests, and plundered their property. In this way, the normal English anti-Catholicism of the seventeenth century—political as much as religious in character—supplanted the proprietor's scheme of toleration.

In Virginia, the assembly also continued to increase its powers. It is obvious that the burgesses relished their authority and seized the initiative in new legislation, opening up the Indian trade to all freemen and revising the colony's laws in 1658-1659; they seem to have also encouraged territorial expansion. In 1658 the assembly renewed its claim to appoint all the colony's officers. In 1660 it even discussed "An Act for the Annihilation of Councillors." The assembly invitation to the royalist ex-Governor Berkeley to be governor again on the news of the death of Richard Cromwell may have similarly appeared as a confirmation of its strength as well as a shrewd anticipation of the restoration of the monarchy in England. Berkeley entered his post in March 1660; news of Charles's Restoration reached Virginia in the autumn of the same year.

Maryland's proprietor regained its government in 1657-1658 through the sympathetic ruling of Cromwell's advisers. The new proprietary governor, Josias Fendall, took office in February 1658. Yet Fendall then threw in his lot with Baltimore's enemies. At the news of the approaching Restoration of Charles II in England, he repudiated the authority of his employer and accepted a new commission from the assembly; that body declared itself to be supreme in the colony, perhaps in the name of the King. But Charles II squashed this new assertion of anti-proprietorial assembly power and confirmed Baltimore's charter and standing.

The result of the civil wars for the Chesapeake then seems reasonably clear. The weakening of the spring of government in the mother country allowed local interests and local factions to assert themselves. They did so mainly through the assemblies, which took advantage of the relative powerlessness and of the preoccupations of the English authorities—central and proprietorial—to strengthen themselves. In New England the situation was much the same. There, the King's defeat brought no protests as it had in the Chesapeake, and no English commissioners had to be sent out. The internal government of each colony, already largely independent of England, proceeded much as it had before, without hindrance. But local interests, even when they conflicted with those of England—over English hostility to New England's religious intolerance or Cromwell's scheme to persuade New Englanders to settle Jamaica—flourished and prevailed everywhere. Rhode Island, too, took advantage of the transfer of power to English Puritans to gain constitutional recognition of its unchartered plantation in 1644. So all in all, the twenty years from the calling of the Long Parliament to the Restoration of Charles II loosened the already weak grip of the English government on North America, providing ideal conditions for the firmer rooting of their local and particular institutions.

Yet it is also true that the same years saw important or vital English developments—or their beginnings—that were to affect North America. Cromwell revived the expansionist maritime spirit of Elizabethan England, seeking an entry into the Spanish monopoly of the South American trade as well as endorsing an anti-Dutch policy aimed at weakening the commercial strength of the United Provinces. In the 1650s came an attack on the Spanish in the West Indies and the seizure of Jamaica as well as the first Dutch War and a renewed English interest in the largely Dutch-dominated East Indies. Englishmen also challenged French privateers and French commerce; in North America this included the capture of Nova Scotia in 1654. Finally, the legislative expression of England's new commercial policy was of the first importance. The Navigation Act of 1651, "the first parliamentary statute that in any comprehensive way defined England's commercial policy," attempted to drive the Dutch out of the colonial carrying trade of Africa and America, although it had little actual effect at the time. While all these developments had little or no immediate result for the American colonies, they began an era in which English commerce and English markets were immeasurably strengthened. Restoration statesmen dismantled most of Cromwell's domestic reforms, but they carried forward and expanded his commercial and colonial policy.

Chapter Two

The English Colonies Established: The Second Phase

A. The Restoration, the English government, and the colonies

Apart from Jamaica seized from Spain in 1655, no important new English colonies were established in the Americas from the settlement of Maryland until after the Restoration of Charles II. The civil wars occupied Englishmen at home, and only in the 1650s was Oliver Cromwell able to turn his attention to the revival of English commerce and overseas expansion. Cromwell's death in September 1658 was followed by another period of great uncertainty, partly ended by the Restoration in 1660. In commercial and colonial matters, the Restoration caused no great break in the development of the past ten years. Many of Cromwell's mercantile and colonial advisers went directly into the employment of the royal government or continued to advocate the same policies to the King and his ministers that they had pressed on the Lord Protector. The Navigation Acts and the anti-Dutch policy that underlay them were re-implemented, and despite the coming of peace with Spain, Jamaica was retained by England. Moreover, the administration of trade and colonies by standing councils and committees, agreed to by Cromwell, was followed by Charles II. Within five years of the Restoration, in large part as a continuation of the mood of commercial and state aggressiveness that predated the return of the monarchy, Englishmen were again founding colonies in North America. A second phase of colonization had begun, during which some of what became the largest and richest English colonies were established.

Charles himself was interested in any method that promised to increase the revenues of the Crown, including the expansion of foreign and colonial trade to the benefit of his customs duties. He left control of these matters in the hands of his ministers and advisers, particularly his brother James, Duke of York, and Edward Hyde, Earl of Clarendon. With the fall of Clarendon in 1667, James's dominance over maritime matters increased considerably, but from 1660 onward both men listened to merchants and courtiers who advocated the development of England's commerce and its corollary, the destruction of Dutch trading power. In particular, James patronized and encouraged English attempts to wrest the African slave trade from the Dutch and sought through the Royal African Company to monopolize the supply of Negroes to English North America and the West Indies. It was among men close to the Duke of York that much of England's commercial and colonial policy during the next twenty-eight years evolved. Here was a difference from the first era of English colonization, when those closest to the Crown had been little interested in these matters and when many colonies had been founded or encouraged by political opponents of the Stuarts. Yet it would still not be true to say that the Crown conscientiously fostered colonial settlement after 1660, as Louis XIV and his minister Colbert did in France. The financing and administration of colonies was not generally the concern of the English state. But many politicians, merchants, and courtiers, men who helped make policy, showed a new awareness of and sympathy for colonial developments.

The extent of anti-Dutch feeling in these years needs to be emphasized as a major element in English attitudes to colonization and overseas trade. Holland had now replaced Spain as both the great example of a successful imperial power and as the supreme rival to be emulated. Both Parliament and Court united in an ambition to weaken and supplant the Dutch seaborne empire. "Delenda est Carthago" was a motto of the anti-Dutch leaders and "What we want is more of the trade the Dutch now have," their war cry. For this reason the House of Commons and the Crown could cooperate to bring about the passage of the most important commercial legislation to affect the colonies since the passage of the 1651 navigation ordinance. This legislation was initiated in an act passed by the Convention Parliament, shortly after the Restoration, and confirmed by the Parliament of 1661.

The first Navigation Act of 1661 reinstated the ordinance of 1651 with important additions. Non-English ships were prohibited from carrying goods to and from England's overseas possessions. For this purpose the colonies—but as an act of 1662 made clear, not Scotland, the Channel Islands, or the Isle of Man—counted as English. Other sections of the act prohibited the export from the colonies of certain "enumerated" commodities, notably sugar, cotton, tobacco, indigo, and various dye woods, unless they were taken directly to England. These were either commodities that English merchants did not want to be forced to buy from European middlemen rivals, that had special importance for English customs revenues, or that could give employment to English workmen. Except in the enumerated commodities, the act did not deny the colonies the right to trade in their own ships to foreign parts. Indeed it benefitted the northern colonies, whose main exports were not among those listed. Two years later, in July 1663, a complementary act (often referred to as the Staple

Act) prohibited the import into the colonies of any goods from any country unless they had first passed through England. Exceptions were allowed only for essential supplies, which included salt for the New England fisheries (but not for the southern colonies, which had to import their salt expensively from their northern neighbors), servants, horses and provisions from Ireland and Scotland, and wines from Madeira and the Azores. This act in effect recognized that the colonies were or could become a valuable market to be supplied by British merchants.

These and later acts provided a link between England and the different parts of her overseas empire. The concept of empire itself would increasingly be identified, not as in the sixteenth century with English dominion over Scotland, Wales, and Ireland and with English freedom from Rome, but with overseas trade and commerce based on maritime strength. In this empire, colonization remained a subordinate though important aim, for trade and defense rather than the planting or the well-being of the English overseas formed the primary objective, a point that Americans later came to resent. The acts also provided a point of departure for the rationalization of colonial administration. Their enforcement necessitated the dispatch, first of instructions and orders to the colonies from central agencies in London, then of a variety of English officials. Finally, together with problems of military offense and defense, they would cause the reorganization of government itself in many colonies. The Restoration state was piecemeal committing itself to a commercial and colonial policy, a significant event for the history of English North America.

This commitment was gradual, not always consistent, and subject to the general weaknesses of English government in the period. In the important immediate post-Restoration settlement, the colonies were in fact regulated very little and were granted political and religious freedoms denied many Englishmen at home. New England, the later bane of high Anglicans and high royalists, was particularly laxly treated. In October 1660 Rhode Island became the first colony in this region to proclaim Charles II king; Connecticut was the second in March 1661. Neither colony had certain title to its lands or governments. The first was the refuge of Baptists and Quakers, often seen in England as little better than seditious levelers, the second, of Congregationalists whose closest allies in England were now being ejected from church and civil office. Yet their agents successfully persuaded Lord Clarendon to confirm these colonies' rights and, indeed, won for them charters that were closely modeled on usages they themselves had developed or on ones similar to those of the Massachusetts charter. Special consideration was given to their religious freedom. Of Rhode Island it was allowed "that noe person within the colonie, at any time hereafter shall be in any wise molested, punished, disquieted or called in question for any differences in opinions in matters of religion . . . but may from time to time, and at all times here after freelye and fullye have and engage in his and their own judgements and conscience, in matters of religious concernments . . . not useing this libertye to licentiousness and profaneness, nor to the civil injurye or outward disturbance of others." Connecticut's charter contained no clauses detrimental to the Congregational system there established. In a strictly legal sense Connecticut was the first Restoration colony, and it was granted a charter based on the colonial practices of the English government in 1629 that made it as independent of England as any other existing colony.

Of the other New England colonies, Plymouth proclaimed Charles II king in June 1661 and New Haven in August 1662. Like Massachusetts, which had not persuaded itself to accept the inevitability of the Restoration until earlier in the same month, New Haven contained a substantial group of influential men who identified the Stuarts with Laud, the Pope, and Anti-Christ and also feared the political consequences of Charles's return. Yet both New Haven and Plymouth were too obscure and of too little consequence for the English government to take much notice of them. New Haven was in fact included in the new charter of Connecticut, though it is doubtful that the significance of this for the New Havenites was appreciated in England. Plymouth remained a separate, unchartered entity until the wholesale reorganization of colonial governments in the 1680s. Massachusetts received more attention and much criticism. Yet its treatment, too, was surprisingly sympathetic. Until 1666 the English authorities sought to persuade the Massachusetts government to stop whipping and hanging Quakers, to rewrite those of its laws that contrary to its charter were not consonant with the laws of England, to grant non-Congregationalists religious and political rights, and to admit legal appeals to the mother country. The colony was slow to respond to these orders but was neither punished nor seriously threatened with the loss of its charter and in fact escaped further action until 1676. From the considerable documentation and activity involving England and Massachusetts in the 1660s it is clear that the English government was quite prepared to tolerate the existence of a Puritan colony, provided it did not actively persecute religious minorities and did not act as a wholly independent commonwealth.

In its treatment of New England, the Restoration government may be said then to have generally accepted the *status quo* and to have preserved the continuity of American colonial establishments. The same was true of its actions toward Maryland and Virginia, the two other North American colonies. Maryland emerged from the interregnum in the control of Lord Baltimore, who had won back his proprietary control under the auspices of certain English Puritans in 1657-1658. By confirming him in his government, the Crown merely accepted the existing state of affairs. This was also the case in Virginia, where the royal governor had withdrawn from office in 1652 and was restored as governor by the assembly in March 1660. Charles regularized the governor's position by giving him a commission, and Virginia again became a royal colony. The political system that had grown up there was not changed; the

English government even refused to accede to a request from Virginia to strengthen, in a novel way, the Church of England there.

Since Maryland and Virginia were adversely affected by the Navigation Acts and the enumeration of tobacco, it can also be said that New England benefitted more from the Restoration than the southern colonies, a point that is paradoxical in view of the often alleged loyalty to the Stuarts of the Chesapeake region and the nonconformist, republican tendencies of the northerners. In fact neither the Chesapeake colonies nor New England had provided the Crown's enemies with effective aid during the civil wars and there were strong pockets of anti-Stuart Puritanism in Virginia and Maryland. It was only after 1660 that the idea of a cavalierish, loyal south as the counterpart of a nonconformist, leveling, roundhead New England was to grow.

Some of the uncertainties of colonial policy sprang from—or were reflected in—the post-Restoration machinery of colonial administration. Although in July 1660 the care of trade and plantations was first entrusted to a single committee of the Privy Council with a membership of ten men, this merely marked the beginning of a succession of councils and subcommittees that functioned from 1660 to 1672. For example, in December 1660, a large Council for the Plantations was established, with forty-eight members, that lasted only until 1664 or 1665. Neither it nor its successors achieved what was recognized in 1660 as desirable: that the trade conditions and governments of all the colonies should be investigated and where necessary made more uniform or more rational. In 1670 the government set up a Council of Plantations, largely along lines suggested by Lord Ashley (later Earl of Shaftesbury) and John Locke. Two years later, oversight of trade affairs and more detailed powers were given to it. It was, the King stated, "a Select Councill, whose employment shall be to take care of the Wellfare of our said Collonyes and Plantations, And of the Trade and Navigation of these our Kingdomes, and of Our said Collonyes and Plantations." It functioned not to make orders but to collect information and provide the Crown with "Opinions and Advice" so that higher authority "may the better be enabled to make such Orders, and give such Directions therein for the good and wellfare of Our People . . ."

The Council of Plantations was abolished in 1674 mainly for domestic political reasons. The range and vigor of its activities had been much greater than its predecessors, and powerful politicians—in particular the Earl of Shaftesbury—frequently attended its meetings. The "instructions given to the Council in 1672 were the most detailed of any issued to trade or colonial councils of the first British Empire" and constituted a prototype for later administrators. They called for the collection of information about the colonies, for oversight of colonial proceedings to make sure not only that trade regulations but the terms of their charters were observed. The Council's successor was an even more powerful body, the Lords Commissioners of Trade and Plantations, holding executive and policy-making powers, for it was a standing committee of the Privy Council. It also had permanent quarters and a secretary and clerks for its day-to-day business. During these years a more consistent, vigorous, and firm colonial policy emerged, in part because of issues raised in America, in part because of a more sustained attention to the colonies on the part of Charles II and his brother the Duke of York, who succeeded him as James II in 1685. There was also growing continuity in colonial administration and colonial business provided by the divergent persons of James himself; of Shaftesbury, who maintained a steady interest from 1646, when he invested money in Barbados, to his exile in 1682; and of influential functionaries associated with trade and colonial administration: William Blathwayt, Sir Robert Southwell, Edward Randolph, and various members of the Povey family, all of whom constituted the beginnings of an imperial civil service.

Commercial considerations—the enforcement of the Navigation Acts—naturally occupied the English authorities. Strictly speaking, enforcement of the acts lay with another branch of the English government, the Commissioners of the Customs, themselves under the jurisdiction of the Treasury. Before 1671 customs officials had not been appointed for America itself, since the Crown's advisors generally assumed that most colonial trade would be carried by ships sent out from England and therefore inspected by the English customs. In the colonies, it was felt, the governors could deal with the collection of revenue and issue of bonds. But the growth of colonial shipping and the evidence that enumerated commodities were illegally taken directly from America to Europe led to the passage of a new Act of Trade in 1673. This gave Parliamentary sanction to the extension of the Customs Service to America, and the appointment of officials for Maryland, the Carolinas, and certain West Indian islands, as well as the reappointment of a collector for Virginia which followed. In 1678 a collector was chosen for New England. During these same years the Admiralty also became increasingly involved with American customs affairs, since royal vessels received instructions to seize offenders against the Act of Trade.

The Lords of Trade concerned themselves primarily with creating conditions under which the acts would be obeyed. This inevitably necessitated discussion of wider aspects of colonial government, especially the weakness of royal power in New England's corporate colonies and in the proprietary colonies. During the 1670s and early 1680s English administrators pressed for the rationalization and centralization of colonial affairs. Royal agents were sent out to enquire into affairs in New England, greater attention was given to appointments to Crown offices in the colonies, and in 1675 royal governors were asked to send a statement about the laws, offices, trades, and military situation in their colonies as well as to submit regular reports to London. Attempts were also made to collect copies of the proceedings of colonial assemblies. The personal interest of Charles II and of his brother in colonial matters (the Crown had an understandable wish to maintain or increase the flow of customs duties from colonial goods into the exchequer) aided these endeavors.

This Stuart involvement in colonial affairs reached its height in the 1680s. It was James who supported a great reform of colonial government, the creation of the Dominion of New England, a unified government of New York and New England under a single royal governor and council. Indeed James encouraged not only the cancellation of the first Massachusetts charter in 1684 but a wholesale attempt by his officials to revoke the charters of all the proprietary and corporate colonies. Ultimately the Crown might have sought to create three general and perhaps unrepresentative governments in northern, middle, and southern North America in the interests of a more efficient bureaucratic control from London, better enforcement of trade regulations, an increase in colonial revenues, and a more rational system of defense. These truly revolutionary designs were underway when James was forced to flee to France after William of Orange's successful invasion of England in 1688. Had the Glorious Revolution not curtailed these activities, James might well have been remembered as the most ambitious and adventurous colonial reformer of the seventeenth century.

B. The new colonies: the background

The years after 1660 also saw the founding of new English colonies in North America. In March 1663 Carolina was chartered; in March 1664, New York; and in June of the same year, New Jersey. The chartering of Pennsylvania in 1681 lies slightly outside of the Restoration period proper, but its origin has many similarities with those of the earlier creations and it may be considered with them for the sake of convenience. In reality seven of the thirteen pre-Revolutionary colonies took on legal identity or grew out of the transactions of the second phase of colonization, for Delaware later split off from Pennsylvania, and North and South Carolina emerged out of Carolina, while New Hampshire was given a royal governor and independent status in 1679. Georgia, the last English colony in North America, was founded in 1732. Carolina, New York, New Jersey, and Pennsylvania were all proprietary colonies, and their government was left in the hands of their owners in the beginning. Moreover, they were mostly large areas of land, with their boundaries loosely and grandly defined. In these ways, the Restoration government acted very much as its predecessors had, following the precedent of Maryland, the last North American colony to be founded before 1660. Yet there were also differences from what had gone before, particularly in the cases of New York and Pennsylvania.

Carolina had close links with the West Indian island of Barbados. One of the prime instigators of this colony's settlement was a Barbadian planter, Sir John Colleton, a civil war royalist exile. In this period the large number of small producers in Barbados were under considerable pressure from the rising population of imported Negro slaves and the engrossing of lands by the richer planters. Colleton's wish was to move the surplus whites to a more promising home and to enrich himself in the process. Fixing on the area to the south of Virginia as suitable in climate and relative proximity to the Caribbean, he formed an alliance with Governor Berkeley of Virginia. The two were both in England at the Restoration. Berkeley himself had observed the migration of Virginians into the Albemarle region (later to become North Carolina) and recognized the attractions of the whole area to the south of his colony. Other men had been attracted from New England to the Cape Fear region. Any owner of these lands might therefore expect a profitable migration of settlers to them from within the Americas, something that would save the expense of transporting colonists from England.

Colleton and Berkeley had useful contacts in England and quickly persuaded a number of important figures to join with them. Besides the Barbadian and the Virginian, there were six other proprietors of Carolina: Sir George Carteret; John, Lord Berkeley; Lord Ashley; the Earl of Clarendon; the Duke of Albemarle; and the Earl of Craven. Clarendon was Charles's leading minister; Albemarle was the ennobled General Monk who had brought the King back to the throne; Carteret and John Berkeley were close to James, Duke of York. These men were also members of the committees and councils entrusted with the administration of commerce, the navy, and colonies; and they were leading promoters of other colonial and commercial enterprises, including the Royal African Company, in all parts of the world. They formed a relatively small but highly influential circle. For the time being at least, new colonies were to be given only to powerful men close to the Crown. The days of the Pilgrim Fathers and the Winthrops and Calverts were largely past. Yet few of these men were driven by any urgent central desire to promote American colonization. Their interest in Carolina, with some exceptions, was that of absentee land speculators who hoped for a return in rents but whose livelihood and main concerns were far from the modest investments they made in Carolina.

The Carolina charter resembled very closely that of Maryland, including the grant of the considerable powers under the "Durham palatinate" clause. It also contained clauses providing for religious toleration and stressing trade and towns, for it was hoped that Carolina would be settled on a township plan, rather than Virginia-style in dispersed plantations, and that it would produce subtropical crops for cash export. The charter itself took the characteristic form of a grant from the King to the proprietors. In order to attract settlers, the proprietors now had to make their own grants to those who would come to the colony.

These proceedings were complicated by the fact that four different groups were at first involved in the colony's settlement. The Virginians in Albemarle were already in possession. Two other groups were Barbadians, and a fourth had New England connections. The latter characteristically sought virtual self-government on the New England model. Their demands were answered by a set of ''Declarations and Proposals'' issued in 1663 as a basis for negotiation that reserved powers of legislative veto, quitrents, and choice of governor, from a list to be prepared by the adventurers, to the proprietors. These Declarations were also sent to the first Barbadian group, and men from both groups settled at Cape Fear in 1664. But the proprietors never formally agreed to regard this document as binding. The other Barbadians proposed to settle at Port Royal further south, and with them a new ''Agreement and Concessions'' was signed in January 1665. This was also declared, with some modifications, to supercede the 1663 Declarations and to apply to Cape Fear and Albemarle as well as Port Royal. In fact, the original Cape Fear settlement did not survive and that of Port Royal never commenced. By 1667 the only English in the Carolinas remained the Virginians in Albemarle.

The importance of the Declarations and the later Agreement lay in the fact that they were the first of a series of such documents which became a familiar part of post-Restoration colonial enterprise, whether for Carolina, New Jersey, or other new plantations. The Declarations of 1663, for example, gave to prospective settlers the right to submit a list of names to the proprietors from whom a governor and council of six would be chosen. After three years, when the colony was established, its freeholders would nominate these officers. Laws would be made by an assembly, but the consent of the governor and council, and of the proprietors in England, would be required for them. Freedom of religion was also granted. Those coming to Carolina received headrights in land: one hundred acres for each freeman, fifty acres for each man servant and thirty acres for each woman servant brought to the colony in the first five years. Servants would also receive land (ten acres for men and six for women) at the end of their term of service, a provision to attract indentured persons. The inhabitants would support their own public administration, and the proprietors would be paid one halfpenny per acre in rents; twenty thousand acres would be reserved for them in each group settlement that was made. Later documents provided a sliding scale of land grants according to the time settlers arrived—early settlers got the most land—and allowed a period of some years before rents were due. The promise of substantial self-government, religious toleration, cheap land, and other privileges may be found in most of the comparable documents of the period.

A second stage in the early history of the Carolinas began in 1669 when the most active of the proprietors, Lord Ashley, undertook the reorganization of the colony. The prologue to these efforts was the famous ''Fundamental Constitutions'' written by Ashley or by his adviser, John Locke, or by both. Ashley also promoted a new headright system designed to compete with that of Virginia and other colonies in attracting settlers and oversaw the dispatch of a number of settlers in 1669 directly from England.

The Fundamental Constitutions and the revised land policy reveal that

Ashley had succumbed to the temptation to treat American territory as a *tabula rasa* on which a new society could be planned, reverting to the utopianism that to some extent was present in many colonial schemes, from those of Gilbert to the New England Puritans. A great Whig magnate with landed and commercial interests, Ashley was attracted throughout his life to the alliance of trading and territorial power that characterized the efficient oligarchies of Venice and Holland. Like other English Whigs of his day, he may also have been a student of the influential political theorist James Harrington, who subscribed to the view that the ideal constitution recognized the connection between political power and wealth and that a governing class not based on material superiority was doomed to failure. Ashley sought to establish in Carolina a mixed society of more numerous and less well-to-do freeholders, representing the democratic side of the political equation, and a smaller and wealthier upper class, a ruling aristocracy. Both freeholders and nobility would be equal before the law, and there would be religious toleration. The nobility would be strong enough to perform its role without either overawing or succumbing to the power of the freeholders. In his ideal scheme of things, he envisaged Carolina as a series of counties, each consisting of forty squares of 12,000 acres. In each county eight squares would be reserved for the proprietors, eight squares for the nobility, and twenty-four squares for the more numerous freeholders who would hold three-fifths of the land. But because they were more numerous, the freeholders individually would hold less property and would not be able to aspire to three-fifths of the power. Precedence in the colony would be held by the nobility: first the proprietors (if there were any in Carolina, or their deputies), then the landgraves (those men who held 48,000 acres each), then the caciques (the Spanish word for an Indian chief—those men who held 24,000 acres each), then the Lords of the Manor (with 3,000-12,000 acres each). Ashley also intended that the Carolina lands should be surveyed and granted in an orderly fashion, with proper provision for laying out towns and planned expansion. There were also provisions for various political devices, including a Grand Council, a kind of House of Lords, that would be comprised of the leading men of the colony and would recommend laws to a legislative body for its consideration. The legislature itself would be a mixture of great landowners and representatives elected by freeholders in possession of 50 or more acres. But to be elected, a representative must possess at least 500 acres. The preamble stated that the Constitutions provided "for the better settlement of the government of the said place . . . ; and that the government of the Province may be made most agreeable to the monarchy under which we live and of which this province is a part, and that we may avoid erecting a numerous democracy."

It has been pointed out that Ashley's elaborate schemes did include several shrewd promotional devices attractive both to men of wealth and to lesser men who might be induced to settle. They were not, as many historians have written, completely fantastic for American conditions. Professor Wesley Frank Craven suggests that the Fundamental Constitutions both allowed for the support of the Church of England and give liberty of conscience in order to attract Anglicans from Barbados and dissenters from elsewhere. That they encouraged the development of Negro slavery was also an inducement to West Indians and others who rightly believed that great fortunes might be built on slavery. Also, rich men were reassured of their political and social position by the institution of a powerful nobility and poor men attracted by very cheap land. The main deficiencies in Ashley's schemes were the elaborateness of the political system and his belief that land grants and settlement could be ordered and controlled in frontier conditions.

In fact the Fundamental Constitutions were never fully implemented, and the structure of government that developed in North and South Carolina soon came to resemble that in other proprietary colonies with a proprietary governor and council and an assembly of freeholders. Only a few landgraves and caciques were created, remaining more of a curiosity than anything else. And although Charleston was laid out in a planned manner, the general rule was for haphazard expansion and development. The political history of the early years reveals that local forces and factions frustrated the halfhearted attempts of the proprietors to implement their constitutions and utilize their legal rights of government.

The geographical division between the northern and southern parts of Carolina was not recognized in the Fundamental Constitutions, and it seems likely that the proprietors would have preferred a single form of government over the two. But from 1664 until 1691 Albemarle County and, from its foundation until the same date, the southern section had separate governors and assemblies. Although a common governor was then appointed, with his seat of office at Charleston and a deputy in Albemarle, the two sections preserved their separate legislative bodies. In 1701 the proprietors recognized the distinction between north and south by giving the former region its own fully fledged chief officer "independent of the Governor of Carolina."

The second new colony of the Restoration period was in many ways the most imposing of all the English colonies. Its creation was linked to high matters of state, and its geographical position made it a focus of imperial policy in the struggle between France and Britain for the control of North America. New York also was virtually a royal colony in the sense that it was established for the brother of the King, the possible heir to the Crown. Although exact details of the process which resulted in the grant to the Duke of York in 1663 are not available, a number of circumstances can be mentioned. The first is its anti-Dutch nature. The grant was indeed to be followed by the English conquest of the New Netherlands. Since the Duke of York was a leading antagonist of the Dutch and in the forefront of commercial warfare against them, the establishment of the English in New York obviously belongs in this wider context of English policy and activities in the 1660s. Indeed, before the charter was granted, a committee in London reviewed the military strength of the New Netherlands. New Englanders, too, had pushed into Dutch territory from the

1640s onward, though how much influence on English plans they had is uncertain; English policy here dovetailed with American realities.

A second important consideration is the size and extent of the territory granted to James. It was considerably more than what the term "New York" now connotes, for it included Maine between the Sainte Croix and Kennebec rivers running to the St. Lawrence, Martha's Vineyard and Nantucket Island, Long Island, and all the region between the Connecticut and Delaware rivers running north to include Fort Orange (later Albany). A later grant included the region on the west bank of the Delaware and to the south of that river (modern Delaware), the subject of controversy with Maryland both before and after it was given to William Penn in August 1682. These grants contradicted several other chartered boundaries and removed the government of Maine from Massachusetts. In all, the establishment of New York can be interpreted as an unthinking grand gesture from a king to his brother, or, though this is a surmise running beyond the evidence, a final royal sharing-out of what was thought to be all remaining ungranted American seaboard land north of the territory under the Spanish shadow.

A final remarkable feature of the ducal proprietary was the charter itself. The shortest of all the colonial charters, it gave its recipient the greatest powers, failing to require that legislation in the colony be passed by an assembly (which was not even mentioned in the grant) and allowing James to undertake at his discretion whatever he thought was necessary for the good of the inhabitants. It also implied that he might disregard claims to or within his territories resting on grants made previously. Yet the New York charter, oddly enough, did not expressly give the Duke the powers of the palatine Bishop of Durham, although these had been included in the charters of Maine, Maryland, and Carolina.

James himself was one of the more efficient English proprietors of the American colonies. He named a deputy governor, Richard Nicolls, for his colony in April 1664 and sent him with three other officials to North America the same year. Their main objective was the conquest of the Dutch, and four frigates and 450 regular soldiers went with them. Their subsidiary task was to sit as a commission of investigation into the affairs of the colonies north of the Delaware, particularly those of Massachusetts, and to bring order out of the situation that existed before 1664 and had now been further complicated by the terms of James's charter. The first was accomplished without pain, for the government of the New Netherlands was weak and uninspired and surrendered quickly, unheroically, and sensibly, in contrast to the second occasion on which English forces destroyed the sovereignty of a European power in North America with the capture of Quebec by Wolfe. The commission's second task was more difficult and was only partly achieved with the agreement of Rhode Island, Connecticut, and Plymouth to an adjustment of their boundaries; in Massachusetts it ran up against an intransigent and self-protective stand by the colony's government.

The organization of a government for New York itself was predominantly the responsibility of Nicolls, whose own main concern was the populous section of his vast territory, the former New Netherlands. He fixed the capital at New Amsterdam, renamed New York City. Unlike most other English colonial governors, he was faced with the problem not of creating order among new settlers but of fixing his authority over a heterogeneous population of established Europeans: New Englanders on Long Island and in Westchester, Dutchmen in New York City and on the Hudson River, and assorted Dutch, Swedes, Finns, and others in the disputed territory west and south of the Delaware. The success of Nicolls and later proprietary governors was mixed. The instability that plagued other American colonies in this period was very evident in New York.

The policy adopted by Nicolls and approved by the Duke recognized from the outset a distinction between Dutch and English. For the former, generous terms of surrender were agreed, including the right to leave the province with their property if they so desired or to stay and take a minimal oath of allegiance that did not oblige them to fight for the English king. Nor were their religious practices disturbed. Dutch law remained in force along the Hudson River, in New York City, and on the Delaware. English law was imposed only in sections where the English seem to have outnumbered the Dutch. Perhaps most important, the dominant group of Dutch merchants were permitted some rights of trading directly with the United Provinces. In 1668 the revocation of this commercial privilege caused considerable resentment.

Uncertainty as to Dutch loyalty was not balanced by full assurances of the English inhabitants' support. Governor Nicolls hoped to placate the New Englanders in the province and attract others with the institution of a code of law based on New England practice and a system of government that had some similarities to what was enjoyed in New Haven and Massachusetts. For the English parts, he proclaimed what are commonly known as the Duke's Laws, which have recently been praised as holding "true to an English standard of law and government, with such modifications as had been suggested by the experience of Englishmen living in America." Those parts of the Duke's Laws that were based on the laws of the two New England colonies included the grant of elected town officials and the right of a town to decide on the kind of church that it wanted and to tax in support of its minister. Town meetings were not allowed by law but may well have been held. The laws, first accepted by a special assembly on Long Island in March 1665, to this extent were conciliatory. But their central omission so far as the Yankees were concerned was their failure to provide for a representative assembly and for taxation by consent. This was a constant provocation to protest and controversy, another source of political instability. Even so, had the Duke granted an assembly at this time, it would likely have come into conflict with the proprietary government!

Another motive behind the Duke's Laws was certainly the wish to attract migrants from New England to New York and swell the proprietary revenue.

Just as the Carolina grantees hoped to induce Americans and West Indians to their territory, Nicolls hoped for considerable and cheap settlement from the north. He was particularly certain that the most fruitful area for new settlement lay west of the Hudson and east of the Delaware—in what was to become New Jersey. Indeed, as early as 1664, the governor deeded an area on the coast (from the Passaic to the Raritan rivers) to men who promised to bring in New England settlers (the Elizabethtown Grant), while in April 1665, by the Monmouth Grant, he performed the same action for land south of the Raritan. In May 1665 he stepped up his promotional activities: a broadside advertising leaflet, *The Conditions for New Planters in the Territories of His Royal Highnes the Duke of York*, was printed in Boston.

What Nicolls did not know was that the land that he was busily arranging to have settled had, in June 1664, passed out of the hands of the Duke of York. In that month James had rewarded two of his most devoted followers, Sir George Carteret and John, Lord Berkeley, with title to the soil of America lying west of the Delaware River and south of a line from latitude 41° 40′ on the Delaware to latitude 41° on the Hudson. It was not a large portion of his extensive dominions, and it is doubtful that he knew the value that Nicolls put on it. In a sense this grant expressed in its purest form what was present in different degrees in all the proprietary grants of the Restoration period: the disposal of a cheap form of patronage to loyal courtiers who naturally expected the Restoration to benefit in one way or another those who had served the Stuarts in exile. Carteret and Berkeley were faithful servitors to James, part of the circle that shared his interest in maritime and colonial matters, and this grant was another (they were already proprietors of Carolina) method of payment to them in times when ready money was hard to come by. The new proprietary was named after the Channel Island where Carteret was born, and Nova Caesaria, as it was grandly known (New Jersey as it was more usually known) came into existence.

Carteret and Berkeley did not receive a charter for their province but merely a deed; nor did they legally possess more than the soil of New Jersey since rights of government had to be granted by the King and could not be transferred by James alone. This omission later caused considerable difficulties but at that moment appeared of no real consequence. In 1665 the two proprietors issued a number of provisions for the government and settlement of their colony and appointed the nephew of one of them, Philip Carteret, as their deputy governor. These provisions, largely modeled on the Concessions and Agreements granted a few months earlier for Carolina, bore the same title. This borrowing, and the fact that after 1665 neither man showed much interest in New Jersey, underlines the large element of speculative casualness in Restoration colonization. The New Jersey Concessions promised liberty of conscience, freedom of trade, immunity from customs, and rights of self-government through an elected assembly. Land was offered in generous quantities to free settlers and to servants at the end of their service, with the proviso that a quitrent of a halfpenny an acre be paid. As in Carolina and New York, it was hoped that the bulk of new settlers would come from within America itself. Like Nicolls, Governor Carteret published an advertisement in Boston. About 30 men recruited in the Channel Islands by Carteret came from the mother country; otherwise, there is little evidence of migration from England to New Jersey in the years 1665-1674, when the colony belonged to its two original proprietors.

During the same years, the two proprietors received few profits and had many problems. Accordingly, and because of his debts, Berkeley sold his part ownership of New Jersey to a Quaker, John Fenwick, in March 1674, who purchased it on behalf of a second Quaker, Edward Byllynge. After involved proceedings, the Fenwick-Byllynge interest in New Jersey passed to three trustees in 1675, again all Quakers: Gawen Lawrie, Nicholas Lucas, and William Penn. By the terms of their trusteeship, one-tenth of the territory involved was reserved for Fenwick's exploitation. The trustees in fact set up a joint stock company in which Fenwick held ten shares and ninety went up for sale. The ninety shares attracted about 120 purchasers, nearly all members of the Society of Friends also. Meanwhile, in 1676, the other proprietor, Sir George Carteret, agreed with the trustees to divide New Jersey territorially to reflect the changed circumstances. This arrangement gave rise to the separate provinces and governments of East New Jersey (Carteret's) and West New Jersey (the Quaker purchase).

These complicated agreements illustrate a further truth about post-Restoration colonial enterprise. Colonization was now tending to become more and more involved with speculation in land as well as speculation in America's envisaged commercial possibilities. Although many of the Quakers who invested in New Jersey were attracted to the idea of founding a colony where their religion could flourish without hindrance, many also seem to have been canny businessmen who hoped that they would make money out of their investments. Fenwick, for example, an old Cromwellian soldier, was a property owner interested in land and estate law.

C. The Quakers and colonization

The Quakers had now become colonial promoters, following the example of other dissident religious groups before them: Pilgrims, Puritans, Catholics. Isolated Quakers had already found their way to America for many years, but there had been no attempt at organized colonization. George Fox, the great Quaker leader, had carried on the tradition of Quaker missionary work in the New World, traveling to the West Indies and North America. William Penn, the other great Quaker chieftain of this period, once stated that he had been interested in America since the 1660s. In England, Quakers were imprisoned and harassed at the Restoration and for many years after, although intermittently and less rigorously than was once suggested. Their notion of America as a place of refuge, particularly in view of the religious toleration usually allowed there, might have been expected. But in the years immediately after the Restoration, the Society of Friends lacked organization and self-confidence. By 1676 a network of local, regional, and national meetings and committees provided a unifying force. Quaker confidence grew as their leaders challenged the treatment of Friends in the courts and as Quaker commercial strength developed. Quakers had never all been of the "mean" quality sometimes attributed to them. Some were respectable gentry, tradesmen, and merchants with increasing amounts of capital at their disposal, interested in the speculative as well as the humanitarian aspects of colonization. The Quakers also had contacts at the highest levels. Penn, the son of Admiral Sir William Penn, a devoted follower of Charles and James, was himself close to both royal brothers. The less-well-known Byllynge, involved in the purchase of Berkeley's share in New Jersey, apparently enjoyed the friendship of the proprietor. So while Quaker colonization reflected a desire to circumvent persecution, it also displayed the growing economic and social vitality of the movement.

Substantial Quaker migration took place to West New Jersey under the promises contained in a typical set of "Concessions and Agreements of the Proprietors, Freeholders and Inhabitants of the Province of West New Jersey, in America" issued in 1677. These embodied the usual terms offered by most proprietors to intending settlers, including a legislative assembly, liberty of conscience, and a system of headrights for free settlers and servants. They also contained stipulations regarding quitrents. In contrast to the eastern province, these seem to have been disregarded later. Yet the West New Jersey concessions were not wholly typical, for they went beyond ordinary promises and suggested the utopian vision found earlier in other ideas of America. The form of law and government in the new settlement, the preamble to the Concessions stated, provided a "foundation for after ages to understand their liberty as men and christians, that they may not be brought in bondage, but by their own consent; for we put power in the people, that is to say, they meet, and choose one honest man for each proprietary who hath subscribed to the concessions; all those men to meet in an assembly there, to make and repeal laws to choose a governor, or a commissioner, and twelve assistants, to execute the laws during their pleasure; so every man is capable to choose or be chosen; no man to be arrested, condemned, imprisoned, or molested in his estate or liberty, but by twelve men of the neighbourhood. No man is to lie in prison for debt, but that his estate satisfy as far as it will go, and be set at liberty for work; No person to be called in question or molested for conscience; with many more things mentioned in the same concessions."

Like Penn's later "Frame of Government" for Pennsylvania, these Concessions testify to the extent to which the Quakers shared and contributed to the more radical political ideas of the later seventeenth century. The emphasis on jury trials held in the accused's own neighborhood and nonimprisonment for debt came from their own experience. While attention to the legal rights of property owners was common enough in seventeenth-century political thinking, the idea of human liberty for every man, irrespective of his status in the community, was not. The Concessions guaranteed annual elections and secret balloting, enfranchised all male inhabitants, and set up a powerful legislature. Although the government of West New Jersey passed out of the hands of the Quakers and the Concessions were later modified, substantial portions of them remained part of the political and legal structure of New Jersey throughout the colonial period.

Circumstances in England and decisions made there also affected the development of East New Jersey, Sir George Carteret's half of the original province. Even before Berkeley's sale of his proprietorship, both men had been forced to alter their original concessions in an attempt to reduce the power of the assembly which had quickly become the focus for the settlers' attack on the proprietary government's powers. The main event in England was, however, the sale of East New Jersey by Sir George's heirs in 1682, two years after his death. Again, the purchasers were Quakers: William Penn and eleven other men. Since many of the eleven were already involved with the development of West New Jersey and since Penn himself was promoting his own ambitions for a new proprietary on the banks of the Delaware, the timing of this purchase suggests the vigor of Quaker enterprise. It seems almost that the Quakers planned to become owners of middle America between New York and Maryland. Yet it is doubtful if any such coherent policy existed; indeed the founding of Pennsylvania shortly afterward diverted settlers from the Jerseys.

The twelve Quaker trustees of East New Jersey disposed of some of their rights in the colony, seeking to reimburse themselves by creating another joint stock proprietorship of the type that had purchased West New Jersey. This proprietorship maintained its control of East New Jersey to 1702. At one stage it attempted to replace the Concessions of 1665 with a set of "Fundamental Constitutions" of great complexity. Like the West New Jersey Concessions, the Fundamental Constitutions had many features of a roughly radical-Whiggish kind, although giving a less generous amount of power to popular representatives than the former document. Of interest also is a tortuous and lengthy clause in it dealing with the problem of Quaker pacificism and public defense. This asked Quakers to speak "as men without respect to one's particular perswasion in matters of religion" when assessing the need for defensive precautions, but allowed them to refuse to contribute money for arms, while asking them to pay extra money toward other charges. These Constitutions, promulgated in East New Jersey, were rejected by the existing colonial assembly. The government of the colony continued much as it had under its two original proprietors with a governor, council, and assembly. Indeed, it is notable that East New Jersey, controlled by English Quaker proprietors for twenty years, felt hardly at all the influence of the Society of Friends' philosophy. It was the western part of New Jersey, whose Quaker proprietors owned it only for some thirteen years, that became a "Quaker commonwealth."

The reason for this lay predominantly in a pattern of migration which English decisions influenced. New England Puritans originally settled East New Jersey since the proprietors, Berkeley and Carteret, did not wish to spend money on promoting English migration and because New Englanders found the area convenient and attractive. When the Quakers assumed control, they handed over promotional activities to a number of Scots—Quakers and non-Quakers. These men were unsuccessful in stimulating a migration of Friends and managed to send over only about 500 settlers, the majority of whom were Scottish Presbyterians. The province's population therefore never became a Quaker one. By contrast, the West New Jersey proprietors sent large numbers of Quakers to their territories.

Other factors in the English background had importance for the tangled early history of New Jersey. The Duke of York never really clarified the relationship of the territories that he granted in 1664 to those that he retained. The original omission of a grant of the government as well as the soil of New Jersey to the two proprietors was never repaired. On several occasions the Duke stated that the government of New Jersey rested with its grantees, but in commissions issued by him to his own governors of New York, James often included, as part of his dominions, the territory south of the Hudson. From 1664 onward New York's governors constantly interfered in the affairs of New Jersey, one of several facts that made government there unstable. Similarly, the English division of East and West New Jersey and frequent changes in their English ownership also produced uncertainty and a lack of settled authority. East New Jersey went from Sir George Carteret's heirs to twelve Quakers, from these Quakers to twenty-four joint stock proprietors, then from 1688 to 1692 into an extensive royal dominion. It then returned to the proprietors until 1702, when it was reunited with West New Jersey as a royal province. West New Jersey passed from Berkeley and Carteret to Fenwick and Byllynge, from them to the Quaker trustees, and from the Quaker trustees to the proprietary joint stock holders. In 1687 Dr. Daniel Coxe, a colonial speculator, purchased it; he later sold it to a group of forty-eight London merchants, most of whom were members of the Church of England and who controlled it until 1702.

William Penn's connection with New Jersey in its Quaker phase has already been mentioned. Pennsylvania, the last English colony of the seventeenth century, Penn named not for himself but for his father, Admiral Sir William, apparently at the behest of the King. Although Penn's father—royalist, Tory, establishment-minded—seems the very model of a careerist sailor, later a naval civil servant, while William was politically and religiously radical, ready to protest against contemporary standards of justice and law and, to some extent, unworldly, the compliment was not an unjust one. Admiral Sir William had been part of the group of expansionists around the King and the Duke of York from which much of the colonizing impetus of the Restoration had come. More to the point, the younger William owed his special privileges, which brought him the grant of Pennsylvania and leadership among the Quakers, to his father's services to the Crown. Because of his father, he had access to the Stuarts and to other great men, and this made him a natural intermediary between the Society of Friends and the English government.

Penn also had courage and fortitude. Born in 1644, he entered Christ Church, Oxford, then the most royalist college in a royalist University, at the Restoration. His father foresaw for him the life of a career-minded English gentleman, a courtier or diplomatist, reaping the rewards of the family's attachment to the Stuarts. At the age of seventeen, William chose the path of sympathy with Puritanism and piety and was expelled for refusing to conform with the rituals of the Anglican church. Dispatched by his angry father on a tour of the Continent to come to his senses, he spent part of 1663 and 1664 in France. But this was not the Catholic France of Paris and Versailles. Penn made his way to Huguenot Saumur, a center of the French Protestantism of the southwest. Here, he studied with the liberal theologian, an advocate of religious toleration, Moses Amyraut. Returning to England, he was for a brief spell at Lincoln's Inn. Then he traveled to Ireland to look into the affairs of his father's estates. In Ireland he renewed former contacts with the Society of Friends. By 1668 he was a convinced Quaker, and he rapidly became a leading member of the Society.

Wide scope existed for Penn's activities as a well-born Quaker, particularly in the field of protecting his fellows from the burden of statutes enforced in different ways by local magistrates and officials to break up Quaker meetings and to imprison Quaker leaders, Penn among them. Neither the King nor his ministers necessarily favored these measures although forced to acede to them by Parliament. Penn was able to use his contacts to some extent to mitigate such persecutions. His legal training and intense interest in the libertarian heritage of English law, as he interpreted it, was used to challenge acts of arbitrary or illegal persecution. By the 1670s he had emerged to join George Fox as the acknowledged Quaker leader.

Penn's position almost inevitably led him toward a particular legal and political philosophy. He disputed the arrest of nonconformists as an attack on "Ancient Fundamental Laws, which relate to Liberty and Property," of which no man should be deprived for the sake of purely religious belief. He achieved some success in the courts on this point and also, for a short time in 1679-1680, took an active political role supporting the Parliamentary campaign of Algernon Sidney, the republican Whig. Penn subscribed neither to the republican ideas of Sidney nor to his advocacy of armed revolution against tyrants but supported those of his views that coincided with what has come to be known as the "country" philosophy. For Penn, this meant that as many limitations as possible should be imposed on the "court" executive and its agencies. At the heart of the country philosophy lay, in his words, the securing "to us our ancient laws by new ones, and, among the rest such as relate to frequent Parliaments, the only true check upon arbitrary ministers, and therefore feared, hated and opposed by them." Often this political ideology was based on a belief in fundamental laws or an "ancient constitution" dating from Saxon or even earlier times, considered to be the heritage of all Englishmen. Penn espoused this view of English history, seeing Magna Carta not as the origin of the rights of the subjects but merely as the ratification of pre-existing freedoms. He also believed that Parliament itself was limited in its powers by such laws and could not alter them. Government rested on a contract, the people accepting their rulers for the purpose of promoting happiness and securing justice and fundamental rights.

Together with West New Jersey's Concessions, which Penn may have had a hand in, and which certainly reflect a similar manner of thinking, the creation of Penn's province expressed the aspirations of the nonconformist radicals in a way that the other post-Restoration proprietaries did not. The parallel with the early New England colonies is obvious and the political utopianism even more pronounced. Penn's own thinking had a striking religious and moral component not unlike that of the Puritans, whose heirs the Quakers were, in some senses. According to him, government should impose a moral code based on biblical commandments to which all men, whatever their sectarian persuasions, could agree. Virtue and order should be promoted to avoid God's wrath against the impious and to encourage a fundamental morality. Drunkenness, luxury, whoredom, fornication, gambling, oaths, cursing, blasphemy, and profaneness Penn saw as "Sins against Nature, and against Government, as well as against the Written Laws of God . . ." So, while avoiding the establishment of particular churches or the denial of men's rights to follow their own consciences in matters of dogma and worship, Penn still saw the state as a kind of super-churchly guardian of basic Christian values, and it cannot be said that he believed that religious and civil spheres of authority should be completely separate. As much as Massachusetts, Pennsylvania was to be a "holy commonwealth."

A further aspect of Penn's thought which was to give Pennsylvania a different complexion from most other American colonies was his internationalism. As a Quaker, his activities had not been confined to England and Ireland; he traveled extensively in northern Europe, acquainting himself with foreign Quakers and other Protestant pietists. Penn came to see his new colony not as an exclusively national foundation but as one where all European Protestants would be welcomed. Especially, it would be a refuge for those fleeing persecution or harsh conditions. To this end he devoted considerable attention to advertising for migrants throughout northern Europe.

Exactly how Penn came to the notion of extending his American interest from the Jerseys to the foundation of his own proprietary is unclear. That powerful economic motives were as important as his idealism is evident. Had Penn wished only to provide a Christian refuge for Quakers and other Protestants, he could have concentrated his attentions on the Jerseys, particularly on West New Jersey, which in 1680 seemed destined to develop in ways that he approved. His subsequent conduct made clear his hope of improving his shaky financial position by raising revenue in the form of land sales and quitrents from an American territory. Also, perhaps with the confidence of his class and his convictions, he wished for the unfettered control of a new territory, rather than the shared proprietorship of West New Jersey, in order to gain a free hand to build the government and society that he favored.

William Penn petitioned Charles II for an American grant on 1 June 1680 and received it in the short time of ten months, on 4 March 1681. Since these were years when English officials showed a growing dislike for proprietary forms of government, and since Penn himself was a controversial figure, his success was noteworthy. It has been ascribed to various motives on the part of the Crown, including the wish to repay debts owed to the Admiral Penn for many years and a willingness to encourage the migration of dissenters.

Changed conditions in English colonial thinking did lead to modifications in Penn's charter. He enjoyed less absolute powers than those of previous American proprietors. The charter contained clauses to make him observe and enforce the Navigation Acts, admit royal customs officers to his ports, and keep an agent in London to answer for breaches of commercial regulations. Moreover, Penn was obliged to send legislation passed in his province to the English government for approval. This provision for royal disallowance of colonial laws, common in royal charters, had not appeared before in those of proprietaries. Another clause allowed legal appeals to royal courts, something similarly unknown. He also had to send a minister of the Church of England if 20 persons petitioned for one. Another clause, double-edged in its implications, allowed the King to impose taxes on the inhabitants of Pennsylvania only with "the consent of the proprietary, or chief governor, or assembly, or by act of parliament in England." Otherwise it did not differ substantially from earlier proprietary charters.

Penn's position under the English government was defined by the charter; he now moved in the usual way to settle the terms on which he would grant land and government in Pennsylvania. Since he continued to be strongly guided by the vision of Pennsylvania as a place in which the religious and political errors of England could be avoided and remedied, this was a task of importance. In England, he wrote, "my understanding and inclinations have been much directed to observe and reprove mischiefs in Government, so it is now [in Pennsylvania] put into my power to settle one. For the matters of liberty and privilege, I purpose that which is extraordinary, and leave myself and my successors no power of doing mischief, that the will of one man may not hinder the good of a whole country." He began to write a constitution for Pennsylvania in 1681.

Penn's "Frame of Government," as it was called, was not easily completed. Seventeen drafts were needed before the final version appeared. Of these, the eighth probably gave the most generous powers to the settlers of Pennsylvania. Penn called it the "Fundamental Constitutions of Pennsilvania," recalling the title of Ashley's Carolina constitution. This provided for legislation by an elected assembly, chosen by the province's freeholders, which alone would propose and pass laws. In addition, Penn introduced a kind of unwieldy direct democracy by which the electors could instruct their assemblymen and by which tax bills would be referred back from the assembly to the freemen of each electoral district. An upper house, or council, of forty-eight men was also elected from among and by the members of the lower house, having no right of veto over lower house bills. Numerous other clauses specified that executive power should be exercised through committees rather than by individuals, provided for the annual elections of justices of the peace, sheriffs, and other officials, and granted considerable legal privileges, including monthly courts and the prohibition of imprisonment for debt. Of course, this eighth draft was never put into effect. The final version emerged in early 1682.

The importance of these revisions, apart from the light they cast on later seventeenth-century views of possible constitutional systems, rests in the reasons for the transformation of Penn's liberal and popular ideas of government to the more conservative and aristocratic shape of his final Pennsylvania constitution. Penn's friends, including Algernon Sidney and the influential and scholarly Quaker Benjamin Furly, noted these changes. Furly complained to Penn that he "wondered who should put thee upon altering them for these. And as much how thou couldst yield to such a thing." The 1682 Frame of Government was less liberal in fact than the West New Jersey Concessions or, surprisingly, than a charter granted New York in 1683 by the Duke of York. It put the power of initiating all legislation except tax bills in an upper house of seventy-two men to be elected from those "most eminent for vertue, Wisdom and Substance" while the lower house had only a nine-day annual session and might merely approve or negate laws. In addition, the proprietary governor and council had full executive and judicial power. Penn, however, stuck to his belief that good government depended on the protection of legal and religious rights and added to the Frame certain "Laws Agreed upon in England" that guaranteed these.

On the basis of strong indirect evidence, the most recent and painstaking study of Penn's Frame of Government suggests that he adapted his political ideas to take into account his great need for the support of well-to-do men. Penn spent about £12,000 in two years to obtain his charter and launch his enterprise. He hoped to sell land in large separate lots to rich purchasers who might be persuaded to move to Pennsylvania. To encourage this, he had to be able to promise these men political and social order. The power given to the upper house ensured influence to "men of substance," the nucleus of a governing class, and served as an inducement to wealthy migrants. In fact Penn rewarded all but three of the largest purchasers (over five thousand acres) with appointments to offices of authority in the colony. Conversely, as Professor Gary B. Nash has demonstrated, "Hardly a position of influence or profit in the early years was conferred on a man who invested in less than 5,000 acres in the province." Penn also linked the allocation of lots in Philadelphia, which he expected to increase rapidly in value, to the purchase of "country" lands by large buyers. His creation of a monopolistic joint stock company to exploit the colony's potential trade, the Free Society of Traders in Pennsylvania, represented another attempt to attract capital; its leading members were also large land buyers.

Ironically then, Pennsylvania, at first conceived as a society in which political and legal privileges would be granted to a very wide portion of the population, began to take shape as an oligarchy. The largest investors in land and in the stock of the Free Society, or in both, were mainly well-to-do Quaker merchants, and they, together with one or two sympathetic Anglicans, received appointments to leading offices. While the laws agreed on in England protected fundamental liberties, power and position clearly went to men of substance. Penn himself defended his final draft of the Frame, and it must be recognized that his prime concern was stability and Christian living rather than democratic experiments. As a Whig, albeit a radical one, he was no leveler. As a Quaker, he believed that the large numbers of his co-religionists in Pennsylvania would create a holy and just community. "Let men be good and the government cannot be bad" was one of his replies to criticisms of his laws.

Penn's other energies were devoted to promoting his colony in less select circles by encouraging a large migration. In this he was hugely successful and, it has been pointed out, the 8,000 immigrants who arrived in Pennsylvania by the end of 1685 represented a larger movement than that to New England in the first years of settlement during the "great migration" of the 1630s. Quantities of promotional tracts, the use of his well-established contacts with other leading Quakers, and the regular system of correspondence that existed within the Quaker organization in the British Isles helped recruit this substantial force. By this time, too, indentured servitude as a method of emigration was commonplace, and probably one-half of the adult males of the early years came in this capacity. Most of the other settlers were drawn from humble but industrious groups, craftsmen or other workers and small yeomen or husbandmen.

Pennsylvania grew at an astounding rate, surpassing that of any other North American colony and telescoping, into a few years, developments that took place over much longer periods in slower-moving societies. Very soon after its settlement, Philadelphia competed successfully as a commercial center with New York. Individual merchants built up considerable businesses within two or three years of their arrival. These circumstances suggest how much Penn's province benefitted from its late foundation. By 1681 there remained little sense of mystery or danger in colonization, especially colonization on the Delaware River, where Europeans had been settling for more than half a century.

Penn's efforts to build his proprietary also included an early extension of the boundaries given to Pennsylvania in the charter. By these, Pennsylvania's access to the Atlantic was overlooked on the one side by New Jersey and on the other by the territory to the southeast, today the state of Delaware. In 1682, in two deeds executed by the Duke of York, he obtained Delaware, then known as the three "lower counties." Although the deeds had a doubtful legality and carried no rights of government, Penn did not hesitate to include the new territory within his political jurisdiction, summoning freeholders from the three counties of Newcastle, Kent, and Sussex to the first proprietary assembly held in Pennsylvania. Lord Baltimore also claimed parts of Sussex and Kent counties, and he and Penn disputed these claims for many years afterward.

The inclusion of the lower counties in Penn's proprietary gave him adequate access to the sea and protected the approaches to the Delaware River and Philadelphia. It also early introduced a discordant note into his government, for most of the settlers of the region—who numbered about 1,000 by the 1680s—were non-Quakers and felt no allegiance to him. Many were Marylanders with no wish to be brought under Penn's proprietary control, having escaped the Calverts to enjoy a loose government under representatives of the Duke of York in the lower counties. With their own officials and local leaders, those men fell outside the pattern of loyalties that Penn had otherwise tried so carefully to construct among the chief land- and officeholders of the province.

Penn's problem with this heterogeneous element in his colony was minor compared with that of other proprietors with their diverse and argumentative populations, for Quakers made up the bulk of Pennsylvania's first settlers. Yet Penn soon came to share the anxieties of all the other American proprietors. Their problems came from a number of sources. The forms of proprietary government and land ownership, adapted from older and not very suitable medieval precedents, could not be easily reconciled with seventeenth-century American realities. Many proprietors, in spite of their vast paper constitutional and economic powers, had neither the political, administrative, nor financial resources to control and build up their American holdings. Their wish to raise rents and revenues from their territories and to spend little themselves led them to policies of open settlement, with most proprietors encouraging migration from within the Americas. The heterogeneous settlers thus attracted could hardly be expected to show much loyalty. Rather, they asserted their own interests, resisting in particular proprietorial attempts to collect rents and taxes. Nor did the often complicated transactions of the proprietors in England with respect to their colonial possessions create confidence or stability in America.

All these factors meant, as we shall see, that like the New Englanders and the Virginians, the inhabitants of Carolina, New York, the Jerseys, and Pennsylvania almost immediately pressed their claims to local self-government and large political powers, continuing in the post-Restoration colonies the process that had begun in Virginia before 1620.

With the foundation of Pennsylvania in 1682, the English were now established along the greater length of the North American seaboard in settlements of varying size, roughly from Saco Bay in the north to Charleston in the south. At the one extremity of northern New England and Nova Scotia, the presence of the French in Canada as well as the rugged inhospitality of the country restricted English expansion. At the other end of America, the Spanish presence still inhibited the establishment of formal settlements beyond South Carolina. Yet if there was little actual colonizing in either of these areas, English traders and explorers pushed into them and into the other unsettled regions to the west of the thin strip of coastal communities. Later, when England's cautiously amicable relations with France and Spain were replaced by conflict, especially during the reigns of William III and Queen Anne, colonial appetite and British policy would coincide to prepare the way for the ultimate mastery of the whole of North America by the Anglo-Americans.

This was the future. Yet even as early as 1660 the great disparity in population and resources between the English, French, and Spanish settlements in North America pointed to what the years to come might hold. In 1660 the population of the English colonies in North America numbered about 70,000. In the same year about 5,000 persons lived in the Dutch New Netherlands, some 3,000 French settlers in Canada and tiny numbers of Spanish in Florida. By 1700 the gap had widened. The 250,000, mainly English and African, found in the British colonies disputed North America with about 7,500 French and Spanish.

Internal disorders and instabilities within and among the English colonies balanced this potential superiority. Until and in some cases beyond 1700, disruptive conflicts, crises of authority, intercolonial jealousies, and disputes between colonies and mother country were prevalent and disturbing. The still fluid social and political structures of many of the colonies and the unrealistic and unattainable powers claimed by proprietors or governors and other officials, or even by particular local groups, made disorder inevitable. Not until an internal political order based on solid economic and social foundations had been established in them did some degree of stability arise in each colony. Even then, problems of government remained, especially when established or rising local elites came into conflict with the authority claimed by royal and proprietary governors.

Chapter Three

Virginia and Maryland After the Restoration

A. Politics and government

In spite of the constitutional distinction between the royal government of Virginia and the proprietary government of Maryland, the many features common to both colonies make it possible to consider the settled area around Chesapeake Bay as a distinct region. Economic and political similarities that led to parallel developments and problems underlay the separate governments of Virginia and Maryland. Foremost among these were the tobacco economy, a settlement pattern of scattered farms and plantations, a system of local government based on counties, and contentions between representative lower houses and appointed governors and councils. In the latter part of the seventeenth century, the introduction of growing numbers of Negro slaves into the Chesapeake region provided another common development provoking parallel responses.

The pattern of settlement around Chesapeake Bay remained much as it had before 1660. By the end of the seventeenth century about 88,000 persons lived mainly on small farms dotting the coastline and the river banks of Maryland and Virginia. This represented more than a doubling of numbers since 1660, but the limits of settlement had hardly reached the fall lines of the rivers that drained into the Chesapeake. Migration may still have played a significant part in population increase, since recent research suggests that large numbers of immigrants arrived in the years from 1650 to 1675. Chesapeake society probably remained young and masculine. Large plantations owned by wealthy men and worked by dozens of white or black laborers were still exceptional and would become more common only after 1700 with a great increase in the number of slaves. In Maryland the average size of plantations may have decreased in the second part of the seventeenth century and economic opportunities lessened because of the pressures of population and a slump in the tobacco trade.

ESTIMATED POPULATION
Chesapeake Colonies

1660–1720
Showing decennial percentage increases

		Maryland	%	Virginia	%	Totals
1660	W	7,668	–	26,070	–	33,738
	N	758	–	950	–	1,708
1670	W	12,036	*57*	33,309	*28*	45,345
	N	1,190	*57*	2,000	*111*	3,190
1680	W	16,293	*35*	40,596	*22*	56,889
	N	1,611	*35*	3,000	*50*	4,611
1690	W	21,862	*34*	43,701	*8*	65,563
	N	2,162	*34*	9,345	*212*	11,507
1700	W	26,377	*21*	42,170	*–4*	68,547
	N	3,227	*49*	16,390	*75*	19,617
1710	W	34,796	*32*	55,163	*31*	89,959
	N	7,945	*146*	23,118	*41*	31,063
1720	W	53,634	*54*	61,158	*11*	114,792
	N	12,499	*57*	26,599	*15*	39,098

W = White Population
N = Negro Population
% = decennial percentage increase

The high incidence of small farms producing a commodity that experience showed could be most economically and profitably grown by gang labor on larger estates had several explanations. One was the easy availability of land, which made every man ambitious to set himself up as a landowner and promised that every indentured servant at the end of his term could do so. Combined with this was a slump in tobacco prices and other economic difficulties, making the purchase of large farms difficult through the two or three decades after 1660. The workings of the English Navigation Acts at first struck very hard at the Chesapeake tobacco region. Forbidden to sell directly to non-English markets, the Chesapeake planters held large amounts of unwanted tobacco, and prices slumped dramatically. Governor Sir William Berkeley led a campaign of vigorous protest to the home government. At the same time, Virginia and Maryland planters attempted to force up the price of tobacco by creating artificial shortages through agreements to grow only limited quantities. These failed, partly because of the attitude of the Maryland proprietor, an early instance of colonial noncooperation. Until the 1680s, when English merchants developed new markets for the re-export of Chesapeake tobacco, reports of grim economic conditions and of real poverty, debts, and distress were heard on all sides. These depressed economic circumstances formed the background for muted social and political unrest in the post-Restoration period in the Chesapeake.

In Virginia Governor Berkeley was reinstalled without difficulty and the resumption of royal government brought no protests. The assembly did revise the colony's statutes in 1662 in such a way as to reinforce the already powerful control of the county courts (of which many burgesses were members) over local government at county and parish levels. If this was designed to safeguard Virginian rights against royal government interference, neither the Crown nor the governor objected. Indeed relations between Berkeley and the burgesses remained cordial. Berkeley continued the assembly without new elections for fourteen years, but there were no protests that this restricted popular rights. In 1670 the assembly itself acted to narrow the franchise by excluding freemen who had no real or personal property in Virginia from voting. This still left large numbers of men with voting rights but indicated a growing consciousness of social and political status in the colony. The burgesses explained that they wished to prevent tumults at elections and to conform to English laws. "Only," they stated, "such as by their estates real or personal have interest enough to tie them to the endeavour of the public good" should vote. As one authority has recently written, this was "the first formulation of the concept that was to prescribe the nature of political right in Virginia."

These years after 1660 reveal, then, no great struggle between governor, council, or assembly. Berkeley was certainly a man of his age, and he had always sought to consolidate his position by creating a stable political machine, a following of loyal officeholders and officials and other allies, bound to him by his patronage and favors. In this he succeeded fairly well, allying himself with ambitious and successful men, many of whom had come to Virginia in the 1640s. By the Restoration these men had seats on the council and in the assembly and were also local officeholders. They were also allied by intermarriage, and it is clear that an elite of propertied and officeholding families was emerging. This elite, widened later, became a powerful presence in Virginia. What is not clear about the fifteen or so years after 1660 is how far other members of the assembly and other officeholders resented or felt their interests challenged by these developments. Was the assembly controlled by the governor, and how far did its members express the opinion of planters outside the governor's circle? If the latter was the case, there is little evidence of widespread discontent in the seemingly pacific record of relations between governor and assembly in the years to 1676. But these questions are of interest. For in 1676 the real or apparent calm was abruptly shattered. Armed revolt was followed by the meeting of an assembly that protested in strong terms about many features of Virginia's political life.

The immediate occasion of the revolt of 1676 against the Virginia government arose from an area of popular discontent—Indian policy. English expansion in both Maryland and Virginia had caused unrest among the Indians of the Potomac River. Forced away from their own lands, the Susquehannocks, until now allies of the whites, avenged themselves in 1676 by slaughtering some thirty-six or thirty-eight persons in the upper Virginia counties. This led to calls for punitive expeditions, but Berkeley finally persuaded the assembly to follow his policy of defensive containment. He favored building expensive forts rather than dispatching inexpensive militiamen who might, however, provoke a very costly general Indian war. Yet his policy was unsuccessful. The Indians carried on killing whites, and by the late spring of 1676 there was rising anger, focused particularly on the high costs of Berkeley's ineffectual measures and on the lack of popular control over the rising taxes that paid for them. At this time the fact that the governor and various members of his entourage benefitted from a monopoly over the lucrative Indian fur trade was linked to Berkeley's failure to lead an army against the Indians as a selfish motive to protect this trade. These were popular grievances in that men voiced them from levels of society that did not influence the county courts or have effective representation in the Virginia assembly, which still supported Berkeley's Indian policy. Discontent spread, feeding on the poverty and distress created by the depressed economic conditions of these years, a situation that made Governor Berkeley fear disorder before 1676.

Leadership of the opposition fell to Nathaniel Bacon, a young Englishman of good family who had come to Virginia as recently as 1674. Because of his relative wealth and his family connections (Berkeley was a cousin by marriage), Bacon had been warmly welcomed and given a seat on the council. His own grievances, like those of his more substantial followers, arose from the frustration of a wish to mount an aggressive war against the Indians. Bacon's plantation was in Henrico County on the Upper James, a "frontier" exposed to Indian depredations. Bacon, backed by popular meetings in the frontier counties, led a volunteer force against the Indians in opposition to the governor's orders. From April to October 1676, Bacon defied the governor, fought both the Indians and Berkeley's own forces, and disrupted the government of the colony. Proclaimed a rebel, he still had wide popular backing. But Bacon died suddenly in October 1676, and his following then dissolved. Governor Berkeley had little trouble in regaining control, and no Baconian faction survived to resist him.

In the field of Indian policy Bacon's rebellion had negligible results. Like many frontier rampages it mainly involved the killing or dispossessing of friendly Indians, some of whom held "good lands" coveted by Bacon's followers. Nathaniel Bacon, in spite of his short stay in Virginia, seemed already to have held the view that "all Indians in general" were enemies and that it was impossible to distinguish between "good" and "bad" ones. He seems to have had no strong political feelings, and it is doubtful that he would have challenged the Virginia political or social system, had it allowed him free rein for his anti-Indian impulses. Yet the rebellion did serve as a catalyst and a release for a variety of grievances expressed in an assembly held in Jamestown in June 1676.

This assembly was summoned by the governor himself by writs that allowed all freeholders to vote for burgesses, a concession that flouted the previous restriction on the franchise. It certainly included many men who had not served as burgesses before and were sometimes described as "Bacon's men." Similarly, the laws passed by the assembly were later and mistakenly described as "Bacon's laws." In fact, Bacon was at the assembly for a limited time, had no evident influence on its members or legislation, and was interested in securing not new laws but a legal military commission to fight against the Indians. The assembly even condemned the kind of "unlawful assemblies routes, riots, and tumults" that had given support to Bacon and provided him with followers.

Yet the assembly was a reforming one and its members protested against many aspects of Virginia's government as they had developed under Berkeley, although there was no attack on the governor personally or on his Indian policy. In particular, an effort was made to check the closed and oligarchical nature of local and colonial government in Virginia. It has been suggested that two groups of interests were represented in Bacon's assembly. The first and "popular" interest was that of the ordinary planter who supported laws to end the restrictions on the franchise, to give the ordinary freeman powers in the election of parish vestries and the right to elect representatives to the county courts, and to ease the position of men in debt. The second interest was that of locally prominent families outside the governor's immediate circle who sought access to greater political power by breaking the monopoly of Berkeley and his friends. Their ambitions resulted in legislation against multiple officeholding, against the right of councillors to sit on the county courts by virtue of their office, for barring officeholding to newcomers of less than three years residence in Virginia, and for placing restrictions on the terms of appointment and office of sheriffs and tax collectors. To some degree, the interests of both groups overlapped. For example, one law made members of the council liable to taxation, something they had previously escaped. A detailed examination of the membership of Bacon's and Berkeley's following, especially of their previous social and political positions, is needed. It seems likely, for example, that many of Bacon's followers were probably the young, unmarried men who still formed a substantial part of the population in 1676.

An investigation of the pattern of local and colonial officeholding from 1660 to the end of the seventeenth century might explain not only much about the events of 1676 but about subsequent political alignments. These alignments suggest that after 1676 the system of local government and the privileged Virginia council weathered the crisis of the rebellion and the governing class, perhaps enlarged by the addition of upward-striving planters formerly checked by Governor Berkeley's policies, consolidated and strengthened its position. The legislation passed at Bacon's assembly, for example, was repealed. One of the reasons for these developments was that the English government, prompted both by Bacon's rebellion and by a general determination to review all colonial matters, first sent over royal commissioners and then a new royal governor. Unlike Berkeley, these men had no family or property connections in Virginia and were under orders to check the growth of local political interests. These English officials were easily made the focus of general colonial resentment. This they provoked after 1676, when the Crown attacked the powers of the Virginia assembly, threatening to deprive the burgesses of even their cherished and fundamental rights of taxation. As a result of this struggle, the assembly did lose certain powers.

Yet the assembly scored one victory. It called on James II for the recall of the governor, Lord Howard of Effingham, who vigorously asserted the claims of the royal prerogative against the powers of the House of Burgesses. This petition was put into the King's hand in September 1688. William of Orange's invasion of England interrupted its consideration. When it was heard in the early months of the new king's reign, the burgesses' complaints received sympathetic consideration. Howard was eventually commanded to remain in England and to commit his authority over the colony to a lieutenant governor, Francis Nicholson. When, after a gap of five years, the assembly again met, it did so without serious conflict with the governor. Virginia, like several other colonies, benefitted to this extent from the Glorious Revolution in England.

Overall, the lower house seems not to have found new strengths in the latter seventeenth and early eighteenth centuries. It did, however, become more responsive to the concerns and needs of Virginia's population and more competent in drafting effective legislation, and this became a source of renewed power after about 1720. It was the council which gained immediately from the royal assault on the assembly, winning several new powers from the Crown. Yet since the members of the council also represented local interests, this was finally of no help to royal government. Governors again faced overmighty subjects on the Virginia council although questions of fundamental political and constitutional rights were not essentially involved in these disputes, and more normal political relations replaced the conflicts of earlier years.

In Maryland the proprietary system had been, as we have seen, vigorously challenged during the English Civil Wars. The restoration of the Baltimore family to its ancient rights resulted in the suppression rather than the obliteration of the colonial interests opposed to it. After 1660 Lord Baltimore placed first his brother Philip, then his son Charles, in the governor's position. Philip was compensated by being made chancellor, chief chancery judge, chief justice of the provincial court, and senior member of the council. A distribution of plural offices to family members characterized Baltimore's proceedings. The proprietor's friends were in exclusive possession of seats on the council and the more important judicial, legal, and fiscal offices. This had the effect of blocking access to positions of power for men who in wealth, or ambition, or education, were or felt qualified to hold them. Since the payment of Maryland's officials was largely made from fees set by themselves, this also led to grumblings about nepotism and extortion.

The proprietor's deliberate policy in fact was to assert his prerogative charter rights to the full and to bolster his position by surrounding himself with loyal officeholders, many of whom were blood or marriage connections. Either men of large estates, or men engaged in using their official positions to build up their land holdings, this proprietary faction was oligarchical, privileged, and predominantly Roman Catholic. Where proprietary office was used to build up a strong economic position by new arrivals in the colony it caused particular resentment among substantial men outside Baltimore's circle. The old anti-Catholicism of the earlier period also asserted itself. Although Baltimore continued to promote a policy of religious toleration—one that encouraged the immigration of English and foreign Protestants—his family and close associates were normally Roman Catholics. Catholics held high office in numbers disproportionate to their incidence among the population as a whole. While Maryland's oligarchy therefore resembled that fostered by Berkeley in Virginia, it stood out as even more distinctly exclusive in a less homogeneous population, and it provoked earlier challenges than those offered in Virginia.

Baltimore's proceedings were by no means illegal or extra-legal, since they arose from the extensive rights conferred on him by his charter. The same charter gave existence to the body that most strongly resented and contested his powers, the Maryland assembly. By 1660 the assembly had tasted power. It was sufficiently chastened at the Restoration to accept Baltimore's reading of the Maryland charter and his assertion of prerogative rights. It may be, in fact, that Baltimore for some years placed his own followers in the assembly by the familiar means of seventeenth-century electoral control. But this short period of amity gave way to one of conflict. In 1669 the assembly issued a statement of seven grievances, reflecting on the proprietor's sovereignty. In his turn the governor lashed its members, who, he informed the lower house, were "not to conceive that their privileges run parallel to the Commons in the Parliament of England, for that they have no power to meet but by Virtue of my Lord's Charter." Their standing, he stated, was like that of an English municipal council such as the Common Council of the City of London.

The assembly's grievances were compounded in 1670 (the same year as the narrowing of the franchise in Virginia) when the proprietor ordered a tightening of eligibility for the franchise, making this dependent on the possession, by freeholders alone, of fifty acres or a personal estate worth £40. This move was followed by restrictions on the number of representatives to be sent from each county to meetings of the assembly, presumably because a smaller electorate and a smaller legislature were thought more amenable to proprietorial influ-

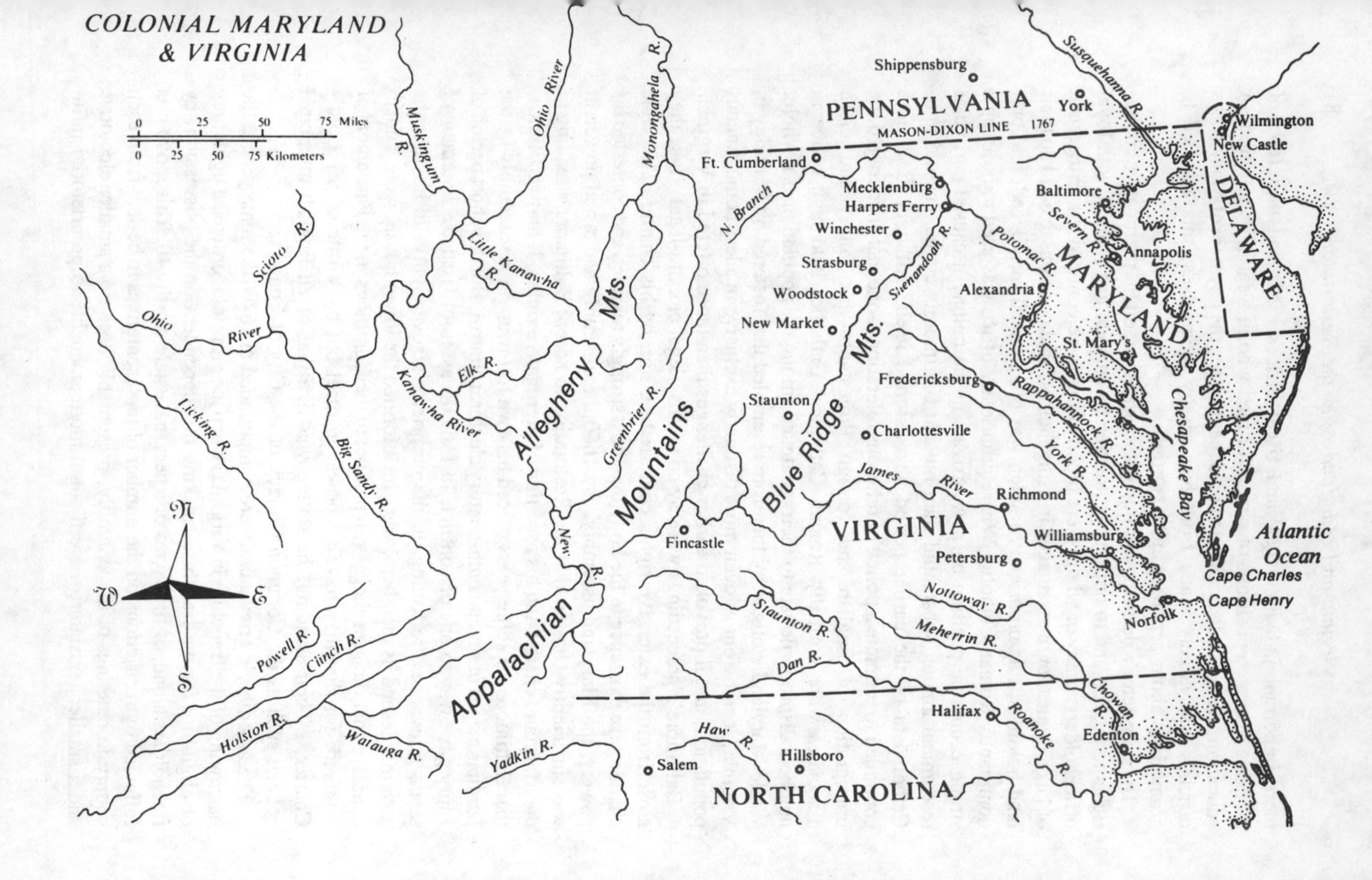
COLONIAL MARYLAND
& VIRGINIA
0 25 50 75 Miles
0 25 50 75 Kilometers
Muskingum R.
Ohio River
Monongahela R.
Scioto R.
Ohio River
Little Kanawha R.
Elk R.
Kanawha River
Licking R.
Big Sandy R.
Allegheny Mts.
Greenbrier R.
Mountains
New R.
Appalachian
Powell R.
Clinch R.
Holston R.
Watauga R.
Yadkin R.
N
W
E
S
PENNSYLVANIA
MASON-DIXON LINE 1767
Shippensburg
York
Susquehanna R.
Wilmington
New Castle
DELAWARE
Ft. Cumberland
N. Branch
Mecklenburg
Harpers Ferry
Winchester
Strasburg
Woodstock
New Market
Shenandoah R.
Blue Ridge Mts.
Staunton
Charlottesville
Fincastle
Baltimore
Severn R.
Annapolis
MARYLAND
Potomac R.
Alexandria
St. Mary's
Fredericksburg
Rappahannock R.
York R.
Chesapeake Bay
James River
Richmond
VIRGINIA
Williamsburg
Petersburg
Atlantic Ocean
Cape Charles
Cape Henry
Norfolk
Nottoway R.
Meherrin R.
Staunton R.
Dan R.
Chowan R.
Halifax
Roanoke R.
Edenton
Haw R.
Salem
Hillsboro
NORTH CAROLINA

ence. Lord Baltimore personally disliked the large franchise and large representation then existing in Maryland and probably attributed to it the lack of cooperation that he received from the assembly.

Baltimore's changes in the conditions of representation touched a highly sensitive issue for the assembly. By the 1670s and 1680s, its members seem to have been men of property who had established themselves in local and county offices but were frustrated by the existence of the closely knit and exclusive proprietary group in any inclinations they may have had to climb higher. For them, the assembly was the only countervailing institution to the proprietary executive, and they focused their political aims on asserting its independence and its claims to provincial authority. They therefore strongly objected to Baltimore's interference and to his later attempts to stress his legal power of veto over their legislation and other implied or stated challenges to the lower house's powers. Naturally enough, many of their arguments and the procedure of their house they borrowed from the strongest legislative body they knew—the English House of Commons. Naturally enough, these claims proved unacceptable to Baltimore whose powers legally exceeded those of the King in relation to Parliament.

Whether or not the assembly members' more basic economic interests also clashed with those of the proprietor is uncertain. On many occasions the assembly agreed with economic legislation initiated by the proprietor promoting trade and commerce. Neither the proprietary system of quitrents and taxation nor the proprietary abolition of the headright system in 1683 stirred up agitation in the assembly. But there were clashes over economic policy in the assembly of 1688. And there was dissension in some parts of Maryland led by men outside the assembly over fiscal and economic matters. In 1676, in Calvert County, sixty men protested against heavy taxation, asserted their Protestantism, and condemned the proprietary system. Two were subsequently hanged without, it appears, provoking any protest from the lower house. In Charles County an old enemy of the Baltimores, Josias Fendall, stirred up trouble in 1676. He was elected as an assemblyman in 1677. Yet his position was exceptional. He had been barred from public office since 1660, and among his complaints was one that the lower house was too subservient to the Calverts. Another agitator of this time, John Coode, served as an assemblyman from 1676 but was expelled at the demand of the council in 1681. These protests from outside the assembly, viewed with alarm by the proprietor, undoubtedly sprang from conditions caused by the poor state of the economy and the influence of Bacon's rebellion in Virginia. Recent studies also reveal that in Maryland (and the same may have been true of Virginia) after 1660, opportunities for poor settlers to achieve land and office declined sharply with the consolidation above them of a sizeable group of men of wealth, education, and status. Poor men and some gentlemanly leaders suggested that these ills would be remedied if only proprietary rule were replaced by royal government, an illogical if understandable feeling.

The culmination of these agitations came in 1689. In July of that year John Coode raised a body of men, captured the state house, the proprietary governor, William Joseph, and Lord Baltimore's plantation. The armed insurgents called a convention of four delegates from each county which confirmed existing officeholders, except Roman Catholics, set up an interim government, then dissolved to await instructions from England. These had not arrived by 1690, and in the spring of that year it was necessary to call another convention to set the provisional government on a firmer footing. The causes of the Maryland revolt of 1689 are fairly well established; its progress to 1692 when the first royal governor arrived has recently been closely analyzed. Similarities between it and an uprising against Governor Andros in Boston and a revolt led by Jacob Leisler in New York are striking. The participants in all three were influenced by uncertainties that arose after news of the invasion of England by William of Orange in 1688 came to America. In Maryland the failure of the proprietary government to proclaim the King aroused serious apprehensions and provided an excuse for action by its enemies. All three involved unfounded rumors of a Catholic-French-Indian plot to overthrow colonial liberties and colonial Protestantism. In Maryland the revolutionaries formed themselves into a "Protestant Association." The participants in all these revolts were political Protestants who genuinely believed that the new Protestant monarch and his government would check what they saw as a growing Catholic threat to North America. All three drew on various long- and short-term economic, social, and political grievances, particularly those arising from the exclusion of rising local men from power. The participants in all three were also willing to leave the final settlement of their affairs to the Crown.

From Maryland, Coode and a companion personally took the complaints of the revolutionaries to England. Like the emissaries from Virginia and Massachusetts, they were sympathetically treated. The English government, anxious for a Protestant government in Maryland and for a share in proprietary revenues, annulled the proprietary charter and sent out a royal governor, reserving to the Calverts only their rights as proprietary landlords. The succeeding political history of Maryland, like that of Virginia, suggests that a certain stability came to the colony after the Glorious Revolution. In part this was because the royal council appointed in 1691 was predominantly Protestant and predominantly representative of the emerging social leadership in the colony. Some of the frustrations experienced by ambitious Protestant planters under the Calverts therefore disappeared. The assembly also escaped from the pressures it had felt under the proprietary system; after 1691 it virtually controlled its own elections, size, and procedures and was not threatened by the Crown. It also seems to have taken over several types of public business from the council and to have played a greater role in the affairs of Maryland in the years after the Glorious Revolution than the more quiescent Virginia assembly did. In 1715, when the Calvert family was restored to its full proprietary rights, Maryland, according to one student, was "in a state of almost perfect quiet and harmony."

Local government in the Chesapeake colonies continued much as it had been established before 1660. In Maryland the three original counties of 1650 had grown to eleven in 1700; four more would be created by 1776. The hundred system also continued and, as the population within the counties increased, new hundreds were created by division and subdivision of the old. As in Virginia, a common feeling existed that advances in prosperity and stability would come more quickly if ports, towns, and even cities could be established. Executive and legislative actions to bring this about were taken on several occasions from the 1660s to the 1720s, but these paper enactments could hardly reshape Maryland's rural society. There were few concentrations of population in the colony, indeed, that could even be given the title of hamlet. The city (by legislative act in 1708) of Annapolis was in reality a small village; St. Mary's, the seat of government until 1694-1695, had only thirty houses scattered around as late as 1678.

Two developments in Maryland's local government did mark the latter years of the seventeenth century. The first was the decline of the manor, of which about sixty had been erected, exclusive of those held by proprietors, by 1675. After this date their creation almost ceased. Records of the holding of manorial courts survive in only one instance for the period from the Restoration to 1672, and it seems unlikely that even before 1675 the manors had much significance as units of local government; after 1675 they seem to have had none. The second development was the provision of a parish system, created by an act of 1692, tentatively establishing the Church of England in the colony. The actual formation of parishes was delegated to the county courts and proceeded very slowly. But by the end of the century they were beginning to function. Of the parish vestrymen, six in number, it was stipulated that after being initially chosen by the freeholders, they might fill their own vacancies. This closed system of appointment, challenged in Virginia during Bacon's rebellion, was modified in Maryland in 1702 to allow voting for vestrymen by taxable freeholders; in 1730 a definite system of rotation in office replaced it. An act provided that vestrymen should not be eligible for re-election for three years after holding office. The vestry had powers of taxation but could not appoint ministers. This was done by the governor. The early Maryland vestries appear to have had less power and prestige than their Virginian counterparts. Unfortunately, the few excellent detailed studies of local government and society in seventeenth- and early eighteenth-century Maryland are not sufficient to support worthwhile general conclusions.

In Virginia the structure of local government further developed but did not fundamently alter after the Restoration. The competition for local office that was perhaps involved in Bacon's rebellion has already been mentioned. The parish vestry had been consolidated by legislation in 1662; it was then stated that vacancies on the vestry, previously filled by freeholders' elections, had to be filled by the choice of the existing vestrymen. This principle was returned to after the attack made on it in 1676. Although the original motive for its application may have been practical rather than political, the result for many parishes became the perpetual domination of the vestry by the same prominent local families who sat on the county courts and had members in the assembly or on the council. Among the significant duties of the vestry—later, perhaps deputed to the sheriff—was the collection of the parish tax. In Virginia, at least during the latter seventeenth century and possibly for most of the eighteenth century, this tax was probably greater than either the county or public tax, a fact that emphasized "the importance of the parish as a religious and secular institution in the colony." But the county and the county court continued as the most important unit. Governor Berkeley reported the existence of some twenty counties containing forty-eight parishes in 1671. The number of counties had grown—often by a process of subdivision—to some thirty by 1735.

One final but essential point about local government in both Maryland and Virginia was the persisting tendency for it to be shaped and controlled by local forces. At the beginning of settlement, the absence of detailed British colonial policy had left the initiative in many matters of administration to the colonists themselves. After 1660 the commercial control of the empire was strengthened but with little interference with local institutions—the parishes and counties of the Chesapeake or the townships of New England. Yet the royal and proprietorial governors did struggle with local groups and interests, represented in the assemblies, over the control of such matters as the establishment of law courts, of profitable local offices and their fees, even over the erection of towns and other units of local rule. From these contests the executives emerged with little success. In Maryland, after 1689, the assembly stripped the royal governor of most of his earlier executive control over local government and took over its supervision and administration. In Virginia virtually the same process took place. As a whole, the colonists' continuing control of local government was crucial to the development of the Chesapeake and other regions of seventeenth-century America.

B. Slavery and society

While the political life of Virginia and Maryland settled in the 1690s to a pattern of relative stability and tranquility, Chesapeake society changed rapidly in other ways. Foremost among these was the transformation of a predominantly English into a mixed African and white population. Africans were first brought in large numbers to North America at the end of the seventeenth century. Virginia's Negro population in 1670-1680 probably numbered 1,000-2,000. By 1710 it numbered perhaps 20,000 and by 1730, 30,000. In Maryland the Negro population in 1700 was about 3,000-4,000; by 1710 it numbered about 8,000 and by 1720, 12,000. With few exceptions, the Negroes were slaves, owned by white masters and subjected to a body of colonial legislation and unwritten laws that defined their position.

CHESAPEAKE COLONIES

Estimated Percentages of Blacks and Whites

1680–1740

	Maryland			Virginia		
	Total Population	Black %	White %	Total Population	Black %	White %
1680	17,904	9.00	91.00	43,596	6.88	93.12
1700	29,604	10.90	89.10	58,560	27.99	72.01
1720	66,133	18.90	81.10	87,757	30.30	69.70
1740	116,093	20.70	79.30	180,440	33.25	66.75

The rapid increase in the importation, purchase, and use of slaves in the Chesapeake is explicable in purely economic terms. The period, especially after about 1700, when the slave ships brought more and more cargoes to the region, was one of renewal in the tobacco business after thirty or so years of stagnant prices and falling production. The turning point probably came in the 1680s. But there are more precise figures that indicate the value of exports to and imports from England after 1697 which, while not totally reliable, are suggestive. In 1697 the value of the Chesapeake colonies' exports is estimated at £227,756 and their imports at £58,796. Although 1698, 1699, 1703, 1705, 1707, and 1715 saw unfavorable balances of imports over exports, the years from 1716 to 1756 were all favorable. In total, for the period 1697-1715, exports were valued at about £4 million and imports at about £2 3/4 million. In the succeeding fifteen years exports totalled about £4 1/2 million and imports about £2 1/2 million. Figures for the importation of slaves in the same years are partly available: from 1699 to 1708 about 7,000 were brought in, a number perhaps greater than the entire slave importations of the seventeenth century. From 1709 to 1726 slaves imported from Africa probably numbered 10,000 and others came from the West Indies. Probably the ability of slaves to produce large quantities of tobacco at low prices first enabled the richer planters to undersell their foreign competitors. This in turn stimulated the import of more black slaves. A combination of low production costs and the re-opening of European markets after the end of the War of the Spanish Succession confirmed the large planters in their development of slave agriculture. But small planters also used slave labor, although adequate details of the relative slave holdings in different Virginia counties are lacking for this period.

The rising numbers of black men and women in the Chesapeake was a new development, but the presence of the Negro and of slavery was not. The first Negroes had come to Virginia in 1619—"About the last of August came in a dutch man of warre that sold us twenty Negars," John Rolfe recorded—and by 1644 about 300 mingled with a total population of some 15,000. From the beginning they were bought and sold. The enslavement of Negroes in the

Caribbean and South America empires of Spain and Portugal (and the traffic in slaves by these nations and the Dutch and the English) was already a fact. Negroes and slavery were therefore associated before the beginnings of slavery in North America. A lack of firm evidence has prevented a sure analysis of the exact development of Negro slavery in either Virginia or Maryland. It can, however, be shown that Negroes were servants for life very early on, and that they were early regarded by whites as different, inferior, and potentially dangerous.

It has been argued that in England and its colonies, anti-Negro prejudice followed rather than preceded slavery—with the implication that present-day racial prejudice will diminish or disappear as the economic and/or civil position of the black improves—but the most exhaustive study of these matters concludes that from "the first, Englishmen tended to set Negroes over against themselves, to stress what they conceived to be radically contrasting qualities of color, religion, and style of life, as well as animality and a peculiarly potent sexuality." Winthrop D. Jordan has isolated assumptions about blackness (equated in English thinking with sin, evil, filth), African religions (which seemed to Christians to be no religions at all) African behavior, the association of Africa with apes, and the belief that Negro women and men were sexually more active and virile than whites as determining the reactions of Englishmen in their contacts with Africans.

This very early racial prejudice, combined with the important fact that Negroes were already bought, sold, and enslaved, explains a great deal about early American treatment of the African. Further, Western Europeans believed that pagans, especially if captured in wars, might be enslaved. Indeed, religious arguments in support of slavery emerged quickly in Puritan New England as well as in the Chesapeake. All these factors combined with the shortage of labor in the colonies, led to Negro slavery. And once slavery developed, racial prejudices were intensified. It is important to remember that servile bondage of varying degrees reinforced by cruel and unusual punishments was not specifically confined to Negroes. White servants and laborers and the "poor" in general received savage treatment in England and, sometimes, in America. The feelings of respectable Englishmen toward their propertyless countrymen or, for example, toward the native Irish, in many ways resembled those they held toward the Negro. As a laborer controlled by others, the African was considered to possess all the defects of the white lower orders, and more. Many whites would have willingly subjected their poorer fellow countrymen to a kind of servitude little better than slavery. Indeed, it has recently been suggested that leading men in the Chesapeake may have welcomed the import of slaves as a way of diminishing the numbers of the volatile, less easily controlled, young white servants in the region.

Early laws on slavery and the Negro were codified in Virginia in 1705 when the growing proportion of blacks in the population made it politic to restate them in a convenient form. In Maryland numerous laws dealing with slaves were passed after 1690. The nature of this legislation is an important commentary on white attitudes, although the existence of legislation is never an entirely sure guide to practice. Broadly speaking, the laws show how the blacks were gradually "singled out for special treatment in several ways which suggest a generalised debasement of Negroes as a group," a debasement that "appeared about the same time as the first indications of actual enslavement." These laws included a recognition of the lifetime servitude of Negroes (Virginia 1670, 1682; Maryland 1664, 1671), the use of Negro but not white women as field laborers (Virginia 1643; Maryland 1654), the denial of the right to bear arms to Negroes (Virginia 1640; Maryland 1704) and the discouragement or prohibition of sexual relations or intermarriage between Negroes and whites (Virginia by 1662 and in 1691; Maryland in 1664, 1681). Later laws reinforced these distinctions and added others, especially those aimed at preventing slave "tumults" and "conspiracies," for although the slave was defined as property, he was also seen to have human yearnings for freedom.

This legislation and other sources also reveal that not all the early Negro population in the Chesapeake were slaves, although the percentage of free Negroes was very small. The early treatment of the free Negro was in part an index of racial feeling; later it also became an index of the degree to which the slave system was felt to be a stable one, able to co-exist alongside a free black class. One result of the increase in the total African population at the end of the seventeenth century seems to have been a diminution in the opportunities for the manumission of slaves and in the status of free Negroes. Although non-slave Negroes could always hold some forms of property in Virginia and Maryland, they were forbidden to own white servants, to possess weapons, to hold any kind of office—"civil, military or ecclesiastic"—or generally to be witnesses in law courts, or in Virginia to vote in 1723 (but nor did they vote in Maryland). This last act brought a protest from the English Attorney General, who wrote that he could "not see why one freeman should be used worse than another merely because of his complexion." The Virginia governor replied that it was necessary "to fix a Perpetual Brand upon Free Negros and Mulattos by excluding them from that great Priviledge of a Freeman, well knowing that they always did, and ever will, adhere to and favour the Slaves. And 'tis likewisé done with design, which I must think a good one, to make the free Negros sensible that a distinction ought to be made between their offspring and the Descendants of an Englishman, with whom they never were to be Accounted Equal."

The manumission of slaves was not only gradually made more difficult for the owner but in Virginia in 1691 the assembly declared that freed slaves should leave the colony. Again, the motive was to protect the slave system, since it was held that free Negroes and mulattoes were sympathetic to Negro slaves. In 1723 manumission was made even more difficult, and it seems that it was now meant only to be given to slaves who had betrayed slave plots or crimes.

In Maryland there was no legislation on manumission until 1752; it occurred but was not widespread before that date. The proportion of free Negroes in all parts of the Chesapeake was minute before about 1770.

The lives of the slaves are not well documented, especially in the earlier eighteenth century. By mid-century, "outlandish" or newly-imported Africans generally served as closely regulated field workers, often on slave "quarters"—small, isolated plantations—in the more remote regions. Here, they were cut off from wider social contacts, fed adequate but uninspired diets, and governed by overseers who were often free from the interference of their employers. Acculturation was therefore difficult; many must have lived and died in those rural solitudes. Typical quarters in Virginia contained about twenty-four slaves, of whom eight were field hands and the remainder women and children. Women, of course, also worked in the fields, as did children over the ages of thirteen or fourteen. Family life of a severely limited nature existed. Ratios of men to women varied in sampled Virginia quarters from two to one, to three to eight. Of the "family" life of these slaves, their customs and habits, we know effectively nothing.

Other slaves, presumably both "outlandish" and native born, worked on ordinary farms and estates. They lived in barns, attics, or in small huts and might labor and live closely with the owner's family. Opportunities for contact with other blacks depended on their master's personality, the nearness of neighbors, and other fortuitous factors. It would probably be wrong to think that their lives, except in abnormal circumstances, were totally circumscribed and bound by inflexible rules, making them robot laborers. For in such circumstances the owners and the slaves must have experienced a closeness in work that led each to experience and adjust to the personalities of the other.

Most generalizations about slave lives must be based on what is known of the larger plantations. On these large estates, slave occupations were not restricted to monotonous field work, for some jobs were available in the household and significant numbers of slaves were trained as artisans. Washington, for example, listed 67 slaves at Mount Vernon including 2 valets de chambres, 2 waiters, 2 cooks, 3 drivers and stablers, 3 seamstresses, 2 house maids, 2 washers, and 4 spinners, as well as knitters, blacksmiths, carpenters, a wagoner, a carter, a stock keeper, a miller, and several coopers. In fact, at least in the Chesapeake, a whole range of occupations existed for slaves by 1750 or 1760. On such estates as well a range of personal and social relationships among the slaves was obviously possible. Large owners tended to be relatively beneficent for both economic and humanitarian reasons. Slaves could make semi-official marriages, raise children, and sometimes indulge in social or festive behavior. Usually, they seem to have been reasonably fed and clothed. Those in the household, although sometimes suffering the whims and neuroses of individual masters and mistresses and cruel and unusual punishments, may have otherwise known reasonable working and living conditions.

The most privileged slave was certainly the artisan, especially when, as was increasingly the case in the eighteenth century, he was hired off the plantation to work in the neighborhood. House carpenters, joiners, coopers, blacksmiths, and the like were in great demand. In acquiring these skills, they also became proficient in English, and by working off the plantation they became knowledgeable in the ways of the world outside, able to manipulate or conform as opportunities presented themselves or circumstances demanded. This mobility and acculturation to non-plantation values, Gerald W. Mullin has suggested, "weakened slavery's hold on the very slaves who were most able to resist it effectively." From their ranks came many of the runaways and those who passed as free Negroes.

This brief discussion suggests some of the intricacies of slave life, although the sources for its reconstruction are scant and partial, and the fact that the great majority of slaves suffered brutish lives as field hands should not be forgotten. What does need emphasizing is that within a basically exploitative and oppressive system, a degree of humanity, sociability, and opportunity did exist. Conversely, a limited form of resistance and manipulation was available to the victims. Some slaves deliberately worked slowly and shoddily, they feigned illnesses, and they pilfered and stole, even to the extent of creating a large black market in food and supplies. Such mute protests suggest a degree of self-possession and self-determination. More overt acts of protest or revenge—arson and running away—were also practiced, but given the savagery with which these were repressed, it perhaps shows a rational caution that riots and rebellions were not. In the southern colonies before 1774, there were only a handful of slave rebellions, the most serious of which resulted in few white casualties but many Negro executions. The gravest rebellions of the colonial period, in South Carolina in 1739 and 1740, resulted in the deaths of about 25 whites and at least 100 blacks. Here, of course, lay bare the iron hand of planter control, always evident under the most velvet of patriarchal gloves. For the ultimate sanctions of slave life remained violence and the will of the master, often coincident realities.

It is important to note the other results of the rise in the number of slaves in the Chesapeake. The most obvious of these was what has been called the undoing of the Virginia "yeoman." First, the import of slaves reduced to a very low level the demand for white indentured servants, formerly a steady stream into Virginia. This removed a source of new recruits into the class of the poorer farmers and checked its expansion, perhaps for deliberate social and political reasons. By 1715 the migration of English men and women, which had amounted to tens of thousands during the previous century, had largely ended. From about 1730 it was to increase again but in limited numbers. Second, the existing small farmer, already badly hit—even to the point of leaving the colony—by the low prices for tobacco after 1660, found further difficulties after the influx of Negroes. The large planter with slaves could produce and sell tobacco at low prices and use his wealth and political influence to buy up large tracts of land. The less efficient of the smaller farmers, unable to compete, sank into relative poverty or moved to areas of greater opportunity, especially in Pennsylvania and North Carolina. The seaboard counties of the Chesapeake at least were gradually largely dominated by the better-off planters. This process brought the new political stability of the later seventeenth and the earlier eighteenth centuries, as established families finally came to exert much of the social and political control they desired.

C. Religious and cultural life

The developments outlined above suggest a society in which economic, social, and political pressures alternated to produce varying degrees of flux and stability. The Virginia planter, beset by the contraction of the tobacco trade in the 1660s and after, by Indian troubles and political dissensions in the 1670s, by the new problems of an expanding economy and the advent of wide-scale slavery in the 1690s and after, had ample outlets for his energies. Since the most influential settlers were also mostly thrusting and ambitious men eager to advance their profits and their status and to hoist themselves into the ranks of a colonial gentry, their main preoccupations became those of business, property, and politics. The Chesapeake society was young, unstable, and materialistic. Many of the old constraints of custom, tradition, and convention did not apply where a new business activity—free enterprise in tobacco planting—became the dominant preoccupation.

The need of Chesapeake society for organized religions, for example, was very weakly expressed. In Maryland, a deliberate proprietorial policy of religious toleration meant there was no formally established church for many years. This feeling was partly responsible for a relative profusion of religious sects. Three-quarters of the inhabitants, the proprietor estimated in 1676, were either Presbyterian, Anabaptists, Independents, or Quakers, "those of the Church of England as well as the Romish being the fewest." Of these, even the groups that accepted the need for an educated clergy were badly supplied. By 1690 there were probably only 20 or so clergy to minister to a white population of 22,000. In Virginia, where the Church of England had been legally established for many years, only some 10 Anglican clergy in 1662, 35 in 1670, 37 in 1702, and 29 in 1724 could be found. The numbers of dissenters—Quakers, Baptists, and Presbyterians were represented before 1700—and of dissenting clergymen were inconsiderable. The presence of the Church of England, as expressed in the ratio of clergy to population, was far less visible in the Chesapeake than in the mother country.

In Maryland the Anglican Church finally emerged as the established church, largely as a result of the anti-Catholic and anti-proprietorial feeling that had found its political expression in the revolt of 1689. The new royal governor,

Lionel Copley, was instructed by the Crown to establish the Church of England in Maryland. In 1692 the assembly passed "An Act for the Service of Almighty God and the Protestant Religion," already referred to in connection with local government and the establishment of parishes. There was little actual religious Anglicanism in Maryland. Indeed, the assembly insisted that a church settlement should be tied to the question of political rights and also rejected the possibility of establishing a high Anglican official to superintend the clergy. Not until 1702 was the act of establishment finally made law, mainly through the efforts of the handful of Anglican clergy in the colony and in spite of the assembly. Among these clergy was now Dr. Thomas Bray, a commissary or representative of the Bishop of London, who had arrived from England in 1700.

Bray's vigor, though he stayed for only a few months, improved the Church of England in Maryland, which also benefitted from a renewed English interest in the Anglican Church overseas dating from the late 1690s and which Bray also helped to promote. Compared with Virginia, the lay vestries in Maryland gave more freedom to the parish clergy, who also received good salaries. Indeed, the question of the supervision and discipline of the clergy played a large part in Maryland politics after 1700, for the natural tendency of the Maryland planters was to seek to establish the authority of the vestries and the colonial assembly over the Anglican church, a move resented by the clergy.

In Virginia a similar situation existed. The first commissary, James Blair, was appointed by the Bishop of London in 1689. As his counterpart in Maryland was to do, Blair struggled to improve the position of the clergy and to free them from overdependence on lay authority. The commissary noted that at the time of his appointment the governor had the legal right to induct ministers and the vestries had the right to present them. Yet it was usual for Virginia's clergy, although many of them served for many years, not to be inducted but to be appointed by the vestry in "a Contrary Custom of making annual Agreements with the Ministers, which may call by a name coarse enough, *viz*. Hiring of the Ministers." Local control in Virginia became even stronger than in Maryland, for Blair soon relaxed his reforming zeal, assimilating the thinking of the Virginia gentry during a tenure of fifty-four years as commissary.

In essence all these facts meant that throughout the Chesapeake region, church, like civil government, was subjected to a large measure of local control. The lay vestries exercised this directly, receiving their sanction from the assembly. It is clear that many Anglican clergy in the Chesapeake would have welcomed a greater assertion of authority by the English hierarchy in order to free them from this dependence. For years, there was talk of sending an English bishop to America to administer the colonial church. But this never happened, a sign of the lack of vitality of the eighteenth-century Church of England. In Virginia the governor and assembly continued to challenge the commissaries in matters of religion, while in Maryland after 1734 the commissary's position was so undermined that no appointment was made to the post, and the lay proprietor claimed final ecclesiastical authority. The reality of lay control was also strong in the dissenting churches.

In these ways the churches in the Chesapeake region became part of the structure of local institutions rather than an effective arm of their English parent bodies. The consequences of this would finally be of some moment. One immediate consequence was the lack of a countervailing force against the interests of the planters as slave owners. While the ecclesiastical (and civil) powers in England to some degree tried to impose humanitarian values and to persuade the planters to Christianize and baptize their slaves, the Church of England clergy in the colonies, in part because of their dependence on the slave owners, could do very little to implement these policies and had largely to accept the values of their slave-holding vestries and congregations.

The intimate connection between religion and learning in sixteenth- and seventeenth-century societies also underlay the development of culture and education in the Chesapeake. Most early colonial populations contained few university graduates, and those few were often clergy. In England the clergy of the Church of England to a large extent staffed the grammar schools and the universities while, after 1660, nonconformist ministers established academies (schools for pupils of twelve to eighteen and some adults) with new syllabuses, offering commerce, technical subjects, military studies, navigation, modern history, and languages as well as the traditional study of Greek, Latin, and philosophy. In the Chesapeake the small numbers of clergy and other graduates only slightly mitigated the influence of the thrusting and ambitious planters, few of whom were men of ideas. For much of the seventeenth century there is little evidence of corporate intellectual life or of the promotion of education.

Part of the reason for this was obviously the dispersed nature of the Chesapeake plantations and the difficulty of communications as well as the uncertain state of the economy after about 1660. In Virginia it also seems that a certain bluff self-interest on the part of some of the more influential men—possibly royalists apprehensive lest education promote "commonwealth" ideas—actively discouraged the founding of free schools or of colleges on English or New England lines. Governor Berkeley, who was certainly conscious of the relationship between some forms of education and political and religious dissent, thanked God that there were no free (i.e. grammar) schools in the colony, and on another occasion is supposed to have said that ministers of religion "should be better if they would pray oftener and preach less." One of Nathaniel Bacon's allegations was that the Virginia authorities had by 1676 promoted no "arts, sciences, schools of learning, or manufactories." And only a certain inertia, if not a positive prejudice, can explain why legislation proposed in 1661 and 1662 to promote grammar schools and a college—the latter, at least, could have been founded irrespective of population distribution—did not then pass the Virginia assembly but had to wait until the later seventeenth century. Nor was there a permanent printing press in Virginia until

1730. In Maryland, although provincial statutes provided for free schools in every county, few existed.

Yet there was, it seems, a generally high level of popular literacy in the Chesapeake, at first reflecting the existing literacy of its English migrants. In England and in the Chesapeake at this time instruction in the family in reading, writing, and arithmetic probably was widespread, and the household indeed was obviously an important transmitter of learning. In Virginia and Maryland it is also likely that there were some simple schools set up in different localities by clergymen and groups of parents. An apprenticeship system did exist, and some laws and court orders referred to schools or the provision of instruction in trades and handicrafts. A number of planters, too, made charitable bequests to found different types of schools. Henry Peasley, for example, left 500 acres of land, slaves, and household goods for the educational benefit of two parishes of Gloucester County, Virginia, and Robert Beverley in 1705 wrote of "schools founded by the legacies of well-inclined gentlemen . . ." managed by the county courts or the parish vestries.

The decisive emergence of an established upper or ruling group at the end of the seventeenth century was to be crucial for the cultural as well as the social and political shape of the Chesapeake region. This group's political and economic ascendancy sharpened the wish for social distinctions, including education and cultural polish. The moneyed Chesapeake planter in particular now began to model himself on his idea of the English gentleman. He imported books and pamphlets to stock his library and possibly subscribed to some English periodicals and newspapers. English fashions in literature and the staple mix of the classics, religious and theological writings, and works of history and travel were duplicated in the Chesapeake libraries of the well-to-do. In addition, manuals or guides to practical problems of medicine, husbandry, and other useful matters found collectors. Law books had an especial importance, and, indeed, various county courts had their own legal libraries by the end of the seventeenth century. Dalton's *Justice of the Peace* and *Office of the Sheriff*, giving simple guidance to the untrained officeholders among the Virginia gentry, were extremely popular. Similarly, medical books were useful in a region with few physicians.

The eventual foundation of a college in Virginia demonstrates some of the characteristics of culture, education, and politics in the colony. New demands for the establishment of a college seem to have come originally less from the ranks of the planters than from the Reverend James Blair, the Anglican commissary. It was to the clergy that he first looked for the endorsement of a plan "for the better encouragement of learning by the founding [of] a college in this country." The new proposals seem then to have been approved at a meeting of "private gentlemen," then by the governor and council, and only finally by the assembly. Money was afterward collected in Virginia and England, and in February 1693 the Crown granted the charter of "the College of William and

Mary in Virginia." The original plan for the college was that it should consist of three sections: a grammar school would prepare boys for two more advanced schools of philosophy and of divinity.

Blair became president of the College of William and Mary; his subsequent career brought him into frequent conflict with Virginia's governors. This was one reason why the college did not flourish. For it seems clear that William and Mary College functioned for many years at the level only of a grammar school. As late as 1724 it was described by a professor as "a college without a chapel, without a scholarship, and without a statute." No statutes indeed were promulgated until 1727. For most of the eighteenth century few students stayed long enough to take a degree. While this was also not uncommon in more celebrated seats of learning, including Oxford and Cambridge, it is obvious from other evidence that the college had many deficiencies and never had the academic respectability of Harvard or Yale in the colonial period. One result was that although the number of schools and school teachers increased in the eighteenth century, the Chesapeake was to be less well endowed with these than the populous northern and middle colonies. In Maryland no firm steps were made to found a college (at Annapolis) until the 1760s.

In the absence of an acceptable educational system—and perhaps contributing to this feature of Chesapeake society—came the growth of private and expatriate education among Chesapeake families. From the late seventeenth century until the Revolution, the better-off planters had their children taught at home by private tutors, then dispatched them to British or European universities or, for legal training, to the English Inns of Court. These contacts with the mother country naturally intensified the cultural links between England and the Chesapeake but removed a stimulus to the development of schools and colleges there. This must have deprived poorer boys of the opportunity for advancement through education that existed, for example, in New England and made the elite planter group more secure in their monopoly of polite culture.

The first native Virginians with cultural interests or achievements therefore tended to emerge from the ranks of the richer planters. William Byrd II, whose diaries provide a picture of Virginia life in the first half of the eighteenth century, read widely in classical and English literature; the scion of a wealthy family, he had received his education at Felsted School in Essex, England. Ralph Wormeley II, another product of planter society, whose library suggests a man of wide reading, also had an English education. Robert Beverley, the author of *The History and present state of Virginia*, published in London in 1705, had been English-trained. Only one or two of the few seventeenth- and early eighteenth-century Virginians and Marylanders with claims to humane learning acquired this wholly in the colonies. Moreover, Marylanders and Virginians wrote relatively little and published even less. Although William Byrd II dabbled in polite literature and left a number of manuscripts, nothing he wrote was printed in his lifetime.

In science, no native of the Chesapeake rivaled the achievements of New Englanders or, later, Pennsylvanians. Several residents sent descriptions of animals and plants to the Royal Society in London, beginning with Edward Digges in the 1660s. William Byrd II, elected a fellow of the Royal Society in 1696, acknowledged in 1706 that "we have not some people of Skil and curiosity among us" and, though an irregular correspondent of the Society, his own interests were those of a virtuoso rather than a precise amateur. The most important scientific communications on the Chesapeake came from observers, often sent out by English scientific patrons to dispatch samples and written comments back to the mother country. Among them, the Reverend Hugh Jones, a Welsh cleric, in Maryland from 1696 to his death in 1701; the Englishman William Vernon; and Dr. David Krieg, a Saxon physician (the latter two visitors to Maryland in 1678), however, seem to have provoked little enthusiasm among the Maryland planters, and "no articulate scientists of consequence developed in Maryland" up to the Revolution. No doubt, in the Chesapeake as a whole, the lack of urban centers where men of some leisure could meet, talk, read, and experiment, as they did in the colonial cities, hindered the development of a visible literary and scientific culture.

Chapter Four

New England After the Restoration

A. The Puritan colonies

The three Puritan colonies of Massachusetts, Connecticut, and Plymouth retained many of their similarities during the seventeenth century, particularly in the spheres of church and civil organization and in the general identity of outlook shared by their leading men. In all the Puritan colonies, a crucial development was the growth of population. This necessarily altered a society in which civil and religious life rested on the idea of small stable communities, organized in towns and churches. An increase in the wealth of the Puritan colonies also had significant results for men and women who by and large were taught that worldly riches presented dangers to the individual and to their religious institutions. For many New Englanders, however, an even clearer threat appeared with the re-establishment in 1660 of the monarchy and the Church of England in the mother country; the menace of a revival of royalist, Anglican authority was deeply disturbing to people who had constructed godly commonwealths during a period of virtual independence of English control.

Estimates of New England population growth show an average decennial increase from 1660 to 1720 of some 74 percent, almost twice that of the Chesapeake. The factors that caused this growth of population, a striking contrast to the Old World, can be stated with some confidence. The birth rate was probably no higher than that in England. But mortality in New England seems quickly to have fallen below that in England and Europe. One scholar has estimated that for Dedham, Massachusetts, the highest the death rate could have been in the period 1648-1700 was about twenty-seven per thousand, compared with some English and French figures as high as thirty-five to forty-one per thousand. Another demographic study suggests that in Ipswich, Massachusetts, where the population increased by 600 percent between 1661 and 1713, a significantly low rate of mortality for infants, children, and adults prevailed in the same years. The reasons for this can be suggested. First, nutrition seems to have been relatively good for all, leading to improved health and resistance to disease. Second, it seems likely that the kind of endemic and epidemic diseases that ravaged the Old World at this time had not yet seriously struck New England. Passengers with contagious illnesses, perhaps, had a chance to pass through their infectious stages on the long seaboard journeys to the New World, arriving in America after the moment at which the illness could be transmitted to those settled there. True, smallpox became a significant scourge in the colonies during the latter seventeenth century, appearing in New England in 1666, and, very seriously, in 1677-1678 and 1689-1690. It reached grave proportions as well on several occasions after this. Yet it may be that neither the incidence of smallpox nor the resulting mortality rate was as high as that in England. More important from the point of view of population increase, the peculiar combination of disease and malnutrition that caused major crises of mortality in Europe do not seem to have appeared in New England. A final point about New England's population growth, at least during the seventeenth and part of the eighteenth centuries, was the slightly earlier ages at which both men and women tended to marry compared with England. Since women conceived very quickly after marriage and then bore a steady progression of children, a decline in the age at marriage of even one or two years could have an important effect on population. Even so, the usual age at marriage was not strikingly low—above twenty-one for women and above twenty-five for men.

The expanding population clearly affected two of the fundamental institutions in New England, the town and the church. For the established towns, population growth meant intensive pressure on town lands. This first resulted in the division and settlement of vacant lands within the extensive existing town boundaries. New hamlets of settlement within the township at a distance of two or three miles from the older village center, as well as many isolated farms, often grew up. In Massachusetts twenty new towns were set up in the twenty years after 1660 and another thirty-seven between 1681 and 1719. In Connecticut the years between 1681 and 1700 saw the foundation of eight new towns, while from 1700 to 1720 a further sixteen came into existence.

This dispersal of population brought conflict between newer and older settlements within the townships, for men living at some distance objected to attending Sabbath services in the old meeting houses or to paying rates for highways and other services that they did not often use. They therefore pressed for the recognition of their hamlets as separate communities, or for some other form of independence from the traditional town authorities. The records for this period reveal numerous contentions between men officially living in the same town but not feeling part of the same community. At the same time, the old system of open field farming generally gave way to enclosed farms, and many inhabitants ceased to live on their "house lots" in the nucleus of buildings that had constituted the original village.

It has been suggested that the growth of population and the resulting pressure

ESTIMATED POPULATION
NEW ENGLAND COLONIES
1660–1720
Showing decennial percentage increases

W = White Population
N = Negro Population
% = decennial percentage increase

		New Hampshire	%	Massachusetts	%	Rhode Island	%	Connecticut	%	Totals
1660	W	1,505	–	19,660	–	1,474	–	7,955	–	30,594
	N	50	–	422	–	65	–	25	–	562
1670	W	1,740	*16*	29,840	*52*	2,040	*38*	12,568	*58*	46,188
	N	65	*30*	160	*–62*	115	*77*	35	*40*	375
1680	W	1,972	*13*	39,582	*33*	2,842	*39*	17,196	*37*	61,592
	N	75	*15*	170	*6*	175	*52*	50	*43*	470
1690	W	4,064	*106*	49,104	*24*	3,974	*40*	21,445	*25*	78,587
	N	100	*33*	400	*135*	250	*43*	200	*300*	950
1700	W	4,828	*19*	55,141	*12*	5,594	*41*	25,520	*19*	91,083
	N	130	*30*	800	*100*	300	*20*	450	*125*	1,680
1710	W	5,531	*15*	61,080	*11*	7,198	*29*	38,700	*52*	112,509
	N	150	*15*	1,310	*64*	375	*25*	750	*67*	2,585
1720	W	9,205	*66*	88,858	*45*	11,137	*55*	57,737	*49*	166,937
	N	170	*13*	2,150	*64*	543	*45*	1,093	*46*	3,956

on land, the splintering of old towns and founding of new ones, weakened the social and political cohesion aimed at by the original founders of the Puritan colonies. In some of the older towns, brother argued with brother, or son with father, about the division of the family's estates. Speculation and attempted profiteering in wilderness or vacant lands also became a feature of Massachusetts life. Many Puritan clergy saw the situation as one of potential chaos and decried the "insatiable desire after Land, and worldly Accommodation," particularly attacking the lack of public spirit and social cooperation in the newer and remoter towns where the inhabitants "were contented to live without, yea, desirous to shake off all Yoake of Government, both sacred and civil." But it is also argued that in the older towns a son's desire to inherit the family lands, and his inability to gain his own there because of scarcity, bound children more closely to their fathers, giving the older men "patriarchal" status and control. The double pull of the secular ambitions of an expanding and contentious society and of the reverence for remembered or imagined past stability and neighborliness may have created in many men a sense of guilt about the development of New England society.

In spite of these pressures, the town survived as the basic unit of government, and the newer towns in time came to resemble the old, embracing the ordinary concerns of their inhabitants and providing the focal point of community life. The Congregational churches and the militia continued to be organized on a town basis, although larger towns had more than one church and more than one militia company. Where they existed, schools also remained the responsibility of the town. Recent studies of town government in Massachusetts in the later seventeenth century have suggested that the annual town meeting was coming to play a greater role in decision-making in town affairs and that the selectmen lost some of their powers. But how far this process occurred generally throughout Massachusetts or in the other Puritan colonies is not known. What seems likely is that in most mature towns a number of influential families were regularly chosen for town and provincial office but that in cases of crisis or extraordinary controversy the ordinary deference given to them might be suspended or withdrawn.

The growth of population led indirectly to major changes in the other distinctive institution of New England life, the church. Early Puritans had hoped that the world would be "remade out of the churches" and that the whole population of the Christian commonwealth, with a few unhappy exceptions, would become full communicant members of the churches. By 1660, and increasingly after that date, many young adults failed to follow their parents and grandparents into full church membership. In many churches, attending but noncommunicating worshippers outnumbered the godly. The situation seemed to be reverting to that of the parish churches of old England where a minority of the truly godly had been surrounded, the Puritans believed, by hordes of the unconverted. This also threatened another cherished Puritan belief—the necessity for the churches to exercise discipline over their communicant members, who were expected to be a majority of the congregation. For many clergy and godly laymen, who set the tone of public life and who continued to maintain that New England was essentially a plantation of religion, the failure of the "rising generation" to enter full church membership amounted to the gravest crisis that the colony had experienced.

The crisis particularly centered on one area—baptism—for here the link between old and new generations in the churches was made. We have seen earlier that strict Congregationalists believed that only the children of full church members (one parent only, if necessary) might be baptized, the position still maintained in most of the churches in 1660. Many of these baptized children had grown up but had never themselves made the declaration of regenerate faith necessary for their communion. What was the position of their children and could they be baptized? This had become the important question in 1660 when the third generation was rapidly increasing in numbers. To deny these children baptism broke the chain of godliness that the older Puritans hoped would link all succeeding generations to the founders of the churches. But to admit these children of unconverted parents to baptism would, according to some clergy and many laity, betray the original and fundamental principles of religion in New England. Whatever was done might be dangerous.

The problem of social and religious order—discipline and the survival of the churches—therefore underlay that of baptism. Even advocates of strict baptismal regulations sometimes anxiously asserted the churches' control over the unbaptized in their congregation. The solution offered by those willing to make innovations in the New England church way was the extension of rights of baptism to the sons and daughters of non-church members if the parents themselves were the "seed" of godly fathers or mothers and would testify to their faith and promise to obey church rules. A substantial number of full church members opposed this accommodation and wished to uphold, unchanged, what they felt to be the vital precepts of Congregationalism. They were joined by a minority of the clergy, though a majority of clergy advocated reform, holding less steadfastly to the old ways than their church members.

Doctrinally, the issue found resolution as far as possible with the opinion in 1662 of a majority of those attending a synod of churches that "confederate seed"—later known as "Half Way" members, had a place in the churches. These nonregenerate but baptized children of the godly, who promised obedience to the government of the church, entered a "Half Way Covenant." They could have their children baptized and they had the rights of full church members, except for communion and voting in church matters. But the opinion of the synod could only be a recommendation to the sovereign local churches, many of whom refused to accept it. The resulting arguments over the Half Way Covenant within and between the churches went on for many years before a majority of churches finally agreed to the new practice. In this way, the churches experienced the same burden of controversy and change undergone by the towns. Indeed, the crisis in the churches was perhaps more severe and more lasting in its effects and accompanied by numerous other church quarrels over matters ranging from the doctrinal to the financial.

Besides the changes in towns and churches, a third internal development of importance occurred in post-Restoration Puritan New England: the growth of trade, wealth, and prosperity. Although some years, especially those of King Philip's War (see Chapter 6), would still bring hardships and shortages, increasing trade and economic diversifications into commercial farming came first to Massachusetts, then to Connecticut. Plymouth did not share this growth, one reason why it was soon absorbed into Massachusetts. After the Restoration, New Englanders continued to trade to the Chesapeake, the Canary Islands, and other areas of older trade, but they also successfully expanded their commerce.

One important area of growth lay with the West Indies, whose carrying trade by 1677 was reported to be largely in the hands of New England merchants. A considerable trade took place with the French West Indies, a connection that persisted in spite of its prohibition by the Navigation Acts and for which New England became notorious in London, especially at times of war between France and England. From the West Indies the New Englanders brought sugar, which they distilled into rum. Much of this was taken to Newfoundland and paid for by fishermen in bills of credit to be drawn in London at a substantial profit. Direct contacts also opened with France. A French Channel Islander who settled in Boston established a substantial commerce not only to the Channel Islands but to the French ports of Nantes and Bordeaux. By 1675 reports even stated that Boston had a glut of French goods. Another development, from which Boston as well as New Hampshire merchants profited, was a growing trade from Portsmouth in naval timber, something that the British navy had come to depend on by 1672. New Englanders also sailed to several English and European ports and by the later seventeenth century had begun to penetrate to the fringes of British commerce in Scotland and Ireland.

The changes brought about by this growth became as significant as those in the towns and churches. Many of the merchants saw the advantages that membership in the British empire held for their commerce and the extent to which their success depended on amicable relations with the British government and with British merchants, providing access to the British trading network and credit facilities. For these and other reasons they proved unwilling to support many of the religious and political practices that disturbed the English government. Native New England merchants did not generally attack these practices outright but usually favored their reform. After the Restoration, a number of more defiantly anti-Puritan English merchants came to Boston, providing an alternative style of life—latitudinarian, secular, cosmopolitan—to that favored in the colony. Although contemporaries among the clergy and the laity noted and criticized the growth of commerce as destructive to religious and social homogeneity, they also recognized it as an important engine of wealth and social mobility. They married their sons and daughters into merchant families. One cynic wrote that they would "marry their children to those whom they will not admit to baptisme, if they be rich." By and large, Boston, by the end of the seventeenth century, was a town in which trading values dominated society, and this must have become true of the whole eastern New England seaboard in the years that followed. In Boston, for example, during these years large numbers of small investors held shares in shipping ventures, although the economy grew in the next century in such a way as to concentrate share holding in fewer hands.

These alterations in town, church, and trade formed the background to New England's political and intellectual life in the post-Restoration period. A further change, and one that became enmeshed with internal developments, arose from the Restoration itself. The English government after 1660 wished both to regulate colonial commerce and to modify the religious and political practices of Puritan New England. Plymouth and Connecticut, suppliants for English favors and barely known in London, were less affected by this policy than Massachusetts. The government of Charles II neither sought to suppress the charter or the congregational system of that colony but modestly intended to ensure that it tolerated Anglicans and Quakers, observed the terms of its charter, and did not discriminate politically in favor of Congregationalists. To many Puritans, these proposals challenged cherished practices thought to guarantee church and civil order and threatened the colony's assumed charter independence. In New England, from about 1662 onward, a division, lasting until the end of the seventeenth century and even to some extent forming the basis of later political factions, existed between a fiercely independent Puritan group and more moderate and conciliatory men willing to cooperate with the English authorities.

In Boston, many political moderates also supported the Half Way Covenant and many political independents resisted half-way practices. This suggests a spectrum of attitudes encompassing religion and politics. Some men wished to defend traditional practices; others more open or more commercially minded were willing to accept political and religious innovations. In general, the inhabitants of the smaller towns, as might be expected, often held traditional and orthodox views while the more cosmopolitan merchants and residents of the ports showed a readiness to admit change. In time a majority of the deputies in the General Court, many of whom represented the smaller inland towns, came to support a policy of noncompliance with English demands. A majority of assistants, many of whom were drawn from the less insular merchant elite, proved more amenable to English wishes. Yet, especially after the passage of an Act of Trade of 1673 adversely affecting merchant interests, and after clumsy attempts to enforce the Navigation Acts by officials sent from England in the 1670s, many merchants came to see the merits of opposition to English authority. This, however, they based on political Whiggism rather than Congregational scripturalism.

Another area of disagreement between the English government and conservative Puritans was the franchise. After 1660 English officials pressed the Massachusetts authorities to repeal the law granting full voting rights only to church members and to give all freeholders the right to vote. The Massachusetts General Court rejected this order, upholding the right of all church members to become freemen, although they conceded that non-church members holding taxable property of £120 and meeting certain other requirements might also vote. The property qualification was a high one, and the number of church members among the adult males had now begun to decline from the high level of the first twenty-five years of the colony's history. By the 1680s probably about 30 to 40 percent of the adult males in Massachusetts held the right to vote. The English government objected not to the shrinking size of the franchise but to political discrimination against Anglicans and other non-Congregationalists. Yet the firm hold on government given by the religious franchise to the orthodox Puritans now appeared doubly important to them in the face of English pressures. Its usefulness became apparent in the 1680s when the church member-freemen voted deputies and assistants out of office for taking too soft a line on relations with England.

The culmination of these controversies between England and Massachusetts came in the 1680s as the determination of the English government to reform the whole colonial system steadily grew. Like several other colonies, Massachusetts had her charter cancelled. A royal president and council were appointed, representative government was abolished, and the town-meetings' powers were curtailed. In spite of a great burst of political activity when the Puritan independents, encouraged by such ministers as Increase Mather and Joshua Moody, gained complete control of the government before the vacation of the charter and spoke of armed resistance to England, there was no overt opposition. In 1686, when effective royal government began, the defeated former rulers conceded a surly, passive obedience to the new regime.

The history of Puritan New England from 1686 to 1691 is one of tightly-packed change. Under James II, the whole region together with New York and New Jersey was incorporated into a single Dominion of New England, and Sir Edmund Andros, formerly governor of New York, became governor, advised by a council of nominated members drawn from the various former colonies and territories. Andros, a dutiful soldier, tried to strengthen colonial defenses, to enforce the Navigation Acts, to regularize colonial administration by laying down set procedures and scales of fees, and to create a uniform system of land titles. Although several colonial administrators recommended against this, James II had also instructed that New England should be governed without a representative assembly. As a good Anglican, Andros patronized the Church of

England and sponsored clergymen and services in Boston. From the beginning, the Puritan independents opposed him; their objections to the lack of a representative assembly and to the suppression of town meetings found wide support. However, the governor did at first have the cooperation of some considerable and influential moderates, many of whom served as members of his council. Their gradual alienation from him, as they saw their economic interests threatened by his reforms, undermined his position. The moderates eventually were pushed into an uneasy alliance with the unreconciled Puritan orthodox.

Early in 1689, news of William's invasion of England reached New England, creating considerable excitement. Dissident colonists could now identify their cause with that of the Whigs and anti-Catholics in England, and rumors flew around accusing Andros of treacherous dealings with the French and Indians and of Tory and Catholic sympathies. Finally, on 18 April 1689, an armed uprising in Boston resulted in the imprisonment of the governor and most of his officials. Whether the uprising was spontaneous or carefully planned remains uncertain. It brought about the formation of a Council of Safety to conduct the affairs of Massachusetts until orders should be received from England; on it moderates and more orthodox Puritans sat uneasily side by side. A few weeks later, the council was abolished as the result of demands from the Massachusetts towns, possibly engineered by the leaders of the orthodox faction, for a return to the old charter and the restoration of the governor and General Court of 1686, the last year in which charter elections had taken place. These events coincided with the outbreak of serious hostilities between the English in the northern colonies and the French and their Indian allies. War forced restraint on opposing political factions, but their divergences found expression in different opinions about the future of Massachusetts. The old "independent" group sought the English government's restoration of the charter of 1629 and the re-implementation of traditional practices. Many moderates sought a new charter or a modification of the old charter, hoping to break the power of the Puritan independents. A strong realization of New England's military dependence on the mother country in time of war now also lessened yearnings after self-government.

Massachusetts in 1691 finally received a new charter that sought to meet the demands of the orthodox group by providing not only for an elected house of deputies but also for the election of the colony's council by the deputies. Yet it brought general conformity with normal English colonial practices and satisfied the anti-independents by making the governor of Massachusetts a Crown appointment, giving him veto powers over colonial legislation and control of the military. Religious toleration was also enjoined; so, too, a franchise based on property rather than religious qualifications. After years as a virtually self-governing community, Massachusetts now approached the status of most other English colonies. This was something of a watershed. Even more so was

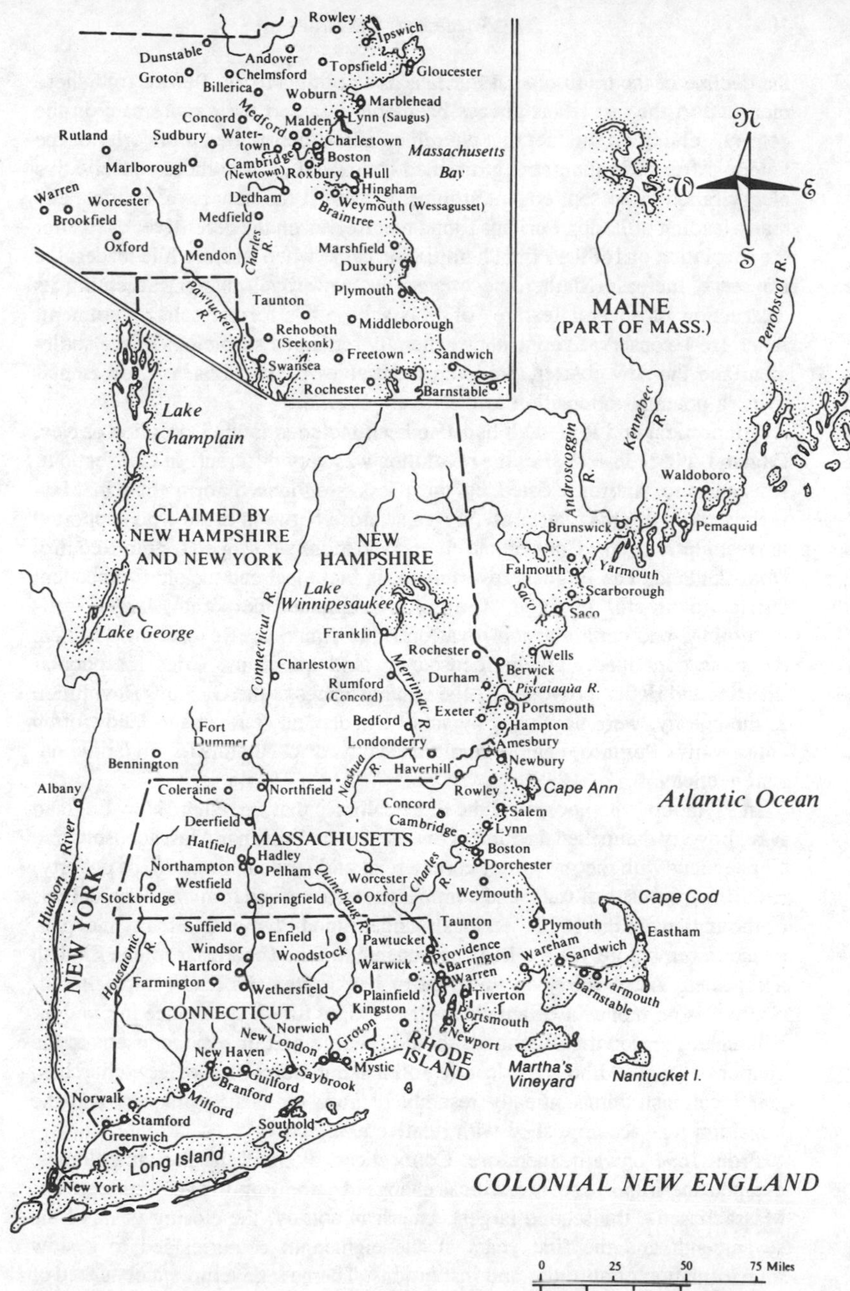

COLONIAL NEW ENGLAND

the decline of the traditionalist Puritans as a political force. Before 1686 these men had in the last resort always been able to assert their supremacy in the colony, relying on the fact that church members constituted a majority of the voters. After 1686 their strength waned considerably. The more conservative clergy failed to present cogent arguments against the new royal charter, and many leading orthodox Puritans found themselves on the defensive, even after the revolution of 1689. A final humiliation came when an erstwhile leader, the Reverend Increase Mather, negotiated the new royal charter, accepting its destruction of several features of Massachusetts's former self-government. After 1691 conservative Puritans generally remained suspicious of the settlement and the new charter, grouping themselves in the House of Representatives, a potential opposition to the royal governor.

Connecticut and Plymouth had also been included in the Dominion of New England, but their fate after the revolution was very different. In Connecticut, resistance to Andros existed but in a less pronounced form than in Massachusetts. After his overthrow, a rivalry arose between those who supported the resumption of the Connecticut charter and those who hoped for more control from England. The English government, in fact, declared the old Connecticut charter to be still in force. The colony remained corporate, largely self-governing, and certainly non-royal until the American Revolution. Political divisions continued, largely focused on land questions. Cries for popular liberties and rights, provoked by the circumstances of the Glorious Revolution in the colony, were now used by small tenants and claimants to lands (often conservative Puritans) against landlords and land speculators (often latitudinarian gentlemen).

In Plymouth, the poorest of the three colonies that shared the New England way, poverty dampened the kind of dissent that had arisen in Massachusetts and Connecticut with the growth of commercial and landed groups. This poverty, resulting from lack of trade and commercial farming and from the depredations of the Indians in the 1670s, seriously undermined Plymouth's shaky independence. Even before 1686 it had been unable to win a charter from the English authorities. After 1689, on the edge of bankruptcy, its leadership faltered. There was no money available to sponsor a fight for independence in London. Whitehall decided that Plymouth should become part of Massachusetts in the charter of 1691. Although it lost its political autonomy, its society, churches, and local institutions already resembled those of its new master, and the transition was accomplished with relative ease.

From 1691 onward, therefore, Connecticut, alone of the Puritan colonies, escaped the imposition of political changes by the English government. For Massachusetts, the second largest American colony, the closing years of the seventeenth and the first years of the eighteenth centuries led to a slow transformation of attitudes and institutions. The new government consisted of the Crown-appointed royal governor, the council elected by the representatives in the lower house—an election subject to veto by the governor—and a

House of Representatives, chosen by all freeholders rather than by the earlier church-based electorate. The fact that the first royal governor and the council had been selected by Increase Mather and were all natives or residents of the colony helped smooth the transition, although the lower house on several occasions vainly supported attempts to restore the old charter. For a time after 1691, the lower house, in which the most conservative, pro-old charter and anti-gubernatorial sentiments could be found, lost influence, much as it did in Virginia in the same years, and the council expanded its importance, initiating most general colonial legislation. A greater turnover of representatives—some 297 different men served as such from 1692 to 1700 compared with only 487 during the whole first charter period—and war-time conditions partly explain this situation.

One important consequence of the new structure of government lay in the strengthening of the Massachusetts county and the relative decline of the town as a political force. Counties and county courts had existed in Massachusetts since the early years, but only after 1691 did the county office of justice of the peace, a royal appointment, become important, providing the governor with a new weapon of patronage. About a fifth of those elected to the House of Representatives in 1720 were J.P.s, and "they provided the nucleus for the governor's party." Indeed, in spite of interludes of assertiveness by the representatives, especially in opposing the grant of a permanent salary to the governor and the existence of "opposition" politicians, royal government found a relatively easy acceptance. The old political divisions between orthodox Puritan "independents," opposing all calls for change from England, and the moderate, merchant-associated group, more amenable to the English connection, faded away. As population grew and the economy became more complex, different interest groups arose and conflicts over finance and administration replaced the simpler struggles of the past. The old Puritan politico-ecclesiastical position merged into a Whiggish hostility to executive power, similar to that found in the other American colonies. Its roots lay in American conditions but its principles derived from Whig and radical English models rather than from New England's Puritan heritage, though the latter now merely receded, remaining fully available to those who wished to draw on it. By the 1720s or 1730s most politically active men had learned to live with, even to cherish, the new Massachusetts charter as the basis of these new Whiggish liberties.

B. The other colonies and territories

The three remaining New England colonies and territories of New Hampshire, Rhode Island, and Maine lacked the density of population, the relatively cohesive religious and civil institutions, and the intellectual and cultural identity of the Puritan colonies. During much of the second half of the seventeenth century, indeed, their Puritan neighbors relentlessly sought to dominate and impose on them the particular imprint of their own society. In the case of Maine and New Hampshire, this was partly achieved. Rhode Island, although bitterly attacked at various times by Plymouth, Connecticut, and Massachusetts, successfully fought off assaults on its territories and institutions and retained a distinctive flavor of religious and political radicalism within its contested boundaries.

Maine had a tiny population and uncertain forms of government during most of the seventeenth century. Such sparse coastal settlements as Kittery, York, and Wells, as well as the Isles of Sholes where rough fishermen lived under rougher justice, were primitive and poor. The Gorges family continued to maintain an ineffectual connection with Maine until 1677 when Massachusetts finally acquired its proprietary rights by purchase. This was virtually a recognition of reality, for since 1652 the larger colony had been active in the government of Maine and had controlled it during many of the years after 1658. Later, the Gorges family sought to reclaim their Maine lands, but these attempts were not supported by the English government. The Crown formally incorporated Maine into Massachusetts in 1691 under the second Massachusetts charter.

This final triumph of Massachusetts was not an unmixed blessing for the Bay colony. In spite of the ambitions of some Boston merchants to develop a profitable fur trade and use Maine as a base for the conquest of Nova Scotia, the province probably proved more of a liability than an advantage. Its few hundred inhabitants lived in scattered hamlets, a settlement pattern ill conceived for defense against French and Indian attacks. These were numerous in the wars of the later seventeenth century, and Maine's tiny communities suffered periodic devastation. Maine, in other words, remained a frontier territory and one that was contracting under enemy pressures before 1714. Yet during the same period, a degree of social and religious order came to it by the efforts of Harvard-trained ministers, financed virtually as missionaries by the Massachusetts government, in order to soften the manners and evangelize the morals—often by hell-fire preaching—of its inhabitants.

New Hampshire, as we have already seen, was also coveted by expansionist Massachusetts. In the years before the Restoration, the Bay colony's government moved in to fill the vacuum left by the Mason family's abandonment of its territory. Massachusetts's jurisdiction over New Hampshire lasted until 1679 when, with partial success, the descendants of Robert Mason revived their claims to his old proprietary. Although the family got back their rights to the soil, the Crown decided to give New Hampshire a royal government, first under a president and council and then under a governor, Lionel Cranfield. This ended Massachusetts's formal control over the region. New Hampshire then became part of the Dominion of New England. After the overthrow of Andros in 1689, it was temporarily reunited with Massachusetts by the vote of a convention of its towns. In spite of strenuous opposition from Massachusetts, the Crown re-established it as a royal province in 1691. New Hampshire then remained separate from Massachusetts, although the two colonies shared the same royal governors from 1698 to 1741.

Coinciding with these changes in New Hampshire's political status was a growing economic prosperity. Portsmouth became the center of a lucrative and expanding lumber trade. In particular, the town became the focus for the supply of masts and other timbers for the British navy and for pipe staves and boards to the West Indies and fish to southern Europe. A ship-building industry was also becoming important by the 1690s. An oligarchy of wealthy intermarried families rapidly consolidated its control of these activities. Before about 1680 these families had mostly been content to leave political affairs to Massachusetts-appointed officials while they pursued their own profit. After that year, increasingly realizing that economic success could be adversely affected by political developments, they assumed control of many important local and provincial offices. This left them free to support or oppose the central authorities—whether the Mason family, officials from Massachusetts, or a royal governor—according to how their interests were advanced or threatened. A classic example of a colonial elite that differentiated itself from the ordinary settlers over the years, such New Hampshire clans as the Waldrons, the Cutts, and the Vaughans—later to be joined by the most successful of all New Hampshire families, the Wentworths—constituted a powerful force in the colony's politics.

Rhode Island was in some ways the most interesting—though strangely it has been the least studied—of the New England colonies. In the post-Restoration period, as before and later, it remained curiously at odds with its neighbors. In these years the Puritan dislike of Rhode Island's policy of religious toleration explains much of the hostility which it faced. Puritan New England wasted few opportunities to represent Rhode Island to the English government as a factious and anarchical anomaly, and Puritan irritation with the colony redoubled when Rhode Island filed counter-accusations, citing Massachusetts's religious intolerance as well as instances of disloyalty to the mother country. The Rhode Islanders were generally successful in defending themselves against these attacks, as their success in gaining a favorable charter in 1663 presaged. Depending on British goodwill to restrain the predatory behavior of Puritan New England, Rhode Islanders were not entirely displeased with the suppression of charters during the Dominion of New England period and did not conclusively reject Governor Andros. They suffered no severe discomforts as part of the Dominion and cautiously reassumed their old government and institutions in 1689-1690. These actions were approved in England. Rhode Island, like Connecticut, remained a semi-autonomous corporate colony until the American Revolution.

Much of the hostility of its neighbors to Rhode Island emerged in the support given at various times by the Massachusetts, Connecticut, and Plymouth governments to assaults on the territory of that colony. Although Rhode Island managed to stave off the majority of these attacks (its boundary difficulties were not settled with any degree of conclusiveness until the next century), they placed a severe strain on its limited financial resources and rather primitive and decentralized government. It became necessary for the colony to maintain agents in London to argue its cause, and the taxes raised to finance these activities caused resentment and factionalism among its inhabitants as well as a depleted exchequer. This political factionalism also involved—though the details are still not clear—the actions of land claimants, rivalry between the towns of Newport and Providence, and controversies between Quaker and Baptist.

Yet for the most part these factional crises seem to have been intermittent and sporadic and not to have brought any fundamental challenge to the shape of Rhode Island's distinctive institutions. In general, for example, a low incidence of attendance by the towns' representatives at the colony's General Assembly seems to have been usual, which suggests a degree of political apathy. This and frequent elections kept the actual influence of the General Assembly limited, although its formal constitutional powers were more imposing. Yet the Rhode Island towns also had powers reserved to them which lessened the status of the assembly over which they continued to maintain a final check, especially in matters of taxation. The governor and assistants provided some continuity of experience and administration, sitting with the towns' deputies during legislative sessions as a single house until 1694. Not only did Rhode Island for many years escape the typical American colonial experience of opposition between executive and legislative branches of government but it maintained the ancient practice—discarded in most colonies—of using the assembly as a judicial court of appeal. In these and other ways its political practices maintained something of the radical coloring that they had taken on in the earlier seventeenth century.

On the whole, these practices could survive because of Rhode Island's poverty and remoteness. Its population in 1710 numbered only about 7,500, and its commerce, though growing in the late seventeenth and early eighteenth centuries, was slow to develop. Although Rhode Island fell afoul of the English authorities in the years after 1690, when it was accused of disregarding the Navigation Acts and harboring pirates and other disreputables, its trade had only ten years before been described as inconsiderable—the export of "Horses and provisions" to the West Indies and the import of a "small supply of Barbados goods for supply of our families." At that time it also was said that there were several men "that deale in buyinge and sellinge though they cannot properly be called Merchants." The great obstruction to the development of commerce was noted indeed as "the want of Merchants and Men of considerable Estates amongst us," although Professor Bridenbaugh has recently shown that a prosperous group of stock-raisers and graziers, who exported animals and carcasses to the rest of New England, New York, Newfoundland and the West Indies, had emerged by 1690. In the eighteenth century the growth of Newport and other commercial and economic developments not only changed this state of affairs but led to the formation of a socially differentiated and politically conventional society more similar to that found in the other North American colonies.

C. Ideas and society

While it has been customary for many historians to write of a "New England mind," it should now be clear that there was no single New England. Outside of Puritan New England, Maine was still a frontier, most of whose inhabitants hardily struggled to wrest a living from the soil, without the desire or resources to engage in intellectual or artistic activity. New Hampshire was barely moving in the latter years of the seventeenth century toward a pattern of society that could support a cultural life; this would be one that was mostly derived from Puritan Massachusetts or from England. Rhode Island's inhabitants could claim to have fostered certain distinctive political and religious ideas, but after 1660 these were hardly enlarged or developed and nothing much was added to the original tenets of its founders. The colony lacked schools, colleges, and, until 1727, a printing press. And, within Puritan New England, in cultural matters Plymouth was an appendage and Connecticut a lesser partner of Massachusetts. In sum, the "New England mind" was in most respects the mind of southeastern Massachusetts. The Bay colony's ascendancy lay in its size and wealth which allowed it to support Harvard, the only institution of higher learning in New England until 1701, when Yale College was founded, and the only printing presses until 1709, when one was set up in New London, Connecticut. Boston was also the center of New England book selling and had the only concentration of men of learning, wealth, and some leisure in New England, although Edward Taylor, the best New England poet until Emily Dickinson (his writings were not published until 1939) lived and wrote in the remote village of Westfield.

The later seventeenth and early eighteenth centuries were as much times of change in this as in other areas. The school system, in spite of its legal existence, actually declined in vigor and quality after about 1660. While the founders of the colony had sought to establish Latin or grammar schools in order to provide the basis for the transmission of traditional European culture, many rural communities were reluctant or unable to pay for this kind of teaching. They preferred their village schools to teach simple English and numbers. More sophisticated communities like Boston maintained a Latin school, while their practical needs were met by the establishment of private institutions offering young men instruction in commercial subjects, French, and navigation. Some girls' education was also offered privately in subjects like needlework, music, and other accomplishments.

The intended pinnacle of New England's intellectual life, Harvard College, also slumped in this period. Throughout the later seventeenth century there were only two or three teaching officers resident in the college, and the numbers of students fell to as few as twenty-five in 1671. A low level of enrollment, mainly due to economic hardships, was accompanied by the unwillingness of any New England minister to assume the presidency of the college, for it was badly paid and the college's problems created an unpleasant atmosphere for its staff. For some time, Harvard was felt by contemporaries to be "sinking to extinction." The college inevitably became a focal point in the religious and political disagreements of the period. Conservative Puritans, for example, resented what they felt was a movement toward a more liberal influence in its affairs, signified by the choice of John Leverett as president in 1708, seeing in this a threat to the production of orthodox ministers and to the continuing preponderance of orthodox religious thinking.

The growth of New England after 1660, therefore, by no means produced a feeling of optimism among Puritans. Indeed it became the conviction of many educated Puritans that the decline of Harvard, of traditional types of learning, of the churches and religion and the changes in town and society, were part of a common pattern. New Englanders were falling away from the virtuous ways and the godly unity enjoined and enjoyed by the early inhabitants. The "little model of the Glorious Kingdome of Christ on Earth" was disintegrating. The rising generation appeared lax and irreligious. The merchants and land speculators introduced new elements of selfishness and luxury into New England. Increasing numbers of jeremiads, sermons and tracts that pointed to this decline in virtue and faith and exhorted men to reformation and revival, were preached and written. A point of belief among many clergy and lay Puritans was the danger to New Englanders of divine punishment if they did not remember as the Reverend John Higginson preached, "that *New-England is originally a plantation of Religion, not a plantation of Trade.*" These jeremiads sincerely expressed feelings of fear, anxiety, and bewilderment during a time of change and controversy. By the eighteenth century, when the experiences of the preceding years had mostly been accepted and assimilated, jeremiads were still preached but often more as time-honored rituals than as indications of perfervid beliefs.

While ancestral voices prophesying doom cried out on many sides, a developing sense of what might be called a confident and incipient nationalism also could be found in Puritan New England. The first settlers of the region had seen themselves as exiles in a harsh wilderness, preserving a godly church away from the corruptions of the Old World and awaiting the last coming of Christ. Their children and grandchildren, while conscious that some Old World corruptions were now finding their way to New England, now saw their American homes as a permanent and complete society, a distinct community identified with certain religious, political, and local institutions. Although continually conscious of the contribution of the founders' ideas to their way of life, the second and third generations constructed on them a powerful new interpretation of the character and meaning of New England, illustrated in the writing of such Puritan intellectuals as the Mathers, particularly in Cotton Mather's *Magnalia Christi Americana*.

A vivid example of this process at work was the idealization of the first Massachusetts charter. After about 1660 many Puritans invested this royal patent with a sublimity and significance that its original grantees had never accorded it. It came to be regarded as a kind of Magna Carta of Massachusetts life, the fundamental bulwark of the religious as well as of the political structure of the colony on whose continuation the whole happiness of New England rested. The charter was seen as no mere revocable royal grant but as a fundamental compact or contract between Crown and colony, unalterable without the consent of both partners. Many ministers even went to the edge of recommending armed resistance to any moves—from within or without the colony—to alter, amend, or destroy this fortress of their religious and civil liberties. Linked to these ideas was a developing interpretation of New England's short history. Massachusetts and Puritan New England were seen as the providentially directed creation of a small handful of poor exiles who had conquered the wilderness by their own financial and material efforts and without any English aid. Having established themselves by these labors, they had the right to direct their lives and enjoy their institutions without interference from the English Crown. The attitude was strengthened after 1660 by the conviction of many clergy that the restoration of the Stuarts to the throne of England was the restoration of Anti-Christ, a grave threat to the future of godliness in England and America. This reading of *Revelations* was confirmed for many by the persecution of dissenters that began in the mother country after 1660. Moreover, many Puritans continued, even into the eighteenth century, to believe that the final coming of Christ and the end of the world was imminent. Cotton Mather set the date for this first in 1697 and then in 1716.

The Puritan interpretation of New England's history as providential and unique continued throughout and beyond the colonial period although it gradually took on a more secularized form, asserting the rights of New Englanders as political beings rather than as godly Christians. A belief in the sanctity of the political and religious rights of Massachusetts and New England became part of the region's general culture and underlay many of the challenges to English authority in the eighteenth century. Yet seventeenth-century political and religious leaders by no means resisted all changes or subscribed to a common orthodoxy. Although the relinquishment of the 1629 charter and its replacement by the charter of 1691—later to be given its own aura of sanctity—brought protests from conservatives who believed that this accommodation was a betrayal of the first principles of New England, many others thought the new arrangement still guaranteed the survival of the churches as well as a reasonable degree of political freedom. Indeed, the 1689 revolt against Governor Andros was something of an intellectual as well as a political watershed, for it revealed that many had come to accept that politics and religion could to some extent be separated and that the disappearance of the old charter and the old political structure meant neither the end of the churches nor Massachusetts's uniqueness. Conversely, an individual's sound religious standing no longer seemed the necessary condition for full civil liberties. Cotton Mather was to write that "A man has a Right of his Life, his Estate, his liberty and his Family, although he should not come up to these and those Blessed Institutions of our Lord." Whiggism, as we have seen in connection with political developments, had begun to displace or build on—though not to obliterate—the old Puritan political ideas.

It seems likely that changes in political ideas found an easier acceptance than some other kinds. For example, tensions between old and new ideas about religion and society are revealed in the famous Salem witch trials of 1692-1693. These sprang from the accusations of several young girls against numerous women and men, beginning in the small and relatively isolated community of Salem Village (now Danvers), Massachusetts. Of the 165 persons accused, 20 were eventually executed as witches in league with the devil or his instruments while scores more confessed to the same indictment. A wave of hysteria seems to have gripped Eastern Massachusetts, reaching up to threaten even Lady Phips, the wife of the governor, before it was checked.

Isolated cases of witch accusations had appeared in New England in earlier years, and at a popular level, in both old and New England at this time, both the existence and reality of witchcraft was accepted. Moreover, Salem Village, where the outbreak began, was criss-crossed by the same kind of local feuds and arguments that, as the fullest studies of seventeenth-century English witchcraft have suggested, provided the social conditions for witch accusations. In Salem Village, one recent study suggests, the witchcraft charges sprang from a group of families engaged in subsistence farming and were directed against members of a more successful and rising section of commercially oriented farming families. There may also have been some connection—although this can only be suggested rather than demonstrated—between the political ferment of the years 1686-1691, the harsh conditions brought about by the French and Indian war that started in 1689 and a smallpox epidemic in the same years, and the rapid and large-scale outbreak of witch accusations. Many inhabitants may indeed have regarded all these painful experiences as justly merited punishments sent by God to chastise New Englanders for their sins.

Yet, from one point of view, what is crucial about the progress of the witch cases is its demonstration that as late as 1692 the colonial government, the judges, and the lawyers for several months all endorsed the popular belief in witches and allowed a large number of executions to take place. The most learned and well-educated men in the colony had overwhelmingly rejected as inadmissible evidence the identity of a witch that was based on the recognition of her (or his) specter or image by the afflicted, but not the existence of witchcraft. By this time in England the governing classes on the whole acted to suppress popular beliefs in witchcraft, and there had been few executions since 1660. In Massachusetts, certainly, the attitude of the Puritan clergy and leading laity, although in advance of popular beliefs, lagged behind those of the educated in the mother country, and the proceedings provide evidence of the extent to which Calvinist New Englanders were isolated from the spreading rationalism and skepticism of the seventeenth-century European pre-Enlightenment. Although Governor Phips in late 1692 and early 1693 increasingly acted to inhibit the law courts and prevent further executions and trials, the damage had been done.

This larger question has indeed occupied a number of writers on later seventeenth- and early eighteenth-century New England society who have tried to measure a Puritan or "New England mind" against a "mind" of the developing Enlightenment, in spite of the fact that neither "mind" can clearly be shown to have existed except in general terms. Nor has a history of the growth of the American Enlightenment yet been written. Still, it is a tribute to the intellectual vitality of New England—a colonial as well as a provincial society—that this question is discussed at all. Few other colonial or provincial societies had reached the point at this time where it would be worth contemplating these questions, and only the claims of New England Puritanism to embrace a coherent world view as well as the remarkable quality of Puritan intellectuals in the early phase of New England history make such an assessment important. In brief, it would seem that in what was essentially a provincial, colonial, and Calvinistic society, educated men moved relatively slowly to admit the growing claims of rationalism and the Enlightenment, and that many Puritans, as they became aware of them, tended to accept these new ideas only in such a way as to blend them with more traditional interpretations. If, as in Scandinavia or Scotland, Calvinism did erect a barrier to rationalism and certain kinds of intellectual development, so did traditional Catholicism and traditional Anglicanism in France and England. And new ideas did penetrate and find an audience, preparing the ground for the nurture and education of thoroughly rational thinkers like Benjamin Franklin. In politics, the watershed had appeared in the 1680s and 1690s; in theological and scientific matters, the process took longer. But from the latter years of the seventeenth century onward, if not earlier, it is impossible to see Puritan New England as a predominantly "orthodox" society in which educated men subscribed to a single range of opinions.

A case in point is the most prolific and best-known Puritan writer and thinker of these years, Cotton Mather. While flirting with the new European learning he continued to hold to a providential and miraculous understanding of history and to deem reason as secondary to revelation. Nor did he embrace a belief in religious toleration on moral or philosophical grounds, advocating it only for political reasons and only in a limited form. But Cotton Mather has also been called the "father of American medicine," and he showed a lively interest in the natural sciences and in natural history. In this he reflected a growing trait in New England society, for as early as 1683 there had been an unsuccessful attempt to found a "philosophical society" in Boston, and by 1715 scientific interests were well established.

Yet Mather, who read and wrote about astronomy, botany, geology, and zoology, as well as medicine, tended to combine rational enquiry with a certain pietistic incredulity. Although many English scientists, including Newton, mixed reason and superstition in their approach to social and historical facts, they did not on the whole set out, as Mather did, to reconcile the new science with a theology that accepted providences, miracles, and divine revelation. In general, therefore, the effect of Mather's brand of New England Puritanism was not to deny the importance of the new science as much as to obscure its philosophical import. Other New Englanders who were drawn to scientific pursuits mainly belonged either to the more liberal Puritan circles or were anti-Puritan. Of the eight New Englanders who were elected Fellows of the Royal Society before 1730, most can be described as hostile to the conservative Puritanism that prevailed among many ministers and laity. By the 1730s, however, the warfare between science and theology had largely ceased to be important and Boston at least had a thriving scientific circle. What is finally suggested by these remarks is the danger of trying to force even Puritan New England into a mold.

Within the churches, other changes were taking place. In the Puritan colonies, Anglicans, Baptists, and Quakers were gradually consolidating or expanding. Anglicans and Baptists were probably about equal in number; the Quakers were probably the more numerous. Connecticut, with its highly organized state churches, had few Quakers, and the Baptists and Anglicans tended to absorb dissidents from Congregationalism. The centers of New England Quaker strength lay first in southern New England, bordering Rhode Island, where dissenters from the established Puritan church had tended to migrate in the latter seventeenth century, and on Nantucket Island, and, second, in Maine and a few places in New Hampshire, where either hostility to Congregationalism or no strong religious bodies existed.

In the Puritan colonies of New England, law and custom continued to give Congregationalism a privileged position. In Massachusetts the Anglicans, Baptists, and Quakers sought relief from the act, reintroduced under the second charter in 1692, that made every inhabitant liable to pay taxes (except in Boston, where the churches were voluntarily supported) for the support of a Congregational minister. True, the government stated that in cases—there were none—where Anglicans made up a majority of a town, they could have a clergyman supported by public taxation. But to the Baptists and Quakers, who did have majorities in some towns, this right was denied. By the 1720s Baptists, Quakers, and Anglicans were contesting the rights of the government—though not in unison and not by advocating general religious freedom—to tax them and were suffering distraint and imprisonment for refusal to pay.

New England Congregationalism also continued to suffer the internal stresses that had racked it in the latter decades of the seventeenth century. Of these we know a great deal insofar as they affected the articulate clergy, provoking crises of authority and opinion. Certainly, a Puritan ideal of church unity and church uniformity was breaking down. Church practices now began to diverge from congregation to congregation. In Connecticut and western Massachusetts (an area of new towns) the whole idea of exclusive church membership was abandoned and the sacraments thrown open to all who seemed to be godly. In Boston, at the end of the century, an influential group of citizens, including the president of Harvard College, founded the Brattle Street Church, stating that the old covenant idea was dead, that any child might be baptized and any person admitted to communion without the necessity of a minute investigation of his conversion experience. Although the Congregational churches remained established and official, they were gradually becoming latitudinarian and accommodating, encompassing a variety of opinions. Shaped more and more by society, they acted less and less as prime movers in that society. This was a fundamental change from the years before 1660.

Of the general institutional history of Congregationalism far less is readily known. What was the ordinary relationship of ministers to their congregations and communities? In Charlestown, Massachusetts, in 1697, for example, the town rather than the members of the church appointed a minister, an attack on the first principles of Congregationalism and a recognition of the fact that the whole town and not merely the church members paid taxes to support the ministers. Were the numbers of ministers sufficient to keep up with the great rise in population? How did Congregationalism function in the newly settled areas of the region? One impression is of clerical defensiveness in the face of congregations that neither hesitated to challenge their general authority nor to strike as hard a bargain as possible in financial matters and other aspects of ministerial livelihood. "A cheap minister is the best, let his qualifications be ever so mean," contemporaries are supposed to have thought. Numbers of clergy had to support themselves by farming or teaching and must have had little leisure for study or reflection. Ministerial laments over the growth of luxury and immorality in New England often mentioned the breakdown of church discipline and reflected the fear of a clerical loss of status and power.

By the end of the seventeenth century, many Congregational ministers looked for new measures to strengthen their authority, especially in areas where the Half Way Covenant had opened wide the doors of church membership. In

Massachusetts five local ministerial associations existed by 1705; in addition, it was customary, Cotton Mather wrote, to hold "a *General Convention* of Ministers (which perhaps are not above half) belonging to the *Province*, at the time of the *Anniversary Solemnity*, when the *General Assembly* of the Province meets . . . *Then* the *Ministers* chusing a *Moderator*, to propose Matters of public importance referring to the Interest of Religion in the Churches; and though they assume no *Decisive* Power, yet the Advice which they give to the People of GOD, has proved of great use to the County." The Mathers indeed led a movement for the establishment of a permanent ministerial convention and an extension of the powers of the ministerial associations. In fact, this was a call for a permanent synod of a kind sponsored in the seventeenth century by the civil power, the General Court. But the eighteenth-century Massachusetts government, with a royal governor, was not likely to acede to these demands, especially since several prominent clergy objected to them. Without civil backing, the scheme could not be enforced. It also produced two important attacks, both by the Reverend John Wise; one of these, *A Vindication of the Government of the New England Churches* (1717), was a restatement of the sovereign rights of local churches and of the rights of church members to participate in their government. In this way any real chance of enforcing a degree of orthodoxy over ministers and churches was lost. In 1725 the government refused to call a synod and later there was consistent political opposition to its summoning any kind of general congregational assembly. So, while Massachusetts Congregationalism continued to benefit from the province's tax laws, it now lacked the support of the civil authorities in a vital area.

In Connecticut the case was different. There, a former minister became governor in 1707, and the General Court itself was sympathetic to calls for stricter ministerial control over the churches. In 1710 the government accepted the recommendations of a synod called at Saybrook and distributed thousands of copies of the platform produced by it. This Saybrook Platform provided for the elders or elder of a particular church to exercise discipline within that church, for county consociations of churches, for annual meetings of a general association of consociation representatives, and for ministerial associations within each county. Its purpose, clearly stated, was "the Better Regulation of the Administration of Church Discipline In Relation to all Cases Ecclesiastical both in Particular Churches and in Councills to the full Determining and Executing of the Rules in all such Cases."

Discipline and order were one problem. Yet for conservative Puritans, disagreements in high places posed as serious a threat. The Mathers, for example, who regarded their opinions as the embodiment of essential Congregationalism, had already suffered a defeat with the founding of the Brattle Street Church in 1698, an institutional expression of liberal Puritanism which offended them both with its policy of open admissions and by the fact that its minister, Benjamin Colman, had received a Presbyterian ordination in London.

They also rightly interpreted Increase Mather's removal from the presidency of Harvard College as a blow to their control over the education of ministerial candidates. Yale College, founded in 1701, was established as a conservative counterweight to Harvard; its creators sympathized with the Mathers and led the movement toward the Saybrook Platform. Out in the Connecticut Valley, too, Solomon Stoddard of Northampton, known as the "Pope" of the area because of his unchallengeable power, practiced open church membership, though in his case he did so in order to make the church a more effective agent of evangelization.

The Brattle Street Church had urban, upper-class members. Theirs was a kind of benevolent and tolerant Calvinism that had developed since the days of the Half Way Covenant among the wealthier, mainly mercantile communities of the eastern seaboard. Theologically speaking, it differed hardly at all from its neighbors. Although disliking some aspects of the Brattle Street Church, even Cotton Mather eventually came to preach much that must have appealed to its members. While he firmly held to the belief that conversion came to men through God's agency and that there was little or nothing they could do to precipitate it, he also asserted that sanctified men would have "a disposition to do good works," so accepting the view of Christians as men dedicated to doing good and probably achieving it for themselves. "Among all the dispensations of a special providence in the government of the world, none is less interrupted than the accomplishment of that word 'Unto them that hath shall be given,'" he wrote. Mather also spoke of the "reasonableness" of Christianity, and there is no doubt that he saw himself as the harbinger of the modern age—which he did not fully comprehend—in Boston. An increasing humanitarianism, an emphasis on human weakness and divine compassion and tenderness that Alan Everitt has linked in English Puritan circles to growing comforts in the home that made suffering and bereavement more painful can be found in Mather's writings as well as in those of Colman.

Chapter Five

The Newer Colonies: The Challenge To Proprietary Rule

A. Patterns of society and local government

Colonies founded after the Restoration were naturally rawer and less stable than those of the Chesapeake and New England, where institutions and social patterns had now developed from the earliest years of English settlement. Some of the newer colonies—the Carolinas, for example, and New Jersey—remained relatively unpopulous for many years; others like Pennsylvania and New York grew rapidly, soon achieving parity with or surpassing some earlier foundations in wealth or population. The first settlers of these post-Restoration colonies did not generally experience the same hardships and privations that had marked the beginnings of Virginia or Plymouth or even Massachusetts. The promoters and organizers, and the first migrants to the Jerseys and Pennsylvania, were undertaking a strenuous but well-mapped route and could draw on experiences and techniques formed in the more heroic age of wilderness conquest. The actual existence and nearness of settled regions to the newer colonial territories provided material assistance. So did a network of world trade, now linking North America to Europe, Africa, and the Caribbean, a benefit that had been only partly available to New England and the Chesapeake in their formative years.

One mark of the late organization of the newer colonies and of the more favorable conditions that they provided was that in many of them settlement had already preceded their formal incorporation. In New York, of course, Dutch inhabitants had already formed a settled community with commercial links to Europe, the Caribbean, and the fur-trading Indians of the Hudson and more distant areas. Besides the Dutch, New Englanders also had established themselves in parts of New York. Hostility between Dutch and English, and between

Puritan New Englanders and the Anglican and Catholic followers of the Duke of York, who arrived after 1664, became a constant irritant in the colony's early development. To a lesser extent, the existing Delaware settlers provided a similar disturbing influence on Penn's plans for the government of Pennsylvania, while the Virginians who had moved into Albemarle (North Carolina) and some inhabitants of West New Jersey occupied tiny areas of those territories even before they were formally taken into English hands.

In other parts of New Jersey and the Carolinas, settlement began roughly at the same time that these regions became English colonies. But even here many of the first immigrants came from other existing English colonies—New Englanders to East New Jersey and Barbadians to South Carolina. Only to Pennsylvania and West Jersey was there substantial migration from the British Isles; Penn's proprietary also benefitted from its proximity to New York, New Jersey, and Maryland and drew migrants from them and from the Chesapeake.

While these circumstances often eased the earliest material and economic development of the newer colonies, they also provoked difficulties. Experienced settlers resisted or challenged the pristine authority of their untried English proprietors while a struggle for status, power and profit among the colonists themselves produced unstable societies characterized by intense factional controversy, riots, rebellions, and even miniature revolutions. In all the newer colonies conflict and dissension marked the first decades.

The Carolinas. The proprietors did not formally recognize the full separation of South and North Carolina until 1701, but the two regions developed very differently from the beginning. A striking feature of South Carolina's early history was the entrepreneurial drive of many of its inhabitants. Both the proprietors and the leading settlers sought prosperity through the development of profitable staples and for some time after 1670 experimented with various crops. Generally speaking, however, the first years of the colony's existence produced no very successful results and it relied on exports—tobacco and foodstuffs to the West Indies—already commonplace elsewhere. But before 1685 two more profitable exports were developed—naval stores and hides bought from the Indians. Naval stores became particularly important during the early eighteenth century when the British government paid a bounty for them; deer hides, and an ancillary traffic in Indian slaves sent to New England and the West Indies, constituted the most profitable exports in the seventeenth and early eighteenth centuries.

After 1685 rice cultivation was introduced into South Carolina. A recent author has suggested that the small number of slaves in the colony at the time may have brought its techniques from their West African homes. Although made an enumerated commodity in 1703, which meant that it could not be shipped directly to foreign markets, it had become the second most valuable export commodity. In 1731 rice was removed from the list of enumerated articles, and the trade picked up enormously. Rice, during most of the colonial

ESTIMATED POPULATION
Colonies Founded After 1660
1660–1720
Showing decennial percentage increases

W = White Population
N = Negro Population
% = decennial percentage increase

		New York	%	New Jersey	%	Pennsylvania	%	Delaware	%	North Carolina	%	South Carolina	%	Totals
1660	W	4,336	–	–	–	–	–	510	–	980	–	–	–	5,826
	N	600	–	–	–	–	–	30	–	20	–	–	–	650
1670	W	5,064	*17*	940	–	–	–	660	*29*	3,700	*278*	170	–	10,534
	N	690	*15*	60	–	–	–	40	*33*	150	*650*	30	–	970
1680	W	8,630	*70*	3,200	*240*	655	–	950	*44*	5,220	*41*	1,000	*488*	19,655
	N	1,200	*74*	200	*233*	25	—	55	*38*	210	*40*	200	*567*	1,890
1690	W	12,239	*42*	7,550	*136*	11,180	*1,607*	1,400	*47*	7,300	*40*	2,400	*140*	42,069
	N	1,670	*39*	450	*125*	270	*980*	82	*49*	300	*43*	1,500	*650*	4,272
1700	W	16,851	*38*	13,170	*74*	17,520	*57*	2,335	*67*	10,305	*41*	3,260	*36*	63,441
	N	2,256	*35*	840	*86*	430	*59*	135	*65*	415	*38*	2,444	*63*	6,520
1710	W	18,814	*12*	18,540	*41*	22,875	*31*	3,145	*35*	14,220	*38*	6,783	*108*	84,377
	N	2,811	*25*	1,332	*160*	1,575	*266*	500	*270*	900	*117*	4,100	*68*	11,218
1720	W	31,179	*66*	27,433	*48*	28,962	*27*	4,685	*49*	18,270	*28*	5,048	*–26*	115,577
	N	5,740	*104*	2,385	*79*	2,000	*27*	700	*40*	3,000	*233*	12,000	*193*	25,825

period, was grown either in open fields fed by natural rainfall or in swamps and paddy fields, the latter formed by building small, gated dams. Its onerous cultivation demanded intensive labor. Not only had areas to be cleared before planting, but the growing plants had to be continually hoed and weeded and the cut rice, threshed, and husked. Undoubtedly, this labor required for rice cultivation created a demand for Negro slaves, and the years when rice growing increased—from 1700 to 1715 in the first instance—were years of constant slave importation. A white population of about 2,500 in 1690 had grown to about 5,000 by 1720. The slave population rose from around 1,000 in the earlier years to 12,000 in the later.

NORTH AND SOUTH CAROLINA

Estimated Percentages of Blacks and Whites
1680–1740

	North Carolina			South Carolina		
	Total Population	Black %	White %	Total Population	Black %	White %
1680	5,430	3.87	96.13	1,200	16.67	83.33
1700	10,720	3.87	96.13	5,704	42.85	57.15
1720	21,270	14.10	85.90	17,048	70.39	29.61
1740	51,760	21.25	78.75	45,000	66.67	33.33

As in the Chesapeake, the legal basis of slavery followed rather than preceded the importation and use of Africans. Here, the influence of the Barbadian settlers seems to have been crucial, for in their previous home, slavery was regulated by custom rather than law, and South Carolina followed Barbadian example. The growing pressure of slave numbers led to the first comprehensive slave law of 1696, largely modeled on one passed in Barbados in 1688. Most of the law concerned the policing and punishment of slaves, declared "barbarous, wild, savage" and "naturally inclined to Disorders, Rapines and Inhumanity." Offences were punished on a sliding scale of severity—whipping, branding, nose-slitting, and emasculation. The law, perhaps here deliberately vague, defined as slaves all "Negroes, Mollatoes, and Indians which at any time heretofore have been brought and sold or now are and taken to be or hereafter Shall be Bought and Sold . . . and their children. . . ." As in the Chesapeake, there may have been more freedom for Africans before the great importations; the number of blacks probably surpassed that of the whites by about 1708. In time, manumission became more difficult and free Negroes were burdened with restrictions. Moreover, the influence of the church was negligible. "Is it possible that any of my slaves could go to Heaven and must I see them there?" asked one master. Following a slave conspiracy in the 1720s, dramatic public punishments were decreed for

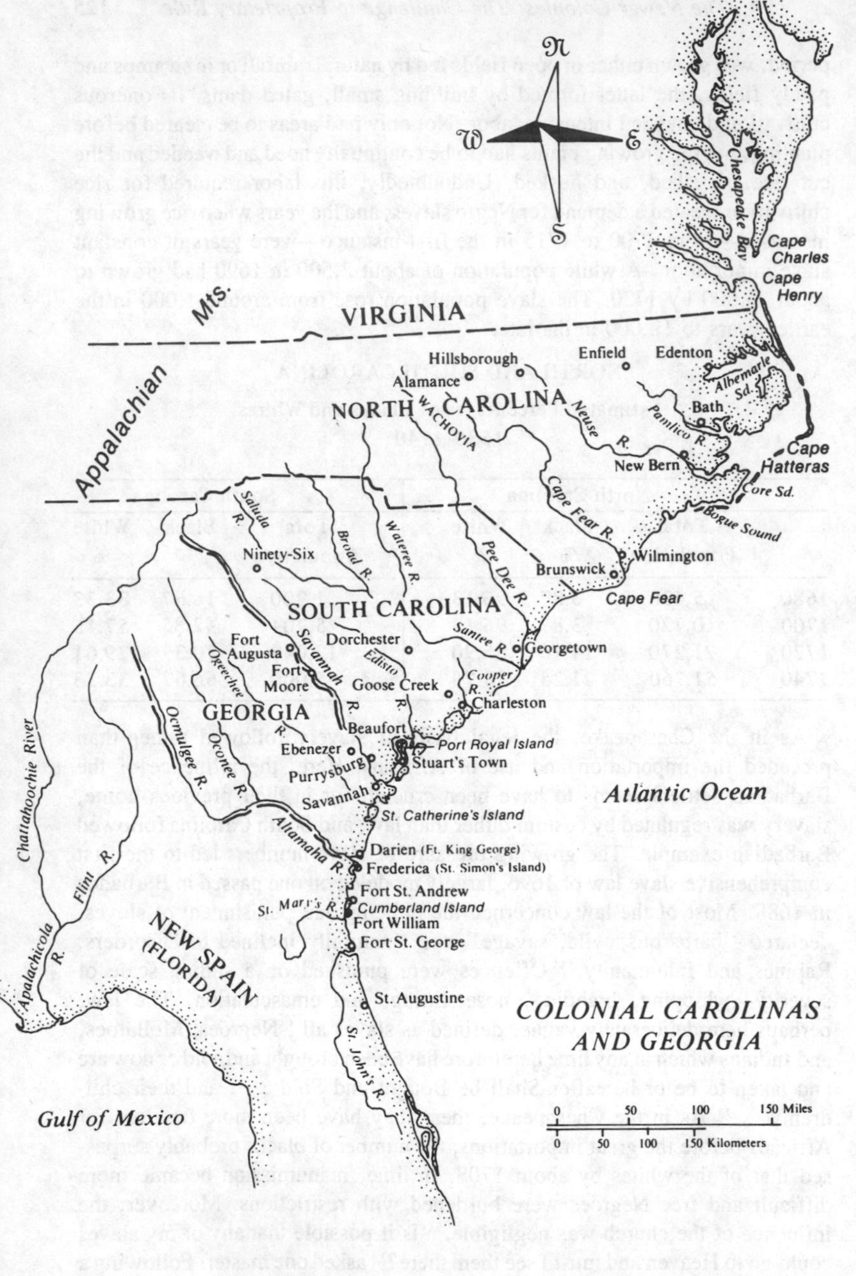

COLONIAL CAROLINAS AND GEORGIA

rebellious slaves. In 1740 an uprising occurred—the Stono rebellion—involving several hundred slaves; in the same year Charleston was badly hit by a fire, rumored to be slave-ignited. During the same years the slave came to be defined—and treated—as a personal chattel and, the foremost student of colonial American slavery has written, suffered the "most rigorous deprivation of freedom to exist in institutionalized form anywhere in the English continental colonies." It may even be that the numbers of births among slaves dropped below the numbers of deaths in the 1730s.

It seems clear that the growth of plantation society at first radically lessened the demand for white servants and made their importation rare. It is also clear that after 1740 the colonial authorities, fearful of the high ratio of slaves to whites, sought very hard to cut down on their import and to encourage renewed white immigration. The same situation also made white Carolinians inward-looking and fearful; the militia acted as a local anti-slave police force and was rarely permitted to join in military operations outside the colony's boundaries. In Maryland and Virginia the introduction of slavery had also resulted in the re-ordering of the social structure, as large plantations absorbed small farms. In South Carolina the proprietorial headright system had provided for relatively generous headrights to numerous individuals, and this had allowed the establishment of many small farms. How far these became absorbed into large plantations is not clear and the information probably cannot be elucidated from the fragmentary land records. But large plantations probably became common in the rich seaboard region. A report of 1726 on St. George's parish, a wealthy, rice-planting, low country area, shows 107 white families of whom about 20 percent owned no slaves and about 8 percent owned a total of 572 or 42.5 percent of the slaves in the parish. About 66 percent of the families owned ten slaves or less per family.

As in the other two southern colonies, settlement in South Carolina was widely dispersed rather than concentrated in towns or villages. Ashley and the other proprietors sought to have compact and planned towns on the New England system established but economic factors prevented this, and only Charleston was laid out and survived as such. Of the five leading colonial American towns, it remained the smallest and least populous. Nor did the proprietors' plans for a carefully ordered system of manors, baronies, and palatines bear fruit. No great feudal domains were effectively founded in South Carolina, and after about 1718 the titles of nobility provided for in the Fundamental Constitutions fell into disuse.

The area that later became North Carolina never received the same attention and care from the Carolina proprietors as the southern part of their province. With a sand-locked coastline and an interior where the large numbers of swamps, creeks, and rivers made communications difficult, North Carolina seemed to offer less obvious economic possibilities than the more attractive southern region. Because of the early settlement of the Albemarle area by

Virginians who extended their tobacco culture southward and the proprietary interest of Governor Berkeley in the Carolinas, the early government of the Albemarle was entrusted to his nominees. During the remainder of the seventeenth century, settlement crept south from the Albemarle to the Pamlico River, but not until 1722 did it reach Core and Bogue sounds. After 1725 more rapid and major expansion came with a movement of South Carolinians into the Cape Fear region on the boundaries of North and South Carolina. Here, in the next two decades, the population increased at a very considerable rate.

Figures distinguishing between natural increase and immigration are not available, though from about 1700 onward growing numbers of Virginians came into North Carolina, driven there by land shortages. Moreover, French Huguenots and Swiss settlers also arrived in these years. These added an ethnic diversity to the already-existing religious one. The Quakers had been strong in Albemarle since about 1672, were well organized, and grew in numbers until the end of the century. Other English settlers were described by Thomas Blair in 1704 as "a great number who have no religion, but would be Quakers, if by that they were not obliged to lead a more moral life than they are willing to comply to" or as "something like Presbyterians which sort is upheld by some idle fellows who have left their lawful employment, and preach and baptize throughout the country without any moral manner of orders from any sect or pretended Church." Blair claimed zealous Church of Englanders to be few in numbers but "the better sort of people." This expanding white population—10,000 or so in 1700 and about 18,000 by 1720—generally lived on small farms and plantations, producing tobacco in the Albemarle region and naval stores, turpentine, and tar at Cape Fear as well as more conventional foodstuffs and livestock. The propertied slave-holding elite that came to dominate South Carolina never emerged with the same force in the north, which lacked the wealth created by rice planting. North Carolinians owned only about 3,000 slaves in 1720.

Local government in North and South Carolina differed considerably. South Carolina's had several peculiarities that distinguished it rather sharply from other southern regions. Foremost among these was the failure of county government to develop. Although legislation in 1682 created three counties, Berkeley, Colleton and Craven, these never became important administrative or judicial units in the manner of the Chesapeake or North Carolina counties. A Berkeley County court was erected in Charleston, also in 1682, but no courts existed in the other counties. An eighteenth-century South Carolina historian even went so far as to write, "For the first 99 years of provincial Carolina, Charlestown was the source and centre of all judicial proceedings. No courts were held beyond its limits, and one provost marshal was charged with the service of processes over the whole province." (Moreover, he added, even the central courts largely shared the same judges; the Court of King's Bench and the Court of Common Pleas for many years had the same single judge, and in

1719 this judge was also sole judge of the Court of Vice-Admiralty and, as a councillor, one of the judges of the Court of Appeal.) By 1730, for example, five precinct courts, established outside of Charleston in 1721, were probably defunct. Not until 1769 were courts again to be set up beyond the capital. Yet justices of the peace were appointed, as were constables, though their geographical locations and actual functions have not yet been sufficiently elucidated.

Parishes were created in South Carolina at the beginning of the eighteenth century with the formal establishment of the Church of England. Until that date, committees of the General Assembly conducted all local affairs. An original ten parishes had increased by subdivision and new creations to twenty-four in 1776. While the parish officers supervised the registration of births, christenings, deaths, and marriages, they had no great responsibilities for other forms of local government. True, they exercised (through a board of overseers) the supervision of the poor after 1712 and of highways after 1721—rare instances of the relinquishment of local government powers by the General Assembly, hitherto responsible in this field. Of incorporated borough towns, no trace seems to exist in South Carolina; indeed, even Charleston itself, in spite of recommendations as early as 1694, never became incorporated, and a committee of the General Assembly carried on its government. A number of "townships" in areas of new settlement existed by 1763 but few had parish vestries or sent representatives to the assembly. The nature of their government remains largely unexplored.

The curious failure of local government to develop in South Carolina as it did in the other southern colonies is not readily explicable and the whole subject still awaits detailed modern research. Why did the General Assembly continue to act as the main instrument of local government rather than delegate its powers to local bodies as was the case elsewhere in most of English America? It seems likely that the old seaboard counties accepted the direct control of the assembly over local government because their leading men controlled the assembly. But with a rapid rise in the number of settlers in areas far away from Charleston, and unrepresented in the assembly, this lack of local organs of law and administration finally created great difficulties and grave feelings of resentment against the South Carolina government.

Local government in North Carolina resembled Virginia's more than South Carolina's. The county system developed rapidly and generally kept up with the expansion of population. The first four "precincts," as the counties at first were known—Chowan, Currituck, Pasquotank, and Perquimans—established in 1670 were followed by Craven, Hyde, and Beaufort in 1712 and Bertie and Carteret in 1722. By 1763 North Carolina had twenty-six counties, each with their judicial and administrative officials. In each county, the wealthier families, the local ruling class, largely controlled its government. The extent of their influence is nicely illustrated by the duties of the office of sheriff that one of their number usually filled. His office, defined in 1739, gave him police powers; he collected taxes for the colony, county, and vestry; he oversaw, and often manipulated, elections. One authority has written that "his influence was felt in nearly every phase of colonial life." In contrast also to South Carolina, incorporated towns with rights of representation in the legislature as well as privileges of local government existed. The parish vestry as a unit of government, although first established in 1701, suffered severe challenges from dissenters and it is unclear how far it became effective, even in the more Anglican counties.

The middle colonies. New York's early settlement flowed up the Hudson River valley from New York City, reaching Albany, a frontier trading post, and Schenectady on the Mohawk, the outpost of the colony's expansion. A second seaborne settlement wave crossed the Sound from New Haven and Connecticut into Long Island with some direct overland movement from New Haven into Westchester County. Although the Dutch had attempted to establish feudal patroonships, of the five of these granted, only one "lasted beyond the first years of the English period." Early settlement consisted of scattered small farms or of townships. English settlers after 1664 moved into southern Westchester and King's counties while Puritan New Englanders dominated most of Long Island. By 1698 the Dutch strongholds lay in the upriver interior counties of Dutchess, Ulster, Orange, and Albany. In Albany they constituted 93 percent of the population. Besides Dutch, English, and New Englanders, French Huguenots had arrived in New York in 1685 and German Palatines in 1710.

This multi-ethnic pattern was even more pronounced in New York City, resulting in a great mixture of nationalities and religious sects, although English influence began to predominate there after about 1700. To what extent the city acted as an early melting pot is unclear. What is more apparent is that the rural areas did not. The Dutch lived in national enclaves while religious sects like the Quakers or ethnic-cum-religious groups like the Moravians were also generally exclusive. Local government, too, reflected diversity rather than uniformity. The New England type of town, first established on Long Island, served as a unit of government in much the same way as its original. It soon spread from Long Island; Westchester, Ulster, and Albany counties all had some townships where population was concentrated enough to support them. In these towns a mixture of English and New England practices existed. The townsmen appointed "trustees" annually as a governing body and elected constables, tax assessors, and other officers. Land divisions in them followed patterns seen previously in New England. New York City and Albany, officially chartered as cities in 1686, had been self-governing for many years before.

The townships co-existed with a system of counties. The assembly established ten of these in 1691. Within the counties, areas too lightly populated to support townships became precincts, with their own elected officers and

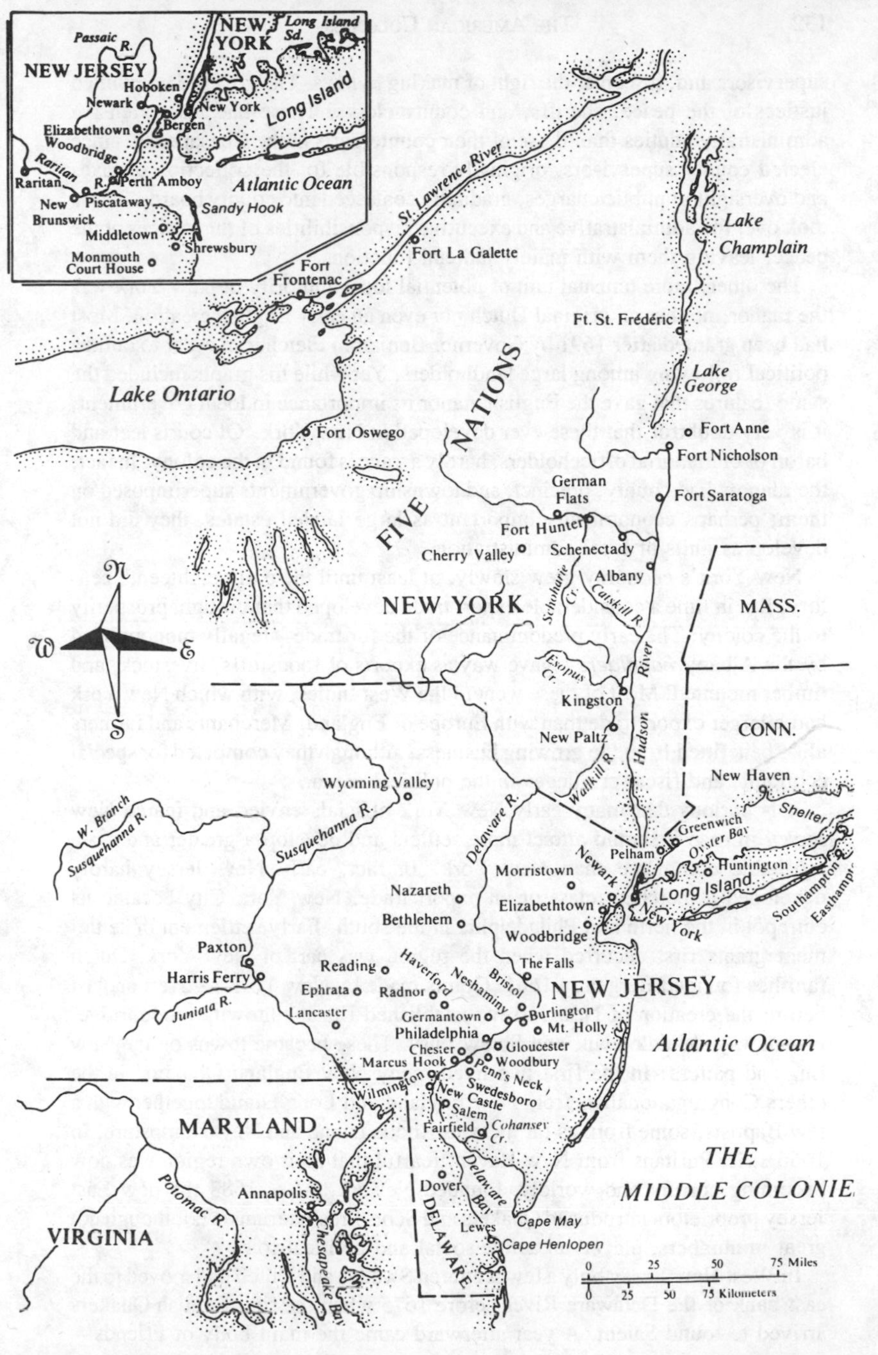

NEW YORK
Long Island Sd.
Passaic R.
NEW JERSEY
Hoboken
Newark
New York
Long Island
Elizabethtown
Bergen
Woodbridge
Raritan R.
Raritan
Perth Amboy
Atlantic Ocean
New Brunswick
Piscataway
Sandy Hook
Middletown
Shrewsbury
Monmouth Court House
St. Lawrence River
Fort La Galette
Fort Frontenac
Lake Champlain
Ft. St. Frédéric
FIVE NATIONS
Lake George
Lake Ontario
Fort Oswego
Fort Anne
Fort Nicholson
German Flats
Fort Saratoga
Fort Hunter
Cherry Valley
Schenectady
Albany
Schoharie Cr.
Catskill R.
NEW YORK
MASS.
Esopus Cr.
Hudson River
Kingston
New Paltz
Wallkill R.
CONN.
New Haven
Wyoming Valley
W. Branch Susquehanna R.
Susquehanna R.
Delaware R.
Shelter I.
Greenwich
Oyster Bay
Pelham
Huntington
Morristown
Newark
Long Island
Nazareth
Elizabethtown
New York
Southampton
Easthampton
Bethlehem
Woodbridge
Paxton
Reading
Haverford
Bristol
The Falls
Harris Ferry
Ephrata
Radnor
Neshaminy
NEW JERSEY
Juniata R.
Lancaster
Germantown
Burlington
Mt. Holly
Philadelphia
Gloucester
Atlantic Ocean
Chester
Marcus Hook
Woodbury
Penn's Neck
Wilmington
Swedesboro
New Castle
Salem
MARYLAND
Fairfield
Cohansey Cr.
Delaware Bay
THE MIDDLE COLONIE
Dover
Annapolis
Potomac R.
DELAWARE
Chesapeake Bay
Cape May
Lewes
VIRGINIA
Cape Henlopen
0 25 50 75 Miles
0 25 50 75 Kilometers

supervisors and, it seems, the right of making bylaws. The governor appointed justices of the peace, sheriffs, and county clerks. These had less extensive administrative duties than those of their counterparts in the Chesapeake, since elected county supervisors, originally responsible for the collection of taxes and oversight of public charges, gradually coalesced into county boards. These took over the administrative and executive responsibilities of the justices of the peace, leaving them with mainly judicial functions.

The other, more unusual unit of potential local authority in New York was the manor, neither an original Dutch nor even an early English creation. Most had been granted after 1691 by Governor Benjamin Fletcher in order to build a political following among large landholders. Yet while his grants included the same features that gave the English manor its importance in local government, it is very doubtful that these ever developed in New York. Of courts leet and baron or of manorial officeholders, hardly a trace is found in the colony. In fact, the manors had county, precinct, and township governments superimposed on them; perhaps economically important as large landed estates, they did not develop as units of local administration.

New York's economy grew slowly, at least until the early eighteenth century. But in time a considerable export trade developed that brought prosperity to the colony. The early predominance of the fur trade—legally monopolized by the Albany *handlaers*—gave way as exports of foodstuffs, livestock, and timber mounted. Most of these went to the West Indies, with which New York had a larger export trade than with Europe or England. Merchants and farmers alike benefitted from the growing business, although they competed for special economic and fiscal privileges in the political arena.

It is curious that many early New York officials envied and feared New Jersey in case it should attract more settlers and develop a greater and more profitable commerce than New York. In fact, early New Jersey hardly developed a merchant class or an export trade. New York City became its entrepôt in the north and Philadelphia in the south. Early settlement or settlement grants first occurred when the region was part of New York. Dutch families founded Bergen in 1661. Grants made by New York's governor, just before the creation of New Jersey, established Elizabethtown, Woodbridge, Piscataway, Middletown, and Shrewsbury. These became towns on the New England pattern. In the first two lived many New England Quakers, in the others Congregationalists from New England and Long Island together with a few Baptists, some from as far away as Rhode Island and New Hampshire. In 1666 strict Puritans from New Haven, fearful that their own region was now becoming corrupt and worldly, founded Newark. After 1683 the new East Jersey proprietors introduced Quakers and Scots Presbyterians who, though not great in numbers, played an active social and political role.

In West New Jersey only a few scattered Swedes and Dutch had moved to the east bank of the Delaware River before 1675 when the first English Quakers arrived to found Salem. A year afterward came the main body of Friends—

mostly from Yorkshire and London—eventually to found Burlington. Later, Irish Quakers came to West Jersey, settling in Gloucester County, to the south of Burlington. By the end of the century, the southward and eastward movement of population had brought a few settlers to tiny hamlets on Cape May and the Atlantic coast. In addition, New England Congregationalists at New Fairfield, New England Baptists on the Cohansey River, and the Lutheran Swedes at Penn's Neck and Swedesboro added to the diversity of population. Moreover, in West and East Jersey, Anglican settlers from England had begun to arrive toward the end of the seventeenth century.

This infant society—New Jersey's total population in 1700 numbered about 15,000—at first remained strictly agricultural, with a little fishing and whaling. In East New Jersey landholdings were originally of moderate size—100-200 acres—and there seems to have been little social diversity. Later the East Jersey proprietors made much larger land grants, and a division arose between small farmers and large speculative landholders. In West Jersey this division did not take place.

Pennsylvania's early history in many ways presents a sharp contrast to that of the Jerseys, predominantly because of its rapid population growth and the emergence of Philadelphia as an important town. The staggering initial immigration into the colony and the beginnings of an early export trade by merchants who came with existing capital and connections in the Old World account for these developments. Experienced traders quickly sent foodstuffs, particularly wheat, flour, and beef, to an expanding market in the West Indies, and Philadelphia became a thriving port. It also served as the entrepôt for the import of English goods and a reception point for the many indentured servants who came to the middle colonies. As the colony's capital, Philadelphia was the focus of public life, officialdom, and administration, inhabited in 1700 by about a quarter of Pennsylvania's 18,000 strong population. Incorporated in 1691, the city was tightly controlled by a Quaker oligarchy that increased in strength and wealth as the years passed. Yet Anglicans and other non-Quakers of education and influence also formed a growing section in the city, a nucleus of dissent from the prevailing politics and culture.

The export trade of the capital and the expansion of the colony's settlement depended on a successful agriculture and forms of rural settlement. As in New York, the flow of settlers moved first along the major river, the Delaware, extending south from Philadelphia into the lower counties and north into Bucks County. After about 1700, a westward movement into the areas north and south of the Schuylkill took settlers in a new direction. By the end of the first decade of the new century a few families indeed had crossed the Susquehanna River into what became York and Cumberland counties. The early settlers were mainly English and Welsh and predominantly, though not exclusively, Quakers. Yet Germans, Swiss, and Scotch Irish arrived at an early date, although the great flood of these nationalities came in the first half of the eighteenth century.

Penn's early plans called for the contiguous settlement of regular divisions or "lots" of land. This careful expansion he, like many early New England leaders, hoped would bring stability, order, and civilization. Some of these lots were set out as he intended; Philadelphia itself was closely surveyed. Yet the proprietor's own need for money led him to make large land grants beyond the line of settlement. He also gave himself substantial "manors"—great reservoirs of land—holding at one time 20 percent of Chester and 11 percent of Bucks and Philadelphia counties. Penn hoped that the basic territorial-social unit would be a village or township community. The plans of Plymouth township, for example, showed 450 acre farms with 50 acre home lots at the center of the village; the farms were enclosed, not open field holdings (as in early New England). After about 1700 these ideas were clearly untenable. Few compact agricultural communities had come into existence; dispersed and sometimes isolated farmsteads had become the rule in Pennsylvania. The growth of a market economy and the availability of land, as well as the absence of menacing Indians, meant that the obligations of communal agrarian life had no staying power or purpose in Penn's province, even when reinforced by the Quaker social ethic of mutual assistance and responsibility.

Local government in Pennsylvania and New Jersey has not been given detailed modern study. Certainly, the county system provided the essential framework. In East Jersey the New England type of town, the earliest unit of local authority, remained important. But four counties were created in 1683: Bergen, Essex, Middlesex, and Monmouth; and county courts in 1684. Somerset and Perth Amboy counties were soon added. In West Jersey four counties and two towns provided the units of local government. Pennsylvania's first three counties, Philadelphia, Chester, and Bucks, had been established as early as 1683. The next county to be formed, Lancaster, was not followed by other new ones until 1749. Although Philadelphia and two or three Pennsylvania boroughs had their own local government, Penn's planned rural townships, or villages, never became strong. The county freeholders either filled county offices by election or the proprietary appointed men to them. After 1722 county commissioners (like those in North Carolina) absorbed most of the nonjudicial functions of the justices of the peace, many of whom had been township rather than county officers. In New Jersey the appointment of freeholders to join the justices of the peace in deciding administrative matters, especially cases of special local expenditure, tended to limit the latter's administrative powers.

B. The disturbed political scene

The establishment of farms and plantations, the growth of agriculture and trade, and the arrangement of a system of local government have often received less attention from historians than the stormy political life of the emerging colonies. Yet these mundane developments obviously had a great relevance to the lives and livelihoods of the great majority of the 70,000 or so persons who inhabited the newer colonies by 1700, perhaps a greater relevance than the dramatic clashes between governors and governed, English proprietors and American settlers, that marked the political life of these societies. The colonial assembly, the most usual area of confrontation, often met infrequently and inconclusively, and even the virtual breakdown of central political authority in several colonies on different occasions must have had relatively little effect on the rhythm of life of many inhabitants. On the other hand, political battles did involve economic and social issues: land tenure and distribution, rents, fiscal policy and trade regulation, rivalries between contending religious groups, matters of local government or of Indian policy that ultimately affected large numbers of settlers. Such controversies also tended to be conducted in language that stressed fundamental constitutional and legal principles; they resulted in political patterns that continued to be important to and beyond the American Revolution. Distrust of the proprietary executives and the establishment of the colonial assembly as its great rival became the two most important patterns.

In South Carolina, early and persistent opposition to the Fundamental Constitutions and the later schemes of the proprietors characterized politics. The first substantial group to oppose the proprietors, the settlers from Barbados, formed a majority of the population by 1680. Concentrated in an area around Goose Creek on the Cooper River, the Barbadians achieved a degree of political unity and a monopoly of lesser government offices that made them formidable enemies, able to block the proprietors' wish to introduce the Fundamental Constitutions and to manage land and Indian policy. Their ascendancy in colonial political life was partly challenged in the 1680s by the arrival of several hundred new settlers from England and several hundred French Huguenots before 1700. There seems no doubt that the English authorities stimulated this immigration in part to create a counterweight to the Goose Creek faction. While the Barbadians were Anglicans, and to some extent royalists and not particularly sympathetic to the proprietors' policy of religious toleration, the new English settlers were dissenting Protestants with strong antipathies to the Stuart monarchy. These English Presbyterians and Baptists located themselves to the south of Charleston in what became Colleton County. About 200 Scots Covenanters attempted to settle Fort Royal in 1684 but their fierce, undiplomatic proceedings finally led to their destruction by Spanish and Indian forces in 1686, unmourned by the other British inhabitants.

Before about 1700 the dissenters allied with the proprietors and occupied provincial offices under them. After this, the proprietors began to give active support to the establishment of the Church of England and incurred the dissenters' hostility, manifested in lengthy accounts of their grievances sent back home to politicians in England. The increasing attention of English politicians and government officials to South Carolina's affairs, encouraged by these proceedings, was also stimulated by South Carolina's strategic position. Not only did the colony's Indian traders become involved in intertribal rivalries and wars but her frontier position as the closest English settlement to Spain's American possessions brought special dangers. Frontier military strength became a matter of concern to the English government. Opponents of proprietary rule could underline this point after England's war with Spain led the colonists to attack St. Augustine in 1702 and then to mount offensives against pro-Spanish Indians. In 1706 the Spanish unsuccessfully counterattacked near Charleston; in 1715 South Carolina faced a costly and dangerous revolt on its southern frontier when the Yamasee and other Indian tribes rebelled with devastating results, in protest against the abuses of the traders.

Although South Carolina put down the Indians, the Yamasee war compounded a fiscal crisis, involving the issue of paper money and increased taxes on merchants. It also led to further confrontations between the proprietors, who had sent no aid to the colony in its time of need, and the merchants and other settlers, most of whom now favored royal intervention. The Crown's policy remained unclear. In 1719 the Commons House of Assembly moved to take over authority from the proprietary governor and declared itself a "Convention, delegated by the People, to prevent the utter Ruin of this Government, if not the Loss of the Province" until the Crown's will should be known. In 1720 the Crown agreed to take over the colony's government temporarily in order to protect the southern fringe of English settlement. Francis Nicholson became the colony's first royal governor. Even so, the proprietors retained their rights to the soil, not selling these to the Crown until 1729.

The clamor for royal government to replace the proprietors in part represented a tactical maneuver by local factions who would, in fact, oppose any strong central authority that did not respond to their wishes. Before 1720 they had whittled away the extraordinary powers of the proprietary governor, reducing these to the level of other colonial governors. The similarly extraordinary Grand Council made up of proprietary nobles and freemen's representatives, formerly charged with initiating legislation, was transformed into a regularly appointed council that also sat as an upper house. In the 1690s the Parliament, the third arm of proprietary government, finally became transformed into a conventional lower house, known as the Commons House of Assembly. Like other lower houses, it provided a center of opposition to proprietary rule. In other words, the new royal governor arrived to face powerful political institutions that the local men of power had already molded from the grandiose English-designed government of the proprietors to suit their own interests.

Early politics in North Carolina resembled those of South Carolina. Dissatisfaction with the proprietors' policies was as strong there as in the south and factions among the settlers as commonplace. Early clashes revolved around quitrents charged on land, the plans of the proprietors for a nobility, and the enforcement of the Navigation Acts, while Bacon's rebellion in Virginia had repercussions in Albemarle. Although many details of the early political history of North Carolina are obscure, it is certain that, as in other colonies, the assembly came to embody the various elements of opposition to the proprietary government. Foremost in this opposition stood the oldest and most successful settlers, who hoped to form policy for the benefit of local rather than proprietary interests. The early involvement of a number of New England merchants complicated Albemarle's affairs. Trading in North Carolina tobacco, which they carried to Boston for illegal (it was alleged) transhipment to foreign countries, the New Englanders seem to have been instrumental in encouraging resistance to proprietary attempts at enforcing the Navigation Acts.

In 1677 an uprising against the proprietors resulted in the imprisonment of several officials and the meeting of an extra-legal convention or "Parliament," as they called it, of eighteen rebels. Known as Culpepper's rebellion, after one of its ringleaders, the uprising was inconclusive. Several years of political factionalism and governmental near-anarchy followed, culminating again in 1688 or 1689 in the deposing of another proprietary governor, Seth Sothel, by the better-off planters. Whether or not the event had any connection with the Glorious Revolution in England is not clear. As a result of this, and of the troubles in South Carolina, came a renewed attempt by the proprietors to check their unruly provinces. Philip Ludwell was appointed governor of both North and South Carolina in 1691. After this date North Carolina still remained troubled. Factional tensions between Anglicans and dissenters ran so high that in 1711 another bloodless, anti-proprietorial rebellion occurred led by Thomas Cary, a dissenting politician. More confusion followed in the same year with an uprising of the Tuscarora Indians provoked—as was South Carolina's Yamasee war—by the chicaneries and brutalities of various traders and settlers. The war and associated epidemics seem to have weakened the vigor of factional strife. After about 1714 came many years of relative political peace with no riots or rebellions or agitations comparable to those in South Carolina. But hostility between a "popular" assembly-based group and the proprietary governor and his officials remained strong. Unlike South Carolina, however, was there no great agitation for North Carolina to become a royal colony, although this happened when the proprietors sold out to the Crown in 1729. The first royal governor, indeed, had a very hard time, plunging immediately into fierce contests with the assembly over fiscal policy, quitrents, and his salary.

In New York, the Duke of York's first deputy governor, Richard Nicolls, attempted, as we have seen, to establish order over the heterogeneous population of his master's proprietary. He gave much early attention to the conciliation of the Dutch, a process that had little immediate success. During the third Anglo-Dutch war, forces from the United Provinces recaptured the colony, occupying Manhattan and Staten islands. The Dutch population eagerly participated in the dismantling of English institutions and laws. After the return of New York to England by the Treaty of Westminster, a third governor, Edmond

Andros, seems to have been instructed to reduce the special privileges previously granted the Dutch and to commence more rigorous and direct measures of Anglicization. These had some effect, particularly since intelligent Dutchmen now realized the impossibility of escaping English rule. The wealthier and more ambitious merchants and several clergy cooperated with the English authorities; from this time forward increasing intermarriage occurred between Dutch and English elites. Yet the bulk of the Dutch settlers—ordinary inhabitants and the minor civil and ecclesiastical functionaries—probably remained suspicious, showing only an uneasy acceptance of the English. Also, the Duke of York's Catholicism, shared by some of his colonial officials, proved as unwelcome to Dutch Calvinists as to the Puritan inhabitants of Long Island.

The division between these New Englanders and the proprietary government found more open expression than that between Dutch and English. Agitation for a representative assembly with the sole power to enact laws and levy taxes flared intermittently during the 1660s and 1670s with petitions for the "liberties of Englishmen" being sent to the proprietary governor and to the King. In 1680 assertions against the Duke's collector of customs included references to  Magna Carta, the Petition of Right, and the "known Ancient and Fundamentall Lawes of the Realme of England," a nice illustration of the extent to which commonwealth and Whiggish political rhetoric had been transmitted to New York—as it had to the Jerseys and Pennsylvania. Moreover, New Yorkers had a precise awareness of the divergence between their form of government and that of the other English colonies, all of which had assemblies.

The Duke of York notoriously disliked parliamentary bodies for their habit, as he said, of assuming "to themselves many priviledges which prove destructive to, or very oft disturbe, the peace of the government wherein they are allowed." But by 1680 it seemed evident that a continuing refusal to allow representation would create a financial crisis, with settlers refusing to pay taxes and duties or leaving the colony for New Jersey. Moreover, James's own officials generally supported granting an assembly since they felt it would make New York more attractive to settlers as well as lessen their tax-collecting difficulties. James gave way. In 1683 a new governor, Colonel Thomas Dongan, arrived in New York with instructions to call an assembly and allow the colonists "such Priviledges and Libertyes as Other Plantations Enjoy only a Fond is Expected to be Provided [by the Assembly] for the Necessary Support of the Government, Maintenance of the Garrison and Payment of Arrears. . . ." The first assembly met in October 1683. Its first statute—with a title obviously influenced by Penn's Pennsylvania measure—was a "Charter of Libertyes and Priviledges."

This document set out a political framework for New York. Governor, council, and "the people mett in Generall Assembly" would exercise supreme legislative authority, though laws might be vetoed by the Duke. The assembly had guarantees of triennial meetings and many parliamentary privileges, including freedom from arrest for its members and servants, the rights of adjourning and assembling at will, and the rights of judging the qualifications of its members. A revenue act, passed the same day, stated the power of the assembly to originate money bills. Voters for assembly representatives included all freeholders, as defined by English law. Executive authority rested with the governor and council, who were to rule "according to the Lawes." The Charter also guaranteed many individual liberties, including trial by jury, no excessive bail, and others taken from Magna Carta and the Petition of Right. A long section granted liberty of conscience, although special privileges were given to the Long Island towns' Congregational churches. These might be established and supported by town taxes as long as two-thirds of the inhabitants agreed.

Had the Charter been implemented it would have placed New Yorkers on an equal—or superior—constitutional standing to the inhabitants of other colonies, possibly giving them the full legal rights of Englishmen. New York's governor and council did accept it and James himself approved it in England. But this move came at a time of change in the Crown's colonial policy, when the wholesale reorganization of colonial government was at hand. James never returned the Charter of Liberties to New York. After he became king in 1685, he endorsed the new policy. New York soon found itself absorbed into the Dominion of New England, an extensive royal government without any representative assembly.

The Dominion government therefore represented a fresh setback to various interests in New York, although many leading merchants and landowners sought and received offices under it. At the same time, economic depression and resentment against monopolies and special economic favors to privileged groups, as well as new threats of French and Indian attack, gave the lieutenant governor, Francis Nicholson, a difficult task. The news of the Boston uprising of 18 April 1689 and the imprisonment of Sir Edmund Andros reached New York in late April. From that point on, Nicholson's authority rapidly declined. The New England settlers in Suffolk County instigated an attack on his powers, and Long Islanders generally threw off his rule during May. In New York City, Nicholson tried to rally support from local leaders, but on 31 May 1689 the New York militia seized the royal fort from the governor's English soldiers. In early June the rebels formed a Committee of Safety. Nicholson fled the colony on 6 June, leaving its government in the ineffectual hands of three members of his council. In fact, the Committee of Safety filled the vacuum. From its ranks emerged a new leader, a militia captain, Jacob Leisler, appointed commander-in-chief of the province on 28 June. Yet Leisler's control was always tenuous and without the relatively united backing from the men of influence that the rebels in Boston, by contrast, enjoyed.

Like the Bostonians, the New Yorkers proclaimed their loyalty to William and Mary, declaring that they rose to save New York from the Catholic government and French and Indian allies of James II. Their political ardor indeed fed on reports of Catholic conspiracies. They feared—since Nicholson, awaiting English orders that never arrived, did not repudiate James II or announce his support for William and Mary—that the old government might remain loyal to the Stuarts, possibly in alliance with the French. The leadership of New York's revolt came to be identified with Leisler, a well-to-do German merchant who had never been accepted by New York's ruling class. Although generally supported by the lower-class Dutch in and out of New York City and in Albany, he proved unable to rally the Dutch leaders of Albany or the English grandees to his cause. These men declared their loyalty to William and Mary but described Leisler and his associates as seditious upstarts. The majority of the leaders of the Maryland and Massachusetts revolts managed to present themselves as the loyal subjects of William and Mary and had their positions confirmed by the new charters granted by the English government. Leisler found himself isolated and unable to achieve this. Agents sent by him to England were virtually ignored. The King appointed a new government for New York headed by Colonel Henry Sloughter, an English soldier, who believed Leisler and his followers to be a disorderly, seditious rabble. Leisler's subsequent behavior—he resisted the first royal officials of the new government to arrive in New York—confirmed this opinion. The new government imprisoned and tried the Leislerians, and Leisler and his son-in-law, Jacob Milborne, were hanged as rebels on 16 May 1691.

For about the next twenty years the political history of New York was profoundly influenced by the aftermath of the Leislerian movement. The second royal governor, Benjamin Fletcher, allied himself with the grandees, the large merchants and landholders who had opposed Leisler, making vast land grants on the Hudson and conniving at illegal trade. His obvious political favoritism attracted the jealousy of those excluded from power and influence. After a brief interlude the third governor, Lord Cornbury, played the same political game, maintaining this factional feeling. Although Governor Robert Hunter (1710-1719), a man of exceptional ability, tried to diminish the older hostilities and built up a large following in the assembly, his rule fostered a new division between merchants and landowners by his imposition of high taxes on commerce and low taxes on land. His successor, Governor William Burnet, savagely attacked the merchant community, expelling their chief men from his council. The politics of these years, therefore, consisted less of powerful local interests vying with royal governors and royal policy than of shifting alliances between English governors and New York factions, as several groups maneuvered for political advantage. At least in terms of our present understanding, New York's politics showed a complexity and subtlety that the political life of the other new colonies probably did not achieve until later in the eighteenth century.

New Jersey's early political history began, like New York's, with the protest of New England settlers against proprietary rule. Generally speaking, the first New Englanders had generous terms of settlement, including control of their local town government, initial freedom from rents and taxes, liberty of conscience, and the power to appoint a minister approved by the majority; joined to these was, of course, the right to a representative assembly, specified in the "Concessions and Agreements." But in addition, they quickly sought permanent freedom from quitrents and resisted registering their lands with the proprietors' officials. In pursuit of this autonomy, the townsmen used to the full all the political devices they had become accustomed to in New England—town petitions, resolutions, and remonstrances particularly. Indeed, by the time the final session of the first New Jersey assembly met in late 1668, its members had already begun to press for more general political rights against the proprietary government. By 1672 arguments became so heated that an illegal convention virtually deposed Philip Carteret. The unhappy governor was forced to sail for England to seek a remedy from his masters.

This episode can serve as an illustration of the general tendency in East Jersey, as in other proprietaries, for initial opposition to economic and fiscal obligations to develop into a political struggle. On the one hand, for example, Governor Carteret secured a modification in England of the original Concessions, gaining the restriction of full political rights to freeholders who held their lands by registered proprietary patent. On the other, a hostile assembly in 1681 went so far as to insist that the original Concessions formed a kind of "fundamental constitution" of which the proprietors' alteration ought "to be made voyd and of none effect" and that "the Inhabitants of this Province [are] not obliged to conforme themselves to." In this fashion the language and ideas of contemporary New England and English political thinking made an early appearance in the infant colony.

The turbulent politics of the early period continued, in fact, for the rest of the seventeenth century. Political instability not only resulted from the proprietary system but increased because of two factors already mentioned. New York's governors claimed authority in East Jersey on the grounds that the Duke's original grant had not included rights of government. Then, East Jersey was owned before 1702 by several sets of proprietors, all of whom made unsettling changes in policy. Among these, the introduction of Quaker and Scottish Presbyterian settlers after 1683 coincided with vigorous proprietary land speculation. A number of factions—proprietorial, anti-proprietorial, Puritan, Presbyterian, and so on—now competed for political and economic power. And at the end of the seventeenth century a growing Anglican element pressed forward in East New Jersey, adding to factional strife.

Faction similarly held sway in West New Jersey. This began with disputes over the implementation of the West Jersey Concessions. Although most of its provisions became law, a single governor rather than a multiple executive ruled the colony, facing characteristic assertions from the residents against proprietary authority. In 1683 the West Jersey assembly voted to strengthen its own powers, usurping the governor's prerogative in actions that have been described as "revolutionary." But the real crisis came after the transfer of West Jersey to the commercial syndicate, the West New Jersey Society, in 1692. Following this, ambitious and fairly well-to-do Anglicans, supporters of the proprietary, arrived in the colony. Broadly speaking, a Quaker, anti-proprietary group opposed these supporters of the proprietary government. Yet many elements, including the proprietary governor, actually favored royal government in New Jersey, petitioning the Crown for this against a background of argument and counterargument. In 1702 both parts of New Jersey were reunited as a royal province.

Royalization did not mean the end of proprietary politics, for the proprietors kept their land rights and sought governmental influence to maintain them. The politics of land thus became one basis of provincial politics in eighteenth-century New Jersey. Not only did landlord and tenant disagree over rents and leases but the proprietors themselves were divided, one group wishing for legislation to allow them to sell off their properties for immediate profit and another preferring "to manage their common holdings so as to produce the greatest profit over a long period." Not until the 1750s did such disputes fade away. Yet with the exception of serious land riots in the 1740s and 1750s, these and other political controversies no longer produced the virtual anarchy that had sometimes prevailed before 1702.

Pennsylvania underwent political stresses and controversies similar to those of its smaller neighbor. Like all other proprietors, Penn discovered the inevitability of conflict between his authority and his subjects' interests. His troubles began almost as soon as he arrived in Pennsylvania. A convention, summoned in December 1682 to ratify the Frame of Government, instead attacked the proprietor's constitution even before it could begin to function. The first regular asssmbly of 1683 followed this up by forcing Penn to diminish his own and his council's prerogatives and to strengthen the powers of the lower house. This early trend generally continued during the rest of the seventeenth and in the early years of the eighteenth century. As in most other American colonies, the lower house quickly assumed an important place in Pennsylvania politics and government.

Land policy formed the single most contentious issue. Penn's wish to recoup his expenditures naturally led him to insist on the payment of rents and taxes and to seek an orderly distribution of land. He charged his chief officers with the task of surveying and recording land grants and collecting payments. Proprietary government therefore functioned in Pennsylvania, as elsewhere, as a hindrance to local and provincial autonomy and—since Penn had been charged by the English authorities with supervision of the Acts of Trade—as an agent of Whitehall. In time many of its leading members became powerful and rich in their own right. Then, even Penn's own officeholders began to challenge his authority. Thomas Lloyd, a Welsh protegé of Penn's, led Quaker opposition to him in the 1680s; his namesake, David Lloyd, Penn's attorney general from 1687 to 1699, also turned apostate and later became the proprietor's most formidable adversary. Since the substantial number of non-Quakers in the lower counties and other groups also disputed his authority, Penn's "holy experiment" turned from a dream of harmony to a nightmare of conflict.

Penn himself slowly awoke to this. He had returned to England in 1684. A series of struggles in which both the law courts and his officials refused to support his orders followed his departure. In 1688 he sent over a deputy governor, a tough Puritan soldier, John Blackwell, a move that brought general condemnation from Pennsylvania's Quakers. Blackwell found the entrenched Friend as ruthless as any other man "praying with his neighbour on First Days, then preying on him the other six." He attempted to imprison his chief opponents, a policy that led to assertions that the "Rights, Freedoms and Liberties of every Freeman [are] broken down, slighted and trodden under Foot", and provoked mob violence. Although in 1689 Pennsylvania, unlike Massachusetts, New York, and Maryland, experienced no colonial revolution, resistance to Blackwell had the effect of one, forcing Penn to sacrifice the governor and to yield political power to powerful local interests.

The 1690s, therefore, saw the dominance of an anti-proprietary establishment, controlled by the larger Quaker merchants and landholders, supported by some of the lesser Friends. This faction suppressed threats to its powers as vigorously as it had the proprietor's claims, fighting off non-Quaker Pennsylvanians and Delawareans and royal officials sent to suppress illegal trade. From 1690 to 1694 the activities of George Keith, a well-educated official who sought to promote a written code of practice among his Quaker coreligionists, seriously divided the Society of Friends; many who supported him did so because they resented the political and economic power of the establishment. The latter generally used the assembly to further its powers, judging this body better able to resist pressure from the proprietary, the English government, or domestic opponents than the smaller and nonrepresentative council.

The main threat now did come from Whitehall, where news of Pennsylvania's troubles joined reports of those in the other proprietaries. There seemed no reason why Pennsylvania should not be made a royal colony. If this happened, its inhabitants could expect a fresh attack on their local privileges and on their profitable but irregular or unlawful commerce, as well as an increase in the powers and numbers of an already growing Anglican element in Philadelphia. A royal government, especially in times of war, as the 1690s were, might also insist on a military policy uncongenial to the pacifistic Quakers. Penn's generosity led him to acede to requests to anticipate such disasters. He returned to Pennsylvania—"this licentious wilderness," he then called it—in 1699. On his departure in 1701 he consented to a revision of government, issuing a virtually new constitution, the "Charter of Privileges" or "Frame of 1701." This conferred many parliamentary privileges on the assembly, weakened proprietary land policy, and allowed the lower Delaware counties legislative autonomy. Penn consented to the Charter, one historian has noted, "because he fully expected Parliament to strip him of his rights of government and hoped that the wide autonomous powers granted the colonists by the new frame of government would shelter Quakers from an arbitrary royal governor."

While the Charter of Privileges had constitutional importance, politically it meant little. For Penn never lost his charter. Anti-proprietary feeling therefore persisted, leading to fresh attempts to strengthen the autonomy and independence of the province at Penn's expense. At the same time, those who wanted a royal government agitated unceasingly, seeking to create grounds for the Crown's intervention. After 1701 Penn's opponents, who usually dominated the assembly, resisted his governors and recruited support among the ordinary inhabitants by deliberate political propaganda, raising the "Popular and Plausible Cry of Standing for liberties and Priviledges."

C. The trend to order

The political struggles just reviewed mostly involved clashes between the plans of English-based proprietors and the aspirations of colonial settlers. In each of the newer colonies, for different reasons and at different times, these struggles produced severe crises and often provoked riots and rebellions. On the whole their outcome favored the colonists rather than the proprietors. The Carolina proprietors saw their powers whittled away, and finally lost their provinces to the Crown. In New York the advent of a normal type of royal government in 1691 proved acceptable to most settlers. In the Jerseys royal government also replaced proprietorial rule, and in Pennsylvania the Penn family retained legal control but lost political authority.

These colonial victories reduced some of the tensions existing in the newer colonies and helped produce a less troubled, more orderly kind of politics in which controversy was contained within an acceptable framework. This trend to order cannot be given precise dates since it took place in each colony according to specific internal developments. It also resulted from other developments than the colonists' triumphs over their rulers, particularly from the growth of a more defined social order in each colony and from a concurrent growing prosperity evident after about 1715.

In South Carolina the trend to order was a late development. Before 1730 political contentions combined with economic depression to produce the virtual collapse of central authority. The 1730s saw a gradual improvement, and the 1740s a great boom in business, lasting more or less to the American Revolution. In these years an established gentry class emerged among the planters, including such well-known South Carolinian families as the Laurens, Pinckneys, Rutledges, and Middletons. One observer wrote that the number of men and women "who have a Right to the Class of Gentry" was relatively larger in South Carolina than in any other part of North America. One recent student has also suggested that, as earlier in the Chesapeake, South Carolina then achieved demographic stability, with a rough equality of men and women providing the basis for normal family development. These developments obviously led to an increase in social and political order, for the colony's habitually troubled politics now gave way to the "harmony we were famous for," as one South Carolinian wrote. In North Carolina the transition to a more ordered political and social life also depended on a growing prosperity and the emergence of a commercial and planting upper class, though this circumstance was perhaps less pronounced and slower to happen. In early eighteenth-century Albemarle, a number of wealthy families associated with the Virginia gentry gained political status and considerable property. After about 1715 many South Carolina families moved north to settle on lower Cape Fear where they introduced rice planting. By the 1730s North Carolina gentry from both areas had begun to intermarry. This formation of a settled social elite, maturing in the 1730s and 1740s, coincided with the shift from a politics of riot and rebellion to one of more peaceful argument and faction that took place gradually from about 1719 to 1745.

The middle colonies also passed from disorder to relative order. In New York, in spite of the persistence of political battles, the most chaotic period of the colony's history ended as early as 1692 with the installation of the royal governor, council, and assembly. Although considered a factious people, eighteenth-century New Yorkers conducted their struggles within an imperial system that all sides accepted and tried to manipulate for their advantage. The New York assembly itself, the most recent analyst of New York politics writes, was a "battleground of faction" but one in which "the defense of Assembly prerogatives and colonial rights were not, properly speaking, the dominant themes." Unlike, for example, the Virginia or South Carolina assembly, it "rarely functioned as a unit." In New Jersey royalization in 1702 found six or seven factions with different interests who divided into two major groups; the royal governor was as likely to be a party to their shifting alliances as an adversary. Here, it is true, the assembly also used its opportunities to limit the governor's prerogatives and patronage powers. But in both colonies a conventional political system, in which politicians aimed less to challenge the executive than to ally with it, or capture it in pursuit of factional ends, had evolved by the first decade of the new century.

In Pennsylvania one turning point came at a precise time. David Lloyd, the Penns' leading opponent, lost control of the assembly in an election in 1710 after about nine years of political instability, years also of war and economic recession. After the election a new orderliness came to government and fifteen important statutes passed. In the same year began a return to prosperity and trade expansion. Political calm and economic prosperity roughly grew together. Indeed, the defeat of Lloyd seems to have resulted from the determination of Quaker and non-Quaker moderates to end the unfruitful quarrels of the previous years and promote political conditions favorable to the growth of trade. The next notable political troubles took place from 1722 to 1726 following a severe depression that began in 1722. After 1726, for more than a decade, increasing prosperity and political stability again went hand in hand.

The new prosperity particularly benefitted Pennsylvania's richer inhabitants, creating a more oligarchical society. As in South Carolina, a distinct and self-conscious upper class emerged, linked by intermarriage and property interests. In particular, Philadelphia merchants now dominated the government and law courts; landowners in the rural areas managed their own local affairs but left most assembly and provincial matters to the merchants. The artisans and common people might still be mobilized to political action, but they were not normally courted or prominent in matters of public debate. While factions within the emerging oligarchy still contested for place and power, they did so without disrupting the social and political framework and rendering government virtually unworkable, as it had so often been from 1682 to 1710.

In Pennsylvania other factors may also have counted. The first Quaker settlers had in England often been schooled to suspect and contest rather than to accept authority. Although advised to stand aside from day-to-day political controversy, they were also taught that many English laws were cruel, of doubtful validity, and wrongly administered. Their leaders, particularly Penn, actively campaigned against their legal disabilities, accusing English magistrates and rulers of cruelty and injustice. It may well be that the period of political stabilization marked the end of this Quaker feeling for protest. Their younger men, who had grown up in Pennsylvania, had never experienced religious persecution; many other Quakers were now rich and politically potent, overlords rather than underdogs. Until the disturbance of this newfound tranquility later in the eighteenth century, many Quakers turned from problems of law, government, and society—even from those of religion—to the peaceful pursuit and enjoyment of wealth and its associated rewards.

This certainly was the view of John Smith, an eighty-year-old Friend who testified to the Philadelphia Meeting in 1764 that "he had been a member of the Society upward of sixty years and well remembered that in those early times Friends were a plain lowly minded people, and that there was much tenderness and contrition in their meetings; that at the end of twenty years from that time, the Society increasing in wealth and in some degree conforming to the fashions of the world, true humility was less apparent and their meetings in general were less edifying; that at the end of forty years many of them were grown very rich—that wearing of fine costly garments and using of silver (and other) watches became customary with them . . . their sons and daughters, and many of the Society made a spacious appearance in the world, which marks of outward wealth and greatness appeared in many in our meetings of ministers and elders, and as those things became more prevalent, so the powerful, overshadowings of the Holy Ghost were less manifest in the Society; that there had been a continued increase in these ways of life even until now and that the weakness which hath now overspread the Society and the barrenness manifest amongst us is matter of much sorrows."

It is also known that from the latter seventeenth century a more hierarchical organization also developed. About this time, the monthly meetings usually appointed overseers, leading Friends whose job was to supervise discipline, behavior, and the social conduct of Quakers. At about the same time preparative meetings of "the more experienced and reliable Friends only" met to fix the agenda and business of the monthly meetings. Indeed, an emphasis on the role of the "overseers, or other weighty Friends," became commonplace in the eighteenth century. Similarly, registered "public Friends" or ministers—those Quakers accepted as particularly edifying witnesses—regularly met apart from the other members of the Society; in 1714 they were joined by "elders," defined as two or more Friends appointed by the monthly meeting who sat "with the ministers in their meetings . . . taking care that the Friends chosen for that service be prudent solid Friends. . . ." Quaker historians agree that usually older, and probably richer, Friends received such appointments and that " 'the meeting of ministering Friends' became a solid force for the status quo, and did little or nothing for a genuine development of fresh and vital ministry."

In all these colonies, then, the trend to order seems to have depended on a mixture of two or three factors. First, the successful establishment of institutions satisfactory to the colonists themselves and the defeat of attempts to impose various schemes of government and other rules and regulations. The parish vestries in Virginia, the county courts and commissioners of North Carolina and Pennsylvania, the city governments of Philadelphia and New York, the colonial assemblies—all flourished largely under the control of the American settlers. Conversely, English limitations attempted in many colonies on the types and the extent of settlement, the enforcement of the collection of rents and dues, plans to diversify agriculture or restrict the growth of slavery had little success. Second, a more visible social order, in which many kinds of political power and authority tended to be held by those colonists with a superior economic and social position, brought a measure of stability. The nature of the colonial elites was more apparent in 1740 than it had been in 1680. Then, the new opportunities of colonial life had encouraged ambitious men to fight for wealth and power, but the outcome of the battle was not known. By 1740 the prize for the successful was clearer—entry into an expanding, propertied group that tended to be not only rich but powerful in government and politics and in the social world. Third, the expansion of colonial wealth, while consolidating the position of an elite group, benefitted large numbers of inhabitants, giving the newer colonies a more ordered, differentiated, and less rancorous population.

Yet in spite of these developments, colonial life contained many areas in which discord could be expected. Governors still received their orders and authority from England. Factional interests sought special advantages in or from government. Ethnic and religious differences remained and would be increased by new immigration. New patterns of trade and agriculture produced new fiscal problems. And the rhetorical phrases of the earliest American political struggles that had so often translated local issues and controversies into constitutional and legal debates about Magna Carta, the Petition of Right, or the liberties of Englishmen—these ideas and all the others that had originated in seventeenth-century English political strife—were not forgotten in any of the colonies.

With the maturing of politics and society in the newer colonies came the growth of cultural and intellectual life. Here the emergence of a colonial elite with money to spend on education, books, and other relative luxuries also had great importance. North Carolina, for example, where prosperity never became generally pronounced and an upper class emerged slowly, seems to have been the least well endowed of the newer colonies in terms of cultural advances. It had no printing press until 1749, and its government showed little interest in providing even rudimentary educational facilities until about the middle of the eighteenth century. Although, as in Virginia, planters left money for educational uses and children received instruction in the household, the only regular teachers in the colony seem to have been Church of England missionaries and, later, representatives of other denominations. Although a number of transitory English visitors studied the natural history and the social and political development of the colony at the beginning of the eighteenth century, there is little evidence of any native North Carolinian scientific or cultural activity before the American Revolution. In South Carolina early attempts at scientific observation also came from English visitors, notably the famous naturalist Mark Catesby. Not until the middle of the century did the development of Charleston and the wealthy planting class bring about the growth of a scientific community. Moreover, outside Charleston there were few schools; even in that city educational instruction largely depended on English Church of England missionaries. No printing press existed in the colony until 1731. The Carolinas, like the Chesapeake, undoubtedly suffered from rural dispersion, planter materialism, and the fact that wealthy families could send their sons to England for education or employ private tutors. With the exception of the one city in the region, little evidence so far has been found of the growth of cultural interests among its inhabitants for many years after 1700.

In the other newer colonies, the development of important towns and a different pattern of settlement brought more rapid cultural development.

Philadelphia had a printing press in 1685, although not a permanent one until 1719; New York's first press was set up in 1694. In 1719 Philadelphia's first newspaper appeared; in 1725, New York's. Several men of cultural attainments settled in both places, including Cadwallader Colden, a Scots-Irish graduate of Edinburgh who came to Philadelphia in 1710 and later settled in New York; James Logan, a man of wide cultural interests, "Philadelphia's first scientist," owner of a fine private library; John Kearsley, a doctor and architect who arrived in the same town in 1717; and James Alexander, an official in New York and New Jersey who cooperated with Colden in scientific enterprises. In the middle colonies, both Anglican and dissenter groups established schools and occasional libraries, and governments gave mild encouragement to the provision of public education. Philadelphia, in particular, was becoming an educational mecca for the middle colonies by about 1730, with large numbers of private schools for boys and girls. A foretaste of its later eminence in the American Enlightenment was the formation of the Leather Apron Club in 1727 by the young Benjamin Franklin "for the discussion of morals, politics, poetry and natural philosophy, and for the interchange of books." This developed later into the better-known Junto and led to the foundation of the Library Company of Philadelphia in 1731.

To discuss culture, education, and intellectual life only in terms of schools, polite learning, and scientific interests—though these provide obvious points for comparison of different colonial societies—is inadequate. An examination of colonial culture, using the words in their broadest sense, should include such topics as the extent of literacy, popular beliefs, customs and superstitions, and other matters related to the whole population. Unfortunately, the sources so far tapped by historians have not yielded much evidence on these questions, though they represent a fruitful field for research. Also, the period so far discussed, roughly to the 1720s, was one of infancy for the new colonies in which only the barest outlines of cultural developments are visible.

Chapter Six

War, Administration, and Trade

In the latter seventeenth century, English links with North America became more or less fixed in ways that persisted until the American Revolution. Trade, as it had since the beginning of the century, underpinned the formal relationships of the royal and proprietary governments with their overseas territories; ships and their cargoes passed and repassed between the Old and New Worlds. Trade linked London, the great colonial metropolis, to a score or more of commercial centers in the Americas, while thriving British outports, first Bristol and later Liverpool, also profited from these maritime connections. Commerce and its instruments—bills of credit, invoices, ledger entries, and merchants' correspondence—not only joined the New and Old Worlds but more than any other single force molded official English attitudes to the Americas. The extent to which Englishmen saw the administration of the American colonies as that of trade rather than of territories or persons is readily apparent. The great parliamentary definition of colonial relationships with the mother country took place in the Acts of Trade; in 1696 the Board of Trade, the English agency specifically charged with colonial affairs, was founded. Poets, politicians, and propagandists tended to define the British empire as an empire of the seas over which a glorious commerce flourished. The theory that writers on economic matters developed to describe and justify English relationships with America essentially constituted a theory of trade in relation to national power and prosperity. Finally, the wars of the latter seventeenth and the early eighteenth centuries—greater than any yet fought—were, where they involved colonial possessions, contests for dominion over or access to commercially valuable territories and for mastery over the seas that linked them to Europe.

A. *English, Indians, and Europeans*

The success of William of Orange gave the throne to an inveterate enemy of Louis XIV and strengthened the generally prevalent anti-French feeling in

England. Many years of Anglo-French struggle (1689-1697 and 1702-1713) followed, into which the North American colonies were gradually drawn. Indeed, the scale and length of these Anglo-French conflicts had important results for British government, administration, and policy, necessitating greater efficiency, greater bureaucracy, and greater expenditure. All these developments also had an impact on the colonies and on colonial administration. War in this period as in others was the midwife of change. Yet if the accession of William coincided with the enlargement of the struggle between France and England, the relationship between English and Europeans in the colonies had, of course, been intermittently a military one since the beginnings of English expansion in the Americas. The outcome of the sixteenth-century raids against the Spanish in the South Atlantic and the Caribbean had been the practical relinquishment of Iberian claims to sovereignty over North America's Atlantic coast and the West Indies. English contests with the Dutch had broken the hold of the United Provinces on the Atlantic trades, though not their supremacy in the East Indies. Englishmen had therefore been able to share in the development of the staple commodities of the Atlantic and Caribbean—cod, fur, tobacco, sugar, and slaves. In their turn, the wars of the late seventeenth and eighteenth centuries would mark an English response to French competition, a contest for supremacy in the West Indies, for access to Spain's American colonies, for the bounty of Canada and the interior of North America.

With these aims the American settlers largely agreed. Their own commercial ambitions and cultural and religious prejudices as well as their fears of Franco-Spanish hostility led them increasingly into the great struggle for empire. Its demands, indeed, held in check tensions between metropolis and settlers so evident in the seventeenth century. The sense of belonging to and needing the protection of the British empire made a degree of subordination to English interests more acceptable. Yet Americans did develop their own views of tactics and strategy. They showed a willingness to act to defend their own particular colonies but less readiness to contribute to the aid of other colonies or to support imperial military schemes with no direct relevance to themselves. Many Massachusetts settlers believed that the Crown and not their colony ought to be responsible for northern New England and often refused men or supplies to defend it. Maryland and Virginia sent few men and little money north for the protection of New York. And when victory over and peace with the French came in 1763, repressed hostilities between England and Americans flourished anew with devastating results for the old imperial pattern.

The first English settlers in America had come prepared for warfare. Virginians knew that the Spanish objected to their presence; they also expected that the Indians might be hostile, as did the early settlers of Plymouth and Massachusetts. The Maryland charter referred directly to the remoteness of the proprietary ''placed among so many barbarous nations'' and to the ''incursions as well of the barbarians themselves, as of other enemies, pirates and ravagers'' and gave the Lord Proprietor ''as full and unrestrained power as any captain-general of an army ever had. . . ." Several Virginia governors were military men while the Pilgrims hired a military adviser, Miles Standish, and the Puritans included a number of men with professional military experience. Muskets, cannon, shot, gunpowder, swords, halberds, and pistols constituted part of the supplies of the early colonists.

Their basic military system, naturally enough, followed English precedents, resting primarily on a militia formed of all the able-bodied males between sixteen and sixty who received periodic training. These men kept their own arms. In New England they at first also elected, later nominated, their own officers in each town; in the Chesapeake these were appointed by the governor, usually from members of the county courts. But in all the colonies local men officered and led the militia, and the notion that a citizen-militia provided the cornerstone of a free government and a protection against tyranny and absolutism was as strong in America as in England. Standing professional armies, besides being expensive, threatened civil liberties. As well as the militia, troops of cavalry and artillery also appeared in most colonies with the growth of a colonial upper class that often preferred service in these semi-exclusive companies to ordinary militia duties. The Boston Artillery Company, for example, founded in 1639, numbered most of the Boston elite by the 1680s. Colonies also built up public supplies of arms and powder. In times of emergency or war, governments could impress militiamen into armies serving under martial law, although in many colonies their charters or legislation specified that militia could not be made to serve outside of them.

The Dutch had been the first victims of British expansion in North America. Their original fur-trading factories had gradually evolved into a colony of quasi-settlement by 1630. Yet the policy of the West India Company, the controlling Dutch authority over the New Netherlands, remained one of creating a trading rather than a colonial empire. It sought to stabilize and protect its foothold in the North American fur trade by establishing an inexpensive and self-sufficient settlement there but largely rejected pleas for a vigorous policy of large-scale colonial expansion and sponsored migration. With numerous other responsibilities throughout the Dutch overseas empire and with a vacillating board of directors, the company gave little leadership. But even had migration been encouraged, it is doubtful that conditions in the United Provinces would have made it popular. Ordinary Dutchmen could only be persuaded to go to America with the bribe of "a great deal of money and promises," wrote one observer advocating the importation of Negro slaves. One reason must have been the relative comfort and prosperity of all classes in the seventeenth-century Dutch Republic, a fact often remarked on by visitors.

Many early settlers were foreigners or foot-loose single men. Although Dutch families came and prospered, considerable resentment grew up in the colony against the West India Company and its restrictive policies in the field of immigration and government, for it allowed little settler participation in local affairs. The governors appointed and sent out by the company had a full measure of executive control. After about 1641 an advisory body from among the leading colonists, with few real powers, met intermittently. Not until 1653, after a remonstrance from the inhabitants, did the company permit any form of municipal government with roots among the settlers. The tensions between company and settlers, the large numbers of foreigners in the New Netherlands, and the menace of the sizeable English population in New England and on the Chesapeake, as well as the relatively formidable forces sent by the Duke of York against New Amsterdam in 1664, all contributed to the colony's downfall. In his justification for the surrender of the colony, its last governor, Peter Stuyvesant, claimed that the whole province could muster less than 300 men capable of bearing arms and that the overwhelming numerical supremacy of the English together with the West India Company's neglect to send "reinforcements of men and ships . . . so repeatedly demanded but not come . . ." had made surrender inevitable.

The English attack on Dutch power in North America took place as part of the general English assault on the commercial strength of the United Provinces. Following the end of the third Anglo-Dutch war came a growing rapprochement between England and Holland. Commercial rivalries persisted but the growing ascendancy of France made these of secondary importance. Military and political alliances preceded and followed the ascent of William of Orange to the English throne. Moreover, Holland declined as England gathered force as a commercial and colonial power, so that the old anti-Dutch slogans gradually lost their relevance.

Spanish claims to the Caribbean and North America gradually faded in the face of international realities. Spain recognized Dutch possession of four tiny islands in the West Indies in the Treaty of Munster of 1648, while the Treaty of Madrid of 1670 gave similar recognition to England's possession of Jamaica. The same treaty also admitted the legality of English occupation of most of North America, although Spain had hardly disputed this, except on paper, since the end of the sixteenth century. Florida remained an impoverished military outpost, valued for the defense of the Bahama Channel used by convoys bound for Europe, and as a link in the chain of outposts that protected Spanish interests in the Gulf of Mexico. In 1700, 323 soldiers guarded St. Augustine and other parts of Spanish Florida, and the two forts in the province were poorly repaired and armed. Given rising English pressure from South Carolina on the region that later became Georgia, the Spanish governors of Florida justly feared that their resources were too small. The Spanish presence elsewhere in North America was negligible, though French activity on the Mississippi provoked later countermoves. Yet the whole Spanish-American empire remained formidable in extent, population, and wealth. From it, aggressive Europeans by 1700 sought not territory but trading rights, viewing Spanish America as a lucrative market for manufactured goods and for the human cargoes of the slave ships, especially since these brought payments in silver, itself necessary for trade to the East Indies. In this, as one writer has remarked, "the myth of El Dorado, modernized and mercantilized, retained its grip on men's minds . . . [they thought] of the Spanish American market as insatiable, of the flow of bullion as inexhaustible. The policies of English, French and Dutch towards Spain and towards one another, were constantly affected by these two illusions."

As first the Spanish and then the Dutch withdrew from North America, the French became England's greatest American rivals. The Anglo-French struggle in North America had had its feeble beginnings as early as the reign of James I with disputes over the possession of Nova Scotia, known by the French as Acadia. In the treaty of St. Germain-en-Laye of 1632 England returned Acadia and territory on the St. Lawrence to France. In 1655 the treaty of Westminster again provided for the restoration of Acadian forts to France after their capture by an expedition originally intended by Cromwell for an attack on Manhattan. These were finally returned to France by the Treaty of Breda (1667) in exchange for the English port of St. Kitts, taken by the French in 1666. Breda ended the second Anglo-Dutch war in which the French, allied with the Dutch, carried the battle into the Caribbean, attacking several English sugar islands. In this war, although there was finally to be no Anglo-French fighting in North America, the British government did order an attack on Canada. European wars and diplomacy and North American rivalries were thus becoming interconnected as the century progressed. An important point came with the failure of the Dutch in North America, which removed a barrier to direct confrontation between English and French in the Hudson Valley. As the English supplanted the Dutch, their fur trappers and merchants moved into greater competition with French woodsmen and their Indian allies, adding a second zone of friction to the first in the Newfoundland-Nova Scotia area, where French and English had intermittently jostled since the 1620s. After 1670 a third area of conflict appeared, with the English incorporation of the Hudson's Bay Company, a direct challenge to French sovereignty over the fur trade of the frozen north. Although James II negotiated a treaty of "American neutrality" with Louis XIV, attempts to exclude the New World from the rivalries of the Old soon vanished. In an age of competition for overseas commerce, when merchants and politicians joined to persuade governments of the need to consider profits as well as power based on those profits, such attempts had no basis in reality.

French survival in North America in 1660 was by no means certain, since at that date the population of Canada amounted to only about 2,500 persons. By about 1680 it had reached about 10,000; by 1720 about 25,000. This testimony to the increasing vigor of New France seems impressive until it is remembered that the population of New England alone in the latter year was about 170,000. Nevertheless, New Englanders and New Yorkers feared the French and their Indian allies as much or more than the French feared them, and British attacks on French possessions in North America had limited success up to the 1760s. The origins of French strength lay with the initial policy of Louis XIV and his chief minister, Colbert, who promoted migration and paid bounties to increase the birth rate. They also reorganized the government of New France and increased military assistance to the colony. Two Canadian officials, Jean-Baptiste Talon, the intendant, and Louis de Frontenac, the governor, provided an efficient administration. Moreover, French expansion to the Great Lakes and into the Illinois region, spearheaded by missionary priests and fur traders, together with the establishment of the colony of Louisiana, testified to the relative vitality of French colonial enterprise. La Salle, the great explorer, dreamed of connecting Louisiana with Canada by a chain of fortified settlements, a project that was not pursued until the eighteenth century. Yet a growing concentration on defense—a natural reaction to the threat of the vast English colonial population—would soon weaken rather than strengthen New France. While considerable sums were spent on fortifications and soldiers, little was done to subsidize vitally needed emigrants. Moreover, the fur trade remained a monopoly, and New France developed little trade either with her mother country or with other parts of Europe.

The history of Spanish, French, Dutch, and English in North America was tragically intertwined with that of the Indian. From the beginnings of European contact with American Indians, it was obvious that superior European organization and technology would lead to European domination. Sixteenth- and seventeenth-century European society was warlike and aggressive, gearing itself through the development of long-range ocean-going ships, armed with powerful cannons, that would carry military men and materials around the world. At the same time, state bureaucracies and groups of moneyed men financed and encouraged this armed expansion. Technological and scientific advances in the same years often sprang from military developments, and governments became more efficient in response to needs created by the struggle of nation against nation or state against state. No grouping of North American Indians had the technological resources or knowledge, the level of organization or the perception of the world, necessary to resist the European advance. And with rare exceptions, no Europeans had the imagination or sensitivity to transcend the general view of primitive peoples as barbarians, devil worshippers, or noble savages to be sacrificed where necessary to the expansion of white settlement, trade, and power.

European demand for furs rather than for territory brought the first significant contacts between Indians and whites in North America and suggested the future pattern of relationships. European fur traders in the St. Lawrence and the northeastern regions caused great rivalries among the Indians for the control of fur-supplying areas, turning tribes from agriculture and hunting to commercial trapping and commercial warfare. This warfare became more lethal and destructive since the Indians now armed themselves with guns and muskets, often accepting the direction of white allies who fought to kill and destroy. The rivalry for furs led to new alliances and groupings among the Indians. The most famous of these, the Iroquois Confederacy, formed about 1570, became extraordinarily aggressive in the seventeenth century, ranging widely from the St. Lawrence to the Ohio, as they sought to control and benefit from the European fur trade, conquering and vassalizing other Indian tribes, some of whom were driven far into the west. Since the time of Champlain, the Iroquois had been enemies of the French, whose alliance with the Huron Indians of the upper St. Lawrence valley gave them a position in the fur trade coveted by the Iroquois. Before 1660 the French turned from attacks on the Iroquois to attempts to ally with them and finally back to an aggressive policy. The Dutch and the English sought their friendship and remained on good terms with them. However, from the 1690s to the 1750s, the Iroquois did not launch any general attack on the French, and this neutrality helped balance French and English power in the interior of North America.

The Iroquois Confederacy consisted of five "nations"—Seneca, Cayuga, Oneida, Onondaga, and Mohawk—joined by a sixth, the Tuscarora, driven from the Carolinas by white forces in 1722. The federative aspect of the league involved a Council of Sachems, hereditary leaders who discussed external relations but had no power over the internal affairs of each nation. Within each tribe matriarchy prevailed; not only did the women own all the property and exercise police powers but only males belonging to a certain matrilineage could be chosen as sachems by the women. Iroquois society was based on villages, protected by log palisades, outside of which maize and vegetable fields provided staple foodstuffs.

Far to the south, another confederacy evolved during the seventeenth century, a union of Muskogean-speaking tribes, led by the Muskogee Indians. This Creek "nation" or confederacy arose from the interaction of Spanish and English influences. Courted by Carolina traders from Charleston and Spanish missionaries from Santa Cruz, the Creeks at first sided with the English, furnishing troops and in 1705 allying formally with Carolina. Doubledealing and fraudulent practices by English traders, however, pushed the Creeks into enmity, and they enlisted the support of the Yamasee Indians of South Carolina. The Carolinians, using Cherokee allies, prevailed. The Creeks then made peace with the English but began a long war with the Cherokees. Their policy toward the Europeans became one of neutrality, and they traded with French, Spanish, and English. The other important Indians of the South consisted of Cherokees, Choctaws, and Chickasaws, the first Iroquois and the others Muskogean. Of these, the Choctaws came under Louisiana-French influence while the Cherokees and Chickasaws were courted by the British. All the southern tribes lived in "towns," growing corn and vegetables and hunting for subsistence. Before the coming of the whites, warfare was mild, and such "Indian practices" as scalping did not exist. But trade between different villages and tribes did, carried on by Indian merchants over forest paths. This pre-existing trade prepared the Indians for the coming of white traders. White demands for deer pelts and Indian slaves then revolutionized the culture of the southern Indians while French and English rivalries made them seek alliances and influence over those tribes who, unlike the Creeks, did not remain neutral in the struggle.

From the Gulf of Mexico north to the Great Lakes and in the western parts of the colonies, European rivalries had then profoundly affected Indian society. Not only did new types of warfare and new alliances and groupings of Indians become prevalent, but traditional crafts and social patterns changed. Guns, knives, axes, hoes, blankets, pots and pans, salt, paint and alcohol, at first novelties, became necessities. Yet here the whites on the whole maintained Indians as useful allies, as customers and suppliers and did not covet their lands. The case in areas of concentrated or advancing colonial settlement was different. There, the native Americans, faced with superior European armaments and tactics, lost the battle for survival. Some became peaceful, detribalized, generally poverty-stricken inhabitants of the white colonies; others moved out of their tribal areas to escape white overlordship; still others died in resisting it. In Virginia Indian numbers had dropped by 1670 to about 2,000-3,000, perhaps some 8 percent of those living there in 1608. In New England, where perhaps 25,000 Indians lived in 1600, European diseases had reduced their numbers, probably by half, twenty years later. As in Virginia, initial and wary friendship was replaced by violence as white land-hunger grew. Nor did Puritan views of the Indians as savages and, in periods of warfare, as Satan's agents lead to harmony. Few Puritan ministers were active missionaries and those who were sought to persuade the Indians to accept white authority as well as white religion. The powerful Pequot tribe of southern New England was decimated in 1636-1637 by an alliance of settlers and Narragansett Indians. In 1675-1676, Metamoc, or King Philip, a Wampanoag Indian, led his people in a major uprising joined by other tribes, devastating first much of Plymouth colony, then the upper Connecticut Valley, and threatening the coastal towns. Several thousand colonists were killed. The Indian attacks faltered, Professor Nash has argued, less because of English victories than from lack of food, disease, and shortages of guns and ammunition. This failure brought the end of Indian resistance throughout Puritan New England, leaving only the northern Indians, the Penobscot and Abenaki in Maine, who sporadically and often with French encouragement harassed the tiny settlements of the English in that region. In the middle colonies, the Leni Lenape or Delaware Indians, a smaller and less well-organized grouping, faced not only the advancing settlers but felt the weight of pressure from the aggressive Iroquois warriors of upper New York. Under their orders, they moved first to western Pennsylvania to form a buffer between the whites and the Iroquois, then to the Ohio. Further south, the Carolinians also broke Indian resistance. The Iroquoian-speaking Tuscaroras, about 5,000 strong and living on the Roanoke and southwards in North Carolina, were forced out by white settlers in the wars of 1711-1713. They moved north to join their fellow Iroquois in the interior of New York. In South Carolina the Yamassees, a Muskogean-speaking tribe, were routed in 1715-1716 and their survivors absorbed into the Creek nation. Where white settlers prevailed, surviving Indians either continued to live as scattered and dispirited remnants or moved away in search of security elsewhere.

Until the 1690s conflicts with the Indians rather than struggles between the English and other Europeans formed the largest part of colonial warfare. King William's War, which began in 1689 and was part of the European conflict between France and the English and the Dutch, known in Europe as the War of the League of Augsburg, was the first to involve a serious inter-European struggle in North America. In the colonies, tension between French and English had built up in the 1680s with the attempts of New York's governor, Thomas Dongan, to stem French expansion and promote English trade in areas extending to the St. Lawrence and the Great Lakes. Dongan negotiated an agreement with the Iroquois that placed them under British protection; gainsaying this, the French governor, the Marquis de Denonville, attacked the Senecas in 1687. The next year, supplied with British arms, the Iroquois besieged Montreal. At the same time, the French and British skirmished in Maine, and the French encouraged the Maine Indians, the Abenakis, to raid English settlements in their territory. In August 1689 the frontier coastal post of Pemaquid (modern Bristol, Maine) was destroyed by the Indians. A month before, the Iroquois, not on this occasion with any overt English support it appears, had attacked Lachine, near Montreal, and massacred several score French. News of the European struggle—war was declared in May 1689 and the colonies ordered to join in—therefore found the northern colonies already near conflict.

The early stages of the war in America coincided with the revolt against Andros in New England and New York; this circumstance dislocated the colonial militias and colonial leadership, particularly connections between Albany, the forward post for negotiations with the Indians, and New York City. Nor could the Albanyites get much aid from New England, which was anxious about the Maine frontier and internally disorganized. The first successful blows came from the French and Indians, inspirited since October 1689 by the arrival of the famous Count Frontenac, reappointed to Canada for the emergency. Of three war parties sent out by him, one surprised and destroyed the village of Schenectady, fifteen miles northwest of Albany, in February 1690. Another killed thirty-four persons at Salmon Falls, New Hampshire, thirteen miles north of Portsmouth. The third, a force of some 500 men, took Falmouth, Maine, in May and then besieged Fort Loyal (Portland, Maine). When the fort surrendered, the Indians massacred about 100 persons, despite a French guarantee of their safety. Here re-appeared an odd conjunction of European politics and American warfare, since the French commander later justified the massacre on the grounds that the New Englanders were rebels against their lawful monarch, James II!

French successes had so far reflected superiority on land. At sea, the New Englanders showed greater strength. Boston merchants with government encouragement, for example, organized a successful marine assault on Port Royal, the Acadia fort, in May 1690, although its capture was not a great feat as the garrison numbered only about sixty men. A far more ambitious plan called for a joint New England-New York two-pronged assault on Canada, by sea from Boston and by land and canoe from Albany. The land expedition failed dismally. Colonial cooperation broke down from the start. A few dozen men in the end assaulted a small settlement, La Prairie, across the river from Montreal, in August 1690, then returned to Albany. The naval attack on Quebec could have succeeded since thirty-four ships and about 2,000 men sailed in the same month. But the fleet did not arrive until October, and the amateur soldiers, having failed to take Quebec by direct assault, withdrew too soon, stricken by smallpox and fearful of the approaching Canadian winter. A great pall of gloom descended on the English colonies after these events, silencing even the Puritan ministers of Massachusetts who had preached a Protestant Anglo-Saxon crusade against the popish French.

The next seven years of war produced few surprises. The New York government attempted to repair its alliance with the Iroquois, launching another attack on the region around Montreal; Massachusetts sent expeditions against the Maine Indians. But in 1692 the French and their allies returned to the assault in northern New England, destroying York and assailing Wells. In 1693 Frontenac moved against the Mohawks. The English responded with military assistance. In 1694 French and Indians again ravaged parts of Maine and New Hampshire. Two years later a naval expedition from Quebec captured a newly fortified English stronghold, Fort William Henry, at Pemaquid; following this, attacks were made on Newfoundland and on the British in Hudson's Bay. While these events took place, Frontenac invaded central New York and ravaged the Onondaga country, an astute move since the English could now raise no money nor troops to go to the aid of these Iroquois allies. Although the French sent a fleet of fifteen ships to America in 1697 for an attack on Boston, this did not take place.

In Europe, in the Peace of Ryswick signed in September 1697, the clauses relating to America were as inconclusive as the war itself. All conquered territories were to be restored to their pre-war owners, except for three Hudson's Bay forts seized by the French before the outbreak of the war and recaptured by the English during it. Their fate would be settled by a special commission. More important for New York and New England was the attitude of the Iroquois Indians. Disillusioned by the failure of the English to assist them against Frontenac's attacks in 1696, they appeared at a great Indian gathering in Montreal in 1701 and signed a treaty of neutrality. Although they also put their lands under the protection of the British Crown in the same year, the net result of these moves was a defeat for the British, for they replaced a long period of Iroquois aid against the French with one of Iroquois neutrality.

In the South, Anglo-Spanish rivalry focused on the area that later became Georgia, where English influence after the foundation of South Carolina pulled the Indian tribes away from Spain. Unofficial English raiding parties had attacked the Spanish mission of St. Catalina on St. Catherine's Island about 100 miles south of Charleston in 1680; three years later a Spanish outpost of St. Augustine was burned by English attackers. In 1686 the Spanish retaliated, destroying the Scots settlement of Port Royal, then threatening Charleston itself. French joined Spanish influence in the South with the establishment of Louisiana in 1698 and the alliance of its settlers with the Choctaw Indians in 1700. English colonists now began to worry that the French might construct a great chain of forts and Indian alliances from the St. Lawrence-Great Lakes region to the mouth of the Mississippi. The construction of Fort Pontchartrain on the Detroit River and the advances of French missionaries into the Illinois region, as well as the French success with the Iroquois, added to these fears. Soon the French had established themselves at Mobile on the Alabama River and at Cahokia on the upper Mississippi.

The Treaty of Ryswick had settled none of the outstanding problems of Europe or America. The uneasy peace gave way to a new conflict in 1702, the War of the Spanish Succession, americanized as Queen Anne's War. The English hoped to prevent the accession of a French king to the Spanish throne, a threat to England's trade with old and new Spain. In America, we have seen the English colonists' increasing fear of French expansion as a danger to their settlements and a barrier to their access to the fur-rich interior. The pattern of the new war in North America very much resembled that of the preceding struggle, for many years consisting of a series of skirmishes fought by local troops. In South Carolina in 1702 Governor James Moore, a tough Indian trader, raised an army of some 500 militia and 300 Indians and sailed south. They sacked the town of St. Augustine but the stone fort and its occupants withstood them. A year later Moore led a private (mostly Indian) expedition against the Apalachee Indians west of St. Augustine, seizing about 1,000 of them as slaves to pay his costs. This attack ended Spanish influence among the Indians in the area north of the St. John's River and promised the transfer of its fur trade to the English. But Florida remained Spanish; an opportunity had been lost. A Franco-Spanish reprisal in 1706 against Charleston brought some five shiploads of soldiers from Cuba and Florida to the colonial capital, but their landing parties were driven off and their ships dispersed by local forces. The next summer the English retaliated, attacking Fort San Carlos at Pensacola; relief came to the Spanish from the French at Mobile. By about 1708 most of the Southeast, except the Florida peninsula, was under English influence, and profits from the Indian fur and slave trade waxed. The Tuscarora Indian attacks against North Carolina in 1711-1713 and the Yamassee Indian attack on South Carolina in 1715, already mentioned, resulted less from French or Spanish intrigue than from the overconfident commercial greed of the successful English.

In the North, the Abenakis again cooperated with the French, striking the English in Maine and northern New England in 1703-1705. The sack of Deerfield in February 1704 became notorious; 38 English died and 111 were captured. A desultory English attack on Port Royal failed in the same year. During this time New York did nothing, fearing to act without its Iroquois allies, who still maintained their neutrality. New Englanders, indeed, believed that Albany merchants traded with French Indians, buying goods seized in the Indian raids on the New England towns. In 1707 a large-scale expedition against Port Royal, organized by Governor Joseph Dudley in Boston, disintegrated. During the investiture of the fort, it became clear that none of the commanders knew how to conduct siege warfare. Only in 1708 did the English government accept colonial pleas for assistance, promising to send warships, a few men, and experienced military commanders to spearhead an assault on Quebec. But these promises produced neither ships nor men, despite elaborate American preparations in which New York now cooperated. The planned invasion force broke up in disgust. In 1710, however, the English sent 500 hundred marines, and Port Royal was finally captured and renamed Annapolis Royal in honor of the Queen.

The climax of this war in North America came in 1711, when a new Tory ministry in England decided to seek triumph in Canada to rival Marlborough's Whig victories in Europe. Five thousand men and sixty ships arrived at Boston, sailing north on July 30 for Quebec. They never reached it. After losing eight ships and 700 men on the rocks at the mouth of the St. Lawrence, the British admiral decided that the American pilots could not be trusted. The British sailed directly back to England. Admiral Walker, the naval chief, was later dismissed, but an expensive fiasco had taken place that did nothing to improve Anglo-American relations.

The Peace of Utrecht of 1713 ended the war. For the first time a European peace reflected a mature awareness of colonies and trade. It gave Annapolis Royal (Port Royal) and Acadia to England; this was expected to protect the Maine coast and displace the French from a potential base for naval and privateering expeditions against New England and Newfoundland. Yet the respite was illusory, for France kept Cape Breton Island to the north of Nova Scotia and there began to construct a great garrison fortress, Louisbourg. Hudson's Bay and Newfoundland went to England, but the French kept fishing rights and rights to maintain unfortified fishing villages along part of the Newfoundland coast. French subjects in the ceded regions could either leave or remain under British rule with freedom of religion. Both countries promised not to interfere with the other's Indian ''subjects'' and to allow them to trade freely.

To Spain, the British promised assistance in maintaining the Spanish-American empire's territorial integrity; this represented an indirect challenge to French expansion in Louisiana.

This brief narrative of the early colonial wars points to several general facts about North American tactics and strategy. Overall, neither France nor England regarded North America as more than a subsidiary sideshow to the main theater of war. This remained Europe, although the West Indies had become increasingly important. The French sent a few men and ships to Canada during the Spanish succession struggle; the English, a relatively big expedition only for the attack on Quebec in 1711. Neither side stationed armies or fleets in North America or devoted much thought to the war there. Colonial militia and Indian warriors rather than European soldiers bore the burden of the struggle. The French had an advantage here, as the more centralized Canadian government had greater organizational powers. The small Canadian war parties of whites and Indians that struck repeatedly at New England spread fear and uncertainty, holding down the English in their village blockhouses or forcing them to dissipate their strength in vain wilderness searches for elusive enemies. The English launched no successful land attacks on Canada. Yet the French could only frighten, even paralyze their opponents; real victory, the conquest of the English, demanded sea power and large invasion forces able to strike at major coastal towns like Boston or New York, and these they could not raise.

The English had this potential, or so the attacks on Port Royal and Quebec suggest. It still remained to be successfully used rather than wasted through deficient organization and lack of professionalism. But the English government provided no effective military leaders, and the colonies let their internal jealousies and differences divide them. That no American really understood siege warfare, for example, illustrates the first point, while numerous incidents could be mentioned to demonstrate the latter. The English settlers also proved less attractive allies to the Indians than the more dashing French, whose young fur trappers often lived with the tribes and whose missionaries lived and died among them. Iroquois neutrality in the War of the Spanish Succession had also seriously hampered the English and had enabled the French to maintain their hold on the St. Lawrence and Great Lakes region and to push south from there.

B. War and administration

In England the Glorious Revolution seemed initially to mark the assertion of local and county interests, of the parliamentary nation, against the centralizing and absolutist tendencies of the later Stuarts. Yet the long period of war with France that ensued brought changes in government and administration which increased the power of the executive. Ministers and bureaucrats came to control more offices, more places, more lucrative contracts and rewards as the machinery of the state expanded to direct the wars. This expansion ultimately had repercussions for the English administration of the colonies, although it never successfully encompassed the reform of colonial governments themselves. And in the colonies more clearly than in England, the immediate effect of the Glorious Revolution was to reassert local interests against those of central government. For in North America one great change followed the Glorious Revolution: the dismemberment of the Dominion of New England and the restitution of modified versions of its former colonial governments. New York became a royal government, Massachusetts received a new charter that gave it certain corporate privileges and a royal governor, and Connecticut and Rhode Island retained the corporate charters granted to them by Charles II. The policy of revoking other charters and forming consolidated dominions also flagged or disappeared. The Jerseys were returned to their proprietors and Pennsylvania remained with Penn. Of the proprietaries, indeed, only Maryland was reformed, becoming a royal colony in 1691. But the Calverts retained their rights as owners of its lands. These decisions, amounting almost to a return to the liberal colonial policies of fifteen or twenty years earlier, may have reflected the Whiggism of the English revolution with its respect for property and corporate rights. On the other hand, colonial policy does not seem to have been a topic on which Tories and Whigs had differences of party opinion. It is more likely that the decisions arose as easy solutions to the peripheral problem of North America in the first years of a war concentrated in Europe and the West Indies. Certainly, English ministers moved slowly and carelessly to deal with North American problems, usually accepting the powerful representations of American agents who came to London to make the best deal they could for their constituents at home. The new king turned out few of the important officials who had served James II. William Blathwayt, indeed, became a close servant of William's, and he and like-minded colleagues continued to press for a policy of bureaucratic centralization. And the central aspect of English colonial policy, the implementation of the Navigation Acts, was not altered.

Perhaps the most important change in colonial administration was the creation of the Board of Trade in 1696 which replaced the Lords of Trade, who had not responded efficiently to the demands of war. The original call for reform arose from a primary concern with commerce. Acute fiscal difficulties, the virtual collapse of government credit, and complaints that French privateers covered "the Sea like Locusts" led to a Parliamentary enquiry in 1695. By mid-February 1696 the Commons had given a second reading to a bill to create a Council of Trade controlled by the legislature, a challenge to the royal prerogative. Probably to counter this threat, the King's ministers held parallel hearings on the same topic, receiving evidence from such luminaries as Isaac Newton, John Locke, and Christopher Wren. Other separate evidence calling for a new body to administer colonial affairs went to Lord Shrewsbury,

Secretary of State for the Southern Department. The government seems then to have combined these suggestions for trade and plantations, proposing their joint oversight by a new Commission for Trade and Plantations. On 30 April 1696 a royal warrant gave life to the Board of Trade. Parliament subsequently dropped its own plans for a trade committee.

The Board of Trade remained active during the rest of the period before the American Revolution as the central English agency for colonial government and administration. Yet the fact of its longevity, after the short lives of former colonial administrative committees, should not obscure the Board of Trade's origins and functions. It was created as an advisory body to the Privy Council, not as an executive authority over the colonies. From this point of view, it had less formal authority than the body that it replaced. The first members included two privy councillors and five experts on trade or colonies. The great officers of state, often *ex-officio* members, rarely attended. The Board's main work was to receive all correspondence from governors and all important official papers from the colonies; these included particularly laws and proclamations, the journals of governors, councils, and assemblies, and petitions. Problems arising from such numerous communications might be dealt with in several ways. Colonial laws, for example, passed from the Board to the Crown's legal officers, who had to make sure that they did not conflict with English law. Matters calling for decisions not covered by known policy or precedent had to be sent on to the Secretary of State for the Southern Department who might place them before the Privy Council or the inner circle of government ministers, now emerging as a kind of cabinet. Moreover, the Privy Council acted as a final court of appeal for disputed legal cases. It or powerful ministers held the power of appointment of all colonial governors and many other colonial officials. Matters affecting colonial customs, or naval and military affairs, had to be placed before the appropriate English bodies—the customs commissioners, the Admiralty, or the War Office. In this way the Board often served as a transmitting agency, although it sent on its own recommendations and was not merely a post office.

This brief description of procedure suggests the multiplicity of agencies with which colonial administration might in some way be involved. In cases involving the Treasury or the Admiralty, for example, the Board could not order action but merely request it, hoping that in any serious disagreements the Crown might take its side. And while the Board obviously had responsibility for matters that fell directly within its own competence—formulating instructions to governors, framing recommendations for policy toward the colonies and advice on the appointment of colonial officials—even here it found its authority formally limited. It could nominate men for governorships and other offices but could appoint only members of the governor's council. It could put forward general policies but these might not be accepted by the ministry or not carried out if Treasury finance was lacking. In all these concerns, the Board's major responsibility was to protect and foster English trade and English power, not to conciliate or represent the interests or the inhabitants of the colonies.

The most recent study of the Board suggests, indeed, that apart from the very early years, it was always in a weak position when it moved from the conduct of routine business to the formulation of policy. By 1700 it had fairly successfully initiated and superintended a campaign against piracy and illegal trade in American waters, attacking the colonial officials and courts which seemed to shelter the malefactors. The difficulties the Board met in dealing with non-royal colonies led William Blathwayt to revive his former policy of seeking to revoke colonial charters. The Board now recommended, remembering James II, not legal proceedings by the Crown against the charters but an act of Parliament to do this. In early 1700 Blathwayt condemned the proprietary and charter governments to the House of Commons. These, he stated, could not be made to act "without some further Provision by Parliament, capable to Reduce them to a more Regular Conduct and complyance with their Duty in reference to the Trade of England." But Parliament was dissolved without taking action on the colonies. In the next Parliament, that of 1701, Blathwayt took up his former charges in the Commons and a bill was introduced in the Lords to weaken the powers of proprietary and charter government. It failed to gain a hearing. In 1702 a similar bill could not be considered owing to the death of the King.

The Board of Trade's attack on the colonial charters therefore failed, mostly because of their lack of importance in the eyes of the King's ministers; they gave Parliament little time to discuss the colonies and Parliament itself showed no great interest. Even so, colonial agents and representatives in England, led by William Penn and other nonconformists, mounted a vigorous campaign in the defense of colonial charters. Here were indications for the future. First, the Board of Trade and the business of the colonies remained in a subordinate position in the hierarchy of government. Second, the Board had to fight not only government indifference but contending colonial interests represented in England, sometimes with powerful allies and often with as much access to ministers and politicians as had the Board.

How had more mundane matters of colonial administration developed by the beginning of the eighteenth century? From the English point of view the colonial governor remained the lynchpin of royal rule. Even in the corporate and proprietary colonies, the governor often stood charged with royal duties, particularly with enforcing the Acts of Trade and attending to matters of defense. In the growing number of royal colonies, the governor's position had become fairly standardized by 1714, as had the manner of commissioning and instructing him. The governor's commission set out his titles, prerogatives, and duties, specified the composition of his council and of the legislature. His instructions elaborated points in his commission and laid down additional rules for him to follow. For example, royal commissions gave governors the power to erect courts of law, but their instructions usually specified that none should be set up without the Crown's direct permission. Some instructions often ordered governors to veto certain kinds of assembly legislation or to guard certain royal prerogatives with special care. In such cases many colonial politicians often denied that a governor's instructions had any standing in law.

The involvement of the Admiralty Board and the customs commissioners in colonial administration has already been briefly touched on. Since the colonies were mostly valued as parts of a trading empire and since colonial commerce grew steadily in the seventeenth and eighteenth centuries, maritime matters assumed increasing importance. Broadly speaking, admiralty jurisdiction in England covered the coastlines and the oceans; admiralty officials could collect certain royal perquisites—royal fish (whales, sturgeon), wrecks, flotsam and jetsam, among others—and royal fees or dues, and admiralty courts until displaced by the common law courts heard cases involving prizes taken by privateers, piracy, mutiny, and crimes at sea as well as disputes over shipping matters. In early charters, admiralty jurisdiction was granted to the proprietors and governors of the colonies, under the final authority of the English Admiralty. During the seventeenth century, however, royal officials constantly complained of the laxity of vice-admiralty jurisdiction or its non-existence and stressed the need for reform. They used the same arguments against the colonial authorities for their failures to enforce the Acts of Trade; moreover, colonial courts, it was repeatedly alleged, usually found against the Crown, notwithstanding the weight of evidence. In 1696 Parliament passed the last great navigation act, the "Act for Preventing Frauds, and Regulating Abuses in the plantation Trade." This act attempted to "perfect the machinery of enforcement" and among many other matters, it sanctioned the use of vice-admiralty courts in the colonies for the trial of offenses against the Navigation Acts, although it also specified that such cases might also still be tried by juries. The novelty of this legislation lay in the fact that admiralty courts in England were not used for customs offenses and, indeed, as civil law courts operating without juries, had been challenged by the common lawyers since the sixteenth century. Americans knew this very well. Although twelve vice-admiralty courts were eventually set up from New Hampshire to Barbados, they functioned ineffectually, under constant fire from colonial lawyers and courts.

The customs service, established in 1673, had taken shape by the end of the century. Its establishment, settled in 1696, provided for payment of annual salaries to customs officers by the English Exchequer. These salaries were supplemented by locally collected fees and perquisites. In 1710, when the service was divided into a northern and southern department—from Newfoundland to the Jerseys and from Pennsylvania to the Carolinas, including the Bahamas and Jamaica—it consisted of thirty-four districts staffed by forty-two permanent officials, many of whom were experienced English officers. In some colonies important local men received appointments in the service, adding substantially to their income and perhaps extending the principle of local control over a royal institution. Complaints about breaches of the Trade

Acts and weaknesses in the customs continued throughout the eighteenth century, but it appears that the customs service, by the standards of contemporary bureaucracies, did not prove unequal to its main objective. This lay not primarily in the collection of revenue or duties but in ensuring that planters, merchants, and ships' captains observed the restrictions on the trade of the colonies that benefitted England.

One or two other English bodies whose responsibilities extended to the colonies must also be mentioned. The Treasury, in fact, controlled the customs service though it left routine matters to the Board of Customs. It also disbursed all moneys raised by Parliament to be spent for or in the colonies and met all expenses that arose in the royal service, including military ones, paying colonial salaries and contracts. Although the Treasury advocated few positive schemes for colonial government or administration, its veto or approval of other departments' policies was of final importance. The Treasury maintained an auditing office to survey and collect revenues owing to the Crown, except revenues under the Trade Acts. The first English surveyor-general and auditor-general of the colonies was William Blathwayt, the second, Horatio Walpole, younger brother of Sir Robert; the English chief appointed deputies in America. Moneys collected included the royal share of receipts from such items as prize dues; vessels and cargoes condemned for illegal trade; and import, export, and tonnage duties as well as forfeitures, fines, escheats, quitrents, and other Crown dues. In New England control of woodlands and timber was vested in a Surveyor of the Woods, whose appointment arose from the direct concern of the English government with the need for materials for the navy and who received instructions from the Board of Trade and the Admiralty.

Finally, by the beginning of the eighteenth century, the Church of England had begun to see the American colonies as a stronghold of dissent, badly needing an infusion of Anglican piety and the extension of Anglican authority. This movement coincided with governors' reports from America that an infusion of Anglicanism would produce a more pliable and less contentious population. It also reflected a new evangelical spirit in England itself, not necessarily linked to such imperial considerations. William Compton, Bishop of London, had first gained recognition of that see's jurisdiction over the Anglican Church in the colonies in the 1670s. From 1685 royal governors had instructions to recognize his ecclesiastical jurisdiction. Among his achievements, he obtained the grant of a bounty of £20 for each minister and schoolmaster going to the colonies and the power of licensing such individuals. While Virginia remained the only colony that could be said to have an Anglican establishment, growing numbers of Anglicans now lived in the Jerseys, New York, and South Carolina. But the beginnings of new royal governments in many colonies meant, of course, sending royal governors, themselves of Anglican sentiments. (Phips of Massachusetts, baptized by Cotton Mather, was a notable exception.)

Of these, Governor Fletcher in New York secured the passage of a bill that provided for raising taxes to support Church of England ministers in four New

York counties—Richmond, Westchester, Queens, and the County of New York—from which an Anglican establishment eventually resulted. In Maryland, the establishment of the Anglican Church has already been traced with reference to parishes and local government. In South Carolina, an act of 1706 established the Church of England, and in North Carolina, one of 1711, both against bitter dissenter opposition, particularly Quaker. Elsewhere, dissenting strength continued too great for their establishment, although Anglican churches competed with those of other sects in all the colonies, especially in urban centers. And of course, even the places where the church had been established, shortages of ministers and the power of dissenter interests considerably limited its authority and effectiveness.

As far as the operation of English colonial administration was concerned, the church had little real power in an increasingly latitudinarian age; it also had to contend with the influence of dissenters on the English government's colonial policy. The Bishop of London had been a member of the Lords of Trade and sat, *ex-officio*, on the Board of Trade; he approved the clauses dealing with religion in governors' instructions and commissions and received copies of the portions of their letters relating to the same subject. Although the bishop's advice might be followed on existing ecclesiastical problems or on minor colonial legislation, he had little weight in formulating policy or obtaining financial or other kinds of help for the established church in America. Indeed, such expansion as the church enjoyed arose from its own efforts. These were largely channelled through a missionary society founded in 1701 under royal charter, the Society for the Propagation of the Gospel. This foundation resulted directly from the persuasive powers of an Anglican commissary of the Bishop of London to Maryland, Dr. Thomas Bray, who had returned to England and suggested that forty missionaries should be sent to America. Although conversion of the Indians and work among Negroes constituted part of the Society's aims, it also supported Anglicans in nonestablished regions and showed an interest in converting dissenters. From the first, Quakers, Congregationalists, and Presbyterians objected strongly to these aspects of the Society's missionary work. The encouragement that royal governors gave to the Society and to Anglican churches reinforced the divisiveness of religion in colonial life. Many colonial Whigs remained strongly nonconformist, seeing the colonial executives as Tories of religion as well as of politics. Since some well-to-do nonconformists now began to embrace Anglicanism as a genteel faith, fears of the Church of England had another justification. Moreover, from 1704 a number of high church dignitaries in England began to press the government for the appointment of bishops in America, and given Queen Anne's concern for the Church of England, this scheme had some chances of success. Although the accession of George I lessened colonial fears of bishops—inevitably dissenters wrote as though Laud was to be reincarnated in America—they contributed another contentious dimension to American life.

C. War and the colonies

To England the wars of this period brought new trade and territory, prestige and debts. They also stimulated economic growth and saw the beginnings of English colonial and commercial ascendancy among the European nations. During the same years, increasing attention was given to colonial questions, especially since one of the reasons for British participation in the War of the Spanish Succession was the fear of losing the valuable English trade with Spanish America to the French. Particular emphasis was placed on the English West Indian colonies, since these served as entrepôts for the Spanish American trade as well as suppliers of sugar. At the same time, the importance of the northern and middle American colonies was becoming more evident, for these areas of increasing population not only absorbed growing quantities of English manufactures but had become great food producers for the West Indies. In 1705 the Board of Trade observed that "if the merchants on the northern continent do forbear trading and carrying provisions to the southern plantations, it would tend to the ruin of those islands, and be of the greatest prejudice to Her Majesty's customs in England." The southern Chesapeake colonies remained vitally important; not only did they absorb quantities of English manufactured goods but English merchants had a large investment in the tobacco trade. The British government therefore spent large sums on the defense of the tobacco fleets and also aided the successful attempts of London merchants to open new European markets to Chesapeake tobacco as well as allowing its wartime export to France in neutral ships.

One or two new developments occurred in these years. Growing pressures came from English manufacturers to ensure a market for their goods in the colonies. In 1699 the Woolen Act was passed by Parliament which forbade the export of colony-made cloth and woolens—not their manufacture—over colonial boundaries. The Board of Trade also discouraged other colonial manufactures including shoes in Pennsylvania, iron in New England and the Chesapeake, cotton and flax in Virginia. Yet both to try to provide New England and New York with a profitable staple and—although to a lesser extent and against the advice of the Navy Board—to diminish English expenditure in and dependence on northern European supplies, vigorous attempts were made at this time to promote a colonial naval stores industry including ship timber, hemp, resin, turpentine, pitch and tar. In 1705 the Naval Stores Act provided for bounties to be paid on a list of such commodities imported from the colonies. Probably neither of these developments had much effect in the ways intended. Manufacturing for an export market was hardly feasible in the capital-starved and primitive market economies of this period of colonial history; where it did later prove possible and profitable, English legislation was ignored. And naval stores never became an important manufacture of the middle or New England colonies; indeed, they were most developed in South Carolina, where the English government did not seek to encourage them.

Of the overall impact of these and later wars on colonial society, no good modern study has been made. Certainly, the wars highlighted both the advantages and disadvantages of the colonial situation. On the one hand, British naval vessels protected the colonies and their trade, and the British government spent relatively large sums of money in America to finance military activities. On the other hand, freight and insurance rates charged by British shippers rose steeply because of new military dangers, while British imports of colonial tobacco fell with the closing of European re-export markets.

The Chesapeake's fortunes in these years of war seem to have been mixed. A rapid expansion of tobacco growing and an increasing importation of slaves after about 1703 suggests that the planters had received good prices for tobacco and remained optimistic. Yet rising costs of freight and insurance during Queen Anne's War lessened profit on their exports and raised the prices of imports from England on which their comforts depended. Moreover, the European market for Chesapeake tobacco contracted in the war period, further cutting sales. Exports to England from Virginia and Maryland totalled £2,000,000 in the years 1701-1710 and £2.8 million in the years 1711-1720. Imports in the same years amounted to £1.3 million and £1.49 million. A major factor in the economy of these southern colonies was their lack of any other source of external income than that from exports of tobacco to England and Europe. The northern and middle colonies could count on returns from the West Indies and southern Europe to meet any unfavorable balance of trade with England. By 1715 the Chesapeake planters had suffered several years of economic distress and could clearly see some of the drawbacks of membership in the British empire; yet they had continued to import slaves and increase production. They were to be mollified by the opening of considerable new markets for tobacco in the following years. In the much less populous Carolinas, the economy expanded until 1700, with a new English wartime demand for naval stores bringing increased production. Queen Anne's War produced military action and Indian troubles, but overexpenditure on slaves and English goods accompanied a probable fall in rice exports. These picked up again, however, in 1709 and later years. One set of figures for the value of exports from the Carolinas to England totals £142,300 from 1701-1710 and £382,000 from 1711 to 1720; total value of imports from England for the same periods rose from £138,000 to £211,000.

The stimulus of war can be most clearly seen in New York, Pennsylvania, and New England. Boston, for example, whose magnitude in "shipping was easily the most important in America, its equivalent was the ancient port of Bristol, second only to London in the British Isles," added considerably to its registered fleet in the years 1698-1714. Some of this growth reflected ship captures by successful privateers, especially in 1702-1703 and 1710-1711, which were exceptional years. But much of the increase consisted of Massachusetts-built ships, reflecting the vitality of its shipbuilding industry. In earlier years ownership of ships was very widely spread, but a group of about sixty individuals held an increasing control of the largest vessels in the fleet. Certainly, in terms of shipping, the wars did not hinder New England's economic growth. Some figures for its exports to and imports from England are also available, revealing exports of £328,146 and imports of £867,828 in the ten-year period 1701-1710 and exports of £512,856 and imports of £1,311,368 in the same number of years from 1711-1720. Figures for New England's important trades to Newfoundland, southern Europe, and the West Indies are not available, but the values involved must have been high since cod exports to southern Europe and West Indies in 1714-1715 were worth about £84,000, while horses sent mostly to the West Indies were probably valued at some £25,000 and lumber and provisions, much of which also went to the Caribbean, at some £43,000.

In Pennsylvania and in New York, trade to the West Indies consisted of wheat, bread, flour, lumber, and horses amounting in value to probably 30 percent of that of New England. The early years of King William's War brought a decline in this commerce, but after 1695, when French privateers were ineffective, "both Pennsylvania and New York reaped handsome profits from their favored position in the West Indies trade." During Queen Anne's War exports to the West Indies again fell dramatically in the early years but picked up after 1710. In New York and later in Philadelphia a growing number of the ships used in the trade belonged to local inhabitants. The trade with England was less important; even so, New York and Pennsylvania exports to England rose from a total of £127,600 in the years 1701-1710 to £240,000 in 1711-1720; imports from England rose from £381,000 to £641,800 in the same years. In 1699 some seventeen English merchants specialized in the trade to New York, about a third of those engaged in New England's commerce. Such figures as these for New England and the middle colonies have led the leading historian of the colonial cities to the judgment that for the major northern commercial centers, "nineteen years of war stimulated general trade, both legal and illegal, and gave rise to the sister activities, privateering and piracy."

It therefore appears that where—as in New England and New York—Americans owned their own shipping, profits from carrying and from privateering could rise steeply and benefit the colonists. In those regions, also, profits were made from trade to the West Indies, to Newfoundland, and to southern Europe. In the Chesapeake, dependence on a staple trade carried in British ships, insured by British money, and sold in Britain and Europe by British merchants, who took a hefty commission, meant that the normal deficit experienced by the colonists became even more pronounced during the war.

Related to and compounded by this wartime economy was a money shortage in North America. British mercantilist policy looked askance at minting money outside of England; the government forbade colonial coining. At the same time, payment for freight charges, insurance, merchants' commissions, and similar items had to be made in cash, resulting in an outflow of money from North America. The northern and middle colonies, enjoying a profitable trade with such areas as Newfoundland, the West Indies, and southern Europe, gained cash or credit there with which to pay off their accounts in London. The Chesapeake, without these sources of money, remained debtors to English and Scottish merchants and saw their supplies of coin drained off as payment. A chronic shortage of coin throughout the colonies led to constant attempts to attract foreign bullion and coins by permitting them to be exchanged at a value above their legal sterling value. The northern and middle colonies, in fact, were allowed to manipulate the value of coin in this way, while the Chesapeake region was not, in the interests of British creditors and the British customs who had no wish to be paid in coin with a greater declared value in America than it could fetch in Europe.

Shortage of coin in America had first been countered by allowing internal taxes and debts to be paid in "country pay" or commodities rather than in coin. Harvard students, for example, contributed corn toward the cost of their tuition. One important result of the wars was the issue of paper money. In Boston plans for a private bank issuing its own bills to investors had been suggested as early as the 1660s and put into effect in 1681. Yet these bills, negotiable only locally, did not appeal to merchants with English debts, and the bank failed. In 1690 the Massachusetts government, faced with the need to pay the suppliers, ship owners, soldiers, and sailors involved in the Quebec expedition, could not raise the necessary money. It then issued paper bills of public credit, declaring these to be legal tender for all debts and pledging to redeem them in the future from tax receipts. Other issues followed until £82,000 was put out before 1702.

The issue of paper money or bills to meet extraordinary wartime expenses quickly followed in other colonies. In South Carolina, Moore's expedition against St. Augustine cost £4,000 more than the assembly had authorized; this and later debts were paid by the issue of bills of credit, amounting to £20,000 in 1711. These early bills, mostly carrying interest and redeemable in a stated time, did not depreciate and provided a satisfactory medium of exchange. But the creation by the colony's government of a land bank in 1712—land was pledged as security against loans—had mixed results. For various reasons, the bank's currency depreciated in value and consequently became unpopular among creditor sections of the community, particularly among merchants trading to England who could not pay off debts there in a local paper currency. By the 1720s the whole question of paper money had become an embittered one in many colonies. Generally speaking, the small farmers at the bottom of the economic ladder approved of paper money since, as debtors, they suffered no adverse effects from its depreciation. At the other extreme, the large merchants, usually creditors, did not wish to have money owing them paid in bills whose legal value bore no relation to their current value. In a middle position, some merchants and landowners favored a paper currency for local business but wished it to be strictly regulated and small in total amount to guard against depreciation. Violent controversies occupied the colonial assemblies and royal governors. The British government, from about 1715, also took a pronounced line on paper money, generally prohibiting its issue without ample security in the form of tax levies and forbidding that it be made legal currency. Colonial inflationists argued for the liberal creation of paper money. Another contentious matter, therefore, joined those already existing on the colonial scene.

The early wars in no way lessened the powers of the colonial assemblies in favor of stronger executive direction, a tendency obvious in many wars in many periods. In fact, the assemblies, generally speaking, exercised considerable jurisdiction over strategy and policy, allocating moneys to raise only the numbers of soldiers that they approved for purposes that they agreed to. Assemblies did not hesitate to refuse requests from Crown or governor. The Virginia assembly in 1699 declined to fortify the colony's coasts or to authorize special emergency wartime powers for the governor and council. It and the Maryland assembly in 1701-1702 declined to obey a royal order to send men and money to the defense of New York. Similarly, Pennsylvania's assembly rejected demands for aid to New England's expedition against Quebec in 1709. In Massachusetts the assembly for many years rejected royal orders to refortify the town of Pemaquid on the Maine coast, provoking a direct but fruitless letter from the Queen. Massachusetts also provides evidence of the positive strength of the assembly in controlling military activities. It attempted to assign stated numbers of soldiers to postings at garrisons and forts and detailed plans of campaigns and the number of troops to be used in them. In these ways it exercised greater powers than the English House of Commons. In New York, Lord Cornbury, the governor, faced a continual barrage of assembly assaults on his lax handling of money for defense and Indian relations, and the House demanded control over the revenue, ordinary and extraordinary, through a treasurer of its own appointment.

The full study of the effects of the period of warfare from 1689 to 1713 still needs to be written. Yet the evidence of the post-war years, especially the years after 1720, suggests that war had no detrimental results for the colonies. It may well have contributed to the growth and expansion that characterized this new phase of American history.

Chapter Seven

Growth and Expansion

A. The colonial population

In 1754 Benjamin Franklin, who had a lively and informed interest in the growth of the colonies, discussed some population figures for West New Jersey. Here, where there was little to attract emigrants either from other parts of America or from Europe, the population, Franklin believed, had risen by the large figure of 600% between 1699 and 1745. A few years later Ezra Stiles, president of Yale College and like Franklin an intelligent student of early America's human arithmetic, wrote with pride of the great growth in New England's population since the first years of settlement to about half a million in 1760. He, too, stressed that this increase could not have been due to immigration because "since that time more have gone from us to Europe, than have arrived from thence hither."

Franklin and Stiles pioneered the collection and interpretation of population figures in early America. Other collections of data and the work of later demographic historians have, on the whole, confirmed their view of America's population growth. Our figures and ideas are now more refined and selective, but the broad outline remains the same. The general picture is that between 1720 and 1760 the white population of the American colonies increased from about 397,000 to 1,267,000, an increase of about 219 percent, and much of that increase was due to natural growth. Refinement of detail demonstrates that the New England growth rate was rather less than that of the rest of America and that the southern increase was slightly greater than that of New England. Back country or newly settled regions showed a higher rate of natural increase than the longer-settled eastern coastal areas. Other calculations suggest that the rate of increase varied from decade to decade and from locality to locality according to specific factors and forces. So, for example, the colonial city may have had a higher number of deaths than births; its numbers were kept up by an inflow of migrants from the colonial countryside and from overseas.

A crucial point about these population figures is their divergence from those of Europe and England in the same period. If, as may be likely, the white colonial birth rate in the eighteenth century was about 45-50 per thousand and

ESTIMATED POPULATION
New England Colonies
1720–1780
Showing decennial percentage increases

W = White Population
N = Negro Population
% = decennial percentage increase

		Maine	%	New Hampshire	%	Massachusetts	%	Rhode Island	%	Connecticut	%	Totals
1720	W	–	–	9,205	–	88,858	–	11,137	–	57,737	–	166,937
	N	–	–	170	–	2,150	–	543	–	1,093	–	3,956
1730	W	–	–	10,555	*15*	111,336	*25*	15,302	*37*	74,040	*28*	211,233
	N	–	–	200	*17*	2,780	*29*	1,648	*203*	1,490	*36*	6,118
1740	W	–	–	22,756	*116*	148,578	*33*	22,847	*49*	86,982	*17*	281,163
	N	–	–	500	*150*	3,035	*9*	2,408	*46*	2,598	*74*	8,541
1750	W	–	–	26,955	*18*	183,925	*24*	29,879	*31*	108,270	*24*	349,029
	N	–	–	550	*10*	4,075	*34*	3,347	*39*	3,010	*16*	10,982
1760	W	–	–	38,493	*43*	217,734	*18*	42,003	*41*	138,687	*28*	436,917
	N	–	–	600	*9*	4,866	*19*	3,468	*4*	3,783	*26*	12,717
1770	W	30,782	–	61,742	*60*	230,554	*6*	54,435	*30*	178,183	*28*	555,696
	N	475	–	654	*9*	4,754	*–2*	3,761	*8*	5,698	*51*	15,342
1780	W	48,675	*58*	87,261	*41*	263,805	*14*	50,275	*–8*	200,816	*13*	650,832
	N	458	*–4*	541	*–17*	4,822	*1*	2,671	*–29*	5,885	*3*	14,377

ESTIMATED POPULATION
Middle Colonies
1720–1780
Showing decennial percentage increases

W = White Population
N = Negro Population
% = decennial percentage increase

		New York	%	New Jersey	%	Pennsylvania	%	Delaware	%	Totals
1720	W	31,179	–	27,433	–	28,962	–	4,685	–	92,259
	N	5,740	–	2,385	–	2,000	–	700	–	10,825
1730	W	41,638	*34*	34,502	*26*	50,466	*74*	8,692	*86*	135,298
	N	6,956	*21*	3,008	*26*	1,241	*–38*	478	*–32*	11,683
1740	W	54,669	*31*	47,007	*36*	83,582	*66*	18,835	*117*	204,093
	N	8,996	*29*	4,366	*45*	2,055	*66*	1,035	*117*	16,452
1750	W	65,682	*20*	66,039	*40*	116,794	*40*	27,208	*44*	275,723
	N	11,014	*22*	5,354	*23*	2,872	*40*	1,496	*45*	20,736
1760	W	100,798	*53*	87,246	*32*	179,294	*54*	31,517	*16*	398,855
	N	16,340	*48*	6,567	*23*	4,409	*54*	1,733	*16*	29,049
1770	W	143,808	*43*	109,211	*25*	234,296	*31*	33,660	*7*	520,975
	N	19,112	*17*	8,220	*25*	5,761	*31*	1,836	*6*	34,929
1780	W	189,487	*32*	129,167	*18*	319,450	*36*	42,389	*26*	680,493
	N	21,054	*10*	10,460	*27*	7,855	*36*	2,996	*63*	42,365

ESTIMATED POPULATION
Southern Colonies
1720–1780
Showing decennial percentage increases

W = White Population
N = Negro Population
% = decennial percentage increase

		Maryland	%	Virginia	%	North Carolina	%	South Carolina	%	Georgia	%	Total
1720	W	53,634	–	61,158	–	18,270	–	5,048	–	–	–	138,110
	N	12,499	–	26,599	–	3,000	–	12,000	–	–	–	54,098
1730	W	73,893	*38*	84,000	*37*	24,000	*31*	10,000	*98*	–	–	191,893
	N	17,220	*38*	30,000	*13*	6,000	*100*	20,000	*67*	–	–	73,220
1740	W	92,062	*25*	120,440	*43*	40,760	*70*	15,000	*50*	2,021	–	270,283
	N	24,031	*40*	60,000	*100*	11,000	*83*	30,000	*50*	–	–	125,031
1750	W	97,623	*6*	129,581	*8*	53,184	*30*	25,000	*67*	4,200	–	309,588
	N	43,450	*81*	101,452	*69*	19,800	*80*	39,000	*30*	1,000	–	204,702
1760	W	113,263	*16*	199,156	*54*	76,888	*45*	36,740	*47*	6,000	*43*	432,047
	N	49,004	*13*	140,570	*39*	33,554	*69*	57,334	*47*	3,578	*258*	284,040
1770	W	138,781	*23*	259,411	*30*	127,600	*66*	49,066	*34*	12,750	*113*	587,608
	N	63,818	*30*	187,605	*33*	69,600	*107*	75,178	*31*	10,625	*197*	406,826
1780	W	164,959	*19*	317,422	*22*	179,133	*40*	83,000	*69*	35,240	*176*	779,754
	N	80,515	*26*	220,582	*18*	91,000	*31*	97,000	*29*	20,831	*96*	509,928

ESTIMATED POPULATION OF COLONIAL CITIES

1720–1770

Showing decennial percentage increases

	Boston	%	Newport	%	New York	%	Philadelphia	%	Charleston	%
1720	12,000	–	3,800	–	7,000	–	10,000	–	3,500	–
1730	13,000	*8*	4,640	*22*	8,622	*23*	11,500	*15*	4,500	*29*
1740	15,601	*20*	5,840	*26*	10,451	*21*	12,654	*10*	6,269	*39*
1750	——	–	6,670	*14*	14,225	*36*	18,202	*44*	7,134	*14*
1760	15,631	–	7,500	*12*	18,000	*27*	23,750	*30*	8,000	*12*
1770	15,877	*2*	9,833	*31*	22,667	*26*	34,583	*46*	10,667	*33*

the death rate for the same time about 20-25 per thousand, these were respectively higher and lower rates than those in England and Europe; on the other hand some have argued that the birth rate was not extraordinarily high but that the death rate was very low. In England, for example, a crude assessment puts the birth rate at 33.8 per thousand and the mortality rate at 32.8 per thousand from 1701 to 1750, while from 1751 to 1780 estimates give a birth rate of 37.2 per thousand and a death rate of 30.4. Indeed the population of England increased very slowly before about 1750. Perhaps the highest average birth rate was about 37.5 per thousand in the second half of the eighteenth century; it dropped later, for the population growth of the later eighteenth and nineteenth centuries is now assumed to have been due not to an increase in the birth rate but to a decline in the death rate, as, among other reasons, food shortages disappeared and diseases became less virulent. The importance of a low death rate was no doubt very great for colonial America, also; almost certainly, infant mortality rates in particular were very low relative to England and Europe, which meant an increase in the number of marriageable persons, given reasonable continued life expectancy, and suggests that women may also have been healthy and less prone to deaths related to childbearing.

A few studies of particular localities provide valuable evidence to flesh out these generalizations. In Ipswich, Massachusetts, the population increased by approximately 200 percent between 1693 and 1713 and between 1714 and 1744 and rose by 50 percent from 1744 to 1790, mainly because of low mortality among infants, children, and women. In Dedham a death rate of about 27 per thousand before 1700 perhaps dropped even more after that date. An interesting point about this Massachusetts town was the disappearance of the ancient European seasonal rhythm of conceptions—high in summer—which was hardly evident there by 1763. In Plymouth women born between 1675 and 1700 had a mean marriage age of 22.3, perhaps one to three years younger than in England at the same time; similar evidence exists for the New England towns Andover, Dedham, and Ipswich. Roughly the same was true of middle-colony Quaker marriages, while in the South women may have married even younger. But during the eighteenth century the age of women at marriage gradually rose in many colonial areas to a European pattern. Marriages among the middle-colony Quakers were long-lived, for few women died at childbirth. When more local studies have been completed—especially, if this is possible, for the colonial cities and the southern colonies—sophisticated generalizations like those now possible for English and European demography of the same centuries will be easier.

A few observations, however, can be made. First, in some areas the total imbalance of men over women, noticeable in the seventeenth century, lessened and then disappeared in the next. But there may still have been a shortage of women of marriageable age. This increased women's opportunities—and the pressures on them—for marriage. Together with the availability of land in the colonies, this meant that young people could and did marry. Second, the average household and family size seems to have been higher in colonial America than in Western Europe, not because of higher fertility but because of lower mortality rates among mothers and children. Third, Americans seem to have broken away from the traditional European pattern of frequent subsistence crises very early on, even in the seventeenth century. Food was obviously more generally abundant, rarely in short supply, and never lacking to the extent of causing great numbers of deaths. Although even in the eighteenth century a contemporary could write that a failure in the maize crop brought hard times for the poor and William Douglass stated that in New England "the general subsistence of poor people (which contributes much to their endemial psorick disorders) is salt pork and Indian beans, with bread of Indian corn meal, and pottage of this meal with milk for breakfast and supper," there is little evidence of demographically significant malnutrition after the initial problems of settlement.

Another contribution to population growth may have been a lessening of the incidence and effects of the epidemic diseases that ravaged Europe and were often linked to a malnutrition which weakened men's abilities to resist or recover from them. Epidemics certainly occurred in the colonies. Smallpox took a heavy toll in Boston in 1677-1678 and 1689-1690; in and after 1721 a major epidemic affected all New England and further outbreaks took place in 1752 and 1764. But the Boston figures seem to indicate a lower rate of mortality from the disease than in England during the same period. All the other colonial cities also suffered from smallpox. It is possible, for example, that 7 percent of the population of Charleston died in 1760. Diptheria, too, reached epidemic proportions in New England in 1735-1740 and spread to the middle and southern colonies in the next fifteen years, returning again to New Hampshire by 1754-1755. In the first New England epidemic, 802 children under the age of ten died in fifteen small New Hampshire towns. Yellow fever from the West Indies came to Boston in 1693, to Charleston and Philadelphia in 1699 and New York in 1732; its most serious outbreaks were generally in Charleston; yet after about 1760 it seems to have disappeared, to reoccur again forty or so years later. Other serious colonial diseases were malaria—endemic to the southern colonies and prevalent as far north as New York—and influenza. No doubt unseasoned immigrants were hard hit—nearly half of the sixty-two missionaries of the Society for the Propagation of the Gospel between 1700 and 1750 either died or returned to England because of ill health. Satisfactory figures on the demographic significance of all these epidemics are lacking. Some data seems to indicate a lower rate of mortality from diseases than that in England in the same period, and it does seem likely that total mortality from all epidemics may have been relatively less than that from comparable diseases in the Old World. Perhaps, compared with Europe, not only the high standard of living in colonial America meant that lack of food did not combine with illness to cause death but lack of concentrated populations lessened the spread of contagions.

Contemporaries grasped at least some of these points. Peter Kalm, a Swedish traveler in America, pointed to the greater availability of land, which he believed led to earlier marriages, as a reason for the faster multiplication of population in colonial America than in Europe. Franklin contrasted an old society where "as soon as the Number of People is as great as can be supported by all the Tillage, Manufactures, Trade and Offices of the Country, the Overplus must quit . . . or perish" with "these Colonies where all can have full Employment, and there is room for Millions yet unborn. When families can be easily supported, more persons marry, and earlier in life. . . . Marriages in America are more general, and more generally early, than in Europe." Stiles believed that "in new-settled Countries, the transported Colonies, by an established Law of Nature, in a good Climate, do increase to a certain patrial Maturity; then they begin to decline." He felt the rate of growth in the more densely settled, seacoast region of New England in 1761 had already begun to slow down, but the great virgin areas of America would sustain millions for "Agriculture and the rural life are peculiarly friendly to increase." As in the past, so in the future: "Free polity, free religion, free property and free matrimony will soon populate a fertile country, in a good climate." The economic opportunities of American life, most contemporaries felt, were the basis of population expansion.

Modern students have accepted many of these observations. A recent writer concludes that the food supply was the crucial factor, as it "became increasingly abundant, allowing population to grow despite all the rigours of the climate and of pioneer life. Above all perhaps it sustained the health of women of child-bearing age and thus kept low the infant mortality rate." We may also look at this another way by noticing that in seventeenth-century England from 25 percent to 50 percent of the population lived at below what historians regard as the poverty line and that eighteenth-century English population growth certainly was associated with an improvement in general living conditions. In the colonies the distribution of wealth was probably less extreme and the number of persons with good general living conditions probably greater than in eighteenth-century England. These differences in general living standards and wealth still await detailed study but would seem to have contributed to the great population growth of the colonies relative to England. Finally, European demographers have discovered a cultural or psychological component in the factors delaying or encouraging the rate of marriages and conceptions. In the New World, a sense of opportunity together with local influences, such as the Puritan dislike of young adults living outside the family, may well have accelerated the marriage and birth rates.

Immigration, of course, did play some part in the population increase. It has been suggested that the total number of white immigrants for the years 1700-

1775 was about 250,000-300,000, or 15 percent to 20 percent of the total increase in white population over these same years. The striking aspect of white immigration after 1720 was its non-English component. Formerly, English official policy had opposed non-English migration. Now the influence of mercantilist economic ideas acted to make emigration from England undesirable since "fewness of people is real poverty for a nation" and led to a consideration of other sources of immigration into the American colonies, whose growth, men believed, would increase the demand for manufactured goods from the mother country. At the same time, the reputation in Europe of such colonies as Pennsylvania (fostered originally by Penn) was still high, perhaps kept alive by reports of the few European migrants who had gone there in the previous century.

SOME ESTIMATES OF WHITE IMMIGRATION

Period	Numbers	From
1. 1707–1775	150,000	Ulster
2. 1718–1775	100,000–125,000	Ulster
3. 1710–1775	100,000	Germany
4. 1763–1775	15,000–20,000	England
5. 1763–1775	25,000	Scotland
6. 1700–1775	250,000–300,000	All countries
7. 1700–1790	350,000	All countries

The first significant non-English groups to migrate to America in the eighteenth century were Palatinate Germans, who went to the Hudson Valley in 1710. These families were triply unfortunate for, victims of war and persecution in their homeland, they next had promised financial aid withdrawn by the British government. Then, once in America, they suffered by the land policy of the colonial government. Although finally they found a hard refuge on the New York frontier, their experiences persuaded other Germans to avoid the colony. The original plan of the British government had been thoroughly mercantilist, envisaging these settlers as producers of naval stores. From about the same time other Europeans—German-speaking Swiss and southwestern Germans and Palatines—began to head for Pennsylvania, which had a considerable trade with Dutch and German ports and a reputation in Europe for liberality. In 1719 some 7,000 disembarked in Philadelphia, while smaller numbers averaging perhaps 2,000 a year continued to arrive over the next half century or so. Other groups went directly to North Carolina, where Palatines and Swiss founded New Bern in 1710; and to South Carolina where Swiss-Germans founded Purrysburg in 1732 and other townships shortly after. Lutheran Protestants from Salzburg, in part migrating to escape Catholic persecution as late as 1734, found their way to Georgia, settling at Ebenezer.

These German-speaking migrants left their homes for a variety of reasons. Early Palatines sought to escape harsh wartime conditions. Various sectarian groups of pietists and pacifists often migrated after their religious opinions had brought them into conflict with their home governments as well as for economic reasons. The Mennonites settled in Lancaster County, Pennsylvania, establishing a distinct religious and cultural style sixty miles from Philadelphia. The Dunkers or Baptists settled in Lancaster and Berks counties; the unusual monastic settlement of Ephrata, founded by Seventh-day Baptists under the leadership of Conrad Beissel, is well known. Some sects were profoundly influenced by millenial, utopian ideas, here resembling the early Puritans and Quakers. But the German "church people"—Lutherans and Reformed (Calvinists)—were more numerous than the sectarians and mostly migrated for secular reasons. In 1766 Franklin probably correctly estimated that one-third of Pennsylvania's population was German. The influence of these Germans and Swiss on their non-German neighbors was limited, either by a sectarian exclusiveness and unwillingness to participate in the social and political life of their adopted colonies or by their very gradual intermarriage and assimilation with the other inhabitants. Perhaps 135,000 Germans and Swiss lived in North America at the time of the American Revolution.

German migration was closely paralleled in time and numbers by that from northern Ireland. Large-scale departures, first occurring in 1717-1718, mainly involved Presbyterian Scots who had been persuaded to settle and establish a Protestant ascendancy in Ulster in the seventeenth century. Few Catholic Irish went, and Catholic migration of any kind to North America was frowned on. Economic hardship was the main reason for this growing Scotch-Irish migration. Not only did British legislation restrict Irish manufacturing and trade but tenants held land on short leases and rents were often raised steeply at their expiration. For those without land, wages were pitifully low. Many families lived in dread of poor harvests, followed by famine and lack of money to pay rents. In addition, the Presbyterian Scotch-Irish objected to rising tithes paid to an alien Anglican church, and ministers often encouraged members of their congregations to emigrate. Between 1717 and 1776 perhaps some 150,000 Scotch-Irish left for America.

The Scotch-Irish who left Ireland in 1717-1718 disembarked in Boston and sought land in New England; an initial welcome turned sour as Congregationalists came to resent and then oppose the establishment of their brand of Presbyterianism. At Worcester, Massachusetts, a mob destroyed a Presbyterian church. The Scotch-Irish then moved toward the frontier, particularly into New Hampshire, into the region that later became Vermont, and into Maine. After about the mid-1720s, they, like the Germans, were drawn to the middle colonies. The great terminus of Scotch-Irish voyages became the Delaware River and the ports of Chester and Philadelphia and of Newcastle and Lewes, Delaware. Most entered Pennsylvania, attracted by the colony's reputation as a land of good fortune for immigrants. There they joined the Germans in Chester and Lancaster counties. They also penetrated beyond the Susquehanna River, and to the Allegheny Mountains, forming a bloc in western Pennsylvania. Others turned south, pushing with the Germans toward and into the Shenandoah Valley. In the 1730s, too, Scotch-Irish sailed directly to South Carolina. Charleston, for the next forty years, became an important port for their disembarkation.

Many of these eighteenth-century immigrants came to the colonies not as indentured servants but as "redemptioners." Between about 1700 and 1725 a new method of financing the migration of poor persons developed among the Germans. Originating at European ports, it soon spread to Ireland and England, though migration under indenture did not disappear in the case of English migrants. The redemptioner signed no articles but contracted to pay the cost of his passage money to the ship's captain within a week or two of his arrival. If then unable to borrow the money, the redemptioner was sold into servitude by the ship's captain. One important difference between the common seventeenth-century method of an indenture signed before departure and the redemption method was that whole families traveled under the latter agreement, one or two of whom would be put to service to pay the balance of the costs of transport for all. Calculations suggest that of the 65,000-75,000 Germans who came to Philadelphia from 1727 to 1776, possibly two-thirds were redemptioners; of the many Scotch-Irish who came, we have no real knowledge of the numbers of redemptioners.

Together, the Germans (and Swiss-Germans) and Scotch-Irish made up the bulk of the non-English immigrants into America in these years. Yet there were others, in much smaller numbers. Those most migratory of persons, the Lowland Scots, came mainly individually to the colonies either as merchants, professional men, or servants. Highlanders moved in family and clan units, usually under the direction of their landlords, clan chiefs, or sub-chiefs. Several hundreds settled in New York while others from Inverness moved to the Altamaha River, Georgia, in 1735. Others were transported for their part in the uprisings of 1715 and 1745. But the total of Highlanders coming to mainland America before 1763 should not be exaggerated; it was only about 700 and the greatest movement came later. Few French Huguenots came after the seventeenth century, but some "Germans" may have been French-speaking with German names. The other significant group of non-English were 2,000-3,000 Sephardic Jews, mostly merchants and traders in the northern seaport towns, who were permitted full citizenship by act of Parliament in 1740. One of the most beautiful colonial buildings was the synagogue in Newport, Rhode Island, erected in 1763.

Although America has been called a nation of immigrants, some commentators have tried to distinguish between "settlers" and "immigrants." For them usually, a settler was a person who arrived before a certain date and helped found the political, social, and economic institutions of the formative period. The immigrant—a word not used until the nineteenth century—came later, entering a society and a country that had already been formed, adapting—or failing to adapt—himself to what already existed rather than creating it. This distinction was refined even further in the later nineteenth century when many Americans, alarmed at the continuing inflow of southern and eastern European Catholics and Jews, attempted to distinguish between the "old" immigrants, roughly those who came before the Civil War, and the "new" immigrants of subsequent years. At the same time, societies and clubs sprang up open only to those whose forebears arrived on the Mayflower, fought in the colonial wars, or participated in the American Revolution or the War of 1812. These genealogical snobberies thinly disguised ethnic and religious prejudices. White Anglo-Saxon Protestant Americans disliked Germans or Irish Catholics; Germans and Irish felt superior to Slavs and Jews.

While English Americans of the eighteenth century made no elaborately calculated distinctions, they, too, were not unprejudiced. In the seventeenth century, suggestions for the intermarriage of whites and Indians to bring harmony between the two and boost the growth of population were rejected. In the same period "aliens," including Scots and Irish as well as other nationalities, had been excluded from holding office in several colonies. During the eighteenth century the increasing numbers of Scots, Irish, and Germans certainly produced stirrings of nativism. Franklin, for example, feared the Pennsylvania Germans and made unpleasant remarks about these hard-working settlers. He also advocated excluding all "blacks and tawneys. . . . and increasing the lovely white and red." By "tawneys," he may have meant all non-Protestant Europeans. The fact that most eighteenth-century immigrants were Protestant northern Europeans facilitated their incorporation into colonial society and their relatively easy settlement.

One category of Americans does not obviously fall into the framework suggested here. Yet the slave population of the southern colonies did not, as in the West Indies, fail to achieve a natural rate of increase. In 1730, the black population of Maryland, Virginia, and North and South Carolina stood at about 73,000. Thirty years later, when at most another 141,000 Negroes had been imported into these colonies, their combined black population together with that of Georgia stood at 284,000, a rate of natural increase almost equivalent to the rate of increase among the whites. In North Carolina, in the years 1755-1767, when few slaves were imported, the black population increased by 87 percent. Possibly the rate of natural increase was lowest in South Carolina, but this is a surmise. However, extensive work on colonial Philadelphia—and it must not be forgotten that the slave population of the middle and northern colonies was significant in the eighteenth century—reveals that the black mortality rate in that city was greater than the black birth rate and slave numbers had to be kept up by importation. The same may have been true of other northern cities. Unfortunately, no comparable data exists for the white population of the colonial cities, whose mortality may also have been high.

The continuation of the slave trade in the eighteenth century provided a significant source of new labor. Slave imports of about 10,000 in the decade 1721-1730 leapt to about 40,000 in the following ten years, followed by about 58,000 from 1741 to 1750, and about 42,000 in the next decade. Perhaps some 40 percent of the slave population in 1770 had been shipped in during the previous thirty years. During the years from 1700 to 1775, some 210,000-255,000 slaves were brought to North America, forming perhaps 43 percent to 50 percent of the black population increase.

ESTIMATE OF SLAVE IMPORTS

1701–1710	9,000
1711–1720	10,800
1721–1730	9,900
1731–1740	40,500
1741–1750	58,500
1751–1760	41,900
1761–1770	69,500
1771–1775	15,000
Total	255,100

B. *The expansion of settlement*

Population growth increased the pressure on land. In the older parts of the colonies the density of families increased, previously unsettled lands were cleared and occupied, and old towns filled up. At the same time, outlying regions that before 1730 had seen only the occasional white hunters and traders now rang with the farmer's ax and the sounds of pioneering. From Pennsylvania south through the great interior valleys of the eastern Appalachians moved one stream of migrants, largely isolated from the existing centers of population on the colonial seaboards. By 1760 the back parts of most of North Carolina had been reached; shortly afterward settlement in South Carolina's interior lands would begin. Other newcomers moved into western Maryland, into the Virginia Piedmont, and into western North Carolina more or less directly from the older parts of these colonies to meet an overspill coming roughly east or southeast from the interior valleys. During the same years central Pennsylvania itself and some regions of New York and Massachusetts, New Hampshire, and Maine attracted settlers. None of these population movements resulted in the creation of new colonies, though schemes for such were put forward. In fact, only one new colony was created in the eighteenth century—Georgia in 1732—in a region that remained unattractive to new settlers for many years.

Much of the pioneering was undertaken by the new German and Scotch-Irish migrants. In Pennsylvania, for example, finding the best lands near the coasts already taken by earlier English and Welsh settlers or too expensive to purchase, they naturally sought cheap and available sites further inland. The Germans tended to move along the Schuylkill River, eventually spreading east and west to form a predominant group in much of Lancaster, Berks, and Northampton counties. They also settled along Neshaminy Creek from its junction with the Delaware, establishing Easton in the 1730s. Scotch-Irish settlements predominated along the remoter parts of the Susquehanna River, and along the Juniata River, where they established themselves in what became Cumberland County. Some of this settlement took place with a degree of orderliness. The siting of new counties and new market towns was a serious matter of proprietary concern, even in the remoter back country. Yet pioneers from the distant Juniata River moved in the 1760s to the lands south of Fort Pitt (modern Pittsburgh) in the Monongahela River country, outside of areas approved by the authorities.

Expansion into Cumberland County and into western Maryland brought settlers to the edge of the great interior valleys that ran south along the eastern edge of the Appalachians. In 1727 enterprising Germans moved into the Valley of Virginia, establishing Winchester in 1731. From this time on a continual stream of Germans pushed into western Maryland and down the valley, reaching the James River by about 1740. This southward movement was accompanied by a more westerly push toward the mountains, roughly due west of Winchester. The Scotch-Irish, after first settling the upper Susquehanna River and its tributaries in Pennsylvania, began to move south about 1738. Soon pioneers pushed through the Germans in the northern parts of the Cumberland Valley, establishing themselves south of Harrisonburg. By about 1754 a great movement of Scotch-Irish into the back parts of North Carolina had taken place. German Moravians purchased the Wachovia tract in the same colony in 1751, and other Germans also entered the North Carolina back country in a stream that quickly took settlement south to its lower border.

The numbers of settlers who took the southern route into the interior valleys, making these in part a "greater Pennsylvania," cannot be calculated. What is certain is that many settlers also spilled eastward through the natural gaps, first into the Virginia Piedmont, then, after about 1745, into the fertile middle lands of North Carolina. In the Chesapeake colonies, other men moved from tidewater to the frontier. As early as the 1730s in Maryland, migrants moving west into northern and western Maryland met southern-moving families from Pennsylvania, and in 1748 the western part of Maryland was organized as Frederick County.

Similarly in Virginia, the middle region between the fall line and the Blue

Ridge was soon granted and settled along the river systems. In the usual Virginia fashion, county organization followed, or even preceded, this process. Henrico (1728) and Goochland (1728) lay on the James River, Prince William (1731) reached out from Stafford, formerly the northern frontier, and Orange (1734) occupied the region between Goochland and Prince William, athwart the Rapidan. In the south, Brunswick County, a huge frontier, encompassed the Roanoke, Dan, and Staunton rivers. Subsequent redivisions had by 1763 increased the number of Virginia counties to fifty-four, of which Frederick (1743) and Hampshire (1754) lay on and over the northern Alleghenies. Augusta (1745) covered the middle of the mountains. Large land grants to many prominent Virginia families—especially members of the Virginia Council—marked this expansion, including early grants in the Valley of Virginia. To give two examples, Robert Carter and a friend secured 50,000 acres in the Shenandoah Valley in the 1720s, and in 1736 William Beverley, Sir John Randolph, and John Robinson patented 118,491 acres. In Maryland, Daniel Dulany, a prominent lawyer-politician, was the prime example of a seaboard gentleman landlord, for he owned important areas of Frederick County. While large land grants were used and defended as a method of delegating to individuals the task of peopling new areas, they obviously enhanced the power and profits of their recipients and bolstered the position of the gentry. Moreover, younger sons and grandsons of gentry families found outlets for their energies and ambitions in building up plantations in the new counties.

By 1749 the whole Valley of Virginia from the Potomac to the James had been settled, leaving only the less attractive, since remote, Staunton-Roanoke region for further expansion. Many Virginians, in fact, moved into North Carolina, since land there was generally cheaper. In that colony the western regions had double the population growth of the coastal parts, and as in Virginia new counties were organized to accommodate western settlements. In 1740 North Carolina had twelve counties. By 1764 another thirteen had been formed, allowing even Lord Bute's name to be used for one of them. South Carolina's government also made large land grants, distributing a million acres in the tidewater in the 1730s and other large amounts in the back country, although from 1733 to 1759 the government attempted to order western settlement by establishing regulated townships.

Expansion in New England was as much a matter of the gradual filling in of population in already settled regions as spectacular movement into more distant territory. Yet Worcester, founded in 1718 by Scotch-Irish families, provided a point from which other townships were settled, including Rutland, Pelham, Warren, and Colerain. From this area, families moved northwest to the Connecticut River, establishing Keene, New Hampshire, in 1736 and Charlestown, New Hampshire, the most northerly village on the river, in 1740. In roughly the same years, a number of communities grew up in the Merrimack River area. Londonderry, settled in 1719 and named in 1723, testifies to the presence of the

Scotch-Irish even in these remote parts, and from it several other townships were established. By 1760 the line of frontier settlements extended as far north as Franklin, about twenty miles above Rumford (Concord) on the Merrimack River. From there it ran east to the Maine border and Berwick, although New Durham stood beyond it about five miles south of Lake Winnipesaukee. Maine's settlement mainly ran close to the coast, sprinkled along the rivers of the region as far as the Penobscot, and Waldoboro, a German community, set up by a Maine speculator in 1740. Even by 1760, however, the Maine settlers numbered only about 20,000 persons.

New York's increasing population mainly filled up areas sparsely settled by the early eighteenth century. There was little movement into the vast uninhabited areas of the province, in part because of restrictive land policies, in larger part because of fears of French and Indians. The first Palatines eventually settled on the Schoharie River in 1712, establishing a few poor hamlets. About ten years later, two tracts in the Mohawk Valley, beyond the then most westerly fort in the area, were granted to Palatine Germans, but the valley lacked many settlers until the end of the 1730s. Cherry Valley, west of the Schoharie, became Scotch-Irish, with some of these families coming from New Hampshire. Along the Hudson settlement reached Saratoga by the 1740s, but the tiny community was destroyed by enemy attack in 1744. More contentious was the movement of New England settlers into the disputed region between the Connecticut and the Hudson rivers. In the 1750s, sporadic border warfare leading to several deaths broke out between New Englanders and New York officials, as the former intruded into the manorial holdings of the Livingstons, a foretaste of border warfare that would erupt again in the 1760s.

What all this eighteenth-century expansion represented was in fact a vast increase in the territory in which white men now made their homes, although the actual density of settlement remained low and some areas within even the older regions had no inhabitants. Nor, as we have seen, were the only new settlements at vast distances from old centers of population. While those in the southern back country were very remote, many pioneers broke land ten or twenty miles from established areas. In Connecticut, for example, thirty-two new towns were founded between 1720 and 1760, as the population increased from 59,000 to 142,000. Indeed, in all of the colonies, the conquest of new land behind the line of settlement as it existed in about 1720 continued long after that date and was as important a factor in colonial expansion as the more fabled advance of the frontier.

Most of the pioneers expected to acquire new land cheaply. Many simply squatted in remote areas, like "the bold and indifferent strangers" who when challenged for title, told a Pennsylvania official that the government had "solicited for colonists and they pay accordingly." Yet the surveying and registration of grants was undertaken with surprising regularity, for the sale or renting of land was expected to make a return for its owners. In New England, governments sold shares in large township sections to eager purchasers, some of whom intended to settle their purchase, some to sell it to others. Speculation in these shares was commonplace throughout the eighteenth century: for a time, in Connecticut, land sales became a mania like the English South Sea Bubble. In Pennsylvania and Maryland, the proprietors disposed of land prior to 1719 at £5 per hundred acres, raised to £15 in 1732, together with a rental; since land was cheaper in Virginia this may have helped cause southward migration. Within Virginia the government sold off or granted huge quantities of land to single or joint purchasers, who then disposed of it themselves. These grants ran into hundreds of thousands of acres by the 1740s. Further south, the northern half of North Carolina—the Granville district—belonged to an English absentee landlord, heir to an original proprietor; land in the rest of the province was granted by the province's government. In both sections, cheap prices and sales in relatively small parcels seem to have been the rule. South Carolina's land policy involved the wish to attract white immigrants to balance the growing number of slaves, and "townships" designed for immigrants were first laid out under the governorship of Robert Johnson from 1721 to 1735. Yet accusations that Johnson's township schemes also involved a "huge land grab" by well-to-do men were made, since fifty acres for every slave were allowed, irrespective of how much land the claimant already had. Moreover, most of the remaining land in the South Carolina tidewater was granted in very large lots in the ten or so years before 1739.

North and south, land had therefore become a commodity often bought and sold in smallish lots for commercial profit and often acquired in large quantities by entrepreneurs for future resale or leasing. Land speculators tended to gain control of remote areas of virgin land at cheap prices, then awaited or promoted their settlement in order to create a high demand and a good price. As the century progressed, interest grew in land west of the mountains. In Virginia, for example, most Piedmont land had been allotted as far as the Blue Ridge, and by the 1740s active attention was directed to the Ohio Valley. Since this region was disputed with the French and under Indian control, speculation soon merged with high politics and diplomacy. Such high-level gambling in many colonies necessitated winning the support of both the English and colonial officials able to make or approve a land grant. In terms of war and peace, it often depended on calculations that French or Spanish influence in the coveted region would not prevent, and that Indian relations would permit, the realization of English settlement. These considerations, as well as human greed, led to fraud, intrigue, and manipulation, including pressures for military activity on remote frontiers. In these ways, the politics and diplomacy of land linked American speculators with British politicians and both with the great European struggle for empire.

Some, if not all, of these components are found in the development of land speculation in several colonies. In New York, where speculation is sometimes difficult to distinguish from large landlordism, five men gained a grant on the Mohawk River (Oriskany patent) in 1708 that would only have become profitable if the French were expelled from control of the Lake Ontario region's fur trade and the Mohawk Indians remained neutral. By 1738, despite Indian claims to ownership, speculators held most of the land along the Mohawk, and rich men increasingly dealt directly with British officials about their claims, often promising suitable returns if their titles were upheld. New York land grants may well have inhibited settlement, since landlords and speculators often accepted only tenant farmers or made sales at high prices. Certainly the pressure from would-be freeholders—themselves, however, often aggressive land grabbers—came only fortuitously when westward-moving New Englanders reached New York's boundaries, for few settlers sought to enter New York as a matter of choice, as they did Pennsylvania or North Carolina.

In New England land speculation was more closely associated with schemes of settlement, and colonial governments regulated grants more closely, often seeking to form newly populated barriers between the French and Indians in the north and the older regions. The Massachusetts General Court, for example, closely supervised the resettlement of Maine after the wars of the first twenty years of the eighteenth century. Here, and more generally, the authorities insisted on land being granted as discrete townships and on attempts at peopling them. Nevertheless, many of those who became proprietors of such areas did so without any intention of moving to them, and land-jobbing by politicians and merchants was recognized as a social problem. Governor Benning Wentworth of New Hampshire reserved substantial tracts of land for himself in each of the many townships that he approved, while in Connecticut groups of prominent men acquired extensive tracts by the purchase of old private titles.

The formation of business partnerships to deal in land prepared the way for a new phase in land speculation, opening in the 1740s, with the organization of semi-public land companies, a development that would accelerate after the end of the French and Indian War. The earliest companies were unchartered and unincorporated. But they had formal rules and limited, often private, trading in their shares. The Ohio Company set up in 1747 consisted of a group of prominent Virginians, together with a few Marylanders and a London merchant, John Hanbury, who supplied goods and represented the company before the Board of Trade; later members included Virginia's governor, Robert Dinwiddie, and Arthur Dobbs, a governor of North Carolina. In 1748 the British government permitted the company a trans-Appalachian grant of 200,000 acres on the Ohio River with the right to another 300,000 acres should it settle 100 families and garrison a fort in the region. Obviously, strategic anti-French considerations could be argued in its favor, and the British government sent cannons to Virginia for the company's use in 1753. The area, however, could not be protected against French and Indian attack, and the Ohio Company saw its early ambitions swallowed up in the outbreak of war in 1754.

By this time the Virginia House of Burgesses had protested against the increasing number of large land grants made by the Virginia government, and the Pennsylvania government had begun to dispute the right of Virginia over the territory in question. Other southern land companies of this period achieved relatively little; their heyday would come after the defeat of the French in 1763. Yet in the north, one land company became a significant factor in politics and westward expansion.

The Susquehanna Company, founded in 1753, embodied the aspirations of a host of Yankee farmers rather than a few southern gentlemen. Land hunger in Connecticut brought great public support to this company whose backers pressed a claim that Connecticut's charter lands extended west of the Hudson River. The company requested the Connecticut General Assembly to grant it the Wyoming valley on the upper Susquehanna, made a dubious purchase of the land there from the Indians in 1754, and sent out surveyors in 1755. Although rumors abounded of thousands of Connecticut men ready to trek out to it, no settlers arrived until the 1760s. The scheme, however, which attracted clerical and political backing in the colony as well as some opposition, led to angry protests from Pennsylvania which rightly claimed the valley, to armed battles between Pennsylvanians and New Englanders in the disputed territory, and to intervention from England because of the threat to Indian relations and colonial harmony. In 1763 Eliphalet Dyer, a prominent lawyer and politician, went to England but was unsuccessful in advancing the company's claims.

The clash between Connecticut and Pennsylvania over the Susquehanna Company was typical of the many intercolonial rivalries over territorial boundaries often precipitated by land claims. Some eighteenth-century expansionists favored the creation of completely new colonies on the western borderlands, partly to escape these complications. Only one new British colony, Georgia, was to be founded in the eighteenth century, however. To some extent its creation reflected internal American pressures for expansion, since South Carolinians, pushing south after about 1700, had frequently petitioned the home government for the establishment of military townships on the Altahama and Savannah rivers to defend both the trade in deerskins and new settlements against the Spanish, French, and Indians. By 1720 the British government had formally endorsed the need for a defensive barrier policy in the southeast, including a military settlement on the southern border of South Carolina. The makeshift Fort St. George was constructed among the mosquito-ridden cypress swamps of the Altahama a year later. In 1730 the Board of Trade instructed Governor Johnson to extend the settlement of South Carolina as far as the river.

The foundation of Georgia as a separate province with a distinct form of government and its peopling by colonists from England grew, however, from English initiatives, beginning with Dr. Thomas Bray's advocacy of the settling of artisans on American frontiers under Christian auspices. Such a project, he argued, would benefit poor Englishmen and help christianize the Indians. Bray had close connections with many pious and philanthropic men in England, including James Oglethorpe, a former army officer who in 1722 was elected to Parliament as member for a constituency controlled by his family. Oglethorpe chaired a House of Commons committee "to enquire into the State of the Gaols of the Kingdom" set up in 1729 and revived in 1730. These committees included several members of the Board of Trade, one of whom was the influential Martin Bladen. In 1730 Oglethorpe suggested—the general idea was not new—that poor debtors and others released from prison as a result of his committee's findings might be transported to America, to settle on frontier lands; in time "they with their families would increase so fast as to become a security and defence of our possessions against the French and the Indians of those parts; that they should be employed in cultivating flax and hemp, which being allowed to make into yarn, would be returned to England and Ireland, and greatly promote our manufactures." This scheme would be financed with charitable funds. Bray endorsed these plans, and members of a charity—the Associates of Dr. Bray, set up earlier and which now included Oglethorpe—began to promote the idea of Georgia as a refuge for the poor. A great publicity campaign began in the press, the King was petitioned, and in June 1732 the Georgia charter passed the seals. It named twenty persons as "Trustees" of the colony. All those named were also Associates of Dr. Bray and many of them had served on Oglethorpe's prison committees.

The charter gave the trustees supreme control for twenty-one years; at their expiry, its government would be surrendered to the Crown. The trustees decided that slavery, strong drink, and representative institutions should not be permitted in Georgia. Recruiting 114 unfortunates as the first settlers, they dispatched them to the Savannah River under the command of Oglethorpe, where they arrived in early 1733. Another 2,500 or so settlers were sent out from 1733 to 1744. Robert Walpole gave Parliamentary backing to Georgia and a grant of £10,000; up to 1752 the government appropriated a further £126,608, no great sum but more than that spent on any other of the thirteen colonies. Particular conditions placed on the colony provided also that the size of individual land grants should be strictly limited.

Georgia did not quickly flourish, but its early inhabitants—and George Whitefield owned land and slaves in Georgia—looked to the example of South Carolina for the way to wealth. Influential men claimed that the restrictions on the size of land grants and on the use of slaves inhibited Georgia's prosperity. In response to their agitation the land grant restrictions were set aside in 1740. The more substantial planters petitioned the English government for the legal introduction of slavery in the late 1740s—having already smuggled in about 1,000 slaves—and in 1750 the anti-slave law was repealed. In the same year the trustees permitted an assembly able to propose legislation to them. Two years later the trustees surrendered Georgia to the Crown and the first royal governor arrived in 1754 to reside, so he later wrote, among "a Lawless anti-monarchial

People." In fact, Georgia below the Altamaha remained a frontier for many years, but around Savannah slavery, rice growing, and large landholdings were rapidly transforming the area, which by 1760 had some 3,500 slaves and 6,000 whites, into a recognizable southern society with a population of perhaps 24,000 whites and 15,000 slaves in 1775. These fifteen years before 1775 in many ways constituted a "boom" period similar to that experienced by, for example, Pennsylvania in the later seventeenth century.

C. Economies

The great majority of eighteenth-century Americans—probably more than 90 percent—made their living on the land. Although the population of the colonial cities grew rapidly, this growth did not match that of colonial society as a whole. In 1720 the population of the five largest colonial cities, Boston, Newport, New York, Philadelphia, and Charleston, totalled about 36,000, some 7 percent of the entire population of the colonies. By 1760 the same cities numbered 73,000 inhabitants, a twofold growth, while the colonial population as a whole had risen almost fourfold. In the older established regions, population increase resulted in a mounting density of families to land, leading to the settlement of new communities within their boundaries as well as to large-scale migration to more distant areas of abundant cheap land. The cheapness and availability of fresh land, and the high cost of labor, a reversal of English conditions, not only remained a central fact of colonial life but determined the development of American agriculture.

In the newly settled areas agriculture naturally provided almost the only activity, except for a certain degree of lumbering in northern New England. During the first few years, land clearing and other pioneer tasks absorbed most energies. The French traveler Chastellux, though writing of a later period, provided a classic account of the early stages of settlement that he claimed to have seen repeated a hundred times. The pioneer first cleared the land by felling the smaller trees and lopping some branches from the larger ones; these were used to fence an area to become a first field. The large trees were then often girdled (stripped off all around of their bark). "These trees are mortally wounded, are the next spring robbed of their honours; their leaves no longer spring, their branches fall, and their trunks become a hideous skeleton. This trunk still seems to brave the efforts of the new colonists; but where there are the smallest chinks or crevices it is surrounded by fire, and the flames consume what the iron was unable to destroy." Cleared of all but the stumps of these large trees, the ground was exposed to sunlight and grass grew which the settler's few animals could graze on in the first year. Ground was then ploughed and sown and later yielded a first large crop of maize or wheat. After one or two years wooden houses and sheds were built to replace the first primitive shacks.

Usually the settler could supplement his own supplies of flour and provisions with game from the forest and wild fruits and nuts, and the forests also provided grazing for his pigs and other animals. The pioneering stage lasted a relatively short time; often new settlements quickly produced cash crops to be transported over water or primitive roads to inland market points. In the southern areas of new settlement, large-scale herding often marked the first pioneering years, gradually giving way to a more settled agriculture.

Tobacco growing in the Chesapeake and rice growing in South Carolina remained the dominant economic underpinning of both these societies. Tobacco production, after stagnating for about half a century after 1670, increased phenomenally from 1725. By 1740 the total volume of tobacco shipped equalled the combined volume of that sent to the world market from the Spanish and Portugese colonies and from Russia and Turkey, the other main tobacco-growing regions of the eighteenth century. This increased production did not involve any improvement in techniques. Aubrey C. Land writes that there was "next to no development in this direction over the first hundred years. On the contrary, even the most elementary correctives in faulty agriculture practice were long in coming." The planters "had brought their tools and habits with them from England, a land of gentle rainfall and for the most part tough soils, to the Chesapeake, where intermittently the clouds pile high, the heavens crash, and rain falls in torrents on light, easily eroded soils. Leaching of the soil by floods of water percolating through the ground compounded the depletion worked by the tobacco plant, greedy for potash and nitrogen." What permitted greater production was, in fact, the importation of more labor and the opening up of new land. Yet many planters remained in areas of old land and did not substantially add to their labor force; these men continued to constitute a large group—about 40 percent of all producers, perhaps—of poor farmers who made tobacco crops of only about 2,000 pounds or so annually and lived near the margin of existence. In their case, tobacco grown for cash must merely have supplemented a mixed agriculture of Indian corn and other foodstuffs, together with the raising of a few pigs and cattle for their own use. Probably fewer than one in twenty planters owned a plough, even by the 1760s.

Indian corn was certainly ubiquitous. "The Bread in Gentlemen's Houses, is generally made of Wheat, but some rather choose the Pone, which is Bread made of Indian Meal. Many of the poorer sort of people so little regard the English Grain, that they might have it with the least Trouble in the World, yet they don't mind to sow the Ground, because they won't be at the trouble of making a Fence particularly for it. And therefore their constant Bread is Pone not called from the Latin Panis, but from the Indian Name Oppone." Beverley's remark on Virginians at the beginning of the eighteenth century, valuable on several levels, probably remained valid for many succeeding years and for other southern areas.

Signs of change in commercial crop growing do begin to appear in the

Chesapeake by the mid-eighteenth century, a mark of innovatory ambitions if not exactly of improvements in techniques. Indigo growing was attempted only on a minute scale, but wheat became well established in parts of the Chesapeake as well as in the southern back country. Wheat, indeed, may have become the dynamic element in the region's late colonial agriculture, for in terms of output per head, tobacco decreased and grain increased substantially between about 1740 and 1770. By the era of the Revolution, some farmers had almost abandoned tobacco and turned entirely to wheat or other cereal crops.

Yet studies by Professor Land and others suggest that few rich men in the southern colonies acquired their fortunes by or remained content with producing commercial staples. In the Chesapeake the well-to-do planter speculated in land, lent money, held profitable local offices, hired out his slaves, traded in wholesale or retail goods, and acted as middleman in purchasing and consigning the smaller farmers' crops. Conversely, prosperous lawyers, doctors, officials and merchants rapidly invested in land and farming. The same was true of the Carolina rice-planting areas, where the most prosperous inhabitants not only grew, sold and traded in rice, but often dealt in slaves and in wholesale and retail goods, an intermingling that sometimes makes it difficult to distinguish between "merchant" and "planter" interests in the South.

In South Carolina rice cultivation spread into the southeastern part of the colony following the settlement of Georgia; at the same time it was moving north toward and over the North Carolina boundary. Here, a number of improvements do seem to have taken place and, of course, South Carolina was probably the richest colony by the middle eighteenth century. By the late colonial period irrigation may have been used increasingly for destroying weeds and insects as well as for providing water to the rice plants. Experimenters sought to improve techniques of clearing, milling, beating, and sieving rice from at least the 1730s, including the use of wind-fans, although how successful and how widely used these were is not very clear. Obviously, slave labor in hoeing and weeding continued to be all-important. The development of a particular variety of rice plant well suited to the colony had also taken place before the Revolution. The exhaustion of rice land may not have been a problem in the colonial period. It is not completely clear how far eastern South Carolina became a completely specialized rice-growing region of large plantations rather than one that, like Virginia and Maryland, also possessed small mixed farms. It seems likely that the specialized large plantation developed to a great extent; certainly, by about the middle of the eighteenth century, the main rice-producing districts imported food from the Carolina back country and from colonies to the north. Indigo production also tended to drive out mixed farming, especially after the introduction of the bounty system in 1748. Although some improvements in crop yield probably took place before the Revolution, total yields and quality were poor compared with that grown in the West Indies, perhaps because of primitive methods of cultivation as well as differences in soil and climate.

North Carolinians, though with a large trade in wood products, had no great agricultural staple like their adjacent neighbors. A little rice was produced in the lower Cape Fear Valley across the border from South Carolina. Similarly, indigo growing had only limited local importance, largely disappearing when English bounty payments ended in the Revolution. Indian corn, however, was exported from an early date; probably thousands of small farmers each produced a tiny surplus for sale. Wheat growing also assumed importance by the 1760s, though mostly in the newly settled western parts, except for some grown north of Albemarle Sound. Tobacco continued to be a cash crop; its cultivation spread from the Albemarle district to the more populous of the southern counties. Although Scottish merchants encouraged its cultivation by direct purchase in the later colonial period, the quantities exported remained minute compared with Virginia's exports, amounting to perhaps half a million pounds in 1769 and 1.7 million in 1771. Animals were probably an important source of farm income. Great quantities of hogs and cattle were driven into Virginia and the middle colonies, as far north as Philadelphia, while barreled beef and pork was sent out by sea, presumably to the West Indies.

The direct harvest of the forest continued to be important for most of the colonial period. North Carolina sent large quantities of tar, pitch, and turpentine extracted from the long leaf pine to Great Britain; the southern part of the colony became the major producing area after about 1750. This industry could be run profitably only with slave labor and large-scale production, and it seems likely that it was more and more carried on by big slave owners. Shingles, staves, and sawn lumber also provided commercial returns on a smaller scale. The large property owners of the southern part of the province provided most of the sawmills and therefore most of the sawn timber, since mills were generally expensive to construct and run. Staves and shingle production was rather greater in northern North Carolina, though whether this production was specialized or widespread is not known. South Carolina also exported some wood products and deerskins.

In the colonies north of the Chesapeake farm life has been most closely analyzed for southeastern Pennsylvania, a significant area since in many ways it was agriculturally the most advanced of the American regions. Here, faint areas of specialization appeared in the eighteenth century with market gardens, dairy farms, and intensive fruit farming taking place near Philadelphia. Moreover, irrigation of meadows to produce better grass and hay was common in Chester County, near the city. This and other lower Delaware River areas were centers for fattening cattle driven from other parts, some quite distant. There was also some commercial hemp production on the richer soils of Lancaster County, a commodity advertised for sale in Philadelphia. But the great cash crop was wheat, exported to the New England colonies as well as the West Indies. Yet wheat growing was neither specialized nor had it given rise to large farm units. It was grown throughout Pennsylvania by numerous small farmers who also took part in general mixed farming. These men, with few exceptions, did not find it necessary to practice many improvements; only some of the richer Quaker and Mennonite farmers seem to have attracted the favorable comments of observers for attempts at crop rotation or dunging of land. The Pennsylvania Germans, it is true, were considered to be among the finest American farmers, but this may have arisen from the neatness of their buildings and their care for animals rather than from their innovations or superior productivity.

It is doubtful if the general agricultural pattern differed much in the other middle colonies from that in Pennsylvania. While wheat was the major cash crop, New Jersey was extolled for its fruit, particularly its peaches, which are "of a fine flavour, and in such amazing plenty that the whole stock of hogs on a farm eat as many as they will, and yet the quantity that rot under the trees, is astonishing. Apples are not cultivated to go to such waste as they make cider in vast quantities, and also export them by the ship-loads to the West Indies." Near New York City signs of specialization appeared similar to those around Philadelphia: Orange County was noted for its dairy products and Ulster County for its "fine Flour, Beer and a good Breed of Draught Horses," while in parts of eastern New Jersey animals fattened for the market on swampy grass land. Besides wheat and a little Indian corn, flaxseed seems to have been the other cash crop of any significance.

New England's farmers grew maize (Indian corn) rather than wheat, which it imported for breadstuffs on a small scale, on generally nonspecialized farms. Distinct dairying regions did emerge, especially in Rhode Island, and sheep farming was more widespread than in the middle colonies, though for poor-quality wool rather than mutton. From about the 1760s some attempts were made to import English rams to improve the breed. Horse, cattle and pig raising provided some parts with cash products; live horses and oxen, sheep and pigs, as well as barreled beef and pork, were characteristic New England exports. Drovers conveyed large herds of cattle from parts of New Hampshire, western Massachusetts, and western Connecticut over well-used trails to markets in Boston. Again, foreign visitors were horrified at the primitive ploughing and at an intensive, soil-exhausting planting, unremedied by manuring or crop rotation.

Similarly, the once rich swamp and forest vegetation grazed by animals in earlier years was soon denuded, and low-lying meadowland became exceedingly scarce in the eighteenth century as the numbers of animals increased. Jared Eliot, one of the first native writers on agriculture, remarked in 1747 "that the necessary stock [of grazing animals] hath outgrown the meadow, so that there is not hay for such a stock as the present increased number of people really need . . ." and noted its high cost. Yet some relief was felt as newer grasses came into the colonies from England. For example, Timothy grass gradually became common in the course of the eighteenth century, allowing the sowing of tilled uplands. Several characteristics of the country scene remind us that the colonists lacked capital: oxen rather than more expensive horses were generally used not only for ploughing but for hauling, and until the Revolution four-wheeled wagons were generally unknown in New England. Nor were many root crops grown in the northern or middle colonies; potatoes, carrots, parsnips, artichokes and beets were uncommon while a few varieties of peas and beans were cultivated.

Throughout the colonies, agricultural production obviously kept up with the growth of population and also provided a surplus for export. On the other hand, farming did not share in the revolution in techniques and productivity then being exhibited in parts of western Europe, remaining relatively unchanged and conservative. European and English travelers in the colonies as well as ostensibly well-informed Americans consistently emphasised the horrors of colonial agriculture, pointing to primitive tools and implements, to poor ploughing and weeding, to lack of care in fertilizing and manuring, to repeated soil-exhausting plantings of the same crops rather than careful rotation, to the poor care of animals, to failure to irrigate land or to use improved grasses, and to a hundred and one deficiencies. Yet they also noted that Americans were well fed, well clothed, and relatively prosperous, and that agricultural products provided important export crops throughout the eighteenth century, both internally from region to region and also to the West Indies and other overseas markets.

Many of these criticisms had justification; the colonists notoriously did not practice the careful management of their natural resources that present-day conservationists rightly uphold. Yet conservation is the product of scarcity, and those were times of abundance not only in land but in timber, fish, and beast. Moreover, the average colonial farmer was untouched by other forces that made it necessary and profitable for his English counterpart to improve his methods, resulting in an English agricultural revolution. The market for American products did not necessarily make it profitable to produce on a large scale. Distances and poor transportation facilities made it unprofitable for many farmers to take goods to marketing points, a situation that improved farming techniques in themselves could have done little to remedy. Internally, the colonies lacked numerous urban areas demanding foodstuffs. Externally, the amounts of agricultural produce that such regions as the West Indies or southern Europe could absorb were not unlimited. While market demand certainly existed and certainly influenced some farmers in deciding what to grow commercially, it did not necessitate new techniques or even encourage or finance large-scale or specialized agriculture. With notable exceptions, commercial crops, even much tobacco, tended to be raised on thousands of small family farms or plantations as commodities for sale or exchange, enabling their producers to acquire what modest necessities or luxuries they thought fitting. These conditions, together with the availability of land and rural conservatism, did not require or provide the capital or motives for expensive new farming techniques.

Great Britain and Ireland, Southern Europe, and the West Indies remained the major direct external markets for colonial products in the eighteenth century. Increasing quantities of the American products imported into England and Scotland were later re-exported to other places. The rough shape of colonial export trade is fairly clear, although precise figures are few in the period before the 1760s. One fact stands out: the enormous importance of tobacco, which constituted the largest though declining percentage of all exports from the thirteen colonies. Rice was the second most valuable single export. However, dried fish from New England and bread, flour, wheat, Indian corn, and grain from the middle colonies, and to a growing extent after 1750 the southern colonies, were all valuable. Certainly, the predominance of tobacco illustrates exactly the importance of foreign markets since, as Jacob Price has shown in magisterial detail, the great eighteenth-century increase in America tobacco production resulted from new demands in France and northern Europe. Similarly the growing slave populations of the West Indies kept up the market for all kinds of foodstuffs and animals as well as for wood products.

The greatest proportion of New England's and the middle colonies' exports went to the Caribbean, although the percentage of the middle colonies' total exports sent there, and their absolute value, fell below those of the New Englanders. Dried fish and spermaceti candles, livestock, and wood products provided substantial returns for the latter, while bread, flour, and wheat were important exports from the middle colonies. Both areas shipped iron, wheat, Indian corn, and barrels of beef and pork. A relatively greater part of the total trade of the middle colonies than that of New England went to southern Europe; middle colony wheat, grains, bread, and flour substantially exceeded the value of dried fish dispatched from New England. The middle colonies also sent growing and valuable quantities of flaxseed to Ireland, a region in which New Englanders had little footing. Great Britain absorbed roughly equal values of northern and middle colony products, particularly whale oil from the former and wheat, at least by 1768, from the latter, though trade to the mother country probably accounted for less than 30 percent of the value of their total exports.

Southern exports of tobacco and rice to Great Britain by far exceeded the value of their commodities shipped to other parts of the world. The growth in bar iron exports to Great Britain during the eighteenth century is also worth noting. From South Carolina, the second largest export to Great Britain was indigo, produced with the encouragement of British bounties, while naval stores and forest products dominated North Carolina's relatively small exports. After about 1750 southern Europe took bread, flour, wheat, and Indian corn in growing quantities from the Chesapeake, as did the West Indies, to which the export of Indian corn was especially important. Carolinian exports to the West Indies were rather larger than those to southern Europe; rice dominated exports to the latter region and also provided the highest-valued single commodity to the Caribbean, where wood products from North Carolina and Indian corn, livestock, bread, and flour also were sent. Ireland provided a small but growing market for the Chesapeake's bread, flour, and wheat but hardly counted as a market for the Carolinas.

These commodity exports obviously pleased British commentators and statesmen, since the colonies were expected to produce raw materials and agricultural goods for the benefit of the mother country. Colonial exports to southern Europe did not compete with those of England, and they provided funds which Americans could use to buy manufactured goods from Great Britain. Yet few Englishmen could have been aware of the value of certain "invisible" earnings and other kinds of capital received by the colonists. Of these, shipping rapidly grew to a place second only to tobacco exports in earning money. By 1768 New England ships probably earned about £296,000 annually, those of the middle colonies about £165,000 and those of the southern colonies about £94,000. Investigation of their routes has suggested that significant sums came from direct voyages to Great Britain, the West Indies, and southern Europe. By the 1760s the legendary "triangular trade" between New England, Africa, and the West Indies, or from the colonies to the West Indies and then to England, was probably of little significance; it may, of course, have been more so earlier in the century. Examination of shipping also reveals it to have been an area of growth and improved productivity, partly as a result of the decline in piracy and privateering after about the 1720s, partly because of the growth of the "more systematic market economy" that characterized the worldwide commercial imperialism of the eighteenth century. In particular, crew sizes and therefore labor costs decreased through the eighteenth century, expenditures on armaments fell, and insurance premiums cost less; at the same time, shorter stays were made in port, and packaging and specialized storage improved. Other invisible earnings came from the provision of insurance services and from commissions charged by American merchants and agents on the goods that they handled—possibly £168,000 in 1768.

So far, we have discussed only earnings from commodities, shipping, and other services arising from the American trade. In addition, it should be noted that the ships built in the colonies and sold overseas brought returns. Before the great expansion of American trade after about 1725, these may have been a greater percentage of total earnings than they became in the 1750s and 1760s. Figures of earnings ranging from £45,000 to £100,000 annually have been suggested. Other sources of capital inflow were payments made by Great Britain for the expenses of civil administration and for defense, which certainly outweighed the revenues collected by the customs service. Finally, a small annual profit accrued to New England slave traders, responsible for the import of a tiny fraction of the Africans brought to the colonies throughout the eighteenth century. Most of the slave trade, however, was controlled by English firms.

The volume of imports into colonial America was large and grew steadily through the eighteenth century. If the figures for the years 1768-1772 provide a relative indication of imports for the earlier years, about 80 percent of total commodity imports came from the British Isles and the remainder from the Caribbean and southern Europe. As in the later seventeenth and early eighteenth centuries, textiles and various metal goods were the most valuable imports from Great Britain, followed by numerous other articles: household utensils, gunpowder and shot, paper, glass, silk, leather, and other English manufactures. Englishmen also re-exported hemp, spices, tea, drugs, and many other European and foreign commodities to North America. Of total British and Irish imports into North America in the 1750s, about 25 percent went to New England, 41 percent to the middle colonies, 23 percent to the Chesapeake, and 10 percent to the Carolinas. From the West Indies and southern Europe, the colonists sought natural commodities that they could not cheaply produce at home, particularly West Indian sugar and its derivatives and coffee, tea, cotton, wine, and salt. New England and the middle colonies spent most on rum and molasses and the southern colonies most on rum and sugar.

Did colonial trade leave the colonists with a favorable or unfavorable balance of payments? Only an educated guess can be made for the years before 1745, when figures are lacking. Two recent scholars, Professors G. M. Walton and J. F. Shepherd, write that it is likely that some surplus in exports to the West Indies and southern Europe over imports from these areas were earned "and they need not have been large to have offset the deficits incurred in the English trade before 1745." They place these surpluses at £150,000 annually in the 1720s and 1730s and about £250,000 annually by the 1750s. Two other recent scholars discuss the period 1720-1745 as one of gradual growth of trade not marked by noticeable disequilibriums.

After 1745 British imports into the American colonies did rise dramatically as manufacturers, enjoying a boom in productivity, sought to sell more abroad. Figures indeed show that after 1745 deficits in the commodity trade with England did become larger. Some have argued that additional invisible earnings and other sources of income appeared that probably balanced these. By the 1760s commodity exports for all the colonies in per capita terms may have earned less than at the beginning of the century. Certainly, the southern colonies, where imports rose steeply after 1745, shared neither in the earnings from shipping nor from other invisibles to the same extent as New England and the middle colonies. Of the totals earned by all thirteen colonies, they received probably around some 15 percent, notwithstanding the enormous trade carried on between them and Great Britain. The reasons for this are clear: there were relatively few merchants or factors in the south who were not dependent for credits on or who were not actual agents or representatives of English and Scottish houses. Up to the 1740s most tobacco was consigned directly to merchants in England in English-owned ships, and most imports were brought in by them. After about 1745 resident Scottish factors, agents of Glasgow merchants, bought tobacco in the colonies and sold manufactured goods there, all the while extending credit in larger amounts than had before been available. By the 1750s the southern planter was probably falling more and more into debt. To the northern commercial centers, where the established colonial merchants operated on their own account rather than as agents for British firms, the rise in imports, it is argued, brought other threats. Established merchants' prosperity was undercut by the mass of cheap goods sold at cut-rate prices by small, new competitors, or at auction, or by direct consignment to shopkeepers. Importers allowed generous credit, but bankruptcies and distress resulted when recessions caused a call on debtors. In general, dependence on British credit was a distinguishing mark of American commerce, tying the colonial economy to trade and financial fluctuations in the mother country.

The shape of the eighteenth-century colonial economy is in fact now the subject of lively investigations and renewed emphasis. One point is the relation of credit, exchange rates, and currency. Well-established merchants, with adequate liquid capital and firm credit, supported a policy of a hard and stable medium of payment—either coin or well-secured paper money. They wished to collect debts owing from their local customers in a medium that would not depreciate against the sterling for which they had to exchange it to pay their British suppliers. The same was true of British merchants resident in the southern colonies. Yet other kinds of traders and businessmen, as well as most farmers, wished for ample paper as legal tender to facilitate local transactions and as a borrowable form of capital. Landholders who wished to borrow capital against their often considerable resources of lands or buildings, or new merchants and speculators hoping to expand their businesses, naturally wanted access to legal tender currency and were willing to risk its depreciation. In most colonies limited amounts of paper notes, secured by colonial governments, were issued and provided a useful medium of local exchange. Nor did British merchants object to them where they did not depreciate, as in the middle colonies.

The question of paper money or bills remained a vexing one in the eighteenth century. Where colonial paper was issued as legal tender for private as well as public debts and depreciated rapidly, both conservative well-to-do colonial and British merchants complained bitterly. This was the case in South Carolina and increasingly in New England. Faced with these problems, the British government generally acted to restrict but not to prohibit the issue of paper money by colonial governments. This protected British merchants' interests and quietened the opponents of paper money, often men of considerable political and economic importance. Moreover, British economic orthodoxy abhorred a depreciating currency. In 1740 colonial governors were ordered under pain of dismissal to approve colonial acts issuing bills as legal tender only if they contained clauses suspending their operation until they had received the royal assent. In 1741 Parliament extended to the colonies a British Act of 1720 eliminating private banks of issue. In 1744 bills were introduced in Parliament that would have drastically limited any colonial government's ability to issue paper money and restricted its use to the payment of public (mainly tax) debts. These did not become law, but in 1751, as a result of petitions from established New England merchants, Parliament passed a Currency Act that applied these two restrictions to the New England colonies. By the late 1750s British merchants involved in Virginia's commerce were pressing the government to extend this act to all the colonies, a movement that would gather force in the next few years and bring Parliamentary action in 1764.

Overseas trade, unlike static colonial agriculture, has been characterized as a dynamic element in eighteenth-century American life, serving "as a vehicle for the dissemination of technical knowledge, of skills and know-how, of managerial talents, and entrepreneurship." American farmers may have attracted the derision of their European counterparts, but American merchants in Philadelphia and New York shared the same skills and enterprise as those elsewhere in the Atlantic world. This was an age of merchants. The colonies, with a large but predominantly rural and dispersed population, with labor costs high, internal communications poor, and technological skills and capital largely lacking, could hardly have produced and manufactured goods for themselves as cheaply as they could be produced in and shipped from England. In fact, the colonies developed no appreciable industries. True, the British government legislated against colonial manufacturing, but even had such legislation not existed the combination of abundant natural resources and poor pre-conditions for industry would have left Americans as exporters of raw materials and importers of manufactured ones. Indeed, of the major statutory prohibitions against colonial manufacturing, only the Hat Act seems to have been effective; slitting mills, for example, existed in Massachusetts in 1758, despite the provisions of the Iron Act.

Localized iron manufacturing in New England, the middle colonies, and the Chesapeake and milling—paper, flour and other forms—around Trenton and Philadelphia were the only signs of potential industry or large-scale manufacturing to have appeared in the colonies by about the 1760s. Massachusetts in 1758, besides its four slitting mills, possessed forty-one forges, fourteen furnaces and one steel furnace, and Connecticut had several plating mills and refining forges. The Principio Ironworks at the mouth of the Susquehanna was founded by a Quaker entrepreneur as early as 1715. In the same area the Baltimore Ironworks, founded in 1731 by Daniel Dulany of Maryland and his partners, had increased fourteenfold in value thirty years later. While shipbuilding was a considerable employment, it seems to have been carried on not by companies employing many men but by two or three associates combining to build one or two ships and employing the requisite labor for the duration of the process. In Boston as late as 1790 the median number of workers in artisan crafts was three. How many were employed in fishing and whaling is also unclear. Contemporary statistics show 180 Massachusetts whalers in 1763, perhaps two-thirds of the total New England fleet. Between 1748 and 1762 whale oil worth around £40,000 was exported each year to Great Britain and £15,000 worth of spermaceti candles sent to the West Indies annually; there must also have been considerable internal trade in these commodities. The size of the colonial fishing fleets are also not available, but New England sent £128,841 of dried fish to southern Europe and the West Indies in 1768—about 12,000 tons in quantity.

Household production in rural areas and very small-scale artisan workshops in towns and cities, at the most a master and a few apprentices and journeymen, were then typical of colonial manufacturing. In the New England and middle colonies, and in the remoter back country, home-produced textiles and linen, together with knitted woolens, clothed many families. And while the colonial cities numbered many artisans and craftsmen-shopkeepers, bakers, blacksmiths, carpenters, coopers, leather workers, tailors, and the like, surprisingly large quantities of items that might have been expected to have been made locally were imported from England. Not until the 1750s or 1760s did skilled makers of luxury goods—silver, clocks, and expensive furniture—begin to compete against English imports.

In the southern colonies household production was no doubt important. Yet a whole range of crafts providing such necessities as the barrels and casks used for the export of tobacco and rice were mostly carried on by slaves or servants, as were carpentering, blacksmithing, and building. In part, this effectively stifled the growth of a free artisan class. Only in Charleston and the upper Chesapeake did a limited range of artisan occupations arise after about 1750, while for highly skilled work, such as architecture and the building of great houses, men were recruited directly from the mother country. The large quantities of English goods absorbed by the southern colonies seem also to have depressed the demand for home production among their large populations. However, by the 1760s at least, the middle colonies were also large importers, perhaps importing more per head of white population than either the Chesapeake or the Carolinas; yet they contained many skilled workers. So, perhaps slavery and the dispersed southern population were the crucial factors in these matters.

It is apparent that the colonies formed a series of regions with distinct, if overlapping, economies and societies. The paucity of data on the interrelationships of these regions arises from the fact that much more is known of their separate characteristics and of their external trade than of their connections. That there was considerable migration from the middle colonies to the back country is, for example, well known, but whether poor South Carolinians ever found work in Philadelphia or Boston is not; similarly only a little is known of trade connections between different colonial regions.

Chapter Eight

Religion and Culture

A. Churches and sects before the Great Awakening

The importance of religion in colonial America has already appeared from our consideration of the founding and early history of the colonies. New England's development would be incomprehensible without an understanding of New England Congregationalism. In the middle colonies, the growth of New Jersey and Pennsylvania was inextricably linked with the Quakers. Elsewhere, the weakness of the Anglican establishment and the vagaries of dissenting groups were of consequence to social and political development. Nor did eighteenth-century developments change this state of affairs. The coming of the Germans and the Scotch-Irish brought new churches and sects to colonial America, while the expansion of settlement posed fresh problems for those already present. Religious conviction and affiliation continued to play an important part in the lives of individual colonists; we know that large numbers of the articulate had personal and deep religious feelings. At the same time, individual churches or congregations provided a social and intellectual focus for their members in a society where other forms of permanent association outside the household and family were relatively few and weak. One of the earliest communal actions in frontier regions was often the building of a meeting house. Moreover, in eighteenth-century America, as in the mother country, religious sensibility underwent significant changes, and the churches emphasized a greater concern for the poor, the weak, and unfortunate, practicing a pious but utilitarian humanitarianism. In matters of public policy, too, particularly those related to education, poverty, social questions, and the like, some churches provided leadership and action. The clergy and other church leaders still provided the most prolific writers of the era, and their activities commanded public attention. Rivalry among different church bodies or schisms within them caused widespread controversy and political maneuvering. In short, eighteenth-century America remained a society in which religious passions and persuasions had the power to move men individually and in groups.

The political importance of religion also remained. The colonies depended on a mother country where, despite the advent of religious toleration in 1689, the Church of England was the established, official church, and dissenters, while often rich, learned, and respected, were largely excluded from the official business of state. They also constituted a small percentage of the population. In America the reverse continued generally to be the case, one source of tension in the colonial relationship. Nonmembers of the Church of England in America outnumbered members by many times and usually shared fully in the official and political life of their communities, often in uneasy partnership with English-appointed Anglicans—royal governors and other officials. Other tensions arose from disputes among the colonial churches themselves. Inevitably, these crosscurrents also swirled the political waters of American life.

In New England the efforts of Anglicans, Baptists, and Quakers to win freedom from religious taxes which supported Congregational ministers continued. From 1727 onward, the Massachusetts authorities gradually yielded ground to all three groups; the general result was that in each town these denominations were allowed to certify the names of their members who then became exempt from taxation. Similar laws were passed in Connecticut by 1729. Certainly, this process was a defeat for the Congregational system; moreover, it increased the tax burden on individual Congregationalists who still had to pay enforced contributions. It may well have caused continuing friction between ministers and congregations over such matters as salaries and public support, a problem since the latter part of the seventeenth century.

By the 1720s and 1730s also, an uneasiness afflicted those New England Congregational ministers who felt that the tendencies of the new century, represented by the Brattle Street Church and discussions of the reasonableness of Christianity, were inimical to a theology that emphasized man's total depravity and God's gift to a predestined elect alone of the ability to respond to the promises of his covenant. God, many books and tracts from England now stated, was benevolent and liberal; all men might be saved if they wanted to be. "Some of our *Young Men*, and such as are devoted to and educated for, the *Ministry* of the *Gospel*, are under *Prejudices* against . . . important Articles of the *Faith* of these *Churches*, and cast a favourable eye upon, embrace, and as far as they dare, *argue* for, *propagate*, and *preach* the *Arminian Scheme*. There are many dark clouds hang over *New-England*, and the *Churches* of *Christ* therein; but I apprehend this to be as dark and as dismal as any," lamented the Reverend John White in 1734.

"Arminianism" was a word that New Englanders tended to use about what they disliked in other churches'—especially the Anglican's—theology. By this date it had come more or less to mean the denial of the predestination of the elect and the assertion that all who strove hard enough might be saved. Few New England Congregationalists were in fact Arminians in this sense. The shift underway in Congregationalism, was more one of sensibilities than of dogma. Yet Anglicanism did appear to be making inroads. In 1722 Timothy Cutler, the rector of Yale College, and six other men announced their conversion to the Church of England. Three of them, including Cutler and Samuel Johnson, a Yale tutor, later sailed to England to receive ordination. News of the apostasy spread rapidly throughout New England. Franklin reported that in Boston "all the people are running mad," and Joseph Webb informed Cotton Mather that "the axe is hereby laid to the roots of our civil and sacred enjoyments, and a doleful gap opened for trouble and confusion in our churches." By 1735 three more ministers had defaulted to Anglicanism and several other young ministers had been accused of irregularities of belief and doctrine.

Those alarmed by the evidence of Church of England growth in New England knew that it had also gained in strength elsewhere in the colonies. The number of Anglican churches in Massachusetts and Connecticut had risen from a handful in 1700 to about thirty-three in 1750, but many were little more than mission houses. In the middle colonies Anglicanism was more firmly settled, with fifty or so churches to be found in New York, New Jersey, and Pennsylvania by mid-century. Yet those who feared the Church feared especially the nature of its expansion. The English bodies set up to foster Anglicanism overseas were now becoming extraordinarily active. The Society for the Promotion of Christian Knowledge sent libraries of books—some of them anti-Puritan—to America while the Society for the Propagation of the Gospel (S.P.G.) in Foreign Parts sponsored about 160 Anglican missionaries and clergy in New England and the middle colonies before 1760. Obviously, critics reasoned, a well-organized and well-financed ecclesiastical imperialism was at work. Although the S.P.G.'s missionaries could not have organized churches without local support and attendance, colonial dissenters believed that its relative dynamism derived from sinister Tory English connections and that its work threatened American liberties.

In the southern colonies Church of England parishes were, of course, established by law. The situation in Maryland and Virginia appeared potentially satisfactory enough to make these the only two colonies not to be supplied with clergy and support by the S.P.G. In Virginia there were about ninety clergy in 1750 for a white population of 130,000 and a total population of 231,000. About the same number served Maryland's white population of 98,000. Such small numbers created difficulties and made the occasional profligate or immoral minister highly visible, but on the whole, the average Chesapeake clergyman seems to have been hard working and long serving. In 1724 in Virginia the twenty-nine known clergy served an average of twenty-one years each. Many ran small schools and some tried, against planter opposition, to give instruction to the slave population. The parish vestries, of course, had considerable civil powers in both colonies, with authority to levy taxes, the duty of caring for the poor and of enforcing morals. In North Carolina, the parish system merely disguised the lack of churches and ministers within the province. Nor was the effort of the S.P.G. very successful; William Byrd claimed that Anglican missionaries had either been "too Lewd for the People" or, more seriously, "the People too Lewd for the Priest. For these Reasons these Reverend Gentlemen have always left their Flocks as arrant heathen as they sent them." Only nine Anglican churches had been established there by 1750. In South Carolina the S.P.G. worked with some vigor and accomplishment, at least in the Charleston area. Seventeen or so churches and chapels had been built by 1750 and the Reverend Alexander Garden, the South Carolina commissary, was to strengthen the Anglican position until his death in 1765. Several Negro schools were opened at different times in Charleston by Anglican clergy. Here, as elsewhere, the general tendency was to emphasize that christianization promoted slave obedience in the face of the slave-owners' belief that it might provoke dissatisfaction or claims for special privileges by the slaves. While the Anglican clergy always accommodated themselves to slavery, they were one of the few sources of intellectual and humanitarian concern for the plight of the Negro.

In another province, a denomination that enjoyed some of the authority of an established religion—for though not legally so, its members had great political and social authority—was the Society of Friends in Pennsylvania. During the eighteenth century, however, the great Quaker expansion that had been so remarkable a phenomenon of the seventeenth largely ceased. In Pennsylvania, Rhode Island, and New Jersey, the areas of particular Quaker strength, the Friends sought and gained few converts but consolidated their own position, stressing more the exclusiveness of their religion than its missionary side. By the 1750s they were on the defensive against the increasing numbers and hostility of other denominations. Beyond these areas, numerous traveling Quaker ministers did encourage the few Quakers in other colonies to organize and solidify but rarely spoke directly to nonbelievers. Such efforts on the whole had comparatively few results. The areas of relative Quaker strength after 1700 were mainly those where Quakers had settled before that date or where other churches were weak. Maine, as a frontier, offered special attractions for Quaker missionaries and was extensively visited in the 1740s, when Samuel Fothergill wrote of the "people flocking into meetings in crowds" and behaving "with great solidity." A Congregational minister noted with alarm, at about the same time, that his church had to keep a day "of fasting and prayer on account of the spread of Quakerism." In the 1770s a second wave of Quaker expansionism took place in the new frontier of south-central Maine.

This tendency of Quakerism to make relative headway only in certain fringe areas is also evident in New York. Many meetings existed on Long Island, where dissident as well as faithful Congregationalists had migrated in the seventeenth century, together with persons described as "singing Quakers" and "ranting Quakers." The Ranters, indeed, survived into the eighteenth century, and part of the function of itinerant Quaker leaders was to condemn these individuals who, one Friend claimed, "hooted like owls and made ridiculous noises as their manner is.'' Outside of Long Island, a few Quaker meetings were found in Westchester, Putnam, and Dutchess counties. Here, too, the frontier region became an area of Quaker activity in 1770s, around Saratoga County. The Society never developed any strength in New York City.

A similar deveopment is observable in the southern colonies, where except in one new area, Georgia, the Quakers made little headway. They were strong in those parts of Maryland which had been open to Quaker influence before 1700. By 1726 Samuel Bowmas, an English traveling Quaker, wrote that the Maryland yearly meeting ''is held four days, three for worship and one for business. Many people resort to it and transact a great deal of trade one with another, so that it is a kind of market or change where captains of ships or planters meet and settle their affairs; and this draws an abundance of people of the first rank to it.'' Similarly, the Albemarle region of North Carolina, visited by George Fox, was a Quaker area. Here there were few other churches before 1700 and, the governor wrote to the Bishop of London, the small number of persons converted by Fox ''continued to grow ever since very numerous.'' A distinct chain of Quaker meetings spread southward through the colony as population expanded. In South Carolina there were ''but few Friends in this Province,'' wrote Thomas Chalkley in 1713, and the same was true of the coastal region sixty years later. But in the back country of the Carolinas and of Maryland, Friends' meetings were to be found in increasing numbers as migration progressed during the eighteenth century, for these represented the movement of middle-colony and New England Quakers rather than the fruit of missionary work.

The reasons for the relative Quaker contraction in the eighteenth century were both internal and external to the Society of Friends. Obviously, the Congregational establishment in New England and the Anglican establishment in the southern colonies posed barriers to further Quaker advances. Moreover, the most numerous immigrants to the middle colonies, the Scotch-Irish Presbyterians and German-speaking Protestants, had pronounced religious views and were neither much open to Quaker influence. And the Friends neither shared in the religious excitement of the 1740s nor sought nor gained converts from it. In the substantial and rich centers of Quakerism, they had become inward-looking and exclusive, even complacent. The numerous itinerant Quakers who continued to feel a special mission to journey and speak of the ''truth'' often confined themselves to practicing Quakers, had little training or encouragement to become proselytizers, and their fervor was not, for good reasons, expressed with the kind of rhetorical flourishes that appealed in the mid-eighteenth century to men and women eager for an exciting message—condemnation of their sinfulness followed by assurances of salvation. The characteristic Quaker meeting involved long periods of silence interspersed with quiet discourse. Until well after the mid-point of the century, Quaker communities exhibited many signs of conservatism. Both Newport and

Philadelphia were increasingly well-to-do trading communities, the former a center of the slave trade. The rural Quakers in New Jersey and Pennsylvania benefitted from the growth of Philadelphia to which they supplied foodstuffs and livestock for consumption and export. Since many Friends had arrived early enough to be advantageously established by the eighteenth century, and since the virtues of diligence, caution, and hard work were inculcated into Quakers, numerous Friends became prosperous. Moreover, as F.B. Tolles has pointed out, unsuccessful Friends might well break Quaker economic rules about using credit and paying bills and be expelled from the Society.

Linked with a decline in religious fervor and a greater attention to the things of the world came the increasing institutional formalization, already noted. One of the functions of itinerant ministers was to maintain among isolated Quaker gatherings a sense of belonging to a wider society and to inculcate standard notions of discipline and practice threatened by this isolation. In this work, they were aided by the continuing practice whereby the various leading yearly meetings sent epistles of advice and information to subordinate meetings; indeed, a chain of visits and correspondence linked Quaker communities in England and America. From Maine to the Carolinas, no matter how remote and distant from the great centers of Quakerism, Friends were informed of the major developments of the day. In Philadelphia the Quakers quickly utilized the printing presses, and books and tracts from these, as well as those imported from England, found their way to many Quakers throughout America. The Philadelphia monthly meeting in 1705 agreed to buy at least one copy of every Friend's book printed in England for inspection. About the same time, a committee was appointed in Philadelphia to approve the printing of books and official documents, though later the yearly meeting exercised the position of "Overseers of the Press."

The Baptists also tended to consolidate rather than expand before 1740, when they had about twenty-seven churches in New England and perhaps about the same number in the middle colonies. In origin, these middle-colony Baptist churches were mainly Welsh. An association of churches had been established as early as 1706, with headquarters in Philadelphia. Outside these areas, Baptist numbers were minute; there were perhaps six or so Baptist churches in the southern colonies by 1740. In New England Baptist growth had been slow before 1700, and the few churches had been divided on certain principles and beliefs. In 1706 a Baptist church was founded in Connecticut; only another two or three were added in that colony by 1735, when Rhode Island and Massachusetts had some eighteen churches. In all, this was little more than the Anglicans, and the leading historian of the colonial Baptists notes that the Quakers were probably the more numerous. The majority of these Baptist churches were Arminian, believing that redemption was possible for all men and not merely the predestined elect. They also contained a high percentage of educated ministers who by the 1730s differed very little from the general run of

Congregationalists in stressing good works, pious philanthropy and moderation in matters of religion. This was particularly true of the urban Baptists, who cooperated with such leading Congregationalists as the Mathers, partly to win the sympathy and respect of the established church, partly in opposition to the Anglicans. The rural Baptists were less inclined to forget the persecution of their forebears by the Puritans or the difficulty with which toleration and freedom from taxation had been achieved. In general, however, New England Baptists before 1740 were very different from the evangelical, Calvinistic Baptists who led the great expansion of the churches for the rest of the eighteenth century.

Congregationalists, Anglicans, Quakers, and Baptists had firm roots in the seventeenth-century colonies. Not so Presbyterians, whose shadowy existence then depended on certain New England ministers, products of the English civil war period, when differences between Presbyterians and Congregationalists were still developing. Congregationalists believed that each independent church was complete of itself, that full membership and communion were open only to the elect, that clergy and laity cooperated in church government, and that ministers could be ordained only by the congregation which they served. Presbyterians broadly believed in the supremacy of presbyteries and synods over individual churches, in a church membership open to all believers, in the clergy's dominant role in church government, and in their permanent ordination by presbyteries. Presbyterian clergy in New England had some latitude in the conduct of their own local congregations, but lack of strength and numbers made them generally conform in other respects to Congregational orthodoxies. Yet, as we have seen, the Saybrook Platform gave strength to the presbyterianized Congregationalism of Connecticut. Moreover, a number of young Harvard graduates also imbibed Presbyterian principles and later served as ministers outside New England.

These New Englanders found their congregations in the middle colonies. Here, a few Scottish and Scotch-Irish Presbyterian settlers had arrived before 1700. The first organized American presbytery was founded in Philadelphia in 1705 or 1706; of the seven ministers who composed it all but one—a New Englander—had reached America from Scotland or Ireland, and all but one ministered to congregations outside Pennsylvania. By 1716, when a synod was formed in Pennsylvania, made up of four subordinate presbyteries, there seem to have been congregations in all the middle colonies and perhaps in Virginia and Maryland. The great migration of Scotch-Irish to the middle colonies began at about the same time. Most of these new settlers were Presbyterians, and from their arrival arose the new strength of the church in America. By 1730 Jedidiah Andrews, minister of the Presbyterian church in Philadelphia, was writing, "Such a multitude of people coming in, from Ireland, of late years, our Congregations are multiplied in this Province, to the number of 15 or 16, which are all, but 2 or 3, furnished with ministers All Scotch and Irish but 3 or 4.

Besides divers new Congregations that are forming by the new comers, we all call ourselves Presbyterians, none pretending to be called Congregational in this Province."

The very nature of this great migration posed special difficulties, as the Scotch-Irish quickly spread themselves over large areas of western Pennsylvania and eventually turned into the back of the southern colonies. Numerous small communities grew up on creeks and rivers. In many of them, the more religious families formed themselves into congregations and bought or were deeded land for burial grounds and churches on which they raised primitive meeting houses. Here, without ministers, they could pray and worship together. Yet if they wished for teaching, for preaching, and for the sacraments, the presence of a minister was essential. In the middle colonies as a whole there were some twenty-five or so Presbyterian ministers in 1716 and some ninety-eight or so in 1758. Yet by the latter date at least 50,000 Scotch-Irish lived in Pennsylvania alone. A perennial shortage of clergy remained one of the severest problems of colonial Presbyterianism, no less than of many other churches.

The shortage of clergy meant in fact that even churches rich or fortunate enough to have an ordained minister could often expect him to be absent as a missionary or supply preacher to congregations without settled clergy. Outside the wealthiest and most thickly settled towns, weekly services conducted by a clergyman, even monthly services, were a rarity. In most congregations a measure of lay control unknown in Scotland or Ireland arose as a necessity out of American conditions rather than as a theory of church government. At the same time many congregations were either too poor or too parsimonious to offer potential ministers an adequate salary, and it became a regular practice for Presbyterian ministers to contract with several congregations to serve each of them on a part-time basis. Other methods taken to remedy the shortage of ministers were the employment of student ministers as licensed visitors and the use of missionaries.

In theory, the Presbyterian Church was highly organized. Together with the minister, the elders of each local congregation formed a powerful disciplinary body, examining a variety of transgressions by church members. In some areas these sessions did meet. On the frontier, indeed, they probably provided a form of government before the civil authorities were established, rebuking, censuring, and even excommunicating members for drunkeness, fighting, fornication, unfair business dealings, and other matters of Christian morality. No detailed study of their frequency, operation or extent, however, exists, and it is hard to generalize about them. More is known of the various presbyteries—groups of ministers within a specified area. By 1763 there were about eight of these covering the middle colonies. Much of their work was aimed at supporting the authority and livelihood of the clergy. The presbytery of Philadelphia, for example, laid down that a minister should be paid at least £60 per annum in salary. That of Donegal specified that certificates of membership in a church should be issued only to those who supported it financially and attended regularly and that only these could receive the church sacraments for themselves and their children. The presbyteries also acted as licensing bodies for candidates to the ministry, supervised the erection of new congregations, supplied vacant ones with ministers and installed and ordained ministers. Their records show a society in which disputes between congregations and ministers, indiscipline within congregations, and a general disorderliness were by no means uncommon.

At the highest level as well, within the Synod of Philadelphia, colonial Presbyterianism suffered from schism and disagreement. By 1721 many of the Scotch-Irish ministers in the synod urged that the colonial church subscribe in full to the Westminster Confession and the Directory of Church Government, two major doctrinal statements of British Presbyterianism. A few other Scotch-Irish and many New England-trained Presbyterians objected to this. After several years of dispute, a compromise followed in 1729, the Adopting Act, in which the synod agreed that the Confession and Directory would be recommended as standard doctrine but that ministers would not be required to subscribe fully to them.

The group that pressed for strict subscriptionism definitely consisted of the mainly Scottish-educated immigrant ministers now arriving in America. These men took a stand on the necessity of continuing the high educational standards of the clergy that prevailed in Scotland and Ulster and on the rights of synods to firm control of the Church. Yet many of their opponents had a similar background. These included a remarkable family of Presbyterian clerics, the Tennents. William Tennent, born in Ireland in 1673 and educated at the University of Edinburgh, had served as an Anglican minister in his native country before migrating to New York, where he became a Presbyterian minister in 1718. In 1725 or 1726 he moved to Neshaminy, Pennsylvania. Of his four sons, all of whom became ministers, Gilbert Tennent, born in 1703, became the most eminent.

Both William and Gilbert Tennent shared the evangelical Puritan zeal that in Britain was beginning to move men like the Wesleys. In 1734 Gilbert asked that candidates for the ministry and for the Lord's supper should be examined as to "the evidences of grace of God in them, as well as their other necessary qualifications." A year or two later his father opened a seminary or college at Neshaminy for the training of native American Presbyterian ministers, in which emphasis was placed on sanctifying grace as well as learning as a necessary condition for the ministry. This "log college," as it became known, and the zealousness of the Tennents and their friends attracted the hostility of many Scotch-Irish clergy who valued an old-world education as a guarantee of orthodoxy as well as of learning and believed that novel practices might easily split the colonial church from its Scottish roots. A few years later these disagreements resulted in open schism.

Like the Scotch-Irish, the Germans brought their religion with them as they arrived in increasing numbers in eighteenth-century America. Mennonites, Dunkards, Schwenkenfelders, Moravians, and several other varieties of Protestant sectarians came in small groups. Conrad Beissel, an immigrant in 1720, founded the semi-monastic Dunkard Ephrata Cloister at Lancaster ten years later; he was to compile the first German hymnal to be printed—by Benjamin Franklin—in North America. Yet the vitality and diversity of the German sects must not blind us to the fact that the majority of the Germans were church people, either Lutherans or German Reformed (Calvinist). Increasing numbers of Lutherans arrived from the time of the Palatines, mostly settling in Pennsylvania. The Salzburger Protestants who settled Ebenezer, Georgia, in 1734 were also Lutherans. At this time the great center of Lutheranism lay at the University of Halle in Germany. A center of pietism, with a reputation and influence felt in England and America, its teaching from the 1730s onward was, however, accused of increasing formalism and legalism. It was to Halle that the lay leaders of German Lutherans in America looked for a supply of pastors and general support. Yet until the 1740s their hopes were rarely fulfilled; in 1739 there was only one pastor in America, and the Lutherans feared for their future "in a country that is full of heresy and sects." One wrote, "as far as religious interests are concerned we are in a state of the greatest destitution . . . the danger is great that, in consequence of the great lack of churches and schools, the most of them [their children] will be misled into the ways of destructive error."

Members of the German Reformed Church also came to America from the second decade of the eighteenth century; by 1730 one contemporary stated that half of Pennsylvania's Germans belonged to it. For a time, the Reformed authorities at Heidelberg assumed responsibility for sending out ministers. During the 1740s the Amsterdam Classis of the Dutch Reformed Church assumed control over the German church, maintaining this oversight until after the American Revolution. The situation in the Reformed Church in many ways resembled that within the Lutheran, since ministers were never enough for the number of congregations and the German sects made constant converts from its members. It was not until after the arrival of Michael Schlatter, a German-Swiss, sent by the Dutch Classis in 1746, that a firm institutional framework for the German Reformed congregations was created.

Both German churches maintained friendly relations with each other. The Reformed Church also had close contacts with the Dutch Reformed Church which, like it, received oversight from the Amsterdam Classis. Despite attempts lasting until about 1709 by Anglican governors to restrict the expansion of the Dutch church, its growth was practically unhindered; it spread from New York to New Jersey, reflecting the migration of Dutch families perhaps attracted to the religious freedom as well as by the agricultural opportunities of that colony. By 1736 there were at least fifty-six congregations of Dutch Reformed in New York and New Jersey, but far fewer serving ministers. The most famous of these was probably the Reverend Theodore Frelinghuysen, who began intensive attempts at conversion among the churches in the Raritan valley after his arrival in 1720. Frelinghuysen exercised a great influence on Gilbert Tennent, stimulating the growth of revivalistic techniqùes among the New Jersey Presbyterians.

This brief discussion of the Presbyterian, the German, and the Dutch churches reveals quite clearly the similar problems that they faced in adapting to the conditions of the New World. A major weakness lay in the shortage of ministers, often a consequence of their inability, or unwillingness, to accept men not educated and ordained in Europe and one that could be met only when these churches achieved organizational independence of Old World ties. Weakened clerical authority led to grave institutional problems; the records of the Presbyterians and German Reformed, for example, are full of mentions of quarrels and controversies especially over discipline, salaries, and the like. Muhlenberg, the Lutheran minister, wrote that every German peasant in Pennsylvania wanted to "act the part of patron of the parish, for which he has neither the intelligence nor the skill" and that "everything depends on the vote of the majority." In the Presbyterian Church a positive anticlericalism developed. One other factor that certainly contributed to the relative weakness of the clergy in all these churches lay in the new provisions that had to be made for the legal ownership of churches and church property. This came to be vested in the hands of lay trustees, who, rather than the state, as in most European countries, therefore held a large measure of ecclesiastical power.

B. The Great Awakening and its results

In early 1736 the Reverend George Whitefield, a "boy parson" aged twenty-two, preached a sermon in the city of Bristol in the west of England. His audience was amazingly large and varied and he wrote "many of all denominations were obliged to return from the churches where I preached for want of room." A few months later he preached again in the same city; in one church "people hung upon the rails of the organ loft, climbed upon the leads of the church and made the church itself so hot with their breath, that the steam would fall from the pillars like drops of rain." In London "the tide of popularity now began to run very high. In a short time, I could no longer walk on foot as usual, but was constrained to go in a coach from place to place to avoid the hosannas of the multitude." In 1738 the young man sailed to Georgia but returned home in the same year. Back in England he consolidated his enormous popularity—though now he found the doors of most Anglican churches barred to him—preaching for the first time in the open air.

Whitefield preached a simple message: no individual could have assurance of salvation unless he or she was "born again" through a profound, disturbing realization of man's sinfulness and God's redemptive mercy. Mere formal churchgoing, mere formal faith, good works, or a moral life could not bring salvation. The churches and ministers of his own day, Whitefield implied or stated, had become easygoing and conventional, neglecting the fundamental truth that to guide each member of their congregations to a personal experience of God's grace was their essential function. To do this the clergy themselves, he would soon stress, had to have had their own experience of salvation; the blind could not lead the blind. These beliefs Whitefield expressed eloquently, dramatically, turning each appearance into a theatrical occasion. He had quickly become the greatest preacher, actor (and would be perhaps the greatest fundraiser) of his time.

In October 1739 Whitefield returned to America, where news of his remarkable successes in England had appeared in the colonial newspapers, to begin an extensive preaching tour that lasted for two years and took him to every center of population in the colonies. For the knowledgeable among his American audiences, his words were, of course, a re-emphasis on the gospel of redemption and saving grace that the great Calvinist divines of the seventeenth century had constantly stressed but which had become obscured in recent years by the tendency to stress good works, rational religion, and outward morality. Nor had the colonies lacked ministers who shared Whitefield's concerns, for there had been isolated religious revivals in New England and the middle colonies for several years before his coming, in which church congregations had been reminded in dramatic and vivid fashion of the need for individual regeneration. In Northampton, Massachusetts, Solomon Stoddard achieved "harvests" in 1670 and 1683 when he wrote that "the bigger Part of the Young People in the Town, seemed to be mainly concerned for their eternal Salvation." Subsequent revivals occurred in 1696, 1712, and 1718. Ministers, Stoddard observed, must have the experience of personal salvation, must "get the Experience of this Work in their own Hearts. If they have not Experience they will be but blind Guides, they will be in a Great Danger concerning a Work of Conversion . . . Whatever Books men have read, there is a great need of experimental knowledge in a Minister . . . it is a great calamity to wounded Consciences to be under the Direction of an unexperienced Minister." This movement culminated in the success of the Reverend Jonathan Edwards, Stoddard's grandson and successor at Northampton, who from 1735 onward instigated a revival there and at several other towns.

In the middle colonies, among the Dutch Reformed churches of the Raritan valley, we have seen that Freylinghuysen's visits to families and preaching had resulted in numerous conversions. Freylinghuysen quickly befriended the Reverend Gilbert Tennent and gave him the use of his meeting houses and other places of worship when Tennent entered his ministry at New Brunswick in 1726. The young Presbyterian undoubtedly absorbed and improved on the preaching methods of the German pietist, and by the late 1720s had fostered revivals among his own flock. Tennent's background had also prepared him for an evangelical career, since his father seems to have stressed the vital distinction between the truly saved and mere formal Christians. William Tennent's other sons, John and William, also conducted evangelical services in the 1730s. By 1738 they and other graduates of the Log College at Neshaminy were disliked among conservative Presbyterians for their stress on conviction and conversion. Nevertheless, these revivals had been local and mainly confined to members of distinct churches. When George Whitefield arrived, he acted as a public minister, preaching to interdenominational crowds in every colony with correspondingly wide results.

This "Great Awakening" began in Philadelphia where, within six days of arriving, Whitefield was preaching "in the evening, from the Court house stairs" to about "six thousand people," a figure he believed had risen to 8,000 on the next evening. Whitefield soon set out for New York, meeting Gilbert Tennent en route, for whom he preached and whom he also heard preach. Tennent, Whitefield wrote, "convinced me more and more that we can preach the gospel of Christ no further than we have experienced the power of it in our own hearts. Being deeply convicted of sin, by God's Holy Spirit, at his first conversion, Mr. Tennent has learned experimentally to dissect the heart of the natural man. Hypocrites must either soon be converted or enraged at his preaching." Whitefield's successes continued in the middle colonies, and in New England, which he visited in September and October 1740, before traveling south again to Georgia at the end of the year. In January 1741 he set sail for England.

Contemporary reports testify that Whitefield's missionary journeys left the communities which he visited in turmoil. "Numbers of almost all denominations," wrote one Philadelphia lady, "and many who had no connection with any denomination, were brought to enquire, with utmost earnestness, what they should do to be saved. Such was the engagedness of multitudes to listen to spiritual instruction, that there was public worship, regularly, twice a day, for a year . . . The city contained 26 societies for social prayer and religious conference. So great was the enthusiasm to hear Mr. Whitefield preach, that many from Philadelphia followed him on foot to Chester, to Abingdon, to Neshaminy, and some even to New Brunswick, in New Jersey, the distance of sixty miles." In New England, "numbers were made to cry out, 'What shall we do to be saved?' " and five persons trampled to death in one meeting house. "Multitudes were greatly affected, and many awakened by his lively ministry. Though he preached every day, the houses were exceedingly crowded; and almost every evening the house where he lodged was thronged to hear his prayers and counsels. Upon his leaving us, great numbers were concerned about their souls; so that our assemblies were surprisingly increased, and the people wanted to hear us oftener than ever," wrote a Boston minister.

In denominational terms, Whitefield had least effect on the Anglican Church in America, his own. Perhaps Whitefield's reputation in England as an irregular clergyman, a vainglorious disturber of the peace, a contemner of a majority of Anglican clergy had preceded him to America. Certainly, he made a point of speaking in the churches and meeting houses of every denomination and found and expressed more sympathy with dissenters than with Anglicans. Many dissenters, indeed, made a point of welcoming Whitefield as a virtual nonconformist, using him to pursue their own quarrels with their Anglican rivals. Nor did his popularity, or that of revivalism, continue with all the clergy and laity of other denominations. Part of the reason for this arose from the disturbances that his messages could bring to church congregations, forcing ministers to alter the habits of a lifetime. More important, the process of the Great Awakening soon gave rise to quarrels, controversies and schism that spilled over from the churches to create social and political tensions. A crucial issue soon arose as some revivalists proclaimed that "unregenerate" ministers might be unfit to hold office, a direct challenge to authority. Whitefield's own preaching did this, but a sermon by Gilbert Tennent, delivered as early as 1740, printed and widely read, "On the Dangers of an Unconverted Ministry," was its most important expression.

Whitefield's visits were followed by a great outburst of evangelical activity by Americans. In Philadelphia Gilbert Tennent and Samuel Blair, a Log College graduate, joined with two other ministers to lead great meetings. From June 1740 there was a great revival at Newark and Elizabethtown in New Jersey, while later in the same year Tennent traveled for two months in south New Jersey, Delaware and Maryland. From June 1741 the Log College-dominated New Brunswick Presbytery organized a team of six itinerant evangelists charged with traveling to the remoter parts of the middle colonies. Early in 1741, at the behest of Whitefield and several New England ministers, Tennent also visited Boston, where, for three months, according to Timothy Cutler, "people wallowed in the snow for the benefit of his beastly brayings." In New England, the revival was also carried on in 1742 by the Reverend James Davenport, a Yale graduate in his twenties, who, having been declared *non compos mentis* in Boston, where he led large singing processions through the streets, retired to his parish at New London, Connecticut. In March 1743 he organized a bonfire of works by such respectable ministers as the late Increase Mather and Benjamin Colman. Davenport's attacks on fellow ministers and the activities at this time of large numbers of lay "exhorters" including, to Charles Chauncy's regret, "Women, Children, Servants and Negroes," brought hostility even from the previously well disposed. Thomas Prince, for example, described this stage of the revival as "an unhappy Period."

What had caused and was causing the Great Awakening? For many historians, the movement is explicable in purely religious terms. In an age of continuing religious belief, but one characterized by a growing laxity, or formalism or dissension in the churches, preachers could stir up great passions with accusations of wrongdoing followed by a message of regeneration. Others have linked the Awakening to general social and economic conditions, particularly to the economic slump and hardships caused by the wartime disruption of overseas trade after 1739 and to the strains created by the population expansion of the decades before 1740. A rapidly increasing population brought social and political strife and competition for land and trade. As parents no longer had respectable properties with which to reward children for making dutiful marriages, and men lacked the economic wherewithal to marry young, pre-marital sexual relations increased in numbers. Guilt over these matters may have prepared the way for the Awakening. Moreover, an epidemic of throat distemper, causing a high mortality among infants and young persons, swept New England and part of the middle colonies in the 1730s, and may have been seen as divine retribution for those evils, also leading to an acceptance of the revivalists' message. Local studies mainly exist for New England. These suggest that the Awakening there may have been most intense in newer, more isolated towns and among young people. Indeed, young adults participated in relatively larger numbers in the Awakening than their elders, which suggests a generational division, even a conflict. But many of the young were from churchgoing families and might have eventually become full church members anyway, although not fervent converts. Certainly the Awakening did not generally represent a revolt of the poor or dispossessed against the better-off, even if the young men, because of their age, were landless and without political power. Whitefield and other preachers addressed themselves to poor and rich and black and white, and there is no evidence of significant social divisions between those who succumbed to and those who resisted their message. Perhaps the important exception to this generalization concerns the lay preachers and the anticlericals—many of whom later became Baptists.

In the Presbyterian church, the divisions present before 1740 merged into those produced by the Awakening. The Tennent group made it clear that they numbered many of their Scotch-Irish opponents as unconverted clergy; for a time the view prevailed that such ministers might be abandoned by their congregations in favor of a godly minister, a position that undermined the fundamental discipline of the Presbyterian church. The conservatives sought to check the activities of the New Side evangelists by placing synodical restrictions on Log College graduates and forbidding members of one Presbytery to intrude into others. These prohibitions were largely ineffectual and in May 1741 animosities became so pronounced that the conservatives, with a majority of votes, expelled the New Brunswick Presbytery from the Synod of Philadelphia. By this time, opposition to revivalist techniques in themselves had become pronounced. Tennent's opponents argued that preaching the terrors of hellfire and working on "the passions of and affections of weak minds" to make individuals "cry out in a hideous manner, and fall down in convulsion-like fits" did not necessarily lead to true godliness.

The result of the schism was several years of bitterness, with many congregations splitting up into New Side (Tennent) and Old Side (conservative) elements and with the eventual formation in 1745 by the Tennent group of the Synod of New York in opposition to the truncated Synod of Philadelphia. For a time, the energy of the New Side preachers led to further expansions of the revival. The founding in 1741 of the Second Presbyterian Church of Philadelphia, to which Gilbert Tennent came as pastor in 1743, brought a New Side center into the capital city of American Presbyterianism. Missions to the Indians, the most famous of which was undertaken by David Brainerd, a Yale College convert of Gilbert Tennent's, in western Pennsylvania, exemplified new attitudes provoked by the revival towards Indians and blacks, hitherto often neglected as potential converts. Other New Side men opened academies and schools. Finally, New Side ministers were responsible for evangelicizing parts of central and eastern Virginia, where they established Presbyterian societies in the midst of the Anglicans.

Many of the New Side Presbyterians drew back from the final extravagances of the Great Awakening. The Tennents never doubted the need for an educated as well as a converted ministry and certainly never encouraged lay preaching by uneducated men. As early as 1742, Gilbert Tennent had been distressed by his encounter with the mystical, enveloping Count Nicholas Zinzendorf, who rejected the Calvinistic tenet of predestination in favor of the possibility of universal salvation, who believed that the saved Christian existed in a state of perfection rather than in the necessity of continued striving, and who made great use of itinerant laymen as missionaries. All three matters represented tendencies which critics had rightly suggested could easily emerge within Presbyterianism as a result of the Awakening. In the same year, Tennent also rejected his former ally, James Davenport, condemning his denunciations of unconverted ministers and lamenting the schism caused by the revivals. By 1749, Tennent was leading the New Side back to reunion with the Old, a process that was formally completed in 1758, although tensions and disagreements between both groups continued for many years afterwards.

In the middle colonies, the era of the Great Awakening was also consequential for the German denominations. Among them, the excitement produced by Whitefield's visit was naturally muted since he preached in English. Yet he did journey in German areas and many Germans listened to him in Philadelphia. He was also closely connected with the Moravians who carried on an awakening in the German churches, sending out numerous itinerant missionaries and causing considerable alarm to the Lutheran and Reformed ministries. During Whitefield's heyday, the ubiquitous and pious Count Zinzendorf, who claimed authority in both the Reformed and Moravian churches and had established the famous Moravian community of Herrnhut on his German estates, visited Philadelphia. Zinzendorf, like Whitefield, believed that the message of the new life should be preached universally without regard to denominational distinctions; unlike Whitefield he also had plans for founding a new religious order to embrace the sects and the German churches. Arriving in December 1741, he participated in seven general meetings of German Christians at Germantown, from which, however, all except the Moravians, Lutherans and Reformed withdrew after the fourth. Subsequently, the two main churches began to see in Zinzendorf's plans the threat of a Moravian takeover and disassociated themselves from his "Congregation of God in the Spirit." Zinzendorf returned to Germany in early 1743.

A major result of Zinzendorf's visit was the firm establishment of the Moravians in the middle colonies, particularly at their great community in Bethlehem, where a communitarian, regulated society reestablished in the Pennsylvania wilderness many of the practices of the Herrnhut original. Zinzendorf also founded Moravian churches in Philadelphia and four other Pennsylvania towns and on Staten Island and in New York City. During the next decades, itinerant Moravian missionaries traveled throughout the colonies, preaching to the Indians and founding other churches in the white settlements. At the same time, an organizational structure was developed for the church as a whole in America. Its great strength lay in its willingness to ordain men (and women) locally, often without regard to their educational background, thus escaping the dependence of the German churches on the few immigrant ministers who came to America.

A secondary result of the establishment of the Moravians was certainly the tightening up of Lutheran and probably Reformed organization in North America. The Lutheran minister Henry Melchior Muhlenberg arrived in Pennsylvania at a time when Zinzendorf was active and moved rapidly to counter the Moravian threat. Under his tutelage, the church managed to organize itself satisfactorily, forming a ministerium (synod) in 1748 and a united synod with the Swedish Lutherans in 1761. Even so, the Lutherans continued to have far fewer ministers than their numbers warranted, especially in the southern back country to which large numbers of Germans were now moving. Not until 1769 was a seminary for the training of American-born ministers suggested, but nothing came of this in the colonial period. Among the Reformed, the first Coetus, or central ruling body, met in Philadelphia in 1745, attended by thirty-one ministers and elders. Like the Lutheran ministerium, this body lacked the authority to ordain ministers and the church continued to be short of them throughout the colonial period. Like the Lutherans, it tended to depend on European churches for money and supplies as well as ministers. Moreover, the Reformed Church also suffered from inner tensions, presumably linked with the revivalism of the Great Awakening period. One faction stressed the need for an educated ministry and a pure liturgy; another tended to press for pious, evangelical ministers whose learning was not to be closely questioned. Despite these difficulties, the zeal of the Reformed ministers, reflected particularly in the strenuous journeys undertaken by them in the middle and southern colonies, created a network of churches.

The Quakers alone seem to have been untouched by the Awakening, possibly because of their highly organized, closed system, evident in the fact that young Friends were encouraged to attend only schools that emphasized Quaker tenets, were taught the exclusiveness of a sect that demanded special conduct in civil as well as religious affairs, and were not allowed to marry outside of the Society. Indeed, in this period, Friends were still criticized for worldliness in dressing finely, paying taxes for military purposes and compromising in civil and political matters. William Beckitt, an English Quaker visiting Philadelphia in 1758, found the elders of the meeting ''too much in the outward court, which is trodden by the Gentiles, or such as are in the spirit of the world; yet a young and rising generation is here . . . whom the Lord hath visited by his power and good spirits in their hearts.''

Was this ''rising generation'' immediately influenced by the Great Awakening? It seems unlikely, since not until the late 1750s did a wave of criticism and reform appear that, continuously until the American Revolution, renewed older Quaker teachings, especially those that emphasized social equality and the reununciation of worldly wealth. They had earlier examples to draw on, like the numerous itinerant ministers who made long and dangerous journeys in the service of their faith. Moreover, it is well known that the first sustained protests against Negro slavery originated among Quakers, though it should also be remembered that it was the prevalence of slave owning among certain Friends that provoked these. John Woolman, born in 1720 in New Jersey, testified, ''though many kept slaves in [Quaker] Society, as in others, I still believed the practice was not right.'' During the next thirty years, he conducted a personal attack on it with the support of many leading Philadelphia Quakers. Woolman also gave much thought to the question of poverty. Although his solution—that rich men should exercise their powers in a spirit of Christian stewardship and charity—was not a particularly novel one, his incidental comments on the oppression of the poor by the rich and his emphasis on God's ownership of all land as limiting the rights of private landlords show a latent social radicalism.

In New England the effects of the Great Awakening were perhaps even more deeply felt than in the middle region, since in the Puritan colonies the legal establishment of the Congregational churches quickly came into question. One group of ministers and laity—the Old Lights—rapidly opposed the assumptions, techniques and effects of the evangelists. Another group—the moderate New Lights—welcomed the revivals in their initial stages but came at varying times to oppose their more extreme manifestations, especially the rise of lay preachers and the attacks on allegedly unregenerate clergy. The radical New Lights, mainly laymen, supported these attacks, forming a nonclerical or anticlerical group willing to break with the established churches in their wish to pursue a godly reformation. Many of these later became Baptists, while some Old Light Congregationalists sought order and stability in the Anglican Church. The involvement of the civil authorities came as congregations chal-

lenged their ministers, as groups within individual churches and parishes disagreed, and as the radicals sought to break away completely from the established order and found their own churches. What position should government take, for the law made the civil power ultimately responsible for ecclesiastical order? In Connecticut divisions caused by the Awakening went very deep, dividing the population and giving rise to two groups that in time exhibited the characteristics of political parties, which took up views on other issues as well.

One case study illustrates a typical process of fission. At Norwich, Connecticut, in the First Congregational Church, the minister Benjamin Lord had favored "vital practical religion" for many years and welcomed the revival of 1740. Ninety-one persons became communicant members of the church from 1741-1744, an astounding increase over previous years and for the first time, writes J. M. Bumsted, the minister "was paid not only what he considered was an equitable salary, but was actually overpaid for the years 1742, 1743 and 1744!" Yet, lay exhorting and itinerant preaching posed a problem for Lord and the new converts did not always meekly follow his advice. Several decided in 1745 to withdraw from the church on the grounds that the minister was "not a Friend to lively Preaching and Preachers." Later, some of them formed a new church in a western part of the township, alleging distance from the old one as a reason. They were joined by many persons who perhaps lacked profound religious opinions but found the location of the new church more convenient than that of the old.

Many churches, of course, remained Old or moderate New Light bodies, committed to the ecclesiastical order; they supported legislation or ministerial declarations against itinerant clergymen and lay preachers and against schismatic separations from standing churches. But by 1754, about fifty-eight Separate-Congregational churches had been formed by radical pietists in Massachusetts, and about thirty-five in Connecticut. These churches were defined as "illegal conventicles" under Massachusetts and Connecticut law. Their members naturally soon came to argue strongly for changes in the establishment, particularly for the support of ministers through voluntary donations and not through taxation. This perhaps gained them other supporters. Yet one should not underestimate the precipitating fact of religious zeal or its continuing importance. Basic to the Separates' position was the dislike of halfway membership, of the fact that laymen could not speak in, nor even if specially qualified by godliness and ability but without formal education become pastors in, the established Congregational churches. The Separates consistently preached against the established ministry, revived the practice of lay ordination and allowed ordinary members to "improve" their "gifts in teaching." In these senses the movement was popular or "democratic," although it did attract men of property and social standing and was not confined to the poor or downtrodden. Yet, it is a remarkable fact that not one college-educated minister and few such laymen joined the Separate-Congregationalists.

Some Separate-Congregationalists later became Separate-Baptists, a sect with distinct beginnings but which soon merged with the old colonial Baptists under the leadership of Isaac Backus, an active Separate who was rebaptized in 1751 and became one of the most vocal religious leaders in the colonies. In the Norwich, Connecticut, Separate-Congregational Church, already mentioned, some members as early as 1746 stated their dislike of "the method of admitting adult persons to Baptism, and of Baptised persons owning the Covenants, and of children to Baptism." In fact, the Baptists gained ground after 1755 as the Separate-Congregationalists declined in strength, losing members either to them or to the established Congregational churches, most of which had reformed themselves along New Light lines by this date. The number of Baptist churches had risen from thirteen in Massachusetts and Connecticut in 1740 to thirty-one in 1760, and would increase by another twenty-two in the next ten years. Much of the impetus in this expansion came from the newly joined Separates, since among the old New England Baptists there was a great deal of resistance to the enthusiasm generated by the Great Awakening.

In the older areas of the southern colonies, the effect of revivalism seems to have been far less pronounced. Whitefield himself wrote of Maryland that ". . . Satan seems to have people captive to his will. The distance of the plantations prevents people assembling together. Here are no great towns, as in other provinces . . . the commonalty is made up of negroes and convicts; and if they are prepared to serve God, their masters, Pharaohlike, cry out, 'Ye are idle, ye are idle.' " Yet on later visits, he rode many hundreds of miles in Maryland and reported some success. "These southern colonies lie in darkness, and yet . . . are as willing to receive the gospel as others." On his first visit to Charleston, he preached in the dissenting church, reporting that "the auditory was large, but very polite. I question whether the court-end of London could exceed them in affected finery, gaiety of dress, and a deportment ill-becoming persons who have had a divine judgement lately sent among them. I reminded them of this in my sermon; but I seemed to them as one that mocked." In Virginia, Whitefield preached but little and seems to have done so among already-converted Presbyterians. Indeed, Whitefield spent relatively little time in the region from Maryland to South Carolina and did not make detailed reports of great triumphs there as he did of his visits in the middle colonies and New England. Yet he did write later that "God seems to be carrying out as great a work in Charleston as in Philadelphia," and of considerable successes in Maryland. In fact, these areas still need investigation.

Ecclesiastically, the effect of any renewal of religion in the South was certainly modest compared with that in the middle and northern colonies. Within the established Church of England, the same hostility that was found elsewhere greeted Whitefield and revivalism generally. In Charleston, the Anglican commissary even summoned Whitefield before a church court. It seems probable that the dissenting churches did benefit, but these were few. In

Maryland, little interest was apparent. Only in Virginia did the Awakening have easily discernible effects, mostly as a result of the missionary endeavors of Presbyterian preachers. Overall, the reasons for southern somnolence in the period lay not only with the counterinfluence of the established Anglican Church, the religious indifference of its leading southern upper-class members, the dispersed nature of settlement and the lack of a powerful Calvinist tradition awaiting revivification, but also with the fear of the effect of religious excitement on the slaves. But nor did Whitefield and other itinerant preachers make the southern colonies a major target of their endeavors. Had they done so, their religious history might have been very different.

In Virginia, an indigenous revival did occur with important results. In Hanover County, perhaps influenced by newspaper reports of the Awakening, a group of persons held private religious meetings for prayer and study which resulted in manifestations of "the power of the Lord, many were convinced of their undone situation, and constrained to seek deliverance with the greater solicitude." The movement spread and many withdrew from their parish churches, attending instead at "Reading Houses" where lay preaching took place. These groups later heard of the activities of New Side Presbyterian preachers in western Virginia and requested a visit from one of them, the Reverend William Robinson, who arrived in July 1743. Although the Virginians had called themselves "Lutherans," they quickly accepted Presbyterian discipline and a succession of New Side ministers arrived, who soon challenged the "morals" and the "public ministrations" of the established Anglican clergy. In 1745, several dissenters were hauled into court; a year later Whitefield "came and preached for four or five days, which was the happy means of giving us further encouragement and of engaging others to the Lord, especially among Church people, who received the gospel more readily from him than from ministers of the Presbyterian denomination." In 1747 the Reverend Samuel Davies settled in Hanover County as a permanent Presbyterian minister; he would play an important part in consolidating New Side Presbyterianism in eastern Virginia, where it grew in strength in several counties until the 1770s.

A greater potential for religious change came to the South, however, as newcomers moved into the back country. Presbyterian Scotch-Irish, after moving into western Pennsylvania and Maryland, entered the Great Valley and the Piedmont of Virginia. In 1738 the Synod of Philadelphia recognized its responsibility for their spiritual welfare and gained Governor Gooch's permission to send ministers and establish meeting houses. Itinerant ministers appeared at the same time, and in 1740 the first settled Presbyterian minister west of the Blue Ridge served the congregation of Triple Forks of Shenandoah, Augusta County. By 1748 there seem to have been four such settled ministers, who were joined occasionally by itinerant and supply preachers. This region was under the control of the Old Side section of the Presbyterians and was generally an area of conservative, nonrevivalistic preaching. Whether the New Sides would have made headway in western Virginia had they not been deflected to Hanover County cannot be known. In fact, after the end of the Presbyterian schism, the Hanover Presbytery assumed responsibility for Virginia as a whole. But Presbyterianism in eastern Virginia rapidly declined in strength and by the end of the colonial period its vital center lay firmly among the Scotch-Irish in the western part of the province. From Virginia, Presbyterians moved to North Carolina, and in 1770 the Orange Presbytery was established to care for the emerging churches of North and South Carolina, mostly located in the newly settled back-country regions.

Presbyterianism, although still weak in numbers of ministers and organized congregations, was nonetheless one of the strongest denominations to be found in the southern back country before the Revolution. After that date, it was largely supplanted by the Baptists and, to a lesser extent, by the Methodists. The Regular Baptists grew slowly in numbers, partly as the result of migration. By the 1760s there were perhaps a dozen Regular Baptist churches in the colonies from Virginia south, all in loose association and with some contacts with the Philadelphia Association. But the most vigorous Baptist growth in the south was a manifestation of the Separate-Baptist explosion of the Great Awakening. In 1754 a number of Separate-Baptists, led by Shubal Stearns, left New England under conviction of a divine call to missionize. These eventually settled on Sandy Creek, North Carolina, from where Separate-Baptists also successfully moved into Virginia south of the James River. After about 1770, the Separate-Baptists expanded in the Carolinas and grew phenomenally in Virginia.

As in the northern colonies, the rise of new religious bodies had wider repercussions. For a time it seemed as if the growth of Presbyterianism would bring conflict within Virginia. However, the Virginia government welcomed Scotch-Irish immigrants into the back country and tolerated Presbyterianism there as soon as it appeared. But ministers in the established Church did object to the growth of New Side Presbyterianism in eastern Virginia, since its luminaries, according to one Anglican parson, took "great pains to vilifie the Clergy of this Colony and have told their followers, both in public and private that they can never reap any benefit by going to hear them because they are not the Servants of God . . ." and its followers withdrew from their churches. Yet the latter point was not so serious as in other colonies, since there was a general shortage of churches anyway. But Samuel Davies gained a ruling that the Toleration Act extended to Virginia and, in 1755, the English Attorney-General ruled that the Virginia government could not put any limit on the number of Presbyterian meeting houses or on the movement of Presbyterian preachers. This was a defeat for Virginia Anglicans who maintained a considerable pamphlet war against the New Sides until the battle was lost. With the Separate-Baptists, the story was to be far different.

The Great Awakening has been viewed as the first great intercolonial movement in eighteenth-century America before the American Revolution. That this was true for the northern and middle colonies seems certain; for the southern colonies the evidence is thinner. And even in the New England and middle colonies, while revivalism may have had the same awakening effects on individuals, its ecclesiastical consequences were different, since the former had established churches and the latter did not. But in general terms, the Awakening further weakened the institutional structures of the colonial churches and the authority of the clergy and led to an even greater denominational variety. It also reinvigorated the religious feelings of many lay persons whose individual piety emboldened them to challenge both clerical and civil authority. These developments culminated in the disappearance of church establishments in the revolutionary and early national periods of American history and in the final subordination of clerical to lay power in the American churches. But perhaps more important, the Awakening brought a new lease on life to the Calvinist, millenarian tradition in America, in decline since the latter seventeenth century. Where this renewed tradition was also reformist and perfectionist rather than inward-looking, it provided a powerful source of support for those who resisted alleged encroachments on American liberties—political as well as religious—or who could identify civil and political changes with moral and spiritual progress.

C. Colonial culture

It has been argued that eighteenth-century revivalism expressed the reaction of the pietistic mind against the growing rationalism and humanitarianism of the time and against a growing secularism. Some of the more extreme pietists distrusted education, championing the unlettered but godly, some equated a retreat from worldliness with a retreat from the world. Conversely, opponents of the revivals published numerous tracts and books after 1740 explaining and applauding "rational religion" and condemning the emotionalism and the unreason of the Awakening. Some of the more pronounced rationalists became deists or agnostics, scorning most organized religions. Yet in general, in both Europe and America pietism and rationalism flowed like two parallel currents in the same river, widely separated at the extremities but mingling in the center. The great majority of revivalists recognized that the regenerate had to live with and in society. What kind of lives should they lead? What kind of society should they seek? The most common answers conflicted surprisingly little with those advocated by skeptics like Benjamin Franklin or anti-evangelical clergy like the influential Charles Chauncy of Boston: good and useful lives displaying benevolent and unselfish attitudes must be no less the concern of regenerate than of rational men. The practical sensibility though not the theology of many religious enthusiasts was similar to that of the proponents of rational religion, stressing particularly utilitarian good works, education, and material progress and improvement. Whitefield himself spent long hours over the affairs of an orphan house that he sought to establish in Georgia and in which poor children were to be taught useful trades as well as brought to God. He later unsuccessfully sought to transform it into an interdenominational degree-granting college.

This involvement of religion with utility is clearly shown in the stimulus given by the Great Awakening to the founding of schools and colleges. Numerous "academies" which attempted to duplicate the considerable achievements of the British dissenting academies were founded. Most were "under the care of skilful and pious Christians" and sought as pupils "pious and experienced youths," but their curricula were broadly based. The Reverend Francis Alison, head of an academy in New London, Pennsylvania, was an expert classicist who taught grammar, composition, belles-lettres, and natural and moral philosophy as well as inculcating sound religious principles. In the southern colonies, less directly influenced by the Awakening, there were no striking increases in the number of schools and academies, and on the frontier the church and the household were often the only institutions of education.

The most striking formal educational development, however, came with a proliferation of colleges offering degrees. In 1746 the first chartered New Light institution of higher learning, the College of New Jersey, was founded at Elizabethtown; in 1756 it moved to Princeton where it was later transformed into Princeton University. In 1756 the Philadelphia Association of Baptist Churches founded Hopewell Academy in New Jersey. By 1764-1765 the Baptists had created their first college, which moved in 1770 to Providence, later becoming Brown University. In 1766 Dutch New Light clergymen, led by the Reverend Theodore Frelinghuysen, founded Queen's College (later to become Rutgers University), which opened in 1771 in New Brunswick. In 1769 an enthusiastic New Light minister, the Reverend Ebenezer Wheelock, provided the impetus behind the founding of Dartmouth College, New Hampshire, which grew from an Indian and missionary school. From the start it was recognized that these institutions, although designed to provide a supply of educated clergy, could not survive as narrowly based seminaries. The College of New Jersey, for example, was open to all denominations and sought to provide a useful education for would-be professional men as well as ministers. Similarly, Queen's College, while its first statement of purpose referred to it as a "school of prophets in which young Levites and Nazarites of God may be prepared to enter upon the sacred ministerial office . . . ," was described by 1771 as providing an "education of youth in the learned languages, liberal and useful arts and sciences, and especially in divinity; preparing them for the ministry, and other good offices."

Such foundations also obviously reflected the competition between the larger religious bodies, all of which recognized that their future strength might depend on their control over the education of the young and their training of ministers in their own institutions. Nor should the understandable self-interest and ambition of the ministers be overlooked, for school and college teaching provided the learned among them with a better career than they could generally find as parish ministers and was usual in the Old World. In this connection the immigration of well-trained and career-minded Presbyterians and Anglicans to America in the eighteenth century was important, as was the return of Americans educated in Europe. Such men brought new ideas and a new professionalism. The teachings of the Scottish enlightenment, for example, flowed into the colonies with the arrival of graduates of Glasgow University; other Scottish- or European-trained men provided a professional medical community and were responsible for founding hospitals and medical schools.

The pietists were not alone in creating new schools and colleges. In New York a college projected in the late 1740s was founded as King's College (later Columbia University) in 1754, mainly under Anglican auspices, and was seen at its beginning as "a Seminary of the Church." Yet Presbyterian and latitudinarian hostility to this development was so powerful that Anglican control was never assured, although the student body was drawn predominantly from the ranks of wealthy Anglican and Dutch Reformed families. The curriculum, heavily classical in the first year, broadened to include logic, natural philosophy, mathematics, and metaphysics, and was very similar to that of Yale College. The college's aim, its president, the Reverend Samuel Johnson, had announced in 1754, was to teach students the learned languages, writing and reasoning, surveying and navigation, and other useful subjects—"everything useful for the comfort, the convenience and the elegance of life"—as well as their duty to God, "themselves, and one another, and everything that can contribute to their true happiness, both here and hereafter."

The other important foundation of the period was the College of Philadephia (later the University of Pennsylvania) founded in 1755-1756 with nonsectarian origins, since its inception lay in a movement promoted by Benjamin Franklin. Its first president, the Reverend William Smith, a graduate of Aberdeen, proposed a curriculum in which religious instruction played a minimal role. Although the Bible was to be "read daily," emphasis was given to ethical and moral philosophy rather than to the scriptures and their commentators; mathematics, natural history, geography, surveying, geometry, astronomy, politics, trade, and commerce as well as rhetoric and the classics were to be studied. In 1765 a medical department was opened. The utilitarian syllabus reflected the spirit of urban Philadelphia, while the middle-colony location of most of the new colleges testified to the general vitality of that region.

This expansion of formal education seems hardly to have affected the southern colonies. Not only did the school system not noticeably improve but no new colleges were founded. Sons of leading families were still sent abroad or, in growing numbers, to northern colleges for their education. Nor did the intellectual achievements of planter society compare with those of the northern and middle colonies. In Charleston a small scientific circle emerged by 1750 but it centered around Scottish-born and educated expatriate medical men, notably Drs. John Lining, Lionel Chalmers, and Alexander Garden, whose interests embraced epidemic diseases, botany, and natural history. Lining wrote the first competent American clinical account of yellow fever. Garden, who came to Charleston in 1752, became the South's leading botanist; the gardenia is named for him. He also tried without great success to interest South Carolina's planters in agricultural improvements. His numerous correspondents included Franklin, Linnaeus, and John Bartram, and he owned an extensive library and collection of scientific instruments. In Virginia British-born and -educated settlers also provided a focus for scientific inquiry. John Mitchell, who left the colony in 1746, was a keen student of botany and zoology; he also wrote a paper on "the Causes of the Different Colours of People in Different Climates." His later writings and his excellent *Map of the British and French Dominions in North America* were published after his return to England. John Clayton, who died in Virginia in 1774, collected material for the "best systematic treatise on American botany," the *Flora Virginica*. He arrived in Virginia about 1720 from England, where he was born and educated. Dr. William Small, who taught at William and Mary College from 1758 to 1764 when he returned to England and became a founding member of the famous Birmingham Lunar Society, helped revivify the college and began a Williamsburg society to encourage scientific experimentation and an interest in arts and manufactures. Small was Thomas Jefferson's teacher, patron, and later correspondent.

Nor did the South produce native-born and -educated men of letters. A recent study of Maryland reveals that its outstanding "men of letters" were not born in the province or in the colonies. Ebenezer Cooke, author of *The Sot-Weed Factor*, had probably arrived from England as a young man; Richard Lewis, the author of the first literary book published in the South, *The Mousetrap*, was born in England or Wales, and had been educated for some short time at Oxford, while the Reverend James Sterling, the best poet of the mid-eighteenth century, had already made a reputation in England before emigrating in 1737. The Reverend Thomas Bacon, the most prolific Maryland writer, was educated in England or Ireland, arriving in the colony in early middle age. One of the best known Marylanders of his day, Dr. Alexander Hamilton, founder of the Tuesday Club, an association of men with literary, scientific, and cultural interests, received his education in Edinburgh before migrating in 1739 at the age of twenty-seven. Another important spirit in Maryland's cultural life, Jonas Green, publisher of the *Maryland Gazette* from 1745, was a native of New England. Similarly, in Virginia not only scientifically curious men but the writing men—sermonizers, poets, essayists, and the like—tended to be British born and mostly British educated.

The southern planters remained consumers rather than creators of scientific and literary culture. More isolated and dispersed than their northern counterparts, they lacked communal facilities and leisure, although several had large libraries. Only in the more populous southern centers were clubs and associations that mixed sociability with practical or cultural ends founded. The Maryland Tuesday Club, organized in 1748, together with medical societies set up in some of the southern colonies before the Revolution, testify to the growing if still minor role of such typical eighteenth-century organizations of polite and learned men. However, by 1750 the printing press was firmly established in the Chesapeake colonies and in South Carolina; in North Carolina a printing press was set up in 1749. Southern newspapers also flourished. The *Maryland Gazette* first appeared in 1726, the *Virginia Gazette* ten years later, the *South Carolina Gazette* in 1734, and the *North Carolina Gazette* in 1751. But given the southern colonies' large population, their wealth, and their age, southern intellectual life lagged behind that of the middle and northern colonies. Not until the era of Thomas Jefferson and George Mason did the South produce native-born men of visible intellectual distinction. Their men of talent read widely, were able lawyers, and participated in government and in politics. They did not speculate or experiment or support an active culture.

In New England, by contrast—although education and cultural life remained Puritan—it was persistent and pervasive. Harvard became increasingly latitudinarian and worldly; Yale, renowned for its orthodoxy, suffered from the divisions of the Great Awakening. Both colleges officially maintained an emphasis on the education of the clergy, although increasing numbers of their graduates had secular careers. Throughout New England, while growing numbers of men and women embraced beliefs that would lead eventually to Unitarianism or to deism and which attempted to reconcile the Enlightenment with the Christian religion, the old compatability between religion, scientific enquiry, and other forms of learning persisted. Isaac Greenwood, a graduate of Harvard in 1721, visited England, where he preached in dissenting meeting houses. There, he also studied mathematics and natural philosophy, returning to Massachusetts to give public lectures on scientific subjects. In 1727 he became Hollis Professor of Mathematics and Natural Philosophy at Harvard and began a vigorous career, promoting Newtonian science. Other native New Englanders also pursued scientific interests. Of these John Winthrop, Greenwood's pupil and successor (at the age of twenty-three) at Harvard in 1739, soon possessed one of the best stocks of scientific books in the colonies and added substantially to Harvard's collection of scientific apparatus. Winthrop introduced the expanding science of the century to four generations of Harvard students. Specializing in astronomy, although he also published works on electricity, meteorology, and other subjects, he organized an expedition in 1761 to St. John's, Newfoundland, to observe the transit of Venus across the face of the sun. At Yale, Thomas Clap, rector from 1739 to 1766, although a strict and authoritarian Old Light Congregationalist who as late as 1754 stated that colleges were "Societies of Ministers . . . ," built up the teaching of science and mathematics, and elucidated "so many of the abstrusest theorems and ratiocina of Newton, that, [one did] doubt not, the whole *Principia* of that illustrious philosopher was comprehended by him." During the eighteenth century, even at Yale, the amount of time spent on the study of divinity gradually shrank.

Even so, the man most generally accepted as the outstanding New England intellectual was a clergyman, a theologian, and a minor philosopher, the Reverend Jonathan Edwards. Edwards's public career was straightforward. Born in 1703, in a prominent clerical family at Windsor, Connecticut, he showed an early precocity. After attending Yale (1716-1722), he spent eight months as a minister in New York, then returned to New Haven as a tutor. In 1726 he joined his grandfather, the Reverend Solomon Stoddard, one of the most powerful clerics of the time, as his assistant at Northampton, Massachusetts, becoming sole pastor on Stoddard's death in 1728. Twenty-two years later, Edwards was sacked by his congregation and spent the years 1751-1757 at Stockbridge, Massachusetts, an Indian mission, remote from the crowded world of the seaboard. Edwards was then invited to become president of the College of New Jersey, arrived there in February 1758, but died after a smallpox inoculation in March of the same year.

Edwards's contemporary reputation among nonconformists in Great Britain and America was high, and in recent years he has attracted considerable scholarly attention from professional theologians, historians, and Christians as a writer and thinker. His first fame came in the period leading up to the Great Awakening, of which he was one of the foremost American promoters. And his first work of real merit, the *Treatise Concerning Religious Affections* (1746), was a psychological study of religious feeling, partly aimed at distinguishing the working of true grace from its counterfeits. The same treatise also announced his return to the position that church membership should be restricted to the elect, a break with the Stoddardean tradition of open communion and one that, together with other controversies, brought Edwards's ouster at Northampton.

Edwards's other major works were written at Stockbridge: *A careful and strict enquiry into . . . Freedom of the Will* (1754); *The Great Christian Doctrine of Original Sin defended*, published in 1758; *Two Dissertations. The Nature of True Virtue and Concerning the End for which God created the World*, printed posthumously in 1765. In addition, two earlier notebooks of Edwards's printed in 1830 as *Notes on the Mind* and *Notes on Natural Science* have been given a special place in his thought, for the first showed a native ability to deal with advanced questions of epistemology and the latter, a mastery of Newtonian science.

Edwards was first and foremost a strict Puritan. Many of his writings reassert the fundamental position of past generations against contemporary critics. Against the Enlightenment belief that men were naturally virtuous and rational once properly educated or freed from the shackles of medieval superstition or unjust social arrangements, Edwards proclaimed that human history was a catalogue of proofs of humanity's innate depravity. In his work on virtue he declared that what the world called virtuous behavior was either instinctual or self-seeking; virtue could arise only in godly men from faith in God. By nature men were not benevolent or perfectible. Against the notion that men could move toward salvation by an effort of will, Edwards upheld the Calvinist idea of total depravity, roundly attacking in his sermons and writings in the period of the Great Awakening all belief that men could find salvation "by any manner or goodness of [their] own." Although he added the metaphysical idea that the will, once grace had been received, could actively combine and act with it, he asserted that man depended utterly on God for redemption. Against the open communion of his predecessors, he preached that church membership should be open only to saved Christians as far as this could be judged.

Edwards's whole view of life was therefore theological. He perceived mankind as God's creation and saw human history only in relation to the divine. He shared the hopes of his pietistical contemporaries that his own time might be one of providential conversion, of the rallying of mankind in a renewed faith. His proposed "History of the Work of Redemption" was at "first sight an uncritical retelling of the 'Christian epic' the Creation, the Fall, Saul, David, and the prophets, the life of Christ, the Reformation; it ends with a prophecy which is simply old fashioned chiliasm—the thousand-year reign of Christ, to be followed by the last apostasy, and then the Day of Judgement and the end of the world in flames." More unkindly, a modern historian, who considers Edwards to have been the "last medieval American—at least among the intellectuals" quotes a review of Edwards's sermons on the same subject, posthumously printed in 1774. They were considered by the English *Monthly Review* to be "pious nonsense," "an attempt to revive the old mystical divinity that distracted the last age with pious conundrums: and, which, having, long ago, emigrated to America, we have no reason to wish should ever be imported back again."

In his concentration on theological questions and his millenial hope, Edwards did stand at the end of a fading intellectual tradition, heroically resisting the sensibilities of the Enlightenment. Yet thousands of American and English nonconformists held these beliefs for decades after Edwards's death, and they were important in forming an ideology even when intellectually bankrupt. The seeming failure of liberalism and liberal theology in the twentieth century has also renewed contemporary interest in Edwards's writings. He possessed a powerful and original mind and spent hours each day in private study, pursuing the philosophical foundations of his beliefs, hoping eventually to produce a great "Rational Account" of the theological system which he espoused. In addition, he was no inconsiderable artist, using a vivid imagery and exhibiting considerable psychological skill. Yet his most profound modern admirer has also admitted that he seemed often to be struggling to free his ideas and that his writings are an "immense cryptogram." In this sense Edwards perhaps was the victim of his provincial situation, a man of great intellectual ability caught up in a system of belief that could not ultimately be set down in the language of reason. For Edwards was in his own eyes a rationalist as well as a believer, rejecting seventeenth-century Puritan scholasticism and its syllogistic reasoning and appealing instead to Lockeian and Newtonian ideas. Locke's epistemology, for example, provided Edwards with an explanation of how men could be said to know God and of the relationship between faith and knowledge. Edwards also claimed that "the mind don't only speculate and behold, but relishes and feels." On this assumption (and drawing on Platonic and medieval thought), he could write of the religious "affections" and support the revivalistic conviction that the Holy Spirit dwells "in the Saints . . . as in his temple . . . And he is represented as being there so united to the faculties of the soul, that he becomes there a principle or spring of new nature and life." But Edwards also warned that the operation of the Spirit was not to be confused with private revelations or secret voices. Many of those who claimed a new nature during the Awakening had been deceived or were deceivers, he wrote. The Word—and this had to be interpreted by authoritative spokesmen—worked equally with the Spirit.

Edwards's vision of Christian faith had by implication a social aspect: faith worked in the world. He wrote, "godliness consists not in a Heart to purpose to fulfill God's commandment but in a *Heart* actually to do it. . . . From love to God springs love to man, as says the apostle . . ." Edwards saw that good works, one scholar writes, "exhibit faith's own liveliness and thereby demonstrate the nature of faith." The new man was therefore a doer rather than a meditator, an ascetic, or a mystic. The Saints had to live in the world and their faith had to manifest itself in charity, acts of benevolence, and a love of neighbors. Although Edwards did little more than write abstractly of good works, his discussion could be fitted to any of the benevolent schemes of the day. His theology recognized the intimate association of practical morality with the aftermath of faith and the assurance of individual salvation.

Edwards symbolized the dominant religious strain in American culture and its practical undercurrents. Examination of the other great American genius of the colonial period, Benjamin Franklin, demonstrates that the growing shift to the secular under way at the same time had religious undercurrents. Franklin was in many ways shaped by the puritanism of his New England childhood and adolescence. He belonged to a generation whose morality of thrift, diligence, hard work, practical education, and outwardly virtuous behavior represented Puritan striving without Puritan faith. John Bunyan's writings and Cotton Mather's *Essays to Do Good* were among his childhood favorites. He confronted questions of religion in early life, found himself to be, and remained, a deist, a believer in good works, social religion, and the immortality of the soul, and an anti-metaphysician. "What is serving God? 'Tis doing good to man'," Franklin later affirmed under the guise of Poor Richard. More strikingly, he provided a secular counterpoint to the later Great Awakening belief in the growing influence for good of the swelling numbers of elect Christians. "There seems to me at present to be great occasion for raising a United Party for Virtue, by forming the virtuous and good men of all nations into a regular body, to be governed by suitable good and wise rules . . . ," he wrote in 1731.

Franklin's easily arrived at deism and his belief in virtue and good works—he was also a Freemason—nevertheless contrast strongly with the tortured metaphyisical analyzings of Jonathan Edwards. Also, while Edwards was introverted, unsociable, uneasy in company, and lacked self-confidence in his practical talents, Franklin had a quick wit, a fund of anecdotes, and an easy social style. He could as equally produce bawdy repartee in the club rooms as polished elegance in the salons. Adaptability, versatility, and self-satisfaction indeed marked his writings and his life, for his was the supreme American success story and he found the world in which he prospered to be good. One of his greatest best sellers was his annual *Poor Richard's Almanack*, first published in 1732, from which he later selected, in his most widely read book, *The Way to Wealth*, a series of proverbs and sayings that in simple phrases set out for the aspiring humble the road to fortune, the road Franklin himself was traveling. This side of Franklin, which advocated moderation, hard work, and the government of the passions by reason, envisaged the end of life as benevolently used worldly success. It typified the optimism of his age.

It was an optimism that together with other aspects of Franklin's mind and character the romantic mind would later find facile, trivial, or ignoble. But the facts of Franklin's own life, together with the experiences of many rising colonists, had produced and reinforced it. Born in Boston in 1706, a poor tallow maker's son, apprenticed at twelve, a runaway at seventeen, his early days were nevertheless spent in confident and useful study. By the age of forty-two he had made a satisfactory fortune in Philadelphia, his adopted home. Nor was it inapposite that Franklin should achieve success in the trade—printing—that brought the world of letters and ideas to the petit-bourgeois society of ambitious artisans in which he first moved. Printing, as well as occupying the central place in the dissemination of the ideas of the Englightenment, also brought Franklin a wider range of contacts—social, legal, and political—than any other trade could have done. Luck, to which successful genius is always tied, therefore early aided Franklin. Along the way to success he became clerk of the Pennsylvania assembly, Grand Master of the Freemasons of Pennsylvania, a justice of the peace, and deputy paymaster of Philadelphia and the promoter of any number of schemes for the improvement of the city. In about 1740 he had invented the Philadelphia fireplace or stove, which he announced to the world in a long pamphlet that characteristically explains the principles of heating as well as the utility of his device.

Residence in colonial Philadelphia was also a stroke of good fortune for Franklin, since its diverse population and rapid growth were associated with an increasingly lively and cultural life, in which Franklin himself acted as a catalyst. In 1743 he proposed the creation of a philosophical society, to be centered in Philadelphia but with members throughout the colonies. This American Philosophical Society would encourage systematic correspondence on useful and speculative subjects ranging from botany, medicine, mines, minerals, and quarries to mathematics, maps, and manufactures. In April 1744 a society was organized in Philadelphia but did not survive. In 1769 a new "American Philosophical Society, held at Philadelphia, for Promoting Useful Knowledge" was organized with 144 local members, 90 from other colonies and 17 foreign correspondents and was for many years the pre-eminent American learned society.

The scientific and utilitarian bent of the society was natural enough. Both the spirit of the Enlightenment and the practical and material needs of a still raw colonial society demanded it. Similarly, Franklin was a prime mover in suggesting the establishment of an academy for boys and youths in Pennsylvania, one that should promote not the classics but useful learning. This was opened in 1751. He also took a leading part in founding a hospital for the sick and insane, opened in 1755, was a director of the first American fire insurance company, and had a large share in equipping the first colonial ship to engage in Arctic exploration, a search for the Northwest Passage—for whose discovery the British Parliament offered a prize of £20,000. Shortly after, he reformed the postal service, speculated on and participated in Indian diplomacy, examined the nature of American population growth in connection with arguments against British Parliamentary legislation, wrote a plan of union for the American colonies, and entered Pennsylvania politics.

Franklin's activities therefore touched most sides of Pennsylvania's life. Yet he was more than a versatile promoter of learning and the public welfare. His earliest European fame came from his discovery of the electrical nature of lightning and other experiments, first recorded in his *Experiments and Observations on Electricity* published in 1751. These have led one eminent historian to declare that in the whole field of colonial science, he was the only American  whose work was "of such major importance that it is worthy of being recorded in every general history of scientific thought." Even so, his middle-colony fellows included Ebenezer Kinnersley, a Baptist preacher turned scientific lecturer and rationalist; Thomas Godfrey, a Philadelphia craftsman who invented an improved quadrant; and John Bartram, Quaker turned deist, a distinguished naturalist. Bartram's activities as a collector of botanical specimens brought him considerable fame and contact with the European scientific community. Indeed, the study of the correspondence of such men as Bartram and Franklin, together with that of natural philosophers in the other colonies, shows the close contacts that developed between British, European, and American scientists. Scores of articles by colonial Americans were printed in the Royal Society of London's *Philosophical Transactions* while a score or so residents of the colonies were proposed or elected as fellows of the society between 1730 and 1776. From this background was to emerge the most distinguished American scientist of the generation following Franklin, the astronomer David Rittenhouse, born near Germantown, Pennsylvania, in 1732.

Accompanying the expansion of schools and colleges, libraries and clubs, and the more learned manifestations of an expanding colonial culture were the voluminous products of the printing press. Many Americans gained their basic education from these, for they received little formal teaching. Washington, for example, seems largely to have been educated at home, while Franklin, who was taught to read at home, attended school only for two or three years and was "almost as wholly self taught as if he had never gone to school." By 1765 most colonies had printing presses; all, with the exception of New Jersey and Delaware, served by those of New York and Pennsylvania, also had newspapers. By the 1740s magazines were also being produced in Boston and Philadelphia, though none were long-lived. The colonial public was, indeed, well provided with imported or reprinted English works of every description, as well as many written at home.

Among the most popular works published in the colonies was the annual almanac, or calendar, which, like its English counterparts, sold in great numbers. Containing at first astronomical and weather information and predictions, chronological tables, practical advice, and details of coming events, they expanded by mid-century to "include the best of English poetry and prose, an infinite variety of essays on topics from anatomy to zoology, a wealth of vigorous political polemic, and every manner of practical advice, from remedies for minor diseases to hints on practical successful farming, from counsel on the management of household accounts to general advice on the conduct of life." By the same time various guides to every trade and vocation also sold well, as did such composite volumes as William Burkitt's *The Poor Man's Help and Young Man's Guide* (Boston, 1731) and Franklin's extremely popular *The American Instructor*. Besides giving information on letter writing, commercial bookkeeping, and other useful skills, such books emphasized an optimistic, secular, and rational view of the world. Young men with ambition were advised to master skills that would enable them to adapt to and make their fortunes in a bustling, business-oriented society. Even pietistic works had a distinctly utilitarian bent either in their purpose—the *New England*

Primer taught the elements of religion and reading at the same time—or in their overt message—Isaac Watts's colonial best seller, *The Improvement of the Mind*, while containing an evangelical stress on Christian conversion and conduct, was also "for all intents and purposes a utilitarian treatise on pedagogy suitable for self-education as well as formal teaching."

What colonial Americans could not read, see, or hear were good poetry, plays, music, and paintings created by their own countrymen. The Boston-born Franklin's achievements in science or the Pennsylvania-born Bartram's in botany were not matched in these areas. Although performances of English plays were held in the colonial cities from about the 1740s, American drama was almost nonexistent. The first American play, by Thomas Godfrey of Philadelphia, *The Prince of Parthia* (1765), set in Arabia, found few successors. Eighteenth-century pre-revolutionary poetry consisted mainly of feeble derivatives from English models, products of labor rather than inspiration. This was true even of Phyllis Wheatley's *Elegiac Poem on the Death of . . . George Whitefield* and her *Poems on Various Subjects*, although she had the distinction of being both a slave and a woman. Colonial painters were not generally remarkable for their talents. Although Benjamin West, born in Pennsylvania in 1728, later achieved great distinction, this was in Italy and England, where he lived from 1760 until his death sixty years later. Gilbert Stuart, born in Rhode Island in 1755, also lived in England for twelve years, returning to America only in 1792-1793. John Singleton Copley, born in Boston in 1738, possibly the greatest colonial painter, did achieve a measure of success in the colonies but left for England in 1775 never to return to America. Similarly, although choirs and chamber-music groups existed in small numbers, there were no American composers of great merit.

Yet this situation was natural enough in a provincial society still in a formative stage. And in political and religious writing, and to a lesser extent in historical writing, colonial Americans showed a greater maturity. The means were at hand to encourage an awareness of the distinct character of the colonists' own society and to extend their awareness of the American environment, especially the political environment. Part of an Atlantic cultural community with access to the classics, to philosophy old and new, to religious, political, and historical works, the educated American also stood on the threshold of perceiving his society as distinct and different from that of the Old World. What deserves comment is less the nonexistence of a high culture than the existence of this practical and generally pervasive emphasis on education, politics, improvement, and the written word.

Chapter Nine

Political Institutions and Political Culture

A. The English background

The Treaty of Utrecht of 1713 and the peaceful accession of England's first Hanoverian king, George I, in 1714 marked the beginning of a new era in English history and in Anglo-colonial relations. For contemporaries, Britain's successes in the War of the Spanish Succession brought new strength and promised further commercial expansion. The growing prosperity of English financiers and of many merchants and traders meant that they sought no great commercial or colonial reforms. Some members of the Board of Trade continued to press for the reorganization of colonial governments along lines suggested in the parliamentary bills of the first years of the century, but they gained little or no support. Indeed, for nearly thirty years neither the King's chief ministers nor Parliament effectively interested themselves in the basic constitutional and political structure of the colonies, and not until the 1760s did they take active measures to change it.

This quietism did not arise solely from growing economic complacency. During Sir Robert Walpole's long office, his skillful use of patronage and place enabled him to buy friends and exclude enemies more effectively than any previous minister. His encouragement of tranquility at home and overseas, of fiscal stability and foreign trade, aimed at diminishing controversy, stilling opposition, and avoiding crises. In colonial matters—-still of little concern to most Englishmen—the government had no need or wish to create political difficulties or disputes in England or America. The earlier policy of trying to reform colonial government and charters was largely abandoned. Walpole and his ministers, particularly the Duke of Newcastle, Secretary of State for the Southern Department from 1724 to 1748, who had formal responsibility for colonial affairs, utilized their positions mainly to serve their domestic political ends, doing little else in colonial matters.

So although the Crown took over the proprietary colonies of the Bahamas

(1717), the Carolinas (1725), and Georgia (1752), this occurred because of, and at the behest of, substantial interests in the colonies themselves rather than any aggrandizing zeal. Maryland and Pennsylvania kept their proprietary charters, and the two corporate colonies of Rhode Island and Connecticut, in spite of frequent criticisms from colonial officials, also remained substantially independent. Even Massachusetts, considered almost republican for its frequent disobedience of royal governors and direct royal commands, suffered no serious challenges. True, Parliament amended its charter in 1726 in order to improve its governor's position against the assembly. Yet nothing came of Massachusetts's constant and sustained refusal to vote a regular income to the governor. Indeed, as long as colonies did not become a burden on the Exchequer—and only Nova Scotia and Georgia received English government money—ministers did little to disturb their internal structure. Walpole, for example, to pacify English as well as American nonconformists, always refused to lend his support to plans to send a bishop to North America in spite of Church of England requests.

From about 1729 Parliament began to legislate with more frequency for the colonies. This does not mean that the legislature rushed in where the executive feared to tread. Parliament's concern was not with the charters or with the political or constitutional position of the colonies but with their commerce. Although proceedings aimed at bolstering the Crown's prerogative in the colonies began in both houses, these were haphazard and on one occasion almost accidental. Thus, attempts in 1734-1735 to pass an act obliging the King in Council to disallow any colonial law found detrimental to the prerogative or to trade, notwithstanding any privilege or limitation in colonial charters, found no general support. Similarly, in 1744 Parliament took no action on another request to strengthen royal power. While the Board of Trade and its officials wished for Parliamentary backing in reforming colonial administration and government, the ministry and, consequently, Westminster showed no anxiety to press for legislation on these requests.

Parliamentary legislation that was passed amended or added to mercantilist policies already established. Politically, this Parliamentary activity had imporance in that it involved the colonies more directly with English affairs. To get Parliament to grant them economic privileges or to resist threatening trade legislation, colonials had to lobby, persuade, cajole, and occasionally bribe. During the eighteenth century it therefore became common for colonies to employ agents to represent them in London, usually Englishmen knowledgeable in the policies and institutions of the metropolis. Temporary agents, of course, had been used by several colonies during the seventeenth century. In the next century British committees also seem to have favored the presence of permanent colonial agents in order to obtain accurate information affecting their administrative decisions. After the Peace of Utrecht the New England colonies and Virginia employed agents more or less continuously, and every colony did so over shorter or longer periods. These agents and representatives visited or were permanently employed in the capital, where they could argue, petition, and give evidence to government and Parliamentary committees. In 1730, for example, largely as the result of several years of pressure from its planters, South Carolina gained the right by act of Parliament to export rice directly to parts of southern Europe. Contrariwise, examples of unfavorable acts illustrate the victories won by English lobbyists over colonial opposition. In 1732 the manufacture of hats was forbidden in North America, and in 1750, the working-up of raw iron. By mid-century, the agents and friends of the colonies constituted North American interest groups that were among many that sought to influence policy and legislation.

On the whole, these North American groups lacked strength; certainly before 1763 they had nothing like the weight of the West Indian sugar interest or the East India Company, with their great wealth, their ability to elect and influence members of the House of Commons, and their friends and connections in the City of London and in government. Indeed, probably the most single important act of this period relating to the colonies represented a victory for the West Indians over other interest groups. The Molasses Act of 1733 laid heavy duties on rum, molasses, and sugar imported from the foreign West Indies into the British colonies. North Americans were prevented from acquiring cheaper sugar in the French West Indies. The act also threatened to lower the price of North American agricultural exports to the British islands, for without the ability to exchange their sugar for foodstuffs the French would no longer be able to compete for these. It also adversely affected London sugar refiners and merchants who expected to pay more for British West Indian sugar since they would be in competition with the American colonists and with Ireland. The reasons for this defeat of the colonists lay as much in the lobbying strength of the islanders as in the nature of their case; North Americans had few allies in high places and a limited direct influence on ministers and politicians.

Among the most effective friends of the northern and middle colonies in England were various individual and associations of religious nonconformists, themselves on the periphery of the English establishment. For example, the Presbyterians, Congregationalists, and Baptists, after various attempts at cooperation before, constituted a "General Body of Protestant Dissenting ministers of the Three Denominations" in 1727 and set up a lay body of "Protestant Dissenting Deputies" five years later that developed close contacts with American dissenters. Similarly, the Quaker London yearly meeting had various committees of a political nature that aided American Friends.

The one area to which English ministers did give attention was filling colonial offices. The number of important places directly available in the West Indies and America—from royal governor down to naval officer—perhaps amounted to some forty in 1702-1704 and some eighty-five by 1750. In addition, others were controlled by the Treasury, the War Office and other military departments, and the Admiralty and, at a lower level, lesser English officials involved in colonial affairs in England used or sought minor American places and profits—army lieutenancies or money in return for favors—to enhance their own positions. All in all, American patronage was a useful addition to the pool of positions at home. The function of patronage in eighteenth-century English politics is well known. Governments mainly used appointments to build, maintain, and encourage political support and to aid the family and personal connections of their members. Sometimes, office even rewarded merit, provided a patron of sufficient strength spoke for the meritorious. Colonial offices can be divided between those that needed the presence of the holder in the colonies and those (patent offices) that could be filled in America by a deputy. Politically, the latter were naturally the most advantageous. The Duke of Newcastle gave the office of Secretary of New Jersey to one of his chief political aides in 1733; the aide continued to work for the duke in England and drew an American salary for doing so; another man was made his deputy in New Jersey, a further bit of patronage. The occasions on which English ministers in the eighteenth century gave out American patent offices as part of their domestic political arrangements were numerous. In general, the choice of many colonial governors and most other officials tended to be determined by the strength and usefulness of their political backing at home. Thus, to take only two examples, offices in the recently royal colony of South Carolina went to friends and clients of Archibald Hutcheson, a man of influence with the newly enthroned George II with whom it was vital that the Walpole ministry continue in favor. Walpole's support north of the border was partly assured by generous gifts of offices to Scotsmen, mainly in the southern colonies.

In times of war, merit and proven ability might tend to count for more than powerful connections. Even in times of peace, governments sometimes favored men of ability with good political support over incompetents with weightier friends. Some colonial officials were highly skilled—Governors Shirley of Massachusetts and Gooch of Virginia, for example. Yet the appointments system did increase the complexity of imperial politics. A colonial governor might find himself without final authority over subordinate officeholders appointed by ministers in London. His own tenure of office might be made difficult or ended by a decline in the political power of his patron at Whitehall. Alternatively, his enemies in the colony might intrigue to have him recalled, using their political contacts in the mother country. Perhaps more serious, a colonial governor found his own powers of patronage limited by the great number of offices filled not by him but by the Crown and the ministry from England. He therefore had few offices to award to possible American supporters, which placed him in an uneasy situation. Moreover, many Americans felt excluded by the official system. Not only did colonial governorships or other high offices rarely go to colonists—partly since they had no political pull in England—but even their exclusion from lesser offices and gubernatorial circles often made up of English-appointed Englishmen made them resentful. They tended, therefore, to form their own political circles in many colonies, often in opposition to the governor's. And precisely because governors could not, as might have been the case in a similar situation in England, buy these men off with office, the process was self-perpetuating. English political stability fed in part on a patronage system that at the same time acted to weaken constituted English political authority in America.

The formal structure of English colonial administration changed little between 1700 and the 1760s. The Board of Trade continued as the central clearing house for colonial business. Yet the Board did not gain further ground in colonial matters or achieve the independent authority that it seemed to be winning before about 1707. This is most clearly seen in the fate of its recommendations for major changes in English policy and governmental practice toward the colonies. It suggested in 1721 abolishing proprietary governments, appointing a chief governor over all the mainland colonies, and ending sinecure offices and those held by deputies, and it requested a right of access by its president to the King, comparable to that enjoyed by the Treasury and the Admiralty. None of these proposals nor a later plan of reform put forward by the Board's leading member in 1739 found acceptance. The Board exercised many important functions as an advisory and supervisory body, but it never achieved parity with the great departments of state.

To describe this situation as the "decline" of the Board of Trade, as some historians have, is perhaps a misnomer. What in fact happened in the first half of the century was that the Board's early influence never developed sufficiently to carry it to the highest position in colonial administration. The Privy Council and its committees and the Secretaries of State retained and extended their authority as the arbiters of colonial policy while the King's ministers retained control of most colonial patronage, leaving the Board in a subsidiary position. In these circumstances, the Board of Trade lost competent members or no longer attracted powerful ones, becoming one among several lesser administrative agencies of government.

Yet there are signs that the 1740s, significant in this way as in so many others, may have been a period of revival for the Board of Trade and may have seen the beginning of a new English approach to the colonies. In 1748 Lord Halifax became president, since the need was now felt for an "efficient man at the head of the Board of Trade." Basic to this development was the growing realization of how the struggle with France was becoming centered in North America; successful military confrontation demanded strong executive control in the colonies, something sadly lacking in past years. These new circumstances now began to push colonial matters more and more into cabinet discussions. Concomitantly, the great value of the colonies to English trade was increasingly realized, and a new generation of imperialist-minded politicians

—Halifax, William Pitt, the Duke of Bedford in England; in America such governors as Shirley of Massachusetts and Dinwiddie of Virginia—urged the importance of America on the British political nation. In these same years a number of other developments took place: Nova Scotia was strengthened and subsidized, a packet boat service was established to facilitate communications with the colonies, governors were urged to greater efficiency and vigor in protecting the prerogative and upholding their instructions, and other reforms advocated. Moreover, Halifax secured greater responsibilities for the Board in 1752 and received the powers of a secretary of state, although without a title or a seat in the Cabinet. (In 1757 he was appointed to the Cabinet.) Colonial matters were taking on a new importance even before the Seven Years' War firmly focused British attention on North America.

B. Government in the colonies: the institutional framework

In the royal and proprietorial colonies by the beginning of the eighteenth century, institutional structures had become more or less standardized. From the point of view of English constitutional lawyers and colonial administrators, they fell into two broad divisions. First, the colonial governor and his council, all appointed by the Crown or the proprietor, shared a large number of directly conferred responsibilities and powers. Associated with them were such other officials as high court judges or naval or customs officers. Second, the colonial assembly, of which the council acted as an upper house, had the British government's recognition as the legislative branch, responsible especially for revenue and tax laws and for locally important matters in each colony. In theory, this mixed government provided its own checks and balances, but also gave the governor, by royal or proprietorial charters or commissions, greater final authority than the council or the assembly. In practice, on the other hand, the council and particularly the assembly had considerable powers, since without their cooperation effective administration and revenue raising could not take place.

The governor occupied the apex of formal power; royal governors' commissions, issued under the great seal of England, were the highest instrument of the royal will. As the King's official representative, the governor also ranked as first gentleman of the colony, entitled to such honors as a seventeen-gun salute and similar official courtesies. In civil matters, he controlled the bureaucracy, holding the colony's great seal, necessary to authenticate public documents, had authority to grant land, and was charged with overseeing the religious and moral life of his province. He also enforced customs and trade laws and could appoint places for fairs and markets. As commander-in-chief, captain-general, and (by a separate commission) vice-admiral, he exercised considerable military and some naval powers. Other rights in which the governor's was theoretically the major voice included the appointment of lesser judges, justices of the peace, and inferior officers and the issue of money from the provincial treasury to meet colonial expenditures.

Yet three facts of colonial life gave the governor great prestige and preeminence rather than great power. The first sprang from English policy in insisting on the appointment of about twelve councillors in each colony with legislative, judicial, and executive functions. The council acted as second house of the assembly, sat with the governor as the colony's highest law court and had responsibility for concurring with him in the exercise of many of his duties—granting land, summoning assemblies, appointing lesser officials, creating law courts, establishing martial law in times of war, and numerous others. In practice, these limitations could work against a governor; sometimes individual councillors caused considerable difficulties, or council majorities refused their support even when a governor sought only to follow his instructions. But since the governor could recommend names for council appointments and suspend refractory councillors, his own position remained predominant. Perhaps more important in weakening the power and influence of councils—and this weakening occurred over the eighteenth century—the Board of Trade itself discouraged them from assuming the role of colonial cabinets, sharing fully in policy or exercising the royal prerogative in conjunction with the governor. The governor alone, the English authorities stressed, had final powers, and these could be touched by the council only when permitted by his tightly drawn instructions. Also, the type of men who sought office as councillors usually had social and official ambitions, and in accepting a council seat they often tied their fortunes to that of royal government. If they then expected lucrative appointments or special recognition, they were advised to cooperate with the governor. Those who expected to oppose could often be more effective as members of the lower house. For all these reasons the council acted as a check but not as a formidable obstacle to the governor.

A second limitation on the governor's authority sprang from his lack of ability to reward friends and supporters, to build a following tied to him by the distribution or anticipation of offices or employments. The institutional reason for this came from the tendency of the home government to deprive royal governors of the power of appointment to most of the better-paid or more presitgious offices. Only occasionally, especially in times of war when military and financial activity led to an expansion of available offices and government contracts for supplies, did conditions exist when governors had adequate patronage at their disposal. Although there were exceptions, like New Hampshire, where Benning Wentworth, governor for twenty-five years, distributed a mollifying patronage in the form of timber contracts for the supply of the British navy, most colonial governors numbered inability to create a strong following among their most severe disabilities. Governor Sharpe of Maryland, for example, facing this problem, wrote that if the English proprietor cared "to leave the disposal of all those offices that are not bestowed on councillors entirely to myself and to signify to those who may apply to him that he is determined to take notice of no application for favor unless they come to him through my hands," he could make some steps to building up an influential following in the colony that would lead to moderation in the legislature.

The lower house of assembly, indeed, provided the third institutional check on the governor's powers. It, like the council, had been sanctioned by the Crown. Apart from the Dominion of New England, no ordinary colony was set up without an assembly; the English government always moved to create such legislative bodies, refusing to give colonial executives any exclusive rights of taxation or general lawmaking. Understandably, English authorities argued that assemblies that originated from Crown grants could be regulated by the Crown. The King's law officers, for example, wrote of New Hampshire that "the right of sending representatives to the assembly was founded originally in the commissions and instructions given by the Crown." To such arguments, many colonists replied that these grants merely recognized the inherent rights of Englishmen to representative government and that the lower house could function and develop its powers without Crown interference or sanction. These conflicting viewpoints, thrown up during arguments over policy, inevitably brought clashes between assemblies and governors, since the latter received minute royal instructions about the conduct and organization of the assembly. In particular, the governor had orders to exercise his rights of summoning, dissolving, and proroguing the assembly, of refusing to sign assembly bills, of accepting a speaker, of deciding on the representation of new districts, and of stating where a session should be held. In effect, such instructions conferred on the governor greater prerogative powers toward the colonial assembly than the King had over Parliament. This invited resistance from American assemblymen, who knew the history of representative government in England and modeled their claims on Parliamentary precedents. The Crown's decision to create colonial assemblies but to deny them full Parliamentary status involved governors in some of their greatest difficulties.

Members of the lower house were generally elected by a potentially wide electorate, although one that seems to have narrowed during the eighteenth century. Throughout New England a forty shilling freehold or a small amount of land usually sufficed for enfranchisement. In Pennsylvania, Maryland, North Carolina, and Delaware the ownership of fifty acres or a specified amount of property conferred voting rights, in New Jersey, a freeholding and property to the value of £50. New York's and South Carolina's voting qualifications were the most onerous, the former requiring a freehold of £40 from 1699 and the latter, very liberal to 1745, was then set at 300 acres of land or other real estate to the value of £60 local currency, widened in 1759 to the ownership of 100 acres of land or the payment of annual taxes of ten shillings. Such figures have been calculated as conferring voting rights on 50 percent to 80 percent of the white adult male American colonists, a large number by contemporary British standards. Yet Whiggish criteria still prevailed excluding servants, tenants, and small property owners from the franchise. Moreover, there is clear evidence that the colonists also accepted Whig notions of deference in returning propertied men again and again as their representatives. Indeed, political liberty remained associated with the rights of property and a franchise of property owners was accepted as part of the nature of things.

Colonial lower houses, in which men of substantial property elected by their peers and by lesser property owners stood forth as the representatives of local interests, therefore rested on powerful foundations. And they maintained or extended their existing powers throughout the eighteenth century. This is seen clearly in two areas. First, in most colonies, the assemblies fought and won lengthy battles with the British government over the governors' salaries. British administrators demanded a permanent grant of revenue to pay these, as existed in Virginia and Maryland, where the governor received money from a tax on tobacco exports. In most other colonies the governor tended to receive annual payments and gifts from the assembly that might be withheld during political disputes. Despite the Crown's fervent efforts, this type of arrangement continued in most colonies. Second, the lower house extended its already powerful control from raising revenue to its expenditure and auditing, earmarking sums for particular purposes, and appointing its own commissioners to supervise fiscal accounts. These actions directly countered British instructions that money should be disbursed on the warrant of the governor with the advice of the council and firmly associated the lower house with the direction of policy.

The whole process has been analyzed in detail by Jack P. Greene for the four southern colonies of Virginia, North and South Carolina, and Georgia. In Virginia the lower house early gained full control over money bills, over fees paid to officers for various services, over the erection of counties and boroughs and the apportionment of their representation, and over the appointment of most of its own officials. In general, governors identified themselves with the colony's dominant gentry, and there were few serious constitutional disputes between the lower house and Crown officials. Those that did occur usually represented novel challenges by a governor against burgess power rather than the reverse, particularly during the term of office of Robert Dinwiddie, from 1751 to 1758. In 1752 a serious conflict took place over fees charged for sealing land patents (the pistole fee) which the governor obtained a right to levy, backed by the Board of Trade. Although the Privy Council upheld the governor's position, it exempted certain patents and otherwise gave ground to the lower house which, for the future, continued to settle the great majority of fees. Dinwiddie also suffered a defeat when he attempted to restore a greater measure of gubernatorial control over church vacancies and to limit the powers of the assembly in setting up and regulating law courts.

The South Carolina Commons House of Assembly also had gained a large measure of control over the colony's government by a relatively early date, before the introduction of royal government; its major battles were fought with the South Carolina Council over framing money bills and supervising expenditures, controversies the lower house had largely won by the mid-century. By 1756 the whole basis of the council's constitutional position was under challenge, an attack that continued for the rest of the colonial period. The Commons House also resisted all British attempts to create a permanent assembly-financed civil list and maintained control over levying officers' fees. It also successfully disputed all moves by governors to control the apportionment of its seats or the creation of new constituencies and virtually nominated and controlled all officers concerned in handling the revenues that it voted. The Commons appointed commissioners to execute a multitude of local public works and services, despite gubernatorial objections, and divested governors of their patronage in church matters as early as 1704-1706. As in Virginia, harmony was broken more by new governors' attempts to alter the prevailing system than by assembly innovations. Governor Lyttleton (1756-1760) unsuccessfully attempted to check the Commons' control over finance so as to lessen his dependence on the house, while Governor Thomas Boone (1761-1764) precipitated a serious crisis in 1762 by challenging the validity of a colonial election in the hope of curtailing the house's powers in that area. The upshot was Boone's removal by the Crown and the vigorous rehearsal of arguments later to be used in challenging British authority before the Revolution.

In Virginia and South Carolina, the powerful planter gentry, the merchants, and the lawyers therefore managed to resist most challenges to an authority that they exercised from an early date through their control of the lower houses of assembly. In North Carolina, where this upper class emerged more slowly and less confidently, disputes seem to have been more equally conducted and more frequent. For three decades after 1729 an inconclusive quitrent controversy involving the governor's salary took place in which the lower house successfully refused to yield its position. Finally the Crown had to pay the governor, beginning in about 1754, from revenue raised in the West Indies. The house also conducted a vigorous opposition to various attempts to reshape and increase the constituencies from which its members were returned. Sectional divisions between the northern Albemarle region and the southern part of the province aided the governor, and the controversy continued from about 1731 to after 1763, with a majority in the lower house defying Crown orders. Other disputes involved the voting of revenue, the issue of paper money, the regulation of fees, and the patronage of church offices. By the 1750s and 1760s, although the North Carolina house had made less formally recognized intrusions into royal prerogatives than those of other southern colonies, it could usually prevent the colony's governors from strengthening their powers and rarely accepted any new policies that it did not approve.

The status of the lower houses was therefore considerable; moreover, they tended to act as other privileged corporate bodies did in the eighteenth century, consolidating and expanding their powers. The punishment and imprisonment of outsiders for insults and breaches of privilege by lower houses occurred more frequently indeed than did comparable attempts to indict political offenders by royal officials. In South Carolina the Commons resolved in 1733 "that it is the Undeniable Privilege of the Commons House of Assembly to Commit into Custody of their Messenger such Persons as they Judge deserve to be Committed" and denied that a writ of habeas corpus could be effective during the session of the house, while on numerous occasions all the lower houses forced critics to kneel and beg forgiveness for offending members. In 1749 the Virginia burgesses imprisoned the printer of the *Virginia Gazette* for publishing what they termed a libel against them. The lower houses had considerable influence over colonial printers whose livelihood might depend on receiving public business by assembly appointment.

In the southern royal colonies, the one exception to the generally powerful position of the lower house lay in the province of Georgia. The reasons for this are not difficult to understand and also underline the nature of the other assemblies' strength. In the Carolinas, the assemblies met and were established before royal government was introduced; in Virginia, the hiatus of the civil war years in the seventeenth century had provided a similar period of freedom from royal control before the resettlement of Governor Berkeley. Thus, through the eighteenth century, it tended to be the governors who challenged lower house strength rather than the lower houses which sought to make inroads on governors' powers. In Georgia no assembly met before the beginning of royal government; one was granted in 1754 simultaneously with the appointment of a governor. Nor did Georgia have a stable and prosperous society with a strong upper class. This and the fact that the British government, learning from its experiences elsewhere, tried to write in permanent limitations on Georgia's lower house, meant that even by 1772 the assembly was still subservient to the governor. The Georgia assembly, in fact, would only gain substantial powers after royal government disappeared from the colony.

North of Virginia royal governors also found themselves at disadvantages with their assemblies. The earliest colonial assembly had met in Massachusetts in 1634. By 1692, when the first regular royal governor arrived, the traditions and institutions of the province were fixed, only to yield slowly or not at all to the new charter government. In New Jersey royal government began in 1702, though the colony had no separate governor until 1738 and the assembly represented an amalgam of that of East Jersey's begun in 1664 and West Jersey's begun in 1675. In New Hampshire, the assembly first met as late as

1680 but its members had absorbed New England political principles and from 1698 it shared a royal governor who gave most of his attention to Massachusetts. No separate governor was appointed until 1741. New York's assembly was the weakest. The body, approved in 1683, existed for only two years. After Leisler's rebellion, the new governor faced an inexperienced lower house, though one whose members had learned from neighboring colonies.

The political history of these governments certainly reveals one or two distinct patterns. In Massachusetts the lower house pressed every governor hard for control of provincial expenditures and defeated every English attempt to gain a salary for him until the issue was dropped by Whitehall in 1735; it also disputed rights of the council in matters of expenditure and intruded itself into the conduct of military matters and Indian alliances. Although in 1743 the assembly lost the right to fix its own constituencies in the case of newly incorporated towns and districts, this hardly mattered since no governor could control even the existing house. Governor Belcher suffered consistent majorities against the Crown's fiscal policy and eventually failed in a desperate attempt to purge his opponents from government. William Shirley, governor for sixteen years to 1757, was successful only because he could conciliate local political interests by concessions in a period of expanding opportunities. At the end of his career, these opportunities had diminished and his successors found renewed problems.

In New Jersey, the assembly met only once from 1730 to 1738 when Lewis Morris became its first separate governor. Summoned in that year, the assembly immediately rejected a plea that he be paid a salary and strenuously defended its exclusive rights to attend to money bills. During Morris's entire administration until his death in 1746, his meetings with the assembly were notable for what each side refused to accept rather than for actual legislation; in one session the only public act passed was for the destruction of crows, blackbirds, squirrels, and woodpeckers in three counties! More common ground was found under his successor, the former governor of Massachusetts, Jonathan Belcher, who served until 1757, but serious conflict between the council and assembly left the government unprovided with tax support for several years. Yet the chief impression given by the detailed study of the colony's political affairs before 1763 is not so much one of constitutionally principled conflict as of rural meanness. Nevertheless, it is certain that in New Jersey no governor who wanted to achieve useful public legislation could afford to encroach on assembly privileges.

In New York by mid-century the lower house had also won formal control over vital areas of government. It consistently refused Crown instructions, abandoned as hopeless in 1755, that the governor be granted a regular salary.  By 1709 its control of specific financial appropriations had reached the point where it "deprive[d] the governor and council of all discretion in issuing warrants." It was soon to appoint its own commissioners to examine the accounts and to seize control of money granted for extraordinary (usually defensive) expenses by requiring that these moneys be lodged with a provincial treasurer appointed by itself. By 1730 assembly control of all revenues was lodged in the house and by 1739 salaries to royal officials were "paid by name and amount, a provision which curtailed the governor's powers of appointment; for, if he did not appoint officers acceptable to the Assembly, that body would grant no salaries." The assembly also had a large influence in military affairs, arising from its control of finances.

In the proprietary colonies, Maryland and Pennsylvania, the proprietors had direct concern in land and fees and some taxes; their colonies represented a business from which they sought to derive immediate profit. At the same time they had to superintend their ordinary administration. Whether this double role made the opposition that they experienced any more severe than that suffered by royal governments can be debated; it certainly did nothing to lessen the strains between proprietors and representative assemblies, who interested themselves in the former's profits as well as their public policies. In Maryland the proprietor, restored to authority in 1715, faced an assembly that had been vociferous since the middle of the seventeenth century and had gained in strength during the period of royal government. Perhaps more than any other North American lower house, that of Maryland self-consciously modeled itself on the House of Commons and even went beyond it in the powers that it demanded, gradually, for example, excluding placemen from the house. Yet part of this self-consciousness may have arisen from an appreciation of the considerable powers of the proprietor in appointing and controlling large numbers of officials to supervise land sales and rentals and his successes in fending off the attacks of the lower house in such basic matters as the appointment of sheriffs, his veto powers, and his attempt to prevent it from maintaining an agent in England. In spite of numerous resolutions and assaults in the previous thirty-five years, the lower house in 1750 had to admit that it enjoyed a less favorable position than did the lower houses in the royal colonies. By 1764, writes a leading authority, "the sixth Lord Baltimore had been deprived of no revenues and no claim of prerogative which his father had had in 1733."

In Pennsylvania, the assembly undoubtedly had greater powers than its counterpart in Maryland, for Penn had been forced to concede large privileges in 1701. Nor did the province have an upper house, for the council had no formal legislative powers. But there is evidence that governors tended to consult it about bills sent to them from the assembly, giving it some extra-constitutional authority. Politically, the assembly was dominated for many years by Quaker politicians, who benefitted from the favorable representation of the eastern counties and from a reputation as defenders of the inhabitants against proprietary threats to their liberties. In essence, the situation resembled that found in most other colonies, with tensions between executive and legislative occasionally resulting in head-on collision, especially at times when the proprietary tried to increase its authority. One key to Pennsylvania politics from about the 1740s onward was, in fact, the renewal of proprietary ambitions to check the powers of local politicians and to promote what was felt to be a "mixed" government in which the lower house's "popular" rights would be balanced by increased executive prerogatives. In turn this led to calls for the final destruction of the proprietary and the creation of royal government.

More fundamental hostilities toward the proprietary government than in Maryland, therefore, seem to have characterized Pennsylvania politics. Yet the situation was more complex than in the relatively homogeneous and closed Chesapeake society. First, Pennsylvania as a center of immigration absorbed large numbers of Scotch-Irish and Germans, who eventually became antipathetic to Quaker rule; second, its location and exposed frontiers by the 1750s created a need for defensive spending that caused great difficulties for the pacifist Friends. Finally, the Penns were effective landlords, owning territory that they neither wished to be taxed nor settled without the payment of rents. Out of these conditions came a factionalism that cut across the simpler opposition between executive and legislative and gave opportunities to all sides for maneuver and counter-maneuver. By 1763 the proprietary government remained in a strong position.

The corporate colonies of Rhode Island and Connecticut escaped the imposed framework of an English-appointed executive working with an American-elected lower house. In both colonies the governor and council were annually elected and had far fewer formal powers than in the other colonies. Nor were they bound by many English instructions. For these reasons, a politics of confrontation was avoided and one of accommodation made easier. Political controversies, in fact, tended not to bring the framework of government into question or pit executives against legislatures but to engulf both. In Connecticut old ideas of deference to godly rulers died hard, and neither governors nor councillors once chosen tended to be voted out of office in subsequent elections. Indeed, in the 100 years after 1689 Connecticut had only eleven governors and ninety-eight different councillors, and only two eighteenth-century governors failed re-election. Yet, political controversies could be violent. In Rhode Island, a similar institutional framework existed, although factionalism began earlier and became more intense, and the same deference did not surround the higher offices of government.

This skeleton survey reveals how the possibility—even the probability—of tension and conflict between executive and legislature was implicit in the structure of most colonial governments. It also demonstrates that assemblies were more confident in their powers, less on the defensive, than governors. Yet tension did not necessarily mean critical instability, nor assembly powers mean gubernatorial impotence. Although colonial governors lacked adequate patronage, frequently complained about the weakness of their prerogatives, and often painted a picture of imminent royal decline in colonial America, they still occupied a central place. Controlling some offices and dignities that ambitious men coveted and successful men expected, they stood as the Crown's representatives at the center of a web of deference and jealousy, of respect and resentment that offered scope for the skillful as well as pitfalls for the incompetent or the unlucky. Their personalities as well as their policies formed an essential component of colonial government. Similarly, the council, no matter what its corporate weaknesses, gave further opportunities and more power to many already well-to-do and established individuals who had even greater access by virtue of their membership to favors, money, and contacts. In Virginia the councillors mainly consisted of members of the leading families for whom office was as much the recognition as the source of influence, and the same was broadly true of all the colonies. Even in Massachusetts, where council membership was elective, councillors tended to be wealthy merchants, lawyers, and property owners and to hold other important civil or military positions.

Governor, council, and lower house constituted the most elevated and have been the most studied elements in the system of colonial government. Nevertheless, the country farmer or the town shopkeeper may have been much more frequently concerned with local government and the law courts. Here, the system seems to have worked relatively well. True, the subject of the tenure of judges became a political issue from about the late 1750s, with colonial assemblies pressing for it to be granted during good behavior, in order to render judges irremoveable for political reasons rather than at the Crown's or governor's pleasure. True, disputes occurred over the erection of new courts, over legal fees, and the manner of appointing judges and justices. Yet the ordinary legal and administrative proceedings of all kinds of courts and their structure attracted little criticism or political hostility, and the law, from a position of umpopularity and disfavor in many colonies in the seventeenth century, became an attractive career for many colonial Americans in the next. With few exceptions, local government and law courts were quickly requested and often quickly extended to areas of new settlement. In fact, while some reforms were sought in the law after the American Revolution, the system of the law courts was hardly changed and provided an essential element of continuity between colonial and independent America.

Similarly, other local government institutions met with little fundamental opposition, molded as they were more by internal American forces than by the Crown. The town meetings and county governments of the northern and middle colonies and the parishes and counties of the southern colonies were not attacked in themselves, except for the incidental abuses to which they sometimes gave rise. What reforms took place in them and in the various kinds of town corporations that existed in the colonies proceeded from the need to adapt them to growing populations and changing practical needs. In particular, the system of appointing special boards and agencies to replace the earlier quasi-judicial, quasi-voluntary organs of local government continued throughout the eighteenth century, paralleling similar developments in England. But these were rarely politically contentious matters.

Overall, it is arguable that for the period before 1763 historians have concentrated too exclusively on the growth of assembly powers, the relative weakness of the colonial governors, and on the strife that seemed to mark the political history of most colonies during the eighteenth century. American politics should not be characterized as a dress rehearsal for the American Revolution, and historians should not seek out only those elements that appeared to portend its coming. In many areas of government and for substantial periods of time assemblies and governors worked together in relative harmony, passing much legislation that met with general approval. Even in the numerous periods of conflict, it is sometimes difficult to draw the line between what contemporaries accepted as a normal and acceptable clash of opinion and attitudes and what may be regarded as abnormal, peculiarly violent, fundamentally unstable. The system, after all, survived and worked for more than a century in which great pressures from a rapidly rising population, warfare, and the expansion of settlement existed. Fewer men expected fewer results from government in the eighteenth than in succeeding centuries. Nevertheless, it is clear that the institutional framework did interact with specific and urgent controversies to give rise to a powerful political culture which emphasized the necessity to limit and check the powers of government. After 1763, new conditions brought the system into crisis.

C. Political culture and political controversy

Most colonists accepted the British constitution as a simple model for their own political institutions. Fully believing that their happiness could be secured by achieving a full measure of English law and liberty in America, they, like their contemporaries at home, saw the British constitution as a mature compromise formed by centuries of struggle and confirmed by the Glorious Revolution and the Hanoverian succession. In the British system of mixed government, the threats of a too powerful Crown or a too powerful popular order were checked by the necessity that both should participate in governing and legislating. Together with this balanced authority, the great tradition of English law, accepted equally by King, Lords and Commons, ensured the liberty of the subject and the protection of his property, administered as it was by independent judges, "one main preservative of public liberty . . . in some degree separated both from the legislative and also the executive power." That the structure of colonial governments to an extent conformed to or resembled this pattern, together with the everyday truth that these governments generally permitted the colonial elites to pursue their own vital interests, explains why for sixty years the colonial assemblies did not seek to annihilate royal or proprietorial prerogatives.

Yet even the acceptance of this simple model of the British constitution caused difficulties and tensions. Acceptance produced the argument that each colonial government was a miniature of the mother country's; by analogy, the powers of the colonial lower houses ought to be as full as those of the Commons and the formal powers of the colonial governors as limited as those of the English executive. But as Bernard Bailyn has recently reminded us, formal Crown powers in America were greater than those in England in ways that directly affected the position of the assemblies. First, as the Crown no longer did in England, the colonial executive could veto assembly legislation, as could the British government itself; indeed, governors were instructed to apply automatic vetoes to certain types of law and to accept some others only with the proviso that their operation be suspended until positive approval came from the imperial authorities. Second, most governors could summon, prorogue, and dissolve their assemblies at will, rights that the Crown had lost over Parliament in England. Third, judges could be dismissed and some types of court erected by the executive alone, without necessary reference to the assembly. These formal differences at times combined with particular issues to create kinds of political conflict that their resolution in England had now made obsolete.

There also existed a positive animus on the part of some colonial governors to the political claims of the colonists. Faced with unruly lower houses, these men did not hesitate to show their hostility, making known to the British government their views that the system ought to be amended. Governor Shute of Massachusetts wrote in 1716 that he "found the House of Representatives, who are elected annually, possessed of all the same powers as the House of Commons, and of much greater . . ." and complained of the "levelling spirit" and "mutinous and disorderly behaviour" of the colonists. Any councillor whose election he negatived, he wrote, was immediately returned as a member of the lower house. "Things can never go well in the colonies whilst the planters are so generally proud, petulant, ignorant, and have the common necessary support of government so much under their thumb," wrote Governor Calvert of Maryland in 1729. Other governors were sure that the colonials drew strength from commonwealth or republican principles. Governor Nicholson in South Carolina complained in 1724 that the "spirit of commonwealth maxims both in state and church is increasing here daily," and Governor Morris, some twenty years later in New Jersey, believed that the assembly adopted "the model of the Parliament of 1641 and that of their neighbours Pensilvania and New England, and that unless some measures are taken in England to reduce them to proper limits I suspect they will not mend much." Certainly, in the less amenable colonies it was a common complaint of officialdom that the lower houses themselves had subverted mixed government by assuming overmighty powers reminiscent of those of the civil war Parliaments in England. "In proportion as a country grows rich and populous," wrote the Reverend William Smith of Pennsylvania in 1755, "more checks are wanted on the powers of the people; and the government by nice gradations should verge more and more from the popular to the mixed forms." Certainly, too, civil servants in England abhorred the reports of legislative tyranny or obstinacy that came constantly from America and prepared several elaborate but unexecuted schemes for remodeling colonial constitutions.

Governors and officials had some grounds for their complaints. For while they stressed the need for authority, obedience, and firm executive action, their opponents characteristically announced that their political power should be limited in order to protect society from oppression and arbitrary rule. The roots of this colonial emphasis on the dangers of overpowerful governors lay in the seventeenth-century origins of the colonies, particularly in the antimonarchical sentiments of the civil war period that had been brought to America by Puritan New Englanders and other Protestant émigrés. And a political ideology appeared in England after about 1675 which was to gain enormous strength in the colonies. This ideology, complex in its different strands, derived from earlier civil war political thinking, particularly from the writings of James Harrington, and from a group of republican or near-republican theorists who drew on historical experience. For these reasons it has been correctly described as "republican" or "commonwealth." Yet many of its creators and those elaborating on it were not republicans but men alarmed by the advances of absolute and arbitrary monarchy in Europe since the fifteenth century, who feared its establishment in England. They therefore drew from the classical-renaissance-republican tradition and from other sources a battery of arguments for limitations on rather than the abolition of monarchical-governmental power. They characteristically stressed, as Penn had done, the existence of an ancient English constitution that at all costs had to be protected from the attacks of state power. Because such arguments usually identified the Court, that is, the administration—the King's ministers, his officials, and their allies among the moneyed men of the City of London—as the powerhouse of expanding absolutism, and because they were often proclaimed by men claiming to represent the independent freeholders of the realm, especially the country gentlemen, the label of "Country" philosophy has been given to them. By the 1690s an identifiable circle of writers and pamphleteers were developing extensive, interlocking arguments against William III's Whig court "which they denounced for governing through influence and standing armies and for boosting the expenses of government in the form of high taxation, national debts, and (yet again) influence and corruption."

The Country philosophy, as summarized by J. G. A. Pocock, saw "Society [as] made up of court and country; government, of court and Parliament; Parliament, of court and country members. The court is the administration. The country consists of the men of independent property; all others are servants." Parliament, Country writers felt, ought to supervise rather than support government—the Whigs believed the reverse, perhaps—since governments by nature seek too much power. In England the executive seduced members of Parliament from their proper supervisory function according to Country philosophers. It "seduces [them] by the offer of places and pensions" and other methods to support administrative measures that increased executive control—schemes for standing armies, national debts, and an excise—and gradually whittled away at liberty. To check this process demanded constant vigilance, the expulsion of placemen, and frequent election of members of Parliament by an uncorrupted electorate. By the time of Sir Robert Walpole, these lines of attack had been fully developed and with some justification. Walpole's government, his many critics argued, consisted of a great conspiracy of ministers, moneyed men, and corrupt officeholders; it manipulated public affairs and it milked the state for private profit. Such a system threatened absolute tyranny since it made the executive irremovable by normal political means, sapping the energies of the political vigorous with a shower of bribes and privileges. Sir Robert, stated Lord Bolingbroke, controlled Parliament by his manipulations of "*honors, titles,* and *preferments* . . . with *bribes*, which are called *pensions*," with "the lean reward of *hopes* and *promises*," with the use of "a set of *party names*, without any meaning, or the vanity of appearing in favor at *court*." Yet these charges, until revived in a different shape and context in the reign of George III, had little power in English public affairs. Country philosophy in England often seemed an outcome of the clash of faction and was swamped by the official Whig philosophy of the day with its emphasis on the perfection of the British eighteenth-century constitution.

In America, as Professor Bailyn has convincingly demonstrated, the case was different. Such ideas did quickly find their way to the colonies, where they became an active ingredient in American political culture. Two of the pamphleteers of early Hanoverian England, John Trenchard and Thomas Gordon, authors of the *Independent Whig* and *Cato's Letters*, "were republished entire or in part again and again, 'quoted in every colonial newspaper from Boston to Savannah,' and referred to repeatedly in the pamphlet literature." These writings together with those by Benjamin Hoadly, the leading low church Anglican Whig theorist, and by Lord Bolingbroke and other lesser-known polemicists were read more widely than the supposedly standard writings of John Locke. They provided the philosophical cum historical foundations for a language of politics that spoke immediately to Americans.

It was a language that defined liberty in terms of an ancient constitution, "the *fundamental* laws and liberties of England . . . a collection of ancient privileges from the common law ratified by the suffrage of the people and claimed by them as their *reserved rights*"—rights that even Parliament could not overthrow—and in terms of the balance of powers within a mixed government. Liberty in America, since executive agencies—British ministers or colonial governors and their officials—always tended to seek larger and larger powers, depended on the steadfast defense of ancient or charter privileges by an uncorrupted people and their elected representatives. Strong also among many Puritan New Englanders from the seventeenth century and growing in the minds of many other colonists throughout the next was the view that America, either because God so willed it or because of its simple new society, was particularly the home of untainted liberty and freedom. Conversely, as James Burgh stated in 1764, following a host of British writers, Britain was halfway down the road to corruption "so great is the influence of the crown . . . so servile the spirit of our grandees and so depraved the hearts of the people." Pride in an uncorrupted Englishness, in the establishment of English liberties in America, and in the undefiled English constitution and a sense of colonial distinctiveness from the growing corruption and venality of English life therefore formed an increasing element in eighteenth-century colonial political culture even in the years before 1763, when the crisis in English-American relationships brought such ideas to a full and general flowering. Yet, the actual threats to colonial liberties were minute. Standing armies were unheard of and the colonial executives were weak and unable to coerce the powerful and vital colonial assemblies. In England, where ministerial government was seemingly onmipotent, such radical sentiments appealed only to a small and powerless although vocal minority. In America, where near popular government seemed well established, "opposition thought . . . was devoured by the colonists. From the earliest years of the century it nourished their political thought and sensibilities."

Part of the solution of this paradox might be that such fears justified the *status quo* in the colonies against the actual or imagined proclivities of royal and proprietary governors, leading back to the fact that the gravest political controversies in many colonies took place when governors attempted to alter the prevailing system. Joined to this was perhaps an often unconscious resentment against the very fact of the limited nature of gubernatorial patronage and the ability to reward. This situation excluded all but a small section of the colonial elite from executive authority and favor, producing suspicion or hostility where largesse might have brought compliance, as it did in England. Nor should the use of the language of opposition as the tool of faction be overlooked, for it was the convention that ambitious young men should seek power by discrediting those in authority, only to defend in office the very prerogatives which they had so fiercely attacked in winning it.

Perhaps more important was the fluid and expanding nature of colonial society. The diversity of religion, the hunger for land, the desire for wealth, and the pressure of a growing population injected highly contentious because fundamental issues into the political system. Questions of religion, land, and money plagued colonial politics in ways not then experienced in the more oligarchical, settled, and stable mother country, where an established upper class had such matters firmly in hand. Many colonies lacked a secure upper class, and in those where an elite existed its interests, for it participated in the controversies arising from an expanding society, often lay as much in challenging certain imperial policies as in supporting them. The imperial authorities could not indeed fully satisfy elite political aspirations for a dominant voice in government without destroying the colonial relationship. Moreover, colonial governors, themselves of diverse backgrounds and skills and often serving for only short terms in any one colony, stood outside the colonial social and political spectrum. Unlike English ministers, they had not gained power by a process of selection within their own society. English ministers benefitted from their birth, wealth, experience, and their feeling for the shape of power, politics, and society in England. Few native Americans became governors of their colonies in a parallel fashion, while the colonial councils which included men of this type were forbidden semi-ministerial responsibilities with the governor.

Although the full political history of the colonies before 1763 has not yet been written, enough evidence exists to show that in times of stress men did draw on the political sources discussed above, sometimes attacking authority with surprising vehemence and hostility. Within New England the political history of Connecticut illustrates that even in a colony with annual elections of the governor, council, and lower house and ample freedom from imperial interference, bitter controversies developed. There, the divisions caused by the Great Awakening, by growing pressure on land from a rapidly expanding population, and by farmer-merchant and popular-gentry antagonisms created several decades of political struggle after 1740. The New Lights, whose strength came from the populous, even crowded, eastern counties won control of the assembly in 1765; in 1766 the electorate turned out the governor and several assistants, an almost unheard-of practice. For Rhode Island and New Hampshire there is no satisfactory study of politics in the earlier eighteenth century. In Rhode Island the farmers demanded paper money, and in Newport, developing as a commercial center, the merchants opposed them. In New Hampshire the assembly resisted Crown prerogatives in the usual manner—rowing with Governor Belcher in 1735, for example, over his attempt to interfere in its judgment of elections and gradually asserting its control over finance as well as refusing to vote the governor a regular salary. But from 1741 in New Hampshire the new governor, Benning Wentworth, began a term of office which lasted for twenty-six years and which demonstrated that a native-born colonial governor who had adequate contacts in his own colony and in England, and adequate patronage, could create as stable a political system as any Walpole. Moreover, Wentworth's long rule does not seem to have inspired a radical opposition. Serious disputes with the House of Representatives lasted only until 1752, and although an unsuccessful attempt was made to oust him in

1747-1748 by political enemies who condemned him as a prerogative man, this campaign was carried out largely by addresses to England and little attempt was made to stir up popular feeling. New Hampshire had no printing press and no newspaper until 1756, which aided court control.

By contrast, the largest New England colony, Massachusetts, saw the earliest use of the political tract and the newspaper, and an early dissemination of opposition ideas. The Reverend John Wise, writing in 1717, for example, displayed an acquaintance with English Country writings including Henry Care's very popular *English Liberties* (possibly written by William Penn), Thomas Gordon's writings, and other obscurer productions. Wise followed their argument that a flourishing society depended on a balanced constitution and that the best government "Clogs Tyranny, Preserves the Subject free from slavery." He felt a vigilant public should ensure that assaults on the "Pillars of English Liberty" were exposed and punished. Wise's Country philosophy lay very near orthodox Puritan political thinking but it lacked the counter-stress on respect for authority. Another early promoter of similar ideas was the weekly *New England Courant*, first published in 1721 by James Franklin. This newspaper announced that the instruction of its readers in their liberties was its first goal. It reprinted numerous extracts from the *London Journal* where Thomas Gordon and John Trenchard were contributing letters under the signature of "Cato." From this time onward opposition to government measures was likely to enunciate and justify itself by reference to radical Country ideas. In 1750 the Reverend Jonathan Mayhew delivered a sermon, *A Discourse Concerning Unlimited Submission*, considered by one authority to be the first political tract of the American Revolution, and denounced by his opponents as a mere plagiarism of Hoadly, Trenchard, and Gordon.

Ideology, of course, arose from clashes on particular political issues, and the strength of opposition, from the inability of government to control a lower house, consisting mainly of the independent representatives of numerous small country towns. In Massachusetts an early division of opinion revolved around the problem of paper money and currency. In 1739-1742 there was a serious political crisis over the question of issuing paper money against the security of land, mortgaged to a Land Bank, which ranged conservative merchants fearing inflation and depreciation against a majority of the House of Representatives. In 1740 the Land Bank's supporters won the election and endorsed the scheme, but it was later vetoed in England. Underlying this controversy, and indeed the political life of eighteenth-century Massachusetts, was a split between farmers and merchants. While conservatives castigated the rural masses as "the debtor part of the country (which is vastly the most numerous) . . . contriving to baulk their creditors by reducing the denominations of money (by their huge and ill-secured emissions) to a small or no value . . . idle and extravagant," the farmers complained that they had subdued the wilderness only to find ruin because of an insufficient money supply and the profits taken by the rich and selfish merchants of Boston. "It's true, Sir, our fore-fathers spent their blood and treasure . . . in subduing this wilderness, and its savage inhabitants; and the land being cultivated is generally exceeding good for so cold a climate; the people orderly, virtuous, and industrious, but want of money has brought them to the pass our author speaks of . . . The truth is this, that the import too much encouraged, or export too much neglected and discouraged, has built up a few on the ruins of many."

On such foundations, since government supported hard money and since one of the sustaining beliefs of Country writers was the corrupt alliance of moneyed men and executive power, controversy flourished. Of course, such ideas were not the property of the rural elements alone. Merchants, lawyers, and clergymen used them when occasion demanded. Other particular issues in the colony included the refusal of the lower house to vote a salary for the governor, the control of provincial funds, the creation of equity courts, and matters involving military service and defense. In 1748-1749, opposition to the governor intensified, partly as a result of economic depression after a period of war combined with discontent over the return of Louisbourg to the French. The opposition used the press. In the pages of the *Independent Advertiser* could be found "verbatim, though without attribution" theoretical statements taken from the perennial *Cato's Letters*. In 1754 a crisis erupted over a scheme for raising money by an excise on rum. The controversy was conducted primarily with arguments lifted directly from those of English opponents of Walpole's Excise Bill of 1733, testimony again to the pervasive borrowing and utilization of English opposition writings.

New York's well-documented early political history reveals a series of factional struggles, with several crises. One erupted in the opposition to Governor William Cosby, who attempted to place his own allies in office after his appointment. In 1733 he suspended the Chief Justice of New York, Lewis Morris. Subsequently, Morris and his allies started the *New-York Weekly Journal*, appointing John Peter Zenger as printer, and also prepared a series of political tracts, both time-honored opposition devices. The *Weekly Journal* from the beginning printed local polemics and the writings of Trenchard and Gordon, labeling the governor and his friends as corrupt courtiers; it also addressed itself to the workingmen and the "industrious poor." In November 1734 Zenger was arrested and tried for libel; in August 1735, defended by Andrew Hamilton of Philadelphia, he was aquitted. The "popular party" in New York, as it was now called, launched further attacks on the governor and drew up a series of demands—annual or triennial elections, courts established by act of assembly, judges appointed during good behavior and not at pleasure, representation according to population, and the "annual Election of Mayors, Sheriffs and other officers of the Corporation by the people" in chartered towns. One spokesman described what was sought as "what Englishmen are entitled to by the original Constitution of their mother country." In 1737 the popular party was in control of the lower house. Though political configurations then altered under a new governor, the Morris-Cosby dispute demonstrated that New York's politicians were in full control of Country rhetoric as well as practical methods of opposition.

New York's factions continued active until the Revolution itself, fueled by the ambition of men for power in a government which controlled fundamental decisions about major sources of wealth—land, trade, and military contracts. Although some leaders in the 1740s and 1750s appealed directly for support to the farmers and small shopkeepers and merchants, these disputes were usually very much the affair of gentlemen. In a second major crisis in 1753-1756 the main protagonists were leading Anglicans and Presbyterians, whose dispute for control of the newly founded King's College broadened out into a wider struggle for power. Again the rhetoric of court and country, influence and corruption, quickly appeared. William Livingston, a leading Presbyterian lawyer, William Smith, Jr., and John Morin Scott established the *Independent Reflector*, which published inflammatory assaults on established authority modeled on Country writings. They also addressed public meetings, circulated petitions, and with the aid of Presbyterian ministers aroused the ordinary members of the congregations. When agitation developed a few years later in the colony about the quartering of British troops and other imperial policies, the opponents of these measures had the vocabulary, the organizing skills, and the experience of opposition; they did not hesitate to use them.

The same was true in New Jersey, Pennsylvania, and Maryland. In the former, a triennial act was passed in 1728, and countless other assaults were made on executive authority. A leading political figure in the colony at this time was John Kinsey, Jr., a radical Quaker lawyer, active in the assembly. Other radical Whigs in New Jersey may have included James Alexander, a lawyer involved in the defense of John Peter Zenger and Samuel Nevill, an English immigrant who had been editor of the *London Morning Post*, both of whom led attacks on New Jersey governors. By the 1740s candidates for the assembly had published political platforms, and in 1754, during a dispute over paper currency, New York papers reported great political struggles in the New Jersey elections. In Pennsylvania the political contentions of the earlier eighteenth century were renewed from the 1740s as the proprietary executive sought to increase its powers. The pretensions of the Quakers also attracted violent opposition. In a series of essays in the *Pennsylvania Journal* in 1758 the author drew on "*Cato's Letters*, Bolingbroke, Sidney, and the Whig historians Rapin, Burnet, Ralph, and White Kennett," warning the public against the demagogues and enemies of liberty who sought to undermine the rights of the people by deceit and corruption. In Pennsylvania the issues again revolved around fundamental questions of land, paper money, and taxation. Maryland, the other proprietorial colony, also experienced grave political infighting. In the 1720s the assembly struggled to gain recognition for the English common law in the province, an anti-proprietorial move which produced one of the earliest southern political tracts, Daniel Dulany's *The Rights of the Inhabitants of Maryland to the benefit of English Laws* (1728). Tobacco and paper money, fees and taxes also provided constant controversial issues which were well publicized in the *Maryland Gazette*.

With the exception of Maryland, the southern colonies seem to have escaped the intense political crises of their northern neighbors. In Virginia from the 1720s to the 1740s there was no vigorous political conflict. Here, Governor Spotswood, after a stormy initiation, cooperated with the Virginia gentry until his removal in 1722. His successor, William Gooch, continued this cooperation. Yet it is clear that one basis of this stability was the respect given by the governors to the prevailing gentry assumption that their political rights rested on the "ancient constitution" of the colony. Moreover, an act against placemen in 1730 clearly showed a Country view of executive power. The first stirrings of rhetorical politics came in 1752 when Governor Dinwiddie announced that the Crown had allowed a number of Virginia laws passed in 1748-1749. Since tradition held that while the Crown might disallow Virginia legislation, it had no right of approving it, this innovation attracted considerable antagonism. Again spokesmen upheld the "ancient constitution and usage of this colony." This shock was followed by the pistole fee controversy. Here, a more radical rhetoric appeared. Richard Bland, for example, wrote of "threats to liberty and property" which "like a small spark if not extinguished in the beginning will soon gain ground and at last blaze into an irrestible flame." The Virginia burgesses resolved against actions that were "illegal and arbitrary, and tending to subvert the laws and institutions of this government." Dinwiddie claimed that the dispute showed "very much in a Republican way of thinking."

The most ample expression of the latent feelings of the Virginia gentry—although inventories of Virginia libraries show numerous Country and Whig volumes to have been owned in the colony—occurred in the late 1750s, with the first serious challenges to its authority. These came not from the governor but from a number of the better-educated and more self-confident Anglican clergy, many of whom taught at William and Mary College, and who had exhibited for some years an increasing restlessness at the gentry-domination of ecclesiastical and educational affairs in the colony. Their dislike was reciprocated by several leading planters, including Landon Carter, who in 1754 swore he would "clip the wings of the whole clergy . . ." but lost a dispute with the minister of his parish by a decision of the Privy Council. In 1755 a number of clergy took violent objection to a temporary "two-penny" act that allowed the payment of cash instead of tobacco at the exchange rate of two pence per pound in settlement of public debts and levies, including parish taxes—the clergy's income—at a time when the real value of tobacco was claimed to be over three pence per pound. In 1758 this act was renewed.

The dissident clergy appealed in strong terms to the Bishop of London, citing not only their loss of income but the act's insult to the royal prerogative in contradicting previous Crown-approved legislation; they also attacked the "gentlemen of the colony." Shortly after, several of the prime actors were dismissed from their posts at the college by the gentry-dominated Board of Visitors, causing considerable ill will. Subsequently in 1763 the Privy Council reinstated the dismissed men; in the meantime it also disallowed the Two-Penny Act and censured the governor for passing it without a suspending clause, contrary to his instructions. At the same time, the burgesses felt under pressure from British merchants' attacks on their paper money policy and also became engaged in a dispute over the appointment of a colonial agent.

The Virginia gentry reacted quickly and confidently to all these major threats to their position. In a series of pamphlets, especially those by Richard Bland, in petitions from the assembly and in the press, the political leaders asserted a large degree of autonomy. Royal orders, Bland stated, had to yield to the good or safety of the people in cases of clear necessity. Moreover, wrote members of the House of Burgesses, the British government was attacking "the very being of the [Virginia] constitution" by insisting on the suspension of ordinary legislative acts until royal approval had been won. Patrick Henry, the fiery young son of a Presbyterian minister, in defending the Two-Penny Act before the Hanover County court, announced that the King by "annulling or disallowing acts of so salutary a nature, far from being the father of his people, degenerated into a tyrant." By 1763-1764 Bland and others were analyzing the whole nature of the Virginia "constitution" and finding both Crown and Parliament to be excluded from the affairs of the colony, "but such as respects its EXTERNAL government" and that "submission, even to the supreme Magistrate is not the whole duty of a citizen, especially such a submission as he himself does not require: Something is likewise due to our country, and to the liberties of mankind." From this time on the gentry, who before had largely supported executive as well as legislative authority, at least in practice, rapidly assumed a posture and a rhetoric of opposition, drawing, as did Jefferson, on sources ranging from classical to Country writers.

In South Carolina, the gentry also controlled the assembly, and the assembly to a great degree controlled the colony. The presence of a vast and feared slave population kept the political temperature cool. Although for twenty years after 1743 a series of constitutional disputes between governor, council, and assembly occurred and questions of defense spending, Indian trade, and paper money provoked disagreements, they did not produce severe factional infighting. Yet it is clear that South Carolinians, like Virginians, were well versed in political theory, and a recent student considers that the prevalent ideology in the colony by the mid-eighteenth century was that of the Country radicals. The *South Carolina Gazette* printed the writings of Trenchard and Gordon, and an examination of books in the Charleston Library Company as well as in the libraries of individual planters shows that these and other pamphleteers, as well as the standard Whig writers, were known and read in the colony. From the 1750s, when numbers of royal placemen rather than substantial South Carolinians were appointed to the council, South Carolinians had definite reason to fear the spreading tentacles of executive control. In 1757-1758 a quartering controversy broke out that led to an assembly defense of civilian property. By 1762, when the South Carolina lower house was faced with a direct challenge to its authority in the Gadsden election controversy, the rhetoric of opposition and the defense of "rights" came easily to its members.

The political record of individual colonies, together with a study of pamphlets and newspaper articles, seem convincingly to show the always latent and often overt attractions of an opposition attitude of mind. In many colonial societies unpopular acts by governors or officials, or the contest of factions for political advantage, often immediately summoned up accusations of intrigue, corruption, influence, and malignant political ambition. Against this background, the logic and the power of immediate resistance, including the articulation of a reasoned ideological position by colonial leaders to the novel measures of the British government in the years after 1760, are comprehensible. "To minds steeped in the literature of eighteenth-century history and political theory, these events, charged with ideology, were the final realization of tendencies and possibilities that had been seen and spoken of, with concern and foreboding, since the turn of the seventeenth century." So writes Professor Bailyn, whose works have brilliantly set forth this view of American colonial politics. And opposition was more than a habit of mind. In the colonial cities, at least, the formation of political caucuses and clubs, the use of propaganda aimed at the general populace, mass electoral meetings, the publication of political platforms and voting tickets were all well known before 1763. Nor were politics restricted to political organizing and campaigning. In moments of high tension, mobs and riots, often controlled by the respectable, brought physical threats to life and property.

Yet, of course, not all colonial politics and government were contentious, not all political controversies were couched in ideological language, and there is some question about the applicability of a general theory of radical ideology to all colonial societies at all stages of their history. The histories of New Hampshire, Virginia, and South Carolina, to mention the obvious, seem to show societies where for many years neither faction, arguments nor violent controversies flourished. Moreover, even in Massachusetts, skillful governors could operate for long periods without experiencing more than the frictions normal in any society. Nor has the political history of New Jersey and North Carolina been discussed in adequate detail to show the extent to which a disruptive ideology held sway. Indeed, for many of these colonies, the older suggestion of the relevance of the struggle between assemblies and governors best fits the present facts, for it was assembly attacks on the particular political claims of governors or vice versa that provoked argument. Of course, it may well be that the lower house members who contested the executives were soaked in ideas of the dangers of court control as well as jealous of the traditional freedoms of their houses. But this point is not yet clearly established. 

Nevertheless it is certain that for a variety of reasons much eighteenth-century colonial political life was turbulent and disorderly, as a constant stream of reports from colonial governors to their English masters testifies. It also seems clear that dissensions grew more and not less pronounced in the two decades before 1760. In these years colonial society was growing in population and in social and economic strength and complexity, creating a variety of claims on resources and a variety of often conflicting interest groups as well as more self-confident colonial elites. At the same time the English government, faced with war in Europe involving its overseas possessions, sought more cooperation and more obedience in the colonies. Her officials were not loathe to suggest methods of procuring these ends, including plans for the reform of colonial governments. By the 1750s the attention of the British government had clearly swung to North America and the expected struggle there with the French. Americans, however, did not respond to British requests for unity and harmony, and they saw in the renewed suggestions for reform the same threats to traditional liberties that they had resisted in the past. War and its consequences, indeed, was the hothouse that nurtured first resistance and then revolution from the seeds of political resentment and suspicion that had been sown in earlier years.

Chapter Ten

Eighteenth-Century Conflicts in North America

A. A continuing struggle

The formal agreements about North America concluded in 1713 at Utrecht related to the possession of Hudson's Bay and Acadia—to furs and fishing. At the same time the peace was signed, England and France made a commercial pact dealing with tariffs, duties, and trade in some American and West Indian products. Further negotiations were arranged to deal with wood, salt, fish, sugar, and tobacco; British merchants hoped that France would eventually provide a populous market for these colonial exports. That all these negotiations mainly involved raw materials and commerce is, of course, evidence of the continuing strength of the new trading interests that had emerged in the seventeenth century. In the eighteenth century they amassed even greater weight as further European expansion into Africa, India, and the Far East brought new profits, and the economies of most western European nations grew with an overall increase in the numbers of ships and merchants. Pressures from commercial interests naturally increased and, since the governments of most European states now realized how important a source of national power and prosperity was trading wealth, found a sympathetic response. In the previous two centuries Europeans had penetrated, traded, and conquered to the end of the world. Now eighteenth-century men found it perfectly feasible to compete for larger and more powerful maritime empires. Those of Spain and Holland, like Rome and Venice, had declined, but France or England might expect in the cycle of history to attain new imperiums, using war as a rational instrument of policy in the design. Not all such ideas were full blown at the beginning of the century, but fostered by the continuation of French and English rivalries across the world, they fructified rapidly. In his epitaph for William Pitt, architect of Britain's imperial position, Edmund Burke approvingly summed up these developments. The Great Englishman's policy, Burke declared, had been to raise his nation "to a high pitch of prosperity and glory by unanimity at home—by confidence and reputation abroad—by alliance wisely chosen and faithfully observed—by colonies united and protected—by decisive victories by sea and land—by conquests made by arms and generosity in every part of the globe—and by commerce for the first time united with and made to flourish by war."

The situation in North America naturally helped shape the course of the wider struggle. Spanish America continued its decline, although to the inhabitants of South Carolina (and of Georgia) the Spanish presence in Florida still seemed to threaten possible attack or invasion, while Floridians feared the continuing encroachment of the English southward into their territory. Rivalry continued between Spanish and English for friendship with or control of the Indian tribes for reasons both of commerce and strategy. These tensions made themselves apparent during the course of the Yamasee War that began in the spring of 1715 on the southern frontier and involved a co-ordinated attack by Yamasees and the powerful island Creek Indians against the English. Contemporaries blamed Spanish intrigues for these attacks although the harsh conduct of the Carolina traders toward the Indians in seizing women and children as slaves to meet Indian debts was probably the precipitating cause. No Spanish forces were involved, and although Indians penetrated to within twelve miles of Charleston their initial impetus was soon checked. When in 1715-1716 the powerful Cherokees sided with the British, the Creek cause was lost; the war soon became a Creek-Cherokee struggle, concluded in 1727. Spanish Florida provided a sanctuary for the defeated Yamasees and Creeks, a further irritant to Anglo-Spanish relations. At the same time relations between South Carolina and Virginia badly deteriorated since the Carolinians believed that the latter had provided supplies to their Indian enemies.

The Yamasee War added to the pressure from America on British officials, felt increasingly since the early eighteenth century, for a more aggressive policy toward Spanish Florida, as did the outbreak of a brief Anglo-Spanish conflict of 1718-19 in the Mediterranean which led to privateering raids and the threat of open warfare—not realized—in the southern American colonies. Spanish claims in the Gulf of Mexico also revived with the construction of Fort San Marcos at the head of Apalachee Bay. As counter to any Spanish upsurge, the British government in 1720 ordered a fort built on the Altamaha River and in 1721 the primeval and deadly swamps were disturbed by the construction of Fort St. George, despite Spanish protests. Seven years later, Carolina militiamen, retaliating against Spanish-protected Yamasee raiding parties on the Altamaha, intruded into Spanish territory to attack the Indian village of Nombre de Dios directly under the guns of the Spanish fort at St. Augustine. The failure of its inmates to retaliate against the British lost the Spanish substantial prestige among formerly well-disposed Indians, while growing British authority among the most powerful nation of southern Indians was symbolized in 1730 with the visit of Cherokee chiefs to London, where they signed a treaty of friendship with the Crown.

Spain's decline in the Americas quickened in these years as she concentrated her waning resources on maintaining her influence in the Mediterranean and in Italy. In 1732 the Spanish had been unable to mount more than a diplomatic protest against the serious invasion of her American territories represented by the founding of Georgia. Indeed, the new colony promised to be a base for British intrusions into Spanish commerce in the Caribbean; its settlement must be viewed in the context of British merchants' increasing ambitions to breach Spain's long-cherished commercial monopoly over her weakened colonial possessions. Not that some Spaniards even then lacked the hope of checking English advances; for example, in 1734 the governor of Florida pleaded for substantial improvements to his defensive capabilities and for the colonization of the Apalache region by settlers from the Canary Islands. Scarcity of resources meant that little came of these plans. But in 1737 the Spanish king finally ordered an attack on Georgia and uncharacteristically strenuous preparations were made at Havana. The expedition was cancelled for diplomatic reasons on the day that it was due to sail. Some troops and supplies did go to Florida and their presence probably saved St. Augustine from capture by Governor Oglethorpe who, after the outbreak of war between England and Spain in 1739, led a major assault south. Oglethorpe's expedition of 1740 faltered during a month-long investiture of St. Augustine.

During the 1740s Spanish privateers mounted an offensive against American and English shipping, even landing small raiding parties in the Carolinas. The failure of an Anglo-American attack on Cartagena in 1741 emboldened the Spanish for a further assault on Georgia, and a fleet sailed from Havana in June 1742, reaching the colony in July. Poor leadership led to withdrawal after an initially successful landing at Jekyll Sound. Similarly, a British naval force which attacked St. Augustine later in the same year also failed to penetrate Spanish defenses, retiring after a storm. In 1743 a mixed force of Indians and English destroyed Fort San Diego in Florida. However, this year virtually marked the end of Anglo-Spanish military activity in the southern colonies, although considerable English colonial resentment remained, directed particularly at Spanish proclamations of freedom and sanctuary for slaves escaping from Carolinian and Georgian masters to Florida. That the Peace of Aix-la-Chapelle in 1748 left the boundary question unresolved now hardly mattered. Spanish Florida remained an isolated outpost of a spent empire, no longer a threat to English possessions or a center of influence among the southern Indians. It played little part in American diplomacy or wars from this time until its cession to England in 1763.

In the Southeast generally, Spain's former influence devolved on the French. Initial enmity between France and Spain over the eastward extension of Louisiana had been settled in 1721. In 1733 the two countries signed a Family Compact, each guaranteeing the colonies and commerce of the other. The French were ambitious to extend a commercial and political supremacy along the Gulf of Mexico based, as most such grandiose European plans in the

NEW YORK — CANADA, 1758-60
NEW FRANCE
Gatineau R.
Ottawa R.
Sorel
Richelieu R.
Montreal
Lachine
Ft. Chambly
Ft. St. John
St. Lawrence R.
Isle-aux-Noix
Adirondack Mts.
Fort Levis
Fort La Galette (La Présentation)
Oswegachie R.
Lake Champlain
Ft. Frontenac
Fort St.-Frederic (Crown Point)
Ft. Carillon (Ticonderoga)
L. George
NEW YORK
Lake Ontario
Fort Oswego
Fort George
Fort Edward
Oswego R.
L. Oneida
Mohawk R.
Fort Stanwix
Fort Herkimer
Fort Johnson
Saratoga
Schenectady
Albany
Hudson R.
0 50 Miles
0 50 Kilometers
Cape Bonavista
Riche Pt.
St. John's
NEWFOUNDLAND
Isle de l'Assomption
Gulf of St. Lawrence
Miquelon I.
St. Pierre I.
Cape Breton I.
Isle St.-Jean
Louisbourg
Fort Beasejour
Beaubassin
Fort Gaspereau
Canso
Tadoussac
Quebec
Penobscot R.
St. John's R.
Grand Pré
NOVA SCOTIA
Annapolis Royal (Port Royal - French)
Trois Rivieres
Pemaquid
Ft. de St.-Castin
NEW FRANCE
Fort Kaministiquia
Lake Superior
Sault Ste. Marie
Montreal
L. Champlain
Salmon Falls
Falmouth (Ft. Loyal)
Dover
Portsmouth
Fort Frontenac
Fort Michilimackinac
L. Huron
L. Ontario
Ft. Oswego
Albany
Deerfield
Boston
Fort Toronto
Schenectady
L. Michigan
Fort Niagara
Fort Massachusetts
Providence
Ft. Presque Isle
Hartford
Atlantic Ocean
Fort Ponchartrain du Detroit
L. Erie
Ft. Le Bouef
Long Island
Ft. Duquesne
Bushy Run
New York
Ft. Venango
Ft. Ligonier
Raystown
Philadelphia
Fort Miami
Ft. Quiatenon
Great Meadows
Fort Crevecoeur
Baltimore
Wabash R.
Pickawillany
Fort Cumberland
Potomac R.
Alexandria
Missouri R.
Fort Vincennes
Williamsburg
N
Cahokia
Ohio R.
James R.
Norfolk
W
E
Fort Chartres
Kaskaskia
Massac
Cumberland R.
Roanoke R.
C. Fear R.
New Bern
Mississippi R.
Fort l'Assomption
Tennessee R.
Fort Prince George
Pee Dee R.
Fort Loudoun
Brunswick
S
Ninety-Six
Arkansas R.
Savannah R.
Fort Augusta
Oconee R.
Arkansas Post
Charleston
THE COLONIAL WARS
Flint R.
Chattahoochie R.
Savannah
St. Catherines I.
Alabama R.
Fort King George
San Luis de Talimali
Jekyll Island
Natchitoches
Fort San Diego
Mobile
Red R.
Biloxi
San Augustin
San Marcos
New Orleans
Pensacola
FLORIDA
0 100 200 300 400 Miles
0 100 200 400 Kilometers
Gulf of Mexico

absence of settlers tended to be, on Indian alliances and fortified posts. English fears of French Louisiana had been heightened in the Yamasee War when French as well as Spanish incitement was alleged among the Indians; conversely, English influence among the Choctaw Indians annoyed the Louisianians. In 1717 the French had begun to construct a fort on the Alabama River, later known as Fort Toulouse, and they later sought to consolidate their position among the fierce Natchez Indians by erecting Fort Rosalie at Natchez. But their security was severely threatened by an uprising of Natchez Indians in 1729 which developed into a wider struggle, involving Choctaws and Illinois Indians on the French, and Cherokees and Chickasaws on the English side. Moves to consolidate Indian support followed. In 1745 Governor Vaudreuil and many Choctaws reaffirmed their friendship at a great conference at Mobile. The Choctaw territory had become a center of Louisianan-South Carolinian rivalry, with the latter's traders penetrating to its towns and seeking its deerskins. A conflict among pro-English and pro-French Choctaws (allegedly begun by a French officer's seduction of a chief's wife) ended in 1751. For about the next nine years the general balance of power among the southern Indians was favorable to the English. The powerful Cherokees and Chickasaws provided a barrier between the southern colonies and the French, while English trading goods, superior in quality and quantity and lower in price than the French, attracted the volatile Choctaws.

Far up the Mississippi from the Louisiana region the French had a more profitable area of influence and minor settlement, centered on Kaskasia near the junction of the river of that name and the Mississippi. Here, by about 1750, six or so weak villages of French, Indians, and Negro slaves (together with a few Jesuits, priests, and soldiers) were valued in part as a wheat-producing area, supplying New Orleans and other French outposts, especially those in the Ohio region. This Illinois territory was also a strategic link between the Great Lakes-St. Lawrence axis and the French line of communications running down to the Gulf of Mexico. East of it, the French had constructed Fort Vincennes, Fort Ouitanon, and Fort Miamis in order to guard communication between Lake Erie and the Mississippi. By 1755 they had also built a powerful stone fort in the Illinois country itself near the site of the old Fort Chartres, guarding the route between the principal settlements.

Northwest of the Illinois country, extending west of Lake Superior, lay a third area of French interest, a region near the rich furs of the virtually unknown interiors. Indeed, enterprising Frenchmen eventually came to hope that they could direct the flow of furs from the south and west away from the posts of the Hudson's Bay Company. From the 1730s the La Vérendrye family supervised the construction of a number of fortified trading posts, including the most westerly French posts. These moves did reduce the inflow of pelts to the Hudson's Bay Company but its agents appeared relatively sanguine about this rivalry. Their own interests were then turning to northern fur areas. For this reason and because of its remoteness, the region did not become a significant factor in Anglo-French rivalry.

Louisiana, Illinois, and the lands west of the Great Lakes were all relatively new areas of French activity, remote from English settlements and largely immune from the intrusions of English traders. The older areas of French settlement or influence lay north and west of the English colonies, mainly south of the St. Lawrence and south and east of the Great Lakes. After 1713 northern New England, Nova Scotia and Cape Breton Island in particular remained a center of contention, for reasons both of commerce—control of fishing waters—and of strategy. Boundary disputes between French and English territories caused innumerable protests, while French influence among the Abenaki Indians, whom they supported in a war against New England settlers in 1722, and the activities of French priests and agents among the conquered French settlers of Nova Scotia suggested a future attempt to regain territory and power in the area. In 1717-1720 the French built a powerful fort, Louisbourg, on Cape Breton Island. The English fort at Annapolis Royal in Nova Scotia was less well maintained.

Elsewhere, French and English antagonisms remained evident. Basic to them was the growing population and commercial expansiveness of the English colonies. English fur traders consistently sought to win over French-linked Indians, and since they had access to more, better, and cheaper trade goods the threat was real, undermining the effectiveness of the French system of forts and fortified trading posts that had grown up since the beginning of the century. Nevertheless, the two mother countries spent relatively little on the military security of their North American possessions. English attention was mainly directed at Spanish America and the Caribbean. Pressure from politicians and merchants had forced Sir Robert Walpole to end his policy of peace in 1739 and declare war on Spain. In 1744 war with France began but it had no American origin and was concerned with the European balance of power and fought largely in Europe. Although William Pitt, who came to minor office in 1746, responded vigorously to representations from North America for an attack on the French there, his endorsement of these proposals carried no weight with the Duke of Newcastle and other powerful political leaders.

King George's War, as the conflict was known in America, was indeed remarkable for its lack of American contests. The first blow was struck by a small French force from Louisbourg that captured the Nova Scotia fishing station of Canso, an insignificant move but one that stirred up New England apprehensions and hit New England pockets. Shortly after, Annapolis Royal was invested by hostile Indians, who dispersed with the arrival of a small force from Massachusetts; stronger French and Indian forces then arrived to assault the ill-garrisoned fort but retired under orders from Louisbourg.

Nova Scotia continued to experience French and Indian raids that were also taken south into northern New England. In October 1744 the Eastern Indians, old foes of New England, refused to ally with the English, and in the following two years Indian attacks erupted in northwest Massachusetts and elsewhere in northern New England. New York suffered less because of Iroquois neutrality, but in November 1745 a French and Indian force from Fort St.-Frederic marched overland to Saratoga on the Hudson, surprising and capturing the undefended post and killing thirty inhabitants. This attack involved about 500 men. An assault on Fort Massachusetts, east of Albany, in August 1746 involved 700. Both were large "armies" for this type of fighting and illustrate the limited character of the struggle in America, one of quickly moving raiding parties. In Nova Scotia, the major engagement was an attack on the English-held village of Grand Pré, involving a few hundred combatants on both sides.

One major undertaking did materialize, a New England assault on Louisbourg, following the tradition of attacking French centers of power near coastal New England that had originated with the expedition against Port Royal in 1690. Again the motives and determination came from commercial interests, anxious to gain the trade and fisheries of the French posts and engage in short-term plunder, as much as the government. New England hatred of French Catholicism also played its part. Supported by the prayers of the clergy and directed by an imperially minded governor, the New Englanders acted at first without the official endorsement of the English government; but news arrived of British naval assistance and in April 1745 British warships joined the colonial forces in Nova Scotia waters.

Louisbourg was captured on 17 June 1745. The troops involved—over 3,000—were entirely composed of New Englanders, amateur soldiers under the command of William Pepperell, a popular Maine militia chief, merchant, property owner and later the first American-born baronet. Rhode Island sent few soldiers, New York, Pennsylvania, and New Jersey, none. The French garrison consisted of about 600 regulars and 900 militia, adequate for its defense. Yet they abandoned a number of heavy cannon to the Americans that were turned on the fort. The failure of a brave amphibious assault in which 300 New Englanders died was followed by the capture of a French relief vessel, for the British naval blockade was successful. Sea power and artillery sealed the fort's fate; after 1,500 cannonballs and shells had poured in and their own ammunition was nearly spent, the French capitulated. A French fleet later sent out to retake Louisbourg with over 3,000 men reached Nova Scotian waters but then turned back, weakened by disease and bad weather.

Peace came officially in October 1748 with the signing of the Treaty of Aix-La-Chappelle. Its terms reflected the nature of the war in that it settled nothing about the fate of North America. If anything, it favored French interests on the continent since Louisbourg was returned to the French in compensation for concessions elsewhere. Outstanding territorial differences were left to an Anglo-French commission that first met in Paris in August 1750 and met intermittently until the rupture of diplomatic relations between the two countries in 1756. The only subjects seriously discussed were the boundaries of Nova Scotia and Acadia and the ownership of certain West Indian islands. The question of the entire frontier between English and French America did, however, receive increasing attention from both governments in direct negotiations between them, suggested first by the English in 1750 and carried on from 1753 to 1755.

Such negotiations obviously testify to the growing awareness and importance of rivalries in North America in European affairs. These rivalries themselves intensified in the same years as the two sides sought to consolidate or improve their positions. The 1740s may also well have seen the awakening of a kind of American nationalism forged by the war against France and by the widely reported colonial participation in the attacks on Cartagena and Louisbourg. Many clergy from New England to Virginia preached of an apocalyptic struggle for Protestant liberty against the French Catholic anti-Christ. Few colonists approved of the return of Louisbourg to France; others disliked the reported condescension of British officers to colonial soldiers. French and English political leaders at home also took positions relating to the colonial situation more and more strongly. In England the Duke of Bedford and William Pitt pressed for a forward policy in America. Indeed, after 1748, the view that maritime, commercial, and colonial strength meant power in European affairs was rapidly reaching an apogee. No European statesman so clearly embodied these views as William Pitt, himself the beneficiary of his grandfather's success as an interloper in the East Indies trade. Pitt's support came from the City of London, the little republic at the center of Britain's imperial expansion. His recall to high political office in 1757 marked the effectual endorsement by court and nation of the view that France was "chiefly if not solely to be dreaded as a maritime and commercial power."

French strength in North America seemed to increase rapidly after 1748. A new program of fort building or improvement included Fort Toronto, the rebuilding of Forts Toulouse and Niagara, the establishment of a fortified mission center at La Présentation near Fort Frontenac among the Iroquois, and the construction of Fort Beauséjour on the Acadian peninsula. Acadia, indeed, still remained a critical area of Anglo-French relations. The French on Cape Breton Island maintained a steady pressure on the French-speaking peasants living under British rule since the cession of 1713. They also established themselves militarily in disputed boundary territory. In 1748 the British government made a countermove, deciding to settle Nova Scotia with English and European Protestant migrants largely at Crown expense, an important alteration in general colonial policy, since only Georgia of all the English colonies had ever before received such financial aid.

In general, the English were also becoming alarmed at what seemed to be growing French strength among the Indians, especially the Iroquois Confederacy, whose previous friendship or neutrality to a great extent maintained a balance of power over large areas from the Ohio Valley northward. Groups of Onondaga, Cayugas, and Senecas were reported in 1750 to have "turned Frenchmen," and many of the Six Nations were said three years later to "have acquired a perfect Indifference [to the English] and give way to those who sollicit best, and in this respect the French, by their situation, frequent Journeys and address, infinitely surpass the English." Even the Mohawks seemed, out of hostility to English encroachments on their land and grudging recognition of French power, about to abandon their traditional English connection. In the Ohio country, claimed by the Six Nations and used by them as a hunting ground, the Iroquois maintained an uneasy neutrality in the face of the intrusions of French and English while the Delawares, Shawnee, Senecas, and other tribes swayed first to one side and then to another.

Yet the French authorities could point to the threat of English expansion, particularly from Pennsylvania and Virginia and particularly into the hitherto quiet Ohio Valley. Unsettled by white men, controlled by the Six Nations (whose jurisdiction had inhibited white advance), but inhabited by numerous groups and tribes of Indians, it was claimed by both French and English by virtue of former explorations and charters. Both also traded extensively in the region from about the 1730s onwards. Pennsylvanians, often agents of ambitious Philadelphia merchant houses, were active in the upper Ohio, while merchants and politicians, like Benjamin Franklin, parlayed for grants of territory from the Indians. In Virginia, the Ohio Company and assorted rivals were granted land west of the mountains in the southern Ohio region and planned to build forts there, all with the sanction and often with the participation of leading colonial and Crown officials. Although not directly athwart French lines of communication, which lay further west, the region's control or settlement by the English would certainly lead to further advances and to the end of Indian neutrality there. For the English, French possession closed westward expansion of their colonies from Pennsylvania south. Commercially, both French and English wished to exploit it as a source of furs. The Ohio, in fact, rapidly became the critical area of Anglo-French tension.

The establishment of a fortified trading house by Indians and colonial traders at Pickawillany on the Great Miami River in 1750 increased French fears of English influence. "If you force the English to leave the region who give us our necessities and particularly the blacksmith who refurbishes our guns and axes, we shall be without any aid and exposed to death from hunger," claimed the Indians at one meeting with the French, exactly testifying to the general European grip on Indian culture. The destruction of Pickawillany by French-led Indians in June 1752 was a "momentous event" toward war. In 1753 the Marquis de Duquesne, the governor-general of New France, began extensive preparations for the affirmation of French sovereignty over the Ohio, constructing Forts Presqu'ile on Lake Erie, Le Boeuf (Waterford, Pennsylvania), and Venango on the Allegheny with the object of excluding English traders and possible settlers. In August of the same year, after a cabinet decision, the

British Secretary of State advised colonial governors to check the advance of French troops "intending as it is apprehended, to commit some Hostilities on Parts of his Majestie's Dominions in America," to resist their building of forts and "to Repel Force by Force." In September the Board of Trade expressed surprise and displeasure about poor colonial relations with the Mohawks and instructed the governor of New York to convene an intercolonial conference to make a general treaty with the Indians.

B. The French and Indian War

This French decision to occupy the Ohio Valley and the English government's willingness to encourage colonial resistance to French moves began the transition from irregular to official confrontation between the two imperial powers in North America. In October 1753 the Virginia Council issued a formal warning to French forces in the Ohio region. George Washington, a young militia officer, undertook the task of delivering the communication, spending three and a half months journeying to and from Fort Le Boeuf on the errand. As expected, the message was rejected; the Virginia government then raised 120 men and hastened the construction of a fort at what would later be the site of Pittsburgh. In London the British government sought a united American effort against the French, even suggesting that a "feint" be made against Canada from New York to relieve the severe pressure on the Ohio expected in the spring of 1754. Yet there was no enthusiasm for an agreed intercolonial strategy. A thousand Frenchmen reached the forks of the Ohio River without interference in April 1754, easily capturing the handful of soldiers and the unfinished Virginia fort there. On its site they began the construction of a new French post, Fort Duquesne.

Washington returned to the Ohio country with the newly raised Virginian militiamen in April 1754, too late to reach the fort before the French attack. Planning to push to the Monongahela River to await reinforcements before seeking out the French, he prepared a temporary base at Great Meadows, Pennsylvania. From here he took a detachment of men to challenge a party of French reportedly watching his movements. On 28 May he engaged them, killing ten and capturing twenty or so. He then constructed Fort Necessity at Great Meadows and received reinforcements but was forced to abandon plans to push forward by the advance of a large body of French and Indians from Fort Duquesne. The enemy attacked Fort Necessity in early July, forcing his capitulation and return to Virginia. The fact that he received little aid from the Indians, while the French had extensive support from them, confirmed the English in their apprehensions of their loss of prestige, authority, and friendship among the Indians generally.

By this time the British-inspired intercolonial conference, ordered in the previous year, was in session. The Albany Congress of June and July 1754, attended by representatives from New York, Pennsylvania, Maryland, New Hampshire, Massachusetts, Connecticut, and Rhode Island but not from New Jersey or Virginia, has been seen as something of a landmark in American history, since it produced the first intercolonial discussion of a serious plan of union for the American colonies. Yet the British authorities had asked it to be summoned for the purpose of treating with the Six Nations and, if possible, for the agreeing by specified colonies of a general treaty with them. This was only achieved in the sense that several colonies separately made certain agreements with the small numbers of Indians who attended—itself a sign of French influence—and that these Indian representatives left the congress on 2 July with thirty wagonloads of gifts, affirming their loyalty to the colonial cause. The other issues discussed arose from the suggestions of the delegates and had not been canvassed by the British authorities. Benjamin Franklin had suggested a colonial union three years previously and his and three other plans were considered. The delegates finally considered a draft plan combining Franklin's ideas and those of Thomas Hutchinson of Massachusetts. It proposed a union under a president-general to be appointed by the Crown and a representative grand council which would mainly concern itself with Indian relations, lands outside the existing colonies, and matters of defense including raising soldiers and building forts. Financing was to come from money supplied by each colony according to an agreed quota. The union was to be statutorily based on an act of the British Parliament. The congress agreed on 10 July that this plan should be, in Franklin's later gloss, "respectfully sent to the Assemblies of the several colonies for their consideration, and to receiving such alterations and improvements as they should think fit and necessary; after which it [is] proposed to be transmitted to England to be perfected and the establishment of it there humbly solicited." Yet the Congress refused at this stage to recommend contributions for practical defensive measures, such as building forts. Nor, of course, did the plan of union materialize. No colonial assembly finally approved it, and the British government, which also attempted but failed to write its own plan of union in the summer and autumn of 1754, did not act on it.

With the spilling of blood in the Ohio Valley, a virtual state of war existed. Yet during the remainder of 1754 neither Pennsylvania nor Maryland agreed to send men for military action, and New York and North Carolina dispatched only a few hundred poorly equipped men to Virginia. South Carolina similarly remained effectively aloof, while Virginia itself failed to raise more militia. All the American colonies, however, continued to assault London, requesting troops and supplies. Nor did the British government retreat from its initial agreement to foster resistance to French measures. Indeed, following news of Fort Necessity it decided in the early autumn of 1754 to send two British regiments and to raise two regiments at British expense in North America, a new departure in imperial policy. Major General Edward Braddock, a veteran of Dettingen and Fontenoy, was appointed as commander-in-chief. Hopes were high for the success of a British-directed strategy to clear the French from the Ohio, Niagara, and Lake Champlain regions. Yet at this stage the British and French still were content to claim that their relatively small forces were merely committed to forcing intruders from their respective territorial claims and that this did not amount, as a contemporary wrote, to an "Infraction of the General Peace." Nevertheless, during the same period, an undeclared sea war was taking place between the two countries, as their fleets maneuvered for tactical advantage.

Braddock arrived in Virginia in February 1755. In April at Alexandria he met with the governors of Virginia, New York, Pennsylvania, Massachusetts, and Maryland and with William Johnson, the New York Indian expert, trader, and leading figure among the Six Nations, to discuss the year's campaigns. Three major thrusts were to be undertaken—against Fort Duquesne by Braddock, against Fort Niagara by Governor William Shirley of Massachusetts, now appointed Braddock's second-in-command, and against Crown Point by Johnson; Braddock after taking Duquesne would aid Shirley. The utility of a separate campaign in Nova Scotia was also agreed. From the first it was clear, as John Shy has succinctly written, that the war in America would be one "in which geography created problems of communications and supply so great that the principal task of generalship was in simply moving a force of moderate size into contact with the enemy . . . The forces of nature were so nearly overwhelming that the French and Indian war had to be a war of organization and administration."

Braddock's army moved first. The route chosen lay across a savage terrain from Fort Cumberland to the Monongahela, and the force, hampered by siege guns, other artillery, and its horse-drawn wagons, achieved only two or so miles a day. In mid-June the army divided. Braddock went forward with a picked detachment of men, leaving half his forces under the command of Colonel Thomas Dunbar. This division, urged by Washington, hastened the march of the forward column, which successfully crossed the Monongahela River and stood about nine miles from Fort Duquesne on 9 July. Up to this day every proper precaution was taken to forestall ambushes and surprise attacks from the French and the Indians, as these discovered in reconnoitering the British advance. But in the afternoon forces from Fort Duquesne attacked the vanguard of Braddock's column, gaining flanking positions in ravines and on a hill that the British had neglected to secure. Other mistakes followed, and the attackers were able to fire at will from cover into the British and American column. More than two-thirds of Braddock's men died or were wounded; Braddock himself fell, expiring later as the remaining troops carried him back toward Dunbar's column.

Braddock's defeat was a serious blow; Dunbar's decision to withdraw immediately to Fort Cumberland, first burning quantities of wagons and supplies, was disastrous. Later he refused to readvance, finally retiring with the regular troops to Philadelphia. The abandonment of the Ohio shattered the cornerstone of the agreed strategy for 1755. It may well have confirmed some British statesmen, New Yorkers, and New Englanders in their belief that a more direct attack on Canada should have received priority. A strike at the heart of France's North American empire, they had argued, would force the retraction of her forces from the Ohio and her other more outlying territories. Braddock's immediate failure seems to have rested on two general factors. First, his army lacked Indian support which could have been used for flanking protection. Second, his march might have been easier and his army have kept together if he had proceeded by a different route to the Monongahela, one known to him and three years later to be taken successfully by General Forbes.

The other campaigns of 1755 achieved little for the English. Those of Governor Shirley in the Niagara region and of William Johnson against Crown Point were organized separately and therefore found themselves in more or less direct competition for recruits, supplies, and Indian allies. Johnson soon came to feel that Shirley sought to hinder his preparations. Shirley found that his greatest enemy was New York's governor, James de Lancey, and his family, who expressed that colony's political and commercial hostility against New England and who allegedly wished to maintain favorable trade connections with the French and Indians rather than support a war. Shirley's main forces had not even reached Fort Oswego when news of Braddock's defeat—and of the death in the same battle of Shirley's own son—arrived. Finally, the New England governor abandoned the plan to assault Fort Niagara but refortified Oswego, leaving garrisons there and at Wood Creek. The third thrust, Johnson's toward Crown Point, also faltered. Johnson arrived at the southern end of Lake George, where he built Fort William Henry, in late August. Here, he mauled a large force of French and Indian attackers but he then withdrew, leaving a garrison behind.

Only in Nova Scotia did English and colonial forces succeed against the French. New England responded with its usual anti-Catholic alacrity, sending 2,000 men in May 1755. The reduction of the powerful Fort Beauséjour and of Fort Gaspereau a few miles northwest of it on the Gulf came with hardly a shot fired, in part due to the treachery of a French official, Thomas Pichon, a complex and fascinating figure whose Voltairean skeptism impelled him to the British side in opposition to the severe Catholic irredentism of his colleagues. But in the aftermath of victory it was the British who acted severely, although in their own eyes justly. The record of most French Acadians since 1713 had been one of passive or active resistance, including acts of war, against their new country. Given a last opportunity to swear a full oath of allegiance to the British Crown in 1755, they refused. Dreadful retribution followed. The French Acadians were ordered to be driven from Acadia and their lands to be forfeited. Marched from the villages, which were then burned, they were put on transports and shipped to other British colonies. The incident has rightly stirred great passions; whatever the argument on each side, the expulsion joins the large list of "sorrows so wantonly inflicted, so bitter and so perennial" that have for different reasons characterized—and still do—the history of the human race.

Despite English setbacks, Shirley, commander-in-chief since Braddock's death, still remained optimistic, summoning a governors' conference in December. His plans for 1756 envisaged a resumption of the three thrusts of the previous year, including a fresh assault on Fort Duquesne, together with a diversionary move against Quebec up the Kennebec River. Yet the colonies from Pennsylvania south favored a defensive war and would not agree to aid any of the schemes. Then, in March 1756 the indefatigable Shirley lost the direction of the war, toppled from authority by the intrigues of his rivals. The new commander, the Earl of Loudoun, a sixty-one-year-old Scot and a blunt disciplinarian, did not arrive at Albany to begin serious campaigning until 28 July. Soon he had decided to rule out an attack on Fort Niagara, although he confirmed orders for the reinforcement of Oswego. His arrival also threw the Crown Point campaign plans into additional disarray, raising questions of the relationship of the mainly militia forces on Lake George to the regulars. But in mid-August he approved an attack on the new French post of Ticonderoga. Very shortly afterward news reached the area of a new and serious British defeat—the fall of Fort Oswego on 14 August 1756. This setback led Loudoun to halt the operations against Ticonderoga and to order the forces near there to a defensive position. By the end of 1756 the advantage lay clearly with the French.

Like Shirley in his planning for 1756, Loudoun remained optimistic in deciding on the operations for 1757. To him, as to William Pitt, now directing operations in England, the loss of the Ohio and of Oswego, and the failure of the British at Lake George, were regrettable but hardly final. The British colonists were vastly more numerous, vastly more wealthy than the French; a direct attack on Canada, where the French had already once lost a major fortress—Louisbourg—seemed entirely feasible. Loudoun even favored Quebec as the target but was persuaded to accept Pitt's preference that the first assault should again be made on the Atlantic fortress in order to deny reinforcements from France to the St. Lawrence. Yet Loudoun's weak administrative abilities together with Pitt's still uncertain control slowed down preparations. By the time an effective force had been assembled for the attack on Louisbourg, a great French fleet had reinforced it. Advised by his naval colleagues that their strength was inadequate, Loudoun, in August 1757, abandoned his planned assault. Nor was this the only British failure of the year. Although the French were repulsed from Fort William Henry in the spring of 1757, Montcalm invested the English outpost in July, forcing its capitulation on 9 August. Even so, it is worth noting that the famous French general could advance no farther and that Fort Edward, the safeguard of Albany and the Hudson Valley, remained untouched. Even at its height, French power seemed limited. It could savage the borders of the English colonies. Could it penetrate to their vitals?

Certainly in 1757, the apogee of French success, Montcalm and others considered plans for breaking out of what was essentially a series of defensive offensives from a fixed perimeter. A seaborne attack on New York was mooted with an optimism heightened by the British failures that seemed inherent and unremediable. The British system of competing colonial governments and weak central control, an intelligent and knowledgeable French observer might justly have pointed out, had not been corrected. Since the defeat of Braddock, the colonies from Pennsylvania south had tended to withdraw from any schemes for united action and had generally refused to aid each other or the region to their north. Indeed, South Carolina had given little support to Virginia since 1754, in spite of her efficient militia and wealth. That colony's jealousy of Governor Dinwiddie's attempt to control southern strategy from Virginia and his attempts to treat directly with the Cherokee and Catawba Indians also incensed her officials and led immediately to their unwillingness to persuade the southern Indians to join Braddock's expedition. South Carolina still remained on the fringes of the war, more concerned to use her own men to guard her plantations against possible slave uprisings and to erect forts on her western boundaries than to assault the French. After Braddock's defeat even Virginia withdrew into a defensive strategy of fort building. Maryland failed to provide Braddock with supplies or horses, refused to countenance a second assault on Fort Duquesne in 1756, and resented the enlistment by recruiting officers of indentured servants. The Quaker-dominated Pennsylvania assembly approved only the erection of frontier defenses, and her merchants traded with the French at least as late as 1755.

This addiction to fortified defensive positions did not spare Pennsylvania and the southern colonies, although few French forces were involved in attacking them. Rather, the Indians learned of English defeats and French successes and quickly opposed the seemingly weaker side. In Pennsylvania in November 1755, Moravians along the Lehigh River were cruelly killed; in 1756 large areas of Cumberland County were deserted by its white inhabitants; in 1757 areas of the Susquehanna were raided. Similar border attacks occurred in Maryland in 1756, in Virginia from 1755 to the end of 1757, and in Georgia. The mobility of Indian warriors is suggested by contemporary reports that some traveled as far as a thousand miles to take part in attacks. North Carolina was relatively sheltered and South Carolina had a more successful Indian policy, together with the protection of a force of British regulars.

Lack of intercolonial cooperation, rivalries, and suspicions between colonials and British and the growing French influence among the Indians must certainly be weighed as causes for British failure after 1754. But had such weaknesses been fundamental, British and colonial authorities would hardly have been in a position to organize substantial direct assaults on the French, which they continued to do, though unsuccessfully. Colonial weaknesses in the struggle arose out of a justified lack of a sense of urgency; the inhabitants of the densely populated, prosperous seaboard regions of the English colonies mostly had little reason to worry about events on remote frontiers. The struggle was not one for their survival or even safety but for territory and prestige useful only in the long term. The fur trade and the fisheries certainly suffered, and in the case of the latter it is noticeable that French interference provoked an immediate and successful response from New Englanders against the French in Nova Scotia. Coastal America, when it thought about the war, considered maritime trade and conquest; thousands joined privateers or contributed in other ways to that struggle. Only exceptionally, as perhaps in crowded Connecticut whose militia turned out in large number for duty against the French, a connection may have been made between conquest and opportunities for settlers in the west. On the whole, however, the struggles on the frontier caused little disruption of every day life or of internal or external trade. The seaports gained new wealth through privateering and wartime spending, the farmers benefitted from the demand for food and supplies from the armies, merchants found lucrative contracts, real wages increased. Moreover, each year brought more promises of financial aid from England. For the majority of Americans the machinery of war ground slowly, but it ground profitably.

The events of 1757 failed to lessen Pitt's or Loudoun's confidence that the following year's campaigning would retrieve the British position. Lord Loudoun prepared a workmanlike plan for the new year before he was recalled—a scapegoat—by Pitt in December 1757 and replaced as commander-in-chief by Major General James Abercromby. Now Pitt himself dictated the grand strategy for the year. About 25,000 British regulars and 25,000 American provincials were to be paid for by Great Britain in order to mount three campaigns. First, an invasion of Canada by way of Lakes George and Champlain, involving the taking of Ticonderoga and Crown Point; second, the capture of Louisbourg; third, the reopening of the Ohio by the capture of Fort Duquesne. Concentrations of troops were to be ready early in the year to avoid the delays that had often previously plagued British efforts. In Europe, the navy was to keep a careful watch on French ports to prevent the dispatch of ships, soldiers, and supplies to Canada. Off Cape Breton, elements of the fleet, by wintering in Halifax, were to be on station as soon as the season permitted to deal with French ships that avoided interception in European waters.

The naval watch succeeded. Only six French warships reached Louisbourg. Then, despite an initial failure to make an early concentration of the assault fleet at Halifax, the British under the command of Brigadier General James Wolfe achieved a lucky yet decisive landing at Cape Breton Island on 8 June and forced a French retreat into their great fortress. Louisbourg, more or less encircled by British artillery, including thirty-two-pounder siege guns, groaned as bombs and red-hot shot crashed into the citadel and its harbor. The French forces capitulated on 26 July. (Two years later on Pitt's orders Louisbourg was mined and blown to pieces.) In late August Wolfe began to land raiding parties at French settlements and villages on the Bay of Gaspé and to make incursions into the St. Lawrence until the approach of winter caused him to withdraw his forces.

Wolfe was one of Pitt's new, young commanders sent out to America in early 1758. His spectacular if mixed successes have placed him firmly among the ranks of military heroes. Major General James Abercromby, Pitt's choice as commander-in-chief, was no young and rising star but a fifty-two-year-old staff officer, apprehensive about the rawness of his provincial troops. His immediate charge, the advance over Lake Champlain into Canada, saw him at Lake George in late June, much later than had been envisaged, and commanding about 16,000 troops rather than the 27,000 planned for by Pitt. Nevertheless, his French opponent, Montcalm, who reinforced Fort Ticonderoga, led only 3,000-4,000 men. Yet Abercromby's campaign failed. Reaching Ticonderoga on 8 July, he retreated precipitately after a seven-hour assault that even the defenders felt must be renewed on the following day. Abercromby blamed the large numbers of raw colonial recruits among his forces and the very high casualties among his regulars for his decision to withdraw; his critics cited it as one of his many tactical errors. His forces returned again to Lake George. The possibility of reopening the offensive in September was discussed but finally rejected. In the same month Abercromby received his recall from England.

The failure at Ticonderoga nullified Pitt's plans for an invasion of Canada in 1758. Indeed, the only campaign east of the Great Lakes with a successful outcome in that year had not even been suggested or approved by him and could not be followed up. This was an attack on Fort Frontenac, advocated by Colonel John Bradstreet to Loudoun in 1757 and reapproved by Abercromby in case the French, emboldened by the Ticonderoga fiasco, should attack the Mohawk settlements. Bradstreet, who had served with distinction at Louisbourg in 1745, moved with great speed. By 26 August he had assembled and led a taskforce to Fort Frontenac. On the following day his artillery bombarded the unprepared post, forcing its capitulation. Although not included in Pitt's war plans, Fort Frontenac had remarkable importance not only as an important staging post and warehouse for the supply of Fort Duquesne and of the French forts in the Great Lakes region but as a strategic position for the control of Lake Ontario and as a center of the fur trade.

Pitt entrusted the return to the Ohio country to the command of John Forbes, formerly a staff officer under Loudoun. A thorough organizer who conquered poor health with determination, Forbes's original intention was to advance on Duquesne along Braddock's former route. But by early May 1758, he had decided to use a more northerly route, beginning at Raystown, Pennsylvania, and proceeding over the Laurel range of mountains to the north bank of the Monongahela, a plan strongly disapproved by Washington and other Virginians. Forbes's campaign was slow but methodical, a conquest rather than a raid, with blockhouses and supply dumps left along the route. The first reconnaissance to the vicinity of the fort came as late as mid-September and resulted in the repulse of the British force with heavy casualties. The French, however, failed to achieve a surprise attack on the British base forty miles from the fort at Loyalhanna (Fort Ligonier). Forbes's final success came very late in the campaigning year, as he did not move close to Duquesne until November. He was then spared an assault, for on 24 November the French blew up Fort Duquesne, retiring to Machault. Crucial to this French defeat was their loss of Indian support, assured by skillful English diplomacy during the preceding months, and, with the fall of Fort Frontenac, their loss of the possibility of reinforcements. Early in 1759 Pitt ordered a permanent English base to be constructed on or near the Ohio.

The English determination that Canada should be invaded had brought successes but not victory in 1758. Louisbourg had fallen but Quebec, a mighty fortress, still stood. Crown Point and Ticonderoga remained in French hands blocking the favored invasion route over Lake Champlain. The breach at Fort Frontenac did not disturb the inner ring of French defenses, and the loss of the Ohio was by no means critical—Montcalm had called Fort Duquesne a "branch that exhausts the trunk." In 1759 Pitt's strategy, however, still stood. Firmly rejecting suggestions from South Carolina for a movement against the southern Indian country and toward eastern Louisiana, he announced that the objective for 1759 was to be the heart of New France. Operations in the Champlain area would continue and English naval supremacy would contribute to force the St. Lawrence and take Quebec. The position at Frontenac might be consolidated by an assault on Fort Niagara but only "as far as the Great and Main Objects of the Campaign shall permit."

In fact, the capture of Niagara was ordered by the new commander-in-chief, Sir Jeffrey Amherst, in June 1759, as it seemed an undertaking that could be speedily carried out, given the fading Indian support in the area for the French. By 4 July 3,000 men, including 1,000 Indians, had landed three miles east of Fort Niagara. These proceeded to rout a powerful French relief force. The fort capitulated three weeks after the first landing. At that time, Amherst, with 7,000 men, was advancing toward Ticonderoga. On 26 July, the French abandoned and destroyed their fort there; five days later they similarly mined the fort at Crown Point. According to prearranged plans, they then left Lake Champlain, retiring down the Richelieu River to an entrenched position on the Isle aux Noix.

Late July indeed was the high season of the campaigning year, when British forces were engaged on all three fronts. For Wolfe on 31 July attempted a landing at the Falls of Montmorency, east of the fortress of Quebec. His great flotilla entered the St. Lawrence in mid-June, reaching the vicinity of Quebec virtually unscathed at the end of the month. From that time until the end of July, although landing a strong force north of the city and reconnoitering the upper river west of it, Wolfe had decided no certain way of penetrating the powerful French entrenchments around Quebec. The landing at the Falls of Montmorency also brought no respite—450 British died in the unsuccessful attempt. Wolfe now anxiously brooded over his next move, even contemplating a prolonged siege lasting over the coming winter, for he feared a bloody repulse if he hurled his forces against the steep and strong defenses. Not until the end of August did he accept a plan prepared by his subordinate officers for a landing west of the city on the north shore of the St. Lawrence. Against their advice, he eventually fixed the exact point at a spot less than two miles from the city at the Foulon Pass. On the night of 13 September his soldiers climbed to the Heights of Abraham above the river, a maneuver that completely surprised the city's defenders. By the end of the morning 4,000 British troops had faced and defeated Montcalm's forces before Quebec in an engagement that took the lives of both the British and French commanders. Quebec itself surrendered five days later. The season was now too late for any further advance up the St. Lawrence.

Amherst in the meantime had made little progress, using August and September to refortify Ticonderoga, build another fort at Crown Point, and construct ships to ensure British naval supremacy on Lake Champlain. Not until 11 October did he march out again from Crown Point, only to march back again eight days later when news of the fall of Quebec and severe freezing weather arrived together. One recent author has written that his behavior "makes sense, granted one assumption: he expected Wolfe to fail, and did not mean to have himself deeply committed in Canada when it happened."

Wolfe succeeded in 1759; victory followed in 1760. Pitt called on the colonies to raise as many men as they had in the previous year and promised the same subsidies. Again the response was good from New England and New York but many soldiers did not arrive until June. By this date the remaining French forces in Canada had already rallied for an assault on the large English garrison that had wintered at Quebec; failing to break the English in a pitched battle at Sillery, they settled down to a siege of the city. The besiegers lacked artillery and sufficient force; nor had appeals to France in 1759 for 6,000 troops to reverse French fortunes been fruitful. The first ships to appear under Quebec on the St. Lawrence flew the British colors. All hopes of French revival disappeared. On 17 May, the besieging forces retreated up the river to join the scanty French garrisons preparing to resist the advance of the English against Montreal. By September three English armies converged there; they had pushed aside all resistance and driven every active French and Canadian soldier into the town. Outnumbered many times by Amherst's armies, deserted by their Indian allies and by most of the Canadian militia, the French military and civil command capitulated peaceably on 8 September 1760. North America seemed won for the English. True, Louisiana remained unconquered but its population and military potential was tiny; nor was France likely to reinforce it. The same was even more true of French outposts on the Great Lakes and in the Illinois country.

C. Problems of war and peace

French power, in fact, did not again pose a serious threat in North America, although France and England remained at war elsewhere. In June 1762 a French fleet attacked Newfoundland attempting to gain a pawn to use in peace negotiations; it was defeated by September. In late 1762 preliminary terms of the peace were agreed between the powers. The final treaty was signed in early 1763. For Great Britain, the formal result of the struggle in North America was almost total supremacy. France ceded Canada and all its dependencies, including the Illinois country and the other western parts. The French retained two small islands in the Gulf of St. Lawrence, St. Pierre and Miquelon, as fishing posts and the right to dry their catches on certain Newfoundland shores. Otherwise, Louisiana remained in French hands, but apart from New Orleans and its environs, its boundary with the British territories was put at the center of the Mississippi River and free navigation guaranteed on it to British subjects. Moreover, in a secret pact of 1762 France had pledged herself to cede Louisiana to Spain, a promise carried out in 1764. So by this time her once extensive North American empire had vanished. Spain herself ceded Florida to Great Britain at the peace and renounced all claims to share in the American cod fisheries. In the West Indies, Africa, and the East Indies, Great Britain had also obtained territories or privileges.

Yet after 1760, for some colonists and British regulars, limited fighting on the continent continued for another four years or so. The Indians, the third party in the "Great War for the Empire," now increasingly realized that the colonists' victory had shifted the conditions under which they lived and might even mean disaster. Indian security in the lands west of the mountains could no longer rest on the elaborate diplomacy that had formerly gained them alliances and guarantees from two opposing European powers. The European practice of giving annual presents to the Indians, of supplying them with arms and gunpowder and of promising, and sometimes supplying, cheap trade goods might vanish in a dependency under one strong but parsimonious imperial power.

Various Indian leaders expressed all these considerations very shortly after the defeat of the French. Nor did the threat of direct white occupation of their territories escape their attention, since colonial negotiations for western lands had been in train for some years and some actual settlement had taken place.

Meanwhile, French agents and adventurers played on Indian apprehensions, pointing to English exploitation and promising the eventual return of French armies to North America. Several of these factors played a part in the first Indian war of the period, the Cherokee War, and probably all of them in the second, the rising of 1763.

The Cherokee War lasted from about 1759 to 1761. Its outbreak marked the temporary ascendancy of an anti-English faction among the Cherokee, a nation traditionally friendly to them. Undoubtedly, the French were active among the Cherokee in the 1750s, promoting their influence by the construction of Fort Massac on the right bank of the Ohio below the Tennessee River. Small bands of French-allied Cherokees raided Rowan County, North Carolina, and parts of western South Carolina in 1759. There were also raids and counter-raids between colonists and warriors returning from aiding Forbes's expedition of 1759. More permanent sources of bad feeling existed in western South Carolina, where white settlement of Cherokee territory and the establishment by the colony of two forts, Loudoun and Prince George, although negotiated with some chiefs, caused resentment among other Cherokee. Nor did the continuing malpractices of the growing number of traders brought to the region by these white advances contribute to stability. Under all these new conditions, many Cherokees increasingly accepted French allegations that the South Carolina forts were meant not to benefit the Indians but to dominate them. Yet the fighting became intense only after the South Carolina governor, William Lyttelton, led an ineffectual punitive expedition among the Cherokees in 1759. In the same year Indian raiding parties advanced to within sixty miles of Charleston. South Carolina's request for regular military aid was agreed to by Amherst, an inveterate if ill-informed Indian hater. In April 1760 a force of regulars arrived at Charleston, marched to and destroyed several Cherokee lower towns but withdrew without crushing all Indian resistance. On 7 August 1760 Fort Loudoun capitulated to a Cherokee force that massacred some of its inmates, and raids continued elsewhere. Peace did not finally come until December 1761, after a second force of British regulars was sent by Amherst and destroyed many of the Cherokee middle towns.

The effects of this war were mostly confined to the frontiers of South and North Carolina and of Virginia. Indeed, on the Cherokee side, the war involved little more than a series of raids; no other southern Indians took part. The colonial decision to call for regular forces against them certainly aided southern expansionists whose territorial ambitions the Cherokees barred. The war does seem to have broken the power of the southern Indian nation, softening them for the rapid advance of settlement shortly to come. The treaty that ended it showed Indian consciousness of the threat of white advances, providing for a permanent line of demarcation between Indian and white territory. The Cherokees could not know how characteristic and useless a feature of so many Indian treaties this would become.

In May 1763 came the military manifestation of northern Indian reactions to the events of the preceding years. An unsuccessful attack on Fort Detroit, which was then besieged by Ottawas, Chippewas, and Potawatomis, was followed by the rapid fall of nine forts in and around the Great Lakes. Other Indian forces gathered in the Niagara region, while to the south in the Ohio Valley Fort Pitt came under attack. The frontier communities of Pennsylvania and Virginia also suffered numerous raids. The scale and intensity of this pan-Indian movement, involving and encompassing the greater part of the Old West, and the fact that it showed evident cooperation between many groups and tribes, made it perhaps the most serious, certainly the most extensive, colonial Indian war. Regular forces had to be used, both in 1763 and 1764, before a general peace could be imposed. The last treaties with the numerous Indian groups involved did not, in fact, come until 1766. Yet it may be noted that the southern Indians, although aware of events north of the Ohio, remained at peace, allowing the British to concentrate their forces.

What led to this war? In the first place, fears of the consequences of English victory had soon spread among the Indians; the most detailed evidence of these appears from the words of a Delaware Indian, the "Delaware prophet," whose emergence in the early 1760s reveals the psychic and material pressures on Indian consciousness. His message seems to have been that the Indians should renounce white culture, including firearms and trade, but his language and symbolism reflected Christian influences. As quoted by Pontiac, one of the leading figures among the hostile Indian warriors, the prophet had communed with the "Master of Life" who had spoken of the intrusion of the English and the French and the sins of the Indians: ". . . if you were not evil, as you are, you could surely do without them. You could live as you did live before knowing them—before those whom you call your brothers had come upon your lands. Did you not live by the bow and arrow? You had no need of gun and powder, or anything else, and nevertheless you caught animals to live upon and to dress yourselves with their skins . . ." The prophet's exact preaching is mainly lost, but he obviously called for an Indian renaissance by the rejection of the whites. From this point of view the movement resembled, though this is difficult to discover, those of other oppressed groups inspired by other millenial dreams.

Other Indian grievances were specific, often contradicting the religious theme. Amherst, for example, had instituted a stringent and mean policy of refusing to allow gifts for the Indians and of depriving them of gunpowder necessary for their winter hunting. This reversal of former European policy, which seemed to justify Indian fears of English victory, the general supported on the grounds of showing the Indians who were their masters. Prices of trade goods increased, rather than lessened as the English had promised. English settlers and traders pressed in, especially in western Pennsylvania and around Fort Pitt on the Ohio. At a conference in Easton in 1761 several of these points were enunciated, and one Indian prophetically bewailed that "We are penned up like Hogs; there are Forts all round us and therefore we are apprehensive that Death is coming on us." At the same time, French dissidents encouraged Indians fears and promised aid.

Naturally, the Indian effort failed. Although those involved showed a limited ability to cooperate for short periods, bravery was no match for well-armed regular soldiers. Henry Bouquet, the Swiss-born general and the best tactician of the time, particularly distinguished himself, dispersing the Indians around Fort Pitt at the Battle of Bushy Run in August 1763.

These Indian wars concluded nearly a decade of struggle that had important consequences for colonial-English relations. One of these was a certain disdain among British officers for the military capacities of the colonials. The wars also raised again the question of the support and assistance that Americans could be expected to give to regular forces. Colonel Montgomery, commander of the British troops in South Carolina in the Cherokee struggle in 1760, complained of the scant support given him there, continuing similar, earlier criticism. Bouquet, for example, in 1757 informed Lord Loudoun that South Carolinians were "*extremely pleased to have Soldiers* to protect their Plantations but will feel no inconveniences from them, making no differences between a Soldier and a Negro." In Pennsylvania the reluctance of the assembly to vote money for frontier defenses became an internal political issue as well as a source of British irritation. Official military dislike of alleged colonial parsimony and unwilling cooperation was evident throughout all the war years. The refusal or inability to meet full demands for soldiers, to provide adequate supplies, to act with any sense of urgency, and the haste with which colonial troops returned home, even before campaigning finished, provoked frequent comments. By 1763 some in England believed that the Americans, indeed, had refused to fight the French until paid by the Crown.

Potentially more serious had been disputes over barracks and winter quarters for British soldiers, particularly in New York and Massachusetts, where quartering was widely resisted as an encroachment on civilian rights and liberties. In December 1757 Loudoun wrote of the latter colony that the assembly, in legislating restrictively about quartering, was attempting both to "take away the King's undoubted prerogative" and opposing "an Act of the British Parliament . . . ," attempting "to make it impossible for the King either to keep Troops in North America, or if he kept them in his Forts to make it impossible for him to march them thro' his own Dominions either for the Defence of these Dominions or for the Protection of the Lives and Property of his subjects." Such reports were not to be forgotten by colonial administrators and contributed to a determination to order American affairs more firmly when the opportunity came. Writing in or before 1763, an advisor to Lord Shelburne stated that "The Provinces being now surrounded by an army, a navy, and by hostile tribes of Indians . . . it may be time (not to oppress or injure them) but to exact a due deference to the just and equitable demands of a British parliament," while

William Knox, an influential official, categorically stated in the same year that "Troops, and Fortifications will be very necessary for Great Britain to keep up in her Colonys, if she intends to settle their Dependence on Her."

Yet it is doubtful if any important British politician subscribed to the view that military forces should remain in America to guarantee colonial subordination or cooperation. Rather, the outcome of the war made some kind of army absolutely necessary. With the need to maintain a sovereign presence over the newly acquired territories in Florida, in Canada, and over the former French forts of the Illinois, Great Lakes, and Michigan-Wisconsin regions and in Nova Scotia and Newfoundland, there could be no return to the position a few years before when there were few regulars in the colonies. The consensus of opinion among Indian agents like William Johnson and among informed military commanders was also that some means had to be found to prevent white settlement west of the mountains which would "infallibly irritate and provoke the Indians, and might be attended with fatal consequences" as well. Nor was settlement alone to be feared, for experience showed that traders' abuses provoked equally grave Indian resentments. From these views came the assumption in British circles that troops should be used to control trade and to police white activities in the interiors. Decisions that regiments should be maintained in North America were made in late 1762 and early 1763 when, Professor Shy has suggested, the only discussion was over the size of the American garrison. The orders given in October 1763 to the commander-in-chief in America for the use of regular troops in peace referred to the prevention of illegal settlement on Indian land, the regulation of the fur trade and the assistance of customs officers. In the same month the English government also issued the famous proclamation that forbade settlement west of the mountains and prohibited the purchase of land from the Indians except by Indian superintendents.

The instruction to the commander-in-chief to assist customs officers in their duties marked another novel aspect of British colonial thinking produced by the war. Initially, the conflict had raised in dramatic fashion the question of illegal colonial trade with the French. Before 1755, it was well known and grudgingly accepted that New England and middle-colony foodstuffs and other provisions found their way to the French West Indies and the islands' molasses came back to America. Evidence that this trade continued, even at the height of hostilities, allegedly more lucratively than in time of peace, was recorded in British files throughout the war. In 1757 Loudoun denounced Rhode Islanders as "a lawless set of smugglers, who continually supply the Enemy with what Provisions they want, and bring back their goods in Barter for them," and in 1760 Pitt condemned colonial smugglers in a circular letter to all British governors. Yet enforcement of trade laws within the colonies provoked a powerful resistance from obviously strong interests. In Massachusetts problems of enforcement became enmeshed in political rivalries between the Hutchinson and Otis families. James Otis, in a campaign against Thomas Hutchinson and his patron, Governor Francis Bernard, argued in 1761 that the use of writs of assistance, allowing blanket searches for suspected smuggled goods, raised great constitutional questions and that they were "instruments of slavery . . . No acts of Parliament can establish such a writ . . . An Act against the constitution is void." In 1762 Otis directed further opposition against the governor, and British legislation, using the language of natural rights to stress the autonomy of Massachusetts in the British Empire. In the same year the British government strengthened the trade acts in a new statute that allowed half of the value of seized articles to accrue to the customs officers. This same act authorized the royal navy to make seizures, giving the crews the same half share. By this date enforcement of the acts of trade seemed even more important because of the vast British public debt created by the war.

British officials and ministers therefore faced problems of military and civil administration and of trade during the years preceding 1763. Yet in other areas potentially disruptive issues between Britain and the colonies were settled amicably. As Lawrence H. Gipson has shown, the British government paid out substantial subsidies to each colony, according to its expenditure on troops and provisions requested for use in the British campaigns, beginning with about £165,000 for the 1755 campaign. In 1758 Pitt's budget included £200,000 for "Compensation to the Provinces of North America, for Expenses incurred by them in levying, clothing, and Pay of Troops raised there" and similar sums were allotted in the two following years, then reduced to £133,333 for 1761 and a similar amount for 1762. Professor Gipson also shows that no colony incurred lasting war debts. After receiving subsidies, Massachusetts's debt, the largest of all, amounted to £490,000 in 1762, which was quickly liquidated; in other colonies as well the public debt had been repaid by the late 1760s.

Liquidation of debts, however, often really meant high taxes and liquidation of circulating paper money, circumstances that coincided with and contributed to the economic consequences of the war. Until the early 1760s, the colonial economy had generally boomed. Yet the boom depended heavily on British credit and wartime spending. Following the active phase of the war at some time in or after 1760, commercial depressions hit most colonies, lasting until about 1765-1766. In the Chesapeake colonies tobacco prices suffered, exchange rates shot up, and creditors called for payment. In 1765 Benedict Calvert of Maryland wrote (admittedly for an English audience on whom he wished to impress the poverty of Americans) that the colony's trade was "ruined, we are immensely in debt, and [with] not the least probability of getting clear. Our gaols are not half large enough to hold the debtors, upon every road you ride you meet people going from different parts of the province to get out of the way of our creditors." In Virginia by April 1765 exchange rates had reached the highest point ever and credit and trade had slackened badly. In Pennsylvania, where early in 1760 one merchant wrote that "the war hath occasioned such a plentiful Circulation of Cash in this and the neighbouring Provinces that the demand of the Inhabitants for European goods is beyond what any Person not full acquainted therewith can conceive," a slump had taken place by the end of the year and trade stagnated until 1765, with business failures continuing after that date in Philadelphia. Similar conditions were reported from Boston and from New York, where the departure of British soldiers in 1761 also cut local profits. The extent of the post-war depression should not, however, be exaggerated. Prices of agricultural products in the northern and middle colonies were high and rose buoyantly after about 1763 in response to new demands from overseas. Rice from Charleston also continued high. The depression, in fact, probably mainly affected the urban merchant class of the colonial towns, which Professor Bridenbaugh believes "had attained its peak by 1760, though the members did not then suspect the fact," and the Chesapeake tobacco trade.

Commerce in America, where it depended on credit, was, of course, shaped by conditions in the mother country. There, the war and its aftermath caused considerable economic fluctuations, including crises in 1762-1763 and from 1765 to about 1768-1769. Yet for America the indirect effects of the transition in Britain from a war to a peace economy were of even greater importance. For William Pitt's financial policy depended heavily on deficit financing: by the end of 1762 the British national debt stood, it has been calculated, at £140 million, twice that of ten years previously. National expenditure, which amounted to £16 million in 1757, had risen to £24 million in 1762. In 1763, the first year of real peace, it amounted to £14 million, of which more than half a million could not be provided by existing taxation. In the minds of many British politicans, rightly or wrongly, it was necessary "to submit to the bankruptcy of their country, or lay fresh taxes in cold blood." That new revenue might be produced from the American colonies on which considerable sums had been spent by Britain in the war years indeed seemed both reasonable and desirable.

Chapter Eleven

The Colonies and the Empire

A. British policies

The sense of financial crisis and urgency that accompanied the end of the Seven Years' War made action imperative for the King's ministers. A ministry that failed to tackle the fiscal problem would certainly lose the vital support of the independent members of Parliament, mainly gentry anxious for a reduction in the tax on land that had risen during the war to 4 shillings on the pound. To such men, often jealous of commercial wealth, trade and colonies were seen as excellent and natural sources of new revenue. At the same time specific colonial issues also awaited attention as a result of the acquisition of vast new territories from the St. Lawrence to the Gulf of Mexico. Henry Fox wrote in 1763 that "the settlement of American affairs has become the greatest and most necessary of all schemes." And as early as April of the same year, a minor politician surmised that "the settlement of America must be the first and principal object [of the administration]. It will certainly be the chief point upon which all future opposition will attempt to throw its colours and rise its battery. It will prove, in a word, the chief engine of faction."

The chief engine of faction! The nature of English political life at the conclusion of the Seven Years' War did not make the solution of vital public issues easy. Pitt, who had the support of the House of Commons during a time of war, had resigned in October 1761. The ministry that carried on the war and negotiated the peace became increasingly identified with the Earl of Bute, appointed Secretary of State and First Lord of the Treasury in May 1762. Bute, although at first enjoying the ardent backing of George III, never won the confidence of Parliament and resigned from office in the spring of 1763. Bute's successor, George Grenville, maintained a precarious hold on George III's favor and, though in the opinion of one recent biographer of the King, Grenville was soon to be "the ablest man in the House of Commons," he only gradually won substantial Parliamentary backing. Pitt's ministry had lasted for one year after George's accession, Bute's as First Lord, for eleven months, and Grenville's was to last for twenty-seven months. Indeed, until the consolidation of Lord North's ministry in the 1770s, a succession of short-lived and divided ministries, vexed as much by the problems of maintaining power as by those of policy, had the responsibility of government. The age was one of faction, and American affairs became grist for the political mill.

Grenville formed his ministry in April 1763. His own forte lay in financial matters, and he had the King's support in his desire for public economy, although George III later stated that his minister had the mind of a clerk in a counting house. Two of Grenville's ministerial colleagues had considerable experience in colonial affairs. Lord Egremont, Secretary of State for the Southern Department, had been responsible for the colonies since 1761 while his colleague the Earl of Halifax, who on Egremont's death in August 1763 moved from northern to southern secretaryship, had formerly been president of the Board of Trade. The ministry continued a thorough review of colonial policy begun before its inception. When news of the Indian war of 1763 began to arrive in England later in the year, threatening fresh expenditures and exposing the weakness of the British position in the west, the review gained greater urgency.

The first substantive acts of the Grenville ministry involved the frontiers and the unsettled territories. Discussions took place during the summer of 1763 and a proclamation of 7 October 1763 provided for the establishment of three new governments in North America—East Florida, West Florida, and Quebec. Other territory south of the St. Lawrence was absorbed into Nova Scotia. The vast western lands outside these areas were reserved to the Indians. Land grants and settlements within them were forbidden, and Indian trade was restricted to licensed men under supervision. Responsibility for law and order and other rudimentary acts of government within the west was left to the British army, and some aspects of Indian relations to the civilian Indian superintendents. This plan had many weaknesses, not least of all its patent unenforceability, except at vast cost. Even as conceived, it was expensive in that it fell mostly to the British army and the British-paid Indian superintendents to operate it. Indeed, only three years later, Lord Barrington, secretary at war, argued for the withdrawal of all British troops from the west, partly on the grounds of expense. Yet the Proclamation of 1763 provided a skeleton policy and the three new governments over the settled areas functioned relatively successfully. Grenville approved certain concessions to French Canadians, while in 1766 the Rockingham cabinet lost office before they could implement new liberal regulations for Quebec, providing for the integration of the conquered French inhabitants and anticipating the more famous Quebec Act of 1774.

For the time being, on paper and as a political matter in England at least, the western question was therefore relatively easily resolved. It did not go before Parliament nor did the House of Commons interest itself in it. Grenville's second line of action on America aimed at tightening up existing trade and customs legislation, something suggested since 1759 and already begun with an investigation of the workings and of the revenue produced by the acts of trade.

The customs commissioners and the Treasury reported in the summer of 1763 that Britain lost thousands of pounds through the collusion of customs officials and merchants in the import of foreign sugar and molasses, and by smuggling made easier by the long American coastline and the absenteeism of customs officers. The government first responded by ordering colonial governors to enforce the trade laws with severity and by requiring absent customs officers to return to their duties. It then prepared to introduce new legislation to attack the root of the problem, accepting recommendations from the permanent officials of the relevant government departments.

The resulting bill dealing with "[his] Majesty's dominions in America" came before the House of Commons in March 1764. Made law in April—it is commonly known as the Sugar Act—it reduced the duty on foreign molasses to 3 pence per gallon, half that laid down in the Molasses Act of 1733. It also placed new duties on other foreign items and repealed certain concessions made to English exporters of foreign goods to the colonies. In total, a revenue of some £45,000 was anticipated; the act itself stated the justice and necessity of raising a revenue from North America for "defending, protecting, and securing the same." Moreover, Grenville, speaking in Parliament, mentioned that it might become necessary to find a new source of American revenue by means of stamp duties on various documents and papers. Similar proposals had been advanced since the 1750s and earlier. Grenville's own interest in a Stamp Act had probably been stimulated by Henry McCulloch, a man familiar with American conditions, who in 1763 claimed that such duties could bring in from £50,000 to £120,000 annually, figures that he later fancifully raised to half a million pounds.

The preparation of a Stamp Act indeed had begun in late 1763. Yet the measure did not become law until March 1765, to take effect in November of the same year. The delay announced the start of important political difficulties for the Grenville ministry's American plans, difficulties that did not cease for the next three years. The questions of the constitutional position of the colonies and their relation to Parliament now emerged from their former obscurity to become a serious issue. Indeed, when Grenville announced the possibility of a Stamp Act to Parliament in 1764, he added that "he hoped that the power and sovereignty of parliament over every part of the British dominions for the purpose of raising or collecting any tax would not be disputed." The apprehensions evident in this statement were justified. For as the views of American agents in England and of their constituents in the colonies on the proposed act were made known to the government, it was evident that they would fight the Stamp Act as a threat to American liberty.

Americans and a few Englishmen also quickly recognized that the act, which sought to raise taxes within America, was innovatory. Although Grenville and his officials could cite several minor acts where this had been done before, he did not argue about precedents but maintained Parliament's absolute sovereignty over all parts of the King's dominions. Yet it is true that English governmental practice had been to concentrate revenue-producing legislation on external commerce, not on internal taxation. Some Americans seized on this distinction between external and internal taxation; others disputed any claim by Parliament to tax Americans at all and included the Sugar Act in their protests. Grenville would certainly have liked to have avoided these debates by obtaining some measures of prior colonial assent to the Stamp Act before its passage by Parliament, which is why he held up its progress. Yet the opinions of the colonial agents and reports of American views confirmed his opinion that prior colonial consent was unobtainable. These facts delayed but did not prevent its passage.

The Stamp Act controversy exposed the great possibilities for discord in the post-war relations of England and her American colonies. English awareness of these was at first very limited. The Grenville ministry did not fear domestic opposition to a strong assertion of imperial constitutional authority, and such opposition on political or constitutional grounds in the House of Commons was slight. The inexpediency rather than the unconstitutionality of the Stamp Act was mainly challenged. On this point the ministry carefully explained that the act was meant at first to raise only the very moderate sum of £60,000 per annum, money that would be collected by American not British officials, used in America, and, they could have added, together with the sums raised by the Sugar Act and other minor measures, would still leave the British government paying over half of the cost of colonial military defense.

Undoubtedly, most British politicians felt the Sugar and Stamp acts to be both fair and fiscally lenient. They were hardly aware of some of the incidental effects of these and other reforms put into effect by the Grenville ministry, or of other matters now troubling Americans. The Sugar Act, for example, had included clauses imposing new restrictions on colonial exports by extending the list of enumerated articles and had raised duties on the important wine trade between the colonies and southern Europe. Moreover, it had further tightened up the administration of the acts of trade, requiring merchants to obtain official documentation for their intercolonial commerce and expensive bonds where the smuggling of foreign molasses and syrups seemed likely. The act also sanctioned the use against offenders of "any court of vice-admiralty which may or shall be appointed over all America"—a reference to a new vice-admiralty court with extensive jurisdiction that was now being set up in Halifax, Nova Scotia. Finally, it reduced the possibility of successful suits for wrongful seizure by merchants against customs officials by making this seizure legal where it could be shown to be based on "probable cause." This tightening up of the customs service in the act ran parallel with the new policy then also being applied in orders of the Privy Council and other non-Parliamentary measures. Previously, Parliament legislated in 1763 to authorize the use of military personnel and ships in aiding the customs authorities.

During 1764 the Grenville ministry also passed a new Currency Act for America, generally extending the provisions of the 1751 act to the colonies outside New England. This enactment met the still growing demands of British merchants involved in the Virginia trade for protection of sterling debts; its most important effect was to ban the use of paper money issued after September 1764 as legal tender for either private or public debts, although the latter provision never found rigorous enforcement in the colonies. This legislation, which in no way solved the problem of an American currency and money supply, occurred at a time when the colonies faced a shortage of specie and a contracting post-war economy. It soon came to be resented among certain important colonial groups as additional evidence of the new harshness of British attitudes toward America.

Other aspects of British policy resulted in more localized irritants, particularly in New England. Among the acts of Parliament on the statute books for some time, but newly and vigorously enforced only in those years, were those reserving certain trees for the navy and those conserving white pine trees. These caused general resentment among substantial men in New England with timber interests. Another bitterly contested English measure was the sanction given to the impressment of colonial seamen by the Royal Navy in American ports, a practice that Americans linked with standing armies and military tyranny. Similar fears were raised with even more force by an act of Parliament of 1765, the Quartering or Mutiny Act, which required the colonies to furnish barracks, or provide other lodgings, and to supply specified items to British troops in America.

A very considerable agitation, first in New England, then in the middle colonies, arose in a way that few English politicians and administrators probably knew or much cared about. Zealous Anglicans in London, mostly associated with the Society for the Propagation of the Gospel and mostly in response to colonial Anglican petitioning, seemed to be attempting to persuade the administration to buttress the Church of England in America. Although the Anglicans scored one victory when in May 1763 the Privy Council disallowed an act of the Massachusetts General Court creating a new missionary society for work among the Indians, their actual influence on government was negligible. Yet a constant stream of English press reports—one in the *London Chronicle* in 1764 reported that an archbishop and twelve suffragan bishops would be appointed to America—and a number of sermons and tracts by important Anglican leaders, together with unsubstantiated rumors, suggested that the establishment of bishops in America and an attack on dissenting institutions there had high priority in the minds of the Grenville ministry. The ministry's relative liberality in its treatment of French Roman Catholics in Canada also was seen as corroborating evidence of its misplaced sympathies.

The Grenville ministry fell in July 1765. By this time, for reasons totally unconnected with America, the King had developed an extreme distaste for

George Grenville, and a fixed determination never again to appoint him to high office became a cardinal point of royal policy, vitally curtailing George III's freedom of political maneuver. During the autumn and winter of the same year Grenville and his followers, anxious in opposition to defend the policies that they had sponsored, increasingly advocated a hard line toward the American colonies as protests against the Stamp Act and reports of disturbances flowed into London. Grenville's successor, the Marquess of Rockingham, and his colleagues at first also showed their resentment against American protests, condemning, for example, the resolves of the Virginia House of Burgesses and of the Massachusetts lower house against the Stamp Act as an "absolute Disavowal of the Right of Parliament of Great Britain to impose Taxes upon the Colonies and a daring attack on the Constitution of this Country." Some members of Rockingham's cabinet, noticeably the Attorney General, Charles Yorke, and his brother, Lord Hardwicke, probably favored enforcement of the Stamp Act; others were undecided; all, like most members of Parliament, resented the violence and, they felt, the irrationality of American protests.

The Rockingham ministry had to proceed cautiously since overready compliance with American demands might lead to defeat in the House of Commons or disputes amongst its members. What finally seems to have decided the ministry on repeal was the growing opposition of English commercial and manufacturing interests, now working in conjunction with American agents in Great Britain, against the Stamp Act on the grounds that American measures were causing "a great and sudden Dimunition and Stagnation" of the export trade. Some of the Rockinghamites fostered this opposition in order to provide a reason for retreat on the Stamp Act. They also awaited the opinion of William Pitt, who had so far held himself aloof from the public debate but whose influence in the House of Commons remained considerable. In January 1766 Pitt made a long-awaited speech before the House. He outrightly condemned the Stamp Act. His attack—stronger than any yet pronounced by a leading politician—probably made repeal inevitable, easing Rockingham's own task in winning support for this policy. Yet Rockingham wished to cite as the reason for it the imprudence of retaining an act that so seriously disrupted commercial relations between England and America. Pitt, by contrast, raised a constitutional point. To many, he seemed to say that the English Parliament could lay external but not internal taxes on the colonists: "Let the sovereign authority of this country over the colonies be asserted in as strong terms as can be desired, and be made to extend to every point of legislation whatever. That we may bind their trade, confine their manufactures, and exercise every power whatsoever, except that of taking their money out of their pockets without their consent." Modern scholars now largely agree that Pitt, like most Americans, "denounced all taxation of the colonists by Parliament but held that this limitation of power did not extend to the imposition of duties framed for the control of trade which might incidentally, but not of intent, produce a revenue."

Nearly all members of the House agreed that should the Stamp Act be repealed, some assertion of Parliamentary authority over America had to be made. Rockingham's ministry provided this before the passage of repeal. In March 1766 the House of Commons, without a division, gave a third reading to a bill which declared that Parliament "had, hath and of right ought to have, full power and authority to make laws and statutes of sufficient force and validity to bind the colonies and people of America, subjects of the Crown of Great Britain, in all cases whatsoever." This Declaratory Act also passed the House of Lords with only five dissenting votes. As between repeal, suspension, modification and enforcement of the Stamp Act, opinions had been divided. The King favored modification of the Stamp Act rather than repeal, but repeal rather than enforcement. Grenville and his ally the Duke of Bedford remained convinced hard-liners, who thought that by repeal English authority would suffer a humiliating defeat. Rockingham and most of his followers now stood for repeal for the sake of conciliation and expediency. Pitt proclaimed his great friendship for America, supported repeal, and seemed to reject Parliament's taxing powers. Yet at the same time he spoke in strong terms of the general right of Parliament to legislate for the empire. On the same day as the Declaratory Act was passed, the ministry's bill for outright repeal of the Stamp Act succeeded in the Commons by 250 votes to 122 on its third reading. Later, a large majority in the Lords voted for repeal. Without the Declaratory Act, it might have failed. And as Professor Morgan has explained, the passage of the Declaratory Act seemed to insist on Parliament's right to legislate for Americans not because, as some Englishmen had previously argued, they had virtual representation in Parliament but because of Parliament's innate legislative sovereignty. Another modern authority suggests that the Declaratory Act was ambiguous since it mentioned Parliament's right of legislation but not, specifically, of taxation. Americans could therefore believe that taxation was excluded from the scope of the act, Englishmen that it was comprehended within it. Certainly, many Americans felt the act to be a mere face-saving device and that the powers proclaimed in it would never be used. They also welcomed a second measure of the Rockingham government, an act proposed in May and passed shortly after that favored the American colonies by reducing duties on foreign sugar and other foreign goods imported into them.

Rockingham's ministry collapsed in July 1766. It had come into office hoping for the support of William Pitt, which it never received. Its youthful leaders lacked experience and self-confidence; when Pitt, now bidding for power, began a serious opposition to them in April 1766, their weak resolution faltered. Hostile to Grenville, disillusioned by Rockingham, George III happily turned to Pitt, for whose service he had hoped during the past years. Pitt seemed still the man who might be able to conduct the government of the country with the general support of Lords and Commons. Moreover, his expressed desire to "form a ministry which should transcend and obliterate party distinctions" accorded with the King's wishes. Pitt, ennobled as Lord Chatham, now became first minister, with the full backing of the Crown. In American affairs a period of moderation was obviously called for and Chatham seemed destined to provide it. He had, after all, emerged during the Stamp Act crisis as the great friend of America, its most powerful English defender. Yet Chatham had also announced his support of Parliamentary sovereignty over America and he was moody, irascible, egotistical, autocratic—and ill.

His ministry, despite the King's support, was politically weak, shored up by the inclusion of politicians of different and sometimes opposing interests—yet no more so than many other eighteenth-century ministries. Nevertheless, Chatham's initial policy was on a grand scale—to produce a revenue from India by reforming the powerful East India Company, an enterprise that was bound to create great political controversy. It has been argued that, as a corollary, Americans were to be left untaxed until, with new Indian revenues flowing in and happy reasonableness prevailing, some mutual agreement would be reached as to a fair method of raising a modest sum of money from the colonies. However, it is clear Chatham's attitude to the American colonies was never wholly conciliatory. During the first months of his government, the New York Assembly vigorously protested against the Quartering Act of 1765, claiming that its demand that the colonies provide billets and supplies for British troops amounted to a new form of taxation, a position Chatham could not accept. And the Chatham ministry from its inception studied the problem of raising an American revenue to pay for the British army there, now costing £400,000 per annum. When these problems became urgent in 1767, Chatham was ill and unapproachable, lying shattered by gout and melancholia, outside of London. He resigned in September 1768 without having returned to lead his administration.

Ministerial decisions about America at first mainly devolved on Lord Shelburne, Secretary of State for the Southern Department. Shelburne had fought for the repeal of the Stamp Act and had opposed the Declaratory Act. In Chatham's absence, he first prevaricated then gradually came to a harsh view of New York's disobedience. Though he distinguished "between *New York* and *America*," he recommended to the cabinet in the spring of 1767 that the province should be cowed by strengthening the Declaratory Act in such a way as to make it high treason for any American to refuse to obey an act of Parliament and a lesser form of treason to write, preach, speak, publish, or affirm that the King and Parliament could not legislate for the colonies. Offenders were to be tried in Britain and the act was to be enforced by the army if necessary. Shelburne's plan was rejected as too autocratic. Charles Townshend, Chancellor of the Exchequer, suggested another scheme. A modification of this became law in July 1767, suspending the New York Assembly from October of the same year unless it voted to carry out the provisions of the 1765 Quartering Act.

A man of oratorical brilliance, Charles Townshend was also devious and unpredictable—even untrustworthy. He was also considered a leading expert on America. "No man in England understands it so well, and consequently nobody would be so agreeable to those who are particularly interested in what relates either to the West Indies or North America," Newcastle wrote to Rockingham in May 1766, recommending Townshend's appointment as Secretary of State for America. This reputation, indeed, had been responsible for several suggestions that Townshend be given high office since 1763. And it is true that he was one of the few leading English politicians who had given any thought to America before that date. In the 1750s he had correctly analyzed the course of American political development, recognizing the paramount powers of the colonial assemblies which had drawn "to themselves the ancient and established prerogative wisely preserved in the Crown" and had dispossessed "the Crown of almost every degree of executive power ever lodged in it. . . ." In March 1763, while president of the Board of Trade, he had, without consulting his colleagues, brought forward a plan for taxing America, thereby greatly displeasing the King—"I think Mr. Townshend's conduct deserves the dismissing of him," George wrote to Bute.

Townshend's political career after that date was a mixture of friendliness and opposition to successive ministries, the latter even when he had a place within them. He first opposed then joined Grenville, supporting the Stamp Act. Yet he was closely consulted by Rockingham on colonial matters. By the time of the debate on the repeal of the act, he supported Rockingham's position, basing his vote on a belief in the act's impracticability and not on opposition to its principles. For Townshend remained convinced in 1766, as he was in 1753-1754, of the need both to tax and to govern America and in this, stood closer to the Grenvillites than to the Rockinghamites. His firmness against New York's disobedience in 1767 was therefore consistent with his whole career.

Yet acceptance of Townshend's claims to speak on colonial matters resulted more from the deficiencies of his colleagues than from their understanding of his real knowledge, especially when the Chatham ministry sought conciliation with America. Townshend proved this in early 1767 when he blandly and unnecessarily mentioned in the House of Commons that he proposed to find an American revenue sufficient to cover most of the costs of the British army there. Moreover, he rejected any distinction between external and internal taxation and praised the principles that lay behind the Stamp Act. In doing this Townshend was acting alone, although the ministry had accepted the idea of raising an American revenue in 1766. His immediate motives are unknown, unless he sought to please the King and advance his political prospects. Of course many members of the house were still ready to support a reduction in English taxation—especially the land tax—by means of American taxation. When Townshend proceeded to produce tax measures, he made it clear that he would resign rather than have them modified. Townshend's full plans were announced to Parliament in the spring of 1767 when he also moved the bill to suspend the New York Assembly. They included the creation of a Board of Commissioners of the Customs in America, a body distinct from the English customs board but with the same powers under the Treasury, and the imposition of new duties on tea, glass, paper, printer's colors, and red and white lead, together with other minor amendments to duties. Colonial courts were to be empowered to issue writs of assistance allowing customs officers to enter and search for goods. Finally, an American civil list was to be created; governors, judges, and other royal officials on this list would be paid directly from revenue and would no longer have to depend on colonial assemblies for their salaries.

This legislation passed by Parliament in June 1767 has recently been described as "inconsequent alike in its premises and in its provisions—a perfect reflection of the man." For although Townshend claimed to see no merit in a distinction between external and internal taxes, he claimed one in the acts and laid duties only on external trade goods at the port of entry. Then, the revenue produced by the new duties was small. Except for tea, the imports taxed were not important ones. Lastly, although the renewal of taxing for American revenue at the beginning had been linked by Townshend to the question of military expenditure, the acts now proposed to use it to make novel payments to British officials by means of the American civil list.

As a plan of taxation, far from burying the political and constitutional issues known to exercise Americans, it resurrected them bodily. Yet Townshend's acts should probably be seen as political in their intention. They embodied a policy not unlike that of Chatham's, in that while maintaining a distinction between external and internal taxation, they aimed to provide conditions in which Parliamentary sovereignty and Crown control over America could be maintained. To believe such a policy could succeed was to misunderstand the nature of American attitudes toward British political authority. But there was little opposition in the House to Townshend's measures, for they probably reflected the mood of the House of Commons and the political nation—one not only of alarm over the fiscal problem in England arising in part from American expenditures but one of hostility toward America. This hostility arose directly from reports of the proud and scornful manner in which many of the colonists had celebrated the repeal of the Stamp Act, declaring it a victory over Parliament, as well as from news of such actions as the New York Assembly's rejection of English authority in the controversy over the Quartering Act. In late 1767 Parliament also passed an act that Townshend had approved, but not initiated, authorizing the substitution of four vice-admiralty courts in America for the one in Halifax; these would be located in Boston, Philadelphia, Charleston and Halifax itself.

In the spring of 1768, a general election took place in England, the first for several years, occupying the government's attention, and delaying action on American grievances and opposition. In the election the previously outlawed

John Wilkes, now under sentence of imprisonment, was returned as M.P. for Middlesex; he presented himself as "opposed to the encroachments of arbitrary power, despising ministerial influence, and maintaining the rights and privileges of the freeborn subjects in a land of liberty." In early 1769, the House of Commons refused to allow him to take his seat there. Wilkes was then re-elected as member for Middlesex on three occasions and three times was refused his seat. The Wilkes affair stirred old and mobilized new demands for Parliamentary reform, heightening political consciousness in London and the provinces, and it occupied Parliament on and off until early 1771. Wilkes had previously clashed with established political authority in England in 1763, but this had attracted little attention in America; the later crisis had wide publicity in the colonies. Like English radicals, with whom they maintained some close contacts, American radicals—and many Americans who had no pronounced radical views—identified Wilkes with the cause of honest, freedom-loving Englishmen and Americans in search of their constitutional rights against a corrupt and tyrannical Parliament and ministry. On the other hand, many Englishmen saw Wilkes and his English and American supporters as clever and unscrupulous politicians bent on weakening Crown and Parliament and overthrowing order and property.

Given these circumstances and the weakness of the ministry, American resistance to the Townshend program—and Townshend himself died in September 1767 before the storm broke—produced little constructive action on the part of the government. Lord Hillsborough, who became American Secretary in early 1768, pointlessly sent a circular letter to colonial governors in April 1768 condemning the Massachusetts lower house for inviting other colonial legislatures to take common action against the Townshend Acts. The governors were told to prorogue or dissolve any assembly that showed "a disposition to receive or give any countenance to this seditious paper." These instructions only further offended the most powerful colonial bodies by the directness of their interference with their basic political freedoms. He also ordered two regiments sent to Boston to aid the authorities. At this stage even Rockingham showed anger at American behavior, proclaiming his firm support of the Declaratory Act. But the ministry still awaited the next meeting of Parliament before deciding on a general policy. Their own position was weak. On 12 October 1768, ostensibly in protest against the impending dismissal of Lord Shelburne which took place a few days later, Chatham resigned, leaving the Duke of Grafton in an uneasy alliance with some of his former political enemies as titular head of the shattered administration. During the Parliamentary session of late 1768 Hillsborough successfully moved a series of resolutions condemning Massachusetts in the House of Lords and approving the dispatch of American "traitors" to England for trial. The Commons soon after concurred in these actions by the upper house. However, a plan placed by Hillsborough before the cabinet in January 1769 for a punitive amendment of the Massachusetts charter was vetoed by the King himself and a substantial minority of the Commons still opposed harsh measures.

In May 1769 it was decided that the Townshend duties would eventually be repealed but not the legislation creating an American board of customs and an American civil list. The conditions surrounding this decision and the subsequent statutory repeal, which occurred in March 1770, differed in important ways from those prevailing at the time of the repeal of the Stamp Act. Although British trade was affected in 1768 and 1769 by American non-importation agreements, their impact was feared much less than in 1765-1766. Moreover, British merchants were becoming disillusioned with America, especially as trade with the colonies had not revived much after 1765. No great alliance of British merchants and manufacturers, similar to that formed by the Rockingham Whigs, exerted pressure on the government. Similarly, the colonial agents, who had been consulted and involved in discussions of repeal of the Stamp Act, had little influence in 1769-1770, a sign of their loss of status and of the breakdown of formerly important links between the colonies, the English government, and English political opinion. In 1766, too, the country gentry M.P.s had not opposed repeal of the Stamp Act, though they profoundly desired a cut in domestic taxation and expected Americans to contribute toward the costs of government. By 1770, the independent members favored a harsh line, believing with Lord North that England ''should not run after America in search of reconciliation'' and that Parliament should enforce English interests. The repeal of the Townshend duties (except that on tea) they accepted as a last concession to ungrateful Americans.

With the reshaping of the original Chatham ministry, its center of gravity shifted as men who favored harsh measures toward America, like Hillsborough and followers of the Duke of Bedford, were brought in and more conciliatory politicians like Shelburne forced out. Grafton's ministry faced Grenvillites, Rockinghamites, and minor opposition groups; in January 1770 Chatham himself, more active since the summer of 1769, spoke against it in the House of Lords. A fortnight or so later, Grafton resigned, an act seen by the King as one of cowardice in the face of an increasingly powerful Parliamentary opposition. George III, at this juncture when men whom he did not want on the terms they offered seemed about to force their way into office, even spoke of abdication. Yet the blow never fell. The King turned to Lord North, Chancellor of the Exchequer since Townshend's death, who accepted Grafton's place as First Lord.

North remained in office until 1782, a surprising development after the succession of uncertain and divided governments up to 1770. His success had several foundations. First, he received the early support of the many country gentlemen, most of whom were always willing to back any efficient government that did not attack their interests and who were by now probably fatigued by the factional struggles of the last ten years. Then, he won the growing confidence of the King, with whom he had an easy rapport. North, too, proved an able dispenser of patronage in the mold of Sir Robert Walpole and Henry Pelham. Finally, the opposition was not really powerful but divided and dwindling, soon to be reduced by deaths and retirements, or deserted by men brought over by North to join his government as the odds against them mounted. When Lord North superintended the repeal of the Townshend duties in 1770, he spoke in terms of a future policy that would emphasize British supremacy over the colonies. The majority of Parliament endorsed his views. Both inside and outside of that body only a few Chathamites and Rockinghamites and a handful of radicals and dissenters could be expected to show continuing forbearance of American opposition.

B. American reactions

The varied and generally localized opposition to unpopular British measures that took place in the American colonies long before the accession of George III to the throne of England has already been noted. Its most regular form constituted part of the normal give and take of administration and politics, involving clashes between lower houses and colonial governors in America or the lobbying and petitioning of officials, politicians, merchants, and religious leaders in England. From time to time this opposition became more ferocious and provoking. The dispute over the Virginia Two-Penny Act, for example, first arose out of the grievances of Anglican clergy against Virginia planters in the colony, then found its way to England by petitions and lobbyists, led to the intervention of the Bishop of London and appeals to the King and finally involved the Board of Trade and the Virginia assembly in a head-on clash. Its further stages produced a full-scale pamphlet attack on the British government's right to tax Americans or interfere in their local government. A similar pattern of events occurred in Massachusetts during the controversy over writs of assistance which started as a lawyers' argument and ended with pamphleteers asserting the possibility that acts of Parliament might be void if contrary to the "British Constitution."

These, and other controversies before 1763, can be cited to illustrate several major features of colonial American politics. First, the existence, long before the new measures of Grenville and Townshend, of a set of political beliefs that kept fresh in the colonists' minds the idea of the legality—and necessity—of resistance to arbitrary power and attacks on liberty. While some men may have expressed these opinions merely as a stylized if useful rhetorical device, it is clear that many colonists genuinely feared malignant corruption and executive tyranny. Second, it is apparent that although this tradition existed to a greater or lesser extent in all the colonies, it did not yet serve to unite them. Although there is evidence that colonial newspapers devoted increasing space to the affairs of all the colonies, and colonial political tracts written in Maryland, for example, might be read in Massachusetts, there was little public intercolonial cooperation. Each colony conducted its political life without reference to its neighbor and viewed its place in the British empire as its own affair.

After 1763 new circumstances gave a fresh dimension to the familiar pattern of colonial politics. First, the new acts of the British government initiated and maintained a reforming pressure on the colonies of a kind that had not before been experienced in America. Both Parliamentary and administrative measures aimed to tighten up imperial control and raise an American revenue. In particular, the powerful colonial assemblies found themselves directly challenged by Parliament. Second, British politics at the same time entered a period of instability and nascent ideology. Now, more and more—though still in limited numbers—Englishmen began to talk again of ministerial corruption, of placemen, and of the need for reform. Americans, already familiar with this language, found a new confirmation of their old beliefs. They rapidly came to identify the measures of English politicians toward America with the alleged attack on liberty in England and America. With this identification, the gateway to revolution was pushed open. Finally, the attack on liberty came at a time of practical economic difficulty and distress. The commercial recession of the post-war years severely affected the colonial elites, creating hardship among northern merchants and southern planters who now found their freedom of action in commercial matters further restricted by British measures.

Even before the Grenville program was known in the colonies, faint murmurings of apprehension, certainly about the consequences of the capture of Canada and possibly about the decision to keep 10,000 troops in America, could be heard. These are comprehensible in the context of the longstanding American fear of standing armies, part of the Country tradition. Moreover, the addition of Catholic French Canadians to the empire brought added fears, and one of the essential components of the American Whig tradition was a violent anti-Catholicism. These now mingled with apprehensions of an Anglican assault, led perhaps by an American bishop, on the dissenters of the New World, particularly in New England where the Puritan clergy identified civil and religious liberty with freedom from Anglican competiton. A tract like Jonathan Mayhew's *Observations on the Charter and Conduct of the Society for the Propagation of the Gospel in Foreign Parts*, published in 1763, spoke of the society's missionaries as false brethren "unawares brought in, who came primarily to spy out our liberty which we have in Christ Jesus, that they might bring us into bondage" and accused it of spearheading the "great design of *espiscopizing* . . . all New-England, as well as the other colonies." After 1763 or so, New England Puritans and middle-colony Presbyterians not only stood in the forefront of opposition to feared British ecclesiastical assault but had also begun to cooperate in the cause of their liberties, a policy most strikingly advocated in 1760 by Ezra Stiles. Yet these murmurings against standing armies and voyaging bishops for the time being remained essentially localized or factional. They do provide firm evidence, however, of the overwhelming disposition of most colonial leaders to distrust and resist British measures that seemed in any way to threaten the shape of colonial societies and the privileges of their elites.

In other words, American opposition to the new British policies was fairly predictable. Yet its scope, character, and violence were not. The first indications of American reactions came in 1764 after the passage of the Sugar Act. This, of itself, brought considerable criticism. Naturally enough, the criticism originated in the New England colonies, the prime importers of molasses, where members of the assemblies spoke of both Parliamentary taxation and of the new juryless vice-admiralty courts as threats to their liberty. It was also heard in New York, New Jersey, and Pennsylvania. Such criticism made no necessary distinction between Parliament's rights to levy internal and external taxes in North America. Arthur Lee of Virginia in March 1764, for example, was already writing of a resolution to oppress North America "with the iron hand of power . . . the House of Commons readily resolved . . . to tax the subject here, without the consent of his representative," while others questioned either the propriety or the constitutionality of Parliamentary taxation. Yet it is often difficult to distinguish between this opposition to the Sugar Act and opposition to the proposed Stamp Act, for the latter had been approved in principle by the House of Commons at the same time as the former was passed.

The deliberate decision of the Grenville ministry to delay proceedings on the Stamp Act was an invitation to Americans to announce their feelings on the bill. The New England colonies, New York, Virginia, and South Carolina quickly sent petitions to London, while other colonies instructed their agents to oppose it. But in spite of these efforts, no generally concerted American plan emerged, and colonial agents in Great Britain warned that "not a single Member of Parliament" would dispute its "Right to lay an internal Tax on the Colonies." It also became a generally known and resented fact in the colonies that the House of Commons refused to receive colonial petitions against the Stamp Act, on the grounds that these could not be heard on money bills.

For a time after the passage of the Stamp Act, opposition in America remained muted, with several colonial politicians accepting stamp distributorships, probably in the hope that these would prove both profitable and a source of patronage and influence. Yet the press was full of condemnations of the act and of predictions of an approaching slavery and tyranny. The first great public pronouncement against it came in May 1765 with the resolutions of the Virginia House of Burgesses, denying that Virginians had any duty to submit to taxation except that laid by the General Assembly and stating that any person asserting the contrary "shall be deemed an enemy to his Majesty's colony." These words at least were printed in the colonial press; what was actually said and passed by the burgesses is not precisely known. But a French traveler present at the Virginia assembly on 24 May 1765 reported that Patrick Henry, "in the heat of passion," declared that "Tarquin and Julius had their Brutus, Charles had his Cromwell and he Did not Doubt but some good american would stand up, in favour of his Country."

This violent language offended many members of the Virginia assembly. By the autumn, when other colonial assemblies had the chance to comment on the Stamp Act—Pennsylvania, Maryland, Connecticut, Massachusetts, South Carolina, New Jersey, and New York eventually did so before the end of the year—the language used was more restrained. The Massachusetts House of Representatives, for example, grounded its opposition to the act on the British Constitution and the colony's charter and affirmed its veneration of Parliament and George III. The culminating event in this growing protest by the constituted political bodies was the meeting of a Stamp Act Congress in New York in October 1765 consisting of twenty-seven representatives from nine colonial assemblies which finally agreed on a declaration of principle, a memorial to the House of Lords and a petition to the House of Commons.

The contents of these petitions and protests by the colonial assemblies and the Stamp Act Congress—an extra-legal meeting of their representatives—is of considerable interest in providing evidence of contemporary American feelings on the part of the propertied classes. Professor Morgan has pointed out that even at this date many of these allowed Parliament only authority to regulate the trade of the empire and not to tax the colonies. Nor did they make distinction between external and internal taxes. Pennsylvania's resolution, for example, asserted "that the taxation of the people of this province by any person whatsoever than such their representatives in assembly, is unconstitutional, and subversive of their most valuable right." English ideas of a distinction between external and internal taxation, particularly Chatham's, arose from representations by a few colonial pamphleteers and lobbyists such as Franklin who portrayed the colonial position as more moderate than it really was.

Important though the resolutions of the provincial assemblies and the Stamp Act Congress were in defining the theoretical elements in the dispute, a crucial development in the crisis lay in the use of violence. This first occurred in Boston on 14 August 1765 when, as Thomas Hutchinson wrote, "an amazing mob" paraded through the streets and through the court house, carrying an effigy of the newly appointed stamp distributor, Andrew Oliver, that had been hung all day on a large tree—subsequently immortalized as the "Liberty Tree"—on High Street. The crowd leveled a small building supposed to be the future stamp office, then burned the effigy; part of the gathering broke into Oliver's own house. Twelve days later another great crowd assembled around a bonfire in Boston, drinking and shouting, "Liberty and Property," and many of them moved off to attack the houses of three royal officials connected with the customs service. They then assaulted the splendid mansion of Lieutenant Governor Thomas Hutchinson, virtually destroying it with, according to

Governor Bernard, "a savageness unknown in a civilised country." They condemned Hutchinson for his support of the Stamp Act (here they were mistaken, since Hutchinson opposed the act) and for issuing writs in vice-admiralty cases. This day's work seems to have been instigated by merchants who had fallen afoul of the Acts of Trade and to have had little to do with the Stamp Act, though it illustrates the climate of Boston at the time. In late August general disturbances took place for three days in Newport, Rhode Island; in November a mob burned the governor's coach and the mayor's house in New York.

These attacks were the most extreme manifestations of opposition to take place during the Stamp Act crisis. Although confined to three of the colonial cities, the threat of violence was felt in many colonies, where large and menacing crowds gathered at critical moments, such as the day of arrival of newly appointed Stamp Act officers. In Virginia a "Concourse of people, I should call a mob did I not know that it was chiefly if not altogether composed of Gentlemen of property in the Colony, some of them at the Head of their Respective Counties, and the Merchants of the Country, whether English, Scotch or Virginian" demonstrated on the arrival of the distributor, reported the lieutenant governor. In North Carolina the Stamp Act distributor, the governor told his English superiors, was "surrounded by several hundred people in semi-military array, with drums beating and flags flying." In Philadelphia and Charleston, crowds gathered to show their hostility to the act, though reportedly with "decency and decorum" and not with violence.

The relative fervor of these demonstrations may have depended on the particular political, social, and economic conditions of the different colonial communities. Yet taken together, they suggest the temper of the time; overt hostilities would have followed any resolute civil or military attempts to enforce the provisions of the Stamp Act. Although some leading opponents of the act denounced the more destructive activities of the mobs, there was also widespread comment in justification of civil disobedience and insurrection against measures that could not be effectively resisted through legal channels. The people, the Reverend Jonathan Mayhew wrote, had the right in certain circumstances "to take the administration of government in some respects into their own hands." Similarly, the *Newport Mercury* in October 1765 supported "a fixed and strenuous opposition to this unconstitutional law," while the final Virginia Resolve, as printed in most colonial newspapers, announced "that any person who shall, by speaking or writing, assert or maintain that any person or persons other than the General Assembly of this colony, have any right or power to impose or lay any taxation on the people here, shall be deemed an enemy to his Majesty's colony." In such phrases, colonial Americans re-enunciated the popular Whig belief that at certain critical moments the people had the right to defend themselves against abuses and to remedy their grievances.

This point of view already widely held found growing support in the colonies over the next ten years. Yet for the time being, many colonists strongly advocated opposition only by pacific means, particularly by a refusal to buy stamps or accept stamped documents or to purchase any English goods. In certain areas groups of merchants and other men associated together, pledging not to buy or sell further English imports. Obviously, here the nature and extent of colonial opposition resulted from the character of the groups hardest hit. Stamps had to be affixed to newspapers—which played a great role in opposition—and to legal and commercial documents. The new customs regulations also adversely affected the merchants. Hence lawyers and merchants, the most articulate and politically skilled colonial groups and the best able to cooperate across colonial boundaries, judged they would suffer severely. Perhaps more important in creating their opposition, the Sugar and Stamp acts were made law at a time of economic distress throughout most of the colonies, when little money was available anyway to pay new taxes and when a glut of English goods filled American shops and warehouses. The nonimportation moves allowed importers to clear their overstocked shelves and in part remedy their depressed economic situation. Moreover, some merchants and men of business looked beyond the immediate crisis. From about 1764 onward numerous suggestions were made in the colonies for schemes to foster domestic manufacturing and to end the expensive dependence on English manufactured imports. In 1764 the *Boston Gazette* reported that "a very great Number of the respectable Tradesmen of this Town, have come to a Resolution to wear Nothing but leather for their Working Habits for the future, and that to be only of the manufacture of this Government."

Economic conditions also spurred colonial protests against the Currency Act of 1764. The assemblies of New York, Pennsylvania, and South Carolina had all petitioned for its repeal by the end of 1766, while in London a number of American agents, with Franklin prominent among them, sought the same end by direct representation to the British government. Besides repeal, several sought a reform of the colonial monetary system, and although their efforts ended in 1768, killed by Hillsborough's obduracy and swamped by the more urgent opposition to the Townshend Acts, the grievances they expressed remained. In individual colonies, forms of protest and action against the Currency Act continued as the currency situation was made more urgent by fluctuations in the availability of British credit and in the supply of money. Together with nonimportation and the encouragement given to the idea of American manufacturing, the reaction to the Currency Act, it is argued, shows that many American merchants and planters were coming to realize that there were sound economic as well as political reasons for protesting against British policies, even to see that economic freedom from Great Britain might outweigh the supposed benefits of the imperial connection.

Religious grievances, too, have also been suggested as a prime force behind resistance to British measures. In the northern colonies, at least, Professor Bridenbaugh has claimed, "the conjunction" of ecclesiastical and civil grievances, rather than civil grievances alone, produced the Stamp Act crisis. As we have seen, the Congregationalists and Presbyterians already had a lively fear of the Church of England and of the British government's religious policy, substantiated when the Anglican clergy in the colonies defended the Stamp Act. Many members of Anglican congregations were British officials, unpopular with colonial patriots. The dissenting clergy, always fearful of the attractions of Anglicanism, by contrast, wrote and spoke on the Whig side, as firm proponents of liberty. This understandable division became deeper as Anglican missionaries appeared to be even more active in attacking dissenters and seeking converts, and constant rumors continued to arrive in the dissenting strongholds of renewed English support for the establishment of one or more Anglican bishops in the American colonies (rumors that often reflected more the wishful thinking of the outnumbered Anglicans of Boston or New York than the truth about what was happening in Whitehall). Nevertheless, it is certain that some dissenters believed, or claimed to believe, that the Grenville ministry intended the Stamp Act and other civil measures to be succeeded by incursions against their religious liberties. In many parts of New England and the middle colonies, the fear of the "ministerial plot" broadened in this way and dissenting clergy and churches became more and more influential in the opposition to British measures, further cooperating across colonial boundaries. Yet with one or two exceptions, these fears did not find expression in the colonial assemblies. Perhaps the situation was made even more tense by reports of unlikely British actions, if the claim of an English woman in New York that the "Credulity of the Common people here is imposed on by a number of Lies raised to irritate and inflame them"—including the lie that a tax on land was imminent—was accurate.

The rise in the colonies of new organized groups that fostered opposition to British measures was of the greatest importance in the unfolding conflict. The emergence of the "Sons of Liberty," as these groups became known, has recently been carefully traced by Pauline C. Maier. The Sons originated in late 1765 and early 1766, not in Boston—so often seen as the "nerve center" of the revolution—but in New York, where a committee was set up that in late October 1765 already corresponded with likely sympathizers in other colonies. In December, two New York representatives visited New London, Connecticut, and by April various groups in Boston, Albany, Portsmouth (New Hampshire), Providence, Newport, New Jersey, Maryland, Norfolk (Virginia), and North Carolina had been organized as Sons of Liberty. Many of the Sons had already been associates in other colonial clubs or bodies, such as the local volunteer fire company of Albany or a social club, the Loyal Nine of Boston. In South Carolina, the members of the Charleston fire company, indeed, operated as Sons of Liberty without forming a separate association. Although "officers and committee members of the Sons of Liberty were drawn almost entirely from the middle and upper ranks of colonial society"—particularly, perhaps, from among the merchants—their aim was to create a broad base of support among the "middling and lower Life" and win the "Confidence of the Populace" as well as to lead local opposition and coordinate intercolonial resistance to the Stamp Act. Many printers were numbered among them and the colonial press provided a vehicle for their ideas. By the time of the repeal of the Stamp Act, some groups of Sons had also made rudimentary plans for military association among colonists.

In 1765-1766 the Sons of Liberty, however, did not constitute a revolutionary cadre anxious to seize authority from the established government. Indeed, many saw it as their duty to aid the civil powers against overaggressive mobs and to restrain overviolent moves and were content to petition and argue. They carefully enunciated their loyalty to Great Britain and the Crown and thought of themselves as the compatriots of the champions of American liberty in England—Chatham, Barré, and the others in the "noble band of patriots" who had opposed the Stamp Act. With repeal, the activities of the Sons subsided and their organization withered. But their practical experience and a heightened awareness of the potential of colonial resistance to British measures remained. Moreover, certain of the more active leaders of the Sons, men who relished their new-found powers and political abilities, stood ready to continue in the fray of ordinary political opposition to governors and crown officers and to take advantage of any new opportunities presented by further unpopular British measures. The Stamp Act controversy also had certainly stirred up political excitement among a large number of colonial Americans, many of whom had probably not been very politically active before.

About fifteen months elapsed between the arrival in May 1766 of news of the repeal of the Stamp Act and tidings in the late summer of 1767 of the passage of the Townshend Acts. Although repeal, greeted with relief and celebration, brought a lessening of tensions throughout the colonies, few interested Americans acceded to the British wishes that they humbly accept the principles of the Declaratory Act and show a boundless gratitude for the ending of the Stamp Act. The Declaratory Act was viewed in America as a mere face-saving device and not as an announcement portending future Parliamentary legislation. Gratitude to British friends of America but not to the British government, together with a large amount of self-congratulatory American rhetoric on the successful conclusion of tough American resistance, prevailed. Pride and a new sense of colonial strength rather than the humble subordination expected by British political and commercial leaders marked American reactions. For example, the Virginia assembly resolved that "we are so convinced of an immediate Connexion between Great Britain and the Colonies, that we cannot but wish that no future Accident may ever interrupt that Union so essential to the Well-being of each of them; and . . . we hope we have Reason now to conclude that the Parliament of Great Britain . . . was actuated by the true Principles of Fellow Subjects with us," while in Boston the House of Representatives on 30 October 1766 set up two committees, the first "to determine whether any acts of Parliament had been inserted in the province law books by order of the Governor and Council; the other to inquire at large into the Practice of issuing Proclamations from the Governor and Council with promise of Reward from the Province Treasury, for enforcing Acts of Parliament."

Nor did opposition to other facets of British authority cease in particular colonies. In Massachusetts and New York, for example, two serious controversies soon took place. The radicals in the New England colony launched an attack on Governor Bernard and Lieutenant Governor Hutchinson, in which James Otis, Thomas Cushing, and Samuel Adams played a leading role. This finally gave the House of Representatives almost complete control over the Massachusetts council. Moreover, Otis seems to have stirred up fresh hatred of the British Navigation Acts, resulting in incidents in which hostile crowds prevented customs officers and civil officials from exercising their authority. In New York at the same time the dispute over the Quartering Act resulted in the governor reminding the assembly of their "indispensable Duty" to "obey the Acts of the Legislature of *Great Britain*" and in the assembly regretting "with Great Concern that we find it impossible to comply with what is now demanded, consistent with our Obligations to our Constitutents . . ." This was followed by a lengthy petition from 240 New York merchants calling for the abandonment of restrictions on American exports and of duties on imports of sugar and molasses and attacking the courts of vice-admiralty. This petition, Chatham wrote, was "highly improper; in point of time, most absurd; in the extent of their pretensions, most excessive; and in the reasoning, most grossly fallacious and offensive." By January 1767, General Gage, British commander stationed in New York, had indeed written to his English superior complaining that the colonies "were taking large strides towards independency" and warning that the mother country must act so as to show them that they "are British colonies dependent on her." In many colonies, serious local disputes between customs officers and merchants also kept discontent with the new British policy of enforcement at a high level.

Against this background, colonial opposition—and resistance—to the Parliamentary measures of 1767 seemed certain. Yet, despite the arrival of news of those in the summer of that year, little agitation appeared immediately in most colonies. In Pennsylvania, John Dickinson began to publish his "farmer's letters" at regular intervals in the press from December onward; these attacks on the British government and the Townshend legislation were widely read and widely reprinted throughout the colonies. But neither the Pennsylvania assembly nor other groups, still pursuing the idea of replacing proprietary by royal government and therefore anxious not to offend the British ministry, took any action, and a similar lassitude seems to have prevailed in other colonies.

The explanation for this lassitude seems to have been economic. If, as many believed, the only response to commercial legislation was commercial resistance—further nonimportation—the merchants were now unenthusiastic. Generally, trade conditions had picked up since about 1767, credit was plentiful, and large numbers of merchants were importing a great volume of British goods that were selling well. The first popular proceedings against the new acts took place in Boston on 28 October 1767. James Otis chaired a town meeting that called for a program of domestic manufactures, nonconsumption of various foreign articles already in America, and the suspension of imports of fifty-four types of foreign goods. The meeting, hoping to renew the cooperation that had marked the Stamp Act crisis, directed that copies of its resolutions be sent to other Massachusetts towns and to the chief towns of the American continent. Some practical effects were felt at once as the restrictions were followed by a series of nonimportation agreements in various New England towns. Also, in these last months of 1767, the New England press published numerous diatribes against the Townshend Acts, condemning Parliament for its assaults on the colonists' "natural and constitutional rights," for its subversion of "the fundamentals of our constitution," for "a mortal stab to our vitals," and for the "introduction of lawless power and arbitrary authority" that would lead to "slavery." Yet the merchants cooperated grudgingly and under duress.

The earliness of Boston resistance to the acts reflected the ambitions and strength of radical politicans already locked in conflict with the governor. In addition, Bostonians had a special concern with those sections of the Townshend Acts that legalized writs of assistance; these writs had provoked hostility in the town since 1761. Writs of assistance never became such an issue in other colonies, especially in the South. Nor were the radicals so well organized, articulate, and numerous outside New England apart, perhaps, from New York. Yet in New York the provisions of the New York Restraining Act do not seem to have roused great passions, for the assembly had decided to comply with the Quartering Act in June 1767, rendering the former act unnecessary. Although New York newspapers reprinted attacks on the Townshend Acts, the colony did not figure prominently in the agitation against them.

The forwardness of Boston is also seen in the early initiative taken by the Massachusetts representatives in petitioning the King for repeal of the Townshend legislation in January 1768 and in sending a circular letter to all the other colonial lower houses in February. This letter spoke of a fixed constitution, and attacked the Crown influence that would arise from applications of the money collected from the Townshend duties. The customs commissioners, for example, residing in America, were authorized "to make as many appointments as they think fit, and to pay the appointees what sum they please . . . from whence it may happen that officers of the Crown may be multiplied to such a degree as to become dangerous to the liberties of the people." It recommended that "the representatives of the several assemblies, upon so delicate a point, should harmonize with each other." Virginia's burgesses, the first members of a lower house to consider the Massachusetts circular letter, decided to petition the King, memorialize the House of Lords, and remonstrate to the House of Commons. They also decided that reports of their actions and their approval of Massachusetts defense of "American Liberty" should be sent to the speakers of all the other colonial assemblies. In the same month, April 1768, New Jersey's assembly voted to send a petition to the King similar to that of Massachusetts. Other colonies delayed action or could take none until their assemblies were called into session. Maryland's and Connecticut's assemblies sent petitions to London in June, New Hampshire's in August, Pennsylvania's and Rhode Island's in September, Delaware's in October, and New York's and North Carolina's in December. These actions of the lower houses in the Crown colonies naturally brought clashes with royal governors, who often prorogued or dissolved them. In South Carolina, the governor dissolved the assembly before it could agree on a petition but not before it had ordered its resolutions against the Hillsborough letter to be printed in the press.

So once again, as in the Stamp Act crisis, the constituted bodies had taken sides against British legislation in a coordinated way. And once again, men calling themselves sons of liberty, or true patriots, or friends of freedom, provided anti-British leadership outside the assemblies. The most obvious manifestation of their strength and influence came with the spreading of nonimportation agreements throughout the colonies, a tactic first used in the Stamp Act crisis and urged by Dickinson in his writings. The original New England movement of 1767 gave way in March 1768 to a larger agreement by Boston traders and merchants to import none but vital supplies to the colony for a period of twelve months, provided that merchants under "other Governments come into the same resolution." Yet although New York merchants agreed to this, the more conservative Philadelphians, proud of their city's commercial supremacy over Boston, refused to enter until the spring of 1769. Other colonies followed in the same year although, as in the case of Virginia and South Carolina, radical elements in the assemblies and among the planters and farmers generally had to put pressure on many merchants to gain the point. Indeed, in the southern colonies particularly, total nonimportation was never achieved; business was good with planters and merchants flourishing and spending on imported goods. In Maryland, for example, Baltimore's merchants, under pressure from Philadelphia, formed an association only in March 1769. In June of the same year a colony-wide movement was launched under the propelling hands of a number of merchants and assemblymen, who were emerging as a clear radical group. Yet in Maryland as elsewhere many merchants viewed these associations with dislike and quickly decided to discontinue them after news of the repeal of the Townshend duties and despite radical protests. In Maryland the radical Country party, led by the young Charles Caroll of Carollton, combined hostility to proprietary measures with hostility to Parliamentary ones. Indeed, their activities provide excellent examples of the interchange between local and imperial politics. In 1766, for example, a lottery set up to provide money for the Maryland agent, Charles Garth, to promote anti-proprietary arguments in England was labeled the "liberty lottery."

Throughout the colonies the radicals were successful in forcing even partial compliance to nonimportation. A noticeable tendency within these movements was for their members, with the support of town meetings or meetings of county freeholders, to coerce and boycott merchants who broke or remained outside the associations, without much interference from the law-enforcement officers. In short, as Pauline Maier writes, "the associations increasingly exercised functions normally reserved to a sovereign state. . . . [and] came to serve as social compacts, analagous to the formal constitutions that would be set up by the various colonies" at a later date.

It seems probable that the years 1768 to about 1770 were crucial ones for both shaping the agencies of opposition and for giving a final gloss to American ideological attitudes. The content of the Townshend legislation itself, with the provisions for an American civil list and for more customs and other officials, reinforced American suspicions of executive attempts to exercise power through placemen and officeholders. Hillsborough's circular letter of April 1768 gave particular credence to these suspicions since it directly attacked the assemblies, denying their rights to free discussion and stressing the power—already disliked—and duty of the governors to prorogue or dissolve them for political reasons. New York's assembly, for example, resolved that "this Colony lawfully and constitutionally has and enjoys an internal Legislature of its own, in which the Crown and the People of this Colony are constitutionally represented; and that the Power and Authority of the said Legislature cannot lawfully or constitutionally be suspended, abridged, abrogated or annulled by any Power, Authority or Prerogative whatever, the Prerogative of the Crown ordinarily exercised for Prorogations or dissolutions only excepted." In the autumn of 1768 British troops and warships arrived in Boston, an obvious threat to one of the capitals of American liberty. This event reinforced American apprehension about ministerial motives and gave radical leaders a fresh opportunity to declaim against the age-old threat of standing armies. When reports came from London of the Parliamentary session of 1768-1769, in which resolutions virtually accusing Massachusetts protestors of treason were passed in both Houses, rumors quickly arose in Boston that such influential men as James Otis, Samuel Adams, and Thomas Cushing were to be arrested and sent to England for trial. Coupled with such speculation came news of the refusal of the House of Commons to admit Wilkes to a seat and the outcry raised there by his supporters, which suggested that the English government had determined to cut down liberty wherever it sought to flourish.

A combination of old American prejudices against executive corruption and tyranny and the new reinforcements and refinements of these attitudes now developed apace. By 1770 many Americans believed, or were informed by the press and pamphleteers, that the English government—or at least a liberty-hating ministerial faction—was conspiring to "enslave a free people." In England it had undermined the independence of Parliament and the law courts so that these bodies now led the attack on traditional liberties rather than their defense. In America the ministers sought the same results by such measures as the Townshend legislation. In New York, in December 1769, Alexander McDougall, a leading Son of Liberty, published a pamphlet that depicted a general assault by the "minions of tyranny and despotism in the mother country and the colonies" against the defenders of freedom. In Rhode Island, where both the Ward and the Hopkins factions tried to outflank the other in claiming the lead in anti-British measures, the *Providence Gazette* reprinted a London letter that asserted that the ministry ruled Parliament by judicious allocation of places and offices, a buying-up of members of the House of Commons. Against this background, such local tragedies as the events of 5 March 1770 in Boston, when British soldiers, provoked by a mob, fired and killed five men (the Boston Massacre), not only engendered fresh anti-British feeling but allowed radicals further to demonstrate what might be expected under growing arbitrary British rule.

Given these developments, the partial repeal of the Townshend duties in April 1770 could hardly contribute to any real reconciliation between American radicals and English authority. Yet repeal did lead—and North perhaps intended this—to the retreat from overt opposition of the more conservative merchants already frightened by growing mob activity and evidence of radical power and soured by a loss of profits at a time of trade expansion. Indeed the collapse of the nonimportation movement by the end of the year revealed the split in the American ranks. Conservatives gradually abandoned all attempts at nonimportation; radicals argued for the continuation of the agreements in order to win even more sweeping political and constitutional concessions from England. Most important, some radical leaders now had a vested interest in opposition. Many had been obscure individuals before 1764 and would not willingly relinquish their newly acquired powers. Samuel Adams, the young tax collector; John Adams, the obscure lawyer; McDougall, a rising New York merchant, the son of a milkman; Patrick Henry, a failure in business before becoming a lawyer; Samuel Chase, a Maryland leader, a parson's son and a debtor, had led where established politicians and the scions of leading families had advocated caution or denounced mob action. The outlook for English governors and their supporters, whatever happened, was unpromising. Meanwhile in England, Lord North, secure in the King's favor and in the House of Commons, had determined not to yield to any American claims. Repeal was to be his one concession. The battle lines remained.

C. Aspects of the colonial scene

American opposition to British reforms may well have gained strength from the frustration of expectations heightened by the victory over France and the acquisition of great new territories. These events had stirred some colonists to paeans of enthusiasm. Some had already maintained that North America had a special position within the British empire and a determining influence on the power of the mother country. Without "the inexhaustible magazine of wealth" provided by the colonies, "Great Britain must not only lose her former lustre but dreadful even in thought! cease to be any longer an independent power," wrote William Livingston of New York in 1758. Englishmen like Chatham obviously held similar views but stated them differently; for them London would always be the great metropolis of empire and American prosperity would depend on English power. Yet Franklin in 1760 had looked far into the future. "I have long been of opinion, that the *foundations of the future grandeur and stability of the British empire lie in America*; and though, like other foundations, they are low and little seen, they are, nevertheless, broad and strong enough to support the greatest political structure human wisdom ever yet erected."

With slight adjustments, such views could obviously support a form of American nationalism. The extent to which the colonists had begun to think of themselves as North Americans within a British empire rather than as colonial Englishmen is difficult to assess, although a study of colonial newspapers suggests a growing awareness in every colony of developments in the others. To a large extent this was a process involving rising political consciousness and feelings of mutual political interests, stimulated by events after 1763. Oxenbridge Thacher, a New England minister, for example, frankly evinced in 1764 that the colonies might expect that "their interests should be considered and attended to; that their rights, if they have any, should be preserved to them; and that they should have no reason to complain, that they have been lavish of their blood and treasure in the late war, only to bind the shackles of slavery on themselves and their children." A year later John Adams restated the feelings of several generations of New England Puritan Whigs. The colonies had been founded by men who "detested all the base services and servile dependencies of the feudal system . . . and they thought all such slavish subordinations were equally inconsistent with the constitution of human nature and that religious liberty with which Jesus had made them free. . . . Is there not something extremely fallacious in the common-place images of mother country and children colonies? Are we the children of Great Britain any more than the cities of London, Exeter, and Bath? Are we not brethren and fellow subjects with those in Britain, only under a somewhat different method of legislation, and a totally different method of taxation? But admitting we are children, have not children a right to complain when their parents are attempting to break their limbs, to administer poison, or to sell them to enemies for slaves?"

The war had opened up new areas for settlement by removing the restrictive human barriers of the French and the Indians. Here was, indeed, the promised land for the millions whom Franklin and other students of America's population confidently expected to be born and flourish under the favorable skies of North America. Nor would this optimism have lessened if the actual rate of population growth had been known. From 1760 to 1770 the total white population of the thirteen colonies increased by about 31 percent, in the ten years after 1770 by about 26 percent. In New England the overall percentage rise in these two periods was 27 percent and 17 percent; in the middle colonies 31 percent and 31 percent; and in the south 36 percent and 33 percent.

Immigration played a larger part than in previous years in this growth, perhaps. The years after 1763 were ones of renewed and growing migration to North America. The highest estimates of white migration suggest large influxes of Ulster Irish, perhaps 60,000 from 1766 through 1776; in the same period perhaps 25,000 came from Scotland and perhaps 15,000 from England and Wales. Four thousand German migrants are recorded in 1765, although other figures are not available. Totals are hard to arrive at; a very high estimate would be 150,000 immigrants between the Peace of Paris and 1776. The total white population growth from 1765 to 1775 was in the region of 468,000, to which immigrants perhaps therefore contributed nearly a third. Black population also increased as a result of large slave imports, with an estimated 84,500 slaves shipped in from 1761 through 1775, an exceptionally high number compared with the rest of the century. These figures suggest a natural increase among the blacks of 33 percent from 1760 to 1775.

The growth of population was not evenly spread. This and other evidence suggests that the cities and long-settled coastal areas were becoming old societies, their demographic and social patterns now bringing them nearer to Old World ones. They show an Old World pattern of later marriages, of numbers of persons not marrying at all, and of a surplus of females in the population. Substantial out-migration from them to the newer areas of settlements occurred and their rate of natural population growth slowed considerably by about 1760. Yet the low mortality rate remained. Socially, there is evidence of a continuing concentration of wealth and property among the better-off. Both in Boston and southeast Pennsylvania the relative wealth of the top 10 percent or so of taxpayers and the relative numbers of those with little or no property seem to have been increasing. In Boston in 1771 about 29 percent of the town's workers owned no property, twice as many as a century before, while in southeastern Pennsylvania the lowest 60 percent of taxpayers, who held 34.8 percent of property in 1748, held 26.8 percent in 1760 and 22 percent twenty years later. For the older areas of southern colonies, there is no direct demographic evidence arising from local studies. Nor do many studies of social change over time exist for these years. The old stereotypes seem to hold up. Wealth in land and slaves was concentrated among the top 6 percent or so of the population who owned 60 percent or more of the slaves and 50 percent or more of the property. Low-country South Carolinians were extraordinarily rich in terms of recorded land and slaves. Some parishes had a majority of very well-to-do planters, a few middling whites, a few more poor whites, and a multitude of slaves. In the Virginia tidewater and in Maryland, however, as many as half the white population may have held no land or have been tenant farmers. Recent studies of four Maryland counties show 44 percent to have been landowners in 1756 and 37 percent in 1771. Overall, this situation is characterized as one of "a growing number of landless" persons who "had no slaves, ate off wooden dishes, possessed extremely limited amounts of clothing and household furniture, and owned very few farm animals and tools." Tenant farming also became increasingly widespread in other southern areas.

All these figures are open to different interpretations; concentration of wealth, for example, was not necessarily incompatible with a rising standard of living for all social groups, and ownership of slaves and lands tells us nothing of indebtedness, mortgages, and shortages of cash among the owners. Nevertheless, it can be argued that late colonial America had some of the characteristics—rapid population growth and increasing density of population in some areas, concentrations of wealth and growing social inequality or social differentiation, and commercial dependence on markets—which mark a society moving from a pre-modern to a modern type. Was this accompanied by an increasing polarization between those who clung to old rural values and ways and those who abetted the changes in social and economic organization? For example, there is evidence of the ending of controls on wages and prices, of demands for the reform of urban organs of local government, and for changes in property, inheritance, and tax laws in some colonies by 1776. Were those who protested against new British legislation after 1763 also engaged in the demolition of internal archaic regulations?

What indeed are the implications of the evidence relating to social and economic structure and changes for political events after 1763? It must be admitted that these have not been convincingly developed. If those years saw a progress toward inequality, evidence that consciousness of this had any early effect on colonial political attitudes is thin. Historians also lack hard facts about unemployment, depressed real wages, or social tensions among the majority of wage earners. One historian sees "a purposeful and radical" opposition to their legal and social status developing among one such group, the merchant seamen, and writes of "pre-" or "sub-political" consciousness among them, but there is little evidence of political or social consciousness among most wage earners, who, anyway, were not numerous even in the colonial cities. Of the artisans and skilled craftsmen, usually self-employed and often small employers themselves, there is proof that they gradually became more and more politically active in the revolutionary years. Their views tended to support a Whiggish concern for property and property acquisition and they sought increased economic and political opportunities. Among small farmers there is evidence of resentment against their lack of money and credit, which after 1776 took on a pronounced political form. This resentment was shared with many better-off merchants and planters. Not a feeling of resentment against the growing inequalities of late colonial America but against uncertain economic, commercial, and political conditions after 1763 probably formed the mainspring of protest and unrest. It was not the growing numbers of the landless and propertyless but the rising artisans, lawyers, merchants, and planters who suffered most evidently and protested most vigorously. For the American economy remained closely tied to that of Great Britain, credit crises in the mother country led to the rapid draining of specie, to slack trade, to depressed demand, and then to less trade and employment. This pattern evident in late colonial America brought bankruptcy and hard times to traders and merchants and increased debts to planters—especially those in the South investing heavily in the slave imports of the period—and to farmers.

One important aspect of late colonial society is apparent—the filling up of the back country and that area's different social characteristics from those of the longer-settled regions. By 1776 in the South, 40 percent of North Carolina's total population and 40 percent of South Carolina's (79 percent of her white population) occupied those provinces' Piedmont regions. In western Maryland, the Great Valley of Virginia and the southwest Virginia Piedmont lived 101,000 persons, some 15 percent of the population of these two colonies. In Frederick County, Maryland, the western third of the colony, population had jumped from about 17,500 in 1765 to 30,000 ten years later. In the North, western New Massachusetts and Maine, both back-country areas, accounted for 72,247 of the 90,500 increase in population in Massachusetts and Maine in the eleven years before 1776. In New Hampshire, of the 20,800 population increase in roughly the same period, two-thirds accrued to its interior counties. In New York, the rate of population increase in the frontier counties was four or more times as great as that in the older-established ones, and the same may have been true of Pennsylvania where by 1780 21 percent of the population lived in areas that were hardly settled twenty or thirty years before. Migration accounted for much of these increases, but some evidence suggests that the natural growth of population was higher in the frontier and back-country regions than in the east. In New Jersey, definite evidence exists of higher fertility in frontier countries than in longer-settled ones. Socially, the back country had large numbers of middling and fewer large or very small property owners than the coastal areas. Yet tenant farming in the back country, north and south, was evident, and parts of the southern Piedmont were already being transformed by the growth of large slave plantations.

In these same years the trans-Appalachian region also attracted settlers. By 1771 the Ohio region around Pittsburgh perhaps had 10,000 families. Further south settlers were established by the 1770s in the Kanawaha River area and in eastern Tennessee. In the same years Kentucky was thoroughly explored by Daniel Boone, agent of the North Carolina politician and land speculator Richard Henderson, and he and other speculators were already taking up land claims there although settlement did not start until the very eve of the Revolutionary War. Indeed in the years immediately before and during the conflict, an ever-increasing stream of migrants entered all these areas, a great folk movement that was hardly touched by the struggle with Great Britain. Nor did the increasing differences between British officials and colonists prevent action in support of expansion. Governor Dunmore of Virginia successfully led colonial militia against the Shawnee Indians in 1774 and forced Indian agreement to the occupation of Kentucky by the Treaty of Camp Charlotte.

Similarly Anglo-American disputes did not initially prevent cooperation among those who sought fortunes as land speculators. In 1768 the British government agreed to move the Proclamation Line of 1763 westward to accommodate Anglo-American speculators and their lobbyists. For a large number of land companies emerged in the 1760s as they had in the 1740s, and their organizers were careful to recruit leading American and British politicians as members. The Illinois Company formed in 1766 was represented by Benjamin Franklin in London; the Indiana Company, which sought land in the Ohio-Monongahela area, included Franklin, his son, William, governor of New Jersey, and leading Pennsylvania politicans. The Indiana Company, which absorbed several other groups and was renamed the Walpole Company after a leading English backer, also included Grenville, Lord Camden, and other influential English politicians. It had great success in gaining Privy Council support for a grant of twenty million acres for the projected establishment of Vandalia, an entirely new colony extending from the forks of the Ohio south to the Greenbrier River and west to the mouth of the Scioto. Acceptance of this scheme against his advice forced Hillsborough's resignation, but it was never to be carried out. Nor was the other pre-revolutionary scheme to form a new colony ever brought to fruition. Transylvania, planned as his proprietary by Boone's patron, Henderson, and announced at Boonesborough in 1775, was never to be consolidated; Virginia quickly assumed control of the region. The problem of the trans-Allegheny west would confront American governments after 1776 as it had the English before that date.

Three colonies, North and South Carolina and Pennsylvania, have a special importance in this period in terms of the growth of the back country. Moreover, events in one of them do demonstrate a consciousness of social deprivation and grievances, though seemingly one that resembles that found in medieval peasant rather than in modern or pre-modern societies.

In North Carolina's western parts local government bodies were instituted to meet the needs of the expanding settlement with some regularity and foresight; nine new counties were set up after 1741, each with sheriffs, local courts, and local officials. Although the more populous western parts were underrepresented in the colony's lower house compared with the eastern section, this does not seem to have been openly resented by contemporaries. What did create tension in the western counties in 1765-1766, against a background of scarce money, was the efficiency, corrupt or otherwise, of local government in

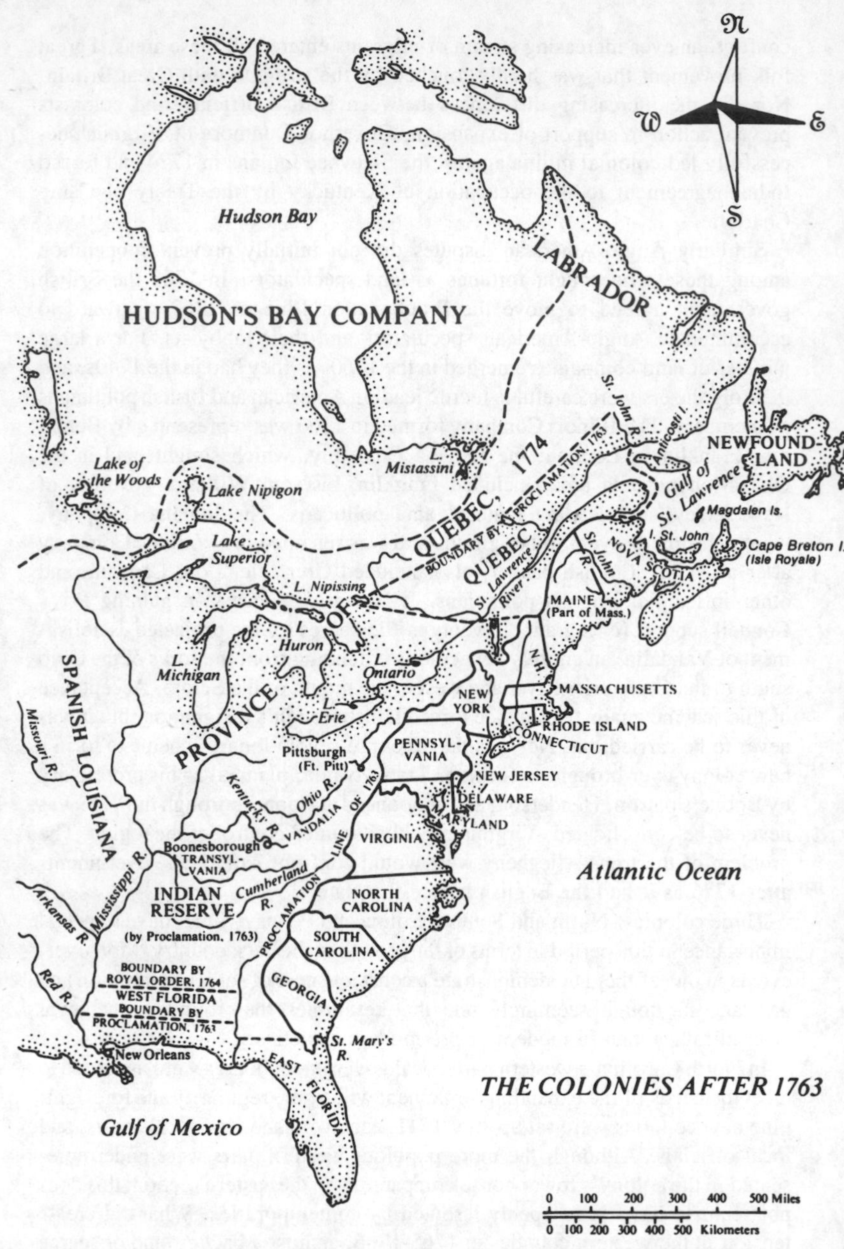

THE COLONIES AFTER 1763

collecting taxes and surveying land, resentment against lawyers and the legal system, and dislike for official fees. In 1767 or 1768, protests in the form of witholding allegedly excessive taxes began, linked to back country dislike of what was considered excessive spending on the governor's new residence and new public buildings in the provincial capital, New Bern. On 4 April 1768 the protestors in Orange County, borrowing the name of "Regulators" from vigilante groups then active in South Carolina, formed an association calling on local officials to publish complete records of their fiscal transactions. The immediate background of this event seems to have been the action of the sheriff in distraining and selling the property of men who refused to pay taxes. Later, armed men attacked the sheriff and interfered with legal processes. In September 1768, Governor Tryon marched to Orange County, at the head of 1,400 militiamen from other counties; 800 Regulators had gathered in the vicinity but dispersed in the face of the superior force. During this first phase of Regulator activity, leaders of the movement petitioned the governor and council for redress of their grievances, citing excessive legal charges and fees, and claiming that previous applications made to the provincial assembly had been ignored. Other documents stressed the poverty and wretchedness of "ignorant men, and at the same time in such necessitous Circumstances that their utmost Industry could scarce afford a wretched subsistance to their Families, much less enable them to engage in uncertain law Suits, with the rich and powerful."

From late 1768 to 1771, the Regulators continued as a potentially disruptive force in certain parts of the North Carolina back country, although they seem to have turned to petitioning to advance their cause. In addresses to the assembly they listed disproportionate taxes on the poor, a lack of currency with which to pay taxes, and extortionate fees and legal charges. Only a reference to the use of ballots in elections showed any interest in general political matters. Their emphasis throughout was on the hardships of "poor industrious farmers" faced with rapacious local officials. Governor Tryon tried to meet their protests about excessive fees in 1768 and was not unsympathetic to their situation. Yet the North Carolina assembly at its meetings of 1768-1769 and 1769-1770 virtually ignored Regulator grievances. Not until its session of 1770-1771, after renewed violence in Orange County, did it pass acts to make the recovery of small debts easier, to fix lawyers' fees, to meet complaints about other unjust fees, and to protect debtors' interests in their distrained property. Yet the same assembly also passed an act that threatened the harsh suppression of the Regulators, including the death penalty for felonious rioters.

The final events in the North Carolina Regulator movement came in early 1771 when attempts to prosecute their ringleaders brought out groups "arrayed in warlike manner" who threatened to march on New Bern and who used violence to make it impossible for the courts to meet at Hillsboro. Tryon then gathered about 1,300 men with artillery and marched into Orange County. Faced with 2,500 or so Regulators, he fought them on 16 May 1771 at the battle of Alamance about thirty miles from Hillsboro. His artillery won the fight; about 300 Regulators were killed but only 10 of his men. One Regulator leader was hanged almost immediately, six more were executed later and six reprieved. After this, the region became tranquil, though many back-country men moved farther west rather than continue under the colony's government.

It is perhaps easier to state what the North Carolina Regulators were not rather than analyze the movement in an entirely satisfactory way. First, they were not representative of the whole back country. In most counties few joined the movement, and the inhabitants provided men to suppress it. Nor were they deeply aware of their grievances as sectional ones, brought about because of their political ineffectiveness in the North Carolina assembly. Political underrepresentation was not mentioned in their protests; they were not proto-revolutionaries or even western Whigs angered by the denial of political rights and liberties. The rank and file seem to have been poor Scotch-Irish settlers protesting, in some cases with reason and in some cases mistakenly, that the costs of government fell too heavily on them and that they were the victims not only of poverty but of extortion. Many were rough and violent, disliking all government. The leaders were men of some education and property, but like some of the participants in Bacon's rebellion in Virginia nearly a century before, excluded from officialdom and status in their counties. Some may have been Baptists or extreme pietists. Regulators resembled a medieval jacquerie or a seventeenth-century French peasant uprising in which poor men with some better-off leaders made a stand against venal officials, lawyers, and others who profited from the established system, and against high taxes. Yet more detailed research needs to be undertaken before the full picture of the Regulator movement in North Carolina can be drawn.

South Carolina also experienced a Regulator movement which has been the subject of a detailed modern study. In this prosperous colony, the well-defined planter-merchant elite firmly controlled the lower house of the assembly and the lower house firmly controlled local government. In contrast to the North Carolina assembly, it had failed to create any new counties, and except for local justices of the peace with restricted powers, there were no civil officers in the back country. After the end of the Cherokee War, a state of devastation and penury prevailed in parts of the back country. With it came lawlessness and crime, with gangs of marauders carrying on organized campaigns of arson and robbery. Although militia companies, justices of the peace, constables, and scattered dissenting churches formed little focal points of order and authority, the lack of sheriffs, county courts, land officers, and other customary sinews of local government left them isolated and ineffectual. Moreover, the social structure of the back country, a younger region than that of North Carolina, was still in a formative stage. The few natural leaders had little official authority in the absence of county offices for them to fill. From such respectable men of property indeed came the stimulus for vigilante action against outlaw groups as a wave of killings and violence became particularly acute in June and July 1767. In October came the beginnings of oath-takings and agreements among hundreds of men throughout the back country. The *South Carolina Gazette* stated on 19 October that "the peaceable inhabitants . . . in a kind of desperation . . . have formed associations, to expel the villains from wherever they can get at them, and to do justice themselves in a summary way."

The low country authorities from the first reacted unsympathetically to the Regulator movement, especially when news arrived that 4,000 men were about to march on Charleston to present their grievances. In fact, a lengthy remonstrance, written by the Reverend Charles Woodmason, a Church of England minister, was handed in peaceably. The remonstrance recapitulated many previous, unheeded petitions to the South Carolina assembly, calling for the establishment of circuit or county courts in the western parts, for the construction of jails and courthouses, and for various legal reforms—including the regulation of official fees and other improvements. Unlike the North Carolina Regulators, those of South Carolina also showed political awareness, calling for representation in the assembly. The most curious aspect of the petition, illustrating both its origin among the propertied respectable elements and testifying to the poverty and vagrancy which, as Woodmason's fascinating account of the area shows, existed there, was a plea for "Coercive Laws fram'd for the Punishment of Idleness and Vice, and for Lessening the Number of Indolent and Vagrant Persons, who now pray on the Industrious" and another for workhouses and the amendment of the provincial poor law. Here, too, the difference from North Carolina is evident, since there the poor and the debtors generally supported the Regulators.

The speed with which the South Carolina assembly acted also contrasted with the slowness of that of the northern province. In 1768 a circuit court act was passed and ranger companies to pursue outlaw gangs authorized; these latter met with considerable success in 1768. Yet in the same year the Regulators took actions that brought them into open conflict with the assembly by deciding to institute their own measures of social control over "all idle persons, all that have not a visible way of getting an honest living, all that are suspected of malpractices" who were to be flogged and made to work. At the same time, apparently because in that year some of those who had suffered at their hands had begun to take legal action against Regulators before the Charleston courts, they decided to prevent the service of low-country writs and warrants in their area, except—and this fact underlines their social standing—writs of debt. About this time some influential back-country men began to question the utility of a vigilante movement that so ostentatiously put itself above the law and whose members sometimes used their powers to pay off grudges, especially after the vigilantes began to flog and harm numbers of prominent local men and to defy justices of the peace. Attempts by Governor Bull to disband the movement had no success until the spring of 1769, when the rise of a counter-Regulator movement in the back country against the growing extremism and arrogance of the Regulators itself finally checked them.

By the end of 1769, indeed, many Regulator demands had been satisfied in law so that it seems probable that only an extreme fringe element remained active. Although the assembly circuit court act of 1768 was disallowed in England, one that anwered to royal wishes passed the assembly in 1769. The same law also met complaints about legal fees, the building of jails and courthouses, and outlaws. And while the back country did not receive a full weight of representation in the assembly relative to its population, the creation of new parishes and the participation of back-country men in elections in low-country parishes gave the area a number of assemblymen in 1768 elections. At this point the Regulator movement infringed on imperial politics since the Crown opposed increases in the size of colonial assemblies. On the whole it seems that the ethos of the South Carolina Regulators was that of youngish, aspiring property owners, many of whom later achieved economic, social, and political prominence. That of the North Carolina movement was of debt-ridden, poor farmers. In neither region did the Regulators—as was once believed—provide disproportionate numbers of Tories; the majority seem to have become patriots.

Pennsylvania was the third colony in which sectional discontent of a sort existed. Here, the growth of back-country feeling impinged on a very complicated political situation in which until about 1766 a movement existed that sought to persuade the Crown to abolish the proprietary government and replace it with a royal one. The rapid progress of settlement in Pennsylvania meant that by about 1763 the first interior county—Lancaster, set up in 1729—was as densely populated as the two original counties of Chester and Bucks. Berks and Northampton counties, established in 1752, contained about nine persons per square mile; only Cumberland, formed in 1750, contained less people. Judicially and administratively, unlike the western parts of some other colonies, these regions were not badly served. Yet they were set off from Philadelphia and the eastern counties by their openness to Indian raids during the French and Indian War and Pontiac's rebellion, by their large Scotch-Irish Presbyterian populations and by a general feeling among their settlers that the colony's assembly was more concerned with the commercial interests of Philadelphia and the fortunes of the Quaker oligarchy than with the prosperity of the western parts. Both General Amherst and William Johnson, had, of course, testified to this latter point, criticizing the assembly for the feebleness of its defense policies during the second half of 1763. The Scotch-Irish had developed an intense suspicion of the Quakers, on whose pacificism and humanitarian concern for the Indian they blamed the red man's aggressiveness and the colony's military timidity.

Feelings among the back settlements erupted on 14 December 1763 when "a Company of People from the Frontiers . . . killed and scalped most of the

Indians at the Conestogoe Town early [that] Morning.'' These were neutral Indians who had lived peaceably in a primitive village at Conestoga, Lancaster County, for many years but were alleged by frontiersmen to have spied for and given shelter to Indian war parties. Thirteen days later it was reported from the county town of Lancaster that ''upwards of a hundred armed men, from the Westward, rode very fast into Town . . . proceeded with the greatest Precipitation to the Workhouse, stove open the door and killed all the Indians . . .'' These Indians were fourteen men, women, and child refugees from Conestoga, who had been sheltered by the government. By the end of January 1764 reports reached Philadelphia that the instigators of these killings, the ''Paxton Boys''—named from the frontier community in Dauphin County where the ringleaders supposedly lived—planned to march on Philadelphia and kill Christian refugee Indians who had been sheltered in the city. In early February about 200 armed and mounted men appeared near the city. They meekly turned back after conferring with a government delegation led by Benjamin Franklin, who promised that their grievances would be examined by the Pennsylvania assembly.

The grievances of the Paxton Boys mainly concerned the ''excessive Friendship, great servility and lack of fortitude'' of the Pennsylvania government toward the Indians, contrasted with the plight of settlers and their families forced from their homes and farms by the Indians. This state of affairs they blamed on ''that Faction which so Long a time have found means to enslave the Province to Indians''—the Quakers. Yet the first grievance listed on a contemporary ''remonstrance'' referred to the sectional political underrepresentation of Lancaster, York, Cumberland, Berks, and Northampton counties, which ''together returned only ten Representatives, while the three Counties and City of Philadelphia, Chester and Bucks, elect twenty-six.'' The same remonstrance also named the Quakers as the source of Indian strength and frontier weakness. It made no mention of sectional judicial or economic resentments. Subsequently, the assembly met some of the frontier grievances but did not allot the western counties more representatives. This latter point continued to be a point of grievance in the western counties, but perhaps because the assembly began to spend money on western roads and public works, no overt continuing sectional struggle occurred after 1764.

Yet Scotch-Irish hostility to the Society of Friends and to the Pennsylvania assembly was an important force. In 1764 the assembly was forced to satisfy western grievances by accepting a supply bill which yielded a long-contested claim to the proprietor—that his lands should be taxed at a very low rate. This gave fuel to the movement for royal government in Pennsylvania that erupted again in Philadelphia. To previous charges against the proprietor could now be added the claim that he might have been in alliance with the Paxton Boys, while it was also argued that royal government would provide greater frontier security. In the spring of 1764, under the guidance of Franklin and his Quaker allies, petitions were distributed calling for the substitution of proprietary by royal government; of the 3,500 odd signers, a majority were Quakers and nearly half inhabitants of Philadelphia and its environs. Rural and western regions contributed far fewer in relation to population than the city. Moreover, the province's Presbyterian leaders disliked the movement, believing that Franklin and the Quakers hoped to reinforce their own position in the colony's government. Fifteen thousand people signed counterpetitions opposing royal government, and its friends lost seats in provincial elections. Later, the Scotch-Irish Presbyterians in alliance with German groups and Whiggish elements assumed the mantle of a patriotic opposition both to royal measures and to proprietary government.

The Regulator movements and to a lesser extent the Paxton Boys illuminated conditions in the increasingly important back country regions. But it is important to note that in the Maryland and Virginia back countries after 1763, the kinds of grievances evident in the Carolinas either did not exist or were not clearly expressed. One distinguished historian has written in this connection that he "searched fruitlessly for evidence that before 1776 political sectionalism—western resentment of eastern over-representation and rule—was an issue, either open or covert, in Maryland or Virginia. Nor were there any undercurrents of back-country economic or social unrest." Yet in Maryland western representatives did show resentment when money payments to the back country were threatened by lower house attacks on the proprietary executive. In both colonies, the extension of local government and law by and large kept up with that of population over the back country; in assembly representation the Chesapeake areas retained their ascendancy, but this seems to have not resulted in protests.

What in fact was the general shape of local as opposed to imperial politics in the colonies after 1763? In Maryland, as in Pennsylvania, a steady opposition to the proprietary executive continued after 1763 but no sentiment arose in favor of royal government. Here, a clear division existed between one part of the planting elite committed to the Baltimores, mainly councillors and important officeholders, and those gentry who dominated the lower house and usually opposed proprietorial measures with the support of lesser and poorer men. Their challenges to the proprietary involving such issues as fees and patronage and the long tradition of hostility to proprietary measures provided both training and arguments for a concurrent resistance to unpopular British measures that developed after 1763 with, indeed, the same men usually combining opposition to both. In Virginia, although shaken by increasing debts and great internal scandals, and soon to face a rapid and unwelcome growth in Baptist strength in the colony, the planter elite still exercised its powerful local predominance, continuing to control both council and the lower house. On local questions, apart from minor and ordinary irritations, relations between the governor and these bodies were never strained. In North Carolina and South Carolina, despite the Regulator movements, conventional political structure changed little after 1763, and relations with the governor and the British authorities were not vitiated by serious conflicts over local matters until the late 1760s.

North of Pennsylvania, in the New England colonies and in New York and New Jersey, local politics increasingly became enmeshed in the disputes with Great Britain. Of the two middle colonies, the politics of New York were the more complex, numbering powerful groups of overlapping interests—merchants and landed gentry, dissenters and Anglicans, and New York City and Hudson Valley residents—and was complicated by the colony's central position in trade, land speculation, and as imperial headquarters for the military. After 1763 the rivalry of two prominent families and their supporters was well recognized. The Livingston and De Lancey factions continued their struggles, but this factionalism among a well-to-do upper class broadened considerably in the struggles over the Stamp Act and the Townshend duties to include more popular elements. In New Jersey, which lacked western lands, overseas commerce, or much internal trade, parochial local issues predominated in the context of a court and country division. But a protracted struggle also went on over the rights of the assembly to issue paper money, and feelings were embittered when in September 1770 a royal disallowance of assembly acts was received.

The same parochialism was found in the small New England colony of Rhode Island, where two factions—the Wards and the Hopkinses—had fought since about 1757 for political predominance and continued to do so until the 1770s, when the Wards lost ground. The factions' objectives were purely to gain power, patronage, and the control of office and involved no issues of principle or broad policy. In New Hampshire, the predominance of the Wentworth family still seemed assured when John Wentworth, nephew of Governor Benning Wentworth, succeeded him as governor in 1767. Internally, the gubernatorial oligarchy increasingly faced a growing sectional feeling among the poor Scotch-Irish and New England settlers who had moved into the Merrimack Valley region. This relatively expanding proportion of the province's small population demanded and was grudgingly conceded in 1769 and under strict conditions the creation of a system of county government. It did not win seats on the council or additional representation in the lower house, which precluded legislative action on western demands for paper money. Western grievances probably continued; indeed, they may have been increased by the fact that the establishment of new counties brought swifter and easier enforcement of contracts and improved the merchants' facilities for debt collecting from the poor families of the interior. Certainly, the area became a center of anti-gubernatorial (and patriotic) feeling in the 1770s.

Connecticut's internal politics after 1763 showed the increasing fusion of internal divisions with imperial issues. The vigorous New Lights, whose solid support came from land-hungry and impoverished eastern farming families, not only continued to challenge the Old Lights by supporting the claims of the Susquehanna Company but challenged the apparent subservience of Old Light gentry leaders to the Stamp Act, voting them from office in 1766. Objections to the Proclamation of 1763 also entered into other disputes with the Crown. Instead of the colonies "sharing in the Honours of Conquest" over the French, "Great Britain possessed all the advantages and not an American entitled to an inch of land," one Connecticut man wrote. Objections were also made to an Order-in-Council of 1766 that revived certain Mohegan Indians' claims to Connecticut lands. Nor did the New Lights and other Congregationalists welcome the apparent successes of the Anglican Church, joining their voices to the opposition to the possible appointment of an American bishop. In Massachusetts, internal political divisions quickly came to reflect differences of opinion over imperial relationships, and we have seen that there, as in many colonies, new men seized the opportunities for leadership presented by the unpopularity of British measures.

Chapter Twelve

American Independence

A. The road to confrontation

Lord North's policy of firmness was announced in the King's speech to Parliament in January 1770 which spoke of efforts to bring back his American subjects "to their duty, and to a true sense of lawful authority." There is little doubt that most members of Parliament also agreed that further opposition from the colonies should not be tolerated. In March, Chatham, out of office, announced that Americans "must be subordinate. In all laws relating to trade and navigation especially, this is the mother country, they are children; they must obey and we prescribe." In April news of the Boston Massacre reached England. The Commons supported a call for an investigation of the incident. But it firmly rejected Edmund Burke's motion that the ill-judged and inconsistent instructions of the administration had caused American grievances. Even Burke, speaking to a crowded house, used the occasion less to defend colonial actions than to attack the ministry, arguing that only an uncorrupted House of Commons could restore tranquility to the empire.

From Parliament's and the ministry's points of view, a kind of tranquility did, in fact, mark colonial matters during the next two or so years. In 1770 Parliament was obsessed with John Wilkes and domestic controversy, in 1771-1772 with fears of war with Spain over the Falkland Islands, with acrimonious controversies over the reform of the East India Company, over marriages by members of the royal family, and over the position of nonconformists. The lack of Parliamentary attention to America also resulted from a lack of extraordinary and major crises in America of the sort that governments usually felt necessary to bring before Parliament. The growing strength of North's ministry also allowed him to deal with American issues administratively without fearing Parliamentary repercussions. Here, the ministry's measures demonstrated a quasi-firmness that did nothing to improve relations with the colonies. In January 1770, Dunmore, the new governor of New York, was instructed to revive his claim to a fixed salary from colonial revenues. In April, the Privy Council annulled the South Carolina assembly's grant in support of Wilkes to the radical London association, the Supporters of the Bill of Rights.

In June it recommended without any result that Parliament should investigate Massachusetts and that British military strength in the colony should be built up. From this time on, the ministry certainly focused more closely on the region as the critical center of disaffection in America, and some very harsh measures were canvassed by the permanent officials of the American Department. In 1771 Hillsborough added to the discontent of American assemblies by a general ruling that only colonial agents approved by the governor and council as well as the lower house might be officially received in England.

Parliamentary inactivity in colonial matters and the relatively minor irritation of these ministerial proceedings obviously did not stir American emotions in the manner of the crises of the 1760s. Yet the early 1770s have been seen as a crucial time for American relations with the mother country. For events in England vividly confirmed and enlarged colonial apprehensions about the fate of liberty in an increasingly corrupt political system. In London in the summer of 1770, Edmund Burke published his *Thoughts on the Causes of the Present Discontents*, which accused the Court of reviving the royal prerogative through an unconstitutional "system of influence." In 1770 and 1771, Wilkeites and other radicals attacked the structure of English politics denouncing the Crown's influence and its use of places and pensions to maintain control of Parliament. The radicals, incidentally, also denounced Burke for not having the courage or independence to take his attack further. Parliament, they suggested, was open not only "to the dangerous designs of a profligate junto of courtiers, supported by the mere authority of the Crown, against the liberties of the constitution" but to "the more complicated and specious, though no less dangerous, manoeuvres of aristocratic party and faction." Triennial elections and other bold reforms were therefore necessary. Americans, who had heard similar ideas for many years, now found growing English affirmation of their suspicions couched in terms of extraordinary relevance to their present situation. The colonial belief in the corrupt nature of the House of Commons, in the undue influence of the Crown, its ministers, or some secret cabal, received fresh sustenance.

In England moderate American observers hoped that the appointment of Lord Dartmouth as American Secretary in August 1772, to replace the stern Hillsborough, promised a more sympathetic hearing of American grievances at Whitehall, for the new Secretary, a Rockinghamite and evangelical Christian, was considered to be a friend of the colonies. Dartmouth, unfortunately, took office only a few weeks after news arrived in England of a fresh affront to British authority. The *Gaspée*, a royal naval schooner, had been attacked and boarded in Rhode Island waters, and towed to Providence, where it was burned in the harbor. This affair, in which the commanding officer of the ship, notorious for his alleged harshness in searching for contraband, was wounded, was considered by the cabinet in the summer of 1772. It ordered an official board of inquiry in Rhode Island and gave instructions that any suspected offenders should be transported to England for trial. The commander-in-chief in America was required, if necessary, to send troops to Rhode Island to support these proceedings.

Colonial radicals quickly and inevitably seized on these terms. The mere fact of a specially commissioned board, it was argued, showed a distrust of ordinary legal procedures and a desire to use star chamber proceedings, "a court of inquisition more horrible than that of Spain or Portugal." The threat to transport those arrested for trial in England "where, whether guilty or innocent, they must unavoidably fall Victim alike to Revenge or Prejudice" both violated the Rhode Island charter and was "shocking to Humanity, repugnant to every Dictate of Reason, Liberty and Justice, and in which Americans and Freemen ought never to acquiesce." Finally, the planned use of soldiers in Rhode Island predictably brought references to military rule and standing armies. Nor were fears for liberty confined to New England; these notions were quickly endorsed in other colonies. On 13 March 1773, the Virginia House of Burgesses resolved that a committee of correspondence should communicate with other parts of America to discover what other actions the British government might have taken to deprive colonists of their rights, as well as to investigate the Rhode Island affair. The house invited the assemblies to erect their own similar committees of correspondence. Between May 1773 and February 1774 every colonial lower house followed Virginia's lead. Such unity among the constituted bodies of all thirteen colonies demonstrated the intense, existing suspicion of British actions among the colonial upper classes.

In many colonies, internal developments reveal this general climate that years of controversy and political-cum-constitutional debate had created. The prime example of this is Massachusetts. There, Governor Hutchinson faced a continual, perfervid frenzy of criticism. In 1771 this had centered on his refusal to disobey royal instructions on various matters that the lower house declared destroyed its charter rights. In 1772 the town meetings expressed violent objections to the purported intention of the Crown to pay judges' salaries from customs revenues, "the last seal of the Despotism they have so long endeavoured to establish here." Later in the year a committee of Bostonians, including James Otis, Samuel Adams, and Samuel Warren, leading opposition politicians, prepared a lengthy report on "the Rights of the Colonists and of this Province in particular, as Men, as Christians, and as Subjects" that summed up every possible grievance against Parliament and the Crown, including objections to mercantilist legislation. From these events came the formation in many New England towns of committees of correspondence to organize and circulate anti-British propaganda. By early 1773 the province was also able to read Hutchinson's letters, written to English contacts in 1767-1769, obtained by Franklin and sent to the speaker of the assembly. They were later printed. One called for "an abridgement of what are called English liberties." The house quickly resolved that "the Tendency and Design of the Letters . . . was to overthrow the Constitution of this Government, and to introduce arbitrary Power into the province." Hutchinson's usefulness was at an end, and the deepest American suspicions of a secret plot against their liberties gained fresh confirmation.

Nowhere had issues emerged so clearly as in the Bay colony. Yet events in England and the other colonies also fueled discontent. From June 1772 and well into 1773, "one of the fiercest financial storms of the century" raged in Great Britain, pulling down banks, causing hundreds of individual bankruptcies, and severely depressing business. Inevitably, the crisis spread to the colonies, hitting the Chesapeake particularly hard since many of the Scottish banks first involved had connections with the tobacco trade. Credit, abundant in the previous two years when massive imports of English goods had taken place, collapsed; creditors called for payment, trade slumped, cases of debt soared, and a fair degree of financial chaos ensued. In varying measure all the colonies, with the possible exception of South Carolina, were badly hit. In Virginia, which had never really recovered from the crisis of the 1760s, many planters found themselves near bankruptcy, and rabid hostility developed against English and Scottish merchants. In Maryland, also, the effects were harsh and coincided with a grave political crisis involving resistance to proprietary fee collections and to payments to Church of England clergy. All the rhetoric of opposition was used by the Country radicals. "Governor—The distributor of posts and places. Government—A confederacy of a few, to enslave the many. Council of State—Ten fools and one knave," pronounced one contributor to the *Maryland Gazette*. Nor did Hillsborough's order that the Privy Council should regularly receive and review Maryland's colonial legislation ease tensions.

In South Carolina other issues produced outpourings of radical rhetoric. The Crown disallowed the establishment of new courts after the Regulator movement unless their judges were appointed during royal pleasure and not during good behavior, a controversy that gave great play to colonial defenders of liberty. And in 1770 perhaps a greater South Carolina political crisis than any before began over the veto of the grant to the Wilkeites, crystallizing the arguments over the standing of a colonial legislature in an imperial system. It soon brought a head-on clash between the lower house and the colony's council. In the deadlock, government almost broke down—as it had in Maryland—and no legislation of any sort was passed from 1771 until the Revolution. In North Carolina, the Board of Trade's support of the council's refusal to concur in the appointment of a colonial agent, unless it shared authority over him, was unpopular. More seriously, the Board also refused to allow North Carolina's courts to attach the property of foreigners (i.e., British merchants) for debt, a decision that led the assembly to refuse to fund the superior courts; it also caused the virtual paralysis of the legal system from 1773 to 1776.

Economic crises and colonial discontents and disturbances certainly made the assemblies receptive to Virginia's call for intercolonial committees of correspondence. During the exact time in 1773 when they were being formed, the British ministry provided fresh reason for colonial anger. On 23 April 1773 Lord North proposed in Parliament that the East India Company—hit hard by the financial crisis of 1772-1773—be allowed to export tea directly to North America without paying British duties on it but still subject to the import tax of 3 pence per pound, payable in America, fixed in the Townshend Revenue Act, and not repealed in 1770. It was calculated that the net reduction in the cost of East India tea would make it lower priced than or at least competitively priced with smuggled Dutch tea and that Americans would therefore accept the duty. Little mention was made of the act in the English press, nor did it attract much attention in Parliament, where there was no comment on it as even an oblique challenge to America. Only a few voices outside Parliament suggested that Americans would not accept it. Yet in the colonies, where accurate news of the act, and of the decision of the East India Company to send tea, arrived in the autumn of 1773, opposition arose and spread quickly.

The bases of American opposition to the Tea Act were that it confirmed the Townshend duty on tea, objected to since 1767, that it presaged further such duties, and that it was the first step in a plan to give the East India Company control of all, or most, imports to America. These reactions can only be understood with the knowledge that since 1770 many Americans had been both predicting and petitioning for the total abolition of the remaining Townshend duty and that many believed that Parliament would make no further moves to tax America. In addition, special measures had been taken to guard against consumption of taxed tea, the single reminder of the hated revenue act. Moreover, many merchants now had a vested interest in smuggling foreign tea into the colonies. Finally, some suggested that the East India Company, a wealthy and oligarchic trading monopoly, was the natural ally of a corrupt government in its sinister schemes and that any large revenue from tea taxes would increase the funds available for the payment of officials and judges in America, a prime reason for nonconsumption. These latter points illustrate how American suspicion now almost automatically slotted every English move into the prevailing ideological framework. All these points gave the colonial radicals a great opportunity for propaganda and action in the four ports where tea was consigned—New York, Philadelphia, Boston, and Charleston. In New York threats of mob violence against the tea's merchant-consignees and against the ships carrying it had grown so warm by the end of the year that there was little hope of landing or selling it. In Philadelphia similar agitation had similar results. In both cities, patriots, Sons of Liberty, and other groups called mass meetings, protesting that recipients of East India tea would be enemies to American liberties, and threatening violence; in both cities the colonial authorities made no move to protect the expected cargoes.

In Boston agitation against East India Company tea took a little longer to develop. Eventually, the town meeting endorsed non-importation, and mobs and public meetings harassed the tea's consignees, who conveniently included

Governor Hutchinson's sons. The situation in Massachusetts was complicated by the facts that thousands of pounds of dutied tea had already been imported since 1768 without protest and that Governor Hutchinson, angered and wearied by a succession of crises, wished to uphold the powers of his government and prevent yet another radical victory. Hutchinson soon found himself powerless, since the Massachusetts council refused to consent to the use of force, and without their concurrence he lacked legal remedies. Hutchinson's backing for the consignees seems to have persuaded them not to resign nor to refuse to accept the tea, although they sought an agreement with the radicals whereby the cargoes would be stored and not sold. When the first tea ship, the *Dartmouth*, arrived in late November 1773, it eventually tied up at a wharf in a town that was controlled by "patriots" and in which the governor's writ hardly ran. Two more ships arrived a week or so later. Town meetings, mass meetings, committees of correspondence, men from outside Boston, all conferred during December.

This was a time of frenzied discussion in which government had become powerless. The patriots could not force the tea ships to leave Boston but had sworn that cargoes should not be landed there; the consignees dared not pay the customs duties on the tea. The stalemate broke on 16 December, after the failure of all plans of compromise, as Samuel Adams addressed a mass meeting. When he announced that he did not know what more the inhabitants could do to save their country, men disguised as Indians rushed from the meeting and, gathering reinforcements on the way, proceeded to the harbor and destroyed the tea. Here was no riot but a carefully coordinated effort, involving the onerous task of hauling up and breaking open large tea chests and dumping 90,000 pounds of tea over the ships' sides. The civil authorities made no attempt to stop the Boston Tea Party, for fear, wrote Hutchinson, of injuring innocent bystanders.

In Charleston, the last of the four ports to which it was sent, tea arrived in early December 1773. Agitation and meetings there made the consignees refuse to accept or to pay duty on it, but the customs officials were allowed to seize and store the tea. (It may have later been sold in 1775 to help the American side at the outbreak of the war.) But the opposition in Charleston split into traditional camps of merchants versus planters. The latter wanted to boycott only English tea; those merchants who had before traded in dutied tea had no wish to see their rivals now bring in the smuggled variety and demanded a ban on all tea.

Of these happenings, the Boston Tea Party, the most dramatic, is naturally the best remembered. Yet the powerlessness of the civil authorities in all four of the major colonial cities in late 1773, the near unanimity of opinion among those who made events, and the actions they successfully took suggest the wider relevance of these months. In four of the cities, many colonists now acted as if they were already independent. Local officeholders, many substantial citizens, many ordinary men supported measures and procedures that deprived royal governors, customs officers, and magistrates of all but the empty shell of power. No matter that most Americans also retained an emotional, or at the least habitual, tie to England, her government, and her king. 1773 had ended with colonial defiance of the highest sort.

Reaction in London, where news of the Boston Tea Party was published by 20 January 1774, at first was muted. Contemporaries gave more attention to Benjamin Franklin's summons before the Privy Council on 24 January to reply to charges connected with the publication of Hutchinson's letters in Boston. Vilified by the Solicitor General, Alexander Wedderburn, in the presence of thirty-five berobed Lords, Franklin received general press sympathy. Increasingly, however, the colorful events in Boston, together with the fact that only there had tea—property—actually been destroyed, attracted public comment to the town. By 1774 many in England had come to the conclusion that an *American* conspiracy now existed, with its headquarters in Boston, a center of anti-English subversion since the days of Charles I and Cromwell, which aimed to foment opposition and rebellion not only in New England but throughout America. From the first, the ministry seems to have determined to isolate the town for punishment. In late January Lord Dartmouth and the government decided to punish "the Town of Boston by removing the Custom House from thence and holding the Assembly in another place . . . as a measure that could be taken immediately by the sole power of the Crown." Other reports show that at this stage the cabinet considered taking legal and executive rather than Parliamentary action. But by the end of February, possibly remembering the futility of executive measures at the time of the *Gaspée* affair, the decision was made to lay the matter before Parliament.

Action followed with great speed. On 7 March Lord North read an address from the King to Parliament calling for the consideration of "what further regulations and permanent provisions may be necessary to be established for better securing the execution of the laws, and the just dependence of the Colonies on the Crown and Parliament of Great Britain." On 14 March the House gave leave for the introduction of the Boston Port Bill; it had passed through all its stages and received the royal assent on 31 March. And on 28 March the House of Commons in committee gave leave to bring in another bill for the "Better Regulating of the Government the Province of the Massachusetts Bay." This act received the royal assent on 20 May. In the interim, on 21 April, a third bill "for the Impartial Administration of Justice" was introduced, which also passed through both houses and received the royal assent by 20 May.

This package of Parliamentary legislation, drawn up and made law with enormous haste for those days, was the most drastic ever aimed at a North American colony. The Port Act made it illegal for ships to load or unload in Boston harbor after 1 June 1774, and the ministry announced that the Customs House would be moved to Salem. The act provided that when the Privy Council decided that "peace and obedience to the laws" had been restored in Boston, the port might be reopened by royal proclamation or an order in council. The

Government Act annulled the Massachusetts colony's charter right of 1691 to choose its council by vote of the lower house and substituted a royally appointed council from 1 August 1774; it also provided that the governor should appoint all judges, the attorney general and provost marshals, justices of the peace and sheriffs, and that jurymen should in future not be elected by the freeholders but effectively be selected by writ of the royal sheriffs. Finally, after 1 August no town meetings were to be held in Massachusetts without the governor's written approval, except the annual town meeting for elections of town and assembly representatives; at these meetings, no other matters could be discussed without the governor's permission. The Justice Act allowed the governor to order the trial of any official or any person acting under the direction of a magistrate or revenue officer and indicted for a capital offense to be held in another colony or in Great Britain if the governor believed he would not receive a fair trial in Massachusetts.

Opposition inside Parliament to these measures was inconsiderable. The independent country gentry supported the ministry in the Commons, believing that the Americans were traitors who would quickly come to heel when threatened with manly action, having "neither army, navy, money or men . . ." Only a handful of members of the Lords or Commons made vigorous speeches, and the opposition proved divided or ill-coordinated as well as outnumbered. Edmund Burke delivered the longest and most impressive speeches, although they revealed less an alternative policy than a desire to wound the government. Barré, who had formerly opposed the Stamp Act, approved the Port Bill, though he spoke against its two fellows. Chatham also indicated distaste for the legislation but support for Parliamentary supremacy and hostility to American actions. He did not choose to speak in the House of Lords. Opposition in the Lords and the Commons came from Chathamites and Rockinghamites; eleven peers signed a dissent from Government Act and eight from the Justice Act. But the highest vote that the opposition in the Lords could rally in any of the divisions on the three acts seems to have been twenty on 11 May. In the Commons the opposition could rarely find more than fifty or sixty votes. When Rose Fuller, a prominent West Indian M.P., moved for the repeal of the Tea Act in April, the occasion of Edmund Burke's famous speech on American taxation, his motion was lost by 182-49 votes. Within the ministry, opinion among the seven men who made up the effective cabinet council revealed only minor divergences on implementing a harsh policy. The Attorney-General and Solicitor-General, the Crown's law officers, also recommended resolute action; so did the two influential under-secretaries for the colonies, John Pownall, and William Knox, a former Grenvillite. Moreover, attempts to rally London and provincial merchants to the colonial cause had no results, and the press published many hostile pieces, condemning Americans for unprincipled disobedience. The King himself, by this time, also vigorously supported drastic action. In all, as William Pulteney, who opposed the Justice Act, said of the three acts, they were "not an error of the Ministry" but "an error of the nation."

The three "Coercive" Acts of 1774 were accompanied, or shortly followed, by other strict measures against Massachusetts. On 31 March Thomas Gage, commander-in-chief in America, was also commissioned as the province's governor. He sailed for Boston on 18 April with four regiments of soldiers and the assurance that he could use force to put down extraordinary civil uprisings without reference to his council. A few weeks later, an amended Quartering Act received the royal assent. This allowed British commanders more latitude in selecting billets for their troops in the colonies, and was seen as another threat to American property and liberty. These measures reflected the temper of the times. Few moderates still hoped for reconciliation and the loud voices called for armed intervention.

One final, important piece of legislation still awaited final Parliamentary action. This was a bill, introduced into the House of Lords on 2 May 1774, "making more effectual provision for the government of Quebec." It contained two main provisions. First, it settled the government of Quebec on an appointed governor and council, but provided freedom of worship and legal and political rights for French Catholics. Second, it extended Quebec's boundaries to include western territories claimed by colonial governments. It has been argued convincingly the bill had little or no relation to the Coercive Acts just passed but represented a long-considered adjustment to the government of Quebec and the Indian territories of the Old West undertaken independently of other colonial developments. Yet the timing of the bill suggested otherwise to contemporaries, and it immediately attracted hostile comment in the House of Commons and the press as an attack both on Protestant and American liberties. French law, Catholicism, a nominated government smacked of absolutism; the ministry sought, Edmund Burke argued, to draw a "line of circumvallation about our colonies, and establish a siege of arbitrary power." Although the government amended it to make it clear that it would not prejudice the western boundaries of the English colonies, the bill provided a red rag to the bull of traditional and often hysterical English radical anti-popery elements as well as—even though it incorporated principles previously agreed to by the Rockinghams—to saner opposition politicians. The Quebec Act became law in June 1774.

B. Committees and congresses

The effect of the four acts in America was immediate and crucial. Americans already believed that the English government had secretly planned to deprive them of their liberties; now the evidence was in the open. John Adams in Massachusetts saw them as "making altogether such a frightful system, as would have terrified any people who did not prefer liberty to life . . ." and believed that they were "all concerted at once" and "samples" of English intentions to take away colonial freedom. Washington, miles farther south, wrote to a correspondent in July that the designs of the ministry were revealed in their acts, "which are uniform and plainly tending to the same point, nay, if I mistake not, avowedly to fix the right of taxation. . . . shall we supinely sit and see one province after another fall a prey to despotism." In particular, the Quebec Act heightened Protestant-radical fears of Tory, Catholic-tinged despotism. Even the King seemed to be involved, for, wrote a contributor to the *Essex Gazette*, a Massachusetts paper, "a prince who can give royal assent to a bill which should establish popery, slavery and arbitrary power either in England or any of its dominions must be guilty of perjury; for it is in express terms contrary to his coronation oath. . . ," a rebuke that would be more generally applied to George III in the months to follow. A kind of unformed nationalism was growing up with more and more men in more and more colonies speaking and writing of an American cause that they largely defined in terms of protecting American liberties against British tyranny.

English ministers knew little of this inflamed state of American feelings or of the pattern of American political ideology as it then existed. Yet even the public events of the last decade should have made it reasonably clear that Massachusetts would not yield to drastic punishment or make the restitution necessary to avoid commercial and political chaos. Since 1765 its radicals had steadily won more and more support and no signs of effective conservative opinion able to temper their influence had appeared, while as the Stamp Act crisis had early revealed, some New Englanders stood ready for armed resistance. Outside of New England, most colonial bodies had willingly harmonized their opposition to British measures, cooperating in the Stamp Act Congress, in the intercolonial bodies of correspondence, and through actions taken by the colonial assemblies. Nor did British officials have the military or police means to enforce punitive decrees. The whole structure of local government, local justice, and the local militia remained in the hands of local leaders, the very men who had generally supported colonial resistance to Great Britain.

In Boston itself, news of the Boston Port Bill arrived on 10 May 1774, a few days before the landing of General Gage. The new governor faced a situation where, so officials stated, effective government had nearly disappeared. In the Massachusetts legislature the radicals held the floor, aiming salvo after salvo against the Crown. In February it had voted articles of impeachment against Chief Justice Oliver for accepting a Crown salary; this, according to the legislature, constituted a "continual Bribe in his Judicial Proceedings." Hutchinson heard himself labeled in an official message from the legislature as a liar who had got himself "advanced to places of honour and profit by means of . . . false representations" and a man "who owed his greatness to his country's ruin." The Parliamentary assault on Massachusetts came, therefore, as an assault on a society that was already heavily and successfully engaged with the enemy. Naturally, Boston took the initiative in the opposition to the Coercive Acts. Its town meeting's committee of correspondence acted as first mover of resistance, proposing in early June 1774 a non-importation, non-exportation and non-consumption movement, reporting their recommendation to committees in New York, Rhode Island, Philadelphia, and Connecticut. Shortly afterward, the Massachusetts House of Representatives, then in session, called for a general meeting of all the colonies and general colonial support for the people of Boston. In July the Boston town meeting voted that a declaration be made to "Great Britain and all the world" and a few days later established a Committee of Safety. At this juncture, Governor Gage banned all town meetings; the only result was that the Boston radicals called for county conventions and themselves organized a Suffolk (Boston and environs) County convention that sat in August and September. These county meetings were soon joined by a colony-wide body, for when Gage refused to summon a newly elected General Court, planned for early October, a number of representatives met anyway as a provincial congress and began to prepare for armed struggle. In other parts of New England, similar developments occurred. In New Hampshire, a provincial congress met on 21 July at Exeter; in Providence, Rhode Island, a town meeting resolved as early as 17 May for an intercolonial congress for "establishing the firmest union" while other Rhode Island towns and the colony's assembly rallied to Boston's support. In Connecticut town meetings and the assembly endorsed the Massachusetts cause, though some local leaders were moderate in their views of the shape that opposition should take.

The reception of news of the Coercive Acts provoked what can only be described as the beginnings of revolution. The most telling and significant feature of this beginning was the wave of activity that swept across the colonies at the level of the local community or district, manifesting itself in the proceedings of bodies that already had a legal or quasi-legal existence. Town and county meetings in the northern and middle colonies and meetings of county freeholders in the southern ones assembled and protested. Other sorts of committee and convention were continually improvised to meet local needs.

In New York old party distinctions were shaken and reshaped. Opposition to the acts was first organized by a combination of Sons of Liberty and Livingston faction members; these, however, compromised with the more conservative De Lanceyites to nominate a committee of merchants—the Committee of Fifty (later the Committee of Fifty-one)—on which the De Lanceyites gained a majority. At this point two popular leaders seem to have appealed to the city's mechanics to provide rival nominees but their nominations were defeated. However, despite continuing disagreements over strategy, the conservative De Lancey group triumphed, making their own nominations to a continental congress and refusing to endorse the resolutions of a mass meeting against the

Coercive Acts. By this time a Committee of Mechanics had emerged which opposed the De Lanceyites. In the rest of the province, inhabitants and freeholders of various counties met and passed resolutions. But a definite split had now developed between the more conservative Whigs, later to become Tories, and those who endorsed vigorous opposition. Soon this split would be repeated within the ranks of the vigorous, as popular and gentlemanly leaders diverged not only over tactics but in their ideas about the shape and style of government. In New Jersey the freeholders of Essex County met on 11 June at Newark and passed resolutions supporting Boston and favoring representation in a continental congress and adopting a non-importation agreement. They also appointed a county committee of correspondence and advocated the calling of a provincial congress. Other eastern county freeholders' meetings quickly followed, and Quaker West Jersey's freeholders also rallied. On 21 July a general meeting of county committees took place at New Brunswick, consisting of seventy-five delegates. This elected five members to a continental congress, supported both non-importation and non-exportation and protested against the "unconstitutional and oppressive" measures of the House of Commons.

The mechanism of protest in the two remaining middle colonies, Pennsylvania and Delaware, was the same. In Philadelphia a mass gathering—but one controlled by the moderates—agreed only to petition the governor for a meeting of the assembly and to express general support for Boston and enter into correspondence with other colonies. Non-importation and non-exportation were not, however, approved. Yet on 19 June a further mass meeting denounced Parliament in strong terms and set up a new committee; it also circumvented the Pennsylvania assembly's possible conservatism by empowering the new committee to elect delegates to a general colonial congress. In its turn, the new committee called a mass meeting of all the county committees of correspondence, which was held on 15 July. Its resolutions favored a non-importation and non-exportation movement. Yet the county convention also finally merely referred these opinions to the Pennsylvania assembly for its consideration, relinquishing to that body the selection of delegates to the general congress. When the assembly met on 18 July 1774, although it elected representatives to the congress, it ignored the more radical demands of the county convention. In Delaware freeholders' meetings took place in the three counties of the colony, followed by a convention of the counties in New Castle on 1 August that appointed three delegates to a general congress.

The county system of the southern colonies gave rise to similar county freeholders' meetings in the Chesapeake and Carolinas. In Maryland at least seven counties held such meetings between 18 May and 20 June and the citizens of the town of Annapolis also gathered. A general convention of the counties followed in Annapolis on 22 June. This approved calling a continental congress, selected five delegates, and gave support to non-exportation, if the other tobacco colonies of Virginia and North Carolina agreed, as well as qualified backing to non-importation. In Virginia the assembly was in session at the time of the crisis. It issued an appeal to the public for the support of Boston on 24 May, was dissolved by the governor two days later, but met as an extra-legal convention on the following day, and its actions were widely reported in the Virginia newspapers. County freeholders' meetings followed, some thirty or so sets of county resolves being passed by 28 July. On 1 August the adjourned Virginia convention met again, adopted an association for the future curtailment of exports and imports and selected representatives to a congress.

In North Carolina Wilmington's inhabitants called for a general meeting of the province's counties to take place in late August. Seventy-one men from thirty counties and six towns assembled on 25 August at New Bern, adopted a commercial association, and chose three delegates for a congress. In South Carolina Charleston was the scene of a gathering of 104 delegates from the counties and parishes of the colony; they were joined by many mechanics and planters living in or near the town. Because of the merchant interest, the meeting did not come out in favor of non-importation and non-exportation. But it did elect representatives to a congress and appoint a committee of ninety-nine men for correspondence and oversight of the implementation of its resolves. The Commons House of Assembly later approved the work of the meeting.

The events of these and subsequent months show clearly that those favoring fresh and more stringent actions against Britain now had the upper hand. They also illustrate John Adams' later dictum that the revolution had already taken place in the hearts and minds of the people before the war began. In many communities men agreed that the final crisis had arrived and that military hostilities might soon commence. Supplies of muskets and ammunition were checked and secured and measures taken to ensure the readiness of the colonial militia. Some Americans still drew back from the brink of open conflict and urged moderation. Yet they sought moderation in resistance, not an end to resistance. Even in Georgia, where royal government remained strong, a group of young, reasonably well-to-do Whigs pressed for firm measures. In the remaining colonies no public meetings, no traditional quasi-political gatherings like the county freeholders and no colonial assemblies, where they had met, considered that concessions should be the order of day. While some individuals and some groups of men, particularly merchants whose livelihood was threatened, still favored legal petitioning and protested against the most extreme resolves, they could not arrange meetings or rally public support to rival the proponents of fiercer measures. In the great majority of cases local officials, local organizations, local churches, local voluntary bodies, and the press and the printers rallied to the American cause. The colonial newspapers, indeed, played a vital part in retailing news and comment, almost unanimously supporting opposition to British authority and printing opinions that went far beyond the official pronouncements of local committees and colonial assemblies. The fact that each newspaper carried reports of proceedings in other colonies meant that not even the most unimaginative colonial groups lacked models for public meetings, standing committees, extraordinary resolutions, and the like.

We have seen that the various bodies that met in the colonies from late May 1774 had quickly appointed delegates to a continental congress. The calling of such an intercolonial body had been suggested in Massachusetts and Virginia in 1773, but the move to convene one had been made by the Virginia convention at its meeting of 25 May 1774. By this time it was felt that such a body should meet, not like the Stamp Act Congress for a specific purpose, but annually "to deliberate on those general measures which the united efforts of America may from time to time require." The first Continental Congress assembled in Philadelphia on 1 September 1774; only Georgia was not represented. The delegates debated American affairs until its session closed on 26 October.

The representatives who came to Philadelphia in September had no doubts that the old ties with Great Britian could not persist. Overwhelmingly, they accepted that Parliament either had no right to legislate at all concerning America or that it could not legislate in any way that infringed on colonial charters or colonial liberties—virtually the same things. Moreover, on 17 September the delegates unanimously approved a set of resolves originally passed in Suffolk County, Massachusetts, which stated in violent terms that no obedience was due to the acts of Parliament affecting Boston and advised the people "to elect the officers of the militia, and to use their utmost diligence to acquaint themselves with the art of war as soon as possible, and for that purpose to appear under arms once in every week." Such sentiments, combined with other actions of the Congress, show that the idea of a fast-approaching military struggle then loomed large. On the other hand, motions that Gage in Boston be attacked before he received reinforcements and that a militia be appointed and provided with ammunition and arms were not carried. Nor, however, did conciliation prove attractive. A plan for the drastic reform of the imperial constitution, suggested by Joseph Galloway of Pennsylvania as a conciliatory move, aimed at "a lasting Accommodation with Great Britain," failed to win the delegates' approval.

The Congress finally agreed on an announcement of colonial rights and grievances and four major addresses, none of which was directed to Parliament. The first declaration of rights and grievances went far beyond the proposals in Galloway's plan of union. It included a denial of the Crown's right to maintain soldiers in any colony without the consent of its legislature or to appoint colonial councils, and it detailed the acts of Parliament that infringed and violated colonial rights. It also attacked the Quebec Act for establishing Roman Catholicism in the province, for abolishing the equitable system of English laws, and for creating a tyranny there. The first of the four addresses appealed directly to the inhabitants of Great Britain, implicity rejecting, as it were, both King and Parliament, in favor of the still uncorrupted body of the nation. Its objective was to rally nonconformist, manufacturing, and trading interests formerly friendly to the colonies, and it made much of the wickedness of establishing popery in America. The second address, to the King, requested his ''royal authority and interposition'' for the relief of America. The third justified the proceedings of the Continental Congress to the inhabitants of the colonies, reviewing the history of the conflict with Great Britain since 1763 and emphasizing Parliament's consistent drive for illegal supremacy. The last went to the French of Quebec, an indication of the role that Canada had already begun to play in the strategic thinking of the congressional leadership. Glossing over the anti-Catholic nature of American opposition to the Quebec Act, it alleged that the British government still withheld political and legal rights from Canadians and promised that, as in Switzerland, Catholics and Protestants in America could live in amity and must unite against oppression.

What gave teeth to these proceedings was a decision for a continental embargo on imports from Great Britain and Ireland and on the use of British goods already in America to take effect on 1 December 1774, and on exports of American goods to Great Britain to take effect on 1 December 1775, unless specified acts of Parliament were repealed by that date. This was accompanied with the publication of a form of association to be signed by all Americans and to be enforced by local committees. The association marked a significant advance in the basic process already apparent in the numerous gatherings of committees and conventions by which a structure of authority and government was emerging to replace the discredited instruments of colonial rule. Local government largely remained in local hands, and these were mainly pro-American—every Virginia justice of the peace was a committeeman, said one British official—and no great upheaval took place at that level. But the new associations furthered the breakdown of official British institutions by offering visible, approved alternatives that could serve as flexible agencies for the radicals to use as overall supervisory committees.

Neither of the addresses sent to England met with any success. Just as the British government gambled and lost with the Coercive Acts, the moderates in the Congress who still thought that commercial coercion might bring a British retreat misjudged the situation in Britain. More extreme elements in the Congress had probably agreed to the addresses in the belief that probable British rejection promised them greater authority in the months to come. By November 1774, indeed, George III already considered that the New England colonies were in open rebellion and by the time that news of the first Continental Congress arrived in London, in mid-December, plans had already begun for a war in North America. The King accepted the Congress's address but merely referred it to Parliament—in other words, ignored it. The address to the inhabitants of Great Britain fell on unfriendly ground. Little pressure from London or the provinces arose to embarrass the government and the Rockingham Whigs failed in an attempt to renew the old petitioning movement of

Stamp Act repeal days. Merchants and manufacturers in London, Bristol, Norwich, in the Black Country and the pottery towns called for measures to alleviate the distress caused by or likely to result from the disruption of American trade. They did not attack the government outright. Other provincial petitioners supported firm British action against America. The "trade and Commerce of Great Britain with her Colonies cannot be effectually restored, and permanently secured, without a due and proper Submission and Obedience to the Laws and Government of this Kingdom," observed several prominent inhabitants of Nottingham. Indeed, merchants and manufacturers were generally cautious toward colonial claims. Still suffering the effects of the crisis of 1772 and fearful that American demands for liberty might destroy the Acts of Trade, they increasingly accepted the sad necessity of coercion. In the summer of 1775 Burke wrote, "We look to the merchants in vain. They are gone from us, and from themselves. They consider America as lost and look to administration for indemnity."

Other moderating or conciliatory pressures were also substantially diminished by this time. The colonial agents, for example, had lost any credibility or influence, although Benjamin Franklin still retained a measure of prestige with some government officials, dissenters, and provincial groups. A move by Lord Dartmouth, and Lord Hyde, Chancellor of the Duchy of Lancaster, representing less extreme opinion in the government, involved an attempt at finding an understanding with the colonies by means of Quaker intermediaries and Franklin. He drew up a draft of "Hints for Conversations upon the Subject of Terms that may probably produce a *Durable* union between Great Britain and her Colonies" in December 1774, and negotiations went on into 1775. Yet the majority of the cabinet was hostile to measures of conciliation. Dartmouth himself and Lord North, the two ministers best disposed to such plans, felt at the same time the necessity of exerting British authority to uphold "the King's dignity and the honour and safety of the Empire . . ." The negotiations had virtually failed by mid-February, for Franklin stressed that American recognition of British authority depended on the repeal of the Coercive Acts and of other Parliamentary legislation, something unacceptable to the government. On 2 March 1775, the day after he finally learned of the uselessness of his efforts, Franklin sailed for America.

Secure in the King's favor—and George III had become a firm protagonist of military action in America by late 1774—sensing little opposition to their measures in the country, and, on the whole, little inclined to listen to moderate voices, the ministers also had no worries about their strength in the Commons. The House had been newly elected in October 1774 in a campaign in which the American issue had played a part in perhaps only twelve to sixteen constituencies. Its members included, according to Lord North's calculations, 321 supporters of the government (of whom 50 might not be present at its sessions for various reasons) and 237 in opposition or of doubtful loyalties. Yet government majorities on American matters in early 1775 usually numbered around 200. The Lords also provided substantial backing. Chatham, so powerful a voice in the repeal of the Stamp Act, now carried little weight. In January and February 1775 he spoke for conciliation through extensive concessions to American sentiment. His plan was voted down in the Lords by 61-32. The high minority vote rested on other factors than genuine agreement with his scheme.

Government measures in early 1775, in fact, amounted to a declaration of war on New England, which a Parliamentary address to the King in February stated to be in rebellion. The sending of more troops and a blockade of its coast, decided in the Cabinet in January, received Parliamentary sanction in the next month, although the former measure was declared to be temporary, until the restoration of amity. The only practical concession offered by the government was a Parliamentary resolution promising that no internal taxes would be levied on Americans if the colonies taxed themselves for purposes of defense, the support of civil government, and the administration of justice in a manner approved by King, Lords, and Commons. Subsequently, the ministry offered a royal pardon to all who had committed treasonable offenses if the offenders would swear an oath to obey all Parliamentary legislation. These heavily qualified gestures meant very little, for they explicitly upheld the sovereign authority of Parliament and ignored American demands for the formal recognition of colonial rights and liberties. As news of additional disorders in America flowed in, the real thrust of the ministry's efforts became clear. In March 1775 a bill was introduced to restrain the trade and commerce of New Jersey, Pennsylvania, Maryland, Virginia, and South Carolina that became law on 12 April. In the same month, the ministry rejected Edmund Burke's attempt to reopen the question of conciliation with an overwhelming majority in the House of Commons. By this time war had broken out in America.

C. War and independence

The first armed clashes between British soldiers and American patriots took place in Massachusetts. Here, one provincial congress had voted in November 1774 to raise troops and money and a second, in February 1775, for taxes to finance the militia and "minutemen" and had approved a set of regulations for the conduct of an army. On 18 April, General Gage, stung by letters from England accusing him of inactivity, sent a detachment of 700 men toward Concord to seize military supplies stored there. His troops were intercepted at Lexington by the village's minutemen, eight of whom died in the subsequent skirmish in the early morning of the next day. Arriving next at Concord, from which all military supplies had been removed by the patriots, the British regulars failed to disperse its embattled farmers, and set out to return to Boston. During the course of the march back, colonial skirmishers continually harassed the British. Almost immediately the countrymen of New England took up arms, and a considerable force assembled to besiege the enemy in their garrison at Boston.

The war spread only gradually. In May 1775 a force of irregulars from Massachusetts under the command of Benedict Arnold and another of Vermont frontiersmen captured—in the name of "the great Jehovah and the Continental Congress," though authorized by neither, it was apocryphally reported—the poorly defended fort of Ticonderoga, an important point on the route between Canada and New York. Canada, indeed, became an American military and political objective, since its conquest or adhesion to the cause would complete continental unity against Great Britain. From New York, Philip Schuyler led a contingent toward Montreal; from New England, Arnold marched on Quebec. The British relinquished the former post but Quebec was not captured; the American siege was lifted in May 1776, and reinforcements began to pour into Canada from Britain. The most dramatic event, however, had taken place two months before this, when the British abandoned Boston and retreated to Halifax, Nova Scotia, to regroup. Shortly before, some of their forces, under the command of General Henry Clinton, had sailed from Boston to the Carolinas, where it was expected that considerable numbers of loyal Americans would rally to the Crown.

This early southern strategy failed. Some Scottish highlanders did rise to the royal cause in North Carolina but suffered defeat at the hands of patriot militiamen at the Battle of Moore's Creek Bridge in February 1776, making pointless any British landing in the province. The fleet, now reinforced by ships and men from England under Lord Cornwallis, sailed on to Charleston, but the city's defenders beat back a poorly coordinated British landing assault in June 1776. Other British activity mainly consisted of bombarding seaport towns from Maine to the Chesapeake. In Virginia Governor Dunmore, in late 1775, had taken to the sea and begun to harry the coastline. His declaration in November of the same year promising freedom to all slaves who would join his forces intensified southern opposition, even among moderates, and would later be included in the early drafts of the Declaration of Independence as an American grievance.

The serious business of war awaited a great fleet under Admiral Lord Howe which arrived in New York in late June 1776. The British had assembled the largest force that "the mother country had ever sent overseas," consisting of 32,000 troops, 10,000 seamen, 400 transports, 10 major warships, and 20 frigates.

Throughout America, from the time of the British evacuation of Boston up to the arrival of Lord Howe, royal authority had collapsed, with governors seeking refuge in forts or aboard ships, waiting either for the opportunity to leave in safety or for relief that never came. Yet while Americans took measures to ensure their military security, they did not rush into conflict. Until

June 1775 the Continental Congress failed to vote to raise an American army for the war in New England. They then commissioned six companies of riflemen and appointed George Washington as commander-in-chief. They also soon voted to emit bills of credit "for the defence of America." In June the Congress issued an important statement of its delegates' current opinion, "A Declaration . . . setting forth the Causes and Necessity of their Taking up Arms" which attacked the British government but denied "ambitious Designs of separating from Great Britain, and establishing Independent States." Two days later, the Congress again petitioned the King, prompted by John Dickinson and other moderates, protesting their loyalty and devotion and asking for reconciliation.

The Olive Branch Petition was not the only evidence that many leading politicians still hoped for reconciliation with Great Britain. At the end of 1775 most state conventions still instructed their congressional delegates to seek an accommodation with the mother country, and substantial numbers of men believed that the colonies should go no further than organizing to conduct a limited resistance to British assaults, all the while pressing for paper concessions. Yet a fiery minority of New Englanders and a few other delegates were now actively resisting these accommodating measures. Although they still hesitated to call outright for independence, it was generally realized that separation or acts that made it unavoidable were what they favored. That the leading spirits were New Englanders hardly helped the cause. For by this time regional feelings among congressional delegates were evident, and many middle-colony and southern gentlemen found plain Yankee talk disconcertingly leveling and democratic. Indeed, there is much evidence that many of those who drew back from the brink of separation, although genuinely pulled by lifelong habits of loyalty to their ideal of king and mother country, also equated independence with the triumph of New England principles, New England principles with republicanism and republicanism with social leveling and the end of a deferential society. In May 1774 Gouverneur Morris of New York stood on a balcony, looking over a mass meeting assembled to protest the closure of Boston, and saw "on [his] right hand all the people of property, with some few dependents, and on the other the tradesmen, etc., who thought it worth their while to leave their daily labour for the good of the country." But those tradesmen and the rest of the generality were not passively content to follow the policies of gentlemen leaders but pressed their own ideas and elected their own sort to committees and the like. For Morris this already represented a breach of social and political order: "the heads of the mobility grow dangerous to the gentry, and how to keep them down is the question." Nearly a year later James Allen of Philadelphia, who proclaimed he loved "the Cause of liberty," also reckoned that the "madness of the multitude is but one degree better than submission to the Tea Act."

Both these men came from the colonial cities, and it was in the cities that the position of the old ruling groups did for a time seem most threatened, both by "mob" activity and by popular meetings. Some of the gentry leaders in New York—imbued with classical Whig ideas—did not believe that the "mechanics" and other artisans could act of their own volition and regarded their activities merely as the result of their mobilization by leaders from outside their ranks. This view may have had some validity, but by the 1770s it is also likely that groups of artisans and skilled workers had developed a consciousness of their own interests that they measured against those of the wealthier merchants and lawyers. In one respect this consciousness was economic. Craftsmen, for example, favored non-importation since it lessened market competition against their own products. They also and sometimes successfully attempted to end internal economic regulations—price controls, building regulations, and the like—that restricted free enterprise. Such actions have led several historians to conclude that "radical" consciousness was in fact the attempt by certain occupational groups to influence public policy in such a way as to increase their opportunities. Politically, too, the radicals seem to have wished not to displace or destroy the leadership of merchants and lawyers but to win a share of the political power that they enjoyed. This led the mechanics of New York to insist that they had the right "to judge whether it be consistent with their interests to accept, or reject, a constitution framed for that state of which they are members" and for a Marylander to write that "every poor man has a life, a personal liberty, and a right to his earnings: and is in danger of being injured by government in a variety of ways: therefore it is necessary that these people should enjoy the right of voting for representatives, to be the protectors of their lives, personal liberty and little property, which, though small is yet upon the whole, a very great object to them." From the angle of die-hard Whigs, resenting any threat to their paternal use of political power, these attitudes represented a democratic challenge by the "vulgar." And considered more broadly, they are one manifestation of the growing revolutionary use of the language of equality. But their challenge was not a sustained one and the rhetoric of equality achieved little in practice.

Elite fears of popular activity increased after about 1774. Also remarkable is the extent to which even firm New England opponents of Great Britain like John Adams felt that the struggle was realizing or provoking social and political attitudes too popular in their implications for him to stomach. Yet other factors than fear of domestic upheavals undoubtedly played as large or a larger part in determining attitudes to the mother country. Neither the Virginia nor South Carolina gentry, for example, were really apprehensive about losing authority at home but the former generally supported and the latter generally resisted the idea of independence. Could the fact of Virginia's economic problems in the empire and South Carolina's economic successes have borne on those attitudes? Similarly, the middle-colony delegates were perhaps the leading advocates of reconciliation, those of New England the leading opponents;

again the middle-colony economy was generally prosperous, that of New England rather depressed. Men may well have been consciously or unwittingly influenced by such conditions. Finally, however, they were driven to independence by British measures and the need to resist them. In October 1775, disregarding the Olive Branch Petition received in August, the King's speech at the opening of Parliament had already prejudged the issue, declaring that rebellion existed in America that was "manifestly carried on for the purpose of establishing an independent empire." On 22 December Parliament passed a further prohibitory act naming all thirteen colonies rebellious, prohibiting all British trade with them and declaring their ships and, indeed, "all other ships . . . found trading" in their ports "forfeited to His Majesty, as if the same were the ships and effects of open enemies." In February 1776 the Continental Congress threw American ports open to foreign ships and a month later sent Silas Deane on a mission to France to seek aid from England's traditional enemy.

With such events, independence became less of a choice and more of a fact. Politically, however, the issue remained complicated since it seemed to be bound up with the necessity of reörganizing American government. Although many Americans believed in a purged political system in which executive power would be strictly checked, they had largely felt this to be compatible with limited monarchy. What they had advocated were increased political and economic liberties within a remodeled empire. Nevertheless, a significant number of American writers since the early 1770s had expressed an increasing disillusionment with monarchy itself, coupled with anger at George III's rejection of colonial petitions and his assent to unpopular legislation. A commencement speaker at Princeton in 1775 criticized the contemporary European monarchies and decided that "the history of Kings and Emperors is little more than the history of royal villainy." At the same time the idea of republicanism—still strongly identified with popular, disorderly, and factional government—began to seem more attractive. By 1776, indeed, Americans could argue that their experience of associations and committees, including the Continental Association of 1774, proved that an authority based on the people could operate without confusion or disorder; despite occasional mob excesses, the "American experience of the mid-1770s," Pauline Maier has written, "suggested that the people were willing to venerate and obey not just hereditary rulers but governments entirely of their own choice, made up of men whom they could 'love, revere, and confide in'. . . ."

On 10 January 1776, a book was published that provided thousands of readers with an opportunity to adjust older perceptions to the novel events of the time. Thomas Paine's *Common Sense* contained an outright call to republican independence. It also marshalled a variety of arguments against hereditary monarchy and aristocracy, linked those institutions to contemporary struggles—"the corrupt influence" of the Crown had "swallowed up the power, and eaten up the virtue of the House of Commons (the republican part of the Constitution . . .'' and condemned George III personally as a tyrant and a brute. At this level Paine's arguments justified parricide. Since the father sought to enslave the children, Americans could be absolved from lingering guilts over undutiful behavior to a loving parent, he reasoned. And, Paine also skillfully argued, if the father was a brute, the other parent was a fraud. Europe, not England, was the true mother of America and would sustain her in her hour of need. At a political level, his evidence suggested that outright republicanism was the purest form of government and that England suffered not only a despotic monarchy but a flabby decadence and lack of military vigor over which Americans could easily prevail. Finally, Paine gave Americans an international destiny as an ''asylum for mankind.'' ''Freedom,'' he wrote, ''had been hunted round the globe—Asia and African had long expelled her, Europe regards her like a stranger, and England hath given her warning to depart.''

If Paine provided many Americans with a psychological release from their dependence on a monarchy that they identified with partriarchal authority, he also flattered and excited them by raising the colonial struggle to the level of a world historical event. And *Common Sense* perhaps sold 120,000 copies in the three months after it appeared—possibly one for every three or four adult white males in the colonies. Contemporaries testified to its influence. Washington observed that ''by private letters, which I have lately received from Virginia, I find that 'Common Sense' is working a powerful change there in the minds of many men.'' The *Connecticut Gazette* resoundingly praised it for declaring the ''sentiments of Millions. Your production may justly be compared to a land-flood that sweeps all before it . . . The doctrine of Independence hath been in times past, greatly disgustful . . . it is now become our delightful theme, and commands our purest affections.'' *Common Sense* also frightened John Adams by its advocacy of single chamber legislatures and its leveling spirit. His *Thoughts on Government* printed in 1776 advocated the retention of elected upper houses and showed a consciousness of the problem of ''the lower class of people'' in a republican society; state education and the desire for their own advancement would bind them to government, he felt. This work would have considerable influence on those making state constitutions in 1776 and 1777.

A movement for formal separation from Great Britain then picked up speed as proponents of independence turned from the Continental Congress to the individual colonies to try to hasten the process. In April North Carolina's provincial congress empowered its congressional delegates to seek independence. In early May Rhode Island declared herself independent of Great Britain; in the same month Virginia's provincial convention unanimously instructed its delegates to the Congress to ''propose to that respectable body to declare the United Colonies free and independent states absolved from all allegiance to, or dependence upon, the crown and parliament of Great Britain." A month later Richard Henry Lee of Virginia moved at the Congress that the colonies "are, and of right ought to be, free and independent States" and that "all political connection between them and the State of Great Britain is, and ought to be, totally dissolved." Although the Congress resolved that this motion should not be debated until the beginning of July, it also anticipated its success, appointing a committee to prepare a "Declaration" that would embody it. Matters then moved quickly, with Pennsylvania and New Jersey declaring in favor of colonial independence and Delaware freeing its delegates to vote as "shall be judged necessary for promoting the liberty, safety and interests of America."

Thomas Jefferson drafted the Declaration of Independence; it was considered by the Continental Congress on 3 July 1776. The day before, however, the Congress had formally approved Richard Lee's motion for independence, so that the completion and signing of Jefferson's declaration was not the occasion of the break with Great Britain but its justification—"the great apologia of the American Revolution," he later called it. Jefferson's own explanation of the necessity for the Declaration of Independence is contained within the document, notably his feeling that "a decent respect to the opinions of mankind" required a statement for European consumption of the causes that impelled the colonists to a separation. Other writers have also pointed out that the Declaration should be seen as a manifesto, or argument, aimed equally at North Americans, a substantial number of whom still hesitated between accepting the necessity of independence or remaining loyal to Great Britain. On both counts, the Declaration served its purpose, embodying as it did a readily comprehensible summary of Anglo-American relations in terms of English infringements of American rights which showed the justice of the colonists' action in dissolving the bonds that linked them to Great Britain. The Declaration also reminded Americans of the kinds of rights enjoyed by sovereign and independent governments—"full power to levy war, conclude Peace, contract Alliances, establish Commerce and do all other Acts and Things which Independent States may of right do"—powers that the colonies would need whatever their declared constitutional positions. Finally, in part directly but mostly by implication, it stated certain political beliefs.

Foremost among these is the idea that power and government proceeds upward from the people and not downward from some superior authority, human or divine. This point was not lost on conservative Americans. Dickinson, for example, had disputed Jefferon's assertion (in a draft of the 1775 "Declaration on Taking up Arms") that the founders of the colonies had "established civil societies with various forms of constitution," substituting instead the phrase, "Societies or governments vested with perfect legislatures were formed under charters from the crown." Now Jefferson again emphasized the Lockeian belief in the constituent power of the people at large, should legislative bodies be annihilated or should a government become destructive of the ends for which it was set up.

Yet it is interesting to note that despite this formulation, the Declaration did not contain an outright attack on monarchical government as such. George III was condemned not because he was a king but because he was a despotic king; Britain was criticized not because of her form of government but because of the abuses in that form—abuses that Jefferson in a draft of the Declaration had stated that the English, although "a people fostered and fixed in principles of freedom," had refused to disavow. "We might have been a free and great people together," he also wrote, "but a communication of grandeur and of freedom, it seems, is below their dignity. Be it so; since they will have it the road to happiness and glory is open to us too; we will climb it apart from them and acquiesce in the necessity which denounces our eternal separation."

Jefferson himself, it should also be noted, had included in his original draft an attack on the King's alleged involvement in the slave trade—"he has waged cruel war against human nature itself, violating its most sacred rights of life and liberty in the persons of a distant people who never offended him, captivating and carrying them into slavery in another hemisphere." In the same draft he also turned on the British people for keeping in power by their free election "the disturbers of our harmony" and "at this very time too . . . permitting their chief magistrate to send over not only soldiers of our common blood, but Scotch and foreign mercenaries to invade and deluge us in blood." The first item was deleted at the request of southerners who knew that their constituents favored the trade and northerners who knew that theirs had taken part in it. The second was omitted, Jefferson wrote, because some congressmen felt that America still had friends in England.

The political creed of Americans as stated by Jefferson is clear enough. It sprang directly from more than a century of traditional English theory, bits of which must then have been familiar to most Americans and all of which to the political leaders of each colony. Representation of the people in the legislatures ("a right inestimable to them and formidable to tyrants only"), a judicial system independent of executive control, legislative control of standing armies, the civil superior to the military power, taxation by consent, trial by jury, a free system of English laws, and fixed forms of government were old ideas. That governments ought to secure life and liberty was also the familiar language of generations of theorists. That it spoke not of property but of equality and of the "pursuit of happiness," however, struck a new, non-Lockeian chord. Indeed, some of Jefferson's readers may well have viewed the whole question of "inalienable rights" in a very different spirit from that of Locke. In England by this date, in writings reprinted in America, several theorists had written of inalienable rights as those known intuitively to conscience or inner light and therefore perceivable by all men, the poor as well as the propertied.

The body of the Declaration, however, listed American beliefs about political rights and government in the most general way. Nothing in it spoke to details or to the social pattern of institutions. It neither defined the "people" nor ventured into such questions as eligibility for holding office or for voting. Did the "people" include the indentured servant, the poor, the propertyless or those of little property? Was their consent necessary to taxation and should their voice be heard in the constituent bodies that might remake government? By remaining silent on all these points, Congress allowed men to make their own interpretations, skirting the controversies that these issues now increasingly provoked among Americans. Nor, of course, did the Declaration address itself either to the forms of government of the independent states or to the problem of the nature of the political relations between the states in the Continental Congress.

Yet this latter point had not been neglected. When the decision to declare independence was made, Congress also set up a committee to draft articles of confederation under the chairmanship of John Dickinson. All three facts were related since Dickinson represented substantial conservative opinion that favored an agreement on central government before or at the same time as independence; otherwise thirteen unconnected, independent states might exhaust themselves in quarrels with each other, tearing the continent "in pieces by Intestine Wars and Convulsions," as Carter Braxton of Virginia wrote. The logic of military activities also demanded some form of central government: in the absence of a continental civil authority, the continental army might swallow up the central direction of affairs. Franklin as early as July 1775, indeed, had with his usual prescience proposed a plan for a confederacy that could be adopted at independence. Under his scheme each colony maintained control over its internal affairs but cooperated in matters of defense and the direction of an army, foreign relations, disputes between colonies, general commerce, monetary affairs, and a post office. A colonial congress, with representatives apportioned according to white male population, would meet annually while executive authority would rest with a council of twelve, elected for three years, with one third of its membership changing annually. At the time of Declaration of Independence, however, Dickinson could only report that his committee, because of sharp conflicts of opinion, could not recommend any plan of union for the colonies.

Chapter Thirteen

From Colonies to States

A. Modes of republicanism

For John Adams, 1776 ushered in a "new World, a young World, a World of countless Millions all in the fair Bloom of Piety." This surge of excitement and optimism stood in deep contrast to the despair with which Adams and others had viewed the recent past. Then English corruption had threatened all; now there was hope. Then tyranny was encroaching in all parts of the world; now everywhere there was a contagion of liberty. Then aristocracy and luxury had produced immorality and decay; now Americans were to live upright, pious, and frugal lives. The intensity of moral hatred developed by significant numbers of the leading men of the day toward British power and corruption stood transformed into an equally intense moral belief in the "regenerative effects of republican government on the character of the people" that would follow the break with Great Britain. Jefferson, for example, had not only the grand design of reforming Virginia's laws and constitution in order to found "a system by which every fibre would be eradicated of ancient and feudal aristocracy, and a foundation laid for government truly republican," but he also contemplated many lesser improvements such as changes in the postal system and methods of collecting vital statistics.

Recent scholars have argued persuasively that this moral or reformist passion constituted a distinguishing mark of the American Revolution. Not all those who supported the revolution felt it deeply and many were pessimistic about the suitability of republican institutions for the vast territories of the New World. But probably none of the intellectually aware escaped it completely and many of the dominant spirits espoused it fully. It was an attitude partly formed in the crucible of radical ideology—the continuing mounting identification of England with corruption and tyranny that had reached a crescendo in the late 1760s. By 1776 republicanism seemed the only alternative to slavery, a republicanism that involved not only the abolition of monarchy and formal changes in the structure of government and institutions but a utopian vision of the future. The function of government was to be the promotion of the good of the whole, and virtue in men, manners and institutions was to be its basis and its end. For those Americans who had often felt awkward or provincial in Old World aristocratic circles, the assertion of republican values no doubt also soothed former feelings of inferiority. Aristocratic traits evident in England and Europe—pride, condescension, arrogance, deceit—as well as the panoplies of hereditary and family privilege were to be cast off. New republican governments and new republican virtues would mutually reinforce each other. Except in one or two particulars, few revolutionary leaders believed that republicanism necessitated—although it might produce—new property or economic relationships.

These republican sentiments rested on a strong neo-classical base. "Having been initiated in youth, in the doctrines of civil liberty, as they were taught by such men as Plato and Demosthenes, Cicero and other renowned persons among the ancients; and such as Sidney and Milton, Locke and Hoadley, among the moderns, I liked them; they seemed rational." So wrote Jonathan Mayhew, and scores of thinking Americans would have approved his sentiments. Yet the republican mood also accorded well with an older American tradition, the pietism shared by thousands of American Christians. For some evangelicals, the revolution was a great religious movement. Israel was to be released from the Egyptian bondage. Right was to triumph over evil. George III, the Pharaoh or the Beast of the Johnian revelation, and the sinful English ministers and officials who surrounded him were to fall, victims of their pride, luxury, and irreligion. America, born in Puritan glory, witness of amazing testimonies of God's love in its prosperity and progress as well as of His chastisements for its backslidings, increasingly filled since the Great Awakening by men and women of elect sanctity, now stood, thought many clergy, at the beginning of a new Christian liberty and unity. The more extreme pietists indulged the contemplation of the fulfillment of millenial hopes. America would become, or had become, one minister suggested "the principal Seat of that Glorious Kingdom, which Christ shall erect upon Earth in the latter Days . . ." It would be "Immanuel's *land*, a *Mountain of Holiness*, a *Habitation* of Righteousness, The Lord's *spiritual Empire of Love, Joy, and Peace*. . . ," enthused the Reverend David Avery, chaplain to the American forces at Bunker Hill and Ticonderoga.

Throughout New England and among some Presbyterians and Baptists in the middle and southern colonies—although it should never be forgotten that many pietists were pacifists or neutrals or quiescent—revolutionary pietism ran high, embarrassing the more latitudinarian Christians and the rationalists. Yet while it can be suggested that republican moral fervor and appeals to virtue rested as much on the evangelical zeal of those, as Adams phrased it, "in the fair Bloom of Piety" as on the generally rationalistic Whig-radical feelings of men like Jefferson and Franklin, it was the latter, the political republicans—shrewd lawyers, merchants, and southern gentlemen, Whig or democrat—who remained dominant. The process of transition from old to new governments showed a spirit of reforming optimism but hardly one of millenial dreams. God was scarcely mentioned in most of the new frames of state government. These grounded the constitutional lives of Americans neither on the Old or the New or the Apocryphal Testaments but on a secular republicanism firmly shaped by a secular curriculum.

The transition from colonial to state governments can be traced back to 1774. In that year it was known that the Continental Congress would not favor any overt attack on the old colonial charters and governments but merely support arrangements that men hoped would be temporary—county committees, conventions, councils of safety, and the like. The first formal call to Congress for guidance came in May 1775 when Massachusetts requested "explicit advice" about the taking up of and exercising the powers of civil government. Congress then recommended the *de facto* authorities only to "write letters to the inhabitants of the several places that are entitled to representation in assembly" to choose representatives, that the representatives should choose a council, and that the "council should exercise the powers of government, until a governor of his majesty's appointment will consent to govern the colony according to its charter." In October, despite the harangues of John Adams, who firmly supported the view that all the colonies ought to "call conventions and institute regular governments," Congress still looked to a settlement with Great Britain. Yet it did recommend to both New Hampshire and South Carolina that their provincial conventions should "call a full and free representation of the people" (a radical victory) to establish as a temporary measure until reconciliation with Great Britain (an expression of moderate opinion) a form of government.

After this date, the issue of government in the individual colonies as seen in Congress joined itself even more closely to the question of independence. Adams and others who supported separation lobbied for a congressional recommendation to the colonies to break from the mother country by adopting new governments; moderates opposed the linked demands for independence and new governments. Not until 10 May 1776 did Congress finally resolve that the colonies might if they felt it necessary adopt governments that "shall in the opinion of the representatives of the people best conduce to the happiness and safety of their constituents in particular and of America in general." Five days later, after heated debates, it added a preamble to this earlier resolution, calling for the total suppression of authority derived from the Crown and for all powers of government to be exerted "under the authority of the people of the colonies." John Adams wrote that this was "the most important Resolution that was ever taken in America"; for him the Declaration of Independence would be a mere formality. Others spoke of "A Revolution in Government," and the religious elements stepped up their preparations for moral and spiritual regeneration.

By the date of this decision three colonies had already made formal constitutional arrangements for new governments. However, the new constitutions of

New Hampshire, approved by its provincial congress on 5 January 1776, and of South Carolina, approved on 26 March, were carefully delineated as temporary measures and preceded by declarations of continuing loyalty to the Crown. They may be properly regarded as expedients, similar to the less formal arrangements made at this date in other colonies to substitute effective authority for vanished imperial supremacies. The first lasted, despite criticism, until 1783, and the second only to 1778. In Rhode Island, too, the spring assembly removed the oaths of allegiance from its charter without reference to Congress. Moreover, the Virginia convention had voted on the same day as the congressional resolution of 15 May for drafting a new and permanent constitution. In the other colonies, news of the resolution and of the Declaration of Independence combined with existing demands to provoke the making of new constitutions. With the exception of Massachusetts, New York, and Georgia, all the colonies had adopted these by the end of 1776.

In the writing of state constitutions some of the now common political principles of the age discovered themselves. All the constitutions, for example, rejected aristocracy as a hereditary or formal order, all imposed the severest limits on, indeed almost annihilated, executive power, placing it firmly in the grasp of the legislatures. Several contained bills of rights, copying that of Virginia which sought consciously to provide written guarantees of conditions likely to produce liberty in the sense that they denied to governments the legal and political powers which in the past had been used, the colonists believed, to restrict individual and other freedoms. Most categorically stated that power must be seen as flowing upward from a consenting people and not downward from some non-popular sovereign. Some—very few—suggested that any representation of the people that was not apportioned to the numbers of those represented was a denial of a desirable political right. Yet all the state constitutions also revealed, despite John Adams's assumption that "in the Great essentials of Society and Government" the colonies were all alike, that the leaders of the new states differed concretely at significant points as they translated their general attachment to a new republicanism into detailed frames of government. The great melody of republicanism could be played in almost as many keys as there were separate states.

In New Hampshire the issue of earlier sectional discrepancies in assembly representation came to a head before the writing of the brief new constitution. Pressure for an end to the inequitable representation of the Wentworth period, when more than half the towns had not been able to send representatives to the assembly, brought victory for the interior. Fuller representation was granted; also an amendment to the franchise allowed every "legal inhabitant paying taxes to be a voter." Yet under the new constitution men of property still had a strong voice in the government. The qualification for members of the assembly was reduced only from £300 to £200 rateable estate. But the constitution provided an indication of the major political drift of the time by virtually abolishing separate executive authority in the state, locating this firmly under legislative control. No mention was made of churches or religion. In practice, the old colonial elite disappeared. The provincial officeholders, often wealthy Anglican merchants, were replaced by Presbyterians and Congregationalists, many of whom came from interior counties and all of whom had been prominent in the struggle against English authority. The same was generally true of the more important judges. At local level where the elected officials had generally supported revolutionary measures, there was little discontinuity. Yet the new men—an incipient elite themselves—were no less averse than the old from using their political positions for economic advantages. Challenges also came to their authority from western New Hampshire where the upper Connecticut Valley towns pressed for additional representation. The basis of these complaints, however, was not the democratic one of representation according to population but the old New England belief that every town, no matter how tiny, ought to have at least one member in the assembly. Yet some democrats did call for the election of all officers by the people rather than their appointment by the assembly, for the ending of property qualifications for officeholding and for frequent rotations in offices, and for a unicameral legislature.

The question of representation was also an early and divisive one in Massachusetts, where political excitement was intense. There, by 1775 the provincial assembly had responded to complaints about geographical inequalities in representation by granting every town with a minimum of 30 voters—often new western ones benefitted—the right to a representative; towns with 120 voters or more could return a maximum of two delegates, except for Boston with four. Complaints of discrimination then came from the larger towns, and in May 1776 a law was passed allowing each town an additional representative for every extra hundred qualified voters. This raised a central problem of representation, particularly since one impulse behind the reform was less that of remedying numerical underrepresentation than the underrepresentation of wealth. The Essex County towns declared that not only were they more populous than others with the same numbers of representatives but that they "paid more than one sixth part of the public tax; and they have not a Right to send one tenth part of the Number of Representatives." Indeed, there is strong evidence that the small rural farmers, often in debt to the merchants of the eastern towns, demanded representation by town rather than by population in the hope of achieving legislative power with which to modify the grip of court-supported tax and debt collectors. Conversely, as "O.P.Q." wrote in the *Massachusetts Spy*, the trading and monied feared oppressive taxation from "the enormous and now increasing influence" of the farmers, themselves profiting, according to the writer, from high wartime prices.

These strains between western and eastern Massachusetts, farmers and merchants, debtors and creditors, expressed themselves in petitions and remonstrances. The small men had imbibed the arguments that their betters had used against British authority and turned them on the revolutionary government itself. They suggested that Massachusetts now stood in a state of nature without a legal government which ought to be created by the formal and deliberate action of the people, a view also shared by some eastern leaders. But the General Court refused to ask the towns to elect delegates to a constitutional convention, requesting them instead to authorize the General Court itself to draw up a frame of government which would then be "made Public for the Inspection and Perusal of the Inhabitants, before the Ratification thereof by the Assembly." The returns of many towns to this invitation of 17 September 1776 reflected what obviously many now believed: that only a properly elected constituent assembly should either make or ratify a new constitution. "That as the End of government is the good of the people So the power and right of forming and Establishing a plan thereof is Essentially in them" and an ordinary assembly could not be entrusted with a task "so pregnant in power," stated the voters of Norton. The General Court could therefore not act in the winter of 1776 but waited for the spring. Massachusetts continued to be governed without a new constitution.

By contrast, the two remaining New England colonies successfully amended their old charters. After removing the oath of allegiance to the Crown from its charter in May, the Rhode Island assembly published the Declaration of Independence on 18 July and declared Rhode Island a state. In Connecticut the general court passed an act in August 1776 containing a "Declaration of the Rights and Privileges of the People of this State," announcing that "having from their Ancestors derived a free and excellent Constitution . . . they have the best Security for the Preservation of their civil and religious rights and liberties." Calvinist millenial feelings were strong in Connecticut, and the act also referred to the "Stability of Churches and Commonwealths" as the "Fruition of Such Liberties and Privileges . . ."

Of the southern colonies, the first to embark on constitution making was South Carolina, where the temporary constitution would last for two years. Here, the ruling oligarchy, "the whole roll of scholars and gentlemen who had guided that State as it entered the Revolution," managed with little difficulty to dominate the convention that framed it and to ensure that its hold on government was not broken. Christopher Gadsden, the radical leader, was rebuked for producing a copy of Tom Paine's *Common Sense*, and attempts to ensure a full representation of back-country areas were defeated. The constitution that emerged gave the low country an overwhelming superiority of representation in the lower house over the upcountry—a clear supremacy of wealth over numbers—and although it specified no actual property qualifications for voting or holding office, the colonial property requirements for both voters and those to be elected were continued. The general assembly was to elect the upper house and the two were to choose a president, who retained veto powers over legislative bills. Local officials, judges, and justices of the peace were to be chosen by the legislature. The constitution made no reference to the Church of England, which continued to be established until 1778.

In Virginia the constitution was almost classically Whig, reflecting the views of its enlightened gentry. Members of an elected upper house were to serve for four-year terms, members of an elected lower house annually. The upper house could not initiate legislation, and a governor, elected by both houses, had no veto power over legislation. Together with a council of state also chosen by the two houses, he did maintain certain final rights in the appointment of militia officers, justices of the peace, and sheriffs. But recommendations to the two latter offices were made by the county courts. Strict provisions were made against placemen and executive corruption. No qualifications were set for holding offices but nor, despite Jefferson's advocacy, was the franchise widened beyond its colonial limits. All in all, the constitution seemed to provide for a continuation of the colonial pattern of gentry rule through the lower house, with the upper house merely providing a check on any of its wilder ventures. The constitution also gave political weight to the tidewater gentry, since seats were allocated by counties and not by white population. Virginia's was also the first constitution to include a bill of rights. This endorsed in rationalistic language "the free exercise of religion, according to the dictates of conscience." But the Anglican Church was not disestablished.

Virginia's convention debated the new constitution in May and June 1776. Some schemes were put forward that show that alternatives to the measures adopted were discussed, including the apportionment of assemblymen according to population. Jefferson had favored this but had also suggested that senators be chosen for nine-year periods or for life, and other leading men had supported either life terms or high property qualifications. The real debate seems to have been between those who accepted the moderate political republicanism that the new Virginia constitution finally reflected and those who wished for a more conservative form of government, which would fully protect property and the control of an upper class.

Conditions in Maryland during the period of transition have, fortunately, been recently explored in much more depth than those in Virginia. Here, proprietary government had held on longer than Virginia's royal government, and the politically dominant merchants and planters seem to have been more divided among themselves. Moreover, serious discontent seems to have existed among the poorer farmers, the indentured servants, and the Negroes, though whether this was created by loyalist agitation or contributed to it is not absolutely clear. Nevertheless, by 1776 some elements in Maryland accused the revolutionary leadership of wishing to substitute their own brand of tyranny and social oppression for that of the British. In their turn, men who had called on every poor planter to oppose proprietor and Crown now themselves feared the resentment of "an ungovernable and revengefull Democracy." This resentment manifested itself in many counties at the time of the election of delegates to draw up a new constitution in 1776, when votes were illegally returned by all soldiers and militiamen and not merely by the qualified freeholders. Yet there were few objections to the basis of representation in the convention—by counties and not by population—and it is evident that some of the discontent was provoked or utilized by a faction of merchants and gentry seeking to grasp power from the existing revolutionary leadership.

These discontents did not ultimately provide a basis for a serious challenge to the men of property. Although a plan of government put forward by the militia of Anne Arundel County proposed an annually elected two-house legislature, the direct election of county officials, the temporary relief of debtors, and a "fair and equal mode of taxation," it did not gain much support in the convention, even among men presumably elected on radical promises. The only marginal votes in the convention, which the radicals lost, concerned their wish further to reduce, or to abolish, the property qualification for voting.

The Maryland constitution, adopted on 11 November 1776, was indeed perhaps the most oligarchical of all the frames of government of the period. It provided for a lower house whose members had to own £500 in real or personal property, an upper house whose members needed £1,000 in property and were specially selected by electors who themselves had to be owners of £500 in property, chosen by the ordinary voters. The ordinary voter's property qualification was set at £30 or fifty acres but he could elect only delegates to the lower house and select the rich electors of the members of the upper house, and at county level, sheriffs. The governor, annually elected by joint ballot of both houses, had to be worth £5,000 and members of the five-man council, also annually elected, had to own land worth £1,000. Finally, the apportionment of upper and lower house was based on counties and not on the numbers of voters. The constitution declared for religious freedom but allowed the legislature to lay a "general and equal tax for the support of the Christian religion," leaving to each individual the power of appointing the payment of the money for the support of any particular place of worship or to the benefit of the poor—a tax never levied.

By the date that Maryland's constitution was completed, three of the middle colonies had also drawn up theirs. Indeed, it may well have been that Maryland's gentry reacted strongly against tendencies evident in the largest and most important middle province, Pennsylvania, where extreme republicans were taking control. This was certainly the case in New Jersey and Delaware, Pennsylvania's other immediate neighbors. New Jersey's provincial convention began to draw up its constitution after the May resolutions of the Continental Congress, completing it on 3 July but declaring, even at that late date, that it should be null if reconciliation with Great Britain took place. Because of the military situation, the constitution was made in great haste. Its tone was straightforwardly Whiggish. An upper and lower house with equal authority in legislation, except over money bills, were to be elected annually on a county basis, although representation might be adjusted numerically in the future. The two houses would annually elect a governor. The governor held "supreme executive power" and commanded the militia, but the assembly chose general and field officers, the highest judges, and justices of the peace. Voters' qualifications were reduced from freeholds to a £50 clear estate in local money.

They were also to elect sheriffs and coroners annually. High property qualifications were demanded of councillors and assemblymen—£1,000 and £500 respectively. The constitution also confirmed New Jersey's traditional religious toleration. In Delaware, where a convention framed the constitution during August and September 1776, this pattern was more or less repeated, except that the governor was named the "president or chief magistrate" and allowed a three-year term of office, and no property qualifications for president, councillors, or representatives were required, nor was there to be any establishment of religion. In both states, substantial portions of old colonial practices were included in their new constitutions and there was little serious controversy.

Far different were conditions in Pennsylvania. There, the seat of the Continental Congress, the transition from colony to state was inextricably and complexly linked to the movement for independence. Two institutions, the old colonial assembly, and a network of provincial committees set up for the emergency, ran in parallel. Both seem to have been dominated by men still favoring reconciliation with Great Britain. Yet a small but active group, including Tom Paine himself, Benjamin Rush, a rising physician, James Cannon, a political schoolteacher, Thomas Young, a New England deist known and complained against in Boston as a firebrand and a rebel not "only against his Sovereign, but against his God," were strongly committed to a final break with England. Paine and some of his associates were also, as he had outlined in *Common Sense*, hopeful of republican governments based on unicameral legislatures and equitable representation. In March 1776 the assembly consented to the creation of seventeen more seats, thirteen for back-country areas and four for Philadelphia, thus heading off criticisms of underrepresentation from these places. Subsequent elections to these seats did not, however, destroy the moderates' majority in the assembly.

Yet events gradually weakened the position of those opposed to independence. In February 1776 radicals had gained control of the Philadelphia Committee of Inspection and Observation, one of the chain of revolutionary committees. Moreover, worsening economic conditions—the British now blockaded the Delaware—and fears of British naval attacks on Philadelphia lessened the attractiveness of moderation, and the radicals won support from and politically organized the militia throughout the colony. They also worked closely with their counterparts among the members of the Continental Congress. The congressional vote of 15 May calling for suppression of British authority—which may even have been aimed at the province—added power to their cause. On 20 May the Philadelphia committee held a large public meeting; this supported the calling of a provincial conference of delegates from the county committees to arrange a constitutional convention and condemned the existing assembly as based on the authority of the Crown rather than of the people. From about this time until 14 June, when it adjourned, never to meet again, the assembly was also crippled by the deliberate non-attendance of radical members, leaving it inquorate.

The provincial conference met in Philadelphia on 18 June. The old politicians now stood discredited as aristocratic supporters of a weak policy of reconciliation and there is little doubt that skillful organization had ensured that those returned to the conference were largely experienced radicals or new men who supported independence and the necessity of new government for Pennsylvania. Voting for delegates to a constitutional convention, they decided, should be open to all taxpaying male members of military organizations. James Cannon shortly afterward recommended his soldier friends to press for a "Government of the Common good framed by Men who can have no Interest besides the Common Interest of Mankind . . . great and over-grown Men will be improper to be trusted." The theme of aristocracy versus democracy rapidly became dominant.

Cannon's views appeared in a broadside, one of many tracts and articles that had appeared by 8 July, the date of the Constitutional Convention's first meeting. Many of these called for the incorporation of the "common people" into the political system and the ending of the semi-automatic assumption that while government sprang from the people, it should be conducted by the best people. Nor was further social analysis lacking. Cannon even suggested during the convention that it should approve the proposition that "an enormous Proportion of Property vested in a few Individuals is dangerous to the Rights, and destructive of the Common Happiness, of mankind; and therefore every free state hath a Right by its Laws to discourage the possession of such Property." The resolve was defeated. Most of the back-country farmers and other "plain country folks" elected to the convention were making or wished to make money and to acquire property.

Yet the convention accepted most of the democrats' political proposals, including an oath to be taken by all voters not directly or indirectly to do anything "injurious to the constitution as established by the convention." It also imposed a religious test on members of the assembly including a belief in God and the Old and New Testaments, evidence of the pietistic spirit of many delegates. The Pennsylvania constitution, completed in September 1776, was condemned by many Americans as fostering the rule of "mobocracy," since it seemed to contain every feature of government objectionable to men of property and caution. Even so, it can be argued that in many ways the constitution looked backward, drawing on the distinctive past of the middle colonies. Although it showed the influence of certain newer eighteenth-century humanitarian ideas, its main emphasis reflected the already radical Quaker traditions found in the region's seventeenth-century constitutions, together with the leading ideas of the great body of Country and radical Whig thinking that had developed over the last hundred years.

The Quaker tradition was represented in provisions for a unicameral legislature, elected by all taxpaying freemen, for the public scrutiny of impending legislative acts and for the local election of justices of the peace, sheriffs, and coroners. The overlapping radical Whig tradition is seen in its provisions for the direct election of the executive by the people, for stringent limitations on officeholding (including rotation in office) and fees, for the exclusion of officeholders from the assembly and the council, and for the commissioning of judges for a limited period. Other clauses provided for limitations on assemblymen's period of office to any four years in seven and for a Board of Censors, elected by the freemen, to be instituted every seven years, to examine the conduct of the whole government and, if necessary, to call another constitutional convention. Eighteenth-century developments revealed themselves in clauses prohibiting game laws, calling for the penal laws to be reformed and for "punishments to be made less sanguinary," for the employment of criminals in prisons open to public inspection and for bail for non-capital crimes.

The constitution lasted until 1789. But as early as October 1776 a great campaign was mounted to revoke it. Whigs and men of property disliked its annihilation of an upper house and correctly felt that, in granting no special privileges to those who felt entitled by wealth, education, and public understanding to a large voice in the conduct of affairs, it aimed at a government of common men. Some refused to participate in public affairs under the constitution, believing that the oath against injuring it amounted to a promise not to try to reform it. Yet many of its provisions largely implemented arguments that Pennsylvania's prosperous classes had used before to oppose proprietary and royal authority.

By the time of the passage of the Pennsylvania constitution in September 1776, New York, North Carolina, Georgia, Maryland, and Massachusetts had remained without new state governments. North Carolina's constitution was drafted in November 1776, after several months of bickering, by a specially elected convention. Despite the attempts of a few weakly organized radicals representing small farmer opinion to win a unicameral legislature and to end property qualifications, the North Carolina gentry prevailed and the state emerged with a bipartite legislature, both houses of which were annually chosen, and whose upper house members needed 300 acres and lower house members 100 acres of freehold land. Voters' qualifications were also different for each house, and the governor, chosen by joint ballot of both houses, was required to own property worth £1,000. Representation was set on a county basis with no census required, and free Negroes and mulattos together with "free persons of mixed blood, descended from negro ancestors, to the fourth generation inclusive (though one ancestor of each generation may have been a white person) . . ." were excluded from voting. As in Pennsylvania, there is evidence of a pietistic mood among the framers. The constitution, while prohibiting an established church, forbade officeholding by any person denying the existence of God, the truth of the Protestant religion, or the divine authority of either Testament. In Georgia the constitution was finally fixed in 1777. The radical Pennsylvania influence was evident in a decision for a unicameral legislature (of Protestant assemblymen) electing an executive council, in very low suffrage requirements, and in the local election of all officials except justices of the peace. Entails were forbidden and, in cases of intestacy, the equal distribution of estates among children provided for. Yet assemblymen had to possess 250 acres of land or property to the value of £250.

New York was the other state that finally adopted its constitution in 1777. There, the fourth provincial congress opened on 9 July 1776, endorsed the Declaration of Independence and began to write a new constitution. But troubled conditions in the colony, with its large loyalist population and active military operations, made progress difficult; nor apparently were the more conservative Whigs anxious to act with speed. Not until March 1777 was a draft of a constitution delivered, drawn up by John Jay with the aid of Gouverneur Morris and R.R. Livingston, all members of well-to-do families. Jay's draft reflected what his son described as his father's favorite maxim, that "those who own the country ought to govern it." Article 36 of the new constitution significantly confirmed all land grants made in the colony before October 1775. Its other terms provided for a powerful four-year senate to be chosen by those "possessed of freeholds to the value of £100" which would share legislative power with an annually elected lower house and with a "council of revision" made up of the governor, the chancellor, and judges of the supreme court. This council had power to return acts to the legislative houses, both of which would have to repass them by majorities of two-thirds if they were to become law. Moreover, the governor was to be elected by the people for a three-year term, had the power of prorogation for up to sixty days and other firm powers. He and a number of senators chosen by the lower house were also made a council of appointment for state officers and judges. These checks to legislative power, unusual at this time, were accompanied by certain more liberal measures, including secret ballots, and no property qualifications were specified for governor, senators, or assemblymen, while a census was to be taken every seven years (after the ending of the war) to adjust representation in both upper and lower houses. Jay's wish to abolish slavery in New York was, however, denied. The free exercise of religion was allowed, the constitution also stated, in accordance with the "benevolent principles of rational liberty." The New York constitution certainly restrained popular legislative activity in accordance with the views of the revolutionary aristocrats of the state, many of whom had pressed for formal oligarchy, including high property qualifications for councillors and a senate elected for life. The mechanic radicals in New York City had vainly demanded popular ratification and opposed the "supporters of oligarchy."

The great common denominator of early American republicanism clearly appeared in all the new state constitutions. Executive power—"ever restless, ambitious, and ever grasping at increase of power"—was to be checked and held captive, wrote a contributor to the *Pennsylvania Gazette*. Hence all contained stringent precautions against the possibility of officeholders exercising influence and patronage, or profiting personally or politically through their positions. Offices of profit, stated the Pennsylvania constitution, create "dependence and servility, unbecoming freemen in the possessors and expectants; faction and contention, corruption and disorder among the people." No Walpole, no Bute, no George III, no Hutchinson nor Dunmore were to rise to power on such foundations. The constitutions mainly sanctioned only the election, direct or indirect—not the appointment—of higher officials, including governors and members of upper houses, and in many cases they erected fixed electoral districts and set residency requirements. They also fixed a term of years on the holding of office and in some cases provided for rotation in office and forbade plural officeholding.

Such provisions checked not only executive political authority but its admixture with aristocracy, since it made the control of elections and of offices difficult even for cliques of wealthy and established families. Indeed, aristocratic political authority, because it seemed especially corrupt and corrupting and a universal foe of liberty, received the severest condemnations. John Adams believed that the revolution meant that "the dons, the bashaws, the grandees, the patricians, the sachems, the nabobs, call them by what name you please, sigh, and groan, and fret, and sometimes stamp, and foam, and curse, but all in vain. The decree is gone forth, and cannot be recalled, that a more equal liberty than has prevailed in other parts of the earth, must be established in America. That exuberance of pride which has produced an insolent domination in a few, a very few, insolent and monopolising families, will be brought down nearer to the confines of reason and moderation than they have been used to."

Yet here a crucial problem arose. For in the end it was the corrupting effect that political authority in itself exercized on all its holders that the state constitutions showed contemporaries to have feared as the greatest danger to liberty. Even the legislative (and executive) supremacy of the popular voice in a single house could itself lead to political abuse. Stable republics needed a defense against the "promiscuous multitude . . . [likely to be] in the execution of government, violent, changeable and liable to many fatal errors," wrote a New Jersey resident. While requirements in state constitutions for annual elections and for assemblymen to be residents of the areas which they represented were designed to keep legislative power from becoming corrupt or overgreat, aristocracy in the form of an appointed and generally upper-class upper house had traditionally been seen as a balancing factor. What was to replace this check on the popular order?

The general answer in the state constitutions was that while old forms of aristocracy were bad, a "senatorial" or "virtuous" aristocracy could replace it. Some may have equated this with the pious, elect Christians—Sam Adams wrote of a Christian Sparta—but most unashamedly meant by it the classes who possessed as William Hooper of North Carolina wrote, "that Weight which arises from property and gives Independence and Impartiality to the human mind." Upper houses had to represent—even if they also, as John Adams and Benjamin Rush argued, confined and isolated—the higher ranks of society and to provide an essential check on the possibility of elective despotism by unrestrained lower houses. In concrete terms, propertied men feared, for example, the use of legislative influence to restrain the collection of debts, to issue vast amounts of paper money, or attack their economic standing. Even Samuel Adams could doubt the propriety of granting political rights to "poor, shiftless, spendthrifty men and inconsiderate youngsters that have no property," who were "cheap bought (that is) their votes easily procured Choose a Representative to go to court, to vote away the Money of those that have Estates." Even the Pennsylvania radicals, much as they feared the influence of men of birth, property and standing, and favored a unicameral legislature, limited the franchise to men with an interest in the community. In 1776 most states met these problems by instituting mixed governments with the two houses effectively resting on different foundations of property. Yet the trend to bicameralism, where the mere juxtaposition of two popularly elected houses in itself was thought sufficient to provide a check on legislative folly (or worse), was evident in those state constitutions where property qualifications were not made a basis of the distinction between upper and lower houses.

To a large extent the making of the state constitutions is the best guide to the controlling forces of the early American Revolution. Certainly, they provided an increase in the number of governmental offices open to popular control and resulted in an enlargement of political opportunities. Some local offices also that were previously appointive were now filled by election. More important, the state lower houses were mainly made larger than their colonial counterparts, while upper house members were now elected rather than appointed. All these tendencies, of course, represented a fulfillment of old colonial radical Whig as well as newer revolutionary republican ideas. Similarly, while blows to the control of wealth and family—to an informal aristocracy, Adams's "nabobs"—may have reflected certain newer ideas in revolutionary Whiggism, the rejection of a formal nobility reflected old colonial realities as well as more recent fears, after 1760, that the British government planned to establish such an order to bind the colonial upper classes more closely to the Crown. Moreover, hostility to religious establishments, another feature of many state constitutions, had also been practically and ideologically dominant in many colonies before the revolution. Finally, who gained power under the new constitutions? A recent study of "higher governmental leaders"—members of councils and the more important officeholders—suggests that the revolution saw the displacement of an older leadership by a newer one. The men who attended the conventions that wrote the new constitutions and who after 1776 were elected as governors and senators and higher officeholders were generally men who were rising economically and potent politically in their own communities and had often been members of colonial lower houses but who had not held the most prestigious colonial offices. These were not "common citizens" but second-level leaders, interested in a stable and balanced constitutional system. The paradox was that they aceded to high offices at the same time that they had destroyed many of their prerogatives, for they were the very Whigs who had criticized and limited executive power.

B. Problems of unity

If independence brought a sense of new freedoms and new opportunities to many Americans, thousands of others remained skeptical, unconcerned or hostile to the change. Many were more or less fixed in the positions of the 1760s, convinced that they had not been well treated by Great Britain but unconvinced that the remedy of independence would not be worse than the disease. If challenged in 1776, such men might well have answered that they could not break the habits and traditions of a lifetime; while some had supported even armed resistance to British measures, they wished to continue to seek British liberties in a British system of government, to maintain negotiations and attempts at compromise. To these and to others less articulate, whose views are undiscoverable, the imprecise term of "loyalist" has been given.

Events from about 1768 onward had increasingly divided the growing numbers of politically aware Americans. Each move toward radical measures, especially the forming of committees, conventions, and associations, had emboldened and attracted support for those favoring a vigorous resistance to British authority. Both the violence of some of this resistance, particularly its disruption of established authority, and the emergence of new, sometimes obscure, political leaders alarmed the conventional. Allegiance itself gradually became a grave political issue after 1773 as their opponents began to urge active disobedience to the new local patriot authorities and to the Continental Congress. For their part the local committees, conventions, councils of safety, and the like made it their task to dig out those disaffected to the "American cause," demanding the signing of oaths of association and the recantation of expressions of dissent and, often, insisting on positive affirmations of support for the "liberties of America." In many colonies numerous if transient internecine conflicts took place in which personal, family, and traditional disputes as well as actual questions of liberty found outlets. By 1775 patriot advances had sometimes resulted in the formation of weak counter-associations and ill-considered conspiracies and plans for armed resistance. By the end of 1776 in Rhode Island, in Connecticut, in New York, in New Jersey, in Virginia, and in North and South Carolina, sequestration or outright confiscation of loyalist property had begun, either with legislative approval or on the initiative of local committees.

In New England, loyalist opposition was limited; most of the region remained quiescent or strongly patriot. In New Hampshire the governor's attempt to form a loyalist association failed miserably, while in Massachusetts a similar association, formed to counter the Continental Association, despite its members' promise to aid each other if threatened by "Committees, mobs, or unlawful assemblies," quickly faded. Outside of Boston, the local patriot committees ran things much as they pleased, ensuring that any unfortunate suspects begged forgiveness and promised obedience to the cause of American freedom. In Boston, where the army maintained order, the loyalists had more security. But when the British evacuated the city in March 1776 about 1,000 men, women, and children sailed with them, fearing to await patriot wrath. In Rhode Island, Governor Wanton advised the assembly against civil war and for a separately negotiated peace with Great Britain. He was forced to resign in 1775. In western Connecticut in 1775 several towns and counties resolved against the measures of the Continental Congress. Several hundred Whig militiamen from the eastern part of the colony curtailed any threat of potential resistance from the area. Connecticut Yankees also obtruded into New York in November 1775, destroying the last loyalist printing press still in operation on the continent.

New York, indeed, has traditionally been described as a hotbed of loyalism, where whole counties refused to support radical American measures and where loyalists in 1775 went about armed. Numerous accounts suggest that a majority (or substantial minority) of the population would not have approved the actions of the Continental Congress if consulted; only five of the twelve counties sent delegates to the provincial congress that assembled on 6 December 1775. Yet despite evidence of loyalist involvement in planning armed resistance to patriot groups, men seem to have been discreetly neutral rather than active in support of the British cause. At the actual moments of political and military crisis loyalist strength vanished. In Queen's County on Long Island, where a majority had earlier signed loyalist petitions, pressure from patriots brought a declaration of neutrality in December 1775. This did not, in fact, prevent Queen's County men from being disarmed by continental forces. A more serious loyalist movement in the western New York, where the Johnson family recruited recent Highland Scottish immigrants, was suppressed early in 1776 by a large army of militiamen led by Philip Schuyler.

In New Jersey up to the end of 1776 the loyalists had no organized strength. Its governor, William Franklin, was not arrested until June 1776, and as in Pennsylvania where the old authorities maintained a degree of visibility until about the same time, men could generally hold aloof from overt activity in an uneasy balance and all shades of opinion could be expressed without arrests and condemnations. By contrast, in Maryland, where Governor Eden attempted to organize armed resistance to the patriots after November 1775, issues quickly crystallized. On the eastern shore armed skirmishes broke out in the autumn of

1775 that lasted for several years. Yet much of this loyalist activity depended on aid from British ships (and in the early period from Governor Dunmore of Virginia) and although it made the eastern shore virtually ungovernable, never seriously threatened the new state's government. In Virginia itself Governor Dunmore was forced to leave in July 1776 after several months of useless attempts to rally support. Many other loyalists also left the colony in 1775 and 1776; others lived in quiet retirement on their estates. While many rumors, and some acts, of individual loyalist disaffection continued, causing treason legislation to be passed in October 1776, the loyalists were never more than an irritant. Their only other alleged strength in Virginia lay among the Appalachian settlers, but nothing came of promises in 1775 that these men would rise in the King's name.

In the Carolinas before the end of 1776 a similar if more pronounced pattern existed. Active loyalist opposition was restricted on the whole to a handful of Scots and English merchants and planters on the coast and to some elements in the back country. The largest loyalist army to assemble in 1776 consisted of 1600 North Carolina Highland Scots and other back-country men, rallied by Governor Martin. Their defeat at Moore's Creek Bridge ended any threat to the patriot movement in the colony for the remainder of the year. In South Carolina, the back country might have rallied to the royal governor, but he remained in Charleston. After desultory fighting in the frontier Ninety-Six district, the loyalists were temporarily disarmed and neutralized. Many supported the patriots when British-provoked Cherokees attacked white settlers along the Carolina frontier in 1776.

Taken together, the evidence of patriot supremacy is overwhelming. Even when numerically outnumbered, they gained and held the initiative, creating both civil and military organizations that in most localities could rally sufficient force to suppress all opposition. As Ralph Wormeley, a great Virginia planter who professed allegiance to the Crown but in practice remained a neutral, observed, the "torrent of violence"—his opponents might have said of moral fervor—"has been strong enough to compel their [loyalist] acquiescence till a sufficient force shall appear to support them." But this sufficient force appeared too late and was too little. During 1775 and 1776, when determined royal governors supported by loyalists and regular troops might have resisted patriot pretensions, little or nothing could be done. Gage was shut up in Boston, and Dunmore, willing to fight in Virginia, had only a hundred or so regulars. In other regions promised loyalist armies could never be organized. Ultimately, the British government failed, for it had neither plans nor power to maintain civil authority. Indeed, the opposite tended to be true since the government instructed its commanding generals to compromise rather than to assert. As Thomas Jones, a virulent loyalist critic of the British conduct of the war, wrote, "the rebels were to be converted, the loyalists frowned upon. Proclamations were to end an inveterate rebellion."

Attempts have been made to measure loyalist numbers in the sense of counting those who in 1776 did not actively approve though they may have passively accepted the assumption of independence. One writer suggests that among "almost all cultural minorities, the proportion of Tories seems to have been clearly higher than among the population at large." These included: Highlanders, many of whom were immigrants, Presbyterians in the Carolinas, Anglicans in the North, Dutch-speaking New Yorkers, and Quaker and German pietiests in the increasingly Presbyterian ambience of Pennsylvania. Both the Quakers and Germans, however, were as much pacifist or neutral as loyalist. John Adams, late in his life, thought that a third of Americans had favored independence, a third had been neutral, and a third opposed. Modern commentators suggest that hardly a tenth of New Englanders, a third or a fourth of southerners, and perhaps half of middle colonists could be described as loyalists. But such calculations rest on conflicting, because self-serving, contemporary evidence and necessitate a whole host of distinctions between active loyalists, passive loyalists, Tory and Whig loyalists, neutral, and latent loyalists. What is known is that by 1783 some 60,000-100,000 former residents of the colonies had gone into exile. In proportion to total population this exodus was almost five times as great as the figure for émigrés from France during its revolution.

Nor do any class differences seem to have separated loyalists and patriots. Some loyalists were extraordinarily prosperous; so were some patriots. Some loyalists were farmers, some merchants, some artisans, some lawyers, some slaves. So were the patriots. Professor Bailyn has recently written that there "are no obvious external characteristics of the loyalist group, aside from the natural fact that it contained many crown officeholders: a multitude of individual circumstances shaped the decisions that were made to remain loyal to England." Obviously, it is possible that further investigations may reveal some relevant social or economic factors—were many lesser loyalists dependent on the custom and patronage of Crown officials, for example? But this seems unlikely.

There was, of course, a bedrock of Crown support throughout the colonies among royal officeholders and Anglican clergy, many of whom were native Englishmen. These men were willing to execute British orders and to write in their defense, and they constituted easy targets for mob abuse. Early favored with the epithet of "Tory" not because they accepted the divine right of kings but either because they actively supported the measures of the English government or because they rejected all arguments for overt resistance to British authority, some also opposed all the constitutional arguments for limitations on Parliamentary authority over the colonies. From their pens, too, came furious denunciations of the low, grasping, and plebian nature of the patriots. "No, if I must be enslaved, let it be by a KING at least," wrote Samuel Seabury of New York, "and not be a parcel of upstart lawless Committee men. If I must be devoured, let me be devoured by the jaws of a lion, and not gnawed to death by rats and vermin."

Yet many who became loyalist fell outside of this category, for they had started and remained Whigs. They had supported and they remained committed to the idea of the defense of American liberties, they had supported provincial conventions, associations, and the Continental Congress, some well into 1776, until at some moment a personal experience, a practical event, or a philosophical doubt caused them to fall away from their patriot colleagues. Some, like the Tories, objected to what they felt were the leveling tendencies in the patriot movement. Others merely continued to believe that further petitions, further negotiations should be tried, or that independence and separation were greater evils than what had gone before. None, Professor Bailyn has suggested, could feel the urgent and "aroused moral passion and the meliorative, optimistic, and idealist impulses that gripped the Revolutionaries' minds . . ." They took Whiggism to its limits in their protests against British actions but could not be remade republicans.

Other groups and issues also presented difficulties to the patriots. The Baptists, the most rapidly growing religious body in America, were by 1775 largely committed to the revolution. Imprisoned and harassed for the nonpayment of church taxes since the middle of the century in New England, they had in 1769 set up a grievances committee to coordinate their legal and political activities. In 1771 they petitioned the Crown against particular Massachusetts laws, winning a royal veto of them and support from Governor Hutchinson. In 1773, in response to continuing imprisonments, they conducted a campaign of civil disobedience. Since their activities brought them into direct conflict with the patriot-dominated general courts of Connecticut and Massachusetts and since they often looked for relief to Great Britain, many Baptists were accused of Toryism. In fact, as Isaac Backus made clear, their prime desire was for religious liberty. This they claimed not with rationalist arguments for toleration but on the basis of their profound scriptural conviction that "God always claimed it as his sole prerogative to determine by his own laws what his worship shall be, who shall minister in it, and how they should be supported." In October 1774 a number of New England Baptists visited the Continental Congress, lobbying the Massachusetts delegation and protesting against the New England religious establishments to the annoyance of its delegates. Isaac Backus wrote that "John Adams made a long speech, and Samuel Adams another, both of whom said, 'There is indeed an ecclesiastical establishment in our province, but a very slender one, hardly to be called an establishment.'" While the original Baptist argument for toleration was not based on Whiggish principles, they quickly seized on the incompatability of revolutionary claims to civil and political liberty with the patriot Congregationalists' denial of religious liberty, a significant broadening of the revolution.

The other center of Baptist struggle was Virginia. There Separate Baptists first arrived in about 1760, becoming more active and successful in each succeeding year and rapidly increasing in numbers between 1770 and 1776. Hostility to their advance was widespread in the Tidewater and Piedmont regions, where Baptist meetings were regularly disrupted. Opposition came from Anglican clergy, elements of the gentry and their supporters, for the Baptists preached a creed at variance with the prevailing culture, attacking luxury, popular recreations and diversions and condemning drink, gambling, and other pastimes enjoyed by many Virginians. That the Baptists themselves were often poor and uneducated and that they appealed to others like them, including some blacks, naturally caused resentment among planters already anxious about their economic and political standing. In 1772 the Virginia assembly passed anti-Baptist legislation; in 1774 and 1775 Baptists and other dissenters petitioned for religious liberty, winning certain concessions about the right of preaching.

Although the Virginia Declaration of Rights of 1776 stated that "all men are equally entitled to the free exercise of religion, according to the dictates of conscience, and that it is the mutual duty of all to practice Christian forbearance, love, and charity towards each other," the Virginia laws remained unchanged. The dissenters rapidly mobilized, flooding the new government with petitions for religious liberty. Jefferson then stood as a champion of religious freedom, advocating the disestablishment of the Church of England in Virginia. His position, however, was opposed by many influential men. The assembly in October 1776 exempted all dissenters from paying taxes in support of Anglican ministers. It continued to impose a general tax for the purpose of supporting all ministers and churches. On 25 December the Virginia Association of Baptists professed that "Preachers should be supported only by voluntary Contributions from the People, and that a general Asesment (however harmless yea useful some may conceive it to be) is pregnant with various Evils destructive to the Rights and Privileges of Religious Society"—notably that state support ultimately meant state control. So in Virginia, the battle for full separation of church and state was under way. Ironically, Jefferson, who championed religious freedom in the rational and secular hope that the free marketplace in religion would result in its moderation and dilution, was about to embark on struggles whose outcome ten years later gave the rapidly growing Baptists the freedom to vote for laws that imposed their own narrow moral views on their fellow citizens.

The other great matter thrown into prominence by the revolutionary stress on natural rights and civil liberty was slavery. Since the 1760s anti-slavery sentiments had begun to intensify in the middle and northern colonies, and by the 1770s even a few influential southerners had begun to express an open distaste for the slave trade and for slavery itself. Two sources of anti-slavery feeling were evident. The religious had its roots among the Quakers and in the Great Awakening and emphasized the brotherhood of man and the immorality of holding humans as property. The secular—its arguments were also used, of course, by religious spokesmen—drew sustenance from the Enlightenment emphasis on benevolent and sentimental humanitarianism, the improvement of human conditions, and the ending of some grosser forms of social oppression. These two streams quickly mingled with revolutionary idealism. As early as 1764, James Otis noted the philosophical difficulty of restricting the defense of liberty to white Americans, affirming that the "colonists are by the law of nature freeborn, as indeed all men are, white or black." By 1776 some friends of the revolution linked the sacred cause of liberty to the ending of slavery, while many of its enemies gloated over the hypocrisy of southern slaveholders pronouncing on the rights of man. Americans, stated one English official, treated Negroes as "a better kind of Cattle" while they bawled about "the Rights of Human Nature."

In the southern colonies, although arguments against the slave trade itself—slave imports were prohibited in the Virginia constitution of 1776—were not uncommon, abolitionist sentiments as such made little headway. Slaves represented an investment of many millions of pounds and constituted, particularly in the coastal regions, a substantial percentage of the population. Abolition would be expensive, would fundamentally change economic and social relations, and would create a huge free population of poor Negroes, feared or despised on racial and social grounds. Jefferson had commented on the "unhappy influence" of slavery "on the manners of our people," remarking that the "whole commerce between master and slave is a perpetual exercise of the most boisterous passions, the most unremitting despotism on the one part, and degrading submissions on the other" and had imagined that he and other southerners favored emancipation, writing that the "abolition of domestic slavery is the great object of desire in those colonies where it was unhappily introduced in their infant state." Yet he was never to press his schemes of emancipation. Not until 1782 was even the general manumission of slaves to be permitted in Virginia. In South Carolina Henry Laurens was "virtually alone . . . in expressing hope for the eventual disappearance of the institution to which the state was so thoroughly committed." Although few men provided a positive defense of slavery, virtually all accepted that emancipation was undesirable or impractical, or both.

The drive for emancipation in the North was less hindered by social and economic considerations, since slave numbers were much lower and free Negroes already numerous. There was widespread agreement that the slave trade should be stopped. By 1776 it had been prohibited in Pennsylvania, Connecticut, Rhode Island, and Delaware, while vigorous efforts had been made to end it in New York and Massachusetts. The Continental Congress's suspensions of the trade in 1774 and 1776 must be seen as expressions of the humanitarian sentiments of some delegates as well as an anti-British economic measure. Attacks on slavery itself also increased. In Philadelphia the Quaker

THE THIRTEEN COLONIES

Estimated Percentages of Blacks and Whites

1740–1780

A = Total Population
B = % of Blacks
C = % of Whites

	1740			1760			1780		
	A	B	C	A	B	C	A	B	C
Maine	–	–	–	–	–	–	49,133	0.93	99.07
New Hampshire	23,256	2.15	97.85	39,093	1.53	98.47	87,802	0.62	99.38
Massachusetts	151,613	2.00	98.00	222,600	2.18	97.82	268,627	1.79	98.21
Rhode Island	25,255	9.53	90.47	45,471	7.63	92.37	52,946	5.04	94.96
Connecticut	89,580	2.90	97.10	142,470	2.65	97.35	206,701	2.85	97.15
New York	63,665	14.13	85.87	117,138	13.94	86.06	210,541	10.00	90.00
New Jersey	51,373	8.50	91.50	93,813	7.00	93.00	139,627	7.49	92.51
Pennsylvania	85,637	2.40	97.60	183,703	2.40	97.60	327,305	2.40	97.60
Delaware	19,870	5.21	94.79	33,250	5.21	94.79	45,385	6.60	93.40
Maryland	116,093	20.70	79.30	162,267	30.20	69.80	245,474	32.80	67.20
Virginia	180,440	33.25	66.75	339,726	41.38	58.62	538,004	41.00	59.00
North Carolina	51,760	21.25	78.75	110,442	30.38	69.62	270,133	33.69	66.31
South Carolina	45,000	66.67	33.33	94,074	60.94	39.06	180,000	53.89	46.11
Georgia	2,021		100.00	9,578	37.36	62.64	56,071	37.15	62.85

yearly meeting, active in condemning slaveholding Friends since the late 1750s, decided on their actual expulsion in 1776. In Massachusetts Negroes themselves had petitioned the General Court in 1773 citing their expectations of "men who have made such a noble stand against the designs of their *fellow-men* to enslave them."

More and more in the North, sentiments of public men and their constituents began to coincide in favor of emancipation. In Pennsylvania Benjamin Rush, a political activist and an abolitionist leader, claimed in 1773 that "three-fourths of the province, as well as of the City of Philadelphia, cry out against it." Yet there is also evidence that Quaker support discredited abolitionism among some patriots, since many Quakers also opposed the revolutionary movement. In New England, where the ending of slavery was canvassed by growing numbers of clergy and public men, there was also evidence of a rising popular feeling against it. Petitions from town meetings supported various—although unsuccessful—legislative attempts to abolish slavery in the 1770s in Massachusetts. In Rhode Island there was an attempt at an emancipation act in 1775. In the northern and middle colonies, as well, successful court cases involving the attempts of individual slaves to win emancipation increased in numbers in the 1770s, and there may have been more manumissions by slave owners. A movement for emancipation was then under way, and in 1776 the Reverend Samuel Hopkins of Rhode Island made sure that all the delegates to the Second Continental Congress knew of it, addressing them in his *Dialogue concerning the Slavery of the Africans*, which argued for complete and immediate abolition. Yet Congress, then as for many years to come, avoided the issue in the interests of sectional harmony and American union.

C. The question of American union

The colonies had looked to the Continental Congress for advice on the matter of remaking their constitutions and had followed its resolution of 15 May calling for the suppression of all authority derived from the Crown and its exercise under popular direction. Dickinson, entrusted with drafting formal articles of confederation in June 1776, seems at first to have looked to the establishment of a new central authority in the colonies as a substitute for the force of British government and to have hoped that this could precede formal independence and the framing of new governments by the states. His feelings that Americans might accept such a new central government may well have been fostered by the very willingness of the different colonies to consult the Congress on such a basic internal matter as the making of individual state constitutions. Dickinson's committee presented its first draft of "Articles of Confederation and Perpetual Union" on 12 July 1776. Some days later eighty copies were printed, and a debate eventually began that would last well into

August and then be resumed for another fifteen months before a vote was taken. Some of this delay arose from disagreements over the form of the articles, some from the difficult military situation, much from the delegates' lack of urgency about the need for a stronger union.

The first draft presented for debate by Dickinson's committee, in fact, provided for a "Confederacy" or "firm league of Friendship" among the "colonies." Its basic provisions clearly applied Whig or republican ideas to the question of union. Annually appointed delegates chosen "in such Manner as the Legislature of each Colony shall direct" were to meet in November each year. No limit was set on their numbers but each colony had only one vote in the assembly. Nine votes were necessary to decide on major issues of war, peace, and finance and seven on other matters. Of the delegates, one from each colony was also to be chosen by the assembled delegates to serve on a Council of State "for managing the general Affairs of the United States, under their Direction while assembled, and in their Recess . . ." Two principles were thus immediately established that had also found expression in many state constitutions—a subordinate executive appointed by the legislative and responsible to it and representation by unit rather than by population. Yet taxation was set according to population; money was to be supplied by each colony "in Proportion to the Number of Inhabitants of every Age, Sex and Quality except Indians not paying taxes . . ."

Dickinson's draft reserved to each colony "as much of its present laws, Rights and Customs, as it may think fit . . . and the sole and exclusive Regulation of and Government of its internal police, in all matters that shall not interfere with the Articles of this Confederation." Edward Rutledge said that this and other clauses involved "the Idea of destroying all Provincial Distinctions and making everything of the most minute kind bend to what they call the good of the whole." Dickinson did give the United States large powers, virtually complete ones over foreign relations, war and peace, admiralty matters, disputes between colonies, coining money, regulating and controlling Indian trade and affairs, post offices, and appointing high-ranking army officers. To most contemporaries in 1776 most of these provisions were acceptable. More controversial was Dickinson's grant to the United States of the virtual power of deciding western boundaries and "assigning Territories for new Colonies either in Lands . . . Separated from [existing] Colonies and heretofore purchased or obtained by the Crown of Great Britain from the Indians, or . . . to be purchased . . . from them." Nor did Congress accept his idea of an incipient form of mutual citizenship between the inhabitants of the states—that the inhabitants of each state should, when in another, enjoy the same rights as its own inhabitants, including commercial rights.

Little can be pieced together about the debate on Dickinson's first draft. But it does seem to have exposed at once certain critical interests of the states. First, in relation to taxation, was population a proper measure of wealth or should land and commerce be separately calculated? What was the position of slaves? If these were to be counted in determining taxes, they ought also to be in settling representation, argued Samuel Chase of Maryland. Here, faintly sounded the "fire bell in the night" whose tones were to ring out with ever-increasing clarity in the years to follow. Nor was another fundamental issue neglected, for John Adams opposed voting rights by states—as the small states desired—and believed that every state should be represented in terms of its population, that "the interests within doors . . . be the mathematical representatives of the interests without doors." To objections that a proportional vote would harm the smaller states, he answered "that an equal vote will endanger the larger."

Perhaps most important at this time was the issue of western lands. Should Congress, as Dickinson suggested, be allowed to settle the boundaries of those states which claimed territory far in to the west that could enrich and increase them to the probable detriment of the smaller states? His own belief, shared by speculators as well as by incipient nationalists, was that the United States should control these regions and dispose of them for the benefit of the Confederation. He also envisaged the settlement of new colonies with "forms of government to be established on the principles of Liberty." Although some Virginians believed that their own republican form of government would be threatened by an expansion in the size of their state, few were at this time willing to yield western claims to Congress.

All these controversial issues would reverberate during the succeeding years. In August 1776 they led the delegates to the Continental Congress to amend Dickinson's committee's draft. The version approved by the Committee of the Whole no longer contained the articles referring to the mutual rights and privileges of the inhabitants of the states or those prohibiting the purchase of land from Indians and regulating Indian affairs "except for those not members of any state." Nor was Congress permitted in the revised draft to ascertain colonial boundaries or meddle with western lands or contemplate the founding of new colonies.

Yet one critical matter had still not been seriously debated—the location of power between the union and the states. Certainly, Rutledge had objected to "the Idea of destroying all Provincial Distinctions," and on 1 August 1776 James Wilson declared that "It had been said that Congress is a representation of states; not of Individuals. I say that the objects of its care are all the individuals of the States . . . As to those matters which are referred to Congress, we are not so many states, we are one large state . . ." John Adams also clearly said that the question of whether the United States would be "A sovereign state, or a number of confederate sovereign states" had now announced itself. But these were isolated instances and did not arise from a lengthy or detailed consideration of questions of sovereignty. In 1776 the revolution still clearly appeared to most men as the clear assertion of the sovereignty of the known—the old colonies now remade as states.

D. *The uncertainties of war*

The war brought new responsibilities for the Continental Congress since that body alone was in a position to grasp the executive control that a united and sustained American effort demanded. Gradually, the Congress, formed to protest against the abuse of executive power, came to exercise that power itself. In September 1775 a committee was established to supervise contracts for the import of powder and munitions; its powers were later gradually extended until by 1777 it had become a fully fledged committee of commerce. In November a committee of correspondence, to be styled in 1777 the committee for foreign affairs, was nominated. In October-November another committee, which would in time become responsible for marine affairs, emerged. In February 1776 a standing committee of Congress was charged with matters of finance, and in June 1776 a war office, supervised by a committee of Congress, was ordered to be established. These committees, uneasily blending executive functions and legislative accountability were, like the Congress itself, adequate but never efficient. Nevertheless, they provided a necessary and ultimately successful direction to a war fought with the strongest power in Europe. Their very origin in and responsibility to the legislature made them acceptable to the many delegates who, because of the experience of the last ten years, would have looked with distaste on any attempts to create more powerful and professional central bureaucratic organs.

The most spectacular successes came to the committee created in November to handle foreign affairs, which for some time functioned as a secret committee to correspond, as Congress resolved, "with our friends in Great Britain, Ireland, and other parts of the world." At about the same time American agents in Europe were asked to discover what possibilities of alliances or aid existed in various foreign capitals. In July 1776 Silas Deane arrived in Paris as the official agent of the American Congress, with instructions to purchase arms and stores. By October a first shipment of gunpowder, of 30,000 guns, of 3,000 tents, 200 cannon with full trains, of 27 mortars, of 100,000 balls and 13,000 bombs was reported as sent to America and other supplies would follow. These often arrived via the French West Indian colonies of Haiti and Martinique or at the Dutch port at St. Eustatius for collection by American ships, after outward dispatch on French, Spanish, and Dutch vessels, whose aid was therefore important to the American cause. Undoubtedly, however, profiteering was already underway. Deane and some of his associates together with Caron de Beaumarchais, the French playwright (and speculator), benefitted privately from these arrangements, dealing commercially in goods that the Spanish and French governments meant the Americans to have as a free gift. In time, other American merchants also became involved in such dealings, continuing the European and beginning the American tradition of making patriotism profitable.

French supplies of matériel reflected only part of the assistance being given or contemplated by that country and by Spain to the American cause. French interest in the growing difficulties between her victorious enemy and the colonies had persisted since the 1760s. When by 1775 it seemed unlikely that war between America and Britain could be avoided, the French foreign minister responded promptly to the urgings of Beaumarchais—then in London as a political agent—for secret aid to America. By May 1776 the King had accepted similar proposals, and his Spanish ally shortly after did the same. Moreover, the French also made it clear that British ships would not be allowed to search French vessels trading between France and her colonies or vessels in colonial French territorial waters, ships likely to be carrying supplies for North America. Both French and Spanish aid ran contrary to their own interests as possessors of colonies. But the wish for revenge on Britain took precedence. A dismembered British empire would immeasurably damage the mother country itself, the trade of America might accrue to France and Spain, and an independent republican America, weak and exhausted by its struggles, would be of little danger to European interests in the New World. These principles, enunciated in 1776, would eventually lead to the open alliance of 1778 between France and the United States.

One other great event also occurred at the close of 1776—the arrival of Benjamin Franklin as an American commissioner to the French court. The America of the enlightened European imagination was a simple, frugal, busy but humane and virtuous society of free, rational, and tolerant citizens, devoid of corruption, luxury, oligarchy, aristocracy, and vice, and Franklin seemed its first citizen. Instrumental in attracting the sympathy of the numerous and influential friends of enlightened ideas in France, his influence grew steadily. Nor was this sympathy restricted to France. Writing in May 1776, an Italian priest considered that "the epoch has become one of the total fall of Europe, and of transmigration into America. Everything here turns into rottenness: religion, law, arts, sciences; and everything hastens to renew itself in America. This is no jest; nor is it an idea growing out of quarrels among the English: I have been saying it, announcing it, preaching it for 20 years and I have always seen my prophecies fulfilled. Therefore do not buy your house in the Chausée d'Antin; buy it in Philadelphia." In October 1776 the Danish foreign minister considered that "the public here is greatly taken by the American rebels not because of any knowledge of their cause but because independence mania has really infected everybody, and because this poison spreads imperceptibly from the works of the philosophers even into the village schools." Liberal circles in other countries also responded to the American cause, although governments remained largely unfriendly. The first foreign volunteers had already arrived to seek employment in the American forces; a few, at least, provided valuable military skills.

During 1776 Congress had in fact already envisaged the possibility of a foreign alliance. The danger that a treaty with France might exchange a Gallic for a British master had been thoroughly explored. John Adams stressed strongly the need to make only a commercial agreement with France and to accept no political bonds, no army, and no naval assistance. In return for American trade France would provide the new states with money and supplies. The model treaty agreed to by Congress on 24 September 1776 and taken by Franklin to Paris therefore enunciated principles of American foreign policy that would find their most famous expression in Washington's Farewell Address but which had their origins in an earlier colonial awakening to the continent's separate interests from those of England and Europe and reflected as well traditional English fears of entangling European alliances. Yet some concessions had to be made to necessity, and Franklin's instructions allowed him and his fellow commissioners a degree of latitude. By December Congress had also optimistically decided that commissioners ought to approach the courts of Vienna, Spain, Prussia, and the Grand Duke of Tuscany for aid.

During all these proceedings, the war continued. It revealed private—or at least sectional—ambitions. Washington's appointment as commander-in-chief had to be balanced by the appointment of a New Englander, Artemus Ward, as "first major-general"; another eleven general officers were appointed to assuage the ambitions of the different states. Moreover, real jealousies and antipathies between the southern states and those farther north had already appeared, symbolized perhaps by the southern discovery that Yankees officers sat and ate with and were often undistinguishable from their men and by the New England agitation to remove Philip Schuyler of New York from his command in 1776, partly on the grounds that his bearing was too aristocratic. Nor was Washington himself yet exempt from criticism, arising from his lack of success and seeming indecisiveness during most of 1776.

On the military front, there was little optimism. Disease among the troops and the fact that they consisted of short-term enlisted men who sought to return to their homes at the expiration (usually each December) of their time threatened the defending forces, as did a shortage of capable generals. "We expect," wrote Washington, "a very bloody summer of it at New York and Canada . . . and I am sorry to say that we are not, either in men or arms, prepared for it." The British evacuation of Boston was the prelude to a regrouping for the occupation of New York. Washington anticipated this move; soon his forces marched from New England to the middle state city, where its patriot defenders had been working on new fortifications for some months. Yet New York City was open on every side to naval assault, and while the British had formidable sea power, the Americans had none. The possibility that the city could be held against the British was remote. Washington later argued for its destruction to deny it to the enemy but his congressional masters forbade such a move as too devastating to American morale.

British forces from Halifax, joined by Admiral Howe's huge reinforcements from England, gathered on Staten Island in the summer of 1776. Not until August did battle commence, with a British landing on Long Island and an assault on the American fortified position at Brooklyn Heights. Just when the position seemed untenable, Howe abandoned the attack. Later Washington moved his army from Brooklyn across the East River to Manhattan in a well-executed retreat. He then divided his forces, garrisoning both New York City and the more easily fortified and defensible Harlem Heights. When New York City was attacked, the Americans resisted only weakly before fleeing in disorder. But again Howe did not follow up his advantage, preferring to land a substantial force. On 16 September some of his skirmishers were beaten back by American troops, a boost to flagging morale. Not for some weeks, did the British move again in strength against the Americans, forcing Washington to abandon his position and move his main army across to New Jersey. But a substantial garrison still occupied Fort Washington on the New York side of the Hudson. The fort fell on 16 November, with American losses of 53 killed and 2,818 captured. Washington then faced grave charges of mismanagement for not evacuating sooner in the face of overwhelming enemy strength. By 19 November the British had also crossed the Hudson into New Jersey. By 24 November Washington's forces retreated to Brunswick in New Jersey; other American troops were left in the Hudson River Highlands under the erratic and vainglorious General Charles Lee. In Canada, a large British army had smashed the American invaders, had taken Fort Crown Point and seemed ready to push its way to Albany.

The next few weeks seemed to bring the Americans near desperation. Thousands of men were preparing to return to their families, despite the military situation. The New Jersey militia refused their aid to the continental army. Washington was criticized by former friends and his orders disobeyed by his subordinates. In early December, Washington, pursued by Howe, retreated across the Delaware; the sight of his bedraggled men made it "the most hellish scene I ever beheld," wrote Charles Willson Peale, the artist. Yet again Howe hung back, leaving garrisons in New Jersey and retiring with the main forces to New York for the winter. It was at this time in late December 1776 that Washington's genius and his steadfast determination asserted themselves, perhaps decisively for the American cause. He recrossed the Delaware and routed Hessian mercenary troops at Trenton, capturing nearly 1,000 together with substantial supplies, a wounding blow to the royal army, since, as Howe remarked, it was astounding that "three old, established regiments of a people who make war a profession should lay down their arms to a ragged and undisciplined militia." In January 1777 Washington repeated his success. Avoiding encirclement near Trenton by British regiments under Cornwallis, he executed a silent night retreat under their guns and marched to Princeton, where he defeated a British brigade, rallying his men from his great white horse in the very forefront of the battle. The American forces then retired to seek winter quarters around Morristown, twenty-five miles west of New York City. Contemporaries regarded these two battles as great victories. In North America they seemed to show that the British, who had generally avoided a head-on assault on the Americans, were rightly afraid of them. In Europe no less an authority than Frederick the Great hailed Washington's successes and they also encouraged those prepared to subsidize the American cause. Washington himself became the idol of his countrymen.

The omens for the British were uncertain. In 1776 Britain commanded the seas and had landed a large army in America. But to operate decisively against all the centers of colonial resistance, British forces probably had to hold the seven strategic ports—Halifax, Boston, Newport, New York, Philadelphia, Norfolk, and Charleston. In late 1776 they occupied only four, a number they were not to exceed in the course of the war. British tactics were also questionable. In the New York fighting, quick decisive action to smash the small American forces had not followed from a superiority of forces. Howe's failure to storm Brooklyn Heights and the delay in moving resolutely against Washington are two examples; similarly, in Canada, the British commander, Guy Carleton, had also moved with slow deliberation. Moreover, Admiral Lord Howe has been accused of poor judgment in not ruthlessly enforcing the blockade of the American coastline, probably because he hoped that leniency might aid reconciliation, for nine-tenths of the gunpowder available to the Americans until the end of 1777 was imported by sea. In fact, the quality of the British command was uncertain. And the rallying of the loyalist population to the victorious British army—which happened in New Jersey and Pennsylvania after Washington's retreat behind the Delaware—was reversed by the American successes at Trenton and Princeton. These successes were also important for their effect on French opinion. Should the British fail in 1777 to achieve quick victory, the French might be willing to enter the war. In that case British resources would be stretched, with fleets and armies needed to defend the British Isles and the Caribbean and the already difficult problem of supplying the huge army in America made vastly more difficult. For the British, confined, as it were, to a number of beachheads, could not live off the land; even in 1776 they imported practically everything, including forage for their horses, from across the Atlantic.

What of the American position? In the first instance, everything depended on the survival of the continental army. Without its destruction, British forces could not win, though they might not be defeated. The auguries for its survival were unsure. On the one hand, with a white population of nearly 2 million, with a countryside in the middle and northern colonies that could easily feed a large army, and with supplies of materiel arriving from Europe, the position was not hopeless. Moreover, the tiny American manufacturing sector already showed signs of accelerating vitality, producing, for example, iron and saltpeter. Finally, in its large merchant fleet, whose ships were also used as privateers—which took 342 prizes in 1776—the Americans had another great asset, always provided the British blockade did not become effective. On the other hand, in military skills and professional training, both American generals and troops seemed to be surpassed by the British. Yet many Americans were volunteers and dedicated men, fighting for their own liberties—and lives. But recruiting, disciplining, provisioning, and supplying the army were never easy, for the whole business had to be organized from nothing. Nor were the farmers whose goods were needed ever very willing to sacrifice profits to patriotism. Although Congress, which had issued $6 million of paper money in 1775, issued another $19 million in the following year, this depreciated rapidly. A dollar in paper money was worth only 66 cents by the end of 1776 and 33 cents by the end of 1777, and prices also rose rapidly. Congress tried to control both prices and the depreciation of its currency but with little result. Given the weak nature of central and state governments, it seemed likely that economic distress might destroy American morale even without a British victory.

Yet in the second instance, should their army be destroyed, Americans had an inestimable strength, conferred by the nature of the war. For if—and nothing suggested it would not—the prevailing hostility to the British continued, their forces might well be exposed to patriot guerilla attacks in an unfriendly countryside, and British control of the colonies would be restricted to a few seaboard localities at an enormous, even crippling, expense to the mother country. At best, a successful but purely military British campaign might be expected to leave a powerful minority of armed patriots at large to harass and conspire, supported by a sullen majority. A British political victory could only rest on a compromise, probably one that conferred virtual independence on Americans. But since the British probably mistakenly believed that military victory would smash the support for American independence, this solution was unlikely. In the end, Britain made a political settlement only after the defeat of her soldiers.

Whether the war might result in defeat or victory for the American cause was uncertain in 1776. Nor could the future development of the United States then be predicted confidently. Yet, in this development, no matter what great and new changes might take place, patterns of ideas, of society, and of institutions arising from the first 169 years of American history would continue to play a part.

Bibliography

The following bibliography both acknowledges the work of the many scholars on which the writing of this book depended and suggests further reading. The first reference to a work contains details of place and date of publication. Subsequent references are by author and short title with a bracketed reminder of the numbered section of the bibliography in which fuller details are set forth. In general, I have listed works published in the last twenty years. Two comprehensive recent bibliographies are highly recommended: *The Harvard Guide to American History*, ed. F. Freidel (2nd edit., 2 vols., Cambridge, Mass., 1973) and the series *Goldentree Bibliographies in American History*, general ed. A. S. Link (Appleton Century Crofts-Meredith Corporation, New York). The value of *The William and Mary Quarterly: A Magazine of Early American History*, published quarterly by the Institute of Early American History and Culture, Williamsburg, Virginia, both for reviews of books and for its articles cannot be overstated. The tables of population figures in the text were taken from U.S. Bureau of the Census, *Historical Statistics of the United States, Colonial Times to 1957* (Washington, D.C., 1960).

Abbreviations

Ag.H — Agricultural History
Ec.H.R. — Economic History Review
H.M.Prot. Ep. Ch. — Historical Magazine of the Protestant Episcopal Church
J.A.S. — Journal of American Studies
J.S.H. — Journal of Southern History
Md.H.Mag. — Maryland Historical Magazine
N.E.Q. — New England Quarterly
N.C.H.R. — North Carolina Historical Review
P.S.Q. — Political Science Quarterly
Va.M.H.B. — Virginia Magazine of History and Biography
A.H.R. — American Historical Review
E.H.R. — English Historical Review
J.A.H. — Journal of American History
J.E.H. — Journal of Economic History
J.Soc.H. — Journal of Social History
Miss.V.H.R. — Mississippi Valley Historical Review
N.Y.H. — New York History
Pa.M.H.B. — Pennsylvania Magazine of History and Biography
Rh.Isl.H. — Rhode Island History
W.M.Q. — William and Mary Quarterly (third series)

Prologue: Europeans and North America to 1620

P.1. For European explorations, see the two magisterial works by S.E. Morison, *The European Discovery of America. The Northern Voyages A.D. 500-1600* (New York, 1971) and *The European Discovery of America. The Southern Voyages A.D. 1492-1616* (New York, 1974). D.B. Quinn, *England and the Discovery of America 1481-1620* (London, 1974) is also useful and cites the same author's other studies of English colonization and his valuable editions of primary sources for the Hakluyt Society. J.B. Brebner, *The Explorers of North America* (rptd. New York and Cleveland, 1963) deals with overland as well as oceanic exploration. J.H. Parry, *The Age of Reconnaissance: Discovery, Exploration and Settlement 1450-1650* (New York and Cleveland, 1963) is excellent. C.H. Cipolla, *Guns and Sails in the early phases of European overseas expansion, 1400-1700* (London, 1965) and J.H. Elliot, *The Old World and the New* (Cambridge, 1970) provide stimulating analyses of different kinds of fundamental problems.

P.2. The following treat national efforts: J.H. Parry, *The Spanish Seaborne Empire* (London, 1966), C.R. Boxer, *The Portuguese Seaborne Empire 1415-1825* (London, 1969), and *The Dutch Seaborne Empire 1600-1800* (London, 1965). There is no good modern treatment of early French overseas expansion, but an older work, C.A. Julien, *Les voyages de découverte et les premiers établissements* (Paris, 1948) is useful.

For the sixteenth-century English background, see K.R. Andrews, *English Privateering during the Spanish War, 1585-1603* (Cambridge, 1964) and *Drake's Voyages: A Reassessment of their Place in Elizabethan Maritime Expansion* (London, 1968), G.B. Parks, *Richard Hakluyt and the English Voyages* (New York, 1930), T.K. Rabb, *Enterprise and Empire: Merchants and Gentry Investment in the Expansion of England, 1575-1630* (Camb., Mass., 1967), and J. Parker, *Books to Build an Empire: A Bibliographical history of English overseas interests to 1620* (Amsterdam, 1965).

P.3. General works on the early British colonies are C.M. Andrews, *The Colonial Period of American History*, (4 vols. rptd. New Haven, 1964), W.F. Craven, *The Southern Colonies in the Seventeenth Century* (Baton Rouge, 1949), and J.E. Pomfret and F.M. Shumway, *Founding the American Colonies, 1583-1660* (New York, 1970).

P.4. Virginia's early history has recently attracted renewed attention. See W.F. Craven, *White, Red, and Black: The Seventeenth-Century Virginian* (Charlottesville, 1971), E.S. Morgan, "The Labor Problem at Jamestown 1607-1618," *A. H. R.*, 76 (1971), and D.B. Rutman, "The Virginia Company and its Military Regime" in D.B. Rutman, ed., *The Old Dominion: Essays in Honor of T.P. Abernethy* (Charlottesville, 1964). There are some important studies in the series *Virginia 350th Anniversary Historical Booklets*, ed. E.G. Swem (Williamsburg, 1957). T.J. Wertenbaker, *The Shaping of Colonial Virginia* (rptd. N.Y., 1958) is still useful.

P.5. The best single treatment of Plymouth is G.D. Langdon, Jr., *Pilgrim Colony: A History of New Plymouth 1620-1691* (New Haven, 1966), and of Newfoundland, G.T. Cell, *English Enterprise in Newfoundland 1557-1660* (Toronto, 1970).

P.6. Early Dutch and French trade and settlement may be approached through V.C. Bachman, *Peltries or Plantations: Economic Policies of the Dutch West India Company* (Baltimore, 1970), T.J. Condon, *New York Beginnings: Commercial Origins of New Netherland* (New York, 1968), and G. Lanctot, *A History of Canada*, vol. I (Toronto, 1963).

Chapter One. The English Colonies Established

1.1. The works cited in P.3, P.4 and P.5 are also valuable for this chapter. R.S. Dunn, ***Sugar and Slaves: The Rise of the Planter Class in the English West Indies, 1624-1713*** (Chapel Hill, 1972) is an excellent and original work on European expansion into the West Indies, superseding most earlier studies. C. Bridenbaugh, ***No Peace Beyond the Line: The English in the Caribbean, 1624-1690*** (New York, 1970) also covers the same general period in a fresh and stimulating fashion. C. Bridenbaugh, ***Vexed and Troubled Englishmen 1590-1642*** (New York, 1967) is the fullest single work on the Great Migration. A.E. Smith, ***Colonists in Bondage 1607-1776*** (Chapel Hill, 1947) is a standard work. M. Campbell "Social Origins of Some Early Americans" in J.M. Smith, ed., ***Seventeenth-Century America: Essays in Colonial History*** (Chapel Hill, 1959) is a pioneering essay; also see T.H. Breen and S. Foster, "Moving to the New World: The Character of Early Massachusetts Immigration," ***W.M.Q.***, XXX (1973).

1.2. For the English background of New England Puritanism, see P. Collinson, ***The Elizabethan Puritan Movement*** (London, 1967), C.H. and K. George, ***The Protestant Mind of the English Reformation 1570-1640*** (Princeton, 1961), W. Haller, ***The Rise of Puritanism*** (New York, 1957), C. Hill, ***Society and Puritanism in Pre-Revolutionary England*** (rev. ed. London, 1969), P. Miller, ***Orthodoxy in Massachusetts 1630-1650*** (New York, 1933), and M. Walzer, ***The Revolution of the Saints*** (Cambridge, Mass., 1965). D.B. Rutman, ***American Puritanism: Faith and Practice*** (Philadelphia and New York, 1970) is an excellent bibliographical essay and a stimulating introduction.

1.3. Books and articles on New England and New England Puritanism are legion. I have listed several that span the period before and after 1660 in the references to Chapter Four. The following studies are particularly useful for the founding and early development of Massachusetts: D. Hall, *The Faithful Shepherd: A History of the New England Ministry in the Seventeenth Century* (Chapel Hill, 1972), G.L. Haskins, ***Law and Authority in Early Massachusetts*** (New York, 1960), Miller, ***Orthodoxy in Massachusetts*** (1.2.), E.S. Morgan, ***The Puritan Dilemma: The Story of John Winthrop*** (Boston, 1958), E. Oberholzer, ***Delinquent Saints: Disciplinary action in the early congregational churches of Massachusetts*** (New York, 1956), D.B. Rutman, ***Winthrop's Boston, Portrait of a Puritan Town 1639-1649*** (Chapel Hill, 1965), R.E. Wall, ***Massachusetts Bay: The Crucial Decade 1640-1650*** (New Haven, 1972), T.J. Wertenbaker, ***The Puritan Oligarchy: The Founding of American Civilization*** (New York, 1947).

Some specialized studies of religious ideas are E.S. Morgan, ***Visible Saints: The History of a Puritan Idea*** (New York, 1963), N. Pettit, ***The Heart Prepared:***

Grace and Conversion in Puritan Spiritual Life (New Haven, 1966), L. Ziff, *The Career of John Cotton: Puritanism and the American Experience* (Princeton, 1962).

S.C. Powell, *Puritan Village: The Formation of a New England Town*, (Middletown, Conn., 1963), P.J. Greven, Jr., *Four Generations: Population, Land and Family in Colonial Andover, Massachusetts* (Ithaca, 1970), K.A. Lockridge, *A New England Town: The First Hundred Years, Dedham, Massachusetts, 1636-1736* (New York, 1970), and J.J. Waters, "Hingham, Massachusetts, 1631-1661: An East Anglian Oligarchy in the New World," *J. Soc. H.*, I (1968) demonstrate the usefulness of local studies.

T.H. Breen, *The Character of the Good Ruler: Puritan Political Ideas in New England 1630-1730* (New Haven, 1970), S. Foster, *Their Solitary Way: The Puritan Social Ethic in the First Century of Settlement in New England* (New Haven, 1971) and L. Ziff, *Puritanism in America: New Culture in a New World* (New York, 1973) are important new studies.

1.4. Connecticut is dealt with in C.M. Andrews, *The Beginnings of Connecticut, 1632-1662* (New Haven, 1934), R.S. Dunn, *Puritans and Yankees: The Winthrop Dynasty of New England 1630-1713* (Princeton, 1962) and, as a factual introduction, M.J.A. Jones, *Congregational Commonwealth: Connecticut 1636-1662* (Middletown, 1962). Also important is D.H. Fowler, "Connecticut's Freemen: The First Forty Years," *W.M.Q.*, XV (1958). New Haven is studied in I.M. Calder, *The New Haven Colony* (New Haven, 1934).

1.5. Works on Plymouth are Langdon, *Pilgrim Colony* (P.5.), D.B. Rutman, *Husbandmen of Plymouth: Farms and Villages in the Old Colony, 1620-1692* (Boston, 1967) and J. Demos, *A Little Commonwealth: Family Life in Plymouth Colony* (New York, 1970).

1.6. More has been written on Roger Williams than on early Rhode Island. For the latter, see Andrews, *Colonial Period*, II (P.3), S.G. Arnold, *History of the State of Rhode Island and Providence Plantations* (2 vols., Providence, 1894) and P.T. Conley, "Rhode Island Constitutional Development, 1636-1775," *Rh. Isl. H.*, XXVII (1968). For Williams, see P. Miller, *Roger Williams: His Contribution to the American Tradition* (New York, 1962), L. Moore, Jr., "Roger Williams and the Historians," *Church History*, XXXII (1963), E.S. Morgan, *Roger Williams: The Church and the State* (New York, 1967), and J. Rosenmeier, "The Teacher and the Witness: John Cotton and Roger Williams," *W.M.Q.*, XXV (1968).

1.7. For northern New England, C.E. Clark, *The Eastern Frontier: The Settlement of Northern New England, 1610-1763* (New York, 1970) brings together much scattered material and provides details of further reading.

1.8. Early commercial development is well treated in B. Bailyn, *The New England Merchants in the Seventeenth Century* (Cambridge, Mass., 1955). Education is considered in L.A. Cremin, *American Education: The Colonial Experience 1607-1789* (New York, 1970), which provides full references to other works, and B. Bailyn, *Education in the Forming of American Society: Needs and Opportunities for Study* (Chapel Hill, 1960). Harvard's early history is lovingly chronicled in S.E. Morison, *The Founding of Harvard College* (Cambridge, Mass., 1935) and *Harvard College in the Seventeenth Century* (2 vols. Cambridge, Mass., 1936).

1.9. Virginia is largely treated in works cited in P.3. and P.4. See also W.M. Billings, "The Growth of Political Institutions in Virginia, 1634-1676," *W.M.Q.*, XXXI (1974), I.D.W. Hecht, "The Virginia Muster of 1624/5 as a source for Demographic History," *W.M.Q.*, XXX (1973), E.S. Morgan, "The First American Boom: Virginia 1618-1630," *W.M.Q.*, XXVIII (1971), W.E. Washburn, *Virginia under Charles I and Cromwell 1624-1660* (Williamsburg, 1957) in *Virginia Hist. Booklets* (P.4.).

1.10 Maryland's founding and early development is summarized in Andrews, *Colonial Period*, vol. II (P.3.). See also W.R. Reavis, "The Maryland Gentry and Social Mobility, 1636-1676," *W.M.Q.*, XIV (1957), R.R. Mennard et al., "Opportunity and Equality: The Distribution of Wealth on the Lower Western Shore of Maryland, 1638-1705," *Md.H.Mag.*, LXIX (1974).

1.11 Pre-1660 English developments relevant to the colonies and to commerce are discussed in C.M. Andrews, *British Committees, Commissions and Councils of Trade and Plantations, 1622-1675* (Baltimore, 1908), G.L. Beer, *Origins of the British Colonial System 1579-1660* (New York, 1908), C. Hill, *God's Englishman: Oliver Cromwell and the English Revolution* (London, 1970), P.L. Kaye, *The Colonial Executive Prior to the Restoration* (Baltimore, 1906), A.G. Olson, *Anglo-American Politics: 1660-1715: The Relationship Between Parties in England and Colonial America* (Oxford, 1973). Also useful is C.H. Wilson, *England's Apprenticeship, 1603-1763* (London, 1965), which is excellent on the Navigation Acts.

Chapter Two. The English Colonies Established: The Second Phase

2.1. Studies of the English background after 1660 may be found in Andrews, *Colonial Period*, vols. III and IV (P.3.), R. Davis, *A Commercial Revolution: English Overseas Trade in the Seventeenth and Eighteenth Centuries* (London, 1967), L. Harper, *The English Navigation Laws* (New York, 1939), P.L. Kaye, *English Colonial Administration under Lord Clarendon* (Baltimore, 1905), R. Koebner, *Empire* (Cambridge, 1961). C.H. Wilson, *Profit and Power: A Study of England and the Dutch Wars* (Cambridge, 1957) discusses Anglo-Dutch relations; his *England's Apprenticeship* (1.11) is also important. Two biographies of the Earl of Shaftesbury should be mentioned; L.F. Brown, *Shaftesbury* (New York, 1933) and K.H.D. Haley, *Shaftesbury* (London, 1968).

2.2. Information on the Society of Friends may be found in W.C. Braithwaite, *The Beginnings of Quakerism* (rev. ed., Cambridge, 1955) and *The Second Period of Quakerism* (rev. ed., Cambridge, 1961), A. Lloyd, *Quaker Social History 1669-1738* (London, 1950), F.B. Tolles, *The Atlantic Community of the Early Friends* (London, 1952) and R.T. Vann, *The Social Development of Early English Quakerism, 1655-1755* (Cambridge, Mass., 1969). A new study of the Quakers after 1660 is badly needed.

2.3. General works on the early history of the new colonies are: Andrews, *The Colonial Period*, vol. III (P.3.) and W.F. Craven, *The Colonies in Transition 1660-1713* (New York, 1968).

The founding and early history of the separate colonies are discussed in the following books and articles.

2.4. Carolinas: C. O. Clowse, *Economic Beginnings of Colonial South Carolina 1670-1730* (Columbia, 1971), H.T. Lefler and W.S. Powell, *Colonial North Carolina: A History* (New York, 1973), E.E. Parker, ed., *North Carolina Charters and Constitutions 1578-1698* (Raleigh, 1963), M.E. Sirmans, *Colonial South Carolina: A Political History 1663-1763* (Chapel Hill, 1963).

2.5. New York: R.S. Dunn, *Puritans and Yankees* (1.4.), D.R. Fox, *Yankees and Yorkers* (New York, 1940), L.H. Leder, *Robert Livingston, 1654-1728, and the Politics of Colonial New York* (Chapel Hill, 1961), M.B. van Rensselaer, *History of the City of New York in the Seventeenth Century* (2 vols., New York, 1909), P.L. White, *The Beekmans of New York, 1647-1887* (New York, 1956). J.M. Murrin kindly gave me his excellent unpublished paper "The Perils of Premature Anglicization: The Dutch, the English and Leisler's Rebellion in New York."

2.6. New Jersey: J.P. Boyd, ed., *Fundamental Laws and Constitutions of New Jersey, 1664-1964* (Princeton, 1964), W.F. Craven, *New Jersey and the English Colonization of North America* (Princeton, 1964), R. McCormick, *New Jersey from Colony to State* (Princeton, 1964). J.E. Pomfret has written *The Province of West Jersey, 1609-1702: A History of the Origins of an American Colony* (Princeton, 1956), *The Province of East Jersey, 1609-1702: The Rebellious Proprietary* (Princeton, 1962) and *The New Jersey Proprietors and Their Lands* (Princeton, 1964).

2.7. Pennsylvania and Delaware: E.B. Bronner, *William Penn's Holy Experiment: The Founding of Pennsylvania, 1681-1701* (New York, 1962), M.M. Dunn, *William Penn: Politics and Conscience* (Princeton, 1967), M.B. Endy, *William Penn and Early Quakerism* (Princeton, 1973), J.E. Illick, *William Penn the Politician: His Relations with the English Government* (Ithaca, 1965), C.O. Peare, *William Penn: A Biography* (Philadelphia and New York, 1957), F.B. Tolles, *Meeting House and Counting House: The Quaker Merchants of Colonial Philadelphia 1682-1763* (Chapel Hill, 1948). Two recent books are very important: J.T. Lemon, *The Best Poor-Man's Country: The Geographical Study of Early South-eastern Pennsylvania* (Baltimore, 1972), and G.B. Nash, *Quakers and Politics: Pennsylvania 1681-1726* (Princeton, 1968). Delaware's early history has received no modern treatment. References to it will be found in studies of Pennsylvania; also useful are H.C. Conrad, *History of the State of Delaware* (3 vols., Wilmington, 1908) and J.T. Scharf, *History of Delaware* (2 vols., Philadelphia, 1888).

Chapter Three. Maryland and Virginia after the Restoration

Craven, *Colonies in Transition* (2.3.) is the best, and most recent, general study with a full bibliography.

3.1. Politics and government: Virginia. Much of the most useful writing on this period is found in the following articles and essays: O.B. Adams, "Virginia Reaction to the Glorious Revolution 1688-1692," *West. Va. H.*, XXIX (1967), B. Bailyn, "Politics and Social Structure in Virginia," in Smith, ed., *Seventeenth-Century America* (1.1.), Billings, "Growth of Political Institutions" (1.9.) and "The Causes of Bacon's Rebellion: Some Suggestions," *Va. M. H. B.*, 78 (1970), J. de Lourdes Leonard, "Operation Checkmate: The Birth and Death of a Virginia Blueprint for Progress," *W.M.Q.*, XXIV (1967), J.C. Rainbolt, "The Alteration in the Relationship between Leadership and Constituents in Virginia, 1660-1720," *W.M.Q.*, XXVII (1970) and "'Stuart Tyranny': The Crown's Attack on the Virginia Assembly 1676-1689," *Va. M. H. B.*, LXXV (1967), W.E. Washburn, "The Effects of Bacon's Rebellion on Government in England and Virginia," *U.S. Nat. Museum Bull.*, 225 (Washington, 1962). Recent books are D.S. Lovejoy, *The Glorious Revolution in America* (New York, 1972) and W.E. Washburn, *The Governor and the Rebel: A History of Bacon's Rebellion in Virginia* (Chapel Hill, 1957). See also C.L. Morton, *Colonial Virginia* (2 vols. Chapel Hill, 1960).

3.2. Politics and government: Maryland. L.G. Carr and D.W. Jordan, *Maryland's Revolution of Government 1689-1692* (Ithaca, 1973) discusses the whole period 1660-1692, and has full references to other articles and works. Also useful are R.H. Gleissner, "Religious Causes of the Glorious Revolution in Maryland," *Md. H. Mag.*, LXIV (1969) and "The Revolutionary Settlement of 1691 in Maryland," *ibid.*, LXVI (1971), M. Kammen, "The Causes of the Maryland Revolution of 1689," *ibid.*, LV (1960), Lovejoy, *Glorious Revolution* (3.1.).

3.3. Slavery and society. The changing tobacco trade is discussed in J.M. Price, "The Economic Growth of the Chesapeake and the European market, 1697-1775," *J. E. H.*, XXIV (1964). The most comprehensive survey of colonial slavery and racial attitudes is W.D. Jordan, *White over Black: American Attitudes Toward the Negro* (Chapel Hill, 1968). C. Degler, "Slavery and the Genesis of American Race Prejudice," *Comp. Studies in Hist. and Soc.*, II (1959) should be read with O. and M. Handlin, "The Origins of the Southern Labor System," *W.M.Q.*, VII (1950) and W.D. Jordan, "Modern Tensions and the Origins of American Slavery," *J. S. H.*, XXVIII, (1962). There are few modern studies of the workings of early slave society in Maryland or Virginia. See R.R. Menard, "The Maryland Slave Population, 1658 to 1730: A Demographic Profile of Blacks in Four Counties," *W.M.Q.*, XXXII (1975) and G.W. Mullin, *Flight and Rebellion: Slave Resistance in Eighteenth-Century Virginia* (New York, 1972). See also T.H. Breen, "A Changing Labor Force and Race Relations in Virginia, 1660-1710," *J. Soc. H.*, VII (1973), R.R. Menard "From Servant to Freeholder: Status Mobility and Property Accumulation in Seventeenth-Century Maryland," *W.M.Q.*, XXX (1973), Reavis, "Maryland Gentry" (1.10). Wertenbaker, *Shaping of Colonial Virginia* (P.4.) is still useful.

3.4. Religion and culture. C. Bridenbaugh, *Myths and Realities: Societies of the Colonial South* (New York, 1963), G.M. Brydon, *Virginia's Mother Church and the Political Conditions under which it grew* (2 vols., Richmond, 1947 and Phila., 1952), Cremin, *American Education* (1.8.), E. Davidson, *The Establishment of the English Church in the Continental Colonies* (Durham, 1936), R.B. Davis, *William Fitzhugh and His Chesapeake World* (Chapel Hill, 1963) and *Literature and Society in Early Virginia 1608-1840* (Baton Rouge, 1973), J.A. Lemay, *Men of Letters in Colonial Maryland* (Knoxville, 1972), N.W. Rightmyer, *Maryland's Established Church* (Baltimore, 1956), P. Rouse, Jr., *James Blair of Virginia* (Chapel Hill, 1971), W.H. Seiler, "The Anglican Parish in Virginia" in Smith, ed., *Seventeenth-Century America* (1.1.), R.P. Stearns, *Science in the British Colonies of America* (Urbana, 1970), L.B. Wright, *The First Gentlemen of Virginia: Intellectual Qualities of the Early Colonial Ruling Class* (San Marino, Calif., 1940).

Chapter Four. New England After the Restoration

4.1. The Puritan colonies: Settlement and population. Demos, *A Little Commonwealth* (1.5.), Greven, *Four Generations* (1.3.), Langdon, *Pilgrim Colony* (1.4.), Lockridge, *A New England Town* (1.3.), Powell, *Puritan Village* (1.3.) are also relevant to the period after 1660. See also the works cited in 7.1. and 7.2. R.L. Bushman, *From Puritan to Yankee: Character and the Social Order in Connecticut 1690-1765* (Cambridge, Mass., 1967) describes the effect of the expansion of settlement in Connecticut; there is no parallel, general study for Massachusetts. But see D.E. Leach, *Northern Colonial Frontier 1607-1763* (New York, 1966), P.N. Caroll, *Puritanism and the Wilderness: The Intellectual Significance of the New England Frontier, 1629-1700* (New York, 1969) and works cited below at 7.4. K.A. Lockridge and A. Kreider, "The Evolution of Massachusetts Town Government, 1640-1740," *W.M.Q.*, XXIII (1966) is important.

The commercial growth of New England is best approached in Bailyn, *New England Merchants* (1.8.). C. Bridenbaugh, *Cities in the Wilderness: The First Century of Urban Life in America, 1625-1742* (New York, 1938) studies Boston and Newport, New York, Philadelphia, and Charleston.

4.2. Religion and politics are sometimes difficult to distinguish. Breen, *Character of the Good Ruler* (1.3.), Dunn, *Puritans and Yankees* (1.4.), and Foster, *Their Solitary Way* (1.3.) are all highly useful. On the churches and religious ideas see also P. Miller, *The New England Mind from Colony to Province* (rptd. Boston, 1961) and *Errand into the Wilderness* (Cambridge, Mass., 1956), R.L. Pope, "New England versus the New England Mind: The Myth of Declension," *J. Soc. H.*, III (1969-70) and *The Half-Way Covenant: Church Membership in Puritan New England* (Princeton, 1969), W. Walker, *The Creeds and Platforms of Congregationalism* (rptd., Boston, 1960).

For political developments see also Viola Barnes, *The Dominion of New England: A Study in British Colonial Policy* (New Haven, 1923), M.G. Hall, *Edward Randolph and the American Colonies 1676-1703* (Chapel Hill, 1960), Lovejoy, *Glorious Revolution* (3.1.), P.R. Lucas, "Colony or Commonwealth: Massachusetts Bay 1661-1666," *W.M.Q.*, XXIV (1967), R.C. Simmons, "The Founding of the Third Church in Boston," *W.M.Q.*, XXVI (1969) and "The Massachusetts Revolution of 1689: Three Early American Political Broadsides," *J. A. S.*, II (1968), Wertenbaker, *Puritan Oligarchy* (1.3.).

4.3. There is a large literature on representation and the franchise. Full references will be found in the following: T.H. Breen, "The Town Franchise in Seventeenth-Century Massachusetts," *W.M.Q.*, XXVII (1970), B.K. Brown, "Freemanship in Puritan Massachusetts," *Miss. V. H. R.*, L. (1954), S. Foster, "The Massachusetts Franchise in the Seventeenth Century," *W.M.Q.*, XXIV (1967), J.R. Pole, *The Seventeenth Century: The Sources of Legislative Power* (Charlottesville, 1969), R.C. Simmons, "Godliness, Property and the Franchise in Puritan Massachusetts," *J. A. H.*, LV (1968).

4.4. Maine, New Hampshire and Rhode Island. See Clark, *Eastern Frontier* (1.7.) and Leach, *Northern Colonial Frontier* (4.1.). Bridenbaugh, *Cities in the Wilderness* (4.1.) discusses early Newport. See also Section 1.6.

4.5. Ideas and society. In addition to works cited in 1.8. and 4.2. see Bridenbaugh, *Cities in the Wilderness* (4.1.), R.E. Middlekauff, *The Mathers: Three Generations of Puritan Intellectuals 1596-1728* (New York, 1971), K.M. Murdock, *Literature and Theology in Colonial New England* (rptd. N.Y., 1963), Stearns, *Science in the British Colonies* (3.4.).

4.6. On witchcraft the most recent study is P. Boyer and S. Nissenbaum, *Salem Possessed: The Social Origins of Witchcraft* (Cambridge, Mass., 1974). See also J. Demos, "Underlying Themes in the Witchcraft of Seventeenth-Century New England," *A.H.R.*, LXXV (1970), S.J. Fox, *Science and Justice: The Massachusetts Witchcraft Trials* (Baltimore, 1968), C. Hansen, *Witchcraft at Salem* (New York, 1969). These works should be supplemented by A. McFarlane, *Witchcraft in Tudor and Stuart England; a regional and comparative study* (London, 1970) and K. Thomas, *Religion and the Decline of Magic* (London, 1971).

Chapter Five. The Newer Colonies: The Challenge to Proprietary Rule

5.1. Craven, *Colonies in Transition* (2.3.) is again invaluable. Other general studies are Cremin, *American Education* (1.8.), J.P. Greene, *The Quest for Power: The Lower Houses of Assembly in the Southern Royal Colonies 1689-1763* (Chapel Hill, 1963), Jordan, *White Over Black* (3.3.), Stearns, *Science* (3.4.). For New York, Philadelphia, and Charleston see Bridenbaugh, *Cities in the Wilderness* (4.1.) and see his *Myths and Realities* (3.4.) for the southern colonies.

5.2. The development of North Carolina can be studied in the works cited in 2.4. For slavery see also E.J. Clark, "Aspects of the North Carolina Slave Trade," *N.C. H. R.*, XXXIX (1962). J.P. Boyd, "The Sheriff in Colonial North Carolina," *N.C. H. R.*, V (1928) and P. M McCain, *The County Court in North Carolina before 1750* (Durham, 1950) are informative. On politics, see also H.F. Rankin, *Upheavals in Albemarle: The Story of Culpepper's Rebellion 1675-1689* (Raleigh, 1962). H.R. Merrens, *Colonial North Carolina in the Eighteenth Century: A Study in Historical Geography* (Chapel Hill, 1964) is extremely important for several topics.

5.3. South Carolina's development is explored in previously cited works of Clowse,

Economic Beginnings (2.4.) and Sirmans, *Colonial South Carolina* (2.4.). In addition, on slavery, see A.W. Lauber, *Indian Slavery in the Colonial Times within the present limits of the United States* (New York, 1913), M.E. Sirmans, "The Legal Status of the Slave in South Carolina 1670-1740," *J. S. H.*, XXVIII (1962) and P.H. Wood, *Black Majority: Negroes in South Carolina from 1670 through the Stono Rebellion* (New York, 1974); on white servitude, see W.B. Smith, *White Servitude in Colonial South Carolina* (Columbia, 1961). See also D. Ramsey, *The History of South-Carolina* (1809, 2 vols. rptd. Spartanburg, S.C., 1959).

5.4. All the previously cited works on New York in 2.5. are still relevant. Also see P.U. Bonomi, *A Factious People: Politics and Society in Colonial New York* (New York, 1971), D.S. Lovejoy, "Equality and Empire: The New York Charter of Libertyes, 1683," *W.M.Q.*, 3rd ser., XXI (1964) and *The Glorious Revolution* (3.1.) and B. Mason "Aspects of the New York Revolt of 1689," *N.Y. Hist.*, XXX (1949).

5.5. New Jersey's development is studied in the works cited in 2.6. In addition, see D.L. Kemmerer, *Path to Freedom: The Struggle for Self-Government in Colonial New Jersey, 1703-1776* (Princeton, 1940) and E.P. Tanner, *The Province of New Jersey, 1664-1738* (N.Y., 1908).

5.6. Pennsylvania and Delaware. In addition to the works cited in 2.2. and 2.7., see F.B. Tolles, *James Logan and the Culture of Provincial America* (Boston, 1957), K.N. Lokken, *David Lloyd, Colonial Lawmaker* (Seattle, 1959) and W.T. Root, *The Relations of Pennsylvania with the British Government, 1696-1765* (New York, 1912). R.M. Jones, *The Quakers in the American Colonies* (London, 1911) is also useful.

Chapter Six. England, Europe and North America

6.1. On English and American trade and trading ideas, see R. Davis, *A Commercial Revolution* (2.1.) and *The Rise of the Atlantic Economies* (New York, 1973), and Koebner, *Empire* (2.1), K.E. Knorr, *British Colonial Theories 1570-1850* (Toronto, 1944), G.D. Ramsay, *English Overseas Trade During the Centuries of Emergence: Studies in Some Modern Origins of the English-Speaking World* (London, 1957), C.H. Wilson, "Mercantilism: Some Vicissitudes of an Idea," *Ec. H. R.*, X (1957) and *Mercantilism* (London, 1958) and *England's Apprenticeship* (1.11). M. Kammen, *Empire and Interest: The American Colonies and the Politics of Mercantilism* (Phila. and N.Y., 1970) treats the years from 1660 to 1776.

6.2. Trade patterns and statistics are detailed or discussed in U.S. Bureau of the Census, *Historical Statistics of the United States: Colonial Times to 1957* (Washington, 1960), R. Davis, "English Foreign Trade, 1700-1774," *Ec.H.R.*, XV (1962-3), E.B. Schumpeter, *English Overseas Trade Statistics 1697-1808* (Oxford, 1960), J.F. Shepherd and G.M. Walton, *Shipping, Maritime Trade and the Economic Development of North America* (Cambridge, 1972).

6.3. For developments in administration and legislation, see T.C. Barrow, *Trade and*

Empire: The British Customs Service in Colonial America 1660-1775 (Cambridge, Mass., 1967), D.M. Clark, *The Rise of the British Treasury: Colonial Administration in the Eighteenth Century* (New Haven, 1960), J.D. Doty, *The British Admiralty Board as a Factor in Colonial Administration, 1689-1763* (Philadelphia, 1930), G.H. Guttridge, *The Colonial Policy of William III in America and the West Indies* (Cambridge, 1922), P.S. Haffenden, "The Crown and the Colonial Charters, 1675-1688," *W.M.Q.*, XV [in two parts] (1968), E.E. Hoon, *The Organization of the English Customs Service 1696-1786* (New York, 1938), Kammen, *Empire and Interest* (6.1.), L.P. Kellogg, *The American Colonial Charter: A Study of English Administration in Relation thereto, Chiefly after 1688* (Washington, D.C., 1904), P. Laslet, "John Locke, the Great Recoinage and the Origins of the Board of Trade, 1695-1698," *W.M.Q.*, XIV (1957), Olson, *Anglo-American Politics* (1.11), I.K. Steele, *The Politics of Colonial Policy: The Board of Trade in Colonial Administration 1696-1720* (Oxford, 1968) and S.S. Webb, "William Blathwayt, Imperial Fixer: From Popish Plot to Glorious Revolution," *W.M.Q.*, XXV (1968) and "William Blathwayt, Imperial Fixer: Muddling Through to Empire 1689-1717," *ibid.*, XXVI (1969).

6.4. On the Church of England and the Society for the Propagation of the Gospel and the colonies, see J.H. Bennett, "English Bishops and Imperial Jurisdiction, 1660-1725," *Hist. Mag. Prot. Epis. Church*, XXXII (1963), C. Bridenbaugh, *Mitre and Sceptre: Transatlantic Faiths, Ideas, Personalities and Politics, 1689-1775* (New York, 1972), A.L. Cross, *The Anglican Episcopate and the American Colonies* (New York, 1902), C.F. Pascoe, *Two Hundred Years of the S.P.G.: An Historical Account of the Society for the Propagation of the Gospel in Foreign Parts*, 2 vols. (London, 1901).

6.5. Dutch, French and Spanish. The history of the New Netherlands until the English conquest is well told in Rensselaer, *City of New York* (2.5.)

The development of New France may be conveniently studied in Lanctôt, *History of Canada*, II, III (P.6)

Spanish fortunes in North America are surveyed in J.L. Wright, Jr., *Anglo-Spanish Rivalry in North America* (Athens, Ga., 1971).

M. Savelle, *The Origins of American Diplomacy: The International History of Anglo-America 1492-1763* (New York, 1967) is a detailed survey of European diplomacy affecting North America.

6.6. The Indians. The most recent attempt to study Indian and white relationships is G.B. Nash, *Red, White and Black: the Peoples of Early America* (Englewood Cliffs, New Jersey, 1974). This work contains a full bibliography. What follows here are a number of general works, guides to further study and bibliographical essays: W.N. Fenton, *American Indian and White Relations to 1830: Needs and Opportunities for Study* (Chapel Hill, 1957), W.R. Jacobs, *Dispossessing the American Indian* (New York, 1972), A.M. Josephy, Jr., *The Indian Heritage of America* (New York, 1968), H.H. Peckham and C. Gibson, eds., *Attitudes of Colonial Powers Toward the American Indian* (Salt Lake City, 1969), R.M. Underhill, *Red Man's America: A History of Indians in the United States* (Chicago, 1953), B.W. Sheehan, "Indian-White Relations in Early America: A Review Essay," *W.M.Q.*, XXVI (1969).

6.7. The early wars, Indian and European, may be studied in P.H. Corkran, *The Creek Frontier, 1540-1783* (Norman, Okla. 1967), V.W. Crane, *The Southern Frontier 1670-1732* (Ann Arbor, 1929). See also D.E. Leach, *Flintlock and Tomahawk; New England in King Philip's War* (New York, 1958) and *Northern Colonial Frontier* (4.1.) and *Arms for Empire: A Military History of the British Colonies in North America, 1607-1763* (New York, 1973), B.C. McCrary, *Indians in Seventeenth-Century Virginia* (Williamsburg, 1967), R.L. Meriweather, *The Expansion of South Carolina, 1729-1765* (Kingsport, Tenn., 1940), H.H. Peckham, *The Colonial Wars, 1689-1762* (Chicago, 1964), A.T. Vaughan, *New England Frontier: Puritans and Indians, 1620-1675* (Boston, 1965). J.W. Shy, "A New Look at the Colonial Militia," *W.M.Q.*, XX (1963) is the best introduction to the subject.

6.8. On some of the consequences of the early wars and related matters, see B. Bailyn, *Massachusetts Shipping 1697-1714: A Statistical Study* (Cambridge, Mass., 1959) and Bridenbaugh, *Cities in the Wilderness* (4.1.) and its continuation, *Cities in Revolt: Urban Life in America, 1743-1776* (New York, 1955); Clowse, *Economic Beginnings* (2.4.), the tables in *Historical Statistics* (6.2.), C. Nettels, *The Money Supply of the American Colonies before 1720* (Madison, Wisc., 1934), Price, "Economic Growth" (3.3.) and Walton and Shepherd, *Shipping, Maritime Trade* (6.2.)

Chapter Seven. Growth and Expansion

7.1. J.A. Henretta, *The Evolution of American Society, 1700-1815: An Interdisciplinary Analysis* (Lexington, Mass., 1973) provides an up-to-date discussion of colonial population trends. A pioneer work is J. Potter, "The growth of Population in America 1700-1860" in D.V. Glass and D.E.C. Eversley, eds., *Population in History: Essays in Historical Demography* (London, 1965). See also P.J. Greven, Jr., "The average size of families and households in the Province of Massachusetts in 1764 and in the United States in 1790" in P. Laslett, ed., *Household and Family in Past Time* (Cambridge, 1972). For table, "Estimated Population of Colonial Cities," see S. Bruchey, ed., *The Colonial Merchant: Sources and Readings* (New York, 1966), 11.

7.2. More specialized studies of demographic questions and of the family include: J. Demos, "Families in Colonial Bristol, Rhode Island: An Exercise in Historical Demography," *W.M.Q.*, XXV (1968), J. Duffy, *Epidemics in Colonial America* (Baton Rouge, 1953), P. Greven, *Four Generations* (1.3.), R. Higgs and H.L. Stetler, "New England Demography: A Sampling Approach," *W.M.Q.*, XXVII (1970), K.A. Lockridge, "The Population of Dedham, Massachusetts 1636-1736," *Ec.H.R.*, 2nd ser., XIX (1966), H. Moller, "Sex Composition and Correlated Patterns in Colonial America," *W.M.Q.*, II (1945), S. Norton, "Population Growth in Colonial America: A Study of Ipswich, Massachusetts," *Population Studies*, XXV (1971), D.S. Smith, "The Demographic History of Colonial New England," *J.E.H.*, XXXII (1972) I.V. Wells, "Quaker Marriage Patterns in a Colonial Perspective," *W.M.Q.*, XXIX (1972).

R. Thompson, *Women in Stuart England and America* (London 1974) studies demography and the family as well as general history.

7.3. For colonial immigration, there is a good general survey in M.A. Jones, ***American Immigration*** (Chicago, 1959) and an economically oriented one in Walton and Shepherd, ***Shipping, Maritime Trade*** (6.2.).

Some selected studies of immigration and ethnic groups are: G.W. Baird, ***History of the Huguenot Emigration to America*** (2 vols., New York, 1885), D. Cunz, ***The Maryland Germans: A History*** (Princeton, 1948), R.J. Dickson, ***Ulster Emigration to Colonial America 1718-1775*** (London, 1966), I.C. Graham, ***Colonists from Scotland, Emigration to North America, 1707-1783*** (Ithaca, 1956), J.G. Leyburn, ***The Scotch-Irish: A Social History*** (Chapel Hill, 1962), J.R. Marcus, ***Early American Jewry*** (2 vols. Philadelphia, 1951, 1953), D. Meyer, *The Highland Scots of North Carolina, 1732-1776* (Chapel Hill, 1962), R. Woods, ed., *Pennsylvania Germans* (Princeton, 1942).

Studies of African slavery in the South are listed in 3.3. and 5.2.-5.3. But see also E.J. McManus, ***Black Bondsmen in the North*** (Syracuse, 1973).

For discussion and reference to the sources for the figures in table "Some Recent Estimates of Immigration" see Walton and Shepherd, ***Shipping, Maritime Trade*** (6.2), 33-6, 139-48 and for table "Estimates of Slave Imports" see P.M. Curtin, ***The Atlantic Slave Trade: A Census*** (Madison, 1969), 136-46, from which the table was taken.

7.4. The expansion of settlement, land speculation, and early land companies are treated in C.W. Alvord, ***The Mississippi Valley in British Politics: A Study of the Trade, Land Speculation, and Experiments in Imperialism Culminating in the American Revolution*** (2 vols. Cleveland, 1917), R.H. Akagi, ***The Town Proprietors of the New England Colonies: A Study of Their Development, Organization, Activities and Controversies 1620-1770*** (Philadelphia, 1924), K. P. Bailey, ***The Ohio Company of Virginia and the Westward Movement 1748-1792*** (Glencoe, Calif., 1939), S.E. Baldwin, ***The American Business Corporation before 1789*** (New York, 1903), J.P. Boyd, *The Susquehannah Company: Connecticut's Experiment in Expansion* (New Haven, 1935), Clark, ***Eastern Frontier*** (1.7.), E.M. Fox, ***Land Speculation in the Mohawk Country*** (Ithaca, 1949), Gipson, ***British Empire***, vols. II, III, IV (10.2), A.P. James, ***The Ohio Company, its Inner History*** (Pittsburgh, 1959), S.B. Kim, "A New Look at The Great Landlords of Eighteenth-Century New York," ***W.M.Q.***, XXVII (1970), Leach, ***Northern Colonial Frontier*** (4.1.), R.L. Higgins, ***Expansion in New York, with Especial Reference to the Eighteenth Century*** (Columbus, Ohio, 1931), L.K. Matthews, ***The Expansion of New England: The Spread of New England Settlement to the Mississippi River, 1620-1865*** (Boston, 1909), Meriweather, ***Expansion of South Carolina*** (6.7.), Morton, ***Colonial Virginia*** (3.1).

7.5. Some works dealing with colonial agriculture and agricultural commodities are: P.W. Bidwell and J.I. Falconer, ***History of Agriculture in the Northern United States, 1620-1860*** (Washington, D.C., 1925), H.J. Carman, ed., ***American Husbandry*** (New York, 1939), H.J. Carman and R.G. Tugwell, eds., ***J. Eliot: Essays upon Field Husbandry in New England, and Other Papers 1748-1762*** (New York, 1935), D. Doar, ***Rice and Rice Planting in the South Carolina Low***

Country (Charleston, 1936), L.C. Gray, *History of Agriculture in the Southern United States to 1860* (2 vols. Washington D.C., 1933), Henretta, *Evolution of American Society* (7.1.), D. Klingaman, "The Significance of Grain in the Development of the Tobacco Colonies," *J.E.H.*, XXIX (1969), A.C. Land, "The Tobacco Staple and the Planter's Problems: Technology, Labour and Crops," *Ag. H.*, XLIII (1969), Lemon, *Best Poor-Man's Country* (2.7.), Merrens, *Colonial North Carolina* (5.2.), C.R. Woodward, *The Development of Agriculture in New Jersey, 1640-1880: A Monographic Study in Agricultural History* (New Brunswick, 1927). *Agricultural History,* XLIII (January, 1969) is devoted to eighteenth-century agriculture.

7.6. Other colonial economic and commercial developments have been most recently studied in Shepherd and Walton, *Shipping, Maritime Trade* (6.2.) which contains an up-to-date bibliography. Other useful works are S. Bruchey, *The Roots of American Economic Growth 1607-1861: An Essay in Social Causation* (London, 1965) and, as editor, *The Colonial Merchant* (7.1), A.C. Land, "Economic Base and Social Structure: The Northern Chesapeake in the Eighteenth Century," *J.E.H.*, XXV (1965) and "Economic Behavior in a Planting Society: The Eighteenth Century Chesapeake," *J.S.H.*, XXXIII (1967), J.H. Soltow, "Scottish Factors in Virginia, 1750-1775," *Ec.H.R.*, 2nd ser. XII (1959), G.R. Taylor, "American Economic Growth before 1840: an exploratory essay," *J.E.H.*, XXVI (1966).

7.7. On paper money, currency and banking, see the following works and their bibliographies: J.A. Ernst, *Money and Politics in America 1755-1775: A Study of the Currency Act of 1764 and the Political Economy of Revolution* (Chapel Hill, 1973), E.J. Ferguson, "Currency Finance: An Interpretation of Colonial Monetary Practices," *W.M.Q.*, X (1953), T.G. Thayer, "The Land Bank System in the American Colonies," *J.E.H.*, XIII (1953).

7.8. On manufactures see A.C. Bining, *British Regulation of the Colonial Iron Industry* (Philadelphia, 1937), C. Bridenbaugh, *The Colonial Craftsman* (New York, 1950), and V.S. Clark, *History of Manufactures in the United States* (3 vols., New York, 1929).

Chapter Eight. Religion and Culture

8.1. General histories of American religion with specialized bibliographies are S.E. Ahlstrom, *A Religious History of the American People* (New Haven, 1972) and S.E. Mead, *The Lively Experiment: The Shaping of Christianity in America* (New York, 1963). E. Gaustad, *Historical Atlas of Religion in America* (New York, 1962) is valuable.

8.2. New England Congregationalism may be approached through the following works: C. Akers, *Called unto Liberty: A Life of Jonathan Mayhew* (Cambridge, Mass., 1964), Bushman, *From Puritan to Yankee* (4.1.), J.W. Jones, *The Shattered Synthesis: New England Puritanism before the Great Awakening* (New Haven, 1973), Middlekauff, *The Mathers*, (4.5.), Miller, *The New England Mind from Colony* (4.2.) and *Errand into the Wilderness* (4.2.),

Pope, *Half-Way Covenant* (4.2.), Walker, *Creeds and Platforms* (4.2.), C.C. Wright, *The Beginnings of Unitarianism in America* (Boston, 1955).

8.3. For the Church of England, there is no good recent general history but Bridenbaugh, *Mitre and Sceptre* (6.4.) is of great value; also Davidson, *Establishment of the English Church* (3.4.)

A few recent specialized studies may be noticed: N.R. Burr, *The Anglican Church in New Jersey* (Philadelphia 1954), Brydon, *Virginia's Mother Church*, (3.4.), S. Erwin, "The Anglican Church in North Carolina," *H.M. Prot. Ep. Ch.*, XXV (1956), Rightmyer, *Maryland's Established Church* (3.4.), Rouse, *James Blair* (3.4.), B.E. Steiner, Jr., "New England Anglicanism: A Genteel Faith?" *W.M.Q.* XXVII (1970), F.L. Weis, *Colonial Clergy of Virginia, North Carolina, and South Carolina* (Boston, 1955). Reference should also be made to Pascoe, *Two Hundred Years of the S.P.G.* (6.4).

8.4. The Society of Friends is studied in S.V. James, *A People Among Peoples: Quaker Benevolence in Eighteenth Century America* (Cambridge, Mass., 1963) and Jones, *Quakers in the American Colonies* (5.6).

See also Tolles, *Meeting House* (2.7.) and *Atlantic Community* (2.2).

8.5. Presbyterianism is examined in G.S. Klett, *Presbyterians in Colonial Pennsylvania* (Philadelphia, 1937), and L.J. Trinterud, *The Forming of an American Tradition: A Re-examination of Colonial Presbyterianism* (Philadelphia, 1949).

8.6. The colonial Baptists in New England have been the subject of a recent, magisterial study, W.G. McLoughlin, *New England Dissent 1630-1833: The Baptists and the Separation of Church and State* (2 vols., Cambridge, Mass., 1971).

The other center of Baptist strength (in the later colonial period) was the southern colonies, and an analytical study is badly needed.

8.7. Other religious groups and sects must be studied in a variety of books, of which the most useful are E.T. Corwin, *History of the Dutch Reformed Church in the United States* (New York 1895), E.T. Corwin, J.H. Dubbs and J.T. Hamilton, *A History of the Reformed Church . . . and the Moravian Church in the United States* (N.Y., 1895), G.L. Gollin, *Moravians in Two Worlds: A Study of Changing Communities* (New York, 1967), A.G. Spangenberg, *Life of Nicholas Lewis, Count Zinzendorf* (London, 1838), J.T. Tanis, *Dutch Calvinistic Pietism in the Middle Colonies* (The Hague, 1967). Also important is M.E. Lodge, "The Crisis of the Churches in the Middle Colonies," *Pa. M. H. B.*, XLV (1971).

8.8. Information about the Great Awakening will be found in works cited in 8.1.-8.7. Similarly, additional information about the churches and sects before the Great Awakening can be found in many of the following studies.

General treatments of the Awakening are few. The following collections of documents are often valuable: R.L. Bushman, *The Great Awakening: Documents on the Revival of Religion, 1740-1745* (New York 1970), A. Heimert and P. Miller, *The Great Awakening: Documents Illustrating the Crisis and its Consequences* (Indianapolis and N.Y., 1967), D.B. Rutman, *The Great Awakening: Event and Exegesis* (New York, 1970). A. Heimert, *Religion and the American Mind from the Great Awakening to the Revolution* (Cambridge, Mass., 1966) mainly treats the New England mind; it has been savagely reviewed by E.S. Morgan, in *W.M.Q.*, XXIV (1967). C.B. Cowing, *The Great Awakening and the American Revolution: Colonial Thought in the Eighteenth Century* (Chicago, 1971), has an excellent bibliography.

8.9. Regional and local studies include: New England: J.M. Bumsted, "Revivalism and Separatism in New England: The First Society of Norwich, Connecticut, as a Case Study," *W.M.Q.*, XXIV (1967) and "Religion, Finance and Democracy in Massachusetts: The Town of Norton as a Case Study," *J.A.H.*, LVII (1971), E.S. Gaustad, *The Great Awakening in New England* (New York, 1957), C.C. Goen, *Revivalism and Separatism in New England 1740-1800: Strict Congregationalists and Separate Baptists in the Great Awakening* (New Haven, 1962), G.F. Moran, "Conditions of Religious Conversion in the First Society of Norwich, Conn., 1718-1744," *J. Soc. H.* V (1972), J. Walsh, "The Great Awakening in Woodbury," *W.M.Q.*, XXVIII (1971). W.G. McLoughlin, *Isaac Backus and the American Pietistic Tradition* (Boston 1967) is a study of a New England Baptist whose importance extended beyond the region.

Middle colonies: C.H. Maxson, *The Great Awakening in the Middle Colonies* (Chicago, 1920), F.B. Tolles, "Quietism versus Enthusiasm: The Pennsylvania Quakers and the Great Awakening," *Pa. M. H. B.*, LXIX (1945).

Southern colonies: W.M. Gewehr, *The Great Awakening in Virginia 1740-1790* (Durham, 1930), R. Isaac, "Religion and Authority: Problems of the Anglican Establishment in Virginia in the Era of the Great Awakening and the Parsons' Cause," *W.M.Q.*, XXX (1973), D.T. Morgan, Jr., "The Great Awakening in North Carolina, 1740-1755: The Baptist Phase," *N.C. H. R.*, XLV (1968)

8.10. Other relevant studies. For Whitefield: S.C. Henry, *George Whitefield 1714-1770 Wayfaring Witness* (New York 1957) and W.H. Kenney, "George Whitefield, Dissenter priest of the Awakening 1739-1741," *W.M.Q.*, XXVI (1969). See also L.W. Labaree, "The Conservative Attitude Toward the Great Awakening," *W.M.Q.*, I (1944).

8.11. Studies of science and education. Science: W.J. Bell, Jr., *Early American Science: Needs and Opportunities for Study* (Williamsburg, 1955), B. Hindle, *Pursuit of Science in Revolutionary America 1735-1789* (Chapel Hill, 1956), Stearns, *Science* (3.4.). Education: Cremin, *American Education* (1.8.) is invaluable also for general cultural developments; R. Hofstadter and W. Smith, *American Higher Education: A Documentary History* (2 vols., Chicago, 1961), B. McAnear, "College Founding in the Colonies 1745-1755," *Miss. V. H. R.*, XLII (1955), R. Middlekauff, *Ancients and Axioms: Secondary Education in Eighteenth-Century New England* (New Haven, 1963), G.P. Schmidt, *Princeton and Rutgers: The Two Colonial Colleges of New Jersey* (Princeton, 1964), P. Sloan, *The Scottish Enlightenment and the American College Ideal* (New York, 1971), R. Warch, *School of the Prophets: Yale College 1701-1740* (New Haven, 1973), T.J. Wertenbaker, *Princeton 1746-1896* (Princeton, 1946).

8.12. Printing: C. Brigham, *Journals and Journeymen: A contribution to the history of early American newspapers* (Phila., 1950), L.C. Wroth, *The Colonial Printer* (Charlottesville, 1964).

8.13. Literature: Davis, *Literature and Society* (3.4.), P. Gay, *A Loss of Mastery: Puritan History in Colonial America* (Berkeley, 1966), Lemay, *Men of Letters*

(3.4.), R.E. Spiller, et al., *Literary History of the United States*, vol. I (3rd ed., N.Y., 1964).

8.14. Edwards and Franklin: C.C. Cherry, ***The Theology of Jonathan Edwards: A Reappraisal*** (Garden City, 1966), P. Miller, ***Jonathan Edwards*** (New York, 1949), V. Tomas, "The Modernity of Jonathan Edwards," *N.E.Q.* XXV (1952); see also Gay, ***Loss of Mastery*** (8.13). A.O. Aldridge, ***Benjamin Franklin Philosopher and Man*** (Philadelphia, 1965), V.W. Crane, ***Benjamin Franklin and a Rising People*** (Boston 1954), N.G. Goodman, ed., ***A Benjamin Franklin Reader*** (New York, 1971), C. Van Doren, ***Benjamin Franklin*** (New York, 1938).

8.15. General reading and biographies. Bridenbaugh, ***Myths and Realities***: (3.4.), C. and J. Bridenbaugh, ***Rebels and Gentlemen: Philadelphia in the Age of Franklin*** (New York, 1942), D. Boorstin, ***The Americans: The Colonial Experience*** (New York, 1955), R.L. Gummere, ***The American Colonial Mind and the Classical Tradition: Essays in Colonial Culture*** (Cambridge, Mass., 1963), L.A. Wright, *The Cultural Life of the American Colonies, 1607-1763* (New York, 1957), J. Ellis, *The New England Mind in Transition: Samuel Johnson of Connecticut 1696-1772* (New Haven, 1973), E.S. Morgan, *The Gentle Puritan: A Life of Ezra Stiles* (New Haven, 1912), L.L. Tucker, *Thomas Clap of Yale College* (Chapel Hill, 1962).

Chapter Nine. Political Institutions and Political Culture

9.1. English colonial policy and relationships have been restudied in the following recent books and articles, which contain relevant bibliographies: Bridenbaugh, ***Mitre and Sceptre*** (6.4), J.P. Greene, "An Uneasy Connection: An Analysis of the Preconditions of the American Revolution" in S.G. Kurtz and J.H. Hutson, eds., ***Essays on the American Revolution*** (Chapel Hill and New York, 1973), P.S. Haffenden, "Colonial Appointments and Patronage under the Duke of Newcastle, 1724-1739," *E.H.R.*, LXXVIII (1963), J.A. Henretta, '***Salutary Neglect***': ***Colonial Administration under the Duke of Newcastle*** (Princeton, 1972), M.G. Kammen, ***A Rope of Sand: The Colonial Agents, British Politics and the American Revolution*** (Ithaca, 1968) and ***Empire and Interest*** (6.1.), A.G. Olson, *Anglo-American Politics* (1.11). There is no modern biography of Lord Halifax.

Useful older studies are C.M. Andrews, *The Colonial Background of the American Revolution* (New Haven, 1931), O.M. Dickerson, *American Colonial Government 1696-1765; A Study of the British Board of Trade in its Relation to the American Colonies . . .* (Cleveland, 1912) and L.W. Labaree, *Royal Government in America, A Study of the British Colonial System before 1783* (New Haven, 1930).

9.2. Information on the institutional framework can be found in several general studies: M.P. Clarke, ***Parliamentary Privilege in the American Colonies*** (New Haven, 1943), E.B. Greene, ***The Provincial Governor in the English Colonies of***

North America (New York, 1898), Greene, *Quest for Power*: (5.1.), E.S. Griffith, *History of American City Government: The Colonial Period* (New York, 1938), Labaree, *Royal Government* (9.1.). B. Bailyn, *The Origins of American Politics* (New York, 1968) studies institutions and ideology. J.M. Murrin, "The Myths of Colonial Democracy and Royal Decline in Eighteenth-Century America: A Review Essay," *Cithara*, V (1965) and P.L. Lucas, "A Note on the Comparative Structure of Politics in Mid-Eighteenth-Century Britain and its American Colonies," *W.M.Q.*, XXVIII (1971) are important.

On representation and the franchise, see R.E. Brown, *Middle-Class Democracy and the Revolution in Massachusetts 1691-1780* (Ithaca, 1955), R.E. Brown and B.K. Brown, *Virginia, 1705-1781: Democracy or Aristocracy?* (East Lansing, Mich., 1964), J. Cary "Statistical Method and the Brown Thesis on Colonial Democracy," *W.M.Q.*, XX (1963), M.M. Klein, "Democracy and Politics in Colonial New York," *N.Y.H.* XI (1954), R.P. McCormick, *The History of Voting in New Jersey: A Study of the Development of Election Machinery, 1664-1911* (New Brunswick, 1953), A.E. McKinley, *The Suffrage Franchise in the Thirteen English Colonies in America* (Philadelphia, 1905), J.R. Pole, *Political Representation in England and the Origins of the American Republic* (New York, 1966), C. Williamson, *American Suffrage from Property to Democracy 1760-1860* (Princeton, 1960). M. Chute, *The First Liberty: A History of the Right to Vote in America, 1619-1850* (New York, 1969) is factually informative.

9.3. Modern studies of local government in the colonies are badly needed. A few existing ones may be cited: Boyd, "The Sheriff in Colonial North Carolina" (5.2.), E.M. Cook, Jr., "Local Leadership and the Typology of New England Towns, 1700-1785," *P.S.Q.*, LXXXVI (1971), J.M. Diamondstone, "Philadelphia's Municipal Corporation, 1701-1776," *Pa.M.H.B.*, XC (1966), L.M. Kay, "The Payment of Provincial and Local Taxes in North Carolina, 1748-1771," *W.M.Q.*, XXVI (1969), McCain, *County Court* (5.2.), A.O. Porter, *County Government in Virginia* (New York, 1947), J.F. Sly, *Town Government in Massachusetts (1620-1930)* (Cambridge, Mass., 1930), A.D. Watson, "Regulation and Administration of Roads and Bridges in Colonial North Eastern North Carolina," *N.C. H. R.*, XLV (1968). Lemon, *The Best Poor-Man's Country* (2.7) has a good discussion of local government. M. Zuckerman, *Peaceable Kingdoms: New England Towns in the Eighteenth Century* (New York, 1970) discusses the New England town in the context of New England's social and political life.

9.4. Studies of the politics of individual colonies are many. The following selected works usually consider political institutions or political controversies, or both. New Hampshire: J.R. Daniell, *Experiment in Republicanism: New Hampshire and the American Revolution, 1741-1794* (Cambridge, Mass., 1970), W.H. Fry, *New Hampshire as a Royal Province* (New York, 1908).

Massachusetts: P.S. Boyer, "Borrowed Rhetoric: The Massachusetts Excise Crisis of 1754," *W.M.Q.*, XXI (1963), Brown, *Middle-Class Democracy* (9.2.), J.A. Schutz, *William Shirley, King's Governor of Massachusetts* (Chapel Hill, 1961), G.B. Warden, *Boston 1689-1776* (Boston, 1970), J.J. Waters, *The Otis Family in Provincial and Revolutionary Massachusetts*

(Chapel Hill, 1968), R. Zemsky, ***Merchants, Farmers and River Gods: An Essay on Eighteenth-Century American Politics*** (Boston, 1971).

Connecticut: Bushman, ***From Puritan to Yankee*** (4.1), R. Sklar, "The Great Awakening and Colonial Politics: Connecticut's Revolution in the Minds of Men," ***Bull. Conn. Hist. Soc.*** XXVIII (1963), Zeichner, ***Connecticut's Years of Controversy, 1750-1776*** (Chapel Hill, 1949).

Rhode Island: M.E. Thompson, "The Ward-Hopkins Controversy and the American Revolution in Rhode Island: An Interpretation," *W.M.Q.*, XVI (1959).

New York: Bonomi, ***A Factious People*** (5.4.), S.N. Katz, ***Newcastle's New York: Anglo-American Politics, 1732-1753*** (Cambridge, Mass., 1968), R.M. Naylor, "The Royal Prerogative in New York, 1691-1775," ***N.Y. State Hist. Assoc. Jnl.***, V (1924).

New Jersey: Kemmerer, ***Path to Freedom*** (5.5.), McCormick, ***New Jersey*** (2.6.).

Pennsylvania: W.S. Hanna, ***Benjamin Franklin and Pennsylvania Politics*** (Stanford, 1964), J.H. Hutson, ***Pennsylvania Politics 1746-1770: The Movement for Royal Government and Its Consequences*** (Princeton, 1972), Nash, ***Quakers and Politics*** (2.7.), T.G. Thayer, ***Pennsylvania Politics and the Growth of Democracy, 1740-1776*** (Harrisburg, 1953), C.R. Young, "The Evolution of the Pennsylvania Assembly, 1682-1748," ***Penn. Hist.*** XXXV (1968).

Maryland: C.A. Barker, ***The Background of the Revolution in Maryland*** (New Haven, 1940), A.C. Land, *The Dulanys of Maryland: A Biographical Study of Daniel Dulany the Elder (1685-1753) and Daniel Dulany the Younger (1722-1797)* (Baltimore, 1955), D.C. Skaggs, *The Roots of Maryland Democracy 1753-1776* (Westport, Conn., 1973).

Virginia: L. Griffith, ***Virginia House of Burgesses, 1750-1774*** (Northport, Ala., 1963), Isaac, "Religion and Authority" (8.9.), Morton, ***Colonial Virginia*** (3.1), C.S. Sydnor, ***Gentlemen Freeholders: Political Practices in Washington's Virginia*** (Chapel Hill, 1952).

North Carolina: Lefler and Powell, ***Colonial North Carolina*** (2.4.).

South Carolina: G.E. Frakes, ***Laboratory for Liberty: The South Carolina*** *Legislative Committee System 1719-1776* (Lexington, 1970) Sirmans, *Colonial* ***South Carolina*** (2.4.), J.P. Greene, "The Gadsden Election Controversy and the Revolutionary Movement in South Carolina," ***Miss. V. H. R.***, XLVI (1959), R.M. Weir, " 'The Harmony We Were Famous For,' An Interpretation of Pre-revolutionary South Carolina Politics," *W.M.Q.*, XXVI (1969).

Georgia: W.W. Abbot, ***The Royal Governors of Georgia, 1754-1775*** (Chapel Hill, 1959) and T.R. Reese, ***Colonial Georgia: A Study in British Imperial Policy in the Eighteenth Century*** (Athens, Ga., 1963).

G.B. Nash, "The Transformation of Urban Politics 1700-1765," *J.A.H.*, LX (1973) discusses political life in the colonial cities. See also P. Maier, "Popular Uprisings and Civil Authority in Eighteenth-century America," *W.M.Q.*, XXVII (1970).

9.5. The most persuasive general treatments of political culture are B. Bailyn, ***The Ideological Origins of the American Revolution*** (Camb., Mass., 1967) and

Bailyn, *Origins of American Politics* (9.2.). Also see R.L. Bushman, "Corruption and Power in Revolutionary America" and E.S. Morgan, "Royal and Republican Corruption" in Library of Congress Symposium, *The Development of a Revolutionary Mentality* (Washington, 1972). Some other recent studies of colonial political culture are: H.T. Colbourn, *The Lamp of Experience: Whig History and the Intellectual Origins of the American Revolution* (Chapel Hill, 1965), L.H. Leder, *Liberty and Authority: Early American Political Ideology 1689-1763* (Chicago, 1968), and E.S. Morgan, *Puritan Political Ideas, 1558-1794* (Indianapolis, 1965).

The English background is discussed in J.G.A. Pocock, "Machiavelli, Harrington, and English Political Ideologies in the Eighteenth Century," *W.M.Q.*, XXII (1965), I. Kramnick, *Bolingbroke and His Circle: The Politics of Nostalgia in the Age of Walpole* (Cambridge, Mass., 1968) and C. Robbins, *The Eighteenth Century Commonwealthman: Studies in the Transmission, Development, and Circumstance of English Liberal Thought from the Restoration of Charles II until the War with the Thirteen Colonies* (Cambridge, Mass., 1959).

A useful bibliographical essay is R.E. Stallhope, "Toward a Republican Synthesis: Emergence of an Understanding of Republicanism in American Historiography," *W.M.Q.*, XXIX (1972).

Chapter Ten. Eighteenth-Century Conflicts in North America

10.1 Works on the English background to expansion are M.S. Anderson, *Europe in the Eighteenth Century 1713-1783* (London, 1961), K. Hotblack, *Chatham's Colonial Policy* (London, 1917), Koebner, *Empire* (2.1.), Savelle, *Origins of American Diplomacy* (6.1.).

10.2. The first nine volumes of L.H. Gipson, *The British Empire Before the American Revolution* (15 vols. New York, 1936-1974) are invaluable for the period c.1748-1763, for both English and American developments. Vols. I, II and III deal with Great Britain, Ireland, and the Colonies. Vols. V, VI, VII, VIII, IX recount the events of 1748-1763, including detailed narratives of military struggles, diplomacy and associated political developments. General military histories are Leach, *Arms for Empire* (6.7.) and Peckham, *The Colonial Wars* (6.7.).

10.3. Studies that illuminate various aspects of the French and Indian War 1754-1763 are: J.R. Alden, *John Stuart and the Southern Colonial Frontier: A Study of Indian Relations, War, Trade and Land Problems in the Southern Wilderness, 1754-1775* (Ann Arbor, 1944), Alvord, *Mississippi Valley* (7.4.), R.L.D. Davidson, *War Comes to Quaker Pennsylvania, 1682-1756* (New York, 1957), Leach, *Northern Colonial Frontier* (4.1.), R.C. Newbold, *The Albany Congress and Plan of Union of 1754* (New York, 1955), A.G. Olson, "The British Government and Colonial Union, 1754," *W.M.Q.*, XVII (January, 1960), Schutz, *William Shirley* (9.4.), J.W. Shy, *Toward Lexington: The Role of the*

British Army in the Coming of the American Revolution (Princeton, 1965), T. Thayer, "The Army Contractors for the Niagara Campaign 1755-1756," *W.M.Q.*, XIV (January, 1957).

10.4. Indian affairs and Indian uprisings are treated in Alden, *John Stuart* (10.3.), Meriweather, *Expansion of South Carolina* (6.7.), H.H. Peckham, *Pontiac and the Indian Uprising* (1947, rptd. Chicago, 1961). See also Nash, *Red, White and Black* (6.6.) and the other works cited at 6.6. and 6.7.

10.5. The immediate effects of the war on administration and policy: Barrow, *Trade and Empire* (6.3.), O.M. Dickerson, *The Navigation Acts and the American Revolution* (Philadelphia, 1951), B. Knollenberg, *Origins of the American Revolution, 1759-1761* (rev. ed. N.Y., 1965), Shy, *Toward Lexington* (10.3.), J.M. Sosin, *Whitehall and the Wilderness: The Middle West in British Colonial Policy, 1760-1775* (Lincoln, 1961), C. Ubbelhode, *The Vice-Admiralty Courts and the American Revolution* (Chapel Hill, 1961). See also J.J. Waters and J.A. Schutz, "Patterns of Massachusetts Colonial Politics: The Writs of Assistance and Rivalry between the Otis and Hutchinson Family," *W.M.Q.*, XXIV (1967).

The socio-economic effects of the war have not been properly investigated. For some general information see Bridenbaugh, *Cities in Revolt* (6.8), Barker, *Background of the Revolution* (9.4.), M.A. Egnal and J.A. Ernst, "Economic Interpretation of the American Revolution," *W.M.Q.*, XXIX (1972), A.L. Jensen, *The Maritime Commerce of Colonial Philadelphia* (Madison, 1963), Shepherd and Walton, *Shipping, Maritime Trade* (6.2.).

Chapter Eleven. The Colonies and the Empire

11.1. For British politics 1763-1770, see J. Brooke, *King George III* (London, 1972), I.R. Christie, *Crisis of Empire: Great Britain and the American Colonies 1754-1783* (London, 1966), P. Langford, *The First Rockingham Administration, 1765-1766* (London, 1973), C.R. Ritcheson, *British Politics and the American Revolution* (Norman, 1954), and P.D.G. Thomas, *British Politics and the Stamp Act Crisis: The first phase of the American Revolution, 1763-1767* (Oxford, 1975).

11.2. British colonial policy 1763-1770 is discussed in the works listed in 10.5. In addition see Barrow, *Trade and Empire* (10.5), R.J. Chaffin, "The Townshend Acts, 1767," *W.M.Q.*, XXVII (1970), J.A. Ernst, "Genesis of the Currency Act of 1764," *W.M.Q.*, XXII (1965) and *Money and Politics* (7.7.), L. Namier and J. Brooke, *Charles Townshend* (London, 1964), Shy, *Toward Lexington* (10.3.), J.M. Sosin, *Agents and Merchants: British Colonial Policy and the Origins of the American Revolution 1763-1775* (Lincoln, 1965) and *Whitehall and the Wilderness* (10.5.), Ubbelhode, *Vice-Admiralty Courts* (10.5.), F.B. Wickwire, *British Subministers and Colonial America 1763-1783* (Princeton, 1966).

11.3. General works on American reactions to British policy include B. Bailyn, *Pamphlets of the American Revolution*, Vol. I (Cambridge, Mass., 1965),

Egnal and Ernst, "Economic Interpretation" (10.5.), J.A. Ernst, "The Currency Act Repeal Movement, 1764-1767," *W.M.Q.*, XXV (1968) and *Money and Politics* (7.7.), P. Maier, *From Resistance to Revolution: Colonial Radicals and the Development of American Opposition to Britain 1765-1775* (New York, 1972) and "The Beginnings of American Republicanism 1765-1775" in Library of Congress Symposium, *Development of a Revolutionary Mentality* (9.5.) and "Popular Uprisings" (9.4), E.S. Morgan, "Colonial Ideas of Parliamentary Power, 1764-1766," *W.M.Q.*, V (1948) and, *The Stamp Act Crisis: Prologue to Revolution* (rev. ed. N.Y., 1963).

11.4. Studies of individual colonies are: New Hampshire: Daniell, *Experiment in Republicanism* (9.4.); Massachusetts: B. Bailyn, *The Ordeal of Thomas Hutchinson*, (Cambridge, Mass., 1974), R.D. Brown, "The Massachusetts Committee of Towns, 1768," *W.M.Q.*, XXVI (1969), Brown, *Middle-Class Democracy* (9.4.), Warden, *Boston* (9.4.) and Waters, *Otis Family* (9.4.); Connecticut: C. Collier, *Roger Sherman's Connecticut; Yankee Politics and the American Revolution* (Middletown, Conn., 1971), Zeichner, *Connecticut's Years of Controversy* (9.4.); Rhode Island: D.S. Lovejoy, *Rhode Island Politics and the American Revolution 1760-1776* (Providence, 1958) and Thompson, "Ward-Hopkins Controversy" (9.4.).

New York: Bonomi, *Factious People* (5.4.) has a full bibliography. Some selected studies are R. Champagne, "Family Politics versus Constitutional Principles: The New York Assembly Elections of 1768 and 1769," *W.M.Q.*, XX (1963), B. Friedman, "The New York Assembly Elections of 1768 and 1769: The Disruption of Family Politics," *N.Y.H.*, XLVI (1965), D. Gerlach, *Philip Schuyler and the American Revolution in New York 1733-1777* (Lincoln, Neb., 1964), A.F. Young, *The Democratic-Republicans of New York: The Origins 1763-1797* (Chapel Hill, 1967); New Jersey: Kemmerer, *Path to Freedom* (9.4.), McMormick, *New Jersey* (2.6.); Pennsylvania: Hanna, *Benjamin Franklin* (9.4.), Hutson, *Movement for Royal Government* (9.4.), D.L. Jacobson, *John Dickinson and the Revolution in Pennsylvania 1764-1776* (Berkeley, 1965), B.H. Newcombe, "The Stamp Act and Pennsylvania Politics," *W.M.Q.*, XXIII (1966), J.J. Zimmerman, "Charles Thomson, the Samuel Adams of Philadelphia," *Miss. V. H. R.*, XLV (1958).

Maryland: Barker, *Background* (9.4.), R. Hoffman, *A Spirit of Dissension: Economics, Politics and the Revolution in Maryland* (Baltimore, 1973), Land, *The Dulanys* (9.4.), Skaggs, *Roots of Maryland Democracy* (9.4.); Virginia: C. Bridenbaugh, "Violence and Virtue in Virginia, 1766: or, The Importance of the Trivial," *Mass. Hist. Soc. Proceedings*, LXXVI (1965), H.J. Eckenrode, *The Revolution in Virginia* (rptd. Hamden, Conn., 1964), J.A. Ernst, "The Robinson Scandal Redivius: Money, Debts and Politics in Revolutionary Virginia," *Va. M. H. Biog.*, LXXVII (1969), E.G. Evans, "Planter Indebtedness and the Coming of the Revolution in Virginia," *W.M.Q.*, XIX (1962), R. Isaac, "Evangelical Revolt: The Nature of the Baptists' Challenge to the Traditional Order in Virginia, 1765-1775," *W.M.Q.*, XXXI (1974), T.W. Tate, "The Coming of the Revolution in Virginia: Britain's Challenge to Virginia's Ruling Class," *W.M.Q.*, XIX (1962); North Carolina: Lefler and Powell, *Colonial North Carolina* (2.3.), C. Sellers, Jr., "Making a Revolution: The North

Carolina Whigs 1765-1775," in J.C. Sitterson, ed., *Studies in Southern History* (Chapel Hill, 1957); South Carolina: P. Maier, "The Charleston Mob and the Evolution of Popular Politics in Revolutionary South Carolina 1765-1784," *Perspectives in American History*, IV (1970), W.R. Walsh, *Charleston's Sons of Liberty: A Study of the Artisans* (Columbia, 1959). Georgia: Abbot, *Royal Governors* (9.4.), Coleman, *The American Revolution in Georgia 1763-1789* (Athens, Ga., 1958).

J.R. Alden, *The South in the American Revolution, 1763-1789* (Baton Rouge, 1957) surveys the colonies from Maryland south.

11.5. Gipson, *British Empire before the American Revolution* (10.2.) is an invaluable narrative. Vols. X, XI, XII, XIII survey the thirteen North American colonies in the revolutionary period. M. Jensen, *The Founding of a Nation: A History of the American Revolution 1763-1776* (New York, 1968) is a general history by an acknowledged authority.

11.6. For information on the beginnings of American nationalism, see R.L. Merritt, *Symbols of American Community, 1735-1775* (New Haven, 1966), M. Savelle, *Seeds of Liberty: The Genesis of the American Mind* (New York, 1948), P.A. Varg, "The Advent of Nationalism 1758-1776," *Am. Qtly.*, XVI (1964).

11.7. For population growth, see Potter "Growth of Population" (7.1.), and K.A. Lockridge, "Land, Population and the Evolution of New England Society," *Past and Present*, no.39 (1968). Population statistics are available in *Historical Statistics* (6.1.). For immigration, see M. Campbell, "English Emigration on the Eve of the American Revolution," *A.H.R.*, LXI (1955), Jones, *American Immigration* (7.3.), G.R. Mellor, "Emigration from the British Isles to the New World, 1765-1775," *History*, XL (1955), Walton and Shepherd, *Shipping, Maritime Trade* (6.2.).

11.8. For studies of socio-economic structure and related questions, see W.F. Bliss, "The Rise of Tenancy in Virginia," *Va. M. H. B.* LXVIII (1950), E.M. Cooke, "Social Behavior and Changing Values in Dedham, Mass., 1700-1775," *W.M.Q.*, XXVII (1970), J.P. Greene, "Search for Identity: An Interpretation of the Meaning of Selected Patterns of Social Response in Eighteenth-Century America," *J. Soc. H.*, III (1969-1970), J.A. Henretta, "Economic Development and Social Structure in Colonial Boston," *W.M.Q.*, XXII (1965) and *Evolution of American Society* (7.1.), A. Kulikoff, "The Progress of Inequality in Revolutionary Boston," *W.M.Q.* XXVIII (1971), J.T. Lemon and G.B. Nash, "The Distribution of Wealth in Eighteenth-Century America: A Century of Change in Chester County, Pennsylvania, 1693-1802," *J. Soc. H.*, II (1968) (which also provides a critique of other findings), K.A. Lockridge, "Social Change and the Meaning of the American Revolution," *J. Soc. H.*, VI (1973), J.T. Main, *The Social Structure of Revolutionary America* (Princeton, 1965), W.S. Sachs, "Agricultural Conditions in the Northern Colonies before the American Revolution," *J. E. H.*, XIII (1953), Skaggs, *Roots of Maryland Democracy* (9.4.), S.B. Warner, *The Private City: Philadelphia in three periods of its growth* (Philadelphia, 1968).

11.9. For the back-country and the trans-Appalachian region, see R.A. Billington, *Westward Expansion: A History of the American Frontier* (third ed., New York, 1967), Bridenbaugh, *Myths and Realities* (3.4.), F.S. Philbrick, *The Rise of the West 1754-1830* (New York, 1965), and J.M. Sosin, *The Revolutionary Frontier 1763-1783* (New York, 1967), which contains a full bibliography.

11.10 On the Regulators in North and South Carolina, see Gipson, *British Empire*, vol. X (10.2.). For the North Carolina Regulators, see Lefler and Powell, *Colonial North Carolina* (2.4.) and W.S. Powell et al., *The Regulators in North Carolina: A Documentary History 1759-1776* (Raleigh, 1971); for the South Carolina Regulators, see R.M. Brown, *The South Carolina Regulators* (Cambridge, Mass., 1963).

For Pennsylvania, see Hanna, *Benjamin Franklin* (9.4), B. Hindle, "The March of the Paxton Boys," *W.M.Q.*, III (1946), and Hutson, *Movement for Royal Government* (9.4.).

11.11. Information on local political conditions may be found in the works cited in 11.4.

Chapter Twelve. American Independence

12.1 British politics, policies and background. In addition to the works cited in 11.1 and 11.2, see I.R. Christie, *Wilkes, Wyvill and Reform: Parliamentary Reform, 1760-1785* (London, 1962), T.S. Ashton, *Economic Fluctuations in England 1700-1800* (Oxford, 1959), B.D. Bargar, *Lord Dartmouth and the American Revolution* (New York, 1965), B. Donoghue, *British Politics and the American Revolution, The Path to War, 1773-1775* (London, 1964), I.D. Gruber, "The American Revolution as a Conspiracy: The British View," *W.M.Q.*, XXVI (1969), G. Rudé, *Wilkes and Liberty: A Social Study of 1763 to 1774* (Oxford, 1962).

12.2. American reactions. In addition to the works cited in 11.3 and 11.4, see R.D. Brown, *Revolutionary Politics in Massachusetts: The Boston Committees of Correspondence and the Towns 1772-1774* (Cambridge, Mass., 1970), B.W. Labaree, *The Boston Tea Party* (New York, 1964), R.L. Sheridan, "The British Credit Crisis of 1772 and the American Colonies," *J.E.H.*, XX (1960) and B. Mason, *The Road to Independence: The Revolutionary Movement in New York, 1773-1777* (Lexington, 1966).

12.3. On committees and congresses and policy debates, see J.P. Boyd, *Anglo-American Union: Joseph Galloway's Plans to Preserve the British Empire* (Philadelphia, 1941), E.C. Burnett, *The Continental Congress* (New York, 1941), J.M. Head, *A Time to Rend: Essay on the Decision for American Independence* (Madison, 1968), W.D. Jordan, "Familial Politics: The Killing of the King," *J.A.H.*, LX (Sept. 1973), B.H. Knollenberg, "John Dickinson vs. John Adams, 1774-1776," Am. Phil. Soc., *Proc.* CVI (1963).

12.4. On the Declaration of Independence, see C.L. Becker, *The Declaration of Independence: A Study in the History of Political Ideas* (rptd. N.Y., 1958). J.P. Boyd, *The Declaration of Independence, The Evolution of the Text* (Washington, 1943), S. Lynd, *Intellectual Origins of American Radicalism* (New York, 1968).

12.5. Popular or "radical" elements in the revolutionary struggle: R. Champagne,

"Liberty Boys and Mechanics of New York City, 1764-1774," *Labor Hist.*, VIII (1967) and "New York's Radicals and the Coming of Independence," *J.A.H.*, LI (1965), B. Friedman, "The Shaping of Radical Consciousness in Provincial New York," *ibid.*, LVI (1970), Hoffman, *Spirit of Dissension* (11.4), J.H. Hutson, "An Investigation of the Inarticulate: Philadelphia's White Oaks," *W.M.Q.*, XXVIII (1971) and J. Lemisch and J.K. Alexander, "The White Oaks, Jack Tar and the Concept of the Inarticulate," *W.M.Q.*, XXIX (1972), M. Jensen, "The American People and the American Revolution," *J.A.H.*, LVII (1970), J. Lemisch "Jack Tar in the Streets: Merchant Seamen in the Politics of Revolutionary America," *W.M.Q.*, XXV (1968), S. Lynd, *Class Conflict, Slavery and the United States Constitution* (Indianapolis, 1967), C.S. Olton, "Philadelphia's Mechanics in the First Decade of Revolution, 1765-1775," *J.A.H.*, LIX (1972), D.C. Skaggs, "Maryland's Impulse Toward Social Revolution 1750-1776," *ibid.*, LIV (1968) and Skaggs, *Roots of Maryland Democracy* (9.4.).

12.6. For early military events, see J.R. Alden, *A History of the American Revolution* (New York, 1969), P. Mackesy, *The War for America, 1775-1783* (Cambridge, Mass., 1964) and H.H. Peckham, *The War of Independence: A Military History* (Chicago, 1958).

Chapter Thirteen. From Colonies to States

13.1 For political, social and religious ideas, see Bailyn, *Ideological Origins* (9.5.), Heimert, *Religion and the American Mind* (8.8.), W.G. McCloughlin, "The Role of Religion in the Revolution—Liberty of Conscience and Cutural Cohesion in the New Nation" in Kurtz and Hutson, eds., *Essays on the American Revolution* (9.1), G.S. Wood, *The Creation of the American Republic 1776-1787* (Chapel Hill, 1969). J.T. Main, *The Sovereign States 1775-1783* (New York, 1973) is a political history with an up-to-date bibliography; it supplements but does not replace A. Nevins, *The American States during and after the Revolution, 1775-1789* (New York, 1924). For the texts of the new state constitutions, see F.N. Thorpe, ed., *Federal and State Constitutions, Colonial Charters, and other organic laws* (7 vols., Washington, D.C., 1909).

13.2. Aspects of the transition to statehood in some individual colonies are to be found in the following. New Hampshire: Daniell, *Experiment in Republicanism* (9.4.); Massachusetts: O. and M. Handlin, eds., *The Popular Sources of Political Authority: Documents on the Massachusetts Constitution of 1780* (Cambridge, Mass., 1966), R.J. Taylor, *Massachusetts: From Colony to State* (Chapel Hill, 1961); New York: Mason, *Road to Independence* (12.2); Pennsylvania: D. Hawke, *In the Midst of a Revolution* (Philadelphia, 1961); Maryland: Hoffman, *Spirit of Dissension* (11.4.); Virginia: Eckenrode, *Revolution in Virginia* (11.4.); North Carolina: R.L. Ganyard, "Radicals and Conservatives in Revolutionary North Carolina: A Point at Issue, The October Election, 1776," *W.M.Q.*, XXIV (1967). Pole, *Political Representation* (9.2) contains a detailed treatment of Massachusetts, Pennsylvania and Virginia.

13.3. Interpretative studies include T.C. Barrow, "The American Revolution as a Colonial War for Independence," *W.M.Q.*, XXV (1968), R. Buel, Jr., "Democracy and the American Revolution: A Frame of Reference," *W.M.Q.*, XXI (1964), E.P. Douglass, *Rebels and Democrats: The Struggle for Equal Political Rights and Majority Rule during the American Revolution* (Chapel Hill, 1955), M. Jensen, "Democracy in the American Revolution," *Huntington Lib. Qtly.*, XX (1957), J.T. Main, *The Upper Houses in Revolutionary America, 1763-1788* (Madison, 1965), J.K. Martin, *Men in Rebellion: Higher Governmental Leaders and the Coming of the American Revolution* (New Brunswick, 1973), G.S. Wood, "Rhetoric and Reality in the American Revolution," *W.M.Q.*, XVIII (1966). See also the works cited at 12.5.

13.4 The loyalists. Recent studies of the loyalists in America include R.M. Calhoon, *The Loyalists in Revolutionary America 1760-1781* (New York, 1973), W. Nelson, *The American Tory* (Boston, 1961), P.H. Smith, *Loyalists and Redcoats: A Study in British Revolutionary Policy* (Chapel Hill, 1964). B. Bailyn in "The Central Themes of the American Revolution" in Kurtz and Hutson, *Essays on the American Revolution* (9.1) makes brief but stimulating remarks on the loyalists; see also M.B. Norton, "The Loyalist Critique of the Revolution" in Library of Congress, *Development of a Revolutionary Mentality* (9.5), and E. Wright, ed., *A Tug of Loyalties: Anglo-American Relations 1765-1785* (London, 1975). Loyalist émigrés are considered in W. Brown, *The King's Friends: The Composition and Motives of the American Loyalist Claimants* (Providence, 1965), and M.B. Norton, *The Loyalist Exiles in England 1774-1789* (Boston, 1972).

A recent article, B.G. Merritt, "Loyalism and Social Conflict in Revolutionary Deerfield, Massachusetts" *Jnl. Am. Hist.*, LVII (1970), suggests the importance of local struggles between old elites and rising men.

13.5. Slavery and the Negro. Relevant works include Jordan, *White Over Black* (3.3.), M.S. Locke, *Anti-Slavery in America, 1619-1808* (rpt. Gloucester, Mass., 1965), D.L. Robinson, *Slavery in the Structure of American Politics, 1765-1820* (New York, 1971), A. Zilversmit, *The First Emancipation: The Abolition of Slavery in the North* (Chicago, 1967). See also D.B. Davis, *Was Thomas Jefferson an Authentic Enemy of Slavery?* (Oxford, 1970) and *Slavery in Western Culture* (Ithaca, 1966), W. Cohen "Thomas Jefferson and the Problem of Slavery," *J.A.H.*, LVI (1969) and E.S. Morgan "Slavery and Freedom: The American Paradox," *J.A.H.*, LIX (1972).

13.6. The Baptists. Isaac, "Evangelical Revolt." (11.4), McLoughlin, *New England Dissent* (8.6) and *Isaac Backus* (8.9). See also D. Malone, *Jefferson the Virginian* (London 1948), J.P. Boyd, ed., *The Papers of Thomas Jefferson*, vols. I & II (Princeton, 1950).

13.7. On continental questions see Burnett, *The Continental Congress* (12.3.) and M. Jensen, *The Articles of Confederation: An Interpretation of the Social-Constitutional History of the American Revolution, 1774-1781* (Madison, 1940). E.J. Ferguson, *The Power of the Purse: A History of American Public Finance 1776-1790* (Chapel Hill, 1961) and C.P. Nettels, *The Emergence of a National Economy, 1775-1815* (New York, 1962) discuss fiscal and commercial questions. S.F. Bemis, *The Diplomacy of the American Revolution*

(Washington, 1935) should be supplemented by R.W. van Alstyne, *Empire and Independence: The International History of the American Revolution* (New York, 1965) and F. Gilbert, *To the Farewell Address: Ideas of Early American Foreign Policy* (Princeton, 1961). L.S. Kaplan, *Colonies into Nation: American Diplomacy 1763-1801* (New York, 1972) provides a recent synthesis with a full bibliography.

13.8. Military events are recounted from the British side by Mackesy, *War for America* (12.6.). The war is seen from Washington's viewpoint by D.S. Freeman, *George Washington: A Biography*, vols. III and IV (N.Y., 1951). J.R. Alden, *The American Revolution* (12.6.), Peckham, *The War for Independence* (12.6.) and Christopher Ward, *The War of the Revolution* (2 vols., New York, 1952) are readable military histories.

Index